HISTORY
of
MEDIEVAL INDIA

HISTORY *of* MEDIEVAL INDIA

Dr Kiran Chandra Chaudhuri MA, LLB, PhD

To be had of

New Central Book Agency (P) Ltd

LONDON

HYDERABAD ERNAKULAM BHUBANESWAR

NEW DELHI KOLKATA PUNE GUWAHATI

NCBA

REGD OFFICE
8/1 Chintamoni Das Lane, Kolkata 700 009, India
email: ncbapvtltd@eth.net

OVERSEAS
NCBA (UK) Ltd, 149 Park Avenue North, Northampton, NN3 2HY, UK
email: ncbauk@yahoo.com

EXPORT
NCBA Exports Pvt. Ltd, 212 Shahpur Jat, New Delhi 110 049
email: ncbaexports@ncbapvtltd.com

BRANCHES

2/27 Ansari Road, 1st Floor
Daryaganj, New Delhi 110 002
email: ncbadel@ncbapvtltd.com

House No. 3-1-315, 1st Floor
Nimboliadda, Kachiguda, Hyderabad 500 027
email: ncbahydb@ncbapvtltd.com

Shop Nos. 3 & 4, Vinayak Towers
681/B Budhwar Peth, Appa Balwant Chowk
Pune 411 002
email: ncbapune@ncbapvtltd.com

GSS Shopping Complex, 1st Floor
Opposite College Post Office, Convent Road
Ernakulam 682 035
0484-4021054/53

Shop No. 15, Bharati Towers, Ground Floor
Forest Park
Bhubaneswar 751 001
email: ncbabub@ncbapvtltd.com

Radhamayee Complex (Second Floor)
Opp. SBI, Panbazar, Jaswanta Road
Guwahati 781 001
email: ncbaguwahati@ncbapvtltd.com

HISTORY OF MEDIEVAL INDIA • Kiran Chandra Chaudhuri

First Published: October 1985
Reprinted: 1996, 2002
Revised Reprint: August 2013
Reprinted: July 2016

PUBLISHER
Amitabha Sen
For and on behalf of
Central Educational Enterprises (P) Ltd
54B Patuatola Lane, Kolkata 700 009

PRINTER
New Central Book Agency (P) Ltd
Web-Offset Division, Dhulagarh, Sankrail, Howrah

PROOF-CHECKING
Rina Basak

PROJECT TEAM
Pradyot Majumder and Pradip Biswas

ISBN: 978 81 7381 205 7

Price ₹ 325.00

CONTENTS

FOREWORD

History of Medieval India is a companion volume of my History of Ancient India and History of Modern India published earlier. This book is intended to meet the needs of the B.A. Honours students of Indian universities as also of candidates preparing for the Indian services examinations.

I shall deem my labour amply rewarded if the book meets the requirements of those for whom it is meant.

It do not claim faultlessness in the preparation of the manuscript and it shall be my endeavour to make improvements, wherever necessary, as soon as occasion for the next edition will arise.

I shall gratefully receive any suggestion for the improvement of the book.

15th October, 1985
Calcutta

Author

1 Introduction

SPREAD OF ISLAM : EARLY CONTACTS WITH INDIA

The vast peninsula called Arabia is about one-fourth of Europe in size and one-third that of the United States of America. It is an arid region of rocks and deserts with a few oases and fertile strips. In Southern Arabia, however, there was sufficient periodic rainfall to warrant a systematic cultivation. Harshness of nature made the people hard working, hardy and stout. Not far from the Western Coast of Arabia is situated the holy city of Mecca where in A.D. 570 was born Prophet Mohammad. He preached the unity of God head. According to him "God is one. He is all powerful. He is the creator of the universe. There is a judgement day. Splendid rewards in Paradise await those who carry out God's commands, and terrible punishment in hell for those who disregard them."

Consecrated and fired by the new task which he felt called upon by **Allah** to perform as His messenger, Mohammad went among the people rousing in them great energy and unbounded enthusiasm. On his death in A.D. 632 the successors of the Prophet called Caliphs (Khalifa) the arms of the Muslims advanced on all sides and the banner of Islam flew out in many countries from Iran to Spain. The Arabs also turned their eyes on the rich ports of the West coast of India and as early as A.D. 637. In that year an Arabian army was sent to Thana near Bombay which was followed by expeditions to Broach, gulf of Debal in Sind and Al-Kikan in the district of Kelat.

In this way, within a hundred years from the death of Mohammad the Arab power spread in all directions. By the early eighth century A.D. the Arab empire spread from the Atlantic to the borders of Sind in India, and from the Caspian to the Nile in Egypt. Spain, Portugal, parts of Southern France, the entire Northern Coast of Africa, the Nile Valley, Arabia, Mesopotamia, Syria, Persia, Afghanistan, Baluchistan, Oxus Valley etc. were within the Arabian empire. Had not the forces of Islam been defeated in the hands of Charles Martel in the battle of Tours in A.D. 732 the banner of Islam would have been carried into the heart of Europe.

By the middle of seventh century Southern Afghanistan fell into the hands of the Arabs. "The Arabs now made repeated onslaughts on the Shah of Kabul, supposed to be a descendant of the great Kanishka, and the **Ratbil** of Zabul in the upper valley of the Helmund river and some adjoining districts". The Arabs followed their success by the conquest of Sind. In Bana's **Harshacharita** Sind is mentioned as one of the territories over-run by Prabhakarvardhana, father of Harsha as well as by the latter. Hiuen Tsang mentions that Sind was under the rule of a Sudra dynasty which was supplanted by a Brahmin family under the leadership of Chach.

Chach was succeeded by his son Dahir. It was during the reign of Dahir that the Arab Governor of Iraq, Al-Hajjaz being incensed by the despoilation of a ship sent for him from Ceylon, by pirates near the Debal port, sent several expeditions against Dahir. It is said that "the King of Ceylon was sending to Hajjaz, the viceroy of the Eastern provinces of the Caliphate, the orphan daughters of Muslim merchants who had died in his dominions, and his vessels were attacked and plundered by pirates off the coast of Sind. According to a less probable account, the King of Ceylon had himself accepted Islam and was sending tribute to "the commander of the faithful". The story that the King of Ceylon despatched eight ships laden with tributes to Hajjaz is not accepted as historical by modern historians.

Whatever might have been the actual nature of the offence given to the governor or the eastern provinces of the Caliphate, the fact remains that he at first sent an expedition against Dahir, under Obeidullah and another under General Budail. But both expeditions having failed miserably and both the leaders of the expeditions having been killed, Hajjaz entrusted the task of punishing the Indian King Dahir to his nephew and son-in-law Muhammad-bin Kasim (A.D. 711). A supporting contingent with arms and ammunitions was also sent by sea route. In the attack on the well protected port Debal, the Arabs made use of a stone-throwing cannon called **balista** which broke the impregnable wall and razed it to the ground. The port Debal was occupied and under orders of Muhammad Kasim all male above the age of seventeen had been done to death. For three days and nights loot and killing went on unabated after which all survivors were forced to adopt Islam. A rule of bayonet was set up in Debal. Kasim then proceeded to conquer the rest of Sind.

After having conquered the forts of Nerun, Sehwan etc. Kasim met Dahir in the field of Rawar. Dahir had assembled an army of 50,000 horse, himself riding his war elephant. The battle was sustained with great valour on both sides but the Arabs used arrows with burning cotton at the tips. One such arrow having struck Dahir's elephant, it fled towards the river followed by the Arabs. The fight was renewed on the river bank and Dahir charged Arabs with great valiance killing many of them until he was struck by an arrow and fell from his elephant. As he was about to mount a horse he was soon cut down by an Arab, his forces fled from the field.

Dahir's wife Rani Bai and her maids immolated themselves at Rawar to avoid falling into the hands of the Arabs.

The remnant of Dahir's army rallied at Bahmanabad and offered determined resistance and gave up when 8000, according to some. 26,000 of them fell fighting in the field. Bahmanabad and along with it Rani Ladi another wife of Dahir fell into the hands of the Arabs. Jai Singh, son of Dahir retired to Chitrur. Muhammad Kasim married Rani Ladi and sent to maiden daughters—Suryadevi and Parmaldevi to the Caliph.

Muhammand Kasim placed a Governor each in Rawar, Sehwan, Nerun. Dhaliyn and proceeded towards Ator. On his way he received submission of people of different places. Ator was defended by a son of Dahir called by the Arabs, Fufi who was under an impression that his father Dahir had fled to Hindustan to bring reinforcement. But Muhammad Kasim sent Rani Ladi, now his wife to Fufi to impress upon him the truth of the death of Dahir and the futility of resistance. Fufi dismissed Ladi with utmost contempt accusing her of joining herself to "the unclean strangers". But being convinced of Dahir's death he fled from Ator by night and the citizens thus deserted by their leader submitted to Kasim. Muhammad Kasim then took Multan. Then the whole of upper Sind and lower Punjab fell to Muhammad Kasim. In this way the whole of the lower Indus Valley was dominated by the Arabs. But Muhammad Kasim had no mind to stop there. He began to carry on minor operations in the neighbouring Provinces. Next Governor was Yazid, who assumed charge in 715 but died within a few days after his arrival at Sind.

The next governor was Juniad who was active and energetic, but extremely unscrupulous. He pursued a more aggressive policy and sent expeditions against Marwar, Mandor, Dahnaj, Broach, Ujjaini, Malwa and Gujarat. The progress of Arab conquest was arrested by the Chalukyas in the south, the Pratiharas in the east and the Karkotas in the north.

The Arab conquest of Sind and certain other areas was a mere episode in the history of India and affected only a small portion of the fringe of the vast country of India. It, however, introduced into one frontier tract of India the religion which was destined "to dominate the greater part of India for nearly five centuries, but it had none of the far reaching effects attributed to it by Todd in the **Annals of Rajasthan.** The tide of Islam, having overflowed Sind and the lower Punjab leaving some Jetsam on the Strand."

SOURCES OF MEDIEVAL INDIAN HISTORY

Source materials for the history of Medieval India are as voluminous as diverse. The writer of this period of Indian history is beset with the difficulty not for paucity of materials but its plethora. He is apt to be confused by the mutually contradictory statements of the panegyrists of the Sultans, foreign travellers and merchants and writers of history of that age, and his task of shifting truth out of these is rendered difficult due to the contradictions. The writer has not to depend on indirect sources at all.

The source materials for the history of medieval India may be considered mainly under five heads, such as : (i) state papers, (ii) writings of the contemporary historians, (iii) accounts of foreign travellers and merchants, (iv) coins and monuments, and (v) writings of the Hindu authors.

(i) State Papers : The state papers of the Sultanate and the Mughal period were the most dependable source materials for the history of the above two periods. During the Mughal period there were very good arrangements for the preservation of the state papers, but much of these papers have been destroyed due to internecine warfare and palace revolutions. In the library of Emperor Akbar there were 24,000 manuscripts, but none of them has been saved from destruction. Yet whatever government and non-government papers have reached us constitute a valuable mass of materials for the construction of the history of the Muslim period.

(ii) Writings of the Contemporary Historians : (a) Al Biruni, a Muslim scholar was originally in the court of Sultan Mahmud of Ghazni. But he came over to Punjab after it was occupied by Sultan Mahmud. While in India Al Biruni learnt Sanskrit language and acquired deep knowledge of Hindu Philosophy. He wrote a book named **Kitabun fi-Tahqiq-i-ma li-l-Hind** i.e. An Enquiry into India, which gives us a wealth of historical materials. In this work he has given an excellent description of the Indian philosophy, astronomy, mathematics, chemistry, geography etc. The work also contains description of Hindu customs, manners and traditions. Al Biruni was deeply influenced by the philosophy of **Bhagabat Geeta.**

(b) Many important historical materials can be had of the works of Minhajus-Siraj and Hasan Nizami. Minhaj was a high government official under Nasir-ud-din. His **Tabaqat-i-Nasiri** is an important historical work depicting the details of the rule of Nasir-ud-din.

(c) Ain-ul-Mulk was a very able administrator, an expert in Muhammadan Law and religion. In his work **Munshat-i-Mahra** he left a detailed description of the administration of Firuz Tughluq.

(d) Amir Khusru or Khusrav was the greatest poet and litterateur of the reign of Giyas-uddin Balban. Later, he became the court poet of Ala-ud-din Khalji. His works not only betray his great poetic genius but also give a good idea of the contemporary history.

(e) Zia-ud-din Barni was responsible for writing the history of the Sultanate from its very beginning till the reign of Firuz Tughluq. His work **Twarikh-i-Firuz-Shahi** is a very important historical work on the reign of Firuz Tughluq. Islami's work **Futuh-us-Salatin** is an excellent history of the period from eleventh century till the middle of the fourteenth century.

(f) **Futuhat-i-Firuz-Shahi,** a work by Firuz Shah himself, recounts the systematic history of the administration of Firuz Shah Tughluq. This apart, important historical materials about the reign of Firuz Tughluq can be had of the works of Shams-i-Shiraj, Ain-ul-Mulk, Amir Khusru, Ahia-bin-Ahmamad, Az-ud-din Khalid Khani etc.

(g) The memoirs of Babur and Jahangir, the **Tajkirat-ul-Wakiat** written by a personal follower of Humayun, and Gulbadan Begum's **Humayun-nama** are replete with historical materials of the medieval period of Indian History.

(h) A detailed history of the reign of Akbar is found in Abul Fazl's **Akbar-nama** and **Ain-i-Akbari.** These two works are indispensable for writing the history of the reign of Akbar. **Mutakhab-ut-Twarikh** and **Tabaqat-i-Akbari** of Badauni and Nizam-ud-din Ahmed respectively are important works on the contemporary history.

(i) Alamgir-nama, Padshahi-nama are two important historical works, the former for the reigns of Shahjahan and Aurangzeb. **Masir-i-Alamgir** is a reliable historical work of the reign of Aurangzeb. Khafi Khan's **Muntakhab-ul-Lubab** contains many secret and historically important information about the reign of Aurangzeb.

(ii) Accounts of Foreign Travellers : During the Sultanate and Mughal period many foreign travellers had come to visit India. Many of them left accounts of their experiences, political, economic and social conditions of the Indians of the time. Naturally, their accounts furnish us with a fund of valuable materials about the contemporary history.

(a) the Italian traveller Marco Polo came to the Tamil kingdom of the South India towards the end of the thirteenth century. His account about his travels contains important historical materials about the flourishing economic condition of South India.

(b) The most important foreign traveller of the Sultanate period was the African traveller Ibn Batuta who came to India in 1334 and was appointed **qazi** by Muhammad bin Tughluq and worked in that capacity for some time. His work **Rehla** i.e. Travels contains abundant information on the judicial, political, social, economic and military conditions of contemporary India. It also throws interesting light on the topics like postal system, roads, traffic, secret intelligence, agricultural products and men and their ideas, court ceremonies, trade, shipping, music etc. The account of Ibn Batuta finds corroboration in the account of Zia-ud-din Barni. While mentioning Ala-ud-din Khalji, Ibn Batuta called him the best of the Sultans of Delhi. He also referred to the great wealth of Bengal and the fertility of agricultural land in Bengal.

(c) Mahuan, a Chinese traveller came to Bengal in the fifteenth century. His account contains a description of the natural wealth and economic well-being of the people of Bengal. He highly praised the quality of the goods produced in Bengal.

(d) Abdur-Razzaq, the Persian Ambassador to the court of the Zamorin of Calicut (1442) visited Vijaynagar and wrote an account of the administration and society of the kingdom.

(e) Nicolo Conti, an Italian traveller, visited Vijaynagar about 1420. He left a detailed account of this kingdom to a Papal Secretary who wrote it in Latin.

(f) The Russian traveller Athanusius Nikitin, Portuguese travellers Paes and Nunitz visited South India. From their accounts the political, social and economic condition of the people of South India can be known.

(g) During the Mughal rule the Jesuit missionaries left a wealth of historical materials in their writings. From the accounts of Ralph Fitch, Thomas Roe, Tavernier, Bernier, Terry,

Manucci, Paelsart, Parkas etc. much historical materials are available for the reconstruction of the history of medieval India.

(iii) The Epigraphic and Numismatic Sources : Although the epigraphic and numismatic sources for the Muslim period are not so important and valuable as for the pre-Muslim period of Indian history, they are of much help in fixing the chronology of events, correcting the list of rulers and fixing their dates, as also in determining the extent of a kingdom. The inscriptions of the Hindu rulers of Orissa, Deccan and South India are of particular importance as they throw valuable and new light on the history of these regions. Edward Thomas' **'The Chronicles of the Pathan Kings of Delhi'** is a standard work on the coins of the period. Lane Poole observes that "As a rule we may look upon Muhammadan coins as the surest foundations for an exact history of the dynastics by which they were issued."

(iv) Monuments : The architectural remains of the Sultanate and the Mughal periods are many and varied and bear testimony to the development of the architectural art with all its ornamental and filigree works. These also show a happy blending of the Hindu and Muslim techniques and styles of architecture.

(v) Works of the Hindu Writers : Among the Maratha historical writings **Sabhasad Bakhr** written during the Mughal period is of special importance. This was the work of a historian of Shivaji's time. Sujan Ray Bhandari's **Khulasat-ut-Twarikh** contains the history from the time of the Ghaznavids till the early part of the Sultanate. The ballads of the Rajput ballad-singers are of particular importance in the reconstruction of the history of the Rajputs. Todd's **Annals and Antiquities of Rajasthan** is based on the Rajput ballads. Although Todd's **Annals and Antiquities of Rajasthan** is not regarded as a work on history, yet it contains various historical materials useful for the reconstruction of the history of the Rajputs. From the **'Granth Sahib'** and other religious works of the Sikhs, the origin of Sikhism is known.

NORTHERN INDIA ON THE EVE OF MUSLIM INVASION

The political condition of India on the eve of the Ghaznavid invasions differed from that before the Arab conquest. In the early years of the eighth century there was no foreign colony far less any foreign power in India except a few Arab merchants on the western coast of India. On the other hand when Sultan Mahmud of Ghazni invaded India there were two foreign kingdoms on Indian soil, namely, Multan and Sind. A large section of the population of these two kingdoms had been converted into Islam. There were also Arab colonies in southern India, specially in Malabar where the Hindu rulers permitted the Arabs to proselytise the local Hindus into Islam, and when Sultan Mahmud of Ghazni invaded India it was natural for these Muslims to have moral sympathy with the foreign invader.

Two Arab kingdoms of Multan and Sind had thrown off the suzerainty of the Caliphate and enjoyed full independence since 871, although because of their peculiar position in a foreign country, they professed seeming allegiance to the Caliph. In the rest of the country there was Hindu rule.

The most notable Hindu Kingdom that extended from the river Chenab to the Hindukush mountain and Kabul was ruled over by Shahiya dynasty which resisted single-handed the Arab inroads for 200 years. The king towards the end of the tenth century was famous Jaipal who was both an intrepid soldier and an able administrator. It was his kingdom, by virtue of its geographical situation had to bear the first onslaught of the Turks from Ghazni.

Kashmir was the next important Hindu kingdom of Northern India. It was under the house of Utpala which was in constant conflict with Kanauj. Under King Shankaravarman Kashmir extended its boundaries in several directions but his death was followed by great confusion in Kashmir and the throne was seized by the Brahmins of Kashmir who placed one named Yasakara on the throne. But this line having come to an end within a short time, Parvagupta became the king. This dynasty ruled over Kashmir till 1003 when the throne passed to Sangrama Raja who founded the Lohara dynasty. When Sultan Mahmud was hammering at the gates of India, Kashmir was under the rule of Dida belonging to the dynasty of Parvagupta and the political condition of Kashmir was not at all satisfactory.

Kanauj : Near about 836 the imperial city of Kanauj had passed into the hands of the Pratihara dynasty. This dynasty claimed descent from Lakshmana, brother of Rama of the Ramayana. But modern historians consider the Pratiharas to have descended from the Gurjaras. The Pratiharas exercised sway over Kanauj and Madhyadesha and fought with varying success with their southern and northern neighbours. But Pratihara King Mahipala was abjectly defeated by the Rashtrakuta king of the Deccan, and lost his capital Kanauj. The Chandela king, however, reinstated him to the throne of Kanauj. The Pratihara power was gradually weakened and the feudatories of the Pratiharas, the Chandelas of Bundelkhand, Chalukyas of Gujarat and the Paramars of Malwa became independent. Rajyapala was the last king of the Pratihara dynasty. He was a feeble ruler and his capital Kanauj was invaded by Sultan Mahmud of Ghazni in 1018.

The Palas of Bengal : King Mahipala of the Pala dynasty was the ruler of Bengal when Mahmud of Ghazni invaded India. Mahipala succeeded in restoring the fortunes of the dynasty to some extent, but a part of Bengal had fallen apart under powerful feudatories who seemingly recognised the overlordship of the Palas. When the North Western India was being laid waste by fire and sword by Sultan Mahmud of Ghazni, the Chola king Rajendracholadeva invaded Bengal and defeated the Pala ruler. Bengal, however, remained safe against the inroads of Sultan Mahmud due to heer distance.

Thus when Mahmud of Ghazni invaded India, the entire area north of Vindhyas was divided into rather small independent states. Naturally, there was not a single monarch in northern India who could successfully stand against the foreign invasion. There was no ruler comparable to Chandragupta, Ashoka, Kanishka, Samudragupta or Harshavardhana whom Sultan Mahmud had to reckon with.

Further, three centuries of immunity from foreign invasion after the Arab conquests of a small part of the country in the north-west, developed a sense of complacency among the Indian rulers who allowed vigilance to sleep. They neglected to fortify the north-western frontier of India and to make necessary arrangements for the defence of the passes through which the invaders entered the country. They also relied on the traditional war tactics which became outmoded and were incapable of facing the shock tactics of the foreign invaders. Prolonged immunity from foreign invasion developed a false sense of security which almost killed the spirit on national ardour and patriotism. A sense of exclusiveness had developed among the Hindus during the period from the eighth to eleventh century. As Al Biruni observed, "the Hindus believed that there was no country like theirs, no nation like theirs, no king like theirs, no religion like theirs, no science like theirs. (the Hindus) were not so narrow-minded as the present (eleventh century) generation". To add to these were the evils of a static society, rigid caste rules, religious conservatism which bred stagnation and a general decadence. Economically the country was rich although the disparity of wealth between the ruling class, nobles, courtiers on the one hand and the common people on the other was great. The temples were repositories of accumulated wealth of the society. Such was the general condition of India on the eve of the invasion of Sultan Mahmud of Ghazni.

REFERENCES

Struggle for Empire (History & Culture of Indian People, Vol. V)

The Sultanate of Delhi : A. L. Srivastava

The Cambridge History of India, Vol. VI

History of Medieval India : Ishwari Prasad

An Advanced History of India : Majumdar, Roychaudhuri & Datta

Thc Oxford History of India : V. A. Smith

A Comprehensive History of India, Vol. J, Delhi Sultanat : Habib & Nizami

2

Sultan Mahmud [971-1030]

THE GHAZNAVIDS

Early Raids : In the early years of the tenth century the descendants of Saman, a Zoroastrian noble of Balkh who had accepted Islam, extended their dominion in Transoxiana, Persia and greater part of Afghanistan. Their empire waned as quickly as it had waxed and their power passed into the hands of the Turkish slaves to whom they would entrust the principal offices of their court and kingdom. One of such Turkish officers Aliptigin rebelled and made himself independent ruler of Ghazni, although his successors would offer lip allegiance to the Samanids who now held their court at Bukhara. Aliptigin was succeeded by his son Ishaq in 963 on whose death the court of Bukhara acknowledged Balkatigin a former slave of Aliptigin (966). Balkatigin was succeeded by Pirai (972). Pirai's five years' reign is remarkable for the first conflict in this region between Hindus and Muslims, the former being the aggressors. The Shahiya king Jaipal whose dominion extended to the Hindukush and included Kabul, was alarmed by the establishment of a Muslim kingdom to the south of the great mountain barrier and invaded the dominion of Ghazni but was defeated.

Pirai's rule became unpopular in the meantime and he was removed from the throne (977) and **Sabuktigin,** a slave to whom Aliptigin had given his daughter in marriage, was placed on the throne of Ghazni. Sabuktigin paid lip allegiance to the court at Bukhara but ruled with full sovereignty. Two years after Sabuktigin's accession Jaipal king of the Shahiya dynasty came to know from some merchants and travellers that Subuktigin had occupied some areas within the borders of Jaipal's kingdom. He therefore advanced with a force to punish Sabuktigin (979). Jaipal met Sabuktigin's forces in a place named Ghuzak. But due to heavy snow fall terms of peace were arranged without resorting to any battle between the two sides. After seven years (986) Sabuktigin after having increased his military strength invaded the kingdom of Jaipal and carried off many captives and much booty. Two years later (988) he again invaded the kingdom of Jaipal and compelled him to surrender Kabul and the neighbouring regions to Ghazni. In 997 Sabuktigin died leaving his unfinished task to his son Sultan Mahmud.

SULTAN MAHMUD (971-1030) :

On the death of Sabuktigin in 997, his famous son Mahmud succeeded to the throne. There was, however, a short war of succession between Mahmud and his younger brother Ismail who was nominated heir by Sabuktigin. Mahmud obtained formal recognition of his occupation of the throne from the Caliph of Baghdad, al-Qadir Billah who sent him a robe of investment and the titles of Yam-in-ud-daulah and Amin-ul-Millah. Hence his dynasty came to be known as Yamini dynasty.

Mahmud gave up the traditional epithet of Amir and assumed the title of Sultan. Now he decided to proceed on 'holy war against Hind'. Utbi says that Sultan Mahmud called a council of his officers "in order to secure a blessing on his design of exalting the standard of religion, widening the plain of right, of illuminating the words of truth and strengthening the power of justice."

In pursuance of his vow he invaded India many times and as to the actual number of his inroads historians differ. According to Sir Henry Elliot Mahmud made seventeen expeditions against India. Modern historians accept the view of Sir Elliot.

The first expedition of Mahmud is said to have taken place in 999 or 1000 when he crossed the Indian border and 'plundered or annexed' some towns and a few fortresses. He appointed a ruler for the newly conquered areas and left with a huge booty.

In the same year (1000) Mahmud 'for the purpose of exalting the standard of religion' and to establish truth, justice etc. proceeded in expedition against Jaipal. Mahmud had 15,000 horses with him and when he advanced near Peshawar Jaipal met him with 12,000 horses, 30,000 foot and 300 elephants. With better marksmanship the followers of Mahmud threw the elephants in disarray and they practically ran amuck and the numerically stronger Hindu army could not stand the impetuosity of the Muslim horsemen and by noon Jaipal's army was in full flight leaving 15,000 dead in the field. Jaipal and fifteen of his high ranking officers, and a large number of his men were captured by Mahmud's troops. The jewels including a necklace of enormous value, worn by Jaipal and his officers formed the part of Mahmud's plunder. Jaipal purchased his and his officers' release on the promise of a fabulous ransom of two and half lakhs of dinars and hundred and fifty elephants. As the full amount of ransom could not be paid forthwith Jaipal and his officers and men were released by keeping a few hostages. Jaipal's son Anandapal made good the deficiency and the hostages were released before Mahmud returned to Ghazni. Jaipal overwhelmed with shame and mortification, having suffered three successive defeats and once a captive, in the hands of the Muslims, considered himself unworthy of the throne and after designating his son Anandapal as his successor mounted a funeral pyre and perished in the flames.

Mahmud renewed his invasion of India in 1004 and after defeating Baji Ray king of Bhera in a desperate battle in which Baji Ray put up a brave fight, carried away all the wealth there as also a large number of elephants. Mahmud made arrangements for permanent annexation of the country and the conversion of the Hindus into Islam. In his fourth expedition Mahmud proceeded against Multan which was under Abul-Fath Daud whose heretical activities had enraged Mahmud. Daud was on friendly terms with Anandapal. Mahmud proposed to Anandapal to allow his army to march through his dominion against Multan. Anandapal, naturally, did not agree to such a proposal from an enemy of his father and against the interest of a friendly ruler. This led to a battle near Peshawar in which Mahmud severely defeated Anandapal who fled to Kashmir. Now it became easy for Mahmud to march his army through the Shahiya kingdom against Multan and besiege the city for seven days and to force it to surrender. Daud was allowed to rule over his kingdom on payment of an annual tribute of 20,000 dirhams, to follow the tenets of Islam and the people of the kingdom were forced to pay an indemnity of 20 lakhs dirhams.

Now Mahmud received news of the invasion of the northern part of his kingdom by Ilak Khan, a Turkish leader. He left Shukhapala or Sevakpala, a grandson of Jaipala who had been earlier converted into Islam and took the name of Nawas Shah in charge of the territories occupied by him in Hindustan. As Mahmud had left India Nawas Shah threw off the allegiance to Mahmud and began to rule as an independent ruler. In 1007 Mahmud marched to India to punish Nawas Shah who fled to the hills but was captured, his treasures were all confiscated and Mahmud left for Ghazni after settling the affairs at Hindustan. Nawas Shah had to pass the rest of his life in prison.

Next year (1008) Mahmud led an expedition against Anandapal in order to punish him for his conduct during the invasion of Multan. Anandapal who had been aware of Mahmud's intention made an appeal to the Hindu rajas for aid and the rajas of Ujjain, Gwalior, Kalinjar, Kanauj, Delhi, Ajmer as also the Khokars of Punjab came to his assistance. The battle between Mahmud and Anandapal took place in the area between Peshwar and Und. The attack of the Khokars on both the flanks of Mahmud's army did such execution among his troops that he was about to retreat when an accident decided the day in favour of Mahmud. The elephant of Anandapal took fright and bore his rider out of the field which gave an impression to the Hindu fighters that their leader was retreating, broke the ranks and fled. Mahmud's troops pursued the retreating Hindus slaying eight thousand. Thus a losing battle was won by Mahmud by an accident. Mahmud took thirty elephants and much other plunder.

Dispersal of the great army of Anandapal opened the way for raid into India and Mahmud advanced towards the fortress of Nagarkot or Kangra, which was famous for its wealth. As the fortress of Nagarkot was most well protected, many of the Hindu rajas and wealthy people deposited their jewelleries and surplus wealth in it. Mahmud forced the fortress to surrender and carried away a booty amounting to "700,000 golden dinars, besides large quantities of vessels of gold and silver and of unworked gold and silver, and jewels" and returned to Ghazni. From Ferishta we know that Mahmud seized control of the treasury "which consisted of 70,000,000 royal dirhams, gold and silver ingots, 7,00,400 **mans** in weight jewelleries, and precious stones. Among the booty were superfine, soft and embroidered cloths and garments, a house of white silver 30 yards in length and 15 yards in breadth, parts of which could be disjointed at will ... provided with two golden and two silver poles and a very costly throne."

On reaching Ghazni Mahmud held an exhibition of the jewels, pearls and rubies, emeralds, diamonds etc. secured from Nagarkot for ambassadors from Turkestan and other foreign countries to see. Acquisition of such a fabulous wealth only whetted the greed of Mahmud. He took upon himself the sacred task of the breaking Hindu idols and Hindu temples. He assumed the titles of **Ghazi,** i.e. Victor, and **Batshikan,** i.e. Idol-breaker.

Next expedition of Mahmud was against Thaneswar. It was his tenth expedition (1014). As Mahmud was preparing for this expedition, the king of Thaneswar having come to know of this, sent an emissary to Mahmud proposing to pay an annual tribute of fifty elephants in order to buy him off. But Mahmud rejected the offer and proceeded towards Thaneswar where he found the famous Thaneswar temple practically without any defence. It was practically without any resistance that Mahmud defiled the temple, broke the idol and carried away the wealth from it. Next he wanted to proceed towards Delhi, but his followers insisted on the conquest of Punjab first and establishment of a military base there before marching towards Delhi. Mahmud saw the logic of the argument and stopped.

In his twelfth expedition Mahmud marched against the sacred city of Mathura. There were magnificent temples within the city and the largest of them stood at the centre. "The Sultan was very much struck by its grandeur. In his estimate it cost not less than 100,000,000 red dinars and even the most skilful of masons must have taken 200 years to complete it. Among the large number of idols in the temples, five were made of pure gold, the eyes of one of them were laid with two rubies worth 100,000 dinars, and another had a sapphire of a very heavy weight. All these five idols yielded gold weighing 98,300 miskals." The city is said to have been within the kingdom of the raja of Delhi. Mahmud pillaged the city for twenty days. All the idols were deliberately broken into pieces and the buildings reduced to ashes.

From Mathura Mahmud marched to Kanauj. On his approach Rajyapal, the king of the Pratihara dynasty fled to the other side of the Ganges, and a large number of citizens deserted the city. In absence of any resistance all the seven forts easily fell into the hands of Mahmud. Under the orders of Mahmud the inhabitants were put to sword and the idols of the temples were broken, and the city was plundered. Rajyapal submitted to Mahmud.

The shameful surrender of Rajyapal to Mahmud without a fight touched the conscience of some of the notable Hindu rajas, the most notable of whom was Chandela raja Vidyadhara, also known as Ganda of Bundelkhand. He organised a league of the neighbouring Hindu rajas to chastise Rajyapal, king of Kanauj. They attacked his kingdom and defeated and killed him. Rajyapal's son Trilochanpal was placed by the neighbouring rajas on the throne of Kanauj. Mahmud considered Rajyapal as his vassal and he marched against the Chandela king Vidyadhara to punish him for attacking Kanauj and killing Rajyapal. Vidyadhara proceeded with a large army to oppose Mahmud, and Trilochanpal also joined him. In the first encounter with Trilochanpal the latter was defeated. Trilochanpal fled and tried to join Vidyadhara but on his way he was killed by some Hindus. Vidyadhara finding that it would be impossible to resist Mahmud fled in the darkness of night. Mahmud easily defeated the army of Vidyadhara and took away 580 elephants and a booty of immense wealth. Next years (1021-22) Mahmud proceeded an expedition against Vidyadhara and on his way attacked the fort of Gwalior then in possession of Kachchapaghata Chief Kirttiraja, who after valiantly defending the fort for four days sued for peace. Mahmud received 35 elephants and some valuable presents from Kirttiraja and proceeded towards Kalinjar fort which he besieged. The siege continued for a long time when Vidyadhara sent an emissary to Mahmud suing for peace. He offered 300 elephants and other valuable presents for raising the siege. Mahmud was very much pleased at the compliments paid by Vidyadhara to him and he reciprocated his friendly gesture by bestowing on the Chandela king the government of 15 fortresses and returned to Ghazni. This episode is mentioned both by Ferishta and Nizam-ud-din.

The most important expedition of Sultan Mahmud was that against the famous temple of Somnath (1024) in Kathiawar. It was on the sea shore of Kathiawar containing a **Siva linga.** Mahmud marched from Ghazni for Kathiawar with 30,000 cavalry and a multitude of volunteers. He first reached Ajmer on his way towards Multan and after having plundered the city of Ajmer moved towards Gujarat and in 1025 reached near the temple of Somnath with his huge cavalary and volunteers. "The Hindus who assembled on the rampart of the port, were passing their time in merry-making, fondly believing that Somnath had drawn the Muslims there only to annihilate them for the sins they had committed in demolishing idols elsewhere. Their morals were high even though their leader had fled away in cowardice with his family to a neighbouring island." The next day the Sultan began his assault driving away the Hindus from the rampart by volleys of arrows. But before the Muslims could consolidate their position they were violently attacked by the Hindus who came out of the temple after prayer for strength and courage. The Muslims were unable to withstand the onslaught and were forced to retreat from the city. They returned next day with great determination and renewed operation with greater intensity and the defence of the Hindus was of no avail. Bands of Hindus came in succession to defend the gate of the temple and 50,000 Hindus sacrificed their lives in this attempt. Mahmud entered the temple broke the **Siva linga** and took possession of 20,000,000 dirhams worth of wealth from the temple. The fragments of the **Siva linga** were carried to Ghazni where they were used to build the steps at the gate of the Jami mosque. The king of Anhilwara fought for the defence of the temple of Somnath. Mahmud therefore attacked Anhilwara and pillaged the capital. But on his way to Ghazni, Mahmud suffered considerable loss due to Jat attacks. To take revenge against the Jats Mahmud proceeded on his seventeeth expedition against India in 1027. The Jats fought bravely against Mahmud but was ultimately defeated. Mahmud then returned to Ghazni where he died after three years in 1030.

Character of Sultan Mahmud's Invasions : Occupation of India on a permanent basis was not the aim of Sultan Mahmud's Indian expeditions. And even "an occupation of India was beyond the means of the forces of Ghazni". In so far as India is concerned Sultan Mahmud was not a ruler, and in fact, he did not want to be so. His annexation of Punjab was prompted by strategic reasons. His repeated entry into India, his line of communication etc. could only be facilitated by his annexation of Punjab. Barring this area he had no design on any other part of India for a permanent occupation. The political disunity of Northern India which was an invitation and cause of success to Sultan Mahmud's expeditions, the same political division also stood in the way of his contemplating any occupation of India. For victory in one war would mean conquest of a small part of the country, and as such the country could only be occupied in piecemeal by being victorious in numerous wars. At least the forces of Ghazni would not be best suited for the purpose. The intrepid Rajput clans could not be perhaps defeated by the Sultan.

Yet it will be a mistake to overlook the contribution made by Sultan Mahmud in founding, however, in an initial manner the Turkish Power in India. He at least had paved the way and left the direction for the establishment of the future Delhi Sultanate.

What then was the real character of Sultan Mahmud's invasions? According to Dr. Smith, Sultan Mahmud was the leader of the fanatical, ruthless Turks of the time. To put to sword the idolators was as much the religious duty of Mahmud and his followers as the pleasure of doing so. Mahmud's real aim in leading repeated expeditions against India was to satisfy his insatiable lust for Indian wealth, his craze for killing the Hindus and defiling and destroying their temples. The glory of victory or motive of proselytising were not his purpose. thus we do not notice any liberal attitude in him that characterises the conduct of a military leader that seeks glory of victory. Mahmud's taking away the necklace of enormous value worn by Jaipal as a part of his plunder, and his destruction of the temple at the centre of Mathura which was the best specimen of architectural skill of ages, in the words of Sultan himself, must have had taken 200 years to construct, were examples of his narrow, selfish and bigoted religious policy. Prof. Habib, however, does not call Mahmud a fanatic. According to him his expeditions were motivated not by religion but by love of plunder.

Factors Leading to Sultan Mahmud's Success : Certain special factors had contributed to the success of Sultan Mahmud's expeditions against India. Mahmud was a brave soldier and a great general with extraordinary personal prowess and intrepidity. An excellent judge of human character, he knew how best to infuse a spirit of unity in his otherwise non-homogeneous force, and to weld it into a powerful unit. His troops comprised Afghans, Turks, Arabs and even Hindus. When his military genius was combined with his high ambition, love of plunder and religious fanaticism, he became an irresistable force. His followers were also lured by the prospect of plunder and killing of idolaters.

As Lane Poole has rightly pointed out, the internal division of India had proved the undoing of India again and again and sapped the power of mere numbers "which alone could enable the men of the warm plains to stand against the hardy mountain tribes and the relentless horsemen of the Central Asian Steppes. To the race and climate, was the added zeal of the Muslim and the greed of the robber. The mountaineers were poor as they were brave, and covetous as they were devout." Although weaker compared to the Turks and other mountainous tribes, yet their number would have decided the issue in their favour. But it was lack of unity on the part of the Indians that made them vulnerable against comparatively small number of the invaders.

In war strategy as well, the Indians were no match for the invading forces. The traditional system of using elephants in battle fields was often the cause of India's undoing. The fleeing of Anandapal's elephant at the moment of victory is an instance in point. Further, the Indian side could not match the shock tactics of the cavalry of Sultan Mahmud.

Character and Estimate of Sultan Mahmud : From court panegyrists and the historians it is possible to draw a fairly complete sketch of the character of Sultan Mahmud. In the writings of the Muslim historians there is often much exaggeration of the personal qualities of the character of the Sultan, but when the writings of all the different writers are compared, it is possible to come to a dispassionate conclusion about his character and achievements. Mahmud was an intelligent, highly religious minded, intrepid soldier and a capable general with a great love for art and literature. Muslim historians regard him as one of the greatest champions of Islam. Speaking generally, he was fair-minded and judicious. But how far his better qualities of character had been overclouded by his raids and masscares and his desire to propagate his faith remains uncertain, for after all Mahmud's character was very complex and a mixture of contradictory traits. His love of religion at times degenerated into blind bigotry, and his love of wealth into greed. Mahmud's court panegyrist Ibn-ul-Athir has mentioned several instances of Mahmud's greed for wealth. In his destruction of Hindu temples in India and his ruthless oppression of different Muslim sects were prompted both by his blind bigotry and greed for wealth. He was "fickle and uncertain in temper and more notable as an irresistible conqueror than as a faithful friend and magnanimous foe." But there is no doubt that he was a brave soldier and a great general.

Mahmud was a clutured patron of art and scholarship. He himself was a poet and a scholar of some skill. According to a writer of repute he "was a just sovereign, a lover of learning, a man of generous nature and a pure faith." He was a Sunni Muslim punctilious in the observance of religious rites of his faith. According to Prof. Habib, Mahmud was not a fanatic and his expeditions against India were not motivated by religious fanaticism but love of plunder. But it may be pointed out that Islam does not sanction the type of vandalism and atrocities committed by Sultan Mahmud in India.

In estimating the achievements of Mahmud, writers often refer to the success of his expedition into India, Persia and Central Asia. These were certainly instances of his rare military genius. But whereas there were many other conquerors in history who led expeditions for spreading their own faith, seldom any one of them had carried on plunder on a scale that Mahmud had carried on in India. For Mahmud the aim was both to put the idolater to sword and to defile and pillage the Hindu temples. At times he could be bought off by a handsome booty. This actually happened when he proceeded against the Chandela king Vidyadhar of Ganda. Mahmud was more concerned with plunder than with the honour of victory. He is said to have been a lover of art, but he did not hesitate to play the part of a wanton destroyer of art so far as India was concerned. It was under his order the most beautiful temple at Mathura was razed to the ground, a temple which was a specimen of excellent art and architecture of contemporary India and the Sultan himself said that it must have had taken the very best of masons at least 200 years to construct the temple.

From the Indian point of view Mahmud was no ruler. As Dr. Smith observes in so far as India was concerned Mahmud was a bandit operating on a large scale. In his own capital Sultan Mahmud maintained a court which was graced by Ferdausi, the author of **Shah-nama,** philosopher Farabi, historian Utbi, story writer Baihaki, poets Ansari, Nunikiri, Dakiki, Ujari, Falruki, Asauzi, Asaditusi, etc. Al Biruni was also in his court for some time. Mahmud established a University in Ghazni. There were 400 contemporary poets who were the students of the University; men of letters regarded Uzari as their preceptor. He also established a library in the university and a museum. He spent the wealth that he carried away from India for the beautification of Ghazni. In Ghazni the Sultan was a patron of art and literature. Due to his patronage Ghazni became one of the most beautiful cities of the East. Yet it was under his orders that the beautiful temple of Mathura was razed to the ground. This kind of expression of love for art and architecture is rarely to be met with. From this, some historians have come to the conclusion that his love of art and literature was more a narrow, selfish show rather than any true or genuine love for art or literature. He himself was illiterate. In his patronage of men of letters he showed his selfishness. He got Ferdausi to write **Shah-nama** promising to pay his sixty thousand gold coins, but after the work was completed he gave Ferdausi sixty thousand silver coins instead.

Lastly, no permanent institution, no nation building is associated with his name. Lane Poole observes that "He left his dominions so ill-knitted together that they began to fall asunder as soon as he was no longer alive to guard them by his vigilant activity."

Yet, it cannot be denied that Sultan Mahmud was a monarch of outstanding ability although not of character. Prof Habib's remark may be mentioned in this connection. He calls him a pre-eminent ruler among his contemporaries due to his abilities and not due to his character. In so far as India is concerned, he was a plunderer, a blind bigot, and perpetrator of vandalism.

Successors of Sultan Mahmud : On the death of Mahmud in 1030 the contest between his two sons Masud and Muhammad was but a repetition of the contest between Mahmud and his brother Ismail. Mahmud in his will left the throne to his son Muhammad who was at Hamdan at the time of the death of his father. As he proceeded towards Ghazni a party of nobles in deference to the will of Mahmud acknowledged Muhammad as their ruler. But soon Masud marched towards Ghazni and he was supported by a section of the nobles. Finding Muhammad's cause lost, those who had supported him earlier changed side and Muhammad was captured and blinded and taken to Balkh which now became the new capital of Masud. Masud summoned the Turkish officer who was placed in charge of Punjab by his father Sultan Mahmud to answer the charges of oppression and extortion of the Indian subjects and retaining with treasonable intent a large part of the revenue. The Turkish officer named Ariyaruq evaded the summons but at a moment when he was drunk, he was persuaded to meet the Sultan at Balkh. Masud as a preliminary to investigation got him arrested, his quarters were broken open and all treasures and belongings, accounts, etc. were seized and Ariyaruq was sent to Ghur where he was put to death. Masud now entered Ghazni and compelled all nobles to disgorge the treasures that had been distributed among them by his brother Muhammad which led to much resentment against him. There was disturbance in Persia and a new governor was sent there. In Punjab no new governor had yet been appointed and the whole of Punjab was in confusion. Niyaltigin, Masud's father's treasurer was sent to Punjab as governor keeping his son a hostage at Ghazni as Niyaltigin was of doubtful loyalty. Niyaltigin quarrelled with Abul Hasan, the **Qazi** and disregarding latter's sane consel led an expedition against Benares in 1033 and carried away large booty in wealth. But Musud soon began to receive news of Niyaltigin's attempts at making himself independent. Masud sent his Hindu Minister Tilak to put him down. In the contest Niyaltigin was killed. Masud now appointed his own son Maudud as governor of Punjab and in 1037 personally came to India and led an expedition against Hansi in 1039, stormed it, massacred many innocent people and enslaved many others, and returned to Ghazni. In the next year he was defeated by the Seljuq Turks and he was compelled to take refuge in Lahore. But on the way he was imprisoned by his own followers who made his brother Muhammad whom he had blinded, as their ruler who as next ruler of Ghazni defeated and killed the governor of Lahore and occupied it. In 1044 Hansi, Thaneswar, and Kangra were wrested from the Ghaznavids by Mahipala, the raja of Delhi. On the death of Maudud there was a long spell of palace intrigues. At Ghazni as well, weaklings came upon the throne for short durations only. By the middle of the twelfth century (1160) Punjab was the only province that remained in the hands of the Ghaznavids.

REFERENCES

The Struggle for Empire : R. C. Majumdar, A. D. Pusalkar, A. K. Majumdar

The Cambridge History of India, Vol. VI

The Sultanate of Delhi : A. L. Srivastava

The Oxford History of India : V. A. Smith

A Comprehensive History of India, Vol. V, *Delhi Sultanate*

An Advanced History of India : Majumdar, Raychaudhuri & Datta

History of India as Told by Her Own Historians, Vol. II

Sultan Mahmud of Ghazni : Muhammad Habib

Medieval India Under Mohamedan Rule : Lane Poole

History of Medieval India : Iswari Prasad

3 Rise of the Muslim Power in India and the Sultanate of Delhi

DYNASTY OF GHUR

Systematic Muslim conquest of India did not begin until the last quarter of the twelfth century, if the frontier provinces of Kabul, Punjab and Sind be kept out of consideration. The first systematic attack began under the chieftain of the obscure principality of Ghur, a mountainous country hidden between Ghazni and Herat. In the tenth century, Ghur was an independent principality but was reduced to vassalage by Sultan Mahmud in 1009. The fortune of the house was made by quarrel with the successors of Sultan Mahmud of Ghazni one of whom named Bahram executed two princes of Ghur. Ala-ud-din Hussain took revenge by sacking Ghazni and putting the city to flames for seven days and nights during which "plunder devastation, and slaughter were continuous. Every man that was found was slain and all women and children were made prisoners". All the palaces of Ghazni were destroyed only the tombs of Sultan Mahmud and two of his relatives were spared. Shortly afterwards Khusru Shah, son of Bahram had to leave Ghazni and take refuge in Punjab due to an incursion by the Ghuzz Turkmans (1160). It was in 1173 that Ghazni was wrested from the Turkmans by Sultan Ghiyas-ud-din of Ghur who made over the territory with its dependencies including Kabul to his brother Muhammad Ghuri.

MUIZZ-UD-DIN MUHAMMAD GHURI

Shihabuddin Ghuri, who later assumed the name Muizz-ud-din Muhammad Ghuri made his early expeditions through the Gomal Pass, west of Dera Ismail Khan and not through Khyber Pass as the former was a shorter route. Multan and Uch which first fell on his way were wrested from the Carmathians in 1175. By 1182 he compelled the Chief of Sumana, of lower Sind to acknowledge his suzerainty. He now attempted to cross the desert into Gujarat acting against the geography of the area and forgetting the experience of Sultan Mahmud. Following the tradition that some Turkish warriors had frequently raided the Rajput kingdoms from that quarter in the twelfth century, but forgetting that all the attacks had been repulsed by the Gujarat rulers, Muhammad Ghuri crossed the desert and reached the foot of Mt. Abu in 1178 with an exhausted and famished army. Mulraja II, the Chalukya king of Gujarat beat off the Turkish army with great slaughter. Muhammad luckily escaped with life. Now the only other route to enter India was through Punjab which he wrested from the Ghaznavids. Now an opportunity offered itself. Chakradeo, ruler of Jammu invited Muhammad for help against Khusrav Malik, the Ghaznavid ruler who was assisting the rebel Khokar tribe against the king of Jammu. Muhammad accordingly proceeded against India and took Peshwar in 1178, and Sialkot in 1185 and the year following captured Lahore by treachery, from Khusrav Malik, the last of the Ghaznavids. The occupation of the whole of Punjab brought the border of the kingdom of Ghur to that of the Chahamanas or Chauhanas. Now Muhammad Ghuri made a bid to Conquer Hindustan. He marched with his well organised army from Ghazni and reached Tabarhinda, identified with Sirhind, which was within the kingdom of Chahamana king Prithviraja. Muhammad's advance as far as Sirhind struck terror into the minds of the feudatories of the Chahamanas and Chandraraja son of Govindaraja, governor of Delhi along with other chiefs came to Prithviraja reporting to him that "Shihab-ud-din had pillaged and burnt most of their cities, defiled their women, and reduced them altogether to a miserable plight. There is scarcely a mountain-pent valley in the country but is filled to suffocation with Rajputs who have fled thither for protection from his tyranny. The noblest of the Rajput families have disappeared before him and he has now established his capital at Multan." Prithviraja was very much excited to hear the tale of owe and readily agreed to render all help. He accompanied by Govindaraja of Delhi and many other Indian princes marched with 200,000 horses, and 3,000 elephants to punish Muizz-ud-din Muhammad Ghuri. The two sides met at Tarain. 14 miles from Thaneswar in 1190-91. When the battle was in progress the two flanks of Muhammad's army broke and fled. Muhammad fought for some time more but Muhammad was severely wounded and was about to fall from his horse but was saved by the timely support given by one of his valiant warriors who took him away from the field. The remainder of his army was at once in disarray and easily overpowered by the Chahamanas. According to **Hammira Mahakavya** Prithviraja took Muhammad Ghuri captive in this battle but released him and allowed him to return to Multan. This seems to be an exaggerated account.

Having defeated Muizz-ud-din Prithviraja pushed ahead towards Tabarhinda, i.e. Bhatinda and besieged the fort. Malik Ziya-ud-din defended the fort for 13 months and then capitulated and Prithviraja took possession of it and thus Chahamana supremacy was reestablished in Punjab.

From Minhaj and Ferishta we know that Muizz-ud-din in order to avenge himself of the disgrace of the defeat at the hands of Prithviraja, organised after strenuous labour an army of one hundred and twenty thousand men and took the road to Hindustan. He came to Lahore via Peshwar and Multan, wherefrom he sent Qawamul Mulk Ruknuddin Hamza to Prithviraja to demand his submission. Muhammad Ghuri's proposal to Prithviraja was that the latter should embrace Islam and acknowledge Muhamad's supremacy to avoid the dreadful consequence of war. Prithviraja treated the proposal with the contempt it deserved and rallied his forces which consisted of 300,000 horses, 3000 elephants and a large number of infantry. Many rajas helped him and one hundred fifty chiefs joined him with the determination either to defeat the Muslims or to die fighting in the battle field. Ferishta gives some details of the incidents preceding the conflict : "Inspired by their first victory with arrogance and pride, they (the rais) sent a haughty letter to Sultan : 'The strength and number of our army will be soon known to you, and reinforcements are coming to us from all parts of Hindustan. Be merciful to yourself, at least to the misguided men you have brought hither. If you repent your venture and go back, we swear by our idols that we will not harass your retreat, otherwise we will attack and crush you tomorrow with more than three hundred thousand horsemen archers beyond all computation and an army which the field of imagination is not wide enough to contain." Prithviraja's reply gave Muhammad an opportunity for playing a trick. He replied that he could not retreat without the permission of his brother in this matter. He, however, agreed to a truce till such time that he received instruction from his brother. The Chahamana army relying on the Sultan's assurances began to bide their time at night in merry-making. Muhammad Ghuri instructed some of his men to keep light in the camp burning giving an impression to the Chahamana army that the Muslim army was in the camp, and ordered the army to attack the Chahamanas from the rear. But Prithviraja although surprised by the army of Muhammad Ghuri beat off the attack with his cavalry. Muhammad began to attack the Chahamana army in small batches repeatedly which were beaten back. In this way when the Chahamana army had became exhausted Muhammad attacked them with the bulk of his army and easily overpowered them. One lakh Hindu soldiers lost their lives in the battlefield. The battle took place in the same place, i.e. Tarain, in 1192, where in the previous year Muhammad Ghuri was completely defeated by Prithviraja. In utter dejection Prithviraja alighted from his elephant and mounted a horse and attempted to escape from the battlefield but was captured near the town of Sarasuti. According to Minhaj he was at once executed but according to Hasan Nizami he was taken to Ajmer and allowed to rule as a vassal of Muizz-ud-din Muhammad Ghuri but was executed on being found guilty of treason.

After his great victory at the Second battle of Tarain, 1192, Muizz-ud-din Muhammad Ghuri conquered Delhi and allowed the Hindu chief to rule over it as his vassal as in Ajmer. He then occupied and garrisoned the military outposts of Hansi, Kuhram, Sarasuti and Sirhind. After these victories he returned to Ghazni leaving his trusted general Malik Qutb-ud-din Aibak with an army at Indarpat, ten miles from Delhi, in charge of his Indian conquests.

Significance of the Second Battle of Tarain (1192) : The second battle of Tarain was one of the decisive battles of India and it ensured the success of Muhammad Ghuri against Hindustan. It was a major disaster for the Rajputs. The Rajput political prestige in general, and the Chauhana ascendancy in particular suffered a serious setback. The Chauhana kingdom now lay at the feet of the invader. The battle of Tarain was a concerted action on the part of a very large number of the Rajput princes, and their defeat in the battle naturally had repercussions which were felt on a very extensive scale and demoralisation became widespread. Immediately following the victory at Tarain, Hansi, Kuhram, Sarasuti etc. which were of strategic importance were conquered and in all the conquered places Hindu temples were destroyed and mosques were erected. In accordance with the Muslim practice Islam was installed everywhere as the state religion. At Ajmer temples of Hindu idols were destroyed and the famous college established by the Chauhana ruler Vigraharaj was converted into a mosque. Demoralisation of the Hindus was most widespread.

Post-Tarain Expansion by Qutb-ud-din Aibak : On Muizz-ud-din's return to Ghazni, there was a serious rising in Ajmer in an attempt to drive away the Turks. Jatwan, a Hindu chief attacked Hansi. Aibak hastened to Hansi relieved the garrison there and defeated and killed the rebel chief. He then captured Bulandshahr from the Dor Rajputs by treachery. While Chandrasena, the Dor chief was putting up a brave fight with Aibak, one of his close relations Ajaipal who was secretly bribed by Qutb-ud-din Aibak fought against Chandrasena in support of Aibak which brought about the ruin of the Dor chief. Next, Qutb-ud-din captured Meerut where he set up a Turkish garrison. He then occupied Delhi on the pretext that the Tomara ruler who was a vassal of Muizz-ud-din Muhammad Ghuri harboured hostile design against the Turkish army stationed at Delhi. After occupying Delhi, Qutb-ud-din Aibak made it his capital (1193). Aibak had already occupied and garrisoned the mighty fort of Ranthambhor. But Hariraja, Brother of Prithviraja recovered both Ajmer and Ranthambhor. As Aibak marched against Hariraja the latter withdrew, but Aibak had to leave Hariraja unsubdued as the disposed chief of Delhi again revolted and Aibak had to hurry back to Delhi. Amidst these confusing pre-occupations Aibak was called away by his master to Ghazni to help him against Khwarazmian menace. The absence of Aibak was not taken advantage of by the Indian rulers by failing to make any effective combination against the foreigners in order to drive them out. The splendid opportunity was thus missed. There were only stray risings and revolts which were easily put down. Soon after Aibak returned from Ghazni and occupied Doab as far as Kol, i.e. Aligarh, where he set up a garrison. Hardly he had completed his work at Kol, Muizz-ud-din Muhammad Ghuri arrived in India with the intention to overthrow the Gahdavala power. After recruiting a strong army at Delhi he proceeded towards Kanauj and Banaras. A tough battle was fought at Chandwar but ultimately Muizz-ud-din came out victorious. Though as a result of the victory the whole of Gahdavala kingdom could not be brought under control, it provided an opportunity for establishing military stations at many places like Banaras, Asni etc. There were important centres, such as Kanauj which could not be annexed till 1198-99.

In 1195-96 Muizz-ud-din again came to India and attacked Bayana. The ruler was compelled to surrender. Thankar and Vijayamandigarh were occupied by Muizz-ud-din and put under Baha-ud-din Tughril. Next he marched towards Gwalior and the Allakhanapala, the ruler, acknowledged his suzerainty.

The Rajputs were not reconciled to the foreign rule and in 1196, the Mers and the Chauhanas (or Chahamanas) invited the Chalukya ruler of Anhilwara to make a concerted effort to expel the turks. They besieged the Turkish garrison at Ajmer. Aibak rushed to the assistance of the Turkish garrison at Ajmer but was himself encircled by the Rajputs and their Allics. Luckily at that point of time a reinforcement arrived from Ghazni and the Rajputs were compelled to raise the siege. Aibak then proceeded against the Chalukya king of Anhilwara and defeated him (Bhim II). Aibak followed up his success by plundering Anhilwara. He appointed a Turkish officer as governor of Anhilwara. It seems this claim was not correct, for the Chalukya kingdom including Abu was under its legitimate ruler till 1240. It is possible that the governor appointed, if at all, must have fled soon after. The next few years were utilised by Aibak in undertaking a number of petty expeditions. He wrested Badaun from the Rashtrakuta Rajputs in 1197-98. Then Banaras was reoccupied by him as it had been lost after its first conquest. In 1197 Aibak reoccupied Kanauj and Chandawar. One important Rajput family still was ruling as an independent house at Bundelkhand. It was the Chandela family of the Rajputs. In 1202-03 Qutb-ud-din invaded Kalinjar, the military capital of the Chandela king Paramardi Deva. The Chandelas fought valiantly but were compelled due to the pressure of numerical strength of the enemies to take shelter within the fort which was now besieged by Qutb-ud-din Aibak. The siege continued for a long time and Paramardi Deva was on the point of accepting the suzerainty of Qutb-ud-din, but before any agreement to that effect could be signed he died. Ajaydeva, his minister withdrew the offer and carried on resistance. Finding the strength of the fort, Qutb-ud-din diverted the course of the stream that supplied water to the fort. The fort went without water and was thus compelled to capitulate. The Rajputs within the fort were allowed to evacuate Kalinjar. Thus Kalinjar, Mahoba and Khajuraho were occupied by the Turks and formed into a military division.

Conquest of Bihar and Bengal : Ikhtiyar-ud-din Muhammad bin Bakhtiyar Khalji was one of the subordinate commanders under Qutb-ud-din Aibak. He was as ambitious as able. But he could not rise in the service in the army commensurate with his ability and ambition. His ungainly looks ugly build of the body stood in the way of his promotion both at Ghazni and Delhi. But with a band of reckless fighters he carried on frequent raids in the province of Bihar, east of Karmnasa river. In one of these expeditions he pushed on as far as Uddandapuri Vihara which he plundered and destroyed. Uddandapuri was a university town and the inhabitants who were Buddhist monks mostly, were put to sword and the town was occupied. The library of Uddandapuri Vihara in all probability was destroyed. Ikhtiyar-ud-din followed up his success by occupying Vikramsila and Nalanda, two other university towns and by constructing a fortress at Uddandapuri (1202-03).

Emboldened by his success Ikhtiyar-ud-din Muhammad bin Bakhtiyar proceeded to conquer Bengal which was then under Lakshmana Sen of the Sena dynasty. According to Minhaj, the Rai (Lakshmana Sena) had been on the throne for eighty years and had made extremely favourable impression on the minds of the people by his justice and generosity. When Ikhtiyar-ud-din was carrying on frequent raids in Bihar, astrologers advised the Rai to abandon the territory to escape the molestation of the Turks. The Brahmanas and inhabitants of the capital city of Nadia left for other cities of Bengal and Assam. But the Rai refusing to accept the advice of a cowardly retreat stayed on. From epigraphic evidence we come to know that in 1203 he performed a great sacrifice called **Aindri Mahasanti** to propitiate the gods for help for averting the impending catastrophe.

In 1204 Ikhtiyar-ud-din Bakhtiyar Khalji suddenly appeared before the city of Nadia. According to Minhaj not more than 18 horsemen could keep pace with Bakhtiyar and the main army followed slowly. Reaching the gate of the city Bakhtiyar proceeded onward "in such a manner that the people of the place imagined that his party were merchants and had brought horses for sale." When he reached the entrance of the palace he drew his sword and started the onslaught. The Rai was then at his midday meal. Bakhtiyar dashed forward through the gateway and the Rai fled barefooted through the backdoor, "the whole of his treasures, his wives and other females, his domestics and servants and his particular attendants were seized". The Rai ruled from Sonargaon for some years over the small remnants of his country.

Nadia was not occupied permanently, as it was not considered suitable as a seat of the government. He selected Lakshanauti as his military base which was nearer to his base in Bihar. Lakshanauti i.e. Lakshanavati was the northern capital of the Senas on the Ganges near the site of Gaur in the Malda district.

Bakhtiyar's phenomenal success in Bengal had whetted his ambition to conquer even Tibet. It is inexplicable why Bakhtiyar Khalji chose to march against Tibet leaving the Hindu principalities within his easy reach. A Koch guide led Bakhtiyar's large army along the Brahmaputra and reaching the spot where the army was to cross the river for the hills the guide took leave. At this point of time Bakhtiyar received a communication from the king of Kamrupa advising him to wait till the following year when he offered to reinforce his army. But Bakhtiyar paid no heed to the advice and reached Tibet where he met with tough resistance and ultimately he had to beat an ignominous retreat losing the bulk of his forces. When he reached the bridge on the Brahmaputra he found that the Assamese army had demolished it. Bakhtiyar was forced to take shelter in a neighbouring temple, but being besieged there fell into the river either to ford or swim across with the remnant of his forces. Many of his men were washed away by current and Bakhtiyar reached the shore with hardly a hundred followers and went back to Devakot. Disaster and disappointed told upon his health and he fell sick and rapidly sank until merciful knife of Ali Mardan, one of his lieutenants relieved him from his agony.

LAST INDIAN CAMPAIGN OF MUIZZ-UD-DIN MUHAMMAD GHURI AND HIS ASSASSINATION

Muizz-ud-din was called back to Ghazni to meet the menace of Khvarazamian house of Central Asia. Instigated by the Caliph of Bagdad and taking advantage of a civil war Khvarazam, the Ghuris had occupied Khurasan, and also captured Nishapur. Tus and Merve in 1201. But soon Ala-ud-din of the house of Khvarazam recovered these places from the Ghuris including even Herat (1201). In 1202 Ghiyas-ud-din elder brother of Muizz-ud-din died and the latter ascended the throne of Ghur. But Hostilities with the house of Khvarazam continued and when Muizz-ud-din returned from his last campaign in India he suffered such a defeat at their hands at Andkhui in 1205 that his reputation and prestige in India received a severe blow.

The Khokars and other tribes in India rose in rebellion and defeated the governor of Multan, plundered Lahore and closed the road link between Lahore and Ghazni. Qutb-ud-din was ordered by Muizz-ud-din to quell the rebellion with a heavy hand but realising that the situation demanded his presence left Ghazni for India on October 20, 1206. Within a short time he defeated the Khokars in a contest between the Jhelum and Chenab rivers. But for the last moment arrival of Qutb-ud-din Aibak with reinforcement, the Khokars would have been victorious. The defeated Khokars were treated with ferocious cruelty. Muizz-ud-din then reached Lahore (Feb, 25, 1206) and after having settled the affairs there, proceeded towards Ghazni, but was stabbed to death in his tent on the bank of the river Sindhu on March 15, 1206. The Ghurid empire did not survive long after him. His nephew and successor Mahmud had to acknowledge the Shah of Khavarazam as his suzerain and rule over the Ghazni dominions a major part of which had passed under the sway of the Khvarazamians. For a short time Taj-ud-din Yildiz, a slave of Muizz-ud-din somehow retained his hold on Ghazni but with his expulsion in 1215 the Ghuri empire in Central Asia came to an end and the Shah of Khvarazam brought the lords of Ghazni under his control. The Indian conquests of Ghuri, however, proved stable. The Indian conquests were placed under the charge of a trusted slave of Muizz-ud-din when the latter left for Ghazni.

CAUSES OF THE COLLAPSE OF THE HINDUS AGAINST THE TURKS

The astounding rapidity with which the Turks first under Mahmud of Ghazni early in the eleventh century then under Muizz-ud-din Muhammad Ghuri at the end of the twelfth century had defeated the Hindu rulers of Northern India brought about an almost complete collapse of Northern India, is rather puzzling to the students of Indian history. It is not easy to explain how within an incredibly short time the invaders gained such a success with power and resources which were hardly equal to those of some of the bigger Hindu states not to speak of their combined strength. Now what were the real causes behind the great political catastrophe that overwhelmed India ? Various speculations have been made as to the real cause of the collapse of the Hindu powers of Northern India in the hands of the Turks.

According to Dr. Smith, Lane Poole, Elphinstone and others, the defeat of the Indians was due to superiority of the Turks who came from the cold, bracing climate of the north, were mainly consumers of meat and used to warfare. This view is rather superficial and does not stand the test of logic. Hindu warriors had fought in battlefields within and without India, under Indian and foreign commands, and in courage and determination they were in no way inferior to the Turks. Cold country and nonvegetarian food made the Turks better painstaking as warriors than the tropical, vegetarian Indians of the Northern India is an argument that does not stand scientific test. It is equally unwarranted to attribute the defeat of the Hindus to social and religious peculiarities of the Hindus."...any solution that we may offer at the present state of our knowledge cannot claim any scientific basis, far less, finality in character".

The causes of the failure of the Hindus may, however, be enumerated as follows : (i) The political disunity was primarily responsible for the undoing of the Hindus. "The false ideals of Kshatriya chivalary made the Rajput princes paralyse one another by perpetual internecine conflicts, and what was more fatal, made them oblivious of a broad national vision and patriotic sentiment." At a time when the country was threatened by grave peril of foreign invasion the rulers of the land devoted the best of their energies in mutual fighting. Temples were built by spending enormous wealth but these the Hindu rulers proved unable to protect. Again the temples were endowed with fabulous wealth which instead of being spent for organising defence of the temples was allowed to lure the foreigners to plunder them.

The Muslim historians like Hasan Nizami, Minhaj-us-Siraj, Fakr-i-Mudabbir are also by and large unhelpful to determine the causes of the Muslim success and the Hindu defeat. They mentioned that "Almighty God gave victory to Islam". Fakr-i-Mudabbir, however, refers to the strength of the Turkish and the weakness of the Indian armies from the military point of view.

Sir Jadunath refers to three characteristic virtues that Islam gave to its followers which no other religion has inspired so successfully. These were : (i) Complete equality, and social solidarity as regard legal status and religious privileges thus sweeping away all distinctions of caste and race and the sect was knit together like the members of one vast family of brothers. This imparted to natural soldiers like the Arabs, Berbers, Pathans and Turks, a wonderful military efficiency. (ii) Fatalism, springing from an absolute reliance on God and belief that what Allah wills must triumph over every human effort, bread contempt of death in fighting. (iii) Freedom from drunkenness. Wine drinking is a sin according to the **Quran** on the other hand wine drinking was the ruin of the Rajputs, Marathas and other Hindu soldiers which made them incapable of farsighted military planning, conducting surprises and guarding their own camps with proper precaution.

According to Prof. Nizami the real cause of the defeat of the Indians lay in their social system and invidious caste distinction, which made the whole military organisation weak and useless. Caste distinctions killed the spirit of unity, social or political. Exclusiveness in matters of religion among the high-caste Hindus made the bulk of the people unresponsive to any patriotic feeling when faced with the Ghurid invaders. "They watched with sullen indifference the fate of the Indian governing classes. The towns consequently, fell like ripe fruits. Only the forts put up some resistance, but they became helpless when the enemy controlled the countryside." These observation of Prof. Habib, to say the least, is over-playing the social and religious causes of the defeats of the Hindus, although it may be conceded that caste-system largely reduced the military efficiency of the Hindus.

More important causes of the failure of the Hindu resistance against the Turks were (i) the Indian armies did not keep themselves abrest of the progress of the art of warefare in Central Asia. The feudal levies from which the bulk of the Indian armies were built up gave them a heterogeneous character which did not conduce to unity of action. (ii) The Indian armies did not possess the mobility of the Turkish cavalry. "It was the age of horse" and a well equipped cavalry with tremendous mobility as the Turkish invaders brought with them could not be matched by the traditional army organisation of the Indians. Sir Jadunath remarks : "The arms and horses of these trans-border invaders gave them indisputable military superiority over the Indians. Their provisions were also carried by fast trotting camels which required no fodder for themselves but fed on the roots and leaves of the wayside, while the Banjara pack-oxen of the Hindu commissariat were slow and burdensome". (iii) The elephants which formed an important part of the Indian army organisation often caused the undoing of the Indian armies. (iv) According R. C. Smail one of the important tactical characteristics of the Turks was their effective archery. They could use the bow from the saddle and while moving which gave an added advantage and superiority to the Turkish cavalry over the Rajput armies.

Added to the above causes were, first, the Hindu rajas did not react to the onslaught that had begun with the Arabs. It assumed formidable proportions under the lead of Sultan

Mahmud. The next century and a half witnessed cessation of the onslaught barring some minor, irregular raids. The Hindu rajas did not use this interval in reorganising their armies during this interval although they had foretaste of what might happen in the future. Even after the first battle of Tarain in 1191, Prithviraja had not taken any adequate measure to prevent any possible resumption of raid by Muizz-ud-din Ghuri. Likewise Lakshmana Sena of Bengal did not take necessary measures to defend his kingdom even after Ikhtiyar-ud-din Muhammad bin Bakhtiyar's raids in Bihar. "While individual courage and bravery were certainly not wanting, there was lack of wisdom and statesmanship, of knowledge of the outside world, and of a desire to keep abreast with the spirit of the time. No realistic adjustment, no far-sighted approach to the problem which had stared them in the face for centuries and threatened their very existence, no improvement in outlook, no elevation of political vision from their petty jealousies and parochial ideals, and consequently no preparation for a concerted defence commensurate with the extent of the danger" were responsible for the undoing of the Hindus.

Muizz-ud-din's Character and Estimate : In assessing the character and achievements of Muizz-ud-din Muhammad Ghuri, it is customary to compare his military leadership and conquests with those of Sultan Mahmud of Ghazni. There is hardly any doubt that he was far inferior as a military conqueror and a leader to Mahmud of Ghazni. While the latter did not sustain any defeat Muizz-ud-din as Professor Habib remarks, was, "hero of three stupendous defeats—Andkhud, Tarain and Anhilwara" but has to his credit the establishment of one of the greatest empires of the middle ages and in that he definitely rises far above Mahmud of Ghazni.

Most striking features of Muizz-ud-din's character were his dogged tenacity of purpose and his grim political realism. No defeat could dampen his spirit, as is evidenced by his defeat at Anhilwara and Tarain. Any other general of inferior mettle would have lost his spirit after a defeat as he had met with at Tarain. But he reorganised his forces with greater zeal and determination and succeeded in the second battle of Tarain. Again he was essentially a builder of an empire. Wealth for its own sake had no attraction for him. In matters of religion, however, he was not tolerant, for after having destroyed the temples at Ajmer he built a mosque in that place. Yet, it must be said in all fairness to him that he was not a religious bigot of the type of Mahmud. He did not allow his political aims and ideals to be overclouded by religious bigotry.

Among Muizz-ud-din's achievements, mention has to be made of his conquest of a vast portion of Indian territories and the foundation of the Turkish rule in India. He had laid the foundations of one of the greatest empires of the middle ages. Muizz-ud-din perceived the difficulty of administering so vast an area extending from Punjab to Bengal and he realising that a direct administration of the conquerred territories was impossible he only liquidated the top-most rais and left the rural areas and small towns in the hands of the ranas and rawats so that the change of the government was not felt by the masses.

Muizz-ud-din was not a mere soldier. His contribution to the cultural development of Ghur was not negligible. He and his brother Ghiyas-ud-din Ghuri brought about a cultural rejuvination of Ghur. Muizz-ud-din patronised scholars like Maulana. Fakhruddin Razi, Nizami Uruzi etc. and helped to convert Ghur into a centre of culture and learning.

DIFFERENCE BETWEEN THE INVASIONS OF SULTAN MAHMUD AND MUIZZ-UD-DIN MUHAMMAD GHURI

Sultan Mahmud and Muizz-ud-din Muhammad Ghuri both had proceeded from Ghazni for expeditions against India. While the former was the Sultan of Ghazni, and latter was the governor of Ghazni under his brother Ghiyas-ud-din Ghuri, Sultan of Ghur.

The difference in the official status of the two naturally contributed to the difference in military advantages of the two. Apart from the difference in advantages, there was fundamental difference in the nature and ideal of the two conquerors.

First, Sultan Mahmud's expeditions were influenced by his religious fanaticism. To kill the Hindu idolaters, to defile the Hindu temples etc. were the natural concomitants of his policy. Muizz-ud-din Muhammad Ghuri on the other hand, although was somewhat influenced by religion in his expedition against India, did not allow his political statesmanship to be overclouded by religious bigotry. Barring destruction of the Hindu temples at Ajmer and construction of a mosque in their place, we do not come across any other instance of his pludering or defiling of any Hindu temple. Ghuri did not make any distinction between Hindus and Muslims in his policy of expedition. He had marched against the Ismailia sect of the Muslims of Multan.

Secondly, the main objective of Sultan Mahmud's Indian expedition was plundering of wealth. Establishment of any permanent rule in India was besides his aim and objective. But from the nature of the repeated wars against the Hindu rulers, even after crushing defeats at times, on the part of Muizz-ud-din shows that the main purpose of his expedition was to establish permanent rule in India. In 1175-76 he occupied Multan and in the year following the occupied Uch. In 1178 he invaded Gujarat without success. But he was not a person to be deterred by defeats. In the next year, 1179, he occupied Peshwar and built a fort at Sialkot. From the building of this fort, it becomes abundantly clear that Muizz-ud-din Muhammed Ghuri sought to protect his conquests.

Thirdly, Sultan Mahmud had repeatedly entered into India through Punjab which gave him control over Punjab. He had no pre-plan to occupy Punjab. But as soon as Muizz-ud-din became the governor of Ghazni he planned to lead expedition against India and sought to implement his plan by raids into India. This explains why even after his humiliating defeat in the first battle of Tarain he did not rest on his oars. He reorganised his army and reappeared in the same battlefield and won victory in the next year. His success in this second battle of Tarain led to the establishment of Muslim rule in India.

Lastly, it may be mentioned here that the repeated expeditions of Sultan Mahmud and pillage of cities and temples had made Northern India economically weak, the advantage of which was taken by Muizz-ud-din Muhammad Ghuri. It was from after Ghuri that systematic conquest of India by the Muslims was undertaken.

REFERENCES

A Comprehensive History of India, Vol. V : Delhi Sultanate

The Oxford History of India (3rd Edn.) : V. A. Smith

The Sultanate of Delhi : A. L. Srivastava

The Struggle for Empire, Vol. V : History & Culture of the Indian People

The Cambridge History of India, Vol. III

An Advanced History of India : Majumdar, Roychaudhuri & Datta

Medieval India : Stanley Lane Poole

History of India as Told by its Own Historians : Elliot & Dowson

4

The Slave Dynasty

QUTB-UD-DIN AIBAK (1206-10)

Muizz-ud-din Muhammad Ghuri had left Qutb-ud-din Aibak in charge of his Indian conquests while returning to Ghazni. Qutb-ud-din was a trusted slave of Muizz-ud-din Aibak who played an important part in his Indian expeditions. He was decidedly the very best and most dependable of the followers of Muizz-ud-din by virtue of his sharp intelligence, his education and ability as a soldier.

Qutb-ud-din was originally a slave who was brought from Turkestan to Nishapur in Persia by the slave traders. The Qazi of Nishapur bought him from the slave traders and noticing his talent taught him literature, archery and the technique of warfare. After the death of the Qazi, Qutb-ud-din had to pass through many ups and downs of fortune and was ultimately sold to Muizz-ud-din Muhammad Ghuri. Under him he got opportunities to give proofs of his worth and gradually became the most trusted of Muizz-ud-din's followers.

Muizz-ud-din died childless. There was a struggle for supremacy between Qutb-ud-din Aibak, Taj-ud-din Yaldiz and Nasir-ud-din Qubacha for deciding the issue on the basis of the survival of the fittest. Qutb-ud-din had, therefore to work hard for getting his position recognised. On the death of Muizz-ud-din, the citizens of Lahore invited him from Delhi to Lahore and requested him to assume the sovereign authority. Qutb-ud-din realised the great danger to which Lahore was exposed and shifted his capital from Delhi to Lahore. Though Qutb-ud-din Aibak was decidedly the ablest of all the senior slaves of Muizz-ud-din Ghuri, there were other ambitious senior slaves who were rivals for the sovereignty of the dominions left by Muizz-ud-din. Among these was Taj-ud-din Yildiz who possessed himself of Ghazni and so felt himself qualified for suzerain status. Qutb-ud-din had married the daughter of Taj-ud-din. Both Qutb-ud-din and Nisir-ud-din Qubacha were opposed to the ambitions of Taj-ud-din Yildiz. Qutb-ud-din's formal change of government from Delhi to Lahore implied severance of India's ties with Ghazni thus forestalling the claims of Yildiz. Qutb-ud-din's accession took place in 1206 but he refrained from assuming the title of Sultan, reading of **Khutba** in his name or striking his own coin till 1208-09 when he received the deed of manumission and royal insignia from his master's successor at Ghur. Ghiyas-ud-din successor of Muizz-ud-din at Ghur also conferred upon Qutb-ud-din the title of Sultan.

Qutb-ud-din as Sultan : Qutb-ud-din ruled for a short period of four years only. Most of this period was consumed in dealing with his chief rivals Taj-ud-din Yildiz and Nasir-ud-din Qubacha. The former was the ruler of the Province of Kirman and the latter of Multan and Uch. Yildiz succeeded in occupying Ghazni after the death of Muizz-ud-din and being jealous at the rise of fortune of Qutb-ud-din Aibak Yildiz proceeded to occupy Punjab but was defeated by Qutb-ud-din who pursued him upto Ghazni and occupied it. Qutb-ud-din, however could not keep his hold on Ghazni for long. His soldiers carried on depredations on the inhabitants of Ghazni which compelled them to secretly invite Taj-ud-din Yildiz to invade Ghazni. In a surprise attack Qutb-ud-din was defeated and had to leave Ghazni. Thus the chance to unite Afghanistan and India was lost. The Shah of Khvarazam was also forestalled by him in the process of the occupation of Ghazni, though for a temporary period. It was also the task of Qutb-ud-din to prevent the Rajputs from recovering their principalities and to put down the pretensions of Nasir-ud-din. Qubacha.

Bengal and Bihar threatened to sever connection with the Delhi Sultanate on the death of Ikhtiyar-ud-din Khalji. Ali Mardan Khan had placed himself as an independent ruler at Lakhanauti but he was ousted by the local Khalji chiefs and Muhammad Sheran was made the ruler. All Mardan escaped and went to Delhi where he succeeded not without difficulty to persuade Qutb-ud-din to accept him as the Governor of Bengal and Bihar on payment of an annual tribute. At the time of his death the Rajputs remained unaffected due to Qutb-ud-din's too much occupation with the north west. He died in 1210 of injuries received as a result of a fall from his horse in a game of polo.

Qutb-ud-din's Character and Estimate : Qutb-ud-din was a great warrior and a military leader. He rose from the obscurity of a poor soldier to the position of power and fame. He was a reliable lieutenant and never betrayed the trust of his master. It was largely due to the service of Qutb-ud-din Aibak that Muizz-ud-din Ghuri succeeded in India. As a ruler he, however, could not make any new conquests because of his pre-occupations otherwise. He had also not enough time to build up a strong government. But he earned the respect of his contemporaries as a wellmeaning, judicious and kind-hearted ruler. Minhaj-us-siraj refers to these qualities of his character. According to Hasan-un-nizami. "He dispended even-handed justice to the people and exerted himself to promote the peace and prosperity of the realm." Qutb-ud-din possessed a refined taste and patronised men of learning among whom were Hasan-un-nizami, Fakhre Mudir who dedicated their works to their royal patron. He was also deeply interested in architecture. He caused two mosques to be built one at Delhi known as **Quat-ul-Islam** and other at Ajmer, known as **Dhia-Din Ka Jhonpara,** out of the materials of the Hindu temples which he destroyed. He had been given the epithet of **Lakh-baksha** due to his generosity. He does not seem to have followed the enlightened policy of religious toleration, although he is said to have twice interceded with Muhammad for the vanquished Hindu Princes.

ARAM SHAH (1210-11)

As Qutb-ud-din died before he had time to put the administration on a firm footing, the foundation of the newly established Turkish state in India became shaky with his death and there was a great confusion among his followers. Aram Shah, according to some was an adopted son of Qutb-ud-din Aibak. The sudden death of Qutb-ud-din at Lahore led his followers to set up Aram Shah on the throne in Lahore, but the nobles at Delhi refused to acknowledge him as ruler, for they felt that at that critical period of the Turkish rule the government should be in the hands of a competent ruler who would be at once a competent administrator and a great warrior. The citizens of Delhi, therefore, headed by the chief magistrate invited Iltutmish, son-in-law of Qutb-ud-din, the Governor of Badaun to come and to accept the crown. Iltutmish naturally accepted the invitation and proceeded towards Delhi with a strong force. As Aram Shah was unwilling to abdicate the throne, he proceeded to oppose Iltutmish with the support of the people of Lahore but was easily defeated and killed.

ILTUTMISH (1211-1236)

Shams-ud-din Iltutmish was born in a family of Turkish nobility of the Ilbari tribe of Central Asia but was sold in his boyhood as slave by his brothers, to a slave trader Jamal-ud-din who took him to Ghazni. Therefrom he was brought to Delhi and sold for a second time to Qutb-ud-din. He was both handsome and talented. Under Qutb-ud-din he received training as a soldier and learnt reading and writing. It is said that Muizz-ud-din was very much impressed by the good presence and talent of Iltutmish and recommended him to Qutb-ud-din in the words : "Treat Iltutmish well, for he will distinguish himself." Soon Iltutmish began to rise rapidly from higher to higher position and Qutb-ud-din took him as his son-in-law. He was made chief in charge of the Gwalior fort after its conquest, then made the Governor of Baran and later appointed Governor of Badaun, which post he held at the time of the death of Qutb-ud-din. It was in 1211 that he became the Sultan. When Qutb-ud-din had invaded Ghazni Iltutmish gave proofs of his extraordinary ability as a warrior and it was his qualities, both as a warrior and an administrator that had won the admiration of the nobles of the court at Delhi for which he was called upon to come and accept the crown.

No sooner Iltutmish had assumed authority as the Sultan than he was faced with a very complex situation. Taking advantage of the confusion during the conflict between Aram Shah and Iltutmish, Nasir-ud-din Qubacha pushed to Multan and extended his hold on Lahore, Bhatinda and even Sarasuti. The Hindu feudatories showed increasing defiance, and Ranthambhor which was under Prithviraja's son ceased to own vassalage. Ali Mardan, Governor of Bengal declared independence. Yildiz although lost ground to the Shah of Khvarazam was yet waxing in imperial pretensions. A section of the Delhi nobles opposed Iltutmish.

Iltutmish, however, acted with circumspection. He suppressed the Delhi nobles who were supporters of Aram Shah and against him were suppressed with difficulty. He then feigned to accept an investiture from Taj-ud-din Yildiz and remained completely neutral when Yildiz drove out Qubacha from Lahore and occupied most of Punjab. But he took advantage of the vacuum and occupied Sarasuti, Bhatinda and Khuram which had been earlier occupied by Qubacha. He began to consolidate his position and strengthen his army, and when in 1215 Yildiz was finally driven out of Ghazni and peremptorily ordered Iltutmish to send reinforcement, the latter met him with great confidence and defeated and captured him in an open battle at Tarain. He took his time to reorganise his army and the newly conquered territories. After two years he moved his troops across the Beas to Lahore. Qubacha hastily fled to Uch. The steady advance of Iltutmish towards the Sindhu basin was halted by the Mongols who drove a huge number of refugees both princes and people into Punjab. The Khvarazami Prince Jalal-ud-din Mangabarni, chased through Khurasan and Afghanistan came into Sind and sought asylum in India. He sent an emissary for the purpose to Iltutmish. It severely taxed Iltutmish's diplomacy to refuse shelter to a brother-in-faith thereby assist the Pagan Mongol cause or to give him shelter and invite a mongol raid. He therefore, tolerated the Mongols' searching for Mangbarni. The latter forced an alliance on the Hindu chiefs of the Salt Range and gathering an army of fugitive tribes caused enormous devastation in the kingdom of Qubacha. The region north of Multan became a no-man's land and therefore sought to be a khvarazamian principality. During his final exit Mangbarni set fire to Uch, seized Sehwan and put the ruler of Debal to flight. The territorial advantages derived thereby, he left Uzbek Pai and Hasan Qarlugh, in charge of the places who were thorns on Qubacha's side. All this advanced Iltutmish's plans against his rival Qubacha. Advancing from Lahore which he occupied shortly after the exit of Mangbarni, Iltutmish forced Qubacha out of Multan and Uch and practically without a battle compelled him to take shelter in the island fortress of Bhakar and eventually to a watery grave in 1228.

Hasan Qarlugh and Uzbek Pai made Sindhu basin an operational area of the Mongols. Iltutmish followed a policy of not assisting them nor liquidating them, as either course would invite unwelcome Mongol raid. He therefore instructed his officers to watch the situation and to reduce the Chenab and Jhelum valleys without giving direct offence to the Mongols. Before Iltutmish died he managed to extend his rule upto Sialkot and Hajner in the north but failed to make much headway in the west.

After the end of the misrule of Ali Mardan in Bengal, the rule had passed to Husam-ud-din Ewaz who assumed the title of Sultan Ghiyas-ud-din Khalji. He assumed sovereign status, gave good government to the people and profitably carried on raids into Hindu states in the neighbouring areas and enhanced his resources. Iltutmish by a show of force succeeded in 1225 in making Ghiyas-ud-din to recognise his overlordship and to relinquish his hold on Bihar. But hardly the troops of Iltutmish had left Bengal, Ghiyas-ud-din declared independence and reoccupied Bihar. Iltutmish had to send his son Nasir-ud-din Mahmud, Governor of Oudh against Ghiyas-ud-din and the latter was defeated and killed in an armed engagement, in 1226. Bengal again became a province of Delhi. Nasir-ud-din Mahmud died soon after, which was a signal for declaration of independence of Bengal under Balka Khalji. Iltutmish had to march on a second expedition against Bengal in which Balka Khalji was defeated and killed in 1230. Now Iltutmish separated Bengal and Bihar into two provinces and appointed two Governors one for each. Ala-ud-din Jani was appointed Governor of Bengal.

In 1231 Iltutmish reconquered Gwalior. He also invaded Malwa and after a long siege took possession of Bhilsa fort. He also invaded Ujjain and destroyed the temple of Mahakal there and carried away the statue of king Vikramaditya to Delhi. In 1236, Iltutmish died.

Character and Achievements of Iltutmish : Iltutmish is regarded as one of the most outstanding rulers of medieval India. "A shrewd, cautious and farseeing statesman, he left permanent mark on the canvas of Indian history. The history of Muslim sovereignty in India, rightly observes Dr. R.P. Tripathy, properly speaking begins with him." It was Iltutmish who gave the country an independent state, a capital, a governing class and a monarchical form of government that lasted for long. Both by his indefatigable energy and power of application to chosen objectives, Iltutmish transformed the loose patches of Ghurid acquisitions in Hindustan into a well-knit state, the Sultanate of Delhi. Iltutmish entered the service of Qutb-ud-din as a slave but within only two decades rose to be the head of the Turkish government in India. With no tradition to guide him, when everything from the theory of kingship to the boundary of the state was in a nebulous undefined condition, Iltutmish gave everything a direction and a definition and laid the foundation of the first Muslim state in India. He gave consolidation to the acquisitions of Muizz-ud-din Ghuri and Qutb-ud-din Aibak. Iltutmish was called upon to shoulder the responsibility of the state at a time when it was faced with multifarious problems both internal and external. He saved it from the internal disruption and also from the terrible Mongol invasion. His circumspection stood him in good stead in trying times like making a choice between giving asylum to the Prince of Khvarazam and avoiding Mongol raids.

Iltutmish was not only a talented military general and efficient administrator, but was also a liberal patron of art and literature. It was during his reign that Khwaja Qutb-ud-din of Unn near Bagdad came to India. Iltutmish had great reverence for this unparalleled man of religion..It was in memory of this Qutb-ud-din that the **Qutb-Minar** of Delhi was built. This **Minar** even today stands as the symbol of Iltutmish's deep respect for religion and leader of religion. Iltutmish was God-fearing man. He would say his prayers as enjoined in Islam. Patronage of men of letters and religion, kind-heartedness etc. have been mentioned my Minhaj as the main features of the character of Iltutmish.

"His greatest achievement was the initiation of a dynastic monarchy, and in utilising it in welding the loosely conquered territories to a political unity. To have preserved the Sultanate's separate entity and escaped the repercussions of earlier affiliations with Central Asia when Chingiz Khan swept through the Continent was a very difficult task which he accomplished with great foresight and skill. It was sheer ability which earned him, an ex-slave, almost sacrosanct right to the crown, and the Caliph's investiture in A.D. 1229, only confirmed the status which his dynasty and state had acquired. Working on the outlines drawn by Aibak, he filled in the details of a military state and richly deserved his position as its first king."

RUKH-UD-DIN FIROZ SHAH (1235-1236)

On the untimely and unexpected death of the Crown Prince Nasir-ud-din Mahmud in 1229, Iltutmish after some hesitation nominated his eldest daughter Raziyya to succeed him in supersession of his other sons. Iltutmish did not consider his second grown up son Rukh-ud-din Firoz Shah competent to succeed him. But the nobles at the Delhi court were not in favour of a woman's succeeding to the throne of Delhi. The nobles proclaimed Rukh-ud-din as the Sultan. He was as inefficient as given to debauchery. Naturally under him in the name of administration there was extravagance and oppression of the people. Taking advantage of this situation, Shah Turkan, mother of Rukh-ud-din Firoz seized the power of the state. She then began to practically torture the Begums of Iltutmish out of jealousy, as she herself belonged to a lower status. As a result of the selfishness, torture and debauchery of both the mother and the son rebellion began all over the country. Badaun, Hansi, Lahore, Oudh and Bengal defied the sovereignty of Delhi. In the circumstances, the nobles of Delhi threw Rukh-ud-din and Shah Turkan into the prison and placed daughter of Iltutmish, Raziyya on the throne of Delhi.

RAZIYYA (1236-1240)

The new sovereign Raziyya received popular acclaim when she asked for a chance to prove her ability **far better than any man.** But the **coup** displeased the **vizier** Muhammad Juniad and a section of the nobility was displeased. The Governors of Lahore, Badaun, Hansi, Bengal, Multan etc. revolted against Delhi. But having been unable to summon reinforcements from loyal provinces Raziyya resorted to the diplomacy of dividing her enemies. She persuaded two of the rebel leaders to join her secretly and betray their comrades and gave out this information to their comrades who fled out of fear when many of them were pursued and killed. The vizier died in the Sirmur hills as a lone fugitive.

The brief rule of three years of Sultana Raziyya constitutes an interlude in a decade of oligarchic misrule worsened by factiousness. She realised the need for vigorous exercise of Crown's authority in an essentially military state and the nature of its function, she sought to compensate the disability supposed to attach to her sex, by kingly demeanour, dress, foresight, firmness hardly expected of a young woman. "She discarded female attire, rode out in public, and held open court; she selected high officers from men of her own choice and, deliberately, not always, from among Iltutmish's freed men who came to be known as **the Forty**." Like Iltutmish Raziyya showed practical wisdom when she turned down very tactfully the invitation to form an alliance with Hasan Qarlugh, the Khvarzami representative who was struggling single-handed against the Mongols in the Western Sind. **The Forty** could not reconcile themselves to the calculated undermining of their position by Raziyya. They began to hatch a conspiracy to depose her or at least limit her liberty of action. The leaders of the conspiracy were the **amirs** and **maliks** at the court and in the provinces. Raziyya had earlier in her reign suppressed the rebellion of the Kiramitah and Mulahid sects of the Muslims led by Nur-ud-din.

Now the leader of the conspiracy Ikhtyar-ud-din Aeitigin who was Raziyya's Lord Chamberlain, and other prominent members like Malk Altunia Governor of Bhatinda and Kabir Khan, Governor of Lahore sought to decoy her to distant place and to finish her off there. In pursuance of this plan Kabir Khan revolted in 1240. Raziyya proceeded to put him down. He was defeated and he took to flight. His progress was, however, barred by the presence of the Mongols near the river Chenab. He therefore could not make good his escape, returned and made his surrender to Raziyya who came back to her capital in triumph. The conspirators, however, did not give up their designs. Within a short time Altunia, Governor of Bhatinda revolted, Raziyya again had to march against the new rebel to put him down. Hardly Raziyya had reached Bhatinda some agents of the conspirators killed Jalal-ud-din Yakut which weakened the Queen's party. The conspirators captured Raziyya herself and put her into prison. They raised the third son of Iltutmish, Bahram, to the throne. Thus the conspirators had their victory over Raziyya.

But disappointment awaited Altunia who did not get what he had expected. He having been thus disaffected vowed to avenge himself. He released Raziyya from the fort of Bhatinda, married her and proceeded with her to recover Delhi. They were, however, defeated and compelled to return towards Bhatinda. Their troops deserted them and near a place named Kaithal they were murdered by some Hindu robbers (October 13, 1240).

Significance of the Rule of Raziyya and her Estimate : The significance of the rule of Raziyya relates to a large extent to her accession. For the first time in the history of the Delhi Sultanate the people of Delhi took decision on the question of succession on their own initiative and the support of the people of Delhi constituted the main strength of her rule. In fact, it was not possible to engineer any palace revolution or any rising against her so long as she did not move out of Delhi.

Raziyya made it more or less a matter of a contract with the people of Delhi who acclaimed her accession that she might be deposed by the people if she did not fulfil their expectations. Her succession also vindicated the choice of Iltutmish who had nominated her superseding the claim of his second son contrary to the accepted rules of succession.

The most significant part of Raziyya's accession was the robustness of the Turkish mind in the unconventional acceptance of a woman ruler. This shows indifference to the Islamic theological objection to the elevation of a woman on the throne.

There was one major lapse in the whole proceedings. While the army and the people of Delhi had placed Raziyya on the throne in preference to the eligible son of Iltutmish, they ignored the provincial Governors who constituted the most powerful section of the Turkish governing class. They naturally felt ignored and humiliated and from the very start began to oppose the rule of Raziyya.

Raziyya was the sole woman ruler in the entire history of the Muslim rule in India. Minhaj credits her with honesty, justice and efficiency in administration. She was as capable a warrior as a patron of literature and men of literature. According to Ferishta Raziyya could read Quran with faultless pronunciation. According to Minhaj Raziyya ruled for 3 years, 6 months only. "That she was the ablest of the successors of Iltutmish can hardly be denied". Her dealings with the recalcitrant provincial Governors, Khvarzamian

Governor Hasan Qarlugh demonstrated her capabilities as a ruler. She showed her diplomatic skill by politely refusing to form a coalition with the Khvarzamian Governor against the Mongols. "This was a political decision and saved the sultanate from a Mongol invasion." It was primarily due to the opposition to the accession of a woman on the throne of Delhi that Raziyya's fall was due.

MUIZZ-UD-DIN BAHRAM (1240-42)

Muizz-ud-din Bahram ascended the throne in April, 1240 when Raziyya was imprisoned at Bhatinda. He was the third son of Iltutmish. He was raised to the throne on the definite understanding that he would allow the Turkish **Maliks** and **Amirs** to exercise all powers of administration. He had also to allow the Turkish nobles to nominate the king's deputy that is, **Naib-i-mamlikat,** a post which was created now. Ikhtyar-ud-din Aeitigin was appointed to this high post. The post of the **vizier** was now relegated to a secondary position. In this way **the Forty**—The **Bandegan-i-Chahelagan** was in complete control of the administration.

Under a king like Iltutmish **the Forty** was loyal no doubt, but under his weak successors its power pushed that of the Sultan into the background. The king's deputy. Aeitigin, usurped much of the power formerly exercised by the Sultan.

Bahram was an intrepid, open-minded unostentatious ruler, but he was not that strong as to keep the reins of government in his own hands. Malik Badr-ud-din, Lord Chamberlain, and vizier Nizam-ul-Mulk held high offices of the state, but Bahram and Nizam-ul-Mulk, both were dissatisfied with Badr-ud-din who secretely tried to depose Bahram from the throne. Nizam-ul-Mulk got scent of the secret plan of Badr-ud-din and told his master all about it whereupon Bahram sent him to Badaun as its Governor. But Badr-ud-din came back to Delhi within a few months without taking permission of the Sultan. For this disobedience he was put under arrest and killed. Badr-ud-din was one of **the Forty** and the circumstances in which he was killed struck terror in the minds of the **amirs and maliks,** for now they apprehended that the life of none of them was safe and they naturally began to conspire against Bahram for his removal from the throne. The Turkish **ulemas** i.e. the ecclesiasticals were also hostile to the Sultan as one of them was put to death under his order. When the situation had become so complex the Mongols invaded Punjab and lay siege of the city of Lahore in 1241. Bahram sent an army for the relief of the city and the vizier who accompanied the army told the officers that the Sultan sent secret orders for the arrest and execution of all of them. The army officers returned with the army filled with rage and vowing vengeance on the Sultan without reaching Lahore. They were determined to depose the Sultan. The people of Delhi fought desperately for some time but were no match for the army under the trained officers. Sultan Bahram fought against the rebellious army from the **White Fort** but was defeated and captured. A few days later he was put to death.

ALA-UD-DIN MASUD SHAH (1242-1246)

Raising Ala-ud-din Masud Shah, the grandson of Iltutmish and son of Rukh-ud-din to the throne after the defeat and death of Bahram signified the defeat of the Crown and complete triumph of the Turkish aristocracy. Ala-ud-din Masud Shah had to agree to abide by the terms of the agreement made by his predecessor, that is, he was to delegate all power to **the Forty** and to reintroduce the post of the deputy king to which post Malik Qutb-ud-din Hasan was appointed. Nizam-ul-Mulk, the **vizier** had earned the displeasure of the **amirs** and **maliks** who got him killed and Nazim-ud-din Abu Bakr was appointed vizier in his place. Malik Ikhtiyar-ud-din Qaraqash was appointed **amir-i-hajib.** Qazi Imad-ud-din Muhammad Shafurqani replaced Minhaj-us-Siraj as Head Qazi.

Adjustments were also made in the assignments held by important **maliks.** Nagaur, Mandor and Ajmer were assigned to Malik Izz-ud-din Balban Kishlu Khan and Badaun to Taj-ud-din Sanjar Qutluq. Baha-ud-din Balban who obtained the title of Ulugh Khan was latter appointed **amir-i-hajib** in place of Malik Qaraqash who was sent to Badaun as Governor.

During the rule of Ala-ud-din Masud Shah, Tughan Tughril Khan was ruling over Bengal as an independent ruler for all practical purposes and even proceeded upto Oudh. It was at the request of Mihaj-us-Siraj that he desisted from his attack on Oudh and returned to Bengal. Within a short time (1245) the Mongols invaded India but were beaten off. Ala-ud-din Masud Shah gradually became pleasure-loving and was given to debauchery. His administrative efficiency naturally began to ebb and as his administrative efficiency began to ebb his oppression of the people began to increase. Ultimately the **maliks** and **amirs** found it advisable to remove him from the throne and to place Nasir-ud-din Mahmud, the youngest son of Iltutmish on the throne (1246).

NASIR-UD-DIN MAHMUD (1246-65)

Nasir-ud-din Mahmud ascended the Delhi throne of June 10, 1246, and two days later he held a **durbar** in the audience hall of **Qasr-i-Firuzah,** and the people pledged allegiance to him. Sultan Nasir-ud-din is usually painted as a man of saintly disposition, who had little or no interest in the administrative or political affairs of the state, being devoted to prayers and religious observances all the time. "This assessment ignores the basic facts of his life. A deeper analysis of the pulls and pressures of the time leads us to the conclusion that if he turned to religious devotions and rites, it was to escape from the terrors of political life. He was essentially political in outlook and that he could keep his head on his shoulders for twenty years under these circumstances is no mean compliment to his political tact and adroitness." (Prof. Nizami). According to Isami, however, "Ulugh Khan served the king and controlled all his affairs; the king lived in his palace and Ulugh Khan governed the empire. It goes without saying that the new king was unambitious, docile and to an extent timid. He kept for himself the mere form of royality while he left the substance of authority to his nobles. He married the daughter of Ulugh Khan, more known as Balban who was instrumental to his rising to the royal position. The Sultan is said to have spent most of his time in copying Quran and doing acts of charity.

BALBAN AT THE HELM OF AFFAIRS (1246-1265)

Nasir-ud-din owed his throne to Balban and naturally he placed all power of the state in the hands of his benefactor, the leader of **the Forty**. Important offices of the state were distributed among the kinsmen of Balban which, however, provoked opposition of the non-Turkish elements headed by an Indian Muslim Imad-ud-din Raihan. Raihan managed to secure the post of **Wakil-i-dar,** i.e. Superintendent of king's Household and then contrived to replace Balban and his kinsmen by his own supporters. The rule of the Indian Muslims being loathsome of the Turks, they began a counter move in which Balban took a leading part. The Turkish officers posted in provinces round Delhi joined their forces and prepared to march on the capital to end the non-Turkish domination. The Sultan was advised to resist the invasion of the capital but at the last moment lost heart and was glad to end the tension by accepting the opponents terms. Raihan and his associates were dismissed from the court and Balban regained his former ascendancy.

Except for a brief interruption when Raihan succeeded in putting his followers in important posts at the court, Balban held all effective power during the whole of Mahmud's reign and even is said to have used the royal insignia. On the death of Sultan Nasir-ud-din Mahmud leaving no heir, Balban assumed the crown, thus a new dynasty was started (1265).

The problems that Balban had to settle before his assumption of the Sultanate of Delhi were as complex as numerous. Bengal gave him repeated trouble. Tughan Tughril Khan, Governor of Bengal, repudiated the authority of Delhi, began to rule as an independent king. He even invaded Awadh, but having been defeated by the raja of Orissa after some time. Tughan was forced to appeal to Delhi for help. This gave Balban opportunity to deal with Tughan. He sent an army under Tamur Khan with instruction to punish Tughan Tughril Khan, although seemingly it was sent for his assistance. Tughan was ousted from his position as Governor of Bengal and Awadh was given him as compensation. Tughan did not survive long to enjoy his new assignment. But Bengal continued to give trouble to Balban. One of Tughan Tughril's successors Yuzbek-i-Tughril Khan declared himself king of Bengal, assumed regal title, read a **Khutba** in his name and struck his own coin in 1255. But fortune did not favour him, for he was killed in 1257 while leading an expedition to Kamrupa. But this also did not end the trouble in Bengal. Within three or four years there was again trouble in Bengal when Arslan Khan, Governor of Kara occupied Lakhanauti and began to rule over Bengal as an independent ruler. Bengal retained her independence till the end of the reign of Nasir-ud-din Mahmud.

The Governors in the north west also became rebellious. Restoration of the authority in that region was far from satisfactory. The constant Mongol pressure Hasan Qarlugh's ambition to extend his dominion to Multan and Sind and the selfishness of the local officers who were always busy in carving out a fortune for themselves and were involved in intrigues with Delhi and Mongols in Persia made for the unrest in the area. In fact, Hasan Qarlugh for a time succeeded in occupying Multan. Kishlu Khan, Governor of Multan and Uch repudiated the suzerainty of Delhi and accepted the vassalage of Hulagu, the Mongol leader of Persia. He then joined Qutlugh Khan of Awadh and made a bid for occupation of Delhi. But their combined attempt failed due to the vigilance and quick action of Balban. It appears that some sort of an agreement was made between Delhi and Hulagu, and the latter sent an envoy to Delhi to assure the Sultan that the Mongols would not infringe the northwestern frontier of India. But all this did not end the trouble in Punjab. In 1254, even Lahore passed into the hands of the Mongols and only south-east part of Punjab remained within the dominion of Delhi and the rest came under the Mongols or under their sphere of influence. Multan and Sind, however, continued to remain parts of Delhi dominion.

The task of supressing the Hindu attempts at independence was perhaps the most trying of all that Balban was faced with. He had to deal with the disaffected Hindus of the Doab first. He defeated Trilokyavarma of the Chandela dynasty, slaughtered a large number of men and carried away women and children to slavery. Next was the turn of Mewat where he perpetrated inhuman brutalities in chastising the disaffected people there. Balban made repeated expeditions against Ranthambhor which he ultimately succeeded in conquering. The Chandela chief of Kalinjar also rose in revolt but it was suppressed with a heavy hand by Balban. Balban also led expeditions against Gwalior, but he did no attempt to extend Turkish hegemony in Malwa or Central India.

GHIYAS-UD-DIN BALBAN (1266-87)

Ghiyas-ud-din Balban was an Ilberi Turk. He was captured by the Mongols in early life and sold to slavery to one Jamal-ud-din who later brought him to Delhi and re-sold him to Iltutmish. Balban was one of Iltutmish's **Bandegan-i-Chahelagan** or **the Forty.** It was by the dint of his merit that Balban became the **de facto** ruler under Nasir-ud-din Mahmud. By giving his daughter in marriage to Sultan Nasir-ud-din he made his power over the Sultan unquestioned and unassailable. Balban's work as **naib** of Nasir-ud-din has already been recounted. On his assumption of the crown he had to deal with problems of establishing an efficient administration, making arrangements for prevention of Mongol raids and to that end to strengthen the frontiers. According to Barni, Balban knowing as he did that fear of punishment generates loyalty to the government, determined to create that feeling among the nobility.

His first task was to organise a strong army. By reorganising the old army of the Sultanate, he increased the efficiency of the infantry and the cavalry. Experienced, efficient and loyal **maliks** and **amirs** were placed in command of the different sections of the army. With the help of this army Balban brought peace and order in the Doab. The marauders of Mewat had made the life of the people upto the outskirts of Delhi insecure. Balban suppressed them with a heavy hand. Kampil, Patiali, Bhojpur were the centres of the Mewati dacoits. Balban proceeded personally against them and by making repeated attacks on their centres liquidated them and thereby made the high ways safe for travels. Suppression of the Mewati dacoits not only brought security to life and property of the passerby, but also largely helped in the development of trade and commerce. In order that the Mewati dacoits might not begin their depredations again, Balban built a fort at Gopalgir and repaired the fort at Jalali. Balban's action against the Mewati dacoits continued to yield good results for more than half a century. Barani writing after about sixty years said that there was no depredations by dacoits in the country.

Balban sought to alter the conditions of the enjoyment of the landed estates by the nobles in order to curb their over-grown power. But he desisted from the plan on the advice of a trusted Lieutenant that such a course would lead to great trouble. But Balban succeeded in curtailing the power of the **Bandegan-i-chahelagan** or **the Forty** and thereby making the administration both strong and respected.

Balban believed in a theory which was similar to that of the Divine Right of Kingship. He expounded his views in his advice to his son Bughra Khan : "The heart of the king is the special repository of God's favour and in this he has no equal among mankind." On a different occasion he stressed the sanctity of the person of the king. Balban also believed in depotism as inherent in kingship, for he sincerely believed that despotism alone could exact obedience from the subjects and ensure security of the state. He copied the Persian model in his court etiquette and introduced the system of **sijda,** i.e. laying prostrate and **paibos,** i.e. kissing the monarch's feet in the royal court as normal forms of salutation. To enhance the splendour of his court he introduced the celebration of Persian Nauroz. Drinking by courtiers and officers was prohibited and a special dress was prescribed for the courtiers. Light moods of laughing or smiling in court were not permitted. In this way, by rigid formalities and enforced dignity and ceremonials Balban restored the reserve and prestige of the Sultanate.

Balban realised that his policy of despotism could not succeed unless he could keep himself informed of the happenings in the different parts of the kingdom. He, therefore, organised an efficient system of espionage by spending much money and time after it. Secret news-writers were appointed in every department and every province, in fact, in every district. He, of course took much care in selecting most loyal persons as secret news-writers, i.e. spies, who had to transmit secret information about important occurrences every day. The news-writer of Badaun who failed to do his duty was hanged near the city gate.

Balban having strengthened his position, proceeded to suppress the tribals of the Jud area. Then he addressed himself to the task of providing security against Mongol raids. Sher Khan was a powerful **jagirdar** of a vast area of Suman, Lahore and Dipalpur.

He was also a close relation to Balban. Sher Khan played a very important part in warding off Mongol inroads, and also in bringing the Jats, Khokars and other tribals under his control. His spectacular success excited the jealousy of Balban and his intentions were suspect. Balban, therefore, got him poisoned to death. But this was highly impolitic step. Balban, however, promptly put his eldest son Muhammad and second son Bughra Khan at Sunam and Saman with strong force for defence of the frontier against Mongol raids. The good result of this arrangement for the defence of the country against Mongol raids were seen in 1279 when the Mongol raid was beaten off with great slaughter by the two sons of Balban. The mongols had to leave the borders after this abject failure.

Taking advantage of the Mongol raids and the preoccupations of the government, Bengal under Tughril Khan declared independence, assumed the title of Sultan, struck coins and caused **Khutba** in his name. Balban sent Amir Khan and Malik Targhi against Tughril Khan in two expeditions against him one after another but both the attempts having failed, Balban himself proceeded against Tughril in a third expedition. Tughril fled his capital out of fear but was pursued and captured and killed. Balban's second son Bughra Khan was placed as the Governor of Bengal.

Hardly the affairs of Bengal were over, the Mongols reappeared in the northwest and attacked Punjab. Muhammad, the eldest son of Balban lost his life in his attempt to drive out the Mongols. This untimely death of his most favourite son was too deep a shock for Balban to withstand and he also died within a very short time in 1287.

Ghiyas-ud-din Balban was far-seeing administrator. He clearly realised that the way to keep so vast a country under control, only a strong army would not do. Efficiency of administration must be the very basis of administration if it were to stand the test of time and win the allegiance of the people. He, therefore, struck a balance between military strength and administrative efficiency. At the top of the administration was the Sultan himself, and nothing could be done without his consent and approval. Even his sons did not enjoy any independence in this regard.

In matters of judicial administration, the principle followed by Balban was one of strict impartiality. His near relations also could not avoid the process of law and justice if they were in any way involved in any act of omission or commission. This had a salutary effect on the **amirs** and **maliks** who now did not venture to maltreat their servants, male or female or even their slaves, for they knew that they could not get away without punishment for their wrong-doings. A certain **malik** got one of his slaves killed by inhuman cruelties. The Sultan came to know of this from the widow of the slave thus killed and ordered the **malik** to be flogged openly for the crime. Haibat Khan, a favourite of the Sultan himself, killed a man and in order to avoid punishment at the hand of Balban paid twenty thousand rupees to the widow of the man as compensation. The institution of an espionage system by Balban has already been referred to. The spies were also to report all cases of miscarriage of justice to the Sultan besides reporting on the occurrences of importance and about high ranking officers, even including Balban's son Bughra Khan, to Balban.

Estimate of Ghiyas-ud-din Balban : Balban held the reins of the government for forty years, both as the deputy of Sultan Nasir-ud-din Muhammad and Sultan himself. Unfortunately his dynasty did not survive more than three years after his death, but the government of Delhi which he had placed on firm footing survived and it is in the context of this institution that Balban's achievements have to be judged.

Zia-ud-din Barani has showered lavish praises on Balban. "By his forts and military posts he established law and order in the main provinces of the empire from Haryana to Bihar. Without this preliminary work, the achievements of the Khalji era would have been impossible."

Throughout the long period that Balban had controlled the state, his chief aim was the consolidation of the Infant Turkish state in Hindustan, in which task he was eminently successful. He gave double protection to the Sultanate, namely, internal peace and protection against the Mongol raids. He developed a defensive arrangement in the north western frontier for the purpose of rendering security to the country against the Mongol raids.

As an administrator he was stern and ruthless, yet honest and just. He meted out justice to all alike, both great and small, high and low without the least partiality. For giving his administration the necessary strength and efficiency he did not hesitate to deal sternly with the Turkish nobility who were the main source of disturbance to the quiet rule.

Balban was a devout Sunni Musalman and was very punctilious in the discharge of religious duties enjoined by Islam. He often held discussions with Muslim divines. He did not believe in religious toleration.

Balban was a noted patron of learning and offered asylum to many learned men and princes from Central Asia who fled from their native lands due to Mongol depredations. In fact, Balban's court was centre of Islamic learning and culture. The famous poet Amir Khusru received the liberal patronage of Balban. Khusru was the best and the most celebrated poet of contemporary India and came to be known by the epithet **Parrot of India.**

For the security of the life and property of the passersby from the Mewati marauders Balban took strong measures against them and liquidated their centres of activities. A series of outposts were built round Delhi for its protection. By rendering the highways safe against the Mewati dacoits, he helped the growth of inland trade and commerce.

Balban was the first Muslim ruler who had his own theory of kingship. This theory was derived from Sassanid Persia, both in form and substance, which gave kingship a supernatural and divine character. The basic principles of his theory were that kingship is the vice-regency of God on earth, and next only to the Prophet in dignity. External dignity and prestige were essential for kingship and Balban carried this dignity to such an exclusiveness that he refused to talk to common people. Official decorum, full regalia and royal paraphernalia were never absent in his appearance before the public or in the court. He also would not forget the distinction of high-born and low-born and he avoided contact with the latter. He used to trace his genealogy to the mythical Afrasiyab of Firdausi's **Shah Nama.** Persian manners and customs, he believed, were a must for kingship and he followed the Persian etiquette in his court. Balban eschewed fresh conquests of the neighbouring Hindu territories, for he believed that, it would impair the strength of his dominion which he was bent on consolidating. He, however, recovered Bengal when it repeatedly tried to make itself independent.

If all the above be the achievements of Balban and reasonably be put on the credit side of his estimate, Prof. Nizami says, that "in all other matters Balban's reactionary attitude did more harm than good". (i) Many Hindu working class guilds of weavers, butchers, elephant-drivers etc. who were converted to Islam did not tolerate an Indian government based on the assumption that all high offices should belong to the Turkish slaves of the Sultan by right of conquest. (ii) Many Hindus had been learning Persian which made it possible for them to undertake enterprises in new fields, particularly the land revenue in which lack of bilingual clerks and accountants had been the main difficulty. But Balban continued to maintain the old state machinery working long after it had lost its utility. "Consequently, the long delayed change, when it came, took a revolutionary form". (Prof. Nizami). According to Prof. Nizami, Balban's failure is best seen in his army. Balban took long six years to crush the rebellion of Tughril Khan of Lakhnauti. He did not challenge any of the great Hindu rais. From Isami, we know that the Mongols had two victories over the forces of Balban primarily due to their superiority in numbers.

Balban's policy of choosing officers from people of high birth for his army stood in the way of raising an army which was inferior in number to that of the Mongols. "Balban with his fad to high birth was quite out of date by the time he died. Both in the civil and the military field Balban and his governing class had been tried and found wanting." (Prof. Nizami).

MUIZZ-UD-DIN KAIQUBAD (1287-1290)

On Balban's death Fakhr-ud-din, the **kotwal** of Delhi set aside the claim of Kai Khushrav and placed Muizz-ud-din Kaiqubad, son of Bughra Khan on the throne. Kaiqubad was then a young man of seventeen or eighteen years of age, 'handsome, cultured and benevolent.' He grew under the strict guardianship of his grandfather and was never allowed to look at any beautiful girl or taste a drop of wine. "He had received instruction in all physical and intellectual arts, including calligraphy, literature, archery spearmanship etc." But no sooner he had ascended the throne than he gave himself up to debauchery and bided his time in wine and venery. The court of Balban which was a centre of religion and culture was soon turned into a centre for the buffoons, pleasure-seekers, dancing girls and musicians. Kaiqubad caused a beautiful palace to be built on the Jumna at Kailugarhi and live there in pleasure and merry-making. According to Isami, "Day and night the king was engaged in his pleasure parties, he had no time for anything else. There were no companions for him all the time except moon-faced maidens with rosy lips. I have heard concerning this king who was a slave of his sex desires owing to his youth."

In such circumstances the burden of the state had to be shouldered by others. Nizam-ud-din Barani writes that "I have heart from Qazi Saraf-ud-din Sarpain that the kingdom could not have lasted for a week had Malik Nizam-ud-din and Malik Qawam-ud-din Ilaqa Dabir not been the pillars of the state." But in fact, Nizam-ud-din sedulously encouraged the youthful king to sensuous pleasures and began to consolidate his dictatorial authority for the final usurpation of the throne which to every one appeared to be inevitable and necessary. Within six months of Kaiqubad's rule Kai Khushrav was murdered and the new **vizier** Khwaja Khatir was removed and a large number of high officials were replaced on trumped up charge of sedition, by Nizam-ud-din's own men.

While Nizam-ud-din was busy in purging the administration of officials he considered undesirable for his fulfilment of ambition, the Mongol chief Tamar Khan invaded India and ravaged the country from Lahore to Multan. Khan-i-Jahan the **barbek** was sent to deal with the Mongols who retreated on hearing the news of the coming of the imperial force. Some Mongols were captured and killed. "Later Nizam-ud-din deceitfully obtained the Sultan's order for the execution of those Mongols (called New Muslims) who had earlier embraced Islam and settled in India." (Prof. Nizami).

Nizam-ud-din's policy made Malik Fakhr-ud-din, **kotwal,** now and old man of ninety apprehensive of Nizam-ud-din's fate. He exhorted him to give up the idea of royalty and to stick to his own business of office. But Nizam-ud-din replied that he had already proceeded too far in the way and to retrace his steps would mean that he would be killed. Bughra Khan, father of Kaiqubad, who was now ruling over Bengal as Sultan Nasir-ud-din, knew that his son was leading a life of dissipation and Nizam-ud-din had made him a cat's paw with the ultimate aim of putting an end of Kaiqubad himself. Bughra Khan in his attempt to save his son from the situation into which both he himself and Nizam-ud-din had put himself, wanted to meet his son. Nizam-ud-din insisted that Bughra Khan must follow the court etiquette with a view to foil the attempt of Bughra Khan to see his son under such humiliating condition. But Bughra Khan followed the etiquette of the court with punctilious care, laying prostrate at the feet of Kaiqubad, kissing the ground and Kaiqubad looking on in stony dignity and kingly unconcern. But at the end Kaiqubad broke down and threw himself at the feet of his father and in tears. Bughra Khan whispered into the ears of his son to get rid of Nizam-ud-din and to refrain from indulging in pleasures.

For a time Kaiqubad corrected himself but the number of young, charming courtesans that surrounded the court soon brought him back to his old ways. Too much dissipation told upon his health and he fell ill. He ordered Nizam-ud-din to proceed to Multan but the latter delayed his departure on various pretexts. The Turkish officers finding the time opportune poisoned Nizam-ud-din. Barani while praising the administrative abilities of Nizam-ud-din expressed his strong disapproval of his ambitious character and unscrupulous methods. On Nizam-ud-din's death the situation became extremely chaotic, although many of the nobles of Balban's court returned to serve Kaiqubad.

Kaiqubad placed Malik Firuz Khalji from Samana in the vacancy caused by the death of Nizam-ud-din. Malik Firuz (later Sultan Jalal-ud-din Khalji) had served Balban for many years along with his brother Shihab-ud-din Khalji father of later Sultan Ala-ud-din Khalji.

Ultimately the conflicts and ambitions of the nobles got crystallised into two hostile groups. The Turkish nobles who looked upon Malik Firuz as a non-Turk soon became hostile to him. The Khalji group was led by Malik Firuz while the Turkish group was led by Malik Aitmar Surkha. Soon after Kaiqubad was struck down with paralysis and the Turkish nobles took the opportunity to raise his infant son under the title Shams-ud-din II (Kayumars) on the throne. They also sought to put Malik Firuz to death, which they did not succeed in doing as Malik Firuz was always on guard. Malik Firuz forestalled the Turkish nobles by occupying Delhi and after having murdered Kaiqubad made himself the regent of the infant king. The regency was nothing but a stop-gap arrangement and was not meant to last for long. Malik Firuz soon after set aside Shams-ud-din Kayumars and put him to death, ascending the throne himself in March, 1290. Thus the so-called Slave Dynasty* of Delhi came to an end.

REFERENCES

The Struggle for Empire, Vol. I : Bharatiya Vidya Bhavan

A Comprehensive History of India, Vol. V : Delhi Sultanate

The Cambridge History of India, Vol. III

The Sultanate of Delhi : A. L. Srivastava

The Oxford History of India (3rd Edn.) : V. A. Smith

An Advanced History of India : Majumdar, Roychaudhuri & Datta

* "This dynasty is usually referred to as Slave Dynasty in Indian history. But of the nine rulers, only three, Aibak, Iltutmish and Balban, began their political career as bond slaves; all others were free men. Among the three it was only Aibak whose manumission followed his accession to sovereign power, Iltutmish and Balban both having obtained their freedom early in their life. None of these rulers in any case assumed insignia of royalty while still a slave. To describe the entire series of these rulers as Slave Dynasty, is therefore, inappropriate, even if it is overlooked that they belonged not to one, to three dynasties or families. And yet they have obvious difference with the later Turkish dynasties,—difference emphasised by domination by freed men grouped round leading members of the same class and functioning as a closed oligarchy and seeking reinforcement only from similar bondsmen." (*The Struggle for Empire,* Vol. I, p. 159, f. n.)

5. The Khaljis : Tughluqs : Sayyids and Lodis

JALAL-UD-DIN FIRUZ KHALJI (1290-96)

About the origin of the Khaljis there is difference of opinion between Nizam-ud-din, Ferishta and Zia-ud-din Barani. According to Zia-ud-din Barani, Jalal-ud-din came of a race different from the Turks and that with the death of Kaiqubad the Turks lost the Empire. But V.A. Smith is of opinion that 'in fact the Khaljis were a Turkish tribe though long settled in Garmsir in Afghanistan. Raverty also is of opinion that the Khaljis could not be classed as Afghans or Pathans, and he assigns to them a Turkish origin. The people of Delhi, however, did not at first welcome Jalal-ud-din Firuz Khalji as they regarded him as of Afghan stock. Modern writers are also of opinion that the Khaljis were originally of Turkish stock but had acquired Afghan character during their long residence in Afghanistan and between them and the Turks there was no love lost.

As Jalal-ud-din was not much liked by the Delhi nobles and people, he had to make Kilokhri the seat of his government, where he performed his coronation ceremony and declared himself as the Sultan. He was an old man of seventy then. Sultan's conciliatory temperament, his excellence of character, his justice, generosity and devotion, gradually removed the aversion of the people and earned the affections of the nobles. His extraordinarily guileless and sincere heart, his childlike lack of equivocation marked him as a saintly ruler, for "by subordinating state-craft to the dictates of heart he showed himself in a perfect and agreeable contrast to the earlier despots." Disposed to rule without blood-shed and oppression he showed most impolitic tenderness towards criminals and even rebels. This naturally led to a recrudescence of intrigues by the nobles and the authority of the Sultan was not being respected.

In August 1290 Malik Chajju Kashil Khan, Balban's nephew and head of old royal family raised the standard of revolt at Kara. He was joined by Amir Ali Hatim Khan, governor of Awadh and other nobles of the old regime. Jalal-ud-din out of imprudent generosity pardoned the rebels.

Sultan's peaceful disposition and undeserved leniency made him unpopular even with his Khalji nobles. Malik Ahmad Chap, the Master of Ceremonies told Jalal-ud-din plainly and bluntly that the king should reign and observe the rules of government or else should relinquish the throne. The only departure was the execution of Siddi Maula, a **darvesh** under Jalal-ud-din's reign, on mere suspicion of treason.

It is needless to say that for such a ruler expansion of territories by conquest was impossible. Naturally his expedition against Ranthambhor proved a failure. He returned from the expedition on the realisation that the fort could not be taken without sacrificing the lives of many musalmans.

According to Prof. Nizami, "Firuz's mildness concealed a seasoned warrior, who could appreciate a straight military challenge." In 1292 a Mongol horde numbering 150,000 invaded India under the leadership of a grandson of Hulagu. Severely defeated by the Sultan's troops the invaders were compelled to make peace. But Ulghu a descendant of Chinghiz and many of his rank and file embraced Islam and settled near Delhi and came to be known as 'new musalmans.'

To the vacant governorship of Kara, Jalal-ud-din appointed his brother's son Ali Gurshasp (later Sultan Ala-ud-din Khalji) whom he had brought up from his infancy and gave his daughter in marriage. The nephew was just the opposite of his uncle, was unscrpulous, aggressive, over ambitious haughty and sharp tongued. He aimed at an independent and glorious existence. To fulfil his ambition he required money which he thought of collecting by raids on the neighbouring Hindu states. With the Sultan's permission he led an expedition in 1293 to Bhilsa via Chanderi. Giving resistance no chance to gather Ali Gurshasp plundered the ancient town and also the temple and carried away 'immense booty, in cattle, precious metal and the inevitable idol to be trampled under the zealot's feet.' (Prof. Nizami). He presented the booty to the Sultan while keeping the more valuable assets to himself, for the purpose of earning greater confidence of the Sultan, who in appreciation of his nephew's loyalty gave him his deceased father's office to **ariz-i-ma-malik** adding Awadh to his governorship. He obtained Sultan's permission to use the surplus revenue of his province for expanding his army for carrying raids on Hindu territories beyond Chanderi. In about a year the equipped himself with men and money and in the winter of 1295 set out in an expedition against Devagiri the Yadava capital with about eight thousand picked cavalry. Rama Chandra Deva was the Yadava King of Devagiri on whose capital Ali Gurshasp descended with the directness of a lightning. Rama Chandra was too unnerved to offer any resistance and he surrendered. But before the invader could collect the ransom, Rama Chandra's son Singhana appeared with the army and attacked the invading army. But was easily defeated. Thus twice defeated the king of Devagiri had to pay for heavier indemnity than before and allow the victorious soldiers to plunder the city. "The resulting gain, in gold and silver, pearl and precious stones, silk stuffs and slaves, elephants and horses exceeded the victor's wildest dreams, for the kingdom had for centuries attracted, through its ports and trading centres, vast overseas wealth. No Sultan of Delhi had ever possessed anything like it."

The news of the exploit of Ali Gurshasp had trickled through to Jalal-ud-din, who although somewhat hurt at the secretiveness of his nephew was pleased at the prospect of so vast a treasure coming to his possession. Jalal-ud-din moved to Gwalior to receive the victorious prince, but when the news reached him of his nephew's direct return to Kara, Jalal-ud-din summoned his Council to deliberate on the course of action to be followed. Ahmad Chap and other realists who knew the prince better, urged strong measure against him for the unauthorised campaign and warned the Sultan against allowing the prince to carry all the treasures to Kara. But Jalal-ud-din's faith in his nephew could not be shaken. Jalal-ud-din returned to Delhi and was hopefully awaiting his nephew to present the spoils of the expedition to him with adequate apology. Ali Gurshasp returned to Kara and sent a report confessing his guilt and asking for pardon, which the Sultan granted through a communication sent per a messenger. Ali Gurshasp detained the messenger who was astounded to find the huge army that the prince had organised at Kara. In the meantime the prince's brother Almas Beg who had earlier instruction to this effect, impressed upon the guileless Sultan that his brother Ali Gurshasp was so desperately weighed down by a sense of guilt that unless the Sultan personally went to give him his pardon it was feared that he would commit suicide. The Sultan decided to see his nephew at once, and disregarding the all counsels of caution Jalal-ud-din proceeded for the trap laid by his nephew. As Zia-ud-din Barani puts it, 'his doom pulling him by the hair' reached Kara by journey down the Ganges by boat. As Jalal-ud-din met Ali Gurshasp the latter ceremoniously threw himself at the feet of his uncle. "Jalal-ud-din affectionately raised him, kissed him on the cheek, and chiding him for doubting his uncle's love drew him towards the barge. The signal was then given. The first blow proved ineffectual, but as the Sultan ran towards his boat a second stroke felled him, and his severed head, raised aloft on a spear, fixedly stared under the setting sun as the faithless nephew quickly spreading the royal canopy over his head, proclaimed himself king."

ALA-UD-DIN KHALJI (1296-1316)

The severed head of Jalal-ud-din Firuz Khalji was still dripping blood when royal canopy was spread over the head of Ali Gurshasp and he was proclaimed Sultan Ala-ud-din. The severed head of Ala-ud-din's benefactor was transfixed in a spear and paraded through Kara and Manikpur and then through Awadh. Ala-ud-din had three younger brothers, Almas Beg, Qutlugh Tigin, and Muhammad but only Almas Beg finds place in history, whom he gave the title of Ulugh Khan. The new king rewarded his followers and brothers with rewards in titles and promotions. But Delhi was still in the hands of Jalal-ud-din's men and Ala-ud-din hesitated to march against Delhi in the rainy season. The widow of Jalal-ud-din thinking a **de facto** king was necessary in that crisis proclaimed the younger son of Jalal-ud-din as King under the title of Rukh-ud-din Ibrahim. Arkali Khan, the eldest son, then in Multan sulked at the news of his brother's assumption of office of the king. His partisans at Delhi, however, refused to recognise Rukh-ud-din as the Sultan. Encouraged by these divisions Ala-ud-din marched on Delhi and his spoils provided him with the means of conciliating the populace. At every stage of his march to Delhi he set up a **balista** with the help of which small gold and silver coins were scattered among the mob. An army was sent from Delhi to oppose him near Badaun, but there was no fight for the army was lukewarm in the cause of Rukh-ud-din and Ala-ud-din's bursting coffers won over the allegiance of the army sent from Delhi. With 60,000 horse and 60,000 foot Ala-ud-din marched on Delhi and Rukh-ud-din Ibrahim after a feeble demonstration fled to Multan with his mother and the faithful Ahmad Chap (Oct. 3, 1296). Ala-ud-din was enthroned in the Red Palace of Balban which became his principal place of residence.

'The new king, having gained the throne by an act of treachery and ingratitude seldom equalled even in oriental annals, conciliated the populace by a lavish distribution of his southern gold, but his example was infectious and attempts to follow it distrubed the early years of his reign" (Wolseley Haig).

Ala-ud-din now sent Ulugh Khan and Hijabr-ud-din with an army 40,000 strong against Arkali Khan in Multan. The city surrendered and the princes Arkali Khan, Ibrahim and others fell into the hands of Ulugh Khan. When they were brought to Hansi Ulugh Khan got them blinded and widow of Jalal-ud-din Firuz was kept under close restraint.

During the early years of his reign Ala-ud-din was faithfully served by his brother Ulugh Khan, Nusrat Khan, Zafar Khan and Alp Khan.

Ala-ud-din's success upto his assumption of the crown and conciliating the nobility and the populace was largely due to the fabulous wealth that he had acquired as a result of his Devagiri compaign the history of which has been already recounted. We may discuss here at some length the significance of Ala-ud-din's Devagiri campaign.

Significance of Devagiri Campaign of Ala-ud-din : The significance of the Devagiri campaign of Ala-ud-din Khalji, before he had become the Sultan (i) was the first Muslim military expedition south of the Vindhyas. This was the beginning of the Muslim domination of South India, (ii) Ala-ud-din's campaign proved that the Hindu rulers of South India were both weak and divided like their counterparts in Northern India and there was no serious, united effort at opposing the Muslim invasions; (iii) it showed the secret ambition of Ala-ud-din to make himself independent of the tutelage of his uncle and benefactor Jalal-ud-din who was practically his foster father and later father-in-law and throws a flood of light on the crafty, ungrateful nature of his character; and (iv) it furnished him with a fabulous booty which helped him to buy off the opposition to his assumption of the Delhi throne, as it also showed the unfeeling character of the Delhi nobles and the populace who cared for money, not for morals.

His Problems : The problems of Ala-ud-din on his assumption of the crown were not merely connected with the task of making his kingship secure, but these arose from other sources. There were internal troubles, rebellions in Malwa, Gujarat, Rajputana, opposition of the Turkish nobility and the Mongol raids. All these problems demanded immediate solution.

His Activities : Ala-ud-din's immediate task was to eliminate the surviving members of the former Sultan's family. We have already noted that Arkali Khan. Rukh-ud-din, Ahmad Chap and few others had been blinded. Their women were all arrested and their slaves and properties were confiscated. Now the sons of Arkali Khan were put to death. The ladies of the **harem** were brought to Delhi along with Ahmad Chap and kept under strict surveillance in the house of Nusrat Khan.

The Mongol raids were the most serious problem that faced the Delhi Sultanate for a long time past. During the reign of Ala-ud-din Khalji, the Mongols invaded India to be fought back every time that they did so. In the successful defence of the country against the Mongol raids, the name of Ala-ud-din Khalji deserves to be mentioned at first. In 1296 the Mongols marched from the Suleiman mountains and crossed the Beas, the Jhelum and the Sutlej. But Zafar Khan, defeated the Mongols with great slaughter. Next year, that is, during the second year of Ala-ud-din's reign the Mongols appeared again under their leader Saldi. This time also it was Zafar Khan who beat them off and captured their leader and about 2000 followers, who were sent to Delhi as prisoners.

In 1299 Qutlugh Khwaja marched into India with a huge number of Mongols and proceeded upto the bank of the Jumna near Delhi. This time their object was not simply plunder but conquest of Indian territories, including Delhi. "Since their object was to conquer and govern the country, they plundered no cities and reduced no forts on their way. Isami tells us that Ala-ud-din had only a week or two at his disposal and perhaps the news of the Mongols reached him after they had crossed the Indus. Ala-ud-din summoned post-haste all officers his orders could reach. "It was a critical hour and Alaul Mulk in strict confidence advised him to follow the precepts of former kings and of text books and not to risk his kingdom on the doubtful result of a single battle." Ala-ud-din was advised to resort to diplomacy by Alaul and to gain some time by negotiations with the enemy. But Ala-ud-din gave his reply by quoting a proverb "You cannot steal a camel and expect to disappear unseen. Similarly you cannot govern Delhi and escape the challenges it entails... If at this moment I show any weakness, neither the mass of the people nor the brave warriors of the land will have any respect left for me." Ala-ud-din and Zafar Khan this time defeated the Mongols under their leader Qutlugh Khwaja. "The battle of Kili "conclusively proved that the Mongols were no longer worthy of the reputation Chaighiz had won for them." The battle, however, cost the life of Zafar Khan. The death of Zafar Khan had removed an extraordinary strong warrior who knew how to defend the country against the Mongols. This naturally made Ala-ud-din's defence against the Mongols somewhat weak, but he was rather happy at the death of Zafar Khan for his suspicious mind was harbouring a fear about the future ambition of Zafar Khan.

The Mongols were not to be deterred by defeats. They raided India for the fourth time in 1304 and proceeded upto Amroha, north of Lahore. But they were completely defeated by the army of the Sultan and had to leave India. But with dogged tenacity they pursued the policy of raiding India and in 1307-08 they appeared for the fifth time under their leader Iqbal Mand and began to proceed into India crossing the Indus. Ala-ud-din sent a strong force against them, Iqbal Mand was defeated and killed in the fight and the Mongols had to leave India leaving a large number of their fellows as prisoners at the hands of the army of the Sultan. This was the last attempt of Mongols against India under Ala-ud-din Khalji's reign. The military ability of the army of the Sultan and the terrible cruelties perpetrated on the defeated Mongols by the Sultan's troops created a fear about India among the Mongols.

Ala-ud-din was not content with defeating the Mongols when they repeatedly raided the country. He wanted to ensure that the Mongols might never again succeed in their attempt in raiding the country. He therefore made adequate arrangements for the security of the north western frontiers. He set up two military out-posts one at Dipalpur and another at Samana. He maintained strong contingents of armed forces in these two places to meet any eventuality at any time. He placed Gazi Malik, the governor of Punjab in charge of the defence of the north-western borders. He also built a line of fortresses along the north-west borders and rennovated the old ones. These arrangements had the double benefit of bringing peace and security to the people of the north-western areas of the country and a sense of relief to the Sultan himself.

The Mongols who had accepted Islam and got settled near Delhi and came to be known as new musalmans, thought that as a result of their conversion, they would be eligible for high administrative posts under the government. But to their utter disappointment they found that they could only be appointed as soldiers and nothing above that. This gave rise to dissatisfaction among them which gradually developed into disaffection. On his return Journey from Gujarat the soldiers in Ala-ud-din's army who had been recruited from the new musalmans became rebellious. Ala-ud-din atonce removed them from his army. This added fuel to fire. The new musalmans now began to conspire to kill Ala-ud-din. When this came to be known to the Sultan, he ordered the mass killing of the new musalmans. 30,000 new musalmans were killed in a day as a measure of revenge for their contumely. In this way Ala-ud-din solved the internal and external Mongol problems.

Ala-ud-din's Campaigns : The spectacular success of Ala-ud-din's campaigns against Malwa and Devagiri had whetted his ambition for territorial conquests beyond measure. "He began to form 'the most impossible schemes' and nourish 'the most extravagant desires." He wanted to 'establish a new religion and creed' and also aspired to emulate Alexander the Great as a conqueror of the world." Qazi Alaul Mulk brought the Sultan to his senses by pointing out that the prophetic office did never appertain to kings, though some prohets have discharged the functions of royalty. He also pointed out to the Sultan that Hindustan still remained to be subdued and there was no **vizier** like Aristotle to govern the state in Sultan's absence. Further, the kingdom was exposed to Mongol raids. The Sultan thus brought to his senses abandoned his wild schemes although he did not hesitate to describe himself as the **Second Alexander**.

In the second half of 1298, Ala-ud-din sent an expedition to Gujarat under Ulugh Khan and Nusrat Khan. It was the wealth and the flourishing ports of Gujarat that had attracted Ala-ud-din's attention. Ulugh Khan invaded Jaisalmer on his march and when Nusrat Khan joined him the two generals made an unsuccessful attempt on Chitor, but they invaded Gujarat and took its capital Anhilwara. The Baghela king Karna offered some resistance near Ahmedabad but being defeated took to flight. His queen Kamala

Devi, and his treasures fell into the hands of the invaders. Gujarati sources, including Merutunga's **Vicharasreni** a contemporary work, ascribes the success of the Muslim attack on Gujarat to the betrayal of Karna's minister Madhava. We cannot be quite definite about the information, although there may be some truth in it.

The Muslim generals then advanced as far as Surat and marched into Saurashtra where they captured the famous city of Somenath and plundered the yet more famous temple of Somenath and its idol, which had been replaced after the original one had been broken by Sultan Mahmud of Ghazni, was taken to Delhi to be trampled under foot by the faithful. Nusrat Khan also plundered the rich port of Cambay where he obtained a rich booty. There he got a young handsome Hindu slave of the name of Kafur who had been originally bought by his master at the cost of one thousand **dinars,** hence known as **Hazardinari**. According to Wassaf, the Muslim invaders pillaged and plundered the country and slaughtered people ruthlessly.

The impregnable fortress of Ranthambhor which had baffled Jalal-ud-din Firuz Khalji, now attracted the attention of Ala-ud-din, precisely for two reasons, (i) its strategical importance as one of the strongest fortresses of Hindustan, and (ii) it had given asylum to Mongol rebels. Ulugh Khan and Nusrat Khan were sent against the Chauhan prince Hamir Deva and the Khalji troops laid siege of the fort of Ranthambhor. Nusrat Khan was fatally wounded in action and this disheartened the Khalji troops who were also forced to retreat due to a surprise attack by the Rajputs. Ala-ud-din now marched in person against Ranthambhor with a large army. On the way there was an attempt on his life at Tilpat only twelve miles east of Delhi by Akat Khan nephew of Ala-ud-din, but the attempt failed.

In the meantime Ulugh Khan had besieged Ranthambhor again when Ala-ud-din was on his march to Ranthambhor. Taking advantage of the absence of Ala-ud-din from Delhi, Umar Khan, governor of Badaun and Mangu Khan, governor of Awadh both nephews of the Sultan, revolted. They were captured by the troops of the Sultan and sent to Ranthambhor where their eyes were gouged in presence of the Sultan himself, and the members of their families were all put to death.

Immediately after the revolt of the nephews of the Sultan, news of an insurrection at Delhi led by Haji Maula reached Ala-ud-din. Malik Hamid-ud-din was promptly despatched to Delhi and he was able to defeat Haji Maula and the rebels and put them to death. Ala-ud-din now carried on the siege of Ranthambhor with vigour and infused fresh courage and enthusiasm into his troops who kept the garrison under siege till the garrison ran short of provisions and Hamir Deva was compelled to send his minister Ranmal to negotiate peace with Ala-ud-din. Ranmal deserted to the enemy with his followers. As there was no hope of any honourable peace, far less of victory the women within the fort of Ranthambhor performed **jauhar** and Hamir Deva and his Rajputs died fighting and the fort surrendered in 1301, July 11. Ala-ud-din put to death Ranmal and those Rajputs who joined him as a punishment to their faithlessness to their master.

Expedition to Warangal : Towards the end of 1302 Ala-ud-din sent an expedition to Warangal under the command of Fakhr-ud-din Jauna and Chajju. K.S. Lal suggests that Ala-ud-din in order to consolidate his position in Northern India sent expeditions against Bengal where Shams-ud-din Firuz had declared independence as also against Telingana. The Muslim chronicles are rather very cryptic in their preference to the results of these expeditions. From the South Indian Hindu sources it is learnt that the Khalji troops penetrated into Telingna and reached the vicinity of Warangal but were beaten off by the Telingana army and were put to flight.

Campaign against Chitor : In 1303, January, Ala-ud-din Khalji sent out on his famous expedition against Chitor. He besieged the fort with a strong army but received strong resistance from the Rajput under their Rana Ratan Singh. Catapults and **balista** were profusely used by the Khalji army but these failed to make any impression on the fort. For seven months the fort offered heroic resistance but ultimately "Epidemic or famine **may have paralysed the garrison**." Rana Ratan Singh surrendered of his own will after the women had perished in the flames of **jauhar.** Thirty thousand Rajputs were put to the sword. According to the Rajput sources Rana Ratan Singh was among those who died on the battlefield, but Amir Khusrav and Isami tell us that the Rana survived the battle and his life was spared by the Sultan. Ala-ud-din stayed at Chitor for sometime when many temples were destroyed and the people suffered from the wanton fury of the Khalji troops. Chitor could not, however, be held under control for long by the Khaljis in the face of 'constant and stubborn resistance of the Rajputs.' Khizir Khan in whose charge Chitor was placed had to abandon it in 1311-12 and then Maladeva brother of the chief of Jalor ruled Chitor as tributary to the Delhi Sultanate.

According to the bardic chronicles of Rajputana invasion of Rajputana was solely due to Ala-ud-din's desire to get possession of Padmini, the beautiful queen of Rana Ratan Singh. Abul-Fazl, Haji-ud-Dabir, Ferishta have accepted this story. Iswari Prasad also remarks 'The immediate cause of the invasion was his (Ala-ud-din's) passionate desire to obtain possession of Padmini, the peerless queen of Rana Ratan Singh, renowned for her beauty all over Hindustan." But modern writers are inclined to reject it altogether, as the episode of Padmini does not find corroboration in any contemporary source.

Malwa : Ala-ud-din's next campaign was against Malwa. He despatched a select army of 10,000 under Ain-ul-Mulk governor of Multan for the subjugation of Malwa.

The Malwa army led by Raja Mahlak Deva and Koka Pradhana met the invading forces of Delhi, but was totally defeated. Koka Pradhana was killed in action. Raja Mahlak Deva took shelter in the fort of Mandu which was besieged by the Khalji troops. Treachery revealed to secret passage into the fort through which the invading army entered at night and surprised the garrison. Mahlak Deva fled, but was caught and slain. Ain-ul-Mulk now reduced Ujjain, Dhara and Chanderi one after another. He was then appointed governor of Malwa.

Devagiri Expedition : It was the gold of South India that had raised Ala-ud-din to the throne of Delhi and he sought to maintain it with the same. His aim in regard to the south was not annexation of new territories but realisation of huge tributes from the Hindu kings with a mere acknowledgement of his suzerainty. Ramchandra of Devagiri had defaulted payment of tributes for several years. Ala-ud-din appointed Malik Naib Kafur with Khwaja Haji as his second in command to lead an expedition to Devagiri. The governors of Gujarat and Malwa Alp Khan and Ain-ul-Mulk respectively were to collaborate with the Malik Kafur with their forces (1307). Malik Naib Kafur joined by Alp Khan and Ain-ul-Mulk reached Devagiri without any opposition and defeated the Devagiri troops, sacked the city, took enormous valuable booty in treasures and elephants and carried Ramchandra with his family and relations to Delhi. Ramchandra did homage to Ala-ud-din and was kindly received. He stayed at Delhi for six months after which he returned to Devagiri with the title of Rai-i-Rayan conferred on him by Ala-ud-din. This was a master stroke of diplomacy on the part of Ala-ud-din, for thereby purchased the loyalty of Ramchandra who rendered valuable service to Malik Naib Kafur in his southern military campaigns.

This second expedition to Devagiri is connected with the last phase of the Hindu rule in Gujarat. The Baghela king Karna about whom mention has already been made before seems to have recovered Gujarat after his defeat at the hands of Ulugh Khan and Nusrat Khan. This necessitated a second expedition against Gujarat for its final conquest. The subsequent history of Karna is not known. The famous poet Amir Khusrav has immortalised the love affair between Khizir Khan, son of Ala-ud-din and Devala Devi daughter of Karna in his poetic work **Ashiqa.**

According to Ferishta Karna after his defeat fled to the court of Ramchandra of Devagiri where he ruled over a small principality as his vassal.

Expedition to Rajputana : Sital Deva, the powerful chief of Siwana refused to submit to the authority of the Delhi Sultan. The Khalji troops kept the fort under siege for five or six years without success. Ultimately Ala-ud-din himself marched against Siwana and pressed the siege with great vigour. The Khalji troops ultimately won victory by entering the fort by escalading the wall. Sital Deva attempted flight to Jalor but was slain (1308). Ala-ud-din returned to Delhi leaving Kamal-ud-din in charge of Siwana. Conquest of Siwana was followed by fortress of Jalor which was initially defended valiantly by its chief Kanhar Deva and when Kamal-ud-din was sent with fresh reinforcement the fortress capitulated and Kanhar Deva was killed in action. With the fall of Jalor-ud-din's expeditions in Rajputana ended, for more prominent Rajput states had already been brought under the authority of Delhi. According to numismatic evidence (1301) Jodhpur had submitted to Delhi although there is no mention of this in the contemporary chronicles. According to Tod mandor, Tonk and Bundi had been occupied by the Delhi troops.

Second Expedition to Warangal : The earlier expedition to Warangal in 1303 had failed. Now, after the success of the second Devagiri expedition Ala-ud-din for the vindication of his prestige prepared for a second expedition against Warangal. In November 1309 Malik Kafur marched from Delhi and taking all sorts of help from Ramachandra of Devagiri, entered the kingdom of Telingana. In spite of valiant resistance the Telingana forces could not resist the attack of Malik Kafur and as usual the women and the children perished in the flames of **jauhar** and men laid their lives in action. Malik Kafur left the fort in charge of the brother of the deceased chief of Telingana on promise of obedience and hastened towards the capital. On reaching Warangal he besieged the fort in 1310. Prataprudra defended the fort with 9,00,000 archers and 20,000 horses against the besiegers who numbered one hundred thousand. "The fort of Warangal was made of stone and surrounded by a strong earthen wall and two deep moats, one protecting the outer wall and the other the inner fort." After repeated and strenuous efforts the Khalji troops were able to fill up the moat and make a breach in the wall and then crossing the inner moat laid siege of the fort. Prataprudra stoutly defended the fort and following scorched earth policy laid waste the enemy's route and communication between Delhi and the invading forces at Warangal was cut off. Over-crowding of the fort created the problem of supplies of provisions and Prataprudra was ultimately obliged to sue for peace. He gave 7,000 horses, 100 elephants and promised to pay an annual tribute to Delhi. "Among the jewels delivered was one 'unparalleled in the whole world' as Amir Khusrav calls it, and this was possibly the Koh-i-Nur or Babur's diamond which, according Khafi Khan and other later chroniclers, Malik Kafur brought from the Deccan."

Expedition to South India : During his siege of Warangal, Malik Kafur came to know of the wealth of the kingdom of the far south. Towards the end of 1310 Malik Kafur set out for Malabar at the extreme south of the peninsula. It was simply the greed of gold that had inspired the expedition and not the propagation of the true faith as some Muslim chroniclers state. Malik Kafur marched via Devagiri where Ramchandra rendered him all possible help, both because of his loyalty to the Sultan of Delhi and because there was no love lost between him and the Hoysala king Ballala III as he had repeatedly encroached upon the territory of Ramchandra. Malik Kafur reached the border of the Hoysala kingdom when Ballala III was absent with his army in Malabar in recovering his ancestral possessions in the Tamil country, taking advantage of a civil war between Vira Pandya and Sundara Pandya, two brothers. The news of Malik Kafur's invasion brought Ballala hurriedly back to his capital and he appealed to two Pandya brothers for help in his peril, although he had just invaded their kingdom shortly before. Vira Pandya sent a reinforcement, but Ballala finding himself no match for the invading forces sued for peace, surrendered his wealth, horses and elephants and agreed to pay an annual tribute.

Malik Kafur did not stay at Dvarasamudra for long, for Malabar was his objective. The Pandya kingdom was known to the Muslim chroniclers as Malabar extending from Quilon to Nellore. Malik Kafur requisitioned Ballal's help in guiding the Muslim forces and after a strenuous journey of five days through mountainous terrain reached the frontiers of Malabar and marched towards Birdhul, the headquarters of Vira Pandya. Due to the civil war betwen Vira Pandya and Sundara Pandya, two brothers, the Pandya kingdom was a house divided against itself. However, the Pandya princes did not take shelter in the forts but avoiding open fight with the enemy began to harass them repeatedly. This ultimately exhausted the invading forces and Malik Kafur failed to secure submission of the Pandya princes. Vira Pandya had left Birdhul before it fell and his position became more precarious because 20,000 of his Muslim soldiers deserted to the enemy. Malik Kafur marched after the fugitive king Vira Pandya, taking Kundur on his way after a severe fight but he could not capture Vira Pandya who made good his escape into the forests. Malik Kafur now arrived at Chidambaram where he massacred the people, razed the golden temple to the ground and its foundations were dug up. With rich plunder Malik Kafur returned to the headquarters of Vira Pandya, Birdhul and sacked all the temples there. The temple of Srirangam and other temples in the vicinity of Kannanur were sacked by Malik Kafur who now suddenly appeared at Madura, the main capital of Pandya country and the headquarters of Sundara Pandya. The Pandya prince had, however, fled with his treasures. Infurated at finding nothing but just a few elephants, Malik Kafur ordered fire to be set to the temple of Sokkanatha. At this stage Sundara Pandya's uncle Vikrama Pandya attacked Malik Kafur with a large force who somehow manage to keep his booty which comprised of 5,000 horses, 512 elephants, 500 maunds of jewels and withdrew in April 1311. The Muslim chroniclers' claim that in the south Malik Kafur had only successes in South India passing over the defeats suffered by Ala-ud-din's army and the Hindu chroniclers' claim of unbroken series of victories have to be taken after much dispassiorate consideration. The facts about the southern campaigns of the Khalji army under Malik Kafur were as related in the foregoing discussions.

Ala-ud-din's Theory of Kingship : Ala-ud-din was a believer in Balban's theory of kingship. He was a staunch believer in the majesty of the monarch who according to him was God's representative on earth. It was Ala-ud-din's conviction that king's wisdom is greater than that of the common people and as such the king's will should be law. Ala-ud-din's idea of sovereignty was that **kingship knows no kingship** and as such all people of the kingdom must be either his subjects or servants. The nobility and the **ulemas** where the two forces that had been exercising influence on the Sultan. But Ala-ud-din was not prepared to allow the nobility or the **ulemas** to influence his policy. He wanted to reduce them to the status of servants of the state fit to be dismissed at the will of the Sultan and to remain in office only so long as they enjoyed the pleasure of the Sultan. Ala-ud-din inspired awe and reverence in the nobles and the **ulemas** in their relation to the Sultan and none dared give him any advice, far less expect to influence his policy. Ala-ud-din was the first Sultan to openly declare that he would not allow the **ulemas to advise** the Sultan in the matter of the administration of the state. The Only person who could presume to advise the Sultan was Alaul Mulk an old friend of Ala-ud-din. Ala-ud-din enunciated his own policy of the state : "I do not know whether this is lawful or unlawful, whether I think it to be for the good of the state or suitable for the emergency, that I decree; and as for what may happen to me on the Day of Judgement, that I know not." It goes to the credit of Ala-ud-din that he was the first Turkish Sultan who brought the Church under control of the state and initiated the factors that might have made the Delhi Sultanate secular in character if his policy were pursued by his successors. He kept the state free from the influence of the **ulemas** but in times of war he took full advantage of Muslim fanaticism in plundering the cities and temples of the Hindu chiefs and kings. He was a devout Musalman and did not act against Muslim law.

Ala-ud-din was too imperious to strengthen his sovereignty by asking for investiture from the Khalifa. But the styled himself as the Deputy of the Khalifa without caring to obtain any sanction from the Khalifa himself. This was done only to keep the theory of relationship of the Delhi Sultanate with the Caliphate alive.

Ala-ud-din's policy towards the Hindus was dictated by settled ideology with which qazi Mughis-ud-din was at one. His policy towards the Hindus was of total repression.

Ala-ud-din's Measures for Suppression of Rebellions : Ever since Ala-ud-din's accession there had been rebellions. He sought the opinion of his confidential council—**majlis-i-khas** as to the causes of the rebellions. The council mentioned four causes : **first,** lack of information of the king about the good and bad acts of the people, **second,** liquor; people having organised drinking parties, talk freely, ally themselves with each other and hatch conspiracies and rebellions, **third,** the unity, affection and relationships of the maliks and amirs and their frequenting each other's houses, so that if one of them is punished, a hundred others join him owing to their blood relationship and ties of affection, and **four,** money ; if there be no money in the hands of the people, they will apply themselves to earning their invelihood and no one will think of rebellion or conspiracy.

This council was held while Ala-ud-din was pressing the siege of Ranthambhor. On his return to Delhi, by a stroke of pen he revoked all grants of lands and pensions and resumed all lands that were held in proprietory rights, gifts, pensions, pious endowments. These lands under different categories were almost exclusively held by the Muslims.

State officials were instructed to extort money from the people with extreme sternness, and according to the contemporary chroniclers this order of the Sultan was carried out so faithfully that except for the big nobles, high officials of the state or wealthy merchants none else possessed any gold. The result was that the people remained so busy in earning their livelihood that they had no time to think of rebellion or conspiracy.

Ala-ud-din's second measure was the institution of a net work of an efficient espionage system through which he kept himself informed of the activities of the nobles and occurrences of importance in the state. Even the activities of the people in the market place were reported to the king.

The third measure of Ala-ud-din was ordering strict prohibition in the state. Use of wine or any kind of intoxicating drugs was strictly prohibited on the pain of severe punishment. Ala-ud-din himself set example by breaking all his drinking vessels and emptying his cellar into the streets. But the fact remains, that despite brutal punishment to drinkers, he could not make Delhi absolutely dry. Ultimately Ala-ud-din permitted private manufacture and drinking of wine ; public sale of wine and its use in convivial parties were stopped.

The fourth and the last measure was the prohibition of all sorts of gatherings in the residences of the nobles and even intermarriages between members of noble families without the Sultan's special permission.

His Measures against the Hindus : In order to check the power of the Hindu officials Ala-ud-din deprived the three classes of revenue officials called the **khut, chaudhri** and **muqadam,** that is the zamindars, the headmen of the parganas and villages respectively of their powers and privileges. "These three classes of people were the hereditary collectors of revenue on behalf of the king, and it was alleged that they appropriated to themselves as much of the state revenue as they could, evaded payment of taxes, and even ignored the government." According to the description of the chroniclers "they ride upon fine horses, wear fine clothes, and go out hunting and hold drinking and convivial parties." The standard of revenue demand was raised to half of the gross produce. The perquisites realised by the chiefs were abolished and all concessions to them withdrawn."...they had to pay land revenue at the full rate and their land was to be brought under assessment ; and all discriminations done away with between the chief and the humblest peasant." The chiefs, i.e. the zamindars and the headmen of the parganas and villages all Hindus were so much impoverished that "no gold or silver was to be found in the houses of the Hindus." According to Barani "The people were brought to such a state of obedience that one revenue officer would string twelve **khuts, muqadams** and **chaudhris** together by the neck and enforce payment by blows." The credit for all this went to the deputy minister of finances Sharaf Qaini.

It may be noted that these regulations operated mainly in the central part of the kingdom and the victims of these measures were Hindus. Some scholars have argued that "when Ala-ud-din had not spared the Muslims or hesitated to deprive them of peculiar privileges, there was no reason why he should have shown any favour to the Hindu officials. "That Ala-ud-din was actuated by communal considerations in his dealings with the Hindus becomes clear from Barani : "Sultan Ala-ud-din demanded from learned men rules and regulations, so that the Hindu should be ground down, and property and possessions which are the cause of disaffection and rebellion should not remain in his house." (Translation by Moreland). Moreland adds that the Hindu referred to by Barani were upper class Hindus and not peasants. Mughis Khan, the Qazi in reply to Ala-ud-din's question about the status of the Hindus uttered two provable lies—lies very dear to Barani's heart, but lies none the less. First, that 'the Hindus were the greatest enemies of the prophet Muhammad and that the Prophet has ordered the Hindus to be killed, plundered and enslaved." The Prophet never came across a Hindu in his life so no such order is found in the six authentic sunni collections of the Prophet's **Hadises**. Secondly, that while Imam Abu Hanifa 'to whose school we belong' has permitted peace with Hindus on the payment of the **Jizya,** other religious scholars have left no alternative for them except 'Islam or the sword.' This again shows a terrible ignorance on Barani's part, which he repeats with greater emphasis in the **Fatawa-in-Jahandari**. (Prof. Nizami).

In order to reduce the Hindus to poverty Ala-ud-din besides his four general regulations meant to ensure against rebellion, rigorously enhanced the land revenue of the Hindus to fifty per cent of the gross produce and also imposed grazing tax on cattle, sheep and goats. Customs, excise and **Jizya** i.e. a poll tax, on non-Muslims, were retained as before. The cumulative effect of all such levies was that the Hindus were reduced to extreme poverty. Evasion of any of the taxes was severely punished. All concessions and privileges enjoyed by high-ranking Hindu officials were now withdrawn. Woolseley Haig remarks that "Hindus throughout the kingdom were reduced to one dead level of poverty and misery, or, if there were one class more to be pitied than another, it was that which had formerly enjoyed the most esteem, the hereditary assessors and collectors of revenue."

Reorganisation of the Army : Ala-ud-din's ambition of territorial conquests, to make himself a Sultan both in fact and name, to enforce the regulations that he had passed to suppress the nobles and above all to keep the country secure against Mongol raids, it was necessary to reorganise the army on a strong and permanent footing. It goes without saying a despotic rule is possible only with the help of an efficient and loyal army. To this end Ala-ud-din undertook certain important reforms in the army. He appointed a minister in charge of the army recruitment, called **ariz-i-mamalik** whose business was to recruit capable soldiers directly to the army. A standing army was created for the first time in the history of the Delhi Sultanate which kept itself always ready for military action under the orders of the Sultan. The army was paid in cash from the royal treasury and the annual salary of a trooper was 234 **tankas** and 78 **tankas** more for a horse. The state bore the expenses of supplying arms, horses and other military stores to the army. The army minister had to maintain a descriptive roll of every soldier so that no body might proxy for the soldier at the time of military review or in the battlefield. Branding of horses was also resorted to in order to prevent production of inferior horses at the time of muster or in the battle-field. Ferishta gives the number of the cavalry as 4,75,000, but while the number of the infantry had far exceeded the number of the horse men, its number was not recorded by the contemporary writers. In order that there might be good discipline, timely supply of equipment to the soldiers and the army always remained in good trim, Ala-ud-din took personal interest in the matter.

Ala-ud-din's Economic Regulations : Zia-ud-din Barani in his **Tarikh-i-Firuz-Shahi** writes that the object of the economic regulations of Ala-ud-din was the maintenance of a strong and efficient army against the Mongols. But Prof. Nizami points out that Barani "after first declaring that the economic regulations were primarily a military measure, explains in some detail how Ala-ud-din regulated the price of the commodities that had no importance for the military ; also the regulations were maintained long after the military need for them had vanished." In this **Fatawa-i-Jahandari** meant for the average king Barani gave advice on price control for combating famines and as a measure of public welfare necessary at all time. However, there is no doubt that Ala-ud-din had to think of the device of price control in order to cheapen the cost of maintaining a vast army. He therefore decided to solve the problem by lowering the price of all essential commodities so that the soldiers could maintain a comfortable standard with a low salary. "The army organiser thus turned to be 'a daring political economist." He fixed the prices of all varieties of food grains, all the different kinds of cloth including silk, cattle, horses, slaves, bread, vegetables, shoes, in fact all articles of daily need. He also controlled the supplies and transport and compelled the merchants to bring supplies of all grains and articles for sale in Delhi. Merchants had to register themselves in the office of the inspector-general of the markets. Peasants of the Doab and areas to a distance of two hundred miles from Delhi had to sell grains to the registered merchants at a fixed rate. The merchants who had to deal in cloth and procure manufactured articles from places beyond Ala-ud-din's control where prices were higher had to sell these at Delhi at fixed rates but Ala-ud-din allowed them a margin of profit. Grains and cloth were stocked in stores to guard against famine and scarcity. Rationing was introduced when necessity arose. Hoarding of grains or other essential commodities was strictly forbidden. All the regulations relating to prices were enforced with all strictness and any infringement of the regulations was brought to the notice of the Sultan by a highly organised espionage system.

The economic regulations of Ala-ud-din which were both bold and original in conception have evoked universal admiration. But these had their short comings which must not be overlooked. (i) The price control and rationing obtained in Delhi and near abouts only, the entire country was not brought under these regulations. (ii) The regulations adversely affected the producers and the traders, for the prices were fixed very near to the cost of production. The narrow margin of profit gave no incentive to the agriculturists nor to the traders and merchants. (iii) The merchants had to keep their wives and children at Delhi as hostages for bringing in continuous supplies. (iv) The peasants had to pay 50% of his gross produce as the land revenue and the rest he had to sell at a fixed price. But he had to buy his daily needs at a much higher price in his local market. Thus while the capital was fed, the rest of the country was starved. "So large a quantity of grain was stored at Delhi that Ibn Batuta, who arrived there in A.D. 1334, consumed the rice stored by Ala-ud-din." (v) The army and incidentally the people of Delhi derived the benefits of the regulations. "Judged by the objective which inspired them, they proved highly successful. Opposed as they were to economic laws, they died with their author."

Ala-ud-din's Last Days : Malik Kafur's return from Malabar campaign in triumph was the climax of Ala-ud-din's imperial expansion. But behind the success lay hidden his decline. "Arduous work, intemperate habits, and advanced years ruined his health and contributed to the rapid deterioration of his personality and ability. According to Barani Ala-ud-din developed dropsy. Amir Khusrav suggests that his disease was of liver and according to Isami the Sultan had grown lean and weak and that excessive pain began to affect his judgment and he had recurring fits of unconsciousness. His failing health and declining abilities led to intrigue for power at the court. One man who profited by the circumstances was Malik Kafur, the hero of the southern campaign.

Malik Kafur the most favourite and powerful of the Sultan's lieutenants had his rivals in Khizir Khan's mother Malika-i-Jahan and her brother Alp Khan. Marriage of Khizir Khan with the daughter of Alp Khan in February 1312 cemented the alliance and the Sultan's declaration of Khizir Khan as the heir apparent made their power and position stronger. It was about this time that Singhana, son of Ramchandra of Devagiri asserted his independence. This necessitated Malik Kafur's expedition to Devagiri. His absence at Devagiri led to the undisputed supremacy of Malika-i-Jahan and Alp Khan at the Delhi court. She now got her second son married to the second daughter of Alp Khan. On this occasion Khizir Khan was also allowed to marry Devala Devi daughter of Raja Karna. The education of the two sons of Ala-ud-din was neglected and they were given to drinking and debauchery. In the meantime the Sultan's health was rapidly declining. Malik Kafur easily succeeded in poisoning the ears of Ala-ud-din against Khizir Khan, his mother Malika-i-Jahan and Alp Khan. But all the same he could not get the sanction of the Sultan to kill Alp Khan. But he got Alp Khan murdered by his trusted follower Kamal-ud-din Gurg. Thus the junta was broken and Malik Kafur became master of the situation. Khizir Khan was removed from Delhi first and then made a prisoner at Gwalior while his mother Malika-i-Jahan was imprisoned in Delhi fort. These happenings at Delhi led to revolt in Gujarat, Chitor, Devagiri etc. In the midst of these troubles "Ala-ud-din Khalji, the mighty king of Delhi, passed away on January 5, 1316."

Character and Estimate of Ala-ud-din Khalji : It is indeed difficult to analyse the character of Ala-ud-din Khalji and come to a definite conclusion about it. His was a complex, subtle and mixed character in which virtues and vices, abilities and weaknesses were so intermingled that it is rather difficult to pass any verdict on his character.

Ala-ud-din was unscrupulous, aggressive, haughty and over-ambitious and as a man he was treacherous and ungrateful. Zia-ud-din Barani calls him crafty and cruel and holds him responsible for shedding more innocent blood than even the Pharoh was guilty of. He was guilty of most disgusting vice. He did not hesitate to get his benefactor, his uncle and father-in-law Jalal-ud-din Firuz Khalji assassinated to satisfy his ambition.

Despite these defects in his character, he was extremely resourceful, of unending energy and capacity for work, unbounded courage, power of cool calculation and a penetrating common sense. He was a valiant general and an unparalleled warrior. He was a master diplomat. As a reformer he was both bold and original and as an administrator he was vigorous, efficient, even ruthless. He understood the value of and prepared the ground for the separation of the state from the church. "Himself almost illiterate, he had nothing but contempt for learning and scholarship, though during his reign Delhi became the 'rival of Cairo and equal of Constantinople' because of the throng of great men of whom the poet Amir Khusrav and Hasan were the most famous." According to Ferishta, however, he learnt reading and writing after his accession as Sultan. Ala-ud-din was the first Muslim imperialist, and the history of Muslim empire and Muslim administration in India, in fact, began with him. Ala-ud-din's career was a distinctive phase in the evolution of the Indo Muslim history. According to Elphinstone Ala-ud-din's reign was glorious despite many absurd and oppressive measures that he undertook. On the whole he was a successful monarch and exihibited a just exercise of his powers. But Dr. Smith does not accept this characterisation of Ala-ud-din by Elphinstone. According to him Ala-ud-din was "a savage tyrant with very little regard for justice and his reign, though marked by the conquest of Gujarat and many successful raids like the storming of the two great fortresses, was exceedingly disgraceful in many respects."

The African traveller Ibn Batuta expressed the opinion that 'Ala-ud-din deserved to be considered one of the best Sultans of Delhi. Zia-ud-din Barani, the historian who gives the full details of his reign refers to his addiction to disgusting vices. Barani observes "He shed more innocent blood than the Pharaoh was guilty of." These are two extreme opinions about Ala-ud-din. True, Ala-ud-din was as crafty, cruel tyrant whose ambition knew no bounds and who could adopt any reprehensible means to fulfil his ambition. He did not hesitate to kill his benefactor and uncle, who was also his father-in-law in order to occupy the throne. He did not falter in killing men, women and children who might in the least be his rival. He was short tempered and sharp tongued and in one day he got about thirty thousand new muslims killed.

Ala-ud-din succeeded in occupying the throne with the help of a large number of the nobles of the court, but on his becoming secure on the throne he did not hesitate to expropriate their estates. Gratitude was alien to his nature. Zafar Khan more than once saved the country from the Mongol raiders, but he was happy at heart when Zafar Khan lost his life in fighting against the Mongols. His suspicious mind always harboured jealousy at the success of others. He took steps so that wealthy Hindu or Muslims were reduced to proverty. He had also fixed the land revenue at 50% of the gross produce of the soil. His fixation of prices of grains and other essential commodities in order to maintain the vast army he had organised brought about economic ruin to the peasants and merchants, for their margin of profits was so small that their work became uneconomic. On the basis of the above facts Barani called Ala-ud-din cruel, vicious ungrateful and ruthless.

Yet there is a brighter side too. He was an intrepid warrior and an able general, a clever diplomat and an excellent military strategist. All his military campaigns were successful. In Northern India, he conquered Gujarat, Malwa, Chitor, Ranthambhor, Ujjain, Mandu, Dhar, Chanderi etc. and in the south he conquered Devagiri, Warangal, Dvarasamudra, Madura and compelled them to accept his overlordship. Ala-ud-din developed the military system of Balban and carried it to its logical conclusion. He also revived the theory of kingship initiated Balban. His greatest achievement was the security arrangements that he had made for the defence of the country against Mongol raids. He was the first Muslim ruler who understood the need for separating state from the church, and therefore, he made his government independent of the influence of the **ulemas**.

For the internal and external security, Ala-ud-din realised the need for developing a standing army and the credit of laying the foundations of a standing army for the first time under the Muslim rule must go to him. He had certain original conceptions which he gave effect to by introducing certain regulations for controlling prices and rationing of the essentials of daily life. Although these measures were undertaken for the maintenance of a vast army at a comparatively low cost, the idea was novel indeed. In order to prevent rebellions he promulgated certain regulations which while impoverished both the Hindu and the Muslim wealthy persons, had the desired effect.

Ala-ud-din while did not give rest to himself because he was keeping himself busy with either military campaigns or affairs of the administration, did not give any rest to his officers. During his reign, there was peace in the country.

Ala-ud-din was the first Turkish conqueror who had carried Muslim arms beyond the Vindhyas and subjugated almost whole of the south, thereby giving political unity to almost the whole of the Indian subcontinent. His consolidation of power at the centre gave the Delhi Sultanate an administrative unity. He was the first Turkish empire builder in India, as also the first Turkish emperor. Rigorous execution of justice under him eradicated the menance of robbery and theft and travelling from Kabul to the Bay of Bengal and from Telengana to Kashmir became absolutely safe.

Ala ud din was a patron of art and learning. Amir Khusrav and Amir Hasan were among the literary lights that adorned his court. His love of architecture can be seen in his construction of **Alai Darwaza,** an extension of Qutbi mosque in Delhi which is the most beautiful specimen of the early Turkish architecture. The fort Siri, the 'Palace of Thousand Pillars' called **Hazar situn,** and many mosques bear testimony to Ala-ud-din's love of architecture.

When a balanced view of the character and achievements of Ala-ud-din is taken, the truth of the remarks of both Ibn Batuta and Zia-ud-din Barani, although apparently contradictory, can easily be realised.

Khalji's Rule after Ala-Ud-Din : When age and ailment had incapacitated Ala-ud-din Malik Kafur made himself the real master of the state. His influence on the old Sultan became so over-powering that he persuaded him to nominate his youngest son Shiab-ud-din to be his successor. On Ala-ud-din's death Malik Kafur placed Shiab-ud-din, the minor son of Ala-ud-din on the throne and began to rule in his name virtually in full sovereignty. The elder sons of Ala-ud-din—Khizir Khan and Sadi Khan were arrested and blinded, and thrown into the prison. The first Begum of Ala-ud-din was also imprisoned. The third son of Ala-ud-din Mubarak Shah was also put under arrest and kept in confinement and everything was made ready to gouge his eyes. But the high-handed policy of Malik Kafur having exceeded all limits of toleration, the nobles and slaves who were still faithful to the Khalji family killed Malik Kafur and placed Mubarak Shah, the third son of Ala-ud-din on the throne of Delhi. Mubarak Shah for a brief period ruled as the regent of his minor brother Shiab-ud-din but after that threw him into the prison after gouging his two eyes. Mubarak Shah now assumed the title of Qutb-ud-din Mubarak Shah.

QUTB-UD-DIN MUBARAK SHAH (1316-20)

Mubarak Shah began his reign with a policy of extreme moderation. Immediately on his accession he declared a general amnesty, releasing all prisoners and permitting the return of all exiled for offences. Mubarak liberally rewarded the soldiers and officers who supported his accession, gave back the **jagirs** which had been resumed under Ala-ud-din, he withdrew the market regulations and reduced the revenue demands, and relaxed the rigours of administration. People who suffered so much under Ala-ud-din now got relief ; the landowing and the peasant classes benefited by reduction of revenue demands.

But soon the "charming and popular king was, however, immersed in drinking, debauchery and pleasure, and the capital, following his example and due to his policy of relaxation, indulged in excesses of wanton sensuality." As Barani puts it : "every house became a tavern." "Bribery, corruption and malversation are into the vitals of administration, which was paralysed." Khusrav Khan, an unknown slave of Gujarat was appointed by Mubarak as his **vizier.**

Rebellions : Administrative laxity at the centre led to rebellions in Gujarat, Devagiri and Madura. Ain-ul-Mulk and Ghazi Malik Tughluq were sent to Gujarat, who quelled the rebellion effectively. Mubarak Shah himself marched against Devagiri whose king Haripala Deva, hearing the news of the arrival of the Sultan fled from his capital. He was, however, captured and flayed alive and his head placed on one of the gates of Devagiri. The Devagiri kingdom was divided into districts each placed under a Turkish officer. Mubarak built a mosque at Devagiri with the materials of the Hindu temples which he demolished. Malik Yaklaki was appointed governor of Devagiri. Khusrav Khan was sent with an army to quell the rebellion at Madura.

Conspiracy to depose Mubarak Shah : On his return journey from Devagiri, a conspiracy to kill Mubarak Shah was hatched by his cousin Asad-ud-din, son of Yaghrush Khan. But one of the conspirators revealed the plot to the Sultan and all the conspirators were arrested and put to death. All the descendants of Yaghrush Khan were ordered to be put to death. Mubarak was much enraged at the conspiracy to take his life and in order not to keep any future chance of any such conspiracy he ordered the killing of his brother Khizir Khan, Shai Khan and Shihab-ud-din. He then took Devala Devi, the widow of Khizir Khan as his wife.

Failure of the Administration : Murder of Mubarak Shah : Mubarak Shah's success in the south appears to have turned his head. Without any apparent reason he ordered the killing of his father-in-law Zafar Khan and his favourite Shahim whom he had left as his regent during his absence in the south. Mubarak again threw himself to sensuality of extreme kind and neglected administration. He took pleasure in indecent remarks and bad gestures of his courtiers and himself at times raised doubt about his sanity. All this naturally denigrating the office of the Sultan in the eyes of the people and the officials and lawlessness began to raise its ugly head everywhere. Malik Yaklaki Khan, governor of Devagiri revolted but was defeated by some of the loyal officers of the Sultan in the south. Yaklaki Khan was sent to Delhi as a prisoner where his nose and ears were cut off. Later he was pardoned and appointed governor of Samana. But all his associates were put to death. The governor of Gujarat Hisan-ud-din who had replaced Zafar Khan revolted but he was also defeated by some of the loyal nobles and sent to Delhi as prisoner. He was forgiven in order to please Khusrav Khan a hot favourite of Mubarak Shah. Khusrav Khan himself was also secretly trying to carve out a kingdom for himself. The news was passed to the Sultan by some of his officers. But the Sultan disbelieved them. He, however, summoned Khusrav Khan to Delhi and punished his accusers with dismissal and imprisonment.

Khusrav finding that his design would not work till he could raise an army of his own, sought the sanction of the Sultan to raise a corps of 40,000 horse from Bharvar tribe of Gujarat to which he himself belonged. The Sultan agreed. After having raised a cavalry 40 thousand strong under his full control, he sought permission of the Sultan that relations of Khusrav might be allowed to enter the palace whenever they would like to meet Khusrav for any urgent business. This permission was also granted, Khusrav now prepared his plan to assassinate the Sultan. A tutor of Mubarak Shah had warned him against allowing too much latitude to Khusrav, but it went unheeded. When the conspiracy had ripened Khusrav's troops entered the palace and cut down the royal guards (April 14, 1320). When this was being done Khusrav was by the side of the Sultan. On enquiry from the Sultan about the noise, Khusrav remarked that some horses had broken loose and the guards were trying to catch them, hence the noise. Soon the murderers reached the royal apartment and the Sultan ran towards the **zenana** out of fear, but was caught by the hair by Khusrav while one of his followers named Jaharia stabbed him to death. Mubarak's severed head was then thrown into the courtyard to cause a feeling of terror among the people around. Thus ended rule of the Khaljis.

NASIR-UD-DIN KHUSRAV SHAH (April 15 to Sept. 5, 1320)

Khusrav summoned the prominent nobles, detained them in the palace till the next morning when he ascended the throne under the tile Nasir-ud-din Khusrav Shah. Barani and other Muslim chroniclers are very hard on Khusrav and treat him with contempt as he was a Hindu convert. Barani sees in Khusrav's **coup de main** the consequence of a Hindu revolution and in his accession "a period of triumph of Hinduism and the downfall of Islam." But a dispassionate consideration will show that Khusrav did never aim at restoration of a Hindu monarchy, nor did he champion the cause of Hinduism. "On the contrary, he had shown the iconoclastic zeal of a Muslim during his campaigns in the south. Khusrav regarded himself as a Muslim, the **Khutba** was recited in his name, and his coins bear the title of Commander of the Faithful." He married the wife of Mubarak Shah.

Khusrav executed some of the nobles who were hostile to him and rewarded those who helped him in his conspiracy. Randhol, his righthand man in the conspiracy was given the title of **Rai-i-Rayan,** some of the prominent nobles were placated by him in order that they might not become hostile to him. With certain exceptions, he retained the services of the old officers and was anxious to secure the support of the nobility. Both Ibn Batuta and Amir Khusrav state that he "did obtain the support and homage of the nobles and governors."

The murder of Mubarak Shah and the consequential orgy of bloodshed had alienated a small section of the nobility who saw in the accession of Khusrav triumph of heathenism and great danger to Islam. The spokesman of this opposition was Ghazi Tughluq whose son Malik Jauna was at the court. Ghazi Tughluq, governor of Dipalpur raised the slogan of Islam in danger, which has often proved so effective a weapon in Muslim history. Malik Jauna, under instruction from his father one day slipped from the court of Delhi to join his father. Ghazi Tughluq appealed to the governor of Uch, Multan Siwastan, Samana and Jalor and even to Ain-ul-Mulk who was at Delhi. Only the governor of Uch responded to the appeal of Ghazi Tughluq. Governor of Samana who was loyal to Khusrav marched against Ghazi Tughluq but was killed by his own men. Governors of Jalor and Siwastan gave half-hearted support. Ain-ul-Mulk secretly assured support, although apparently maintained neutrality. Ghazi Tughluq could not also get the moral support of the great saint Nizam-ud-din Auliya. The true nature of the rebellion was to dispossess Khusrav and to seize power, the slogan of Islam in danger was a mere pretext.

Khusrav Khan sent a force 40 thousand strong against Ghazi Tughluq. But it failed to take Sarasuti. The army proceeded towards Dipalpur against Ghazi Tughluq but was totally defeated. Ghazi Tughluq now proceeded on march to Delhi and despite desperate attempt made by Khusrav to oppose him at the battle of Indarpat he was defeated (Sept. 6, 1320). Ain-ul-Mulk had deserted Khusrav and left for Malwa. Totally defeated Khusrav Khan took shelter in the garden of Shadi Khan at Tilpat. The next day he was captured and beheaded. On September 8, 1320, Ghazi Tughluq ascended the throne under the title Ghiyas-ud-din Tughluq Shah.

THE TUGHLUQS : GHIYAS-UD-DIN TUGHLUQ SHAH (1320-25)

Ghiyas-ud-din's Ethnic Origin and Early Life : Ghiyas-ud-din Tughluq, also called Tughluq which Amir Khusrav in his **Tughluq Nama** mentions as the personal name of Ghiyas-ud-din. Wolseley Haig and some other historians take **Tughluq** to be a tribal cognomen. There is also no unanimity of opinion among the historians with regard to the time of Tughluq's arrival in India. Ibn Batuta and Afif place it during the time of Ala-ud-din Khalji, but according to Amir Kusrav Tughluq after searching for livelihood in Delhi for a long time, was taken into the service of the imperial guard by Jalal-ud-din Khalji. He earned his first distinction at the time of the Ranthambhor campaign under Ulugh Khan. It was, however, under Ala-ud-din Khalji that Ghiyas-ud-din Tughluq, then known as Malik Tughluq, rose in position and prestige. He rendered meritorious service as governor first of Multan and then of Dipalpur. He checked the Mongol inroads into the country and effectively garrisoned the frontier towns. According to Amir Khusrav there was a brief interval of obscurity in the career of Malik Tughluq after the death of Jalal-ud-din Khalji. He then entered the service of Ulugh Khan, brother of Ala-ud-din Khalji as personal attendant. After Ulugh Khan's he joined the service of Ala-ud-din Khalji. He was the governor of Dipalpur when he was called to the throne.

Internal Policy : Ghiyas-ud-din Tughluq's task after his accession was to restore administrative order by removing the abuses of the previous regime. The finances of the state was in a deplorable condition due to the extravagances of Mubarak Shah and Khusrav. Ghiyas-ud-din, therefore ordered a strict enquiry into the claims to Jagirs. Unlawful grants were expropriated and the resentment that this measure had evoked was removed by Ghiyas-ud-din by his conciliating and beneficent measures for the welfare of his subjects including the nobles. He appointed honest and upright persons as governors of provinces and reduced the burden of land revenue by bringing it down to one-tenth or one-eleventh of the gross produce of the soil and strictly prohibited official extortion. He gave up the practice of survey of land to ascertain the state demand of revenue, as it did not work satisfactorily in the hands of officers and it required technical staff which the state did not possess. Land revenue was to assessed by the collectors in person. Collectors of revenue were not to receive any commission on the collection but land grants which were free from taxation. Thus the system of fixing revenue after measurement of land and payment of commission on the collection to the revenue collectors followed under Ala-ud-din were thus abandoned. Ghiyas-ud-din believed in the theory that the surest method of enhancing the revenue of the state was by extension of cultivation and not by increase of the revenue demand. The result was the improvement in the condition of the ryots which reflected itself in the improvement in the revenue collection. Ghiyas-ud-din caused much fallow land to be brought under cultivation and canals were dug for irrigation and gardens were planted. Many ruined villages were gradually re-populated.

Ghiyas-ud-din improved the means of communication by clearing and reconstructing the roads, constructing bridges and digging canals. Forts were built for defensive purposes. The postal system which existed in India from time immemorial was perfected by Ghiyas-ud-din. Postal runners were stationed at every two-third of a mile and postal horse-men were stationed at a distance of every seven or eight miles.

The judicial department had fallen into decay under the rule of Mubarak Shah and Khusrav. Debtors to the state were tortured for the realisation of debt. Ghiyas-ud-din prohibited torture for recovery of such debts, but revenue defaulters, thieves and peculators were, however, tortured and treated with cruelty.

Ghiyas-ud-din retained the restrictions put on the Hindus by Ala-ud-din Khalji and ordered that Hindus should not be permitted to amass wealth. They were, however, allowed to retain just sufficient of the fruit of their labour to keep themselves in moderate comfort. If the Sultan did not over-tax the Hindus, it was with a view not to make them desert their lands or business out of despair (Barani). Generally speaking the lot of the people during the reign of Ghiyas-ud-din Tughluq was not happy.

A Sunni Musalman himself, Ghiyas-ud-din was very much devoted to his faith and observed the injunctions of his religion with punctilious care. It may be recalled that he ascended the throne as an orthodox Muslim and his religious attitude was very near to that of a fanatic. Manufacture of liquor was forbidden by him and religious ordinances of Islam were strictly enforced on the Muslims. Although not a persecutor of other religions, Ghiyas-ud-din did not hesitate to destroy temples and break idols in the temples during the course of his military campaigns.

Military Campaigns : Although he had ascended the throne at an advanced age, Ghiyas-ud-din proved to be an able ruler. One of his first concerns was to restore the authority of the Sultan in the Deccan. Kakatiya ruler Prataprudra of Warangal threw off the yoke of the Delhi Sultanate taking advantage of the disorder at Delhi. He not only refused to pay the stipulated tribute but also extended his territories by conquests. But he lacked diplomatic foresight. He either ignored or under-estimated the Muslim power and instead of organising a united front the Hindu rulers of the Deccan and the South India, he was leading campaign after campaign against them. He had to pay for his folly and lack of political wisdom as soon as Ghiyas-ud-din Tughluq ascended the Delhi throne. In 1321-22, that is in the second year of his reign he sent his son Juna Khan or Jauna Khan, also known as Ulugh Khan against Warangal. The Muslim army under Jauna Khan laid siege of the fort of Warangal. Prataprudra offered heroic resistance and the Hindus mustered strong and fraustrated the attempt of the Muslims to capture the fort. The siege dragged on for long and there were heavy casualties on the side of the invaders. Jauna Khan had to return to Delhi without achieving anything. But in the next year the Sultan sent Jauna Khan on a second expedition to Warangal. This time fortune favoured Jauna Khan and he compelled the Kakatiya king Prataprudra to surrender with his family and nobles to the enemy. Prataprudra was sent to Delhi "with his elephants and treasures, relations and dependants." According to Barani the name of Warangal was changed to Sultanpur and "all the country of Tilang was conquered." But modern historians consider the claim of Barani as an exaggeration for in an inscription dated 1326. Prataprudra is referred to as the ruling king. "It is therefore very likely that even if he were taken as a captive to Delhi, he must have been released and was allowed to rule as a subordinate chief or asserted his independence. "One thing that the Muslim chroniclers have ignored is the reconquest of Malabar (Madura) in 1323. Barani includes Madura in the dominions of the Delhi Sultanate during the region of Muhammad bin Tughluq at the time when he transferred his capital to Devagiri in 1327. Thus only pertinent conclusion is that Jauna Khan after his victory at Warangal had carried his expedition to the southernmost limit of India after his victory over Prataprudra.

After the conquest of Warangal Jauna Khan proceeded on an expedition to the eastern coast. Barani simply mentions that he marched towards Jajnagar and captured forty elephants. From an inscription in a mosque at Rajahmundry, it is found that the mosque was built in 1324 during the regime of Ulugh Khan. This leaves us in no doubt that Jauna Khan had advanced as far as Rajahmundry, wherefrom he proceeded towards Orissa. Bhanudeva II, king of Orissa sent a large army to defend his frontiers against the attack of Jauna Khan. But as Isami observes, the Orissa forces were defeated and Jauna Khan plundered their camp and took a large booty. But the inscriptions of Narasingha IV credit Bhanudeva with victory over Ghiyas-ud-din Tughluq. The presumption is that Ulugh Khan suffered some reverses and his Orissa expedition was not as successful as Isami describes it to be. This is also borne out by a cryptic refererence to it by Barani that Jauna Khan suddenly retired after a victorious campaign, which strikes rather unusual to the modern historians.

Jauna Khan's triumphal return to Delhi was an occasion for much jubilation which was, however, married by the news that the Mongols had crossed the Sindhu and invaded Samana. An imperial army was at once despatched which won two victories over the Mongols, drove them out and took many of them prisoners. This was followed by the suppression of a rebellion in Gujarat.

Ghiyas-ud-din now turned his attention to Bengal which had thrown off the yoke of Delhi after the death of Balban and become independent. At the beginning of 1324 the Sultan started with an army to assert his authority over Bengal, leaving Jauna Khan in charge of Delhi. The Sultan of Bengal then was Ghiyas-ud-din Bahadur. Ghiyas-ud-din Tughluq succeeded in defeating the Bengal Sultan and to bring him captive to Delhi. While eastern and southern Bengal with their capitals at Sonargaon and Satgaon were annexed to the Delhi Sultanate North Bengal was placed under Sultan Nasir-ud-din with his capital at Lakhnauti. Bahram Khan, the adopted son of Ghiyas-ud-din was placed in charge of eastern and southern Bengal.

It was in the course of his Bengal expedition that Ghiyas-ud-din defeated the Raja of Tirhut. Harisimha, king of Tirhut offered a stubborn resistance to the army and Ghiyas-ud-din started for Delhi before Tirhut was completely subdued.

Afghanpur Tragedy and Ghiyas-ud-din's Death : After successful completion of Bengal and Tirhut campaigns the Sultan proceeded towards Tughluqabad, which according to Isami, was founded on the eve of his eastern expedition. Jauna Khan hastily raised a wooden pavilion at Afghanpur village at a small distance from the new town of Tughluqabad in order to welcome the Sultan. Here the Sultan was to rest for sometime till an auspicious moment for entry into the new town. After all formalities of welcome were over, food was served which the Sultan partook of along with some of his courtiers. Then according to Barani "When the Maliks and Amirs came out to wash their hands, a thunderbolt of calamity from the sky descended upon the people of the earth, and the roof of the pavilion under which the Sultan was seated, fell all of a sudden, crushing him and five or six others to death." The tragic event has been the subject of great controversy. Ibn Batuta's account holds Jauna Khan responsible for the tragedy. The problem has been discussed in all its details by Sir Wolseley Haig and Iswari Prasad who hold Jauna Khan responsible for the tragedy. But Dr. Mahdi Hussain and Dr. Moinul Huq, placing their reliance of Ferishta, Jai Muhammad Qandhari etc. have come to the conclusion that the fall of the pavilion was not the result of any conspiracy but only an accident. Prof. Nizami concludes that "Sultan Muhammad's complicity in the death of his father cannot be proved or disproved merely on the basis of positive or ambiguous statements of contemporary or later historians...it would be quite fair to accept the versions of Ibn Batuta and Isami that the pavilion collapsed because it had been hurriedly constructed and its foundations were not strong. In fact, it was a temporary structure for temporary purpose. But the motive attributed to Ulugh Khan by these historians cannot be accepted. They are unnatural and militate against circumstantial evidence."

Estimate of Ghiyas-ud-din Tughluq : Ghiyas-ud-din Tughluq's reign covered nearly five years from 1320 to 1325. During a reign of less than five years he showed all round ability as a ruler. When he had ascended the throne he was already an able administrator and a successful general. He had earned a reputation for his loyalty and ability as a successful warden of the marches. His revenue policy replenished the treasury which had been almost completely depleted due to the extra-vagances under the reign of Mubarak

Shah and Khusrav. He realised the great economic truth that it was not the ease with which revenue was collected that showed the prosperity of the agriculturists, but the ease with which they could pay the revenue. He reduced the land revenue to one-tenth or one-eleventh of the gross produce. He resumed the **jagirs** and grants of lands which were found to be illegal on enquiry. He took special care so that the state officials might not exact the peasants beyond their legitimate dues. His government was based on justice and moderation and inspired by a desire of welfare of the people. State officials were selected on the basis of merits, loyalty and honesty, and they were paid sufficiently well so that they might not go corrupt.

Ghiyas-ud-din was above the contemporary vices of drinking and debauchery. He built a new capital and named it Tughluqabad. To him belongs the credit of restoring the power and prestige of the Delhi Sultanate which had sunk too low and revitalising the administrative system, which had almost collapsed during the reigns of his two predecessors.

Ghiyas-ud-din was particularly careful about the administration of justice. He held his court twice each day. In matters of justice he made no distinction between high and low, rich and poor.

The army received special attention of the Sultan. The military machine reared up by Ala-ud-din Khalji was retained by him. With this army he restored authority of Delhi on Warangal, Bengal, Madura; conquered Orissa and Tirhut, and beat off the Mongols.

Ghiyas-ud-din was Sunni Musalman and faithfully followed the injunctions of the Islam. Although not particularly intolerant to other religions, he was very strict towards the Hindu and he did not allow them to amass wealth.

Ghiyas-ud-din was a patron of architecture. It was under his orders that Tughluqabad was built which was a palace-fort and intended to be his capital. Within the enclosures of this palace-fort his palace and other buildings were built. His main palace was built of gilded bricks which were so bright that none could look at them for long because of their glaze. We know from Ibn Batuta that in one of his treasure rooms there was a cistern in which molten gold was poured so that a solid mass of gold might be formed. He maintained poets and literary men in his court.

MUHAMMAD BIN TUGHLUQ (1325-51)

Three days after the death of his father Jauna Khan, also called Ulugh Khan ascended the throne (Feb or March, 1325) under the title Muhammad bin Tughluq. His accession to the throne, whatever might have been his part in the death of his father, was accepted by all without demur. "Perhaps no other Sultan of medieval India has excited so much curiosity about himself and provoked so much criticism of his policies as Muhammad bin Tughluq. His reign of twenty-six years is a fascinating but tragic story of schemes and projects correctly conceived, badly executed and disastrously abandoned."

According to Barani all people "men, women, young and old, children and grown-ups, free-born and slaves, Muslims and Hindus, shouted praises and blessed Sultan Muhammad and filled their handkerchiefs **(dastarchas),** purses and pockets with coins of gold and silver. Delhi looked like a garden profusely blooming with white and yellow flowers." Such pageantry and extravaganza as also display of generosity were not seen at the accession of any Delhi Sultan except Ala-ud-din Khalji. Both Isami and Barani have used this happy inauguration of Muhammad bin Tughluq's reign "as a contrast-background to the delineation of the subsequent atmosphere of horror and hatred that prevailed during his regime." On his accession, as we know from Isami, he declared that he would follow the footsteps of his father. He also declared that "Every old man in my territory is like a father to me and every young man is like (my brother), Bahram Khan, in my affection."

Character and Concepts

Character : Muhammad bin Tughluq was one of the most striking personalities of medieval India. His intellectual attainments won universal admiration. He, by virtue of his merits stood far above his contemporaries. His personal life was chaste and he was free from the vices that tarnished the character of the medieval monarchs. "There was hardly any branch of medieval learning in which he had not achieved something—literature, history, philosophy, rhetoric, poetry, logic, mathematics, medicine, astronomy and caligraphy." He had also workable knowledge in Arabic. He had committed to memory the whole of Quran and a part of Hidaya. He possessed a prodigious memory; his intelligence was sharp and penetrating and his power of conversation was unrivalled. With a well-built body, smart soldierly bearing he possessed a dauntless spirit of courage and chivalry. He initiated an era of cultural contacts with African and Asian countries. "People from Khurasan, Iraq, Sistan, Herat, Egypt, Trans-Oxiana, Tangiers etc. visited his court and he acquired first-hand knowledge about the literary and cultural development in those lands.

Contemporary historians such as Barani and Ibn Batuta have expressed opposite views about his personality, virtues and vices. Modern European historians also hold opposite judgements on his character and achievements. Elphinstone went to the extent of doubting whether he was not affected by some degree of insanity. Elphinstone's view has been supported by Havell, Edward, Thomas and Smith. Gardiner Brown has, however, taken an altogether different view and paints him in bright colours exonerating him from the charge of madness and blood-thirstiness. There are other scholars who have dealt with the character of Sultan Muhammad bin Tughluq, but the controversy about his character still continues.

Despite the excellent qualities of head and heart that Muhammad bin Tughluq possessed, he had certain defects which contributed to his failure. He was at times cruel, frivolous, capricious and had an unshakable belief in his own ideas and views of things. Any opposition or failure would make him lose his balance and he would start taking false steps. He was intolerant of wiser counsel and often would allow his excellent plans to fail completely due to lack of pragmatic outlook. He had good ideas no doubt, but he had not the capacity to execute them. "This was best exemplified in his ambitious projects like change of capitals, issue of token currency and foreign expedition, and the appointment of new classes of officials. All these indicate a want of judgement which is undoubtedly a great defect in the character of a ruler." As it has been suggested by some writers his character was "a mixture of opposities."

Concepts : Muhammad bin Tughluq possessed unusual originality of mind and was never satisfied with stereotyped solution of problems. Barani referred to this quality of the Sultan in different contexts. Politically Muhammad bin Tughluq desired to achieve political and administrative unity in India. This kind of unity was not visualised by any ruler after Asoka. He sought to liquidate the political and intellectual barriers between the north and the south. Under him "from Delhi to Daulatabad it was now one world." When Muhammad bin Tughluq ascended the throne the Central Asian scene was in a state of flux. The power of the Khans had declined and Timur was not yet born. The vacuum was sought to be filled in by imperialistic expansion for which he mooted the Khurasan project. Muhammad bin Tughluq was a believer in economic, cultural and diplomatic contacts with the outside world. His remission of duties on imports from foreign countries in 1340-41 was largely influenced by this idea. Embassies from different parts of Asia came into his court. To name some of such countries were Iraq, China, Khvarazam, Syria etc. Sultan Muhammad bin Tughluq sent Bighdan, one of his private secretaries to Sultan Abu Said of Iraq with one crore **tankas** for distribution in the sacred towns of Iraq. Having been an ardent student of religion and philosophy, the Sultan had experienced all forms of religions including atheism and agnosticism and ultimately rationalism became the sheet-anchor of his religious thought. Barani, an orthodox theologian, looked upon this rationalistic approach of the Sultan as tantamount to a denial of religion. But this did not mean that he had lost faith in Islam. On the contrary Ibn Batuta tells us that the Sultan constantly urged the people to perform obligatory prayers. Muhammad bin Tughluq participated in religious discussions with ulemas, jogis and Jain scholars. While punctilious in the performance of prayers and other religious rites enjoined by Islam, the Sultan was tolerant to other religions. "He is perhaps the first Sultan of Delhi about whose participation in the Hindu festival of Holi there is clear contemporary evidence." The Sultan caused the construction of **gow math** i.e. cow temple at Batihagarh. "This religious cosmopolitanism of the Sultan provided a pretext for men like Isami to bring charges of heresy and innovation against him."

Muhammad bin Tughluq did not subscribe to the view of the mystics that state did not represent religion. He declared that "religion and state are twins." He was influenced by **sufism** and wanted the **sufis** to make their talent available to the state in its plans and projects.

The Sultan believed in the basically democratic principle that career should be open to talent. Birth was nor taken into consideration by him in raising people to high official positions. Merit and ability were the criteria on the basis of which he had promoted many low-born persons to high position. For instance, Aziz the vinter, Firuz the barber, Laddha the gardener etc. were raised to high status and gave them office and estates.

Muhammad bin Tughluq believed in giving his administration a broad base. "If all sections of the Muslims had to be taken into the administration, it was equally necessary to admit Hindus to the highest offices of the government." With this notion he appointed Hindus to some of the highest offices of the state. "Hindu scholars and poets were patronised by him and there were a thousand poets of Arabic, Persian and Hindu at his court."

INVASION OF TARMASHIRIN (1327-28)

Within two years of the accession of Muhammad bin Tughluq the Mongols under the Chaghtai chief Tarmashirin who was originally a Buddhist but later converted to Islam, invaded India. According to Ferishta. Tarmashirin marched with a huge army towards India and after subduing Laghman, Multan and other regions rapidly advanced towards Delhi. Sultan Muhammad bin Tughluq was taken by surprise and humiliated himself by buying off the invader with a huge quantity of wealth. Tarmashirin returned plundering Gujarat and Sind on the way and taking many prisoners. According to earlier accounts, the Sultan pursued the Mongols after they had retreated, as far as Kalanor in Gujarat, and though there was no engagement between the parties Tarmashirin has been stated to be a vanquished party. Iswari Prasad and some modern historians accept the account of Ferishta to be most probable. Sir Wolseley Haig accepts the story of the invasion but rejects the Sultan's attempt to buy him off. Dr. Hussain is of opinion that Tarmashirin having suffered defeat at the hands of Amir Chhan near Ghazni fled with a part of his army to Punjab and came to Delhi via Multan. The Sultan gave him 5,000 dinars by way of help. But Dr. Hussain's view has been regarded by modern historians as very much speculative and unsupported by any evidence.

Enhancement of the Taxation of the Doab : One of the earliest administrative measures of Muhammad bin Tughluq was the enhancement of the taxation in the Doab. According to Barani the enhancement was to the tune of ten and twenty times. Besides the revenue collectors exacted **abwabs** i.e. extra cesses. The collection was made with such rigour that the **ryots** were reduced to "impotence, poverty and ruin." There were rebellions on all sides, the land was ruined and cultivation largely diminished. The result was a famine in Delhi and its neighbourhood and the Doab. Failure of rains added to the famine condition. "Thousands of people perished and when they tried to escape, the Sultan led punitive expeditions to various places and hunted them like wild beasts." Barani is the only contemporary writer who referred to the ill-conceived policy of the Sultan and the manner of its execution which led to utmost distress of the people and devastation of a large part of the kingdom. It also brings into prominence the inhuman cruelty of the Sultan. But Barani's description raise doubts about its accuracy. He does not mention the exact amount of tax that was levied and Ferishta who says that it was increased three or four fold is probably nearer the truth. According to Badauni, the enhancement of taxation was both a punitive measure and a step to replenish the treasury. Sir Wolseley Haig accepts Badauni's view. Gardiner Brown is of the opinion that taxation was not heavy and Barani's statement about the cruel deeds of the Sultan is highly exaggerated. According to Gardiner Brown, the sufferings of the people were more due to failure of rains for several years rather than to heavy taxation. The people who suffered severely sought to escape from their homes and hearths and were mercilessly punished for that. But Barani's statement that they were hunted like wild beasts was an over-exaggeration. However, on the whole the conclusion is unavoidable that steps taken by the Sultan were highly reprehensible and the method of execution was cruel.

Transfer of Capital to Devagiri : Barani, Ibn Batuta and Isami—three contemporary writers give us detailed accounts of the transfer of the capital from Delhi to Daulatabad or Devagiri (1326-27). According to Barani making deogir (Devagiri) his capital under the title Daulatabad was ruinous to Delhi and distressing to the chief men of the country. "This place held a central situation : Delhi, Gujarat, Lakhnauti, Sonargaon, Tilang, Ma'bar. Dhurasamundar and Kampila were about equi-distant from thence, there being but a slight difference in distances. According to Barani Delhi which rivalled Baghdad and Cairo for 170 or 180 years was completely ruined. So complete was the ruin that 'not a cat or a dog was left among the buildings of the city, in its palaces or in its suburbs.'

Ibn Batuta writes in the same strain. The cause of the transfer of the capital from Delhi to Daulatabad was, according to him, the scurrilous writings which included abuses and scandals were addressed to the Sultan and thrown into his audience hall. "So he resolved to lay Delhi waste." There was then a proclamation that on one should remain in Delhi after three days. He had in the meantime purchased all the houses and dwellings from all the inhabitants of Delhi and paid the price. While many had left some lingered and the Sultan ordered a search for such stragglers. A cripple and blind man were found and brought before the Sultan and the crippled man was thrown up in the air through a **balista** and the blind man was dragged by leg to Daulatabad. His body tore off on the road during the forty days' journey and only his leg reached Daulatabad. The Sultan mounted the roof of his palace at night and finding that there was no smoke, no light anywhere remarked 'Now my heart is pleased and my soul is at rest.'

To the descriptions of Barani and Ibn Batuta, Isami agrees. But the modern historians are of the opinion that the account given by Barani, Ibn Batuta and Isami is highly exaggerated. It has been pointed out by them that in 1334, that is three years before return to Delhi from Daulatabad, Ibn Batuta describes the city of Delhi to be populous. This contradicts the descriptions of Barani, Isami and even Batuta himself that Delhi was altogether deserted. It has also been pointed out that "constructive works were designed and carried out in Delhi by the Sultan during the very years in which he is supposed to have removed all the inhabitants of Delhi to Deogiri." According to Dr. M. Hussain the city of Delhi did never cease to be the capital and was never depopulated and deserted.

Prof. N. B. Roy remarks "The old capital was not however, reduced to utter desolation, it continued to remain a seat of administration and a mint town, coins being issued from Delhi in 728, 729, 730 A.H. (A.D. 1327-30)." The city, however, showed a deserted appearance and Ibn Batuta visiting Delhi six years afterwards found it 'empty and depopulated.' It may therefore be concluded although the city might not have been absolutely depopulated and deserted, 'the story of the removal of the people **en masse** and the incalculable magnitude of suffering caused thereby cannot be doubted.'

Different motives have been ascribed by different historians to Muhammad bin Tughluq's transfer of capital to Devagiri. According to Barani the reason behind the transfer of capital from Delhi to Devagiri was that the latter place was more centrally located. But Barani did not consider the point that if Devagiri could not be controlled from Delhi, the latter could not be controlled from Devagiri. Nevertheless Barani's observation is helpful to the extent it implies effective administrative control of the south.

Ibn Batuta pointed out the Sultan's revenge motive to be the only cause behind the transfer of capital as the people of Delhi were throwing scurrilous writings about the Sultan in his audience hall. If that was the motive why should he have purchased the dwellings and houses of the residents and paid in full for them?

Isami observes that the Sultan was suspicious of the people of Delhi and he wanted to break their power. He is at pains to prove his theory and is not acceptable to the dispassionate historians.

In all probability Muhammad bin Tughluq realised the urgent need of a strong administrative centre in the south after his campaign against Baha-ud-din Gurshasp. His councillors suggested Ujjain, but the Sultan's decision was in favour of Devagiri. To him the population of Delhi "was a fine social and economic unit for a southern capital and he would take it there." According to Gardiner Brown Muhammad bin Tughluq when he embarked upon his Deccan experiment, "he simply acted as an agent of certain economic forces, which were actively operating in the life of the country and demanded the transfer of the capital to a region economically more prosperous to sustain the structure of an all-India government."

Barani's account, leaving out its exaggeration abundantly proved that the transfer had proved a calamity for the upper classes, although the exodus was not a mass exodus but a limited one. But an exodus, although limited, is bound to provoke strong reactions, and Muhammad bin Tughluq's transfer of capital has actually done that. The exodus having taken place in hot summer month, the sufferings of the people knew no bounds. The immediate effect was wide-spread resentment against the Sultan who forfeited once for all the confidence of the people. But its remote effect was that the barriers which separated the north from the south broke down. The rise of the Bahamani kingdom was possible by the influx of Muslim population in the south not all of whom returned to Delhi.

Token Currency : Next to the Devagiri experiment of Muhammad bin Tughluq was the introduction of the token currency by him. In those days there were silver coins called **tanka** and copper coins called **jitals.** The Sultan issued a bronze coin and demanded its acceptance as a token coin equivalent to the silver **tanka.** The metal used in the token coin was copper according to Barani and bronze according to Ferishta. On the token coin the inscription in Persian was "minted tanka current during the days Muhammad bin Tughluq." Obviously the token coin was to have its value due to the fiat of the Sultan, not to its metallic value. In modern times token currency whether paper or base metal carry its value due to the fiat of the government. The basic conditions for the success of token currency are that it must be the legal tender and secondly, its manufacture must be government monopoly and done in secrecy. Thirdly, heavy punishment must be given to persons counterfeiting such coins. Fourthly, to the foreign merchants, token currency had no value. If the state would guarantee exchange of token coin with silver coin at a given ratio the permanent value of the token currency would be assured. But Muhammad bin Tughluq did not take these concomitant measures as a result of which the token currency was being widely counterfeited. The foreign merchants refused to accept the token currency in return for their goods. Ultimately, the Sultan had to recall the token currency from the market by giving standard coins, i.e. **tankas.** Experiment in token currency was nothing new in Asia. Token currency was introduced in China by Qublai Khan with success and by Kaikhatu Khan in Iran. The Iranian experiment, however, failed. The motive behind Muhammad bin Tughluq's introduction of token currency was, according to Barani, to replenish the treasury which had been depleted as a result of his project to conquer foreign land and his boundless munificence; 'it was a device to face the crisis of bankruptcy.' But it was only one of the motives. The other more important reason was the scarcity of silver. Nelson Wright remarks : "But apart from Bengal the sources of silver supply in India were scanty." The problem of shortage of silver was aggravated due to the establishment of new mints in the extensive empire and the enormous expenditure incurred on military expeditions and Devagiri experiment.

The experiment proved a failure because there was fraudulent minting of the token coins. In the words of Barani every Hindu house became a mint. Forged minting became possible because no specialised method nor any special machine was used by the government in its mint. Use of ordinary tools and ordinary workmen naturally could not prevent easy forged minting. Prof. Habib points out that in those days the gold and silver coins would be weighed and tested on the touchstone for detecting the correct weight and metal. But the token currency of a special bronze alloy having been of baser metal nobody cared to test it on any kind of touchstone. This made it possible for the forged coins to get mixed with the government minted coins it was one of the major reasons for its failure. Gold and silver coins were being hoarded and only token currency was left in circulation. Land revenue was being paid in token currency most of which had been spurious. Foreign merchants refused to bring their wares into India and foreign trade received a serious setback. The Sultan had to withdraw the token currency and offered genuine gold and silver coins in retrun. The whole experiment proved a complete failure.

Khurasan Expendition : Muhammad bin Tughluq's Khurasan expedition is counted among his wild projects. According to Barani the Sultan raised an army of 370,000 soldiers for the conquest of Khurasan and Iraq. "Deceived by the people of other lands, he lavishly squandered his resources. He could not conquer those lands while he weakened his control over his own territory." But Barani does not refer to the motive behind the expedition. Ferishta, however, gives us an idea of the motive behind the Khurasan expedition of the Sultan. According to him a large number of princes and maliks, who had arrived in his court from Iraq and Khurasan, convinced him that the conquest of Iran and Turan would be an easy walk-over. There was a political vacuum in Central Asia and Persia in the period between the vanishing of the power of the Il Khans and the establishment of Timur's authority. He also entered into a series of alliances for this purpose. The Sultan of Egypt promised to help him in this expedition. But a serious break in these alliances, however, made him change his mind. The abandonment of the project and the disbandment of the army created 'frustration, unemployment and disgust.'

Qarajal or Qarachil Expedition : The Himalayan tract in Kulu in the Kangra district of Kumaon-Garhwal area is identified as Qarajal region. Ibn Batuta states that Chinese encroachments on the independent Rajput kingdoms became a cause of concern to Muhammad bin Tughluq. Security of this region was the part of the border policy of the Sultan and he decided to complete the chain of fortifications in the north. Barani's statement that Qarajal mountain stood on the shorter route to Khurasan, Muhammad bin Tughluq wanted to conquer it first. But as Himalayas did not obstruct the way to Khurasan, the statement of Barani is meaningless. The motive of the Sultan was to secure the frontier areas and to consolidate his position in a region of strategic importance by compelling the chiefs of the hilly area to recognise his overlordship. An army of 10,000 was sent under the leadership of Khusrau Malik. The army succeeded in occupying Jidya and the Sultan sent a qazi and intimated his decision that Jidya should be integrated with his territory and that the army must not proceed beyond Jidya. But his instruction was disobeyed by Khusrau Malik in the flush of victory and proceeded towards Tibet and was completely routed by the hill people. According to Barani only ten persons survived, but according to Ibn Batuta only three soldiers returned to tell the story of their misfortune. It will be a mistake to think that Qarajal expedition yielded no result except loss of men and money. But we know from Ibn Batuta that after this the Sultan made peace with the inhabitants of the hills that they should pay him some amounts since these people held possession of the territory at the foot of the hills and could not use them without his permission. Both Ibn Batuta and the author of **Masalikul Absar** say that "The people of the country of Qarachil are subject to this Sultan. They have from his protection and security on account of taxes which are brought to him from them and are a source of wealth." Thus the common notion that the Quarajal expedition was waste of men and money is not borne out by the actual results. The Sultan had no desire to conquer China or Tibet as is held by some writers.

Conquest of Nagarkot (1337) : The fort of Nagarkot was situated on the Kangra hill in Punjab. It was a strong fort which had been defying the Turkish forces since the time of Sultan Mahmud of Ghazni. Even Ala-ud-din Khalji who had succeeded in conquering almost the whole of India could not bring this fort under his occupation and it remained under its Hindu prince. In 1337 Muhammand bin Tughluq led an expedition against this fort. The raja offered stiff resistance but ultimately submitted to the Sultan. The Sultan restored the fort to the raja accepting his vassalage.

Rebellions : The first decade of the reign of Muhammad bin Tughluq was pre-eminently successful and his administration extended over areas more extensive than those under Ala-ud-din Khalji. The first of the series of rebellion was that of the Sultan's cousin Baha-ud-din Gushasp, governor of Sagar near Gulbarga. The rebellion was put down effectively and the rebel was flayed alive. Next came the rebellion of the Hindu chief of Kondhana, modern Singh-garh near Poona. He was put down and was compelled to become a vassal of Delhi. The third rebellion in succession was that of Bahram Aiba of Multan who also held Uch and Sind. He was also defeated and put to death.

The above rebellions were the result of the ambitious designs of the chief who rebelled. But later a plethora of rebellions began to raise their ugly heads due to Sultan's oppressive policy of enhancing the taxes and his ruthless punishment of the people. Some of these rebellions were due to the Sultan's transfer of capital and introduction of token currency as a consequence of which he became unpopular the advantage of which was taken by ambitious persons.

(i) Masud Khan, the Sultan's step-brother. The Sultan got his mother stoned to death on the charge of adultery and this created a great resentment in the mind of Masud. Two years later when he was supposed to be preparing for rebellion he was executed. (ii) Rebellion in Sunam and Samana was in the nature of a peasant revolt. The peasants stopped payment of land tax. The Sultan marched against them personally and captured the leaders of the rebels and brought them to Delhi. (iii) Nizam Main of Kara raised the standard of revolt. He assumed the title of Sultan Ala-ud-din and declared independence. He was defeated and flayed alive. (iv) In 1338-39 Tajul Mulk Nusrat Khan also known as Shihab Sultani rebelled in Bidar in order to cover up his failure to pay the stipulated land revenue. He was defeated and captured. (v) Next year, Ali Shah Nathu rebelled at Gulbarga but was defeated and deported to Ghazni. (vi) The rebellion of Ain-ul-Mulk was a close friend and associate of Muhammad bin Tughluq. He was governor of Awadh and Zafrabad. He did excellent work during the days of the famine in the Doab. His success and popularity with the people made the Sultan jealous and even suspicious. The Sultan's suspicion was confirmed by the asylum given to the officers who were guilty of embezzlement and he contemplated to transfer Ain-ul-Mulk to Daulatabad, for Qutlugh. Khan was not equal to the task. The order of transfer was taken by Ain-ul-Mulk as a preliminary to his destruction and he rebelled, but he was defeated and taken prisoner; he was dismissed and subjected to indignities but his life was spared. (vii) Shahu Afghan, a rebel, killed the governor of Multan and occupied the city. Muhammad bin Tughluq personally proceeded against him whereupon Shahu fled to the hills. (viii) Sayyid Jalal-ud-din Ahsan rebelled in Malabar (1335). The Sultan marched against the rebel in person but failed to put down the rebellion. Malabar thus became independent. (ix) The governor of Lahore, Amir Hulaju, was one of the powerful chiefs to revolt. He was defeated and killed. (x) Taking advantage of the unpopularity of Muhammad bin Tughluq Malik Hushang, son of the governor of Daulatabad raised the standard of revolt in 1335-36. After some time, however, he submitted and was pardoned. (xi) The widespread rebellious condition and the unpopularity of Muhammad bin Tughluq offered an opportunity to the Hindus of Southern India to make themselves independent. Harihar, a Hindu leader, laid the foundation of the kingdom Vijayanagar in 1336. He also gave secret support to Krishna Nayak who revolted against Delhi in 1343-44. These rebellions could not be put down and a large part of South India passed to the Hindu chiefs. (xii) In 1345, the people of Devagiri rebelled against the Delhi rule due to the extrotionate collections and repressive treatment of the people by the local officers. According to Ferishta, "the people rebelled in all quarters and the country was devastated and depopulated in consequence." (xiii) The **Amiran-i-Sadah,** the name by which the foreign nobles were known became rebellious. These foreign nobles enjoyed certain special privileges, but taking advantage of their position they embezzeled money, secretly assisted the rebels and took to plunder whenever there was any disturbance or confusion in the south. Muhammad bin Tughluq ordered Aziz Khummar to adequately punish foreign nobles. Aziz Khummar treacherously put many of the foreign nobles to death which created great resentment and disaffection among the foreign nobles. The foreign nobles in Gujarat raised the standard of revolt, captured Aziz Khummar and put him to death. The Sultan proceeded in person against the rebels and defeated them near Dabohi and the **Amir-i-Sadah** were suppressed the foreign nobles at Devagiri being afraid of the fate that might as well overtake them rebelled and occupied Devagiri. The rebellion also spread to Berar, Khandesh and Malwa. The Sultan had to go to Devagiri to put down the rebellion. But before his task was complete there was another rebellion in Gujarat which necessitated the Sultan's presence. This gave rebels in Devagiri their chance. They repudiated their allegiance to Delhi and laid the foundations of the Bahamani kingdom. The rebellion in Gujarat was very formidable. The Sultan, however, hunted down the rebels and their leader Taghi was pursued who fled and took shelter in Thatta in Sind. For three years the Sultan remained Gujarat in order to reorganise the administration of the province and to conquer Girnar. He then proceeded to Sind to punish Taghi but there he was taken ill. He died on march 20, 1351. Thus "the king was freed from his people and they from the king" (Badauni).

Estimate : Muhammad bin Tugluq was one of the most striking personalities of medieval India. He possessed a character that made him stand head and shoulders above the contemporaries. For a man of his profound learning and wide range of interest, the expected liberality of disposition and catholicity of taste were naturally there (See his character, **ante**).

But he failed in his main attempt which was to build up an all-India administration. As a ruler and an administrator, Muhammad bin Tughluq was a failure. The achievements of his long twenty-six years rule were extremely meagre. If we consider the greatness of a ruler from the point of view of his high intentions, Sultan Muhammad bin Tughluq was indeed great. For, his ideas were original and in most part reasonable. His transfer of capital to Devagiri which was more centrally located and far removed from the Mongol approach, was intended to break the barrier between the north and the south. Influx of the Muslims in Devagiri indirectly paved the way for the rise of the Bahmani kingdom of the south.

His introduction of token currency was not unreasonable in itself, but its failure was due to its faulty execution. Khurasan expedition was abandoned and a huge waste of money, energy was the result. But it was due to the failure of the alliances with foreign countries and the refusal of the Sultan of Egypt to redeem his promise of help. Otherwise the situation in Central Asia called for such a project for any ambitious ruler, Quarachal expedition was a failure in the sense that the army was totally destroyed, but it was due to the disobedience of the commander who was asked not to proceed beyond Jidya. But the hill people entered into an agreement with the Sultan for payment for the use of the land in the foot-hills of the Himalayas. The enhancement of the taxation in the Doab was both a punitive and a measure for the enhancement of revenue. But the rate of enhancement has been exaggerated by the contemporary writers.

The Sultan had almost confessed his failure long before his death. He told Barani : "I visit them (people) with chastisement upon the suspicion or presumption of their rebellious and treacherous designs, and I punish the most trifling act of contumacy with death. This I will do until I die, or until the people act honestly, and give up rebellion and contumacy. I have no such **wazir** as will make rules to obviate my shedding blood. I punish the people because they have all at once become my enemies and opponents. I have dispensed great wealth among them, but they have not become friendly and loyal." This is obviously a confession of his own failure.

Some modern historians hold the opinion that Muhammad bin Tughluq was not personally responsible for his failure, but he was a victim of the circumstances. The people of the time were backward and prejudiced and could not accept the reforms introduced by the Sultan which were far in advance of time. Although there is some element of truth in such contention, yet much of the reason for the failure lay in the character of the monarch himself. He lacked balance, practical judgement and strong common sense which alone could make his administration a success. He was scholarly and too much bookish in his knowledge; he lacked insight into character. Not being worldly wise, and given to fits of rage when opposed or faced with failure, he took more wrong steps. He was generous but at times cruel, he was original in his ideas but lacked practical statesmanship. He was after all an unfortunate monarch, comparable to Joseph II of Austria. He was not an atheist as Barani would have us believe, and the charge of insanity against him is definitely untenatable.

FIRUZ TUGHLUQ (1351-88)

Firuz Tughluq was the son of Rajab and a Hindu lady, daughter of Ranmal Bhatti. As Muhammad bin Tughluq left no son, his cousin Firuz Tughluq ascended the throne as Sultan. Rajab was the younger brother of Ghiyas-ud-din Tughluq.

Muhammad bin Tughluq gave Firuz a thorough training in all the civil departments of the government, state policy, administration, account keeping, appointments etc. Firuz obeyed his Sultan-cousin loyally and faithfully and retained affection for him even after his death. Firuz was present in the royal camp when the Sultan died and the royal army being greatly harassed by rebellious Taghi and the Mongol mercenaries decided to select a leader to lead them in the difficulties. A small section was in favour of the minor son of Muhammad bin Tughluq's sister. But most of the nobles wanted a grown up man at the time of the crisis and they offered the crown to Firuz who refused it initially but ultimately accepted it under the pressure of the nobles and the **ulemas.** His coronation took place in the camp near Thatta on March 23, 1315.

Immediately on his accession Firuz restored order in the army and after three days he sent his army against the Mongols which defeated and drove them away and freed the Indians who had been captured by them. At Siwistan where the new Sultan and his army stopped for few days **Khutba** was read in the name of Firuz Shah Tughluq and proclamation of his assumption of the crown was sent all over the country. Special messengers with robes of honour were sent to officers in different parts of the country. The body of Muhammad bin Tughluq was put into a coffin and placed on an elephant and sent to Delhi. The army proceeded to Bhakkar and thence to Uch. Hardly it started from Uch information reached the Sultan that Khwaja-i-Jahan, the deputy of the late Sultan at Delhi had proclaimed a boy as Sultan and gave out him as the son of the late Sultan. At Multan Firuz held a council of the nobles and the Muslim jurists. The council refused to admit that the late Sultan had any son and the jurists pronounced that Khwaja-i-Jahan's candidate being a minor was not qualified for the position of the Sultan. In Muslim law sovereignty was not an inherited right and it was useless to consider the legal aspect of the question whether the boy had any right or not. The circumstances of the time also needed a grown up man at the helm of affairs of the state.

Historians also differ as to the claim of Firuz to the throne of Delhi. Sir Wolseley Haig is of the opinion that the boy proclaimed as the Sultan by Khwaja-i-Jahan was 'not a supposititious son' but an issue of Muhammad bin Tughluq's body. Therefore according to him Firuz was a usurper. Other historians, however, maintain that there is no record or proof that Muhammad bin Tughluq had a son. In any case, the accession of Firuz was sanctioned by the will of the electors—the nobles and the jurists. Dr. R. P. Tripathy says that accession of Firuz revived the principle of election which has been gradually receding to the background.

Firuz reached Delhi, allowed Khwaja-i-Jahan to go back to his fief at Samana but was put to death by a follower of Sher Khan, governor of Sunam and Samana. He appointed Malik-i-Maqbul his prime minister and gave him the title of Khan-i-Jahan. Malik Maqbul was a brahmin who had been only recently a convert of Islam. He was an able administrator and his appointment as prime minister proved to be a great asset to the administration. Firuz Tughluq's first task was to conciliate his subjects and with this end in view he remitted all their debts to the government. With the support of the people of Delhi, particularly the sunni Muslims, whose confidence he had the good fortune to enjoy. Friuz succeeded in bringing peace and order out of the prevailing confusion which resulted due to the disturbances towards the end of the reign of Muhammad bin Tùghluq. Firuz looked upon himself as a mere trustee of the state responsible for the security and welfare of the people. He was a believer in theocratic government and considered himself as the sovereign of the Muslim section of his subjects for the moral and material welfare of whom he did everything possible. Thus he had a dual sovereignty, a temporal sovereign of all subjects under him and spiritual sovereign of the Muslim subjects under him.

Next task of the Sultan Firuz was to raise the "Delhi Sultanate from the state of decrepitude and demoralisation into which it had fallen since the closing years of his predecessor's reign." This could be done by spectacular military achievements and by recovering the Deccan, Bengal, Sind and Rajasthan.

Firuz's Attempt at Recovery of Areas Lost to the State : Dakhin or Deccan : During the last years of the reign of Muhammad bin Tughluq, Dakhin, i.e. South India, had torn off from the Delhi Sultanate and became independent. Firuz was advised by his counsellors to reduce Bahamani kingdom. Firuz Tughluq who followed a vacillating military policy, evaded the issue on the plea that he was against shedding of Muslim blood which was bound to take place if any attempt to recover Bahamani kingdom was made. But in case of Rajasthan, there was no question of shedding Muslim blood. But he did not evince any willingness to bring Marawar and other Rajput states back to the Delhi empire.

Bengal : In 1338 Bengal had declared herself independent of Delhi. Haji Iliyas, who assumed the title of Shams-ud-din Iliyas Shad, had brought the whole of the province of Bengal under his rule by 1352. Iliyas Shah even invaded Tirhut. Firuz Shah marched against Iliyas Shah in order to bring Bengal under the rule of Delhi. Iliyas Shah took shelter in his well protected fort Ekdala. Firuz Shah failed to take the fort and retired with his army. According to Shams-i-Shiraj Firuz Shah returned without reducing the Ekdala fort on hearing the wails of the women and children within the fort. According others Firuz Shah had to return to Delhi on the onset of the rains. Whatever might have been the real cause of his withdrawal from Bengal, this expedition revealed the lack of military talent on the part of Firuz Shah (1353).

Firuz Shah again invaded Bengal in 1359. The ruling Sultan of Bengal Sikandar, like his father, fled to fort Ekdala and ultimately Firuz Shah had to recognise his independence and return to Delhi without achieving anything.

Expedition to Jajnagar (Modern Orissa) : On his return journey from Bengal, Firuz Shah spent some time at Jaunpur. He then decided to march against Jajnagar. His motive was to occupy the famous Jagannath temple of Puri. On the arrival of the Delhi army, the king of Jajnagar fled. Firuz ordered the defilement of the temple and the idol was thrown into the sea. The Raja bought peace with the Sultan by offering submission to him and sending him twenty elephants as tribute. Firuz Shah returned to Delhi in triumph.

Conquest of Nagarkot : During the closing years of the reign of Muhammad bin Tughluq Nagarkot in Kangra had torn off from the Delhi empire. Sultan Firuz Shah led an expedition against Nagarkot in 1360. After a prolonged siege of six months the fort surrendered and the Raja submitted to the Sultan. He was received honourably by the Sultan. The Sultan acquired a great booty which included 1,300 Sanskrit manuscripts, some of which were got translated by the Sultan into Persian.

Conquest of Sind : In 1361-62 Sultan Firuz Shah Tughluq proceeded with 90,000 horses, a large number of infantry and 480 elephants, supported by a navy of many boats. Jam Babaniya, the ruler of Sind opposed the Sultan with an equally strong army. In the engagement, the Sultan's army suffered great loss and he was compelled to retreat to Gujarat for reinforcement. But he was misled by the guides into the Rann of Kutch. It took long six months for the Sultan and his army to emerge from the Rann of Kutch and there was no information about him during this period in Delhi. In 1363, Firuz Shah again attacked Thatta with reinforced strength sent from Delhi by his prime minister, Kha-i-Jahan Maqbul. The jam was compelled to agree to the payment of a tribute and the Sultan returned to Delhi.

Mongol Raids : The reign of Firuz Tughluq was free from the Mongol menance. It is said that there were only two raids during his reign by the Mongols but both were beaten off.

Firuz Shah Tughluq's Revenue Policy : One of the factors that had contributed to the stability of Firuz Shah's government was his revenue settlement. He appointed Khwaja Hisam-ud-din Juniad as assessor who made extensive tours for six years with a large staff and "fixed the income of the whole realm at six crore and seventy five lakhs of tankas." Although the state demand of the revenue was not made on the basis of measurement of land or any estimate of the actual produce, the land revenue was fixed more or less on a permanent basis which in itself was a creditable achievement. The Sultan stopped the practice of levying benevolences which the provincial governors had to pay and the time of their appointment and annually, because the burden of this payment used to be passed on to the shoulders of the people by the governors. Due to excavation of irrigation canals a vast area was brought under cultivation which had been hitherto fallow lands. As a result of this and also due to 10% increase in the revenue for the use of the irrigation canals, the state revenue increased by two lakhs of **tankas**, "Thriving villages were to be seen in the vicinity of Delhi, besides twelve hundred gardens which contained an incalculable number of fruitbearing trees." The sale proceeds of the fruits from these gardens brought one lakh eighty thousand **tankas** to the royal treasury annually. The promotion of trade and agriculture was the most distinctive feature of the reign and despite expenditure on military expeditions, suppression of rebellions etc. there was no need of enhancement of revenue. According to Afif, there was all-round prosperity everywhere in the country and prices of food, cloths, and other things were cheap and low. Necessaries of life were abundant and grains continued to be cheap throughout the reign of Firuz Tughluq "as in that of Ala-ud-din Khalji, but without any effort i.e. without any regulations."

Public Works and Irrigation : Firuz Tughluq was a lover of buildings and he is credited with building 300 towns. This is, obviously, an exaggeration. Among the towns founded by him the most important ones were Fatehabad, Hissar, Jaunpur, Firuzabad etc. Firuzabad was the Sultan's favourite residence. It was crowded with buildings, eight large mosques, each large enough to accommodate 10,000 devotees.

Firuz Tughluq is specially credited with the construction of five irrigation cannals. The longest and the most important of these was 150 miles long and connected Jamuna and the town of Hissar. One that connected Ghagra and Sutlej was 96 miles long. Two others connected Firuzabad with Ghagra, Firuzabad and Jamuna. The fifth canal connected Sirmur Hills with the town of Hansi. Sir Wolseley Haig observes : Firuz Shah is still remembered as the author of schemes of irrigation and traces of his canals yet remain. He also sank 150 wells for the purpose of irrigation and for the use of the travellers and indulged in a passion of building which equalled, if it did not surpass, that of the Roman Emperor Augustus. According to Ferishta, Firuz Shah was responsible for the construction of 50 dams across rivers for the purpose of irrigation, 40 mosques, 30 colleges with mosques attached to them, 20 palaces, 100 caravan serais, 200 towns, 30 reservoirs or lakes for irrigation, 100 hospitals, 5 mausolea, 100 public baths, 10 monumental pillars, 10 public wells and 150 bridges besides numerous gardens. He had transhifted two Asokan pillars one from Merrut and another from Khizirabad to Delhi by an extremely laborious process described in details by Shans-i-Siraj.

Other Reforms : Firuz Shah abolished internal tariffs so that the products of one part of the country might easily find market in other parts. The rapid growth of trade and commerce as also industries was the good result of this policy of the Sultan. The fall in prices of the commodities of daily use made the life of the common people easy.

Firuz Shah had also introduced certain judicial reforms. He abolished the practice of amputation of hands, legs etc. as a mode of punishment. He prohibited this kind of inhuman punishment and made the penal system more humane. For solving the problem of unemployment, Firuz Shah set up an employment Bureau. For the treatment of the poor he instituted **Dar-ul-Shafa,** that is free treatment for them at the cost of the state. For giving alms to the poor and indigent section of the people Firuz Shah opened **Diwan-i-Khairat,** i.e. Alms house. He also had improved the currency system by introducing **Adha** and **Bikh**—two types of coins of mixed metal.

Assignment of Land Revenue to the Army : Firuz Shah re-introduced the system of revenue assignments to the military and civil officials. In such assignments he was very generous. "He made assignments of 10,000, 5,000 and 2,000 **tankas;** and the whole army paid by assignment of land revenue." Ala-ud-din was against assignment of land revenue to officers, for it some of them would combine, this would lead to trouble. But Firuz Shah revived the old system of revenue assignment, that is **Jagir** system. Prof. Nizami points out that when revenue assignment was given on paper the officer in charge of revenue collection would pay to the assignee only half the amount assigned retaining the other half for the state. As a result if the revenue would increase due to improvement in cultivation the share of the state would also increase. According to Afif, a large number of soldiers used to receive their salaries in cash.

Taxation : Firuz Shah levied four kinds of taxes as mentioned in the Quran. These were Karaj, or land tax, Zakat, that is benevolence to the government. **Jizya** a poll tax on non-Muslims, Khams, i.e. a levy of one-fifth of the produce of the mines. These apart, an irrigation tax called Sharb as well as a part of the booty were realised by the state. There were many other cesses illegally realised from the people. But Firuz Shah prohibited their realisation.

Religious Policy : Firuz Tughluq owed his throne to the **ulemas** and prominent nobles. Having been born of a mother who was originally a Hindu, Firuz Tughluq must have thought it necessary to demonstrate that he was no less a devout Musalman than one born of Turkish parents. He therefore followed the policy of restoring the prestige and power of the **ulemas** and unlike Ala-ud-din and Muhammad bin Tughluq he consulted the **ulemas** in matters both political and religious. Under the influence of the ulemas who were, narrow, orthodox Muslims Firuz Shah developed a narrow, bigoted outlook and became a champion of **true faith,** i.e. Islam. He repressed the Hindus and encouraged them to embrace Islam. In 1374-75 Firuz Tughluq went to pray at the tomb of Salar Masud Ghazi at Bharaich. It is alleged that he saw Salar Masud in a dream and after that he "became definitely cruel, communalistic and fanatical." A Brahmin who was alleged to have converted a Muslim into Hinduism was brought before Firuz Shah who gave the Brahmin two alternatives, either to accept Islam or death. The Brahmin opted the latter one. Afif asserts that Firuz Shah imposed **jizya** on the Brahmins of Delhi. Of his fanatical activities reference may be made to the destruction of three Hindu temples, one at the pond of Malwa, the second at Salihpur and the third in the town of Gohana. Firuz Tughluq also punished the Shias and burnt their religious books. Muslim women were ordered not to come out of their houses or to go to tombs outside Delhi. Firuz ordered the execution of Ahmad whom his followers called **God,** Rukn who claimed to be the Mahdi, and a servant of Ain-i-Mahru who declared as **Truth** (Haq). He granted four-fifths of the spoils of war to the soldiers as laid down in the Quran. Firuz Shah held the Caliph of Egypt in high esteem and twice received investiture and robes of honour from him.

Patronage of Learning : Firuz Shah was a great patron of learning. He granted liberal allowances to scholars and established many schools and colleges and placed them in charge of learned men who were paid from the state handsomely. Each mosque had an educational institution attached to it. Zia-ud-din Barani and Shams-i-Siraj Afif enjoyed his liberal patronage. **Twarikh-i-Firuz Shahi** and **Fatwah-i-Jahandari** were the important historical works written during his reign. The latter was the work of Barani. Firuz Shah wrote his autobiograpy which is entitled **Fatuhat-i-Firozshahi.** He caused the Sanskrit manuscripts at least some of them, which he had found in the Kangra fort to be translated into Persian. Theology, jurisprudence and Islamic law were studied during his reign due to his personal interest.

Firuz Shah and the Slaves : Firuz Shah took great interest in increasing the number of his slaves. He issued instruction to the governors in different parts of the kingdom to send him slaves. Under him the number of slaves totalled one lakh eighty thousand out of which forty thousand had been put in the service of the Sultan's palace. A separate officer with necessary staff was in charge of the slaves and a large sum of money was allocated for the expenses of this department. Slaves would also be posted in different provinces. Firuz Tughluq made arrangements for the education and training of the slaves but the system was positively pernicious as the slaves like the **ulemas** began to interfere in the administration and eventually became at least one of main causes of the disintegration of the Delhi Sultanate.

Last Days of Firuz Shah : The last years of Firuz Shah's rule and life were not happy. He lost his eldest son Fateh Khan, whom he had nominated as the heir apparent, in 1374. What for old age and what for the shock of the death of his eldest son the Sultan lost much of his power and judgement. He now nominated his second son Zafar Khan as his heir, but he also died. The third son Muhammad Khan was the next choice but no formal nomination was made in his case. In the meantime the prime minister Khan-i-Jahan Maqbul had died and his son had become prime minister. The new prime minister persuaded the Sultan to believe that the prince was conspiring with the nobles to seize power and got the Sultans permission to punish the Prince's partisans. But the prince Muhammad Khan met the Sultan Firuz in disguide and convinced him that the Khan-i-Jahan, i.e. the prime minister was trying to destory the royal family to clear his way to the throne. Firuz Shah permitted Muhammad Khan to punish Khan-i-Jahan who getting the sense of the situation fled to Mewat. Muhammed now began to assist his father Firuz Shah in the administration and was allowed to share the royal title. He was now formally declared heir-apparent (1387). Soon after the prince got Khan-i-Jahan killed and assumed all power of the state in his own hands. But instead of looking into the administration he gave himself upto pleasure. The administration naturally become lax and everything was in confusion. Some of the nobles who were loyal to the crown tried to rouse Muhammad Khan to his responsibilities, but to no purpose. They therefore organised a rebellion Muhammad was now obliged to throw off his lethargy and fight the nobles. But the nobles brought the old Sultan Firuz Tughluq to the battle field and brought a sense of nervousness on the side of Muhammad Khan who fled for life. Firuz Shah now appointed Ghiyas-ud-din Tughluq Shah son of his eldest son Fateh Khan as the heir apparent and conferred on him the royal title. Firuz Shah died on Sept. 20, 1388.

Character and Estimate of Firuz Shah : Historians have diametrically opposite views about the character and personality of Firuz Shah Tughluq. Contemporary writers like Shams-i-Siraj Afif, Zia-ud-din Barani have called him the most just, merciful and benevolent ruler since the days of Nasir-ud-din Muhammad. Henry Elliot and Elphinstone went to the extent of calling him Akbar of the Sultanate period. But Iswari Prasad and Dr. Smith reject the opinion of Elliot and Elphinstone. Iswari Prasad observes : "Firoz had not even a hundredth part of the genius of that great-hearted and broad-minded monarch who preached from the high platform of public interest the gospel of peace, good-will and toleration towards all sects and creeds." Dr. Smith regards the praise of Elliot and Elphinstone as absurd. Sir Wolseley Haig's opinion is that the 'reign of Firoz closes the most brillant epoch of Muslim rule in India before the reign of Akbar.' Needless to say, the above are the two extremes of opinions and the truth is that his character and personality occupy a middle position.

Firuz was both a patron of learning and an accomplished scholar himself. The teachers of **madrasa,** schools and colleges that he had established were liberally paid by him. He encouraged learned men to reside in different parts of the country so that instruction might be imparted to people of the different parts of the kingdom. He caused some of the Hindu books, the manuscripts of which he found at Kagra, to be translated into Persian.

Firuz Shah possessed qualities of heart, if not much of head. He acted sincerely upto his convictions and really wished the welfare of his people. No ruler of the Delhi Sultanate did so much for the material welfare of the people. His revision of the revenue policy encouraged agriculture and brought comfort and life of ease to the vast majority of the people. His irrigation system, uniquc during the Sultanate period, developed agriculture considerably. His abolition of internal tariff encouraged trade and commerce which brought prosperity to the state and the people, and brought down prices of the essentials of daily life. It is by the quantum of material prosperity that the people judge a ruler and they saw much prosperity under Firuz Tughluq which earned for him the golden opinion of the people, and historians both contemporary and modern. Firuz Shah's numerous acts of charity, his attempt at solution of the unemployment problem, his setting up of a free hospital and alms house speak well of his liberal attitude towards his subjects. His generous treatment of the state employees, arrangements for the comfort of the travellers and the holy men were proofs of his regarding himself as the trustee of the welfare of the people. He abolished inhuman punishment for criminal offence, forbade extortionate realisation by the revenue officers and maintained law and order more effectively than many of the Sultans.

Yet taking the age in which he ruled into consideration, it must be remarked that the prestige of the Sultan depended much on his military efficiency and exploits. But here Firuz Shah failed. His Bengal expeditions, his wandering in the Rann of Kutch for six months etc. were not to his credit. He was timid and timorous and his military expeditions did not bring any gain or prestige to the Sultanate.

His benevolence was at times indiscriminate and bestowed on undeserved persons which injured the interests of the state. It is said that he once paid a gold **tanka** to a trooper who was found to despair his lot that in the muster his horse would not be passed as fit for military service. The Sultan gave him the money for bribing the officer who would inspect the horses at the muster so that the unfit horse might be passed. His system of revenue assignment to the civil and military officers led to much malpractices as these assignments were sold by the assignees to the brokers at a cheaper price, and as a result the latter became very rich.

The Sultan's fondness for the slaves increased the number of the slaves to one lakh eighty thousand and a regular department had to be maintained at a great cost to manage the slaves. The slaves began to interfere in the administration as did the **ulemas** which injured the interest of the state.

Firuz Tughluq restored the **ulemas** to their old position of power and prestige. He for the first time under the Sultanate made proselytising a state policy and encouraged the Hindus to accept Islam by proclaiming that such converts would be exempt from the payment of **jizya.** A large number of poor Hindus accepted Islam to avoid payment of **jizya.** Firuz Tughluq earned the good opinion of the Sunni Muslims by his orthodox religious policy. He did not hesitate to persecute the **Shia** section of the Muslims. It was the irony of Firuz's fate that the very qualities for which he had earned the praise of the people were the very causes that were largely responsible for the weakness of the Delhi Sultanate.

THE LATER TUGHLUQS (1388-1414)

All the Tughluq rulers that succeeded Firuz Shah were utterly incompetent persons without any ability to rule or any force of personality or character. All of them were virtually puppets in the hands of their unscrupulous and ambitious nobles who were busy in lining their coats at the cost of the state.

On the death of Firuz Shah in September, 1388, his grandson Ghiyas-ud-din, son of Fateh Shah, eldest son of Firuz Shah ascended the throne. He was as inexperienced as given to pleasure and merry-making. The **maliks** and the **amirs** were all offended at the conduct of Ghiyas-ud-din and they combined to depose him. They placed Abu Bakr, son of Zafar Khan, second son of Firuz Shah on the throne of February 19, 1389. But Firuz's third son Muhammad Khan reappeared to assert his claim to the throne. With the support of some powerful nobles he proclaimed himself king at Samana on April 24, 1389. A struggle for the throne of Delhi began between the two claimants and ultimately Abu Bakr was compelled to leave the throne to Muhammad in 1390. Muhammad's intemperate life and excessive indulgence told upon his health and he died in January 1394. He was succeeded by Humayun under the title Sikandar Shah who could rule for barely a year, for he died in March 1395. He was succeeded by the youngest son of Muhammad who was the last ruler of the Tughluq dynasty. Nusrat Shah, a son of Fateh Khan disputed his claim to the throne and for some time both of them became Sultans on at Delhi and the other at Firuzabad. According to Badauni, they lived and quarrelled like the kings of a game of chess. The weakness of the situation was taken advantage of by the Muslim governors and the Hindu chiefs who threw off their allegiance to the Delhi Sultan and proclaimed their independence. The vast empire built by the labours of successive Sultans from Qutb-ud-din to Muhammad bin Tughluq began to fall apart. Malik Sarvar under the title Sultan-us-Sharq made himself independent at Jaunpur and founded the Sharqi dynasty. Zafar khan, governor of Gujarat sapped his relation with the Delhi Sultanate. Both Khandesh and Malwa became independent kingdoms. The Khokars of north-eastern Punjab who had never been subdued completely rose in rebellion. Rajasthan and Gwalior became independent. The Hindus of the Doab who hardly paid revenue except under pressure from the government even under Muhammad-bin-Tughluq and Firuz Shah tried to shake off their yoke of dependence. A new Muslim state was founded at Bayana and the example was followed by Kalpi. In this way the Delhi Sultanate had been disintegrated and its fall was only a question of time. When the internal situation was such desperate, Timur invaded India in 1398 which dealt a death blow to the Sultanate.

AMIR TIMUR AND HIS INVASION (1398-99)

Timur was born in 1336 in Samarqand in Transoxiana, the territory between the Oxus and the Jaxartes. He belonged to the Barlas Turkish clan which ruled over the town of Keech and its surrounding area. In course of a fight he got wounded in his leg and after that he limped for the rest of his life and came to be called Timur the lame. The Europeans corrupted the name into Tamerlane.

Timur rose from an humble position to be the ruler of a vast empire comprising Transoxiana, part of Turkistan, whole of Afghanistan, Persia, Syria, Qurdistan and the major part of Asia Minor. Towards the end of his career he decided to lead an expedition against India. The object of the expedition to slay the infidels of India and thereby to become a **ghazi.** In some places he himself referred to a twofold objective of his expedition, namely to war with the infidels and thereby to claim reward in the after life, and to plunder the wealth and valuables of the infidels. "As a matter of fact, the combined in himself the savage ferocity of Chinghiz Khan and the fanaticism of Sultan Mahmud." There is difference of opinion about the expedition sent under Timur's grandson Pir Muhammad. According to some writers, Timur sent an advance guard of his army under his grand son Pir Muhammad in 1398, himself starting from Samarqand the same year after some time. But according to others before Timur had launched his expedition he received information that his grand son Pir Muhammad, governor of Kabul, Qandahar, Ghazni and the neighbouring regions, had already sent an expedition against India which crossed the river Sindhu, captured Uch and besieged Multan. Timur starting either in March or April, 1398 reached Afghanistan when a large number of Muslims complained to him of the ill-treatment they received at the hands of the infidels of Kator. Timur readily proceeded against Kator, a place between Kashmir and Kabul. The fort of Kator deserted by the people was razed to the ground and the houses in the city were all burnt to ashes. The infidels who took refuge on the hills were pursued, defeated and many of them were put to death. Some of the infidels who held out for three days were given the alternative of death or accepting Islam by Timur. They opted for the latter, but soon recanting attacked the regiment of the Muslim soldiers during night. But they were defeated and many of them taken prisoners only to be put to death later. At the day break Timur ordered plunder of the properties of the infidels and to capture their women and children. After this order was faithfully executed, towers on the skulls of the infidels were built. Timur then sent troops to retrieve his position in the Siyah-poshes. But his troops could not succeed completely against Siyah-poshes and these were left alone.

Timur crossed the river Sindhu in September in 1398, crossed Jhelum and Ravi besieged Talamba seventy five miles to the north-east of Multan. Here he was informed that Pir Muhammad had captured Multan. Now the two armies under Pir Muhammad and Timur joined and proceeded via Park Patan, Dipalpur, Bhatner, Sirsa, Kaithal plundering and burning the country and massacring the people on the way. Timur now reached the vicinity of Delhi. Sultan Nasir-ud-din Mahmud Tughluq and his prime minister Mallu Iqbal came out to oppose Timur. But Timur finding that the prisoners whom he had captured on his way to Delhi were embarrassing his war efforts, butchered one lakh of them, all Hindus, in cold blood. In the battle that followed (December 17, 1398) Sultan Nasir-ud-din was defeated. The Delhi army comprised forty thousand infantry, ten thousand cavalry and hundred and twenty elephants. But it fell easily before the invading army of Timur. The Sultan fled to Gujarat and the prime minister to Bulandshahr.

On December 18, 1398 Timur occupied Delhi where the citizens led by the **ulemas** waited on the conqueror and begged quarter. Although Timur is said to have agreed to spare the citizens, the oppressive conduct of the soldiers of Timur left no alternative before the Delhi citizens but to stand in defence. Timur enraged because of this, ordered a general massacre and plunder of the citizens which lasted for several days. Thousands of Delhi citizens were put to sword and thousands taken prisoners. According to one historian "High towers were built with the heads of the Hindus, and their bodies became the food for the ravenous beasts and birds." Those who were still alive were made prisoners.

Timur took immense booty and there was not a single soldier who did not become rich overnight and did not possess at least twenty slaves. Timur picked the master artisans of Delhi and sent them to Samarqand for building his famous **Friday Mosque.**

For fifteen days Timur stayed in Delhi and left Delhi on January 1, 1399 for Samarqand. He had no desire to rule over Delhi. He passed via Firozabad and reaching Merrut stormed it. Near Hardwar he was opposed by two Hindu armies whom Timur had to defeat before resuming his journey. He then plundered Kangra and Jammu.

Everywhere he slaughtered people like a butcher slaughters cattle. Before leaving India Timur appointed Khizir Khan the expelled governor of Multan, Lahore and Dipalpur to run the government of the bordering area. Timur recrossed Indus on March 19, 1399, after inflicting greater misery and causing more deaths than any other conqueror had inflicted in a single campaign.

Effects of Timur's Invasion : The effects of Timur invasion were : (i) the country was laid prostrate and bleeding. Lakhs of inhabitants, including women and children were butchered and the entire tract of north-western provinces including Rajasthan and Delhi had been pillaged, ravaged and plundered and laid waste. (ii) Timur's journey with his large army upto Delhi and back had laid waste the fields of agriculture on both sides of the route of their march. Standing crops were destroyed, granaries were looted, trade and commerce virtually ceased for the time being. The city of Delhi was depopulated as a result of massacre of the citizens and capture of citizens as prisoners and desertion by others out of fear and having lost everything due to plunder the Timur's soldiers. A terrible famine broke out in Delhi and its suburbs followed by pestilence that stalks the land in the wake of famine. (iii) The Delhi Sultanate already shrivelled up had been now confined to the capital and a few districts around it. For some months there was no Sultan in Delhi. In March, 1399 Nusrat Shah Tughluq returned to Delhi only to be expelled by his prime minister Mallu Iqbal. He then invited Mahmud Khan, Nusrat Shah's rival to the throne to Delhi and began to rule over Delhi himself keeping Mahmud only as a puppet. Prime Minister Mallu Iqbal sought to recover some of the lost areas of the Delhi Sultanate but was killed in action against Khizir Khan of Multan (1405). This freed Mahmud from the galling tutelage of his prime minister but he was incapable of consolidating his authority. He died in 1413 and with his death the Tughluq dynasty came to an end.

The Delhi nobles put one of themselves named Daulat Khan in charge of the state, but he did not assume royal title or dignity. He failed to restore order or to put down rebellion all over the country. In the circumstances Khizir Khan of Multan came and besieged Delhi. Daulat Khan after a few months resistance surrendered. He was captured and sent to Hissar. Khizir Khan became the ruler of Delhi on May 28, 1414 and founded the Sayyid Dynasty of the Delhi Sultanate.

THE SAYYIDS (1414-50)

KHIZIR KHAN (1414-21)

According to Yahya Sirhindi author of **Tarikh-i-Mubarak Shahi** Khizir Khan was a descendant of the Prophet of Islam and as such styled himself as Sayyid. Yahya Sirhindi bases his conclusion of Jalal-ud-din Bukhari's account, but on no substantial evidence. It is, however, certain that he belonged to a family that had come from Arabia. Khizir Khan was appointed governor of Multan by Firuz Tughluq but was driven out from there by the brother of Mallu Iqbal Khan. Khizir Khan took shelter in Mewat for a time and reemerged to cast his lot with Timur. It is believed that Timur left him as his viceroy at Delhi but Khizir Khan could re-establish himself at Multan, Dipalpur and Sind. He defeated Mally Iqbal Khan who had usurped power at Delhi and killed him. It was by defeating Daulat Khan who was placed in charge of the state by some Delhi nobles that he entered Delhi in June 1414.

Khizir Khan's first task on assumption of power was to reorganise the administration by distributing important offices of the state to his trusted followers; but he treated the nobles of Muhammad Tughluq's reign with kindness and made liberal grants and endowments to the poor for their resettlement. The capital thus began to recover from the political disorders and sack by Timur that had taken place before his accession.

Khizir Khan believed that he owed his power and prestige to Timur's patronage and therefore he did not assume any royal title and continued his allegiance to Timur's son Shah Rukh and preferred to be addressed as **Rayat-i-Ala.** Three years afterwards (1417) he obtained permission of Shah Rukh to suffix his name to that of Shah Rukh. This acknowledgement of foreign supremacy was nothing more than a formality and he actually functioned as an independent king. He also did not strike coins in his own name. He used the type of coins that were popular in the immediate past by altering their date. This was obviously a sign of his weakness.

India at that time was split up into a number of independent states and the Delhi Sultanate had been considerably reduced both in size and power. Bengal and the Deccan were lost long before. This was followed by the rise of independent kingdoms of Jaunpur, Gujarat, malwa, Khandesh etc. during the confusion of the last years of the fourteenth and early years of the fifteenth century. A number of smaller chiefs of the Doab were trying to throw off their allegiance to Delhi. Khizir Khan's authority extended beyond Delhi over only a few districts. Khizir Khan attempted to recover Etawah, Katehar, Kanauj, Patiali and Kampil but was able to recover only some fertile areas in the vicinity of Delhi and with regard to other places he had only temporary success. Almost every year he would undertake expedition for plunder and return with some booty.

In spite of Khizir Khan's conciliatory policy the rule of the Syyids was not acceptable to the Turkish elements. In 1416 a group of Turkbachchas created troubles in Sirhind and assassinated Malik Sadhu Nadira, deputy of Prince Mubarak who was in charge of the administration there. The royal army drove them out but they rose in arms next year as well under a new leader Tughan Rais who was also defeated. Tughan attacked Sirhind again but this time failing in his attempt effected a junction with the Khokaras of Punjab and assumed threatening proportions in the next reign.

Mahabat Khan, another Turkish noble, **amir** of Badaun who was seemingly loyal made a surprise attack on Khizir Khan when he was returning from Katehar. Khizir Khan besieged the fort of Badaun and when after prolonged siege of six months the fort was about surrender, Khizir Khan had suddenly raised the siege due to the treachery of some Turkisha slaves. The traitors were, however, executed after Khizir Khan's return to Delhi. In 1419, an imposter who posed as Sarang Khan, brother of Mallu Iqbal Khan led a rising in the Bajwara mountains. Sarang Khan had expelled Khizir Khan from Multan. But the imposter who falsely gave himself out as Sarang Khan was defeated by Khizir Khan's able general Sultan Shah and driven to the mountains. Next year Sarang was captured by Tughan Rais who killed him for his properties.

On an appeal from the Muslim ruler of Nagaur for help against the aggression of Ahmad Shah of Gujarat Khizir Khan undertook the distant campaign towards Nagaur. The place temporarily submitted only to transfer its allegiance to Gujarat two years later under the threat of an invasion by Malwa. On his return journey from Nagaur Khizir Khan realised customary payments from Gwalior and Bayana. In the last year of his reign Khizir Khan raided Mewat and destroyed the fort of Kotla. He also ravaged Gwalior and received tribute from Gwalior and received submission of the Raja of Etawa. During this campaign Khizir Khan fell ill and died on his return to Delhi (May 20, 1421).

Estimate : Khizir Khan, according to Ferishta was a just and generous ruler. He possessed laudable traits of character which endeared him to the people. He was also wise and benevolent. He was free from the vices of the contemporary rulers. Although his record as a ruler was not impressive, his conquest of Delhi was a creditable achievement. It was, however, not possible for him to settle the numerous problems of the country which was in virtual anarchy after the invasion of Timur. But during the period of his rule he tried to restore the power and prestige of the Delhi Sultanate in Punjab, Doab, Rohilkhand and parts of Rajputana, but the odds against him were so stupendous that he could not achieve anything substantial.

MUBARAK SHAH (1421-34)

Khizir Khan had nominated his son Mubarak Khan as his heir. Mubarak Khan ascended the Delhi throne under the title Mubarak Shah and the nobles apparently acclaimed his accession although in reality they did not support him. Like his father Khizir Khan, Mubarak Shah had to undertake expeditions to different parts of the kingdom to suppress rebellion and disorder. Although he succeeded in putting down the rebellions at Bhatinda and the Doab, his attempt to suppress the Khokars of Punjab did not succeed. Jasrath, the leader of the Khokars was an aspirant to the throne of Delhi. Mubarak Shah, however, did not make any attempt to recover any territory lost to the Delhi Sultanate. In one respect his reign was a departure from many of his predecessors, for he appointed one or two Hindus to his court. Under him some of the Muslim and Hindu nobles led by Sarwar-ul-Mulk, the **wazir,** hatched a conspiracy against the Sultan. The conspirators fell on him unawares when he was supervising the construction of a town on the bank of the Jamuna and killed him (February 19, 1434).

In **Tarikh-i-Mubarak Shah** a fairly detailed account of the reign of Mubarak Shah as also that of his predecessor can be had. This Persian work was compiled by Yahya Sirhindi during the rule of Mubarak Shah.

MUHAMMAD SHAH (1434-45)

On Mubarak Shah's death, his brother's son Muhammad Khan ascended the throne under the title Sultan Muhammad Shah. For about six months all powers of the state were usurped by Sarvar-ul-Mulk who had become Khan-i-Jaha by persuading the Sultan to appoint him to that post, he appropriate the treasures, stores and elephants of the state which he kept in his own possession. He then filled all the high offices of the state with his own nominees and assigned important fiefs like those of Bayana, Amroha, Narnaul, Siddhipala to his friends and followers who played an important part in the assassination of Mubarak Shah. One of the nobles Kamal-ul-Mulk who was loyal to the house of Khizir Khan feigned loyality to Sarvar and was appointed commander of the royal forces and sent to suppress the revolt at Bayan. Kamal-ul-Mulk proceeded quietly and after reaching Ahar enlisted the support of rebel **amirs** (1434). The united force then marched towards Delhi to punish the regicides. Sarvar finding himself outwitted made an attempt on the life of the new Sultan Mahmud Shah but was immediately killed by the body guards of the Sultan. All the companions of Sarvar met with the same fate. The liberating army which kept the city under a siege for three months was welcomed into Delhi and all the nobles renewed their allegiance to Muhammad Shah. Kamal-ul-Mulk was appointed the prime minister. Freed from the tutelage of Sarvar Muhammad Shah now became a Sultan both in name and fact. As the nobles were now unitedly supporting him he had an excellent opportunity to reorganise the affairs of the state but unfortunately Muhammad Shah preferred enjoyment of pleasures to kingly duties. The result was that rebellions and disorders broke out everywhere, and when the situation went from bad to worse Jalal Khan a Mewati Leader, his companions and the elites of Delhi sent invitation to Sultan Mahmud Khalji of Malwa to come to Delhi. As the Sultan Mahmud Khalji encamped near Delhi at a place called Tilpat, Muhammad Shah finding the situation beyond him called Buhlul Lodi, the chief of Sirhind to come to his assistance. Buhlul Lodi came with 20,000 mounted soldiers and fought at the vanguard of the Delhi forces as the virtual commander Muhammad Shah without consulting any one unilaterally decided after the indecisive battle of the first day to sue for peace. Sultan Muhammad

Khalji who had some distrubance at his own camp accepted the offer readily and withdrew to Mandu. Buhlul Lodi felt the conduct of Muhammad Shah nothing short of betrayal and in order to retrieve the prestige of his army attacked the forces of Sultan Muhammad Khalji from the rear killing many and capturing their baggages. Mahmud Shah was now full of praise for Buhlul and called him a son and conferred on him the title of **Khan-i-Jahan.** Buhlul later occupied the major part of Punjab and Muhammad Shah asked him to subdue the rebellious Khokars and their leader Jasrath who was clever enough to come to terms with Buhlul Lodi. With his power and prestige increased manifold Buhlul Lodi attacked Delhi in 1443 without success.

The last years of Muhammad Shah saw the rapid decline of his kingdom; Multan becoming independent, Sharqis annexing some parganas in the east, many fief-holders stopping payment of tributes and even **amirs** making bid for independence. Before his death in 1445, Muhammad Shah nominated his son Ala-ud-din and called him from Badaun and breathed his last.

ALA-UD-DIN ALAM SHAH (1445-51)

Ala-ud-din ascended the throne with the title Ala-ud-din Alam Shah. He was perhaps the most incompetent king of his line. His reign saw the transfer of power from the Sayyids to the Lodis.

Buhlul Lodi was at that time holding more extensive territories under his control than the Sultan himself had. The Delhi Sultanate for all practical purposes had become non-existent and its place had been taken by petty tribal kingdoms whose boundaries verged on the borders of Delhi. Morally perverse, incapable and worthless, Ala-ud-din realised his incompetence and retired to Badaun where he gave himself up to pleasure and enjoyment. The vacuum thus created in Delhi was soon to be filled. Buhlul Lodi had in the meantime made a second attempt on Delhi, but was not successful (1447). But his opportunity came when Ala-ud-din Alam Shah's minister Hamid Khan invited Buhlul Lodi and Qiyam Khan either of whom he thought would agree to be puppet in his hands and he would enjoy all power of the state. This Hamid Khan did out of fear that some powerful neighbour might forcibly occupy Delhi. Buhlul being nearer at Sirhind than Qiyam Khan at Nagaur, rushed to Delhi and assumed power. Qiyam Khan who reached Delhi late returned disappointed. Buhlul got rid of Hamid Khan after a short time and informed Ala-ud-din Alam Shah that he had assumed power as Sultan of Delhi. Ala-ud-din Alam Khan was, however, allowed to remain in Badaun during the rest of his life. Thus was the Sayyids supplanted by the Lodis.

THE LODIS (1451-1526)

BUHLUL LODI (1451-89)

Buhlul Lodi belonged to an important branch of the Afghans. His grandfather, Malik Bahram, came over to Multan during the reign of Firuz Tughluq and token service under Malik Mardan Daulat, governor of Multan. Among his five sons Malik Sultan and Malik Kala had acquired some fame. Buhlul Lodi was the son of Malik Kala who had defeated Jasrath, the leader of the Khokars and made himself an independent chief. Sultan Shah, Buhlul's uncle was appointed governor of Sirhind by Sultan Khizir Khan (1419) and conferred on him the title of Islam Khan. He united and organised the Afghans of Punjab and thereby strengthened his position. Before his death Sultan Khan also known as Islam Khan, nominated his nephew Buhlul Lodi as his successor in preference to his son Qutb Khan. On his death Buhlul became the governor of Sirhind. Buhlul was both clever and ambitious, and as a means of fulfilment of his ambition he increased the number of the troops under him and soon was reckoned as one of the first ranking governors of the kingdom. When Mahmud Khalji of Malwa threatened his master Muhammad Shah, he hastened to his assistance and saved the situation for which the Sultan gave him the title of **Khan-i-Khanan.** But Buhlul's ambition was not to be satisfied with the position of the governor of a province. His opportunity came when the next Sultan Ala-ud-din Alam Shah had differences with his minister Hamid Khan and attempted to take his life. Infuriated Hamid Khan invited Buhlul Lodi to Delhi to take over the command of the army. The Sultan Ala-ud-din Alam Shah had in the meantime, finding the situation gone out of his control he took himself to Badaun. The power of state now passed into the hands of Buhlul.

Immediately after his occupation of Delhi, Buhlul wrote to Sultan "Your Majesty's father brought me up. I have been acting as your deputy...without expunging your name from the **khutba**." The Sultan replied "As my father used to address you as his son, I look upon you as my elder brother and I resign the kingship to you. I shall live contented at Badaun."

The throne to which Buhlul was raised was no bed of roses. It did not add to his possessions, but increased his responsibilities manifold. His problems were : (i) to consolidate the Sultanate by recovering the neighbouring territories, (ii) to bring back to submission its rebellious fief-holders, (iii) to wage war against Jaunpur, and (iv) to improve and remodel administration with the interests of the Afghan nobility in mind.

The most outstanding achievement of Buhlul was the conquest and annexation of Jaunpur which not only brought back to the Delhi Sultanate the territory lost to it in 1394, but also strengthened the foundation of the Lodi dynasty.

The Sharqis considered themselves legitimate successors to the Sayyids due to matrimonial relations with them. Occupation of Jaunpur by Buhlul came as a disappointment to them. Mahmud the Sharqi king attacked Delhi but was beaten back by Buhlul. Mahmud fought Buhlul at Etawa and Shamsabad but before the engagements came to any decisive conclusion Mahmud died. His son Muhammad Shah made proposal for peace to Buhlul Lodi but the latter would not agree till his brother-in-law who had been taken prisoner by Mahmud, was released. The war therefore was renewed and Muhammad Shah's brother was captured by Buhlul Lodi's troops. A fratricidal war kept Muhammad Shah engaged at home in which he was killed by his brother Hussain who was himself ultimately defeated by Buhlul Lodi.

Pacification of the Doab and Mewat was urgently needed so that the chiefs of these areas might not join the Sharqi king. Buhlul therefore led a number of expeditions against Mewat, Bhongaon, Sambhal, Kol, Sakit, Etawa, Rapri and Gwalior. The chiefs of these places initially submitted to Buhlul but began to waver in their loyalty. But once the Sharqis were finally defeated these chiefs unreservedly submitted to Buhlul. In Multan and in his raid against Alhanpur. Buhlul did not succeed.

Before his death Buhlul had distributed his territories among his relatives and **amirs.** Punjab, Delhi and most part of the Doab were given to his son Nizam Khan (later Sultan Sikandar Lodi) whom he nominated as his heir apparent. Buhlul died in 1489.

Character and Estimate : Buhlul Lodi was a man of lofty personal character and although a devout Muslim was not intolerant to other religions. He was kind and charitable and would never turn away a suppliant from his door empty-handed. His generosity did not exclude even his bitterest enemy. Buhlul Lodi was an intrepid warrior and a successful general. He had the vision of a political realist and a dogged tenacity of purpose guided all his activities throughout his life. He, however, did not hesitate to have recourse to treachery, chicanery, fraud or any other foul means if that would suit his purpose. He did not hesitate to bribe Darya Khan Lodi in the battle field of Narela. He was, however, not devoid of chivalry and twice he restored the wife of the Sharqi ruler whom his troops captured to her husband with all dignity and respect. As a king Buhlul was not at all ostentatious. He considered himself **primus interpares** i.e. the first among the equals with the Afghan lords. "It was no time to reform or discipline the uncouth Afghans, but by respecting their clannish feeling and their instinctive sense of freedom, he managed to win and retain their allegiance, and ultimately succeeded in laying the foundations of the dynasty on a firm basis."

Buhlul deserves the credit of having revived the Sultanate and extended its boundaries, and rehabilitated its declining power and prestige. Conquest and annexation of Jaunpur was one of his chief achievements. Although keen about the welfare of the people, his military pre-occupation did not permit him much time for administrative reorganisation. He won the allegiance of both the Muslim and non-Muslim friends and feudatories and subjects. Buhlul succeeded in laying the foundation of the Lodi dynasty on a firm basis.

SIKANDAR LODI (1489-1517)

On Buhlul's death the nobles of the court were divided on the question of succession. One group supported succession of Nizam Khan, whom they got nominated by Buhlul Lodi before his death as the heir-apparent, the other group favoured the succession of the eldest son of Buhlul, Barbak Shah, who was at the time of the death of Buhlul at Jaunpur. Nizam Khan's mother boldly intervened on behalf of her son and he was crowned king on July 15, 1489. He took the title Sikandar Shah. He was, in fact, the ablest among the surviving sons of Buhlul and proved worthy of the choice as king.

Sikandar's first task was to secure his own position by reducing his rivals to submission and strengthening his own followers. His uncle Alam Khan was an aspirant to the throne besides some others. Alam Khan was making preparations to assert his independence at Rapri and Chandwar. Sikandar marched against him, besieged Rapri and put him to flight. Isa Khan who was opposed to the succession of Sikandar gave asylum to Alam Khan and both now thought of taking the field against Sikandar. But Sikandar by his conciliatory policy towards Aalam Khan won him over and granted him a fief at Etawa. Isa was then defeated. Azam Humayun, a cousin of Sikandar was also a candidate for the throne. Sikandar dispossessed him of his fief at Kalpi and bestowed it upon Muhammad Khan Lodi. Another opponent of Sikandar was Tatar Khan Lodi but Sikandar generously allowed him to remain in possession of Jhatra on his acknowledging Sikandar's suzerainty. Thus within a year Sikandar succeeded in pacifying or subduing his opponents and rivals and thereby consolidating his power.

Sikandar's ideal of kingship did not admit of any divided monarch. He therefore would not allow his elder brother Barbak Shah to rule in Jaunpur in complete independence. He, therefore, tried to bind Barbak in a subordinate alliance, and to that end sent a mission to him. But due to the influence of Hussain Shah, the ex-king of Jaunpur, Barbak rejected the proposal. This made it necessary to subdue Barbak by military force. Sikandar marched against him upon which Barbak fled to Badaun where he was besieged and ultimately compelled to surrender. Sikandar restored Jaunpur to Barbak as a titular king there but divided the kingdom into a number of fiefs which he distributed among his followers. Sikandar also placed his trusted men in Barbak's court and even in his household. Soon after the zamindars of Jaunpur rebelled against Barbak at the instigation of Hussain Shah which compelled Barbak to flee to Dariyabad near Lucknow. Sikandar at once marched against the rebels, crushed them and reinstated Barbak to his kingdom. But Barbak, being inherently a weak ruler proved incompetent to run the administration whereupon Sikandar removed him and put him into confinement and appointed a governor at Jaunpur.

Sikandar and the Nobility : Sikandar was determined to bring the Afghan nobles under proper discipline and control. Although he did not make any fundamental change of the existing system of administration, he took measures to curb the individualistic tendencies and tribal independence of the Afghans and to make them contribute to the welfare of the entire Afghan community in India. He instituted the system of proper audit and accounting of the income and expenditure of the governors and officers of the state. Defalcation and embezzlement were visited with most deterrent punishment. One of the chief nobles, Mubarak Khan Lodi who was in charge of the revenue collection of Jaunpur was punished and compelled to disgorge the defalcated amount. Unlike his father, Sikandar did not consider him to be a **primus interpares** but cent percent a sovereign. He insisted on formalities in the court. Discourteous conduct was severely punished by Sikandar. The nobles did not like the strict observance of courtesies and discipline and conspired to depose the Sultan and to place his younger brother Fateh Khan on the throne. The conspiracy was, however, divulged and the Sultan banished twenty-two of his nobles guilty of conspiring, from the royal court. Royal **farmans** had to be received by the nobles all sanding before the Sultan in the Court. Such steps restored discipline and courtesy among the nobles. The success of Sikandar was largely due to the efficient system of espionage that he maintained. He borrowed the idea from Sultan Ala-ud-din Khalji. He kept himself abreast of the happenings in the kingdom so much so that he was commonly believed to possess supernatural power.

Sikandar's reign was marked by material prosperity. With the restoration of law and order, trade and commerce thrived, abolition of duties on grains made grains cheaper. Food and cloth and other necessaries of daily life became cheap, making people happy and contented.

Sikandar was a religious bigot. He prohibited the Hindus to bathe in the sacred tank of Thaneswar and in the river Jamuna. He followed the policy of destroying Hindu temples and building mosques in those sites. The idol at the **Jwalamukhi** temple at Nagarkot was broken and its pieces were given to the butchers to use as weights to measure meat. He was responsible for the destruction of many temples at Mathura, Mandrail, Utgir, Narwar, Chanderi and other places. Bodhan a Hindu was put to death under his order for no other offence than saying that Hinduism was as true a religion as Islam. Like Firuz Tughluq he followed the policy of converting the Hindus into Islam.

Conquests : Sikandar's ambition prompted him to recover as much of the territories lost to the Delhi Sultanate as possible. His annexation of Jaunpur brought him in conflict with Bihar which was a part of Bengal then. Some of the rebellious zamindars of Jaunpur had close contacts with Hussain Shah Sharqi who had been ousted from Jaunpur in the previous reign. Hussain was living in Bihar wherefrom he was instigating the Jaunpur zamindars. In order to suppress the zamindars Sikandar led an expedition to Phaphamau near Allahabad whose ruler Raja Bhil was the leader of the disaffected zamindars. But the Raja could not be subdued completely, on the contrary his expedition of the year 1494 caused considerable loss to the cavalry of the Sultan. Raja Bhil who was in league with Hussain Shah invited the latter informing him that in the condition of terrible loss suffered by Sikandar it would be easy to defeat him. Hussain proceeded with his army and in the engagement near Benaras Hussain was defeated and had to take to flight. Sikandar pursued the retreating army of Hussain and occupied Bihar. He then stayed in Bihar for some time and raided Tirhut which was compelled to agree to pay an annual tribute to the Delhi Sultan.

Ala-ud-din Hussain Shah, king of Bengal considered Bihar a part of his kingdom and Hussain Shah as his protege. He sent his son Daniyal to oppose the Delhi army but both Sikandar and Ala-ud-din Hussain Shah came to sign a treaty without a fight, stipulating that no party would invade the territory of the other. The king of Bengal also agreed not to give shelter to enemies of Sikandar. In this way the eastern frontier of the Sultanate was pushed to the frontiers of Bengal.

Ambition of Sikandar was not to be satisfied without conquering Gwalior and Dholpur. He led an expedition against Dholpur and after a prolonged fight he succeeded in capturing Dholpur from its Raja Vinayak Deo (1502). But the conquest of Gwalior was beyond his ability and strength. He led successive expeditions against Gwalior but could not succeed against the ruler of that great fortress Man Singh. In order to facilitate his expedition against Gwalior, Dholpur and Malwa Sikandar had made Agra his capital. But years of exertions bore fruits by the way of capturing Dhoplur, Mandrail, Utgir, Narwar and Chanderi. But Gwalior remained unconquered. Malwa was also could not be conquered by him. These military conquest although not very brilliant, yet had raised the prestige of the Delhi Sultanate and of Sikandar.

On his return from Bayana where he had gone in order to lead an expedition against Malwa, Sikandar fell ill and died on November 21, 1517.

Character and Estimate : Endowed with extraordinary physical charm, rare quality of eloquence, and ability as a poet, musician, Sikandar Lodi in many respects was a striking figure of medieval India. 'He gave a new orientation to the Afghan Polity in India and considerably raised the status and dignity of office of the Sultan.' Sikandar was an able administrator and a clear-headed politician who could make clear analysis of the situation that faced him and vigorous in the enforcement of his orders. Highly educated, Sikandar was fond of literature and poetry and himself wrote verses in Persian under a pen name **Gul Rukh.** As he was born of a Hindu mother, he was very anxious to show to his co-religionists that he was a devout Muslim, not inferior to any pure Afghan Muslim. It was his daily practice that after the morning prayer and recitation of the Quran he would begin his administrative activities. He dispensed much in charity. He was also a good warrior and a successful commander.

As a ruler Sikandar attained more than ordinary success. His ideal of kingship was very similar to that of the Turkish and the Hindu conceptions of sovereignty rather than to that of the Afghans. But it may be pointed out that his attempt at royal absolutism, although necessary at that time, was perhaps premature and became a policy of repression, unaccompanied by measures to strengthen the administration necessarily failed. At a time when the danger of external invasion was looming large in the north-west, he alienated his powerful nobles. This betrayed his lack of foresight. Although kindly in disposition and friendly with the saints, divines and his subjects, he was not tolerant of other religions. During his reign, there was an abundance of crop and the people in general lived happily in the midst of plenty and cheap prices. His chief achievements were the conquest and annexation of Bihar, Dholpur, Narwar, Chanderi and a part of Gwalior. His chief defects being his narrow-mindedness and fanaticism in religious matters.

IBRAHIM LODI (1517-26)

On the death of Sikandar Lodi, Ibrahim Lodi, his son, was elevated to the throne without any opposition. Dual monarchy which Sikandar Lodi had ended, was revived under Ibrahim Lodi who installed his brother Jalal Khan as the independent ruler of Jaunpur. But soon he repented his folly and on the advice of some wiser **amirs** deputed an agent to persuade Jalal Khan to come to Delhi, but Jalal Khan refused to come. Ibrahim Lodi sent secret instructions to chief nobles and governors not to recognise Jalal Khan's authority. In the circumstances, Jalal Khan was compelled to leave Jaunpur and return to his old fief of Kalpi, but soon by winning over the important **amir** Azam Humayun Sarwani to his side, he succeeded in recovering Awadh. But when Ibrahim Lodi marched to oppose Azam Humayun he came over to the side of the Sultan leaving the side of Jalal. Jalal in desperation proceeded towards Agra when Ibrahim Lodi's general Malik Adam persuaded him to accept permanent assignment of the fief of Kalpi and to surrender his claim to sovereignty. But the arrangement was not ultimately agreed to by Ibrahim Lodi and Jalal fled to Gwalior, thence to Malwa. Being unwelcome there, he fled to the Gonds who betrayed him to the Sultan. Ibrahim sent him to Hansi where his other brothers were imprisoned, but was killed on his way.

Jalal Khan was given temporary asylum at Gwalior which was the pretext for completing by Ibrahim his father's project of conquering this important Rajput state. Ibrahim Lodi sent an army comprising 30,000 horses, 3000 elephants under the leadership of Azam Humayun Sarwani, governor of Kara to lay siege of the fortress. In the meantime Raja Man who had defied Sikandar died. His son Vikramjit, unable to withstand the pressure of the Sultan's forces surrendered at last. This was indeed an outstanding military achievement on the part of Ibrahim Lodi. But his attempt against Rana Sanga of Mewar failed totally.

Jalal Khan's rebellion was a lesson to Ibrahim Lodi. He now decided to suppress the Afghan nobility with a heavy hand. While his father Sikandar was circumspect in his asserting royal authority on the Afghan followers, Ibrahim insisted on strict observance of court ceremonial and decorum by the Afghan nobility brushing off their minds all thoughts of equality and racial affinity with the Sultan. While the transformation might have been slowly and gradually effected, Ibrahim wanted to effect it all on a sudden. Without realising that his success as ruler depended much on the support of his nobles, Ibrahim decided to destroy the very same men whose help he needed most. Even Azam Humayun Sarwar who contributed to Sultan's victory over Gwalior was recalled from Gwalior and put in chains. Mian Bhuwah, who rendered meritorious service as **wazir** since the time of Sikandar was imprisoned.

The tyrannical conduct of the Sultan led to revolt of Azam Humayun Sarwar's son Islam Khan at Kara. He was supported by two Lodi chiefs. Ibrahim Lodi sent an army against the insurgents but it was defeated. "Ibrahim upbraided the commanding nobles and called upon them to crush the revolt on pain being considered otherwise as traitors." The insurgents who had raised an army 40,000 strong demanded Azam Humayun Sarwar's release but Ibrahim refused to do so despite intercession of a Muslim saint. Ibrahim ordered Darya Khan Lohani, governor of Bihar, Nasir Khan Lohani, of Ghazipur, and Shaikh Muhammad Farmuli to join the royal army with their forces and the battle that followed 10,000 Afghans fell and the insurgents were defeated and Islam Khan was killed. This victory made Ibrahim more ruthless instead of teaching him the lesson of the need of conciliation of the nobles. Mian Bhuwah was put to death and Azam Humayun Sarwani who died in captivity is supposed to have been killed under orders of the Sultan. Mian Hussian Farmuli was done to death at Chanderi. All this created a feeling of insecurity and consternation among the nobles who now contemplated a desperate course for their safety. Important Lodi and Farmuli **amirs** as well as Darya Khan Lohani whom Ibrahim decided to degrade next, organised themselves, Darya Khan cast off his allegiance to Ibrahim Lodi. But on his sudden death his son Bahar Khan took the leadership of the disaffected nobles. He assumed the title of Shah Muhammad and occupied the country from Bihar to Sambhal and after about two years had **khutab** read in his own name. He was joined by Nasir Khan Lohani, governor of Ghazipur, who was erstwhile supporter of Ibrahim, Fath Khan another son of Azam Humayun Sarwani and Sher Khan Sur, the later Sher Shah.

While Ibrahim Lodi was busy in fighting the rebellious **amirs** of the eastern provinces, Daulat Khan Lodi, governor of Punjab opened negotiations with Babur. As he was not able to organise revolt as that of the Afghan nobles of Bihar he preferred to turn to Babur for help sent his son to Kabul for the purpose. Almost at the same time Ibrahim Lodi's uncle Alam Khan who had biding his time in Gujarat was requested by the disaffected **amirs** to replace Ibrahim Lodi. He also arrived at Kabul to seek Babur's help. Babur who was eager to annex Punjab seized the opportunity and led an expedition in 1524 to Lahore where he defeated Ibrahim Lodi's army under Bahar Khan Lodi. Daulat Khan who had fled towards Multan from where he came to Dipalpur to meet Babur. Babur instead of reinstating Daulat Khan appointed his own officials at Lahore assigning only a few small districts to the latter. Daulat Khan found that he had invited not a friend but a master. This infuriated him and on Babur's retirement to Kabul joined Alam Khan in an attempt to capture Delhi on condition that Babur would be allowed to retain Punjab in full sovereignty." In 1525 Alam Khan and Daulat Khan's combined forces attacked Delhi but were easily defeated by Ibrahim Lodi. Babur realising that neither Alam Khan nor Daulat Khan could be relied on set out for a final and decisive invasion of India. The armies of Babur and Ibrahim Lodi clashed with each other at Panipat on April 20, 1526, and Ibrahim despite overwhelming superiority in numbers was defeated and slain. This historic victory was due to Babur's superior fighting tactics and skilful deployment of trained cavalry and a massive store of artillery.

Estimate : Endowed with courage and bravery, Ibrahim had qualities of an excellent warrior, but he was rash and impolitic in his decisions and actions. He was both honest and diligent and applied himself to public business with zest. His attempt at royal absolutism was premature and his policy of sheer repression unaccompanied by measures to strengthen the administration and increase the military resources, was sure to prove a failure. He lacked foresight and he alienated the nobles at a time when external invasion loomed large in the north-west.

Ibrahim's private life was beyond reproach and he was kindly towards his subjects and saints. He took steps for the improvement of agriculture and both the state and the nobles received their share in produce of the soil. People lived a happy life due to plenty and cheap prices.

REFERENCES

The History and Culture of the Indian People : *The Delhi Sultanate* : Bharatiya Vidya Bhavan

A Comprehensive History of India, Vol. V (*Delhi Sultanat*) : Habib & Nizami

An Advanced History of India : Majumdar, Roychaudhuri & Datta

The Cambridge History of India, Vol. III : Wolseley Haig

The Sultanate of Delhi : A. L. Srivastava

The Oxford History of India (3rd Edn.) : V. A. Smith

6 Defence and Administration under Delhi Sultanate

THE MONGOL MENACE AND THE DEFENCE OF THE NORTH-WEST FRONTIER

The Mongols were a scourge of the Delhi Sultanate from the early days of the Sultanate. Iltutmish, acting with great circumspection, allowed Yildiz and Qubacha to consume their strength in mutual struggle, and ultimately proceeded against Qubacha (1217) and succeeded in putting him to flight and occupying Lahore.

Iltutmish's steady advance towards the Indus basin received a serious set back because "like an avalanche, the Mongols of Tartary swept across Central Asia and drove an incalculable number of refugees—princes and peoples alike—into safety of the Punjab."

The Khvarzami empire was rolled up in the process and the Khvarzamian crown prince Jalal-ud-din Mangbarni pressed by Chinghiz Khan, also known as Temuchin, came flying across the Indus through Khurasan and Afghanistan. Chinghiz stopped on the border of the Indus in the wait for the fugitive prince. "He sent his emissaries to Iltutmish, perhaps to ensure that Mangbarni did not receive any help from Delhi. Nothing is known about the way Iltutmish received the Mongol envoys, but his policy shows that he took good care not give the Mongols any cause of complaint. But so long as Chinghiz was alive—he died in 1227—Iltutmish did not try to extend his authority in the cis-Indus region. "The Mongols drove Hasan Qarlugh and Uzbek Pai, two representatives of Khvarazamian prince Mangbarni to lower Sind. For thirty years after the death of Iltutmish Delhi Sultanate was too much pre-occupied in dealing with internal strife and was unable to maintan continuity of action against the Mongols.

Raziyya was approached by Hasan Qarlugh, representative of the Khvarazam house, who was then struggling single handed against the Mongols for an alliance. But like her father, she showed a realistic prudence by firmly yet tactfully turning down the proposal. The Mongols were then operating in Western Sind and Sagar Doab.

In 1214, the Mongols advanced on Lahore and Bahram, the Sultan sent the **wazir** against them, but he betrayed the Sultan and instead of containing the Mongols returned to Delhi, defeated and killed Bahram and Iltutmish's grandson Ala-ud-din Masud was placed on the throne.

It was under Ala-ud-din Masud Shah that Balban who was made **amir-i-hajib** dominated the nobles of the court called the 'Forty' and diverted their attention from mutual quarrels to campaigns against the Mongols as also the Rajputs. His policy was so successful that Masud's reign enjoyed comparative tranquillity for some years. In 1245, however, the Mongols reappeared in the Punjab and even laid siege of Uch but Balban sent an army from Delhi which compelled the Mongols to abandon the siege.

Under the Sultan Nasir-ud-din Mahmud, Balban became the **de facto** ruler and had to deal with rebellions of governors. Kashlu Khan, governor of Multan and Uch had repudiated allegiance to Delhi and became a vassal of Hulagu, the Mongol ruler of Persia.

He entered into an alliance also with Qutlugh Khan of Awadh and thus strengthening his position made an attempt to occupy Delhi. But due to the diplomacy of Balban the attempt failed, for, an understanding was arrived at between Delhi and Hulagu who sent an emissary to Delhi to assure the Sultan that the Mongols would not disturb the north-western frontier of India. But trouble continued in Punjab and even Lahore passed into the hands of the Mongols in 1254.

On his assumption of the crown, Balban was in a better position to deal with the Mongols. In fact, it was due to the Mongol menace that Balban could not follow a policy of conquests. By repeated raids the Mongols had brought Lahore under their control, and only Multan and Sind remained in the hands of Delhi. Balban placed Sher Khan Sanqar in charge of the entire region of the north-west who struck terror in the hearts of the Mongols. But Sher Khan died in 1270 and Balban placed his son prince Muhammad and the younger son Bughra Khan in charge of the defence of the north-west frontier. Prince Muhammad effectively checked the Mongol advance. In 1286, the Mongols reappeared and prince Muhammad in fighting them lost his life. Balban, however, did not relax his efforts to secure the north-west frontier. He even succeeded in re-occupying Lahore. Barring this, his success was not very spectacular. Delhi's authority did not extend beyond Lahore and the region west of Ravi continued to be under the Mongols.

Ala-ud-din's reign was greatly disturbed by a series of Mongol raids which threatened not only Punjab, Multan and Sind but even the capital Delhi, and the fertile tract of the Doab. Ala-ud-din is said to have repelled a dozen Mongol invasions. From the very beginning of his reign till 1308, the Mongols constantly disturbed Delhi and gave him little repose.

It was in 1296 when Ala-ud-din was only a few months on the throne, the Mongols invaded India. Zafar Khan beat them off. The next year the Mongols reappeared and captured Siri a fortress very near Delhi. Zafar Khan again proved more than a match for the Mongols and drove them back with great slaughter. Their leader and 1700 Mongols with their wives and children were taken prisoners. In 1299 the Mongols reappeared under the leadership of Qutlugh Khwaja with two lakh strong force, and marched upto the vicinity of Delhi. Ala-ud-din and Zafar Khan led the royal army and inflicted a defeat on the Mongols but Zafar Khan lost his life in action.

When Ala-ud-din was busy in the siege of Chitor and when his army had suffered reverses at Telingana, the Mongols invaded the country with 1200 strong army under their leader Taghi. The Mongols came and encamped near Delhi. Ala-ud-din had to take shelter in the fortress Siri which was besieged by the Mongols for three months. In the meantime the Mongols plundered the country around Delhi and even carried their raids into the streets of Delhi. But due to lack of experience how towns are captured, the Mongols withdrew after three months.

It was after noticing that the Mongols had marched near Delhi unhindered that Ala-ud-din took measures to protect the north-west frontier against future raids by the Mongols. Old forts were repaired and new forts were built and army was posted in Punjab, Multan and Sind. A warden of the Marches was appointed for the security of the north-west frontier.

But all this did not deter the Mongols. Under Ali Beg, their leader, who was a descendant of Chinghiz Khan, the Mongols raided Punjab and evading the frontier garrison appeared near Amroha, burning the pillaging the country through which they had passed. Malik Kafur and Ghazi Malik were sent to oppose the invaders. The Mongols were intercepted on their return journey with immense booty they had collected. They were defeated and their leaders were trampled to death under the foot of the elephants. Fifty thousand of the invaders including their leader were taken prisoners and later put to death.

The last Mongol raid during the reign of Ala-ud-din Khalji took place in 1307-1308 under their leader Iqbalmand. They crossed the Indus but could not proceed further as they were defeated by the Delhi forces. Iqbalmand was killed. A large number of the Mongols were taken prisoners and taken to Delhi where they were put to death. The Mongols did not distrub Ala-ud-din any more.

In 1324 when prince Jauna Khan, later Muhammad bin Tughluq, was absent in the Deccan, the Mongols invaded Northern India but were thoroughly defeated and their leader captured and brought to Delhi. There was no further Mongol raid during the reign of Giyas-ud-din Tughluq Shah. But when prince Jauna ascended the throne as Muhammad bin Tughluq, the Sultanate was threatened with a series of Mongol raids which took place after the Sultan had ordered the transfer of the capital from Delhi to Devagiri. Tarmashirin the Mongol leader appeared with a vast army and ravaged the country from Lahore and Multan upto the vicinity of Delhi. The Sultan taken by surprise, is said to have bribed the Mongol chief and persuaded him to retire. This encouraged further invasion and the same method was applied to buy them off. This was, to say the least a very unwise policy for it exposed the weakness of the policy of Muhammad bin Tughluq of not resisting the invaders as Balban and Ala-ud-din had done.

Defence against the Mongols : We have seen in the preceeding section how the Mongol meance pursued the Delhi Sultanate from the early days of the Sultanate. The Delhi Sultans, barring Balban and Ala-ud-din Khalji did not make any permanent, systematic arrangements for the security of the north-western frontier of India crossing which the Mongols repeatedly came to invade the country. Iltutmish and Raziyya had recourse to diplomacy in getting rid of the Mongol invasion, but did not think it necessary to evolve out any policy to offer permanent security to the north-west frontier. They had, ofcourse, no time to do so either.

It was not until we come to the time of Balban that we find any policy of defence against the Mongols was actually evolved. Balban clearly saw that to protect the Sultanate from the Mongol raids some permanent arrangement had to be made. He, therefore, placed Sher Khan Sanqar in charge of Multan, Sind and Lahore regions so that the Mongols might not easily cross that area into the territories of the Sultanate. Sher Khan was a capable commander and he struck terror into the hearts of the Mongols. But he died in 1270. But Balban was quick in filling in the vacuum by dividing the frontier region into two parts and placing his two sons in charge of each of them. In one part comprising Multan, Sind and Lahore, he placed prince Muhammad and in the other comprising province of Sunam and Samana he placed his second son Bughra Khan. Prince Muhammad was very capable administrator and an excellent military commander. He took effective measures to check the advance of the Mongols, but the latter ravaged the upper Punjab and succeeded in crossing the Sutlej. Both Muhammad and Bughra Khan sent their troops to oppose Mongols who were defeated and driven out. But the Mongols reappeared in 1286 and in the contest with the army of Prince Muhammad, the latter was killed. This was a great loss both personal as well as in regard to the defence against the Mongols, of Balban. But Balban despite the shock of the death of his eldest son, re-occupied Lahore which the Mongols had occupied after the death of Muhammad. Under Balban the authority of Delhi did not, however, extend beyond Lahore and the regions west of the river Ravi continued to be under the control of the Mongols.

Apart from the defence measures taken by Balban against the Mongols the only other Sultan who took the policy of defending the country against Mongol raids was Ala-ud-din Khalji. Ala-ud-din's reign saw a series of Mongol invasions which threatened Punjab, Multan, Sind and even Delhi. Ala-ud-din is said to have repelled a dozen Mongol invasions. He noticed that twice early in his reign the Mongols succeeded in reaching the vicinity of Delhi without any hindrance. He therefore, took effective steps to protect the frontiers in order to prevent future Mongol raids.

He repaired the old forts in Punjab, Multan and Sind and built a series of new ones. All these forts were garrisoned with strong forces. Apart from these garrisons, he appointed additional army with specific charge of defending the frontier against the Mongol invasions. A special governor—a Warden of the Marches was appointed for the same purpose.

These defensive measures were, however, not sufficient to prevent the Mongols from making repeated raids but the effect of these measures could be seen in the defeat of the Mongol raiders every time they invaded India. It was in 1308 that the Mongols had raided India for the last time and the country remained immune from Mongol invasions during the rest of the reign of Ala-ud-din's and many more years.

The defence measures of Ala-ud-din was not maintained in subsequent reigns of the Delhi Sultans. Under Muhammad bin Tughluq the defence of the north-west frontier became so lax that the Mongols easily reached the vicinity of Delhi and surprised the Sultan. Muhammad bin Tughluq, of necessity, had to buy them off with a fat bribe which encouraged them to make repeated raids which meant more money for them.

Towards the end of the Sultanate, however, the Mongol pressure was relaxed and Delhi was relieved of its greatest scourge. But Timur came to deal the tottering Delhi Sultanate its death blow.

EVOLUTION OF THE IQTA SYSTEM

The **iqta** system occupied a pivotal place in the administrative arrangements made by Sultan Iltutmish. The term **iqta** literally means 'a portion' ; technically it was the land or revenue assigned by the ruler to any individual. According to Mawardi there were two types of **iqtas,** viz; **iqta-i-tamlik** and **iqta-i-istighlal.** The former related to land, fallow, cultivated or having mines ; the latter related to stipends. The **iqtas** of the former type, i.e. **iqta-i-tamlik** is only relevant to our discussion on **iqta** system.

"In the development of Islamic politico-economic institutions, the **iqta** has a long and interesting history. It existed since the early days of Islam as a form of reward for service to the state, and passed through various phases of development...The early Turkish Sultans of Delhi, particularly Iltutmish used this institution as an instrument for liquidating the feudal order of the Indian society and linking up the far flung parts of the empire to one centre." Through this system collection of revenue in newly conquered areas was ensured, despite communication difficulties. Besides, maintenance of law and order, tacking of local problems, **iqta** system proved useful.

Iqtas were both big and small. The small **iqtadars** held neither any administrative nor financial duty towards the centre. They held land in lieu of military service. The large **iqtas** (provinces) which were given to men of status, carried administrative responsibilities with them and the assigness had to maintain law and order and supply contingents to the centre in times of emergency.

Iltutmish granted **iqtas** to the Turks on an extensive scale, for his purpose was intensive control of the conquered territories and the liquidation of Indian feudal institution. But curiously enough, **iqta** system had in it elements which could develop feudal characteristics. Iltutmish strictly discouraged localism in administration and rejected the feudal concept of the legal immunity of the overlord. He infused a bureaucratic form in the **iqtas** by the institution of transfer of the iqtadars from one assignment to another. Iltutmish also realised the economic potentialities of the Doab and granted **iqtas** to two thousand of his Turkish soldiers there.

In the evolution of history of the **iqtas** Balban's reign needs special mention. Balban instituted an enquiry into the conditions and tenures of **iqtas** given to the Turkish soldiers. Iltutmish had granted **iqtas** both big and small besides two thousand small **iqtas** to the Turkish soldiers for a two-fold purpose : (i) to reward his Turkish soldiers for their services to the Turkish government in India, and (ii) to utilise them for the consolidation of the Turkish rule in the most prosperous part of the country. The **iqtadars** in the Doab were to realise revenue from the land assigned to them for their military service. But they being all small **iqtadars** had no administrative duty in their locality, nor any financial responsibility to the centre. The dangers inherent in **iqta** system were almost similar to those of the feudal system of the Continental Europe. But Iltutmish's careful and vigilant control of the administrative machinery eliminated the dangers of the **iqta** system.

But during the anarchy that followed the death of Iltutmish, the **iqta** administration broke down and the **iqtadars** assumed an attitude of defiance towards the central authority. The **iqta** system which was intended to be a centripetal force tended to degenerate into a centrifugal force, threatening distintegration and decentralisation of the central authority.

Balban's ideal of kingship did not permit this kind of an attitude towards decentralisation. He instituted an enquiry into the terms and conditions of the grant of the **iqtas** of the Doab. The enquiry revealed that the original **iqtadars** having died or become too old to render military service, the very purpose of making the original grants became useless. The sons of the deceased **iqtadars** claimed hereditary rights over the **iqtas** and with the connivance of diwan-i-arz retained hold on the **iqtas.** Balban's view was that the grant was personal in nature and on the basis of a contract for rendering military service. Thus with the death of the original assignee, the grant became null and void. After a full enquiry, Balban issued order for the resumption of these **iqtas,** with payment of compensation in certain cases. He also granted pension of 20 to 30 **tankas** as compensation in certain cases, where the soldier was too old or infirm. Balban's order caused great resentment among the grantees. Some of the Turkish leaders approached Fark-ud-din, the famous **kotwal** of Delhi and through his intercession succeeded in getting the order withdrawn.

REVENUE ADMINISTRATION UNDER THE SULTANATE

Land revenue was the most important source of income of the Delhi Sultanate. The total income from this source was next in quantum, to plunder and booty acquired in times of war. For the purpose of land revenue administration there were four classes of land that were taken into consideration namely, (i) the **khalisa** territory, (ii) land divided into **iqtas** and held by **iqtadars** either for some years or for life, (iii) principalities of the Hindu chiefs in alliance with the Sultan, (iv) land given away to the scholars and saints such as **milk, inam** or **waqf**.

The **khalisa** was directly administered by the central government. But the state dealt with the local revenue officers like **chaudharis** and **muqaddams** and not with the individual ryots. There was an **amil,** i.e. revenue collector in every sub-division who would collect revenue from the **chaudharis** and **muqaddams,** who used to collect the revenue from the ryots. The state demand of revenue was not based on any calculation or actual produce of the soil, but just a summary assessment.

In **iqta** the administration including assessment and collection of revenue was in the hands of the **muqti** who paid to the central government the surplus after deducting his own dues. It was naturally his interest to show as little surplus as possible and keep as much more for himself and to evade payment on one pretest or another whenever possible. The Sultan, therefore, on the advice of the **wazir** appointed an officer called **khwaja** in each **iqta** to keep watch over revenue collection and to exercise check on the **muqti.** There was still possibilities of collusion between the **khwaja** and the **muqti** for which the Sultan appointed an elaborate espionage system and the spies had to report about the activities of the local officers directly to the central government. The Hindu chief and rajas who were in tributary alliance with the Sultan enjoyed autonomy in their respective states subject to the payment of the tribute. The zamindars also paid a fixed amount as revenue to the government and the ryots recognised nobody else's authority other than that of the zamindar within whose jurisdiction they lived. Land given in gift as **inam** or **waqf** were free from assessment of revenue and allowed to become hereditary possessions of the grantees. The above system continued to be in force till the time of Ala-ud-din Khalji who introduced certain vital changes in the revenue policy and revenue administration. He had two main considerations for making these changes, viz ; (i) to increase the income of the state to the optimum limit, and (ii) to keep the people in poverty so that they might be mindful to earn their daily bread and have no time to indulge in any conspiracy for rebellion or insubordination. He therefore, (a) confiscated the estates of the Muslim grantees and religious land held as proprietory right **(milk),** free gift **(inam)** or endowment **(waqf)**. While some of the grantees were left untouched, most of the land of the above description was appropriated by the state. (b) The privilege so long enjoyed by the Hindu **muqaddams, khuts** and **chaudharis** was withdrawn and they were obliged to pay taxes as on other land held by them. They had also to pay housing tax and pasture tax. (c) The state demand of the land revenue was enhanced to half of the gross produce of the soil. (d) A few more taxes in addition to those which were current, were imposed by Ala-ud-din. **Jizya,** customs duties, and **zakat** which were levied by earlier Sultans were continued to be realised under Ala-ud-din. (e) He introduced the system of measurement of land in order to ascertain the actual produce and **patwari's** records were consulted to fix revenue settlement. (f) While efficient machinery was established to make rigorous collection of revenue of all kinds, he took care so that no damage was caused to the agricultural crops due to natural or accidental cause. It is true that under Ala-ud-din measurement of land could not be done in all provinces, but his aim was to increase the revenue income considerably and make all classes of the society, the peasants and the landlords, merchants and the traders bear the burden of taxation.

Ala-ud-din's revenue policy was too rigid and very strictly enforced. Naturally it was unpopular. While a Sultan as powerful as Ala-ud-din could enforce such rigid revenue policy, it could not be followed by his weak successors. Many of the rigid and harsh regulations of Ala-ud-din Khalji were allowed to fall into decay but the rate of revenue fixed remained unaltered. Ghiyas-ud-din Tughluq while lessened the rigours of the revenue policy and administration of the time of Ala-ud-din Khalji, did not reduce the revenue demand of the state which continued to remain one half of the gross produce of the soil. But he ordered remission of revenue for damages due to natural calamity or any accidental cause. He also allowed the **khuts, muqaddams** and **chaudharis** to enjoy exemption from payment of tax on their land and their grazing animals. Ghiyas-ud-din also ordered that the revenue demand from any **iqta** must not be enhanced more than one-tenth or one-eleventh of the standard assessment in a year. Ghiyas-ud-din, however, gave up the scientific practice of assessing the revenue after measurement of land and reverted to the policy of fixing revenue on guess. He also abandoned the practice of payment to the civil and military officers and resumed the old custom of granting assignment of revenue to civil and military officers.

Muhammad bin Tughluq wanted to systematise the revenue administration of his realm. In order to introduce a uniform standard of land revenue, he instructed the department of revenue to compile a comprehensive register of income and expenditure of the Sultanate. He also instructed the revenue department to see that no village went unassessed. But this work could not be finished during his reign.

Under Firuz Tughluq there was marked change in the revenue policy of the Delhi Sultanate. He paid much attention to the revenue matters with a view to fostering material prosperity of his subjects. One of the first things he did was to write off the **taqavi** loans that his late cousin Muhammad bin Tughluq had granted to the agriculturists of the Doab when they had been driven to miserable state due to heavy taxation besides 50% land revenue, and also due to famine and pestilence. Firuz increased the salaries of the revenue staff so that they might not coerce the ryots to pay more than their legitimate dues to the state. He strictly prohibited physical coercion of the ryots by the governors and revenue officials for realisation of revenue. The revenue of the **khalisa** land was fixed on a permanent basis after careful and proper examination of local revenue records. The vexatious taxes like house tax, grazing tax and such other taxes numbering twentyfour altogether, were abolished by him. He levied only five kinds of taxes besides the land revenue as permitted by the Quranic law, namely, **kharaj, khams, jizya, zakat** and irrigation tax. He also tried for the improvement of agriculture and encouraged cultivation of commercial crops like sugar cane, poppy, oil-seeds etc. He also encouraged horticultural development in the gardens that he had constructed. Firuz's measures not only enhanced the revenue income of the government, but contributed much to the material prosperity of the people.

But Firuz Tughluq's revenue policy suffered from three major defects, namely, the farming out of the land revenue, assignment of the revenue to civil and military officers who were permitted to sell out the assignments to brokers and the rigorous realisation of jizya. Yet it must be said that speaking generally, Firuz Tughluq's revenue administration was generous yet efficient on the whole. But it fell into negligence under his successors and although the essence of the system continued to exist under the later Tughluq and the Sayyids, under the Lodis the **khalisa** land was greatly reduced and the land in the country was divided among the powerful Afghan families. The revenue administration became extremely slack and inefficient. Sikandar Lodi made an attempt to revive the system of measurement of land for the purpose of fixation of land revenue, but barring this solitary instance to pay attention to revenue administration there was nothing done after the time of Firuz Tughluq.

ADMINISTRATION, SOCIETY, ECONOMY, EDUCATION, ART AND LITERATURE UNDER THE DELHI SULTANATE : THEORY OF STATE

The Delhi Sultanate was a theocracy and the religion of the state was Islam. The political theory on which the Delhi Sultanate was based was the Quran. The Quran laid down the principle of solidarity and unity among all Muslims and condemned any attempt to break away from the organised community. A natural corollary was that the entire Muslim world should offer allegiance to one single head. After the death of the Prophet, it was the Caliph, who was that single head. Muslim jurists as well as thinkers like Ibn Khaldun emphasise that Caliphate is a canoncial necessity, and therefore allegiance to the Caliphate is demanded by the law of Islam. The Sultans of Delhi pursuant to this Islamic law owed a nominal allegiance to the Caliph but for all practical purposes, they were independent rulers. This fiction of allegiance to the Caliph was kept alive even after the real Caliphate came to an end when the last Abbasid Calip Mustasim was put to death by Hulagu, the Mongol leader in 1558. In conformity with this tradition the Delhi Sultans called themselves deputies of the Caliph and received investiture from the Caliph and inscribe his name on the coins and read his name in the **khutba** along with his own. Ala-ud-din Khalji was the first Sultan to make a departure from the practice of offering allegiance to the Caliph. His son Qutb-ud-din Mubarak not only refused to believe in the fiction of the Caliphate, but himself assumed the title of **Khalifa** (Caliph) for himself. The fact remains that no Delhi Sultan really believed in the sovereignty of the Caliph, but they thought it advantageous to maintain a formal relation with the Islamic world outside and earn the unstinted support of the religious-minded Muslims in India.

Administrative Organisation : The head of the state under the Delhi Sultanate was called the Sultan. Islamic law and philosophy both recognised him to be the representative of the Caliph. According to the Islamic jurists the Sultan had to protect the Faith to settle disputes between his subjects, to defend the territories of Islam and to keep the highways and roads safe for the travellers, to maintain and enforce the criminal code, to strengthen the frontiers of the Muslim territory against possible aggression, to wage holy war against those who act in hostility to Islam, to collect rates and taxes, to apportion the shares of those who deserve an allowance from the public treasury, to appoint officers to help him in his public and legal duties, and to keep in touch with public affairs and the condition of the people by personal contact. These functions are, obvious enough, the executive functions of the head of the state. The Sultan had responsibility towards his non-Muslim subjects as well which has been carefully defined by Muslim law. By accepting the suzerainty of the Sultan and payment of taxes the non-Muslims acquired the right of protection, the maintenance of their rites and worship and observance of their social code of conduct and enforcement of their personal law.

Although theoretically the Sultan's authority was despotic, in practice his authority and political power had serious limitations. He was subservient to **Shar** for he had to depend on the Muslim soldiery and open breach of **Shar** would lead to serious consequences. He could not interfere with the personal law of any group of his subjects. The Sultan had to depend on the active support of the nobles, and also ensure the cooperation of a fairly large number of **ulemas.** Further, there were many wise and experienced public servants whose administrative experience and technical knowledge the Sultan could not ignore, nor could the Sultan forget the cultivators, the Hindu peasants and the tribal chiefs. The ultimate force of the state and for the matter of that the power and strength of the Sultan consisted of the Muslim fighters and no monarch could venture to alienate this section without peril. These diverse constraints served as limitations to the authority of the Sultan.

Although the usual practice of the Sultanate was hereditary succession, yet majority of the Muslim jurists are of opinion that a monarch elected by the most influential men at the capital is entitled to the allegiance of the people. This naturally gives sanction to the election of the Sultan whenever necessary. The right to dethrone a monarch is therefore a logical corollary. During the period of the Sultanate of Delhi, both election and deposition of Sultans took place.

The Sultans maintained a great splendour in their court which had great utilitarian value. The Turkish Sultans preferred Persian etiquette in their courts. The Sultans discharged their formal duties in public **darbars** and matters requiring deliberations would be dealt with in the council chamber where those officers were admitted whose advice was required.

Officials : The diverse nature of the business of the state and the maintenance of ceremonial assembly of the royal court necessitated the appointment of a large number of officials. The dignity of the monarch required that everything should be done smoothly; order of predence of the officers to be strictly maintained and even manner of salutation at the court to be formally prescribed. Thus a big staff of officers, ushers and heralds was necessary. Besides, the Sultan had his personal staff, his body guards, palace guards, personal attendants and host of other workers who were all under the charge of **waki-**

i-dar who also supervised the paymet of salaries of this personal staff. **Amir-i-hajib** also called **barbak** was the master of ceremonies at the court. There were **karkhanas** in the royal household for the manufacture of articles for the royal household and the court. There were **karkhanas** also for manufacturing arms, ammunitions and armours. The royal court also served as the patron of learning and fine arts and was instrumental to the promotion of culture.

Ministers : At the top of the civil government was the **wazir** who under weak Sultan enjoyed almost unlimited authority. But where the Sultan was strong and capable, he was only a very powerful officer. The immediate concern of the **wazir** was the central finance, but he was also responsible for the activities of the other officers at the headquarters. He appointed and superintended the civil servants, and organised the agency for the collection of revenue. He also exercised control over expenditure. The assistants under him examined all the accounts submitted by different departments and it was in his department that all financial statements were compared, checked and passed. The wazir at times took humiliating and unpleasant measures against local officials to recover the money spent illegally. From his department stipends to scholars and men of learning, doles to the poor and needy were paid. "No branch of public administration was outside his purview, and every subject from the mightiest governor to the lowliest peasant in the land had dealings with him or his assistants." The department of the **wazir** was called **diwan-i-wazirat**; it mainly dealt with finance. There was a **naib-wazir** to assist him.

Next to the **wazir** and **naib-wazir** was **mushrif-i-mumalik** who was the accountant general of the empire, and **mustafi-mumalik** was the auditor general. Originally the **mushrif** used to enter the accounts that he would receive from the provinces and the **mustafi** would audit the account. Under Firuz Tughluq their work was redistributed and the **mushrif** dealt with income only while the **mustafi** dealt with expenditure. **Mushrif** was assisted by a **nazir** and **mustafi** by a **waquf**.

There were three other ministers which, together with the **diwan-i-wazirat** were compared to four pillars that supported the vault of the state. The next in importance was **diwan-i-ariz**, which was the office of **ariz-mumalik**, who was the controller general of military establishment. His main functions were to recruit troops, to maintain the descriptive rolls of men and horses and to hold muster of men and horses for the purposes of review. The Sultan being the commander-in-chief of the royal army, **ariz-in-mumalik** was not usually required to command the army and if he would, he only commanded a part of the army. He looked particularly after the discipline and equipment of the army and their deployment in the battlefield. The department being very important, Ala-ud-din Khalji would at times look after the department personally.

The next important minister was **sadar-us-sudur** whose office was called **diwan-i-risalat**. He was in charge of religious matters, pious foundations, stipends to deserving scholars and men of piety. According to Dr. Habibullah, he was a minister of foreign affairs. The **sadr-i-sudur** was also the **qazi-i-mumalik** and in this capacity he controlled the department of justice. The third ministry was **diwan-i-insha** which was under the **dabir-i-khas** and dealt with state correspondence. The **dabir-i-khas** was also the confidential clerk of the state. All the correspondences, confidential or otherwise, between the Sultan and rulers of other states or his own tributaries or officials passed through this department. Another minister was **barid-i-mumalik** who was the head of the state news agency. The headquarters of every administrative subdivision had a local **barid** who sent regular news letters to the central office.

The ministers were servants of the crown, held office during his pleasure and responsible only to him. There was no question of any team work among the ministers, or any opposition to the Sultan's wishes. They only exercised their authrority as experts and heads of well organised bureaucratic departments. An office called **naib-ul-mulk** was filled in from the nobles which meant **Lord Lieutenant of the Empire** whose authority varied according to the ability and personality of the Sultan. When the Sultan was weak the **naib-ul-mulk** held absolute authority, but when the Sultan was capable and strong, the **naib-ul-mulk** was a mere title.

Financial Administration : Besides land revenue, which has been discussed under a separate section, and which formed main source of income of the state, the income of the state also came from the sources of other taxes. A capitation tax called **jizya** was levied on the Hindus at the rate of ten, twenty or forty **tankas** per annum according to the wealth of the assessee. "**Jizya** was charged in lieu of military service which was theoretically compulsory for all Muslims...." There is also evidence that the cultivators also did not pay **jizya**. The other sources of income were the import duties, the state share of the spoils of war, imposts on mines and on treasure-troves if they contained coins of pre-Muslim days. "The import duties ranged from $2\frac{1}{2}$ to 10 percent, the rate of demand under the other heads being uniform twenty per cent." The Muslims had to pay a poor tax called **zakat**.

The Army : The Delhi Sultanate was based on force and not on the habitual allegiance of the people. It had, therefore, to maintain a large force which comprised (a) regular soldiers who were permanently maintained in the Sultan's service, (b) troops in permanent employ of the provincial governors and nobles, (c) troops appointed temporarily during wars, and (d) Muslim volunteers who were recruited in the name of holy war, i.e., **Jihad**. In Delhi there were two categories of troops, viz., those in the service of the Sultan and those in the service of the nobles, ministers, and high officials. The Sultan's body-guards, troops of the capital constituted the standing army of the Sultanate and it was reinforced by the contingents sent by the provincial governors as also by the contingents of the Hindu troops in times of need. It was under Ala-ud-din Khalji that a standing army in the proper sense and diectly recruited, paid and officered by the central government was organised. The number of the standing army under Ala-ud-din was 475,000 horse and vast number of foot. The system of standing army continued till the time of Muhammad bin Tughluq. But Firuz Tughluq feudalised the army and made it dependent on land grants. Under the Lodis, the army was organised on tribal basis and thus became organisationally very weak. There were no fixed rules of recruitment, training, payment or promotion. In times of holy wars, that is wars against Hindu rulers, that **maulvis** and **ulemas** were sent out to encourage the Muslim population to join in the **jihad.** The volunteers were not paid any slary but were given a share of the booty.

The army under the Sultanate was not a national army, for it consisted of soldiers belonging to different nationalities, such as the Turks, the Tajiks, the Persians, the Mongols, the Afghans, the Arabs, the Abyssinians, the Indian Muslims and the Hindus. It was neither a homogeneous body, nor scientifically trained.

The army had three divisions, namely, the cavalry, the infantry and the elephants. It goes without saying that the cavalry comprised the most powerful arm of the army. The cavalry was divided into two grades, those troopers who had two horses each, and those who had only one horse each. There was yet a third grade which was not regarded as proper cavalry although troopers of this group possessed a horse each. The foot soldiers who were mostly Indian Muslims, Hindus and slaves were armed with spears, swords and bows and arrows. The elephant had **hauda,** i.e., a wooden structure which could accommodate several fighters, on the back of each elephant. There were also incendiary arrows, javelins, naptha balls, fireworks, rockets and hand grenades. There was also a sort of a mechanical artillery for discharge of fire balls, fire arrows, stones etc. on the enemies. The Sultans maintained a number of boats for both river battles and transport of troops by waterways.

The Sultan was the commander-in-chief of the army. The army ministry called **diwan-i-ariz** under **ariz-mumalik** that looked after the army. But in view of the importance of the armed forces, the Sultan himself would look after the organisation and upkeep of the army.

There used to be general muster of the soldiers and the horses from time to time. But there used to be proxy men in the battle or military review and production of the same horse for more than once for review at the time of the muster. To do away with this corruption Ala-ud-din instituted the system of muster roll of the troops and branding of horses. But this salutary system was abandoned at the time of Firuz Tughluq. Under Ala-ud-din the soldiers were paid in cash. But Firuz Tughluq revived the system of payment by assignment of revenue to the soldiers.

Judiciary : The Sultan was the fountainhead of justice, and justice in the state emanated from him. He was responsible for upholding, maintaining and enforcing the Quranic laws. There was a judicial department called **diwan-i-qaza** and a chief **qazi,** i.e., **qazi-ul-qazat**. But in fact the chief justice did not function independently ; he assisted the Sultan in both the religious and secular cases. The chief **qazi** discharged the functions of the **sadr-i-sudur** while the Sultan dealt with religious cases and advised him with his expert knowledge. As the posts of the **sadr-i-sudur** and **qazi-ul-qazat** were held by the same person, in his capacity as chief **qazi** he would advise the Sultan in secular cases. But when the Sultan was not in session, the chief **qazi** functioned as the highest court of justice, but his decisions were liable to be revised by the Sultan. The Sultan appointed provincial and district **qazis** perhaps on the recommendation of the chief **qazi**. In important cities and equivalent post called **amir-i-dad** would be appointed by the Sultan. The chief **qazi** held his court at Delhi, heard appeals from the provincial courts and was assisted by the legal interpreter called the **mufti**.

The penal laws under the Sultanate was very severe and the punishments were often mutilation and death. Torture of various kinds were resorted to extort confession. There was no police system under the Sultanate but in important cities an officer of the name of **kotwal** used to be appointed, whose duty was maintenance of peace and order. There was another officer appointed in every province and every important town, named **muhtasib** whose duty was to see that Islamic regulations were observed by the Muslims, five prayers were said by them daily, as well as to control the market and to regulate the weights and measures.

Provincial Administration : Under the Sultanate there was no uniform distribution of provinces. While the direct influence of the Sultan was limited to the areas within striking distance of his forts and outposts, the distant provinces were placed under viceroys called **naib Sultans.** The number of provinces under the Sultanate varied from twenty to twenty-five. The province was divided into smaller portions which were in charge of **muqtas** or **amils,** and these smaller portions were again subdivided into further smaller units each under a **shiqdar.**

Each province under a **naib Sultan** was a replica of the empire and head of the province exercised executive, judicial and military functions within his jurisdiction almost as a despot subject to the control of the Sultan. The power and authority of the heads of provinces varied according to the strength or weakness of the Sultan. Under Muhammad bin Tughluq the provincial viceroys declared themselves independent taking advantage of the confusion and weakness of the central government. The viceroy would pay the surplus of the revenue collections after meeting the local expenditure to the Sultan. He maintained his own troops and in times of need would be required to send contingents to the assistance of the centre. The efficient working of the provincial government was hindered by the intrigues and the selfish pursuits of the nobles and there was no peace and order in most of the provinces. Besides the imperial provinces, there were hereditary Hindu chieftains who paid tributes to the Sultan and were allowed to rule their ancestral territories without any interference so long as they paid the tributes in time. The villages being more or less self-sufficient remained unaffected by changes of the government at the centre.

SOCIETY

Muslim Society : During the Sultanate period the Muslim society in India fast became Indianised. The Sultan was at the top of the Muslim society and below him stood the priviledged classes, viz., the nobles and the **ulemas,** who held fiefs and estates under the Sultan. The slaves, in spite of their degraded social position, one way may be regarded as a privileged class for, they were well cared for and there was a department to look after them. Some of the slaves exercised great influence on their royal masters. "This is clearly shown by the examples of Malik Kafur, the lieutenant of Sultan Ala-ud-din Khalji, and Malik Khusrav, the favourite of that monarch's son, Qutb-ud-din Mubarak Shah." The Muslim nobles were usually of foreign origin, the Persians, Turks, Afghans, Sayyids, Arabs etc. There was some arrogance in the aristocratic classes and there gradually developed a sort of exclusiveness and caste system which were contrary to the spirit of Islam and perhaps the result of Indian influence. Thus Turk, a Pathan or a Sayyid would never think of any matrimonial relationship with any family of lower rank.

There was practically no strong or prosperous middle class in those days, and as a result, the wealth and splendour of the upper classes stood in great contrast with the poverty and squalor of the masses both Hindu and Muslim.

The **purdha** system or seclusion of women had already become a common practice. **Purdah** was, however, unknown among the lower classes, particularly in the rural society. How far the rigidity of **purdah** system was the result of the Rajput influence cannot be definitely determined. "What is certain is that peculiar social conditions in India were largely responsible for the development of this system which was unknown in other Muslim countries in medieval times."

Polygamy or keeping of concubines was not a common practice. This sort of luxury could be afforded by privileged few. In most cases the much spoken of **harem** was nothing more than a separate living quarter for the women folk of the family. **Harem** with large number of women was, however, maintained by some Sultans and nobles.

Sultans' use of costly royal dresses, the gilded and studded swords and daggers, colourful umbrellas, richly caprisoned elephants were all typically Indian royal paraphernalia of pomp and grandeur. The old Indian practice of chewing betel-leaf was adopted by the Sultans and the grandees.

While the Muslims adopted the head-gears called **chira** and the **pag** of the Rajput origin, the tight fitting cloak for men and tight-fitting trousers for women were of foreign origin and adopted by the Rajputs. The use of neckchain, ear-rings, rings etc. by Muslim men was due to Indian influence ; these vanities were prohibited in Islam. Fine cotton fabrics, silk cloth for which India was famous were used by the Muslim gentry.

On festive occasions an amazingly large varieties of dishes were served which showed the luxurious and refined tastes of the Sultan and the well-to-do people.

About the cultivation of music there are two contradictory opinions among the Muslim Jurists. According to one school music is not permissible under Islamic law, but according to another school it is permissible. Khwaja Muin-ud-din Chishti's band of **qavvals** used to sing every evening. Iltutmish put a ban on music, but a member of the Chishti order persuaded him to withdraw the ban. Ghiyas-ud-din had also banned music but the ban was withdrawn by Muhammad-bin-Tughluq.

The lowest stratum of the Muslim society comprised the peasants and cultivators, workmen, artisans and domestic servants.

Hindu Society : The Hindu society consisted of four primary castes, namely, the Brahmans, the Kshatriyas, the Vaisyas and the Sudras. There was an indefinite number of the so-called mixed castes of varying social status, and finally a despised class at the bottom of the society. A uniform pattern of social structure as described above was, however, not to be found everywhere. There were local differences in different regions. Besides the above social divisions there were slaves among the Hindus. While the Muslims took delight in enslaving Hindu women **en masse** from the highest to the lowest rank and even making presents of male and female Hindu slaves, from Nizam-ud-din we come to know that the "even Musalmans and Sayyid women were taken by the Rajputs and were turned into slave girls." Sultan Muhammad-bin-Tughluq sent "one hundred male slaves and one hundred slave songstresses and dancers from among the Indian infidels" to the Chinese Emperor.

Smriti authorities of this period emphasised perpetual subjection of women and their lifelong tutelage under their male relations at successive stages of their lives. Before marriage they were to be under the tutelage of their father, next under that of the husband and lastly under the son.

High standard of living of earlier times seems to have prevailed at least at the upper level of the society during the most part of this period. Except under Ala-ud-din Khalji when well-to-do Hindus were reduced to miserable state, during the rule of most of the other Sultans this was true.

The condition of the peasants, workers, artisans etc, was similar to that of their Muslim counterparts.

Hindu-Muslim Relations : The political and religious condition under which the Hindus were forced to live under the Muslim state of the Sultanate, raised a barrier between the two communities. Under the Islamic theory there could be only one faith, one people and one over-all authority. "As for the Hindus and Zoroastrians, they had no place in such a political system. If their existence was tolerated, it was only to use them as hewers of wood and drawers of water, as tax-payers, **khiraj-guzar,** for the benefit of the dominant sect of the Faithful. They were called **zimmis** or people under a contract of protection by the Muslim state on condition of certain service to be rendered by them and certain political and civil disabilities to be borne by them to prevent them from growing strong. They very term **zimmi** is an insulting title." The Quran calls upon the Muslims to fight the non-believers 'till they pay **jizya** with the hand in humility." **Jizya** was a poll tax payable by the Hindus for permission to live in their ancestral homes under a Muslim ruler. The social and religious differences and the political condition under which the Hindus were forced to live led to an uncompromising spirit of animosity between the Hindus and the Muslims in India in the thirteenth century.

But two factors led to some reciprocal influences between the Hindu and the Muslim communities, namely, a vast majority of the Indian Muslims must have been decendants of Hindu converts, and the Muslims who claimed descent from foreigner or foreign immigrants into India lived as close neighbours of the Hindus for generations. Many of the social practices of the Indian Muslims, such as marriage, class distinction, and some of their ideas and beliefs, were probably due to the influence of the Hindu society. Reciprocal influence can be noticed, particularly in Northern India, with regard to dress, food, language, music, art and architecture.

In religious ideas while Sufism influenced the Hindu religion, the doctrines of medieval Hindu saints on the other, influenced the Islam. The Muslim saints, particularly the mystics, were revered by the Hindus and the Hindu **yogis** and astrologers were held in high esteem by the Muslims. Some local cults, such as that of **Satya pir** became popular with the rural people of both communities. In minor matters, such as setting out for any journey or any important work auspicious day would be chosen even by the Muslims according to the Hindu customs.

In both scholarship and literature there was considerable understanding between the two communities. While the Muslim scholars studied Hindu philosophy and sciences, such as **Yoga, Vedanta,** medicine, astrology etc., the Hindus learnt from the Muslims, geography, arithmetic and chemistry. Again, while some Muslim scholars wrote in Indian vernaculars, many Hindus learnt and wrote in Persian.

It may, however, be mentioned here that all these only touched the fringe and external elements of life and were confined to comparatively small section of the society. But the chief features of the culture of the Hindus or Muslims were not imbibed by the Muslims or the Hindus. The ultra-democratic social ideas of the Muslims were strictly confined to the Muslim community and the Hindus despite the example of the Muslim community before their eyes did not relax their social rigidity. "Nor did the Muslims every moderate their zeal to destroy ruthlessly the Hindu temples and images of gods, and their attitude in this respect remained unchanged from the day when Muhammad bin Qasim set foot on the soil of India till the eighteenth century A.D. when they lost all political powers. The Hindus combined catholicity in religious outlook with bigotry in social ethics, while the Muslims displayed an equal bigotry in religious ideas with catholicity in social behaviour."

In conclussion, it may be pointed out that reciprocal influences were too superficial in character to affect materially the fundamental differences between the two communities.

Economic Condition : During the Sultanate the village following the traditional pattern was more or less a self-contained unit and the backbone of India's economy. But due to the centralised administration of the period, the ancient self-governing village assemblies decayed. The economic life of the towns and cities was maintained as of old in full vigour during the period. Ibn Batuta found great cities with rich markets in upper Gangetic valley, in Malwa, Gujarat, in Bengal and the Deccan as well as in Malabar.

In the early sixteenth century the sea ports of Gujarat, Deccan, Malabar and Bengal used to handle extensive inland, coastal and overseas trade. During the fifteenth and the sixteenth centuries the city of Vijaynagar with its large population and rich **bazars,** skilled craftsmen, and dealers in a remarkable varieties of articles including precious stones, impressed foreign travellers such as Dominigo Paes and others.

The foreign travellers of this period described the extensive cultivation of food grains and other crops, raising of domestic animals etc. They often refer to the exceeding fertility of the soil. We learn from Ibn Batuta that there were seven varieties of autumn crop raised every year, and four varieties of spring crops. Rice was grown thrice in a year. His list of Indian fruits include mangoes, jackfruits, oranges, black-berries, pome-granate, etc. Sesame and sugar cane which were cultivated with autumn crops. At Daulatabad grapes were grown. Chinese writers Wang Ta Yuan, Ma Huan, Fei Hsin and Husang Sheng-tseng and travellers like Abdur-Razzaq, Barbosa, Paes etc. corroborate the statement of Ibn Batuta with regard to the production of agricultural and horticultural crops during the period.

According to Barbosa, in Bengal with its sea-port at Satgaon there were many cotton fields, sugar-cane, ginger and pepper plantations as well as gardens of orange, lemons and other fruit-trees. There was also an abundance of cows, horses and fowls.

The textile industry appears to have flourished in this period, as during the preceding centuries. From the account of Barbosa it appears that by the beginning of the sixteenth century Gujarat led the way in the volume of textile manufacture. Cambay was particularly noted for the manufacture of woven white cotton fabrics, printed cotton stuffs, silk cloth, coloured velvet, satins, thick carpets, beautiful quilts etc. Cambay cloth found markets in Western Europe by East African route, Burma, Malaya and Indonesian islands.

Shaliyat, near Calicut, Coimbator and cities of Malabar were famous for cotton fabrics, silk cloth, coloured cotton stuff, chintz, etc. The printed cotton cloth of Pulicat found a good market in Malabar, Gujarat and in countries outside India, such as Burma, Malacca, Sumatra etc.

In Eastern India, Bengal was famous for the abundance and variety of finer cotton textiles and silk cloth. When Ibn Batuta visited Bengal in 1346, finest cotton cloth was being sold at a very cheap price. Ma Huan writing in the middle of the fifteenth century refers to six varieties of fine cotton stuffs, besides silk brocaded kerchiefs and head-coverings woven with gold. The Chinese writer of the fourteenth and fifteenth centuries as well as Barbosa in the sixteenth century speak of the Bengal cotton stuffs in the same strain.

The lavish display of jewellery and pearls besides ornaments of gold and silver testified to the advanced condition of the work in precious metal as well as in precious and semi-precious stones, ivory work, and polishing of pearls. The Hindu and Muslim rulers of the time made use of costly ivory in the decoration of their furniture and palaces. Gujarat craftsmen stood pre-eminent in the ivory industry. In the city of Cambay best workmen of every kind were found and a great amount of work was done there in coral, carnelian and other stones. The Pearl fisheries in Kayal were worked by the local fishermen. At Pulicat, in Vijaynagar, and particularly at Calicut and other cities of Malabar there existed a great industry of cutting and polishing stones like diamonds, sapphires, and rubies which were imported from Ceylon and Pegu, as well as from the Deccan in India.

From the accounts of the foreign travellers, we come across direct evidence of the large volume of India's inland and coastal trade during the period under study. Ibn Batuta called one market in Delhi to be the largest in the world. Delhi was the common market for fine rice from Sarsuti, sugar from Kanauj, finest quality of wheat from Marh, and betelleaf from Dhar. The Hindu merchants of Daulatabad dealt in pearls specially, and were very wealthy. The very good roads connecting big cities facilitated the development of inland trade during that period. The insecurity of travel by the highways, and the constant confusion due to insurrection often disturbed the movement of the internal trade.

From Barbosa we come to know that from the inland town of Limodara in Gujarat, carnelian beads were carried in large quantities to Cambay sea port for export to Europe and East Africa. Copper was imported from abroad to the port of Dabhol in huge quantities and sent to interior areas where from cloth, wheat, millet and pulses were obtained in return. The sea port of Rander in Gujarat was the largest centre of trade in that region to which products from Malacca and China were imported. Goa which had passed into the hands of the Portuguese in the sixteenth century was the port to which horses from outside were imported and Vijaynagar purchased horses from the Portuguese at a very high price. Bhatkal in the vicinity of Vijaynagar kingdom was a very great trade centre.

From the narrative of Ibn Batuta and also from that of Barbosa we have come to know that during the period under discussion there was a chain of sea ports with excellent harbours which was used for the purpose of coastal trade. Among these ports Diu in Gujarat, Goa in the Deccan, Calicut, Cochin and Quilon in Malabar appear to be most important according to Barbosa's description. The highly profitable trade between Gujarat and Malabar was monopolised by the malabari merchants. The list of imports from Malabar included cocoanuts, cardamoms, different kinds of spices, emery, wax, iron, palm sugar, sandal-wood, silk and other articles and export list included cotton, cloth, wheat, other grains, carnelians, horses etc. The coastal trade of the Deccan ports was, however, shared both by the Gujarati and Malabari traders. Gujarat imported cotton cloth, silk, opium, wheat, horses etc. and exported cotton linen fabrics. Malabar imported areçanuts, spices, drugs, palm-sugar, emery, wax, copper, quick-silver and exported cotton goods, rice, wheat, millet, gingili oil, muslin and calicos. The Ceylon market in the neighbourhood was largely controlled by the Indian merchants. The coastal trade of the Vijaynagar kingdom was carried on the Hindu and Muslim merchants from the cities of Malabar.

The overseas trade of India during the period was carried on with Western Asia especially. The Indian merchandise was carried along the Persian Gulf wherefrom by overland route through Mesopotamia to the Mediterranean coast. The second route was through the Red Sea ports to Egypt and thence to the Mediterranean coasts. The merchandise was thereafter distributed to west European countries by the Venetian and Italian merchants. From Ibn Batuta we learn that in the early part of the fourteenth century Ormuz was the entrepot of the trade from Hind and Sind. Indian merchandise was carried from Ormuz to two Iraqs, Fars and Khurasan. Aden was the port where the Indian ships arrived from Cambay, Thana, Quilon, Calicut, Fandarina, Shaliyat, Mangalore, Farkanor, Hinawar, Sindabur and so forth,. A colony of Indian merchants grew up in Aden. From Barbosa we learn that in the beginning of the sixteenth century a highly profitable trade was carried on between the Indian ports of Diu, Chaul, Goa, Bhatkal, Calicut etc. and those of Arabia and Persia, such as Jiddah, Aden, Esh-Shihr and Ormuz. India exported pepper, cloves, ginger, cardamoms, sandal wood, saffron, indigo, wax, iron, sugar, rice, cocoa-nuts, precious stones, benzoin, porcelain, cloth, Bengal muslin. Import comprised Arabian horses, dates, rasins, salt, sulphur, coarse seed-pearls.

Literature and Education : Amir Khusrav declared with pride that Delhi was an intellectual competitor of Bukhara, the famous university-city of Central Asia. During the Sultanate period, the Muslim rulers patronised the Persian scholars who croweded into their courts from other parts of Asia due to the pressure of the Mongol raids. They also established institutions of Muslim learning at places like Delhi, Jullundur, Firuzabad, etc. A big library was founded at Delhi of which Amir Khusrav was appointed librarian. The Sultans and Amirs of Delhi and the Muslim rulers and nobles of the provinces encouraged literary activities in Persian. Amir Khusrav was the most famous of the contemporary scholars whose works covered poetry, prose in Persian, as well as music. He enjoyed a pretty long life and had risen into fame under Balban, was the tutor of Prince Muhammad, court poet of Ala-ud-din Khalji and enjoyed the patronage of Ghiyas-ud-din Tughluq. Shaikh Nizam-ud-din Hasan, popularly known as Hasan-i-Dihlavi was another poet of the time whose fame spread beyond India. About the patronage that the great men of different nationalities received from Ala-ud-din Khalji, the observation of Barani is worth quoting. "The most wonderful thing that people saw in Ala-ud-din's reign was the multitude of great men of all nationalities, masters of every science and expert in every art. The capital of Delhi by the presence of these unrivalled men of great talents became the envy of Baghdad, the rival of Cairo, and the equal of Constantinople." Nizam-ud-din Auliya, the pious man and scholar and several other scholars, flourished during Ala-ud-din's reign. Muhammad bin Tughluq, a man of much accomplishments, was a patron of learned men. Sultan Firuz Shah was responsible for writing his own memoirs named **Fatuhat-i-Firuz Shahi** which reveals his great zeal for education. He established one college to each of the several mosques built by him. Qazi Abdul Muqtadir, Maulana Khwajagi and Ahmad Thanesvari were among the eminent learned men who enjoyed Firuz Shah's patronage. Sikandar Lodi was himself a poet and gave encouragement to learning. Most of the ruling dynasties of Bijapur, Ahmadnagar, Golkunda, Malwa, Jaunpur, Bengal and Multan were patrons of literature. The Muslim writers of the period showed their skill in a branch of study, namely, history, which was neglected by the Hindus. "They wrote several first-rate historical books in elegant prose." Minhaj-us-Siraj's **Tabaqat-i-Nasiri,** Amir Khusrav's historical **mesnevis** and his **Tarikh-i-Alai** are valuable historical works. Zia-ud-din Barani was the most celebrated historian of the period and contemporary of Muhammad bin Tughluq. **Tarikh-i-Firuz Shahi** of Shams-i-Siraj Afif, Ahmad Sarhindi's **Tarikh-i-Mubarak Shahi** are historical works of value.

The Sultanate period was not entirely barren in regard to important Sanskrit works, both religious and secular. Parthasarathi Misra was responsible for several works of which **Sastra Dipika** was very important and studied widely. Some works on Yoga, Vaiseshika and Nyaya philosophy were produced during this period. Jay Singh Suri's **Hammir-mada-mardana,** prince Ravivarman's **Pradyumna-abhyudaya, Prataparudra Kalyan** of Vidyanath, **Parvati Parinaya** of Vamana Bhatta Bana, **Vidaghdhamadhabha** and **Lalita-madhabha** of Rupa Goswami, minister of Hussain Shah of Bengal, Smriti and grammatical works of Bengal and Mithila of the period by famous writers like **Padmanabha Datta,** Vidyapati Upadhyaya and Vachaspati of Mithila and Raghunandan of Bengal deserve special mention. Sayana and Madhava Vidyaranya of Vijaynagar were two famous Sanskrit scholars of the time. There were also few Muslim scholars who possessed knowledge of Sanskrit language and literature.

Religious reformers of the period preaching to the unlettered masses spoke in a language which could be easily understood by the ordinary people. Ramananda, and Kabir preached in Hindi, Namadeva in Marathi, Mira Bai in **Brajabhasha,** Nanak in Punjabi and Gurmukhi. Muslim rulers in Bengal engaged scholars to translate the Ramayana and Mahabharata into Bengali. Vidyapati was the court poet of the Hindu king Siva Singha. Vaishnava poet Chandidas born towards the end of the fourteenth century in Nanur in Birbhum is still held in high esteem for his lyrics. Maladhar Basu, Srikar Nandy, Krittivasa were the famous writers of Bengal of the period.

Art and Architecture : According to Fergusson and some others the architecture of the Sultanate period was Indo-Saracenic or Pathan. Havell on the other hand calls it entirely Indian in soul and body. But the fact remains, the architecture of the period was a happy blending of Indian and Islamic styles as is noticed in certain other aspects of the culture of the time. Sir John Marshall observes that the Indo-Islamic art was not a local variety of the Islamic art, nor is a modified form of the Hindu art. The Indo-Islamic architecture, he points out, derives its character from both Indian and Islamic sources though not always in equal degree. It has to be mentioned as in India at that time there were Brahmanical, Buddhist and Jaina styles, so also in Islamic style there were Arabian, Persian and Turkish characteristics. The mingling of these diverse styles and influences gave rise to the Indo-Islamic style of architecture during the period. While in the Delhi architecture Islamic influences predominated, the styles of architecture in provinces had their local variations. Thus there were Jaunpur, Bengal, Bijapur, Gujarat styles.

The mixture of the Islamic and Indian styles of architecture was due to various factors such as, use of the Indian craftsmen and sculptors who were naturally guided by the existing art traditions of the country. It was also due to the use of the materials of the Hindu and Jaina temples for the purposes of the construction of mosques. Further, there were adaptation by minimal changes of non-Muslim temples to convert them into mosques. There were, however, certain factors which were common to the Indian and the Islamic architecture, namely, open court encompassed by chambers or colonnades both in the cases of temples and mosques. Again, both the Hindu and the Islamic art were ornamental and decorative.

The best specimen of the Delhi architecture of the period is the Qutb Minar. **Jama' at Khana Masjid** and the **Alai Darwaza** at Qutb Minar of the time of Ala-ud-din Khalji reveal preponderance of the Muslim ideas over those of the Hindu architects. The Tughluq architecture was prosaic and devoid of splendour. The Lodis tried to revive the brilliance of the style of the Khalji period.

In Jaunpur many new buildings were built with the materials of the Hindu temples. The **Atala Devi Masjid** (1377) is one of the best specimens of the Jaunpur architectural style. In Bengal as well there grew a mixed style of architecture. Use of Bricks and adaptation of Hindu temple style and Hindu decorative designs in imitation of lotus were characteristic of the Muslim architecture of the period in Bengal. **Adina Masjid, Chhota Sona Masjid, Bara Sona Masjid** and **Qadam Rasul** are specimens of architecture of the period in Bengal. Gujarat evolved an excellent architectural style. It was an indigenous style which had developed there even before the coming of the Muslims and the buildings of the Muslim conquerors bear unmistakable influence of that style. Fine wood-carvings, delicate stone lattices and ornamental decorations are the effects of this influence. In Malwa **Jami Masjid, Hindola Mahal, Jahaj Mahal,** Hushang's tomb, Baz Bahadur's and Rupamati's palaces, mostly built of marble and sand stones, are excellent specimens of the architectural work of the period.

In the Bahamani kingdom of the south, the architectural style betrayed a mixture of Indian, Turkish, Egyptian and Persian characteristics. **Jami Masjid** of Gulbarga and **Chand Minar** of Daulatabad and the college of Mahmud Gawan at Bidar bear testimony to this mixed styles. Many of the buildings in Bahamani kingdom were built on the site of old temples and with the materials of those temples which gave unavoidably a Hindu look in the style.

At Bijapur the native art began to reassert itself and the Adil Shahi buildings which were constructed by the Indian artists and craftsmen bore an Indian style. Sir John Marshall remarks that "it was inevitable that Indian genius should rise superior to foreign influence and stamp itself more and more deeply on these creations." Thus the impact of Hindu and Islamic civilisations was leading to harmony and understanding in the diverse spheres of society, art and culture.

REFERENCES

The History and Culture of the Indian People, Vol. VI : *The Delhi Sultanate* : Bharatiya Vidya Bhavan

An Advanced History of India : Majumdar, Roychaudhuri & Datta

The Delhi Sultanat : *A Comprehensive History of India* : Habib & Nizami

A Comprehensive History of India, Vol. III : Wolseley Haig

The Sultanate of Delhi : A. L. Srivastava

The Oxford History of India (4th Edn.) : V. A. Smith

7 Disintegration of the Delhi Sultanate : Rise of Provincial Kingdoms : Rajputana and the South

DECLINE AND FALL OF THE DELHI SULTANATE

The fall of the Delhi Sultanate was the logical conclusion of the decline that had set in during the last days of Muhammad bin Tughluq. The indiscretion of Muhammad bin Tughluq brought into play a process of disintegration which was accelerated by the weakness and the impolitic steps of his immediate successor Firuz Shah Tughluq, such as the revival of the system of **jagir,** inordinate expansion of the number of the slaves, imposition of **jizya** on the non-Muslims and the persecution of heretical Muslim sects. This process of decline could not be checked by the weak Sayyids and the impolitic Lodis. The Lodis had some military successes to their credit but could not breathe any vitality in the administration nor could stop the policy of official repression of the people. The Delhi Sultanate lacking the force and vitality was tottering to its inevitable fall.

The Delhi Sultanate depended on the personality, ability and military efficiency of the Sultan himself. It being the rule of the sword primarily, did not grow up on the habitual allegiance of the subjects on whom the Sultan ruled. Naturally the foundations of the Sultanate was weak. Where the Sultan was personally powerful and efficient, for example, under an Iltutmish, a Balban or an Ala-ud-din, the administration was effective and Sultan's orders were obeyed. But whenever the Sultan was weak and incapable, the nobility of the court, the provincial governors and other nobles became busy in pursuit of self interest. The inherent defect of the Sultanate which followed the system of granting **jagirs** except under Ala-ud-din especially, and which kept the central authority busy in suppressing rebellions, was that whenever the centre was weak the centrifugal tendencies came into play. The big estate holders, **jagirdars, amirs** and **maliks,** provincial governors and nobles who were the pillars of administration held much local influence ; and whenever there was any sign of weakness or inefficiency at the centre, they would raise the standard of rebellion.

The huge number of the slaves, further expanded under Firuz Shah Tughluq who opened a regular department for their maintenance, became not only a burden on the finances of the state but would in various ways interfere with the administration as did the army. At the beginning of the Sultanate period there emerged from among the slaves capable administrators and rulers like Qutb-ud-din, Iltutmish etc. but this class of efficient and devoted slaves could not be found later.

The life of luxury, drinking and debauchery lived by the nobles and the highly placed officials of the state led to their utter inefficiency and the administration became stagnant and ineffective. Ala-ud-din took some severe measures to stop the rot, but this was not followed under his successors.

Discriminatory treatment of the non-Muslims, particularly the Hindus, the corruption and want of discipline among the officials, and a general tendency among the revenue officials to speculation and extortionate collection from the subjects contributed to the weakening of the administration. In a country with vastly Hindu population establishment of a theocratic state and demolition of temples, imposition of **jizya** and all that, precluded the Delhi Sultans from becoming the national kings of the country. This wide gap in habitual allegiance of a vast majority of the people naturally contributed to the fall of the Sultanate.

When the internal maladministration and confusion, selfishness and struggle for the throne had made the situation extremely serious, Timur the lame invaded India, entered Delhi, plundered it and put many to the sword and thereby administered a deathblow to the Delhi Sultanate.

The subsequent history was one of mutual quarrel among the Lodis themselves and when selfishness got the better of the country's good foreign assistance was invited by Daulat Khan Lodi and Alam Khan Lodi, rivals of Ibrahim Lodi, and the result was the first battle of Panipat, 1526, and the foundation of the Mughal rule in India in place of the Delhi Sultanate.

Provincial Kingdoms : The centrifugal tendencies which were inherent in the administrative structure of the Delhi Sultanate began to be manifest in the assertion of independence by quite a few of the provinces of the Delhi Sultanate after the death of Firuz Tughluq. Jaunpur was one of the earliest to assert its independence.

Jaunpur : Firuz Tughluq founded the city of Jaunpur which he named after his cousin Jauna or Juna Khan, i.e. Muhammad bin Tughluq. Malik Sarwar, a eunuch, was the governor who took the name of Sultan-ush-Sharq and threw off the allegiance of Delhi taking advantage of the confusion of the time of Timur's invasion and began to rule as a **de facto** king. His dynasty came to be known as Sharqi dynasty. Sarwar had extended his authority over Awadh and over parts of the Doab as far as modern Aligarh. Tirhut and Bihar also came under his sway. Sarwar ruled as a king but refrained from assuming the title of the king.

On Sarwar's death in 1399, his adopted son Malik Qaranphul succeeded him and assumed the title of Mubarak Shah. He was the first member of the Sharqi dynasty to assume royal title, to strike coins and read **khutba** in his name. It was during his reign that Delhi sought to recover Jaunpur without success but this was (1401) the beginning of a contest between Jaunpur and Delhi which lasted for long years. On Mubarak Shah's death in 1402, his brother Ibrahim Shah succeeded him. Ibrahim was the greatest king of the Sharqi dynasty and ruled for nearly 34 years. He was not only an able ruler, but himself was a cultured prince who established schools and colleges, endowed them liberally and many learned men enjoyed his patronage. He invited scholars and theologians from different parts of the country and extended them his patronage. During his reign many scholarly works, both theological and secular, were produced. Under Ibrahim many beautiful mosques were built in Jaunpur and the Sharqi style of architecture took its name from the style introduced during his reign. The famous **Atal Devi Masjid** bears testimony to the excellent architectural work of the reign of Ibrahim. The Jaunpur mosques betrayed in their style of architecture the prevalent Hindu art.

During the reign of Ibrahim the relation between Jaunpur and Delhi became bitter. Mahmud Tughluq once had to take shelter in Jaunpur due to the tyranny of Mallu, but Ibrahim did not treat Mahmud Tughluq as his sovereign. For this Mahmud on his return from Jaunpur forcibly occupied the district of Kanauj from Jaunpur. Ibrahim also came into conflict with Khizir Khan. Ibrahim was a powerful warrior and an ambitious ruler. He attempted without success to conquer Bengal. On his death in 1436, his son Mahmud Shah who succeeded in conquering Chaunar but failed in his attempt to take Kalpi. He even invaded Delhi, but was defeated by Buhlul Lodi. He died in 1475 and his son ascended the throne under the title Muhammad Shah. He was as unscrupulous as he was tactless. He soon alienated his nobles, quarrelled with them and they in their turn murdered him and raised his brother Hussain Shah to the throne. Hussain Shah was the last ruler of the Sharqi dynasty. During his reign, the conflict between Jaunpur and Delhi came to a head and a longdrawn war ensued between the two. In 1458 a four-year truce was signed between Jaunpur and Delhi. After this, the respite he got gave him an opportunity to suppress the zamindars of Tirhut and carrying on a plundering raid against Orissa and thereby compelling the Raja of Orissa to pay him a rich indemnity. His next expedition was against Gwalior which he failed to occupy but Man Singh was compelled to pay him a heavy indemnity. It was soon after this that Buhlul Lodi proceeded against him, defeated him and compelled him to take shelter in Bihar. Buhlul Lodi subjugated whole of Jaunpur and placed his son Barbak Shah on its throne. Hussain Shah began to incite rebellion among the Jaunpur zamindars which ultimately made Sikandar Lodi, Successor of Buhlul Lodi to annex Jaunpur as an integral part of the Delhi Sultanate. With the death of Hussain in Bihar as an exile in 1500 A.D. the Sharqi dynasty of Jaunpur came to an end. Under the rule of the Sharqi dynasty Jaunpur attained material prosperity and became noted for educational and cultural activities.

Gujarat : It was in 1297 that the rich province of Gujarat was conquered and annexed to the Delhi Sultanate by Ala-ud-din Khalji, and continued to remain a province of the Sultanate till 1401. In 1391 Zafar Khan, a son of Rajput convert, was appointed governor of Gujarat by Muhammad Shah II Tughluq. The invasion of Timur gave Zafar Khan the opportunity to throw off the allegiance of Delhi and make himself independent (1401). Zafar Khan was for a time deposed by his son Tatar Khan who occupied the throne as Nasir-ud-din Muhammad Shah but he was put to death by his uncle Shams Khan. Zafar Khan now recovered his throne and assumed the title of Sultan Muzaffar Shah and ruled upto 1411. His reign was marked by a prolonged conflict between Gujarat and Malwa in which Husang Shah was defeated. Muzaffar Shah succeeded in capturing Dhar. On his death his grandson Ahmad Shah became the ruler of Gujarat (1411) who ruled till 1442. He was a good warrior and an ambitious ruler and extended his kingdom by conquest. He waged wars against Malwa, Asirgarh, Rajasthan and other neighbouring states. With ambition, energy and power of organisation, he first reorganised the administrative system of the kingdom, then he built the modern city of Ahmedabad on the site of the old town of Aswal and made it his capital. He built several stately buildings in this new city, also a grand mosque which exists till today. He is noted for his liberality, munificence and impartial justice. But he was a religious fanatic and was intolerant towards his non-Muslim subjects. On his death in 1442, the throne passed to his son Muhammad Shah after whom the successors were both weak and incapable. Of the last two successive weak kings, Daud was deposed by the nobles who raised a grandson of Ahmad Shah to the throne who took the title of Mahmud Begarha.

Mahmud Begarha was the ablest and the greatest king of the dynasty. He possessed a huge physique and his appetite was unusually great. He was an intrepid warrior, a successful conqueror and an efficient administrator. He added 'glory and lusture' to the kingdom of Gujarat. His rule was of an inordinately long period of fifty-three years during which he put down the recalcitrant courtiers who conspired to put his brother Hasan Khan to the throne. He then launched upon a career of conquests. He defeated the chiefs of Kutch, conquered the forts of Junagarh and Champaner. He suppressed the pirates of Dwarka. He took the side of Nizam Shah Bahamani against Mahmud Khalji of Malwas whom he defeated signally. The boundaries of Gujarat extended to the extreme limits under him. In alliance with the Sultan of Egypt he defeated the Portuguese who had monopolised the sea-borne trade in the Indian ocean. But after their initial defeat the Portuguese recovered their position by defeating the allies near Diu. Mahmud Begarha was obliged to grant them a site for a factory at Diu. Mahmud Begarha died in 1511 and was succeeded by his son Muzaffar Shah II who fought with the Rajputs under Medini Rai and succeeded in restoring Mahmud Khalji of Malwa to the throne. His death in 1526 was followed by the succession of two incompetent rulers for a few months after which Bahadur Shah, another son of Muzaffar II, became king. He was one of the ablest and most capable rulers of the dynasty and was endowed with courage, valour and love of adventure. He embarked on a career of conquest soon after his accession and defeated Mahmud II of Malwa and annexed it to Gujarat. He then invaded Mewar and stormed the fort of Chitor. But he got involved in a conflict with the Mughals by giving shelter to Humayun's rebellious cousins. Humayun defeated him and Malwa was taken away from him. Later he was driven out of Gujarat also. But Humayun had to withdraw his troops from Gujarat which gave Bahadur Shah opportunity to recover Gujarat. He then began to follow the policy of driving the Portuguese out of Gujarat, for, they did not help him against Humayun. The portuguese governor Cunha beguiled Bahadur Shah on board a ship and got him drowned treacherously. He was succeeded by a number of weak successors and taking advantage of their weakness Gujarat was annexed to the Mughal Empire by Akbar.

Malwa : Malwa was annexed to the Delhi Sultanate by Ala-ud-din Khalji in 1305 and it continued to be under the authority of Delhi till 1398 when it became independent, like other provinces of the Sultanate, taking advantage of the disorder and confusion that had resulted from the invasion of Timur. It was Dilawar Khan Ghur, probably appointed governor of Malawa by Firuz Shah Tughluq, who made himself independent of the Delhi Sultanate in 1401 although he did neither formally threw off the allegiance of Delhi nor assume royal title. During Timur's invasion of India when Sultan Mahmud Tughluq sought asylum in Gujarat but was not received there with the dignity of the sovereign by Muzaffar Shah of Gujarat, he came over to Malwa and stayed there for about three years. He was received with all honour and dignity of the sovereign by Dilawar Khan which irked his son Alp Khan who retired to Mandu and laid the foundations of a fort there which later became one of the strongest forts of Malwa. On the return of Sultan Mahmud Khan Tughluq to Delhi, Dilawar Khan at the instance of his son Alp Khan assumed the paraphernalia of royalty. On Dilawar's death, his ambitious son Alp Khan succeeded him and assumed the title Hushang Shah. Alp Khan was a brave, restless, ambitious ruler who remained engaged in adventurous enterprises and wars all throughout the period of his reign. In 1422 he appeared before Orissa in the guise of a merchant and made a surprise attack on the Raja who had to buy him off by giving him seventy-five elephants. On his return journey he captured Kherla and took the Raja of the place as a prisoner with him. He fought against the Sultans of Delhi, Jaunpur, Gujarat and of the Bahmani kingdom but met with defeat and disaster. On his death in 1435, his son Ghazni Khan ascended the throne as Muhammad Shah. His incompetence and lack of attention to the business of state led to his deposition by his minister Mahmud Khan who assumed the title Shah and founded a new dynasty known as the Khalji dynasty of Malwa. His usurpation of the throne was opposed by a section of the nobles and Ahmad Shah of Gujarat who supported Muhammad Shah's son as the rightful claimant to the throne. But Mahmud Khalji succeeded in overcoming the opposition.

Mahmud Khalji was an intrepid warrior and a successful commander. He fought against Ahmad Shah of Gujarat, Muhammad Shah of Delhi, Muhammad Shah III Bahmani and Rana Kumbha of Mewar. He was defeated in his contests with the Muslim Sultans and his war with Rana Kumbha was indecisive and both sides claimed victory and while Rana of Mewar erected a tower of victory. Mahmud Khalji built a seven-storeyed column in Mandu in commemoration of the victory. But Mahmud Khalji was decidedly the ablest Sultan of Malwa. He extended the territories of Malwa upto the Satpura range in the south, to the border of Gujarat in the west, to 'Bundelkhand in the east and Mewar and Harauti in the north'. His fame spread beyond India and the Sultan of Egypt, i.e. the Caliph. Recognised him as Sultan; he also received a mission from Sultan Abu Said. According to Ferishta, "he was polite, brave, just and learned and during his reign his subjects, Mohammedans as well as Hindus, were happy and maintained a friendly intercourse with each other. Scarcely a year passed when he did not take the field, so that his tent became his home and the field of battle his resting place. His leisure hours were devoted to hearing the histories and memoirs of the courts of different kings of the world." He was a just, impartial and active administrator. He died in 1469 after long thirty-four years of rule.

Ghiyas-ud-din succeeded his father in 1469. He was a highly religious minded man and passed his time in prayers. He was a devout Muslim, said his daily prayers, did not touch wine or food prohibited by Islam, He was a peace-loving man but his last days were rendered unhappy by the quarrels of his two sons. He was poisoned to death by his eldest son Nasir-ud-din who seized the throne in 1500. Nasir-ud-din was given to drinking and debauchery, and he maintained a **harem** of 15,000 women. In a fit of drunkenness he one day fell into a lake and was drowned (1510) and was succeeded by his second son Mahmud II. Mahmud II called in Medini Rai, a Rajput chief, to crush his recalcitrant nobles, and appointed him his prime minister. The ascendancy of the Rajputs in the court gave rise to jealousy among the Muslim nobles who invited Muzaffar Shah II of Gujarat against the powerful Rajput prime minister. But Medini Rai defeated them including Mahmud II himself with the help of Rana Sanga. In this war Rana Sanga took Mahmud II as a prisoner. But the Rana treated him very generously and restored his kingdom to him. But despite this generous treatment the hostility between Malwa and Mewar did not come to an end. Mahmud II led an expedition against Ratan Singh, the successor of Sanga, who retaliated by invading Malwa and defeating Mahmud II. Mahmud also gave offence to Sultan Bahadur Shah of Gujarat by giving shelter to his brother Chand Khan for which Bahadur Shah captured Mandu, the capital of Malwa and thus the independence of Malwa came to an end (1531). Malwa continued to remain a part of Gujarat till it was invaded and made a province under the Mughal empire by Humayun in 1535. It was also a province of Delhi under Sher Shah who appointed Shujaat Khan as its governor. But on Shujaat Khan's death his son Baz Bahadur assumed the title of Sultan in the confusion that followed the death of Sher Shah. It was Akbar who defeated Baz Bahadur and annexed Malwa to the Mughal empire (1562).

Kashmir : A Muslim adventurer from Swat, named Shah Mirza, had entered into the service of the Hindu Prince of Kashmir in 1315. The Hindu prince died shortly afterwards and Shah Mirza seized the throne setting aside the claims of the descendants of the Hindu prince and himself assumed the title of the king. He was, however, a wise and generous ruler. He died in 1349 and was succeeded by his four sons one after another who ruled for a total period of forty-six years. After the death of the fourth son Qutb-ud-din (1394) his son Sikandar ascended the throne.

It was during his reign that Timur invaded India and Sikandar exchanged envoys with him, but the two did never meet each other. Sikandar was a powerful ruler and a patron of Islamic learning. Scholars from Arabia, Persia and Mesopotamia were generously welcomed in his court. But his general attitude was not at all liberal. He was a blind bigot and persecuted the Hindus, and drove away the Brahmanas from Kashmir who refused to be converted into Islam. He allowed only eleven Brahamana families to remain in Kashmir. He demolished Hindu temples the most important of which was the Martand temple of Mattan. On his death in 1416, his eldest son Adil Shah reigned for a few years but was deposed by his brother Shahi Khan and himself ascended the throne in 1420 under the title Zain-ul-Abidin.

Zain-ul-Abidin was the greatest Muslim ruler of Kashmir. He was highly enlightened, liberal and benevolent, for which he was known as the Akbar of Kashmir. He allowed the Kashmiri Brahamana families who had been banished during the reign of Sultan Sikandar to return. To eradicate robbery, theft and other crimes in his kingdom, he made the village communitics responsible for the crimes in their respective jurisdictions. He regulated the prices of commodities, reduced the burden of taxation and rehabilitated the currency which had been greatly debased during the reigns of his predecessors. He admitted Hindu scholars to his society, abolished **jizya,** showed remarkable toleration to the followers of other faiths. He had a good knowledge of Persian, Hindi and Tibetan besides his own language Kashmiri. He was a patron of literature and art, painting and music. He caused the **Mahabharata** and **Rajatarangini** to be translated into Persian. Likewise several Persian and Arabic books were translated into Hindi. After an eventful reign, he died in 1470 and was succeeded by his son Haidar Shah.

After Zain-ul-Abidin's death there ensued chaos and anarchy under the rule of the nominal kings who ascended the throne. Haidar Shah was a fairly competent ruler, but his successors were so incompetent that in 1540 a relative of Babur, Mirza Haidar, conquered Kashmir. Although he acted as a representative of Humayun, in practice he ruled independently. But he was driven out by the Kashmiris in 1551, but the nobles began to quarrel over the question of occupation of the throne. In 1555, the Chakk tribe acquired ascendancy and one of its members ascended the throne of Kashmir. In 1586, Akbar conquered Kashmir and annexed it to the Mughal empire.

Orissa : The kingdom of Orissa was consolidated by Anantavarman Choda Ganga who ruled from 1076 to 1148. The kingdom extended from the mouth of the Ganges to the Godavari in the south. He was not only a great warrior and a conqueror but also a patron of religion and literature. The famous Jagannath temple was built by him. He successfully repelled the Turkish onslaught. After his death his dynasty began to decline. About 1434 this dynasty was supplanted by Kapilendra who founded a new dynasty. The Kapilendra dynasty ruled over Orissa for about a century. Kapilendra was a king of great ability and courage. He ably defended his kingdom against the invasion of the Bahmani and Vijaynagar rulers. Kapilendra was succeeded by Purushottama during whose reign the kingdom became weak and lost the southern half of its territory. He was succeeded by his son Prataprudra (1496-1540) who was compelled to surrender a part of his territory south of the Godavari to the Vijaynagar ruler. In 1522 the Sultan of Golkunda invaded Orissa and compelled Prataprudra to agree to humiliating terms. In 1441-42, the Kapilendra dynasty was supplanted by Bhoi dynasty whose founder was Govinda. This dynasty was overthrown in 1559 by Mukunda Harichandan who tried his best to save Orissa from the Muslim invaders. He died in 1568 and his kingdom was now sought to be occupied by the Mughals as well as by the Karrani Sultan of Bengal. Suleiman, the king of Bengal, annexed it to his kingdom in 1568.

Kamrupa and Assam : During the early years of the thirteenth century the Brahmaputra valley was divided into a number of independent principalities the most important of which was Kamrupa. It was then called Kamta kingdom and was flanked on the east by the Ahoms and on the west by the Sultans of Bengal. In the fifteenth century the Khens established their rule over Kamrupa with its capital at Kamtapur. The ruler named Nilambar of this dynasty was overthrown by Ala-ud-din Hussain Shah in 1498. After some years Vishwasinha of the Koch tribe set himself as the ruler of Kamrupa in 1515. The greatest Koch ruler was Nara Narayan. Under him the Kamta kingdom reached its zenith of power and greatness. But due to internal dissensions the country was divided between Nara Narayan and his nephew Raghudeva. The two parts came to be known as kooch Bihar and Kooch Hajo respectively. But the division of the kingdom did not end the mutual hostility of the two kingdoms, taking advantage of which the Ahoms and the Muslims intervened. In 1639 the western portion came under the supremacy of the Muslims and the eastern portion under the Ahoms.

The Ahoms were a section of the Shan tribe who came to Assam early in the thirteenth century (1215) and gradually consolidated their position and set up a strong monarchy which lasted for nearly six hundred years. During the period of the Delhi Sultanate, the Ahoms successfully checked the eastward expansion of the kingdom of Kamrupa and of the Sultans of Bengal. It was only after the Muslims had succeeded in subjugating Kamrupa that the Ahom Kingdom became vulnerable to the Muslim attacks. It was Ala-ud-din Hussain Shah of Bengal who led an expedition against the kingdom of the Ahoms when it was ruled by Suhenpha. The Muslim forces were initially successful, but the expedition ended in a disaster. For thirty years to follow there was no Ahom-Muslim conflict. Then a second phase of the expedition of the local Muslims of Bengal began against the Ahoms but their attempts also failed (1533).

THE RAJPUT STATES

Mewar : The disruption of the Turko-Afghan Empire had stirred some of the Rajput states with the spirit of revival, the most important of which was the Guhila principality of Mewar. It was in Mewar that the Rajput genius had found best expression in the succession of brave generals, capable and prudent rulers, heroic leaders, intrepid warriors and some briliant poets. Ala-ud-din Khalji besieged and captured Chitor, the capital of Mewar but it was delivered from the hands of the Muslims by Hamir who was one of the wisest and most gallant of the princes of Mewar. The exact date of the recovery of Chitor cannot be ascertained but it seems possible that it took place during the widespread rebellion during Muhammad bin Tughluq's reign. On Hamir's death, his son Kshetra Simha succeeded him in 1378, who in his turn was succeeded by his son Lakha. On Lakha's death, his son Mokala ascended the throne but was assassinated by two of his uncles. The next Rana of Mewar was Kumbha who was one of the most famous Rajput rulers in history of India. According to Tod Rana Kumbha "with Hamir's energy, Lakha's taste for arts, and a genius comprehensive as either or more fortunate, succeeded in all his undertakings, and once more raised the 'crimson banner' of Mewar upon the banks of the Jhaggar." Rana Kumbha fought against the Muslim rulers of Malwa and Gujarat and though he was not successful in all his enterprises, he could all the same hold his position aginst his ambitious neighbours. Kumbha was a great builder and many of the finest monuments of Mewar were built during his reign. Of the eighty-four fortresses built for the defence of Mewar, as many as thirty-two were crected by Kumbha. The fortress of Kumbhagarh was the most brilliant monument of his military and constructive genius and "was second to none in stategical importance or historical renown." His **Jayastambha** or **Kirtistambha** is another monument of his constructive genius. He was also a musician, poet and a partron of learning. He was assassinated by his son Udaya Karan in or about 1469 which horrified the nobles of the court who placed Udaya's younger brother Rayamalla to the throne. On the death of Rayamalla there was a struggle for succession among his sons and one of them named Sangrama or Sanga as he was popularly called, ultimately succeeded to the throne of Mewar in 1509. Sanga was rare military genius and was the hero of hundred battles. "A hero of a hundred fields, he bore the scars of eighty wounds on his body in addition to having an eye blinded and a leg crippled." He fought with success against Delhi, Malwa and Gujarat and organised a large army and a strong treasury with a view to building the supremacy of Mewar on the break-up of the Delhi Sultanate. A fierce contest with Rana Sanga was, therefore, inevitable on the part of any body that would seek to establish supremacy in Northern India and the battle of Khanua was the logical conclusion.

Marwar : The next important Rajput state was marwar. The period which witnessed the gradual development of the Sisodiya state of Mewar, also saw the establishment of the Rathor states of Marwar and Bikaner. The modern Rathors as also the Rajput traditions claim that the Rathors are descondants of the Gahdavalas of Kanauj. Sinha is regarded as the founder of the Rathor dynasty sometime in the first half of the thirteenth century. Sinha died in 1273. The Rathor family after its foundation in Kher was guided by a natural impulse of expansion which involved it in a struggle with its neighbours Muslims and the Bhattis. By first decade of the fourteenth century the greatest of the Delhi Sultans. Ala-ud-din Khalji, had conquered the whole of the eastern part of modern Mewar and Gujarat, and Kher found itself surrounded on three sides by the mighty Muslim power. A struggle for its very existence followed. During the greater part of the fourteenth century the throne of Delhi was occupied by three prominent Sultans—Ala-ud-din. Mohammad bin Tughluq and Firuz Shah Tughluq when it was difficult for the rathor state to make much headway. The weakness of the Delhi Sultanate must have afforded opportunity to the Rathors to follow a policy of expansion.

The modern history of the Rathors begins from the time of Chunda who ruled from 1394 to 1421. His successor Jodha, his grandson, founded the new city of Jodhpur and made it his capital. It was called Jodhpur after the name of its founder Jodha and continued to be the capital of Rathors of Marwar. Jodha at first lost Rathor lands to the Sisodiyas who established garrisons in important places to hold the country under subjection. Jodha was compelled to take shelter in the desert. Jodha made some attempts at recovery of his territories without success. But soon there was a war between Malwa and Mewar which continued from 1443 to 1458. Jodha obtained important success against Mewar during this phase of the struggle between Malwa and Mewar. Sisodiya **sardars** were driven away from one position after another. Choksi, Kosano, Mandor, Sojhat, Merta and Ajmer fell into the hands of Jodha. The reign of Jodha forms an interesting landmark in the evolution of the Rathor state into its modern shape. Jodha also built the fort of Mandor. His reign lasting for nearly fifty years, brought Rathor state into great prominence.

Jodha's death in 1448 was followed by a struggle among his sons for succession. The eldest of the seventeen sons of Jodha having died leaving no male heir, the throne was sought to be given to next brother but as he was found demented, the next brother Satal was placed on throne but he died shortly afterwards. One of the brothers, Bika made an attempt to seize the throne, but he failed and another brother Suja secured the throne. Bika, however, founded the Rajput state of Bikaner. Suja failed to assert his authority on the collateral branches of Marwar, like Metra, Bikaner etc.

The most important ruler during the period under study was Maldeva (1532-62) under whom the Rathor power reached its height. He came into conflict with Sher Shah who had to ultimately sign a peace treaty with Maldeva.

SOUTHERN INDIA

Khandesh : Khandesh was a province under Muhammad bin Tughluq. Firuz Shah Tughluq appointed Malik Raja Faruqi as the governor of the province but during the confusion that followed the death of Firuz Shah Tughluq Faruqi declared himself independent of the Delhi Sultanate as did many other provincial governors and local chiefs. Faruqi was a generous ruler and a man of peaceful disposition and he treated his subjects Hindus and the Muslims alike. On his death in 1399, his son, Malik Nasir, succeeded him. Nasir made himself the sole master of Khandesh by defeating his brother Hasan. He also captured the fortress of Asirgarh from its Hindu chief but he himself was defeated by Sultan Ahmad Shah of Gujarat when he made an attempt to capture Nandurbar and compelled him to swear allegiance to the Sultan of Gujarat. Malik Nasir was a very ambitious man and he even attempted to defeat his own son-in-law, Ala-ud-din Ahmad of the Bahmani dynasty but met with disaster. He died soon after in 1437-38. He was succeeded by his son, Adil Khan, who was in his turn succeeded by his son, Mubarak Khan I, in 1441. These two reigns were as weak as eventless. On Mubarak Khan's death in 1457, his son, Adil Khan II, ascended the throne of Khandesh. He was an able and vigorous ruler and restored the administrative order in the kingdom. He also extended the authority of Khandesh over Gondwana. As he died without any issue in 1501, the throne passed to his brother Daud who died in 1508 after an inglorious reign. He was succeeded by his son Ghazni Khan who was poisoned to death within ten days of his accession which was followed by a struggle between two rivals, one supported by Ahmad Nizam Shah of Ahmadnagar, and the other by Mahmud Begarha of Gujarat till the latter succeeded in occupying the throne under the title Adil Khan III. He was not a worthy ruler and on his death in 1520 his successors were weaker still and incapable of saving the kingdom from external attacks. It was in 1601 that Akbar annexed Khandesh to the Mughal Empire.

The Bahmani Kingdom : Bahmani kingdom of the Deccan was by far the most powerful independent Muslim kingdoms that arose as a result of the eccentric policy of Muhammad bin Tugluq. The Deccan nobles driven to desperation rose in rebellion and seized the fort of Daulatabad and proclaimed one of themselves, Ismail Mukh the Afghan, as the king of the Deccan under the title of Nasir-ud-din Shah. Ismail Mukh was an old man and found himself unequal to the task of ruling the country. He voluntarily abdicated in favour of a more energetic and worthy young leader. Hasan, bearing the title Zafar Khan who was declared king by the nobles in 1347 under the title Abdul Muzaffar Ala-ud-din Bahman Shah.

ALA-UD-DIN BAHMAN SHAH (1347-58)

There are various stories about the origin of Ala-ud-din Bahman Shah. According to Ferishta, he was originally a menial in the service of a Brahmana astrologer of Delhi named Gangu, who enjoyed the favour of Muhammad bin Tughluq and it was due to Gangu that Hasan rose into prominence. But Ferishta's story does not find corroboration in the writings of any Muslim chronicler, nor supported by coins or inscriptions. Tabataba author of **Burhan-i-Maasir,** and Nizam-ud-din, author of **Tabaqat-i-Akbari,** both of whom wrote before Ferishta gave credit to the story that Hasan had descended from the hero Bahman, son of Isfandiyar, and therefore, the dynasty is called Bahmani.

Soon after his accession ceremony at Daulatabad Bahman Shah elected Gulbarga as his capital and renamed it Hasanabad. Bahman Shah founded the Bahmani dynasty of Deccan and this dynasty ruled for next two hundred years. His first task was to impose his sovereignty over many dissident elements that had grown up in the Deccan during the period of confusion before his elevation to the throne. He therefore launched upon a career of conquest which was marked by success. By incessant warfare Bahman Shah extended the limits of his kingdom from Daulatabad in the west to Bhongir in the east and from the river Wainganga in the north to the river Krishna in the south. For effective administration of the kingdom he divided it into four **tarafs** or povinces, namely, Gulbarga, Daulatabad, Berar and Bidar. In every province there was a trusted governor who maintained an army, made appointments to civil and military posts under him. Bahman Shah was an efficient administrator and kept the provinces under strictest control so that there was no outbreak of any rebellion during his reign. Tabataba, author of **Burhan-i-Maasir**, praises the Sultan by saying that "Sultan Ala-ud-din Hasan shah was a just king and the cherisher of his people and pious. During his reign his subjects and his army used to pass their time in perfect case and content; and he did much towards propagating the true faith." Bahman Shah's dominion had two Hindu neighbours, which, like itself, had emerged on the break-up of the Tughluq empire. One was Warangal on the south and the south-east and the other Vijayanagar, a more powerful state than Warangal on the south and south-west. The proximity of two powerful Hindu kingdoms explains the chronic warfare that characterised the history of the Deccan for a hundred years from the time of Bahman Shah.

Bahman Shah created and aristocracy by bestowing titles like **khan, malik** on most of his high officials and the most influential and powerful officers were decorated with the distinctions like **Qutb-ul-Mulk, Khvaza-Jahan** etc. Ala-ud-din Hasan Bahman Shah died in 1358 and was succeeded by his son Muhammad Shah I.

MUHAMMAD SHAH I (1358-75)

Muhammad Shah I strengthened his position as the sovereign of the Deccan by formally obtaining the sanction for the use of **kutba** and **sikka,** that is the right of mentioning his name in Fariday prayer and of striking coins in his own name, from the Abbasis Caliph of Egypt.

Practically, the whole reign of Muhammad Shah was consumed in continuous struggle with Vijayanagar and Telingana. Bukka, king of Vijayanagar in an ultimatum demanded Krishna-Tungabhadra Doab on the ground that it traditionally belonged to Vijayanagar. Kapaya Nayak, king of Telingana in a similar ultimatum demanded the fortress of Kaulas whic had been wrested from him earlier. It became clear to Muhammad Shah I that Telingana and Vijayanagar had entered into an alliance. Muhammad Shah, however, rejected the ultimatum whereupon Kapaya Nayak sent his son Vinayaka Deva with a large army reinforced by a Vijayanagar contingent 20,000 strong. The latter invaded the Raichur Doab. But the combined forces of Telingana and Vijayanagar were defeated by Muhammad Shah's army near Kaulas, Kapaya Nayak was pushed upto Warangal and was compelled to sue for peace by offering a large indemnity and twenty-five elephants. But the peace did not last long and hostilities broke out again and by a surprise attack on Palampet Muhammad Shah defeated the Prince Vinayaka and put him to death by inhuman cruelty. Muhammad Shah himself had also got wounded and many of his followers were killed. But this did not end the hostilities between Bahmani kingdom and Telingana and both sides were making preparations for a show down. Secret news reached Muhammad Shah that Kapaya Nayak had invited the assistance of the Delhi Sultan Firuz Tughluq. He at once marched against Golconda and compelled Kapaya Nayak to cede Golconda and a huge amount as indemnity. Golconda was fixed as the permanent boundary between the two kingdoms. A turquoise throne was presented to Muhammad Shah by Kapaya which henceforth became the throne of the Bahmanis.

Muhammad Shah I now turned his attention towards Vijayanagar. He drew a formal draft on Vijayanagar for payment to three hundred singers from Delhi who had come to Gulbarga, capital of Bahmani kingdom, to attend the marriage ceremony of Prince Mujahid. Bukka was naturally very much incensed and replied at once by invading and capturing Mudkal. But with the appearance with Muhammad's army Vijayanagar army took to flight. Muhammad's army crossed Tungabhadra and entered the Vijayanagar territory. "This campaign is remarkable for the fact that we hear of the Europeans serving an Indian ruler on Indian soil." At Kautalam a great battle took place (1366) resulting in the complete rout of the Vijayanagar army under Bhojmal Rai. He next marched to Adoni wherefrom he moved on to the capital of the southern state. He had to face the guerilla forces of Vijayanagar and retreated to his own territory and after gathering strength he again attacked Vijayanagar and defeated its army. The Raya laid down his arms and sent his envoys for peace to Muhammad Shah. Muhammad Shah simply asked for the payment of the draft drawn on the Vijayanagar treasury. It was also decided that in future wars only the combatants should be killed, not even the prisoners of war should be molested. At this stage a rebellion broke out at Daulatabad and Muhammad Shah pursued him upto Patan. Soon after the Sultan Muhammad Shah I died (April 21, 1375).

Muhammad Shah I was one of the greatest rulers of the Bahmani dynasty and was also a statesman. He succeeded in consolidating his rather loose heritage left to him by his father. He was very much punctilious in his court etiquette and did not spare even his father-in-law from standing before him while he was holding his **Darbar.** He was highly religious in his habits and easily gave up drinking at the behest of his preceptor. The author of **Burhan-i-Ma'asir,** however, states that Muhammad Shah "showed signs of an irreligious manner of living, which threw him on the bed of helplessness."

His great work was political reorganisation of his kingdom. He divided it into provinces—Berar, Bidar and Gulbarga which also included Bijapur. The provinces centred round Daulatabad. He had likewise reorganised his military forces. On his death he left a strong and compact state for his successor and states of Telingana and Vijayanagar as its neighbours.

ALA-UD-DIN MUJAHID SHAH, DAUD KHAN (1358-78)

Muhammad Shah was succeeded by his son Ala-ud-din Mujahid Shah. His short reign was covered by war against Vijayanagar which ended with the defeat of Bahmani Sultan. Hardly he ascended the throne, Ala-ud-din marched in person against Vijayanagar but having failed to capture the city was compelled to make peace with the Raya. Soon after Daud Khan, a near relative of the Sultan had done away with him and occupied the throne. But the usurper got himself assassinated by Parwar Agha, a foster sister of Ala-ud-din Mujahid Shah (1378) and placed Muhammad Shah II, son of Mamud Khan, the fourth son of Ala-ud-din Bahmani.

MUHAMMAD SHAH II (1378-97)

Muhammad Shah II was a peace-loving ruler whose reign was free from foreign wars except some skirmishes with Vijayanagar and capture of Rangini by Vijayanagar. He was devoted to learning and caused the establishment of schools for the orphans, and he invited learned men from all over Asia to his court. He was also a great builder and ordered the building of several beautiful mosques. Even before his death his two sons, Ghiyas-ud-din and Shams-ud-din Daud, began intrigues to secure the throne, and on his death in 1397 they fell out in a bitter fratricidal conflict. Taking advantage of the troubled and inglorious reign of two brothers for only a few months, Ala-ud-din Hasan Bahmani's grandson Firuz seized the throne and became the ruler of the Bahmani kingdom under the title Taj-ud-din Firuz Shah.

FIRUZ SHAH (1397-1422)

According to Burhan-i-Ma' asir, Firuz Shah was "a mighty monarch and expended all his ability and energy in eradicating and destroying the tyranny and heresy and took much pleasure in the society of **shekhs,** learned men and hermits." His eventful career was marked by three campaigns against Vijayanagar and despite Ferishta's eloquent description of his brilliant success in his first campaign (1398) culminating in the siege of Vijayanagar, doubt has been cast by the silence by all other Muslim writers which indicate that in all possibility Firuz Shah did not gain much success in the campaign. There were two subsidiary campaigns, first was against Berar which offered stubborn resistance but having not received any assistance from any of his neighbours, ultimately submitted to Firuz. The second campaign was against Telingana where two rival factions, the Vemas and the Velamas, were supported by Vijayanagar and Bahmani Kingdom respectively. In spite of Ferishta's claim of great success of Firuz, in fact, he achieved very little, and in the conflict between the forces of Bahmani and Vijayanagar that of the latter won complete victory. After conclusion of treaty with Vijayanagar, Firuz proceeded against Telingana but after some initial success the Bahmani commander Ali Khan was defeated.

Second campaign (1406) of Firuz against Vijayanagar began with a romantic love episode of Deva Raya I's daughter, which as Ferishta's account tells us, ultimately led to Sultan's marriage with Deva Raya's daughter. But absence of reference to the episode in Nizam-ud-din's account which gives a different story throws doubt on the account of Ferishta.

Third campaign (1417-20) which centred round the siege of Pangal fort of Vijayanagar by Firuz ended in his defeat. He left the field and his territory was laid waste by fire and sword. The long drawn struggle of Vijayanagar and Bahmani kingdom remained unsettled and Raichur Doab, the bone of contention between the two, remained under Vijayanagar. The Vijayanagar troops occupied the southern and eastern districts of the Bahmani kingdom.

The defeat and disconfiture of Firuz undermined his prestige and mental strength so much so that he offered the throne to his brother, himself abdicating. His successor Ahmad Shah Bahmani occupied the throne in 1422 (Sept. 22).

BAHMANIS OF BIDAR

AHMAD SHAH BAHMANI (1422-36)

Ahmad Shah Bahmani, successor of Firuz Shah, was regarded as a saintly Sultan. He shifted the seat of the Bahmani kingdom from Gulbarga to Bidar. The expansion of the Bahmani kingdom towards the east had made Bidar the most centrally and strategically situated place of the kingdom. Besides, three linguistic areas of the kingdom converged on this city. But there was also a political consideration. "This change of seat of government was really symbolic of the revolution which was taking place in the Bahmani state. What the shrewd Sultan wanted was to put the throne on a sounder pedestal than was possible in the intriguing atmosphere of Gulbarga where regicides abounded and uncertainties of succession prevailed. It is remarkable how the right of primogeniture became firmly established in Bidar." It may be mentioned that before Muhammad bin Tughluq had made Daulatabad one of the capitals of the empire. Bidar was the capital of the Deccan.

Immediately on assumption of the throne Ahmad Shah declared war against Vijayanagar king, Deva Raya II. in fulfilment of the unfinished wishes of his brother. According to Ferishta, Deva Raya was compelled to sue for peace. The Raja of Warangal who sided with Deva Raya and then deserted him, paid heavily for his folly. He was defeated and slain, and Warangal was annexed to Bahmani kingdom with Khan-i-Azam as its Governor at Telingana.

In 1426, Ahmad Shah advanced into Gondwana, reduced Ellichpur, captured Gawil and repaired the fort Narnala. But his attempts against Mahur did not succeed. Ahmad Shah was interested in preserving his lines of communications with Gujarat. In his conflict with Malwa, he came out victorious and Bahmani flag was carried there and during the rest of his reign there was no trouble between the two kingdoms.

In Gujarat, Ahmad Shah got himself involved in war by siding with a Hindu chieftain who had revolted against Gujarat Sultan. In 1429 Bahmani troops were sent to help the rebels but were beaten back. Next year (1430) another Bahmani army was sent under an able commander named Khalaf Hasan Basri to occupy Salsette. But this attempt also failed. In this campaign the **Deccani-pardesi** conflict came to the surface and all the Deccanese men and officers deserted Khalaf Hasan giving an easy victory to Gujarat. The Island of Mahim and some other territories south of Mahim were annexed to Gujarat in this campaign. Ahmad Shah now got an alliance struck with Khandesh by solemnising the marriage of his son Ala-ud-din with the daughter of Khandesh Sultan Nasir Khan Farruqi. Ahmad Shah died in 1436.

ALA-UD-DIN AHMAD SHAH II (1436-58)

Ala-ud-din Ahmad Shah succeeded his father Ahmad Shah in 1436. He caused a magnificent tomb to be built on the grave of his father which with its decorations in painting, and calligraphic devices excite the admiration of the visitors even today. "The colours of these paintings, specially of those on the ceiling, are still fresh and bright, as if they were done only a few years ago. These paintings are considered unique in India for their beauty and elegance."

The year of Ala-ud-din's accession saw hostilities with Vijayanagar This was caused by the non-payment of tribute which had fallen into arrears for five years. Besides, Deva Raya II had seized Anegundi on the south-western bank of Tungabhadra. Ala-ud-din Ahmad Shah sent his brother Muhammad to demand the tribute by force which was realised forthwith. But instigated by some enemies of the Bahmanis Prince Muhammad, brother of Ala-ud-din, demanded half the kingdom from the latter and actually occupied Raichur, Mudkal and Naldrug. But Muhammad was defeated by Ala-ud-din and ultimately pardoned and placed with the jagir of Rajachol. Ala-ud-din's Prime Minister Dilwar Khan defeated the Rai of Sangameswar and brought the Rai's daughter with him, whom the Sultan married and gave her the title of **Zeba Chehrah,** that is, beautiful of face. The greater influence of **Zeba Chehrah** excited the jealousy of Agha Zainab, the other queen of Ala-ud-din, who happened to be the daughter of the ruler of Khandesh. Nasir Khan Farruqi, ruler of Khandesh, on the complaint of his daughter invaded Bahmani kingdom with the help of the Sultan of Gujarat and the Raja of Gondwana. The combined forces were successful initially and the Bahmani commander of Berar was shut up in the fort Narnala.

At this stage an acute party rivalry had begun at Bidar, the capital of Ala-ud-din, between the **Dakhinis** and the **Afaqis,** the former laying the blame of the defeat on the latter, at the hands of Nasir Khan. Now Ala-ud-din sent Khalaf Hasan, an **Afaqi,** against Nasir Khan and the latter was completely defeated.

In the meantime Deva Raya of Vijayanagar increased his military strength by recruiting a large number of Muslims in his army and when he felt him self sufficiently strong, he invaded Tungabhadra in 1444, marched across Raichur Doab and captured

Mudkal and plundered Nusratabad, Sagar and Bijapur. Ala-ud-din marched against Deva Raya in person and in a fierce battle at Mudkal defeated him completely. Deva Raya paid the arrears of tribute and pledged not to cross Tungabhadra again.

Now Ala-ud-din ordered Khalaf Hasan to march westward. Khalaf Hasan made Chakan his headquarters and was trying to convert the local chief Shankar Rao Shirke who had promised to pay tribute to Sultan Ala-ud-din and to show the way to Sangameswar. But one night when Khalaf Hasan lay sick and his army was at rest, Shankar Rao surrounded his camp and cut off the very pick of his army. The Dakhini army who were inimical to the **Afaqis,** is order to save their heads from the Sultan's wrath for the debacle betook themselves to the jungles and even wanted to give themselves up to the Hindus. All this meant a heavy loss to the Sultan's army. When the news of the defeat reached the Sultan he was in a highly drunken state. He ordered that all the surviving **Afaqis** must be put to sword, which was done by their enemies the **Dakhinis.**

The last years of Ala-ud-din Ahmad Shah were consumed by sporadic rebellions of his brother-in-law Jalal Khan who proclaimed himself Sultan at Nalgonda. Jalal's son Sikandar allied himself with Mubarak Khan of Khandesh and proceeded towards the Bahmani border on a false rumour that Ala-ud-din was dead, but discovering that it was untrue he retreated. At this stage Mahmud Gawan, who proved so important in the history of Deccan, took over charge of the Bahmani army. Gawan secured royal pardon for both Jalal Khan and his son and the rebellion ended. This was how Mahmud Gawan, the greatest Bahmani minister and one of the greatest figures of medieval India, first comes into notice.

Ala-ud-din Ahmad is noted for his service to his people. He set up a large hospital in his capital early in his reign and made adequate provisions for metting the expenses of medicines, salaries of the physicians and the diet of the patients. The physicians comprised both Hindus and Muslims. During the last four years of his reign he suffered from a festering would which is said to have been the cause of his death. There is, however, no reference to the cause of the death of the Sultan in the writings of Tabataba and Ferishta.

HUMAYUN SHAH (1458-61)

The late Sultan appointed his eldest son Humayun as his successor. He was of harsh temperament and cruel nature. His short reign which saw numerous rebellions in the kingdom and among his Hindu vassals whom he sought to subdue with utmost cruelty earned him the sobriquent **zalim** i.e. cruel. The author of **Burhan-i-ma'asir** also wrote in a disparaging language about the Sultan; these, however, do not find corroboration in the letters of Mahmud Gawan.

NIZAM SHAH BAHMANI (1461-63)

Humayun Shah was succeeded by his son Nizam Shah Bahmani at the age of eight which necessitated the appointment of a council of regency. It was headed by the dowager queen Nargis Begum and other members were Khwaja-i-Jahan, Mahmud Gawan. The affairs of the state were carried on by the queen-mother. She was one of the most remarkable women that had appeared in the ruling dynasties of medieval India. Although remaining behind the **purdah** she kept close contact with day to day administration of the state and made her son sit in Durbar in the audience hall according to set routine.

In this way while the internal administration of the country was strengthened, the king of Orissa, thinking that kingdom under a boy king was naturally likely to be weak, made an alliance with Telingana and marched against Bahmani kingdom reaching the outskirts of Bidar. But the invading army was beaten off by Mahmud Gawan and Khaja Jahan. A second invasion of the kingdom took place under Mahmud Khalji, Sultan of Malwa who succeeded in occupying Bidar. In this calamity Gawan appealed to the Sultan of Gujarat who sent a contingent and the combined forces of Gujarat and Bahmani kingdom compelled the enemy to retreat to Malwa. Next year (1465) Mahmud Khalji again invaded Bahmani kingdom only to retreat on the news of the approach of Gujarat army to the assistance of the Bahmanis. Nizam Shah Bahmani died young in 1463 at the age of ten, on the very day of his marriage and was succeeded by his younger brother Muhammad Shah III.

MUHAMMAD SHAH III (1463-82)

The council of Regency continued to administer the country on behalf of the new Sultan who was also a minor. The regency continued till 1466. In the meantime Khwaja Jahan turned disloyal and was got murdered by the queen-mother in the open court and Mahmud Gawan was made the Deputy of the kingdom, **Vakil-us-Sultanat,** in other words the Prime Minister and remained in that position till his murder in 1481.

During the period of fifteen years that Mahmud Gawan administered the affairs of the state, the fought with success against the kingdom of Orissa and enlarged the boundaries of the Bahmani kingdom from Orissa to Goa. The conquests of Hubli, Belgaum and Bagalkot which brought the entire area of Bombay-Karnataka under the Bahmani rule were the most remarkable military exploits of Gawan. He also consolidated Konkan and occupied Goa. Sultan Muhamud Shah III was himself a great military leader and took part in all these campaigns which earned for him the title of **Lashkari**.

The addition of the new territories enriched the resources of Bahmani kingdom. The Russian traveller Athanasius Nikitin who visited Bidar in 1470 described it to be the chief town of the whole of Mohammadan Hindustan. The life and living of the nobility and of the common people of the city of Bidar, its buildings, gave him an impression of luxury and well-being of the people and their wealth. The royal palace was wonderful. On an Id-day he saw the Sultan in a bejewelled dress and there was a large diamond on his head-dress. He was riding on a horse with a golden saddle. To the wealth of the city was added the scholarship by founding a **madrasah** by Gawan and a school equipped with a library and housed in a glittering building with glazed tiles on the outer walls. Gawan's administrative reforms had "excited the envy and jealousy of the Deccanis which finally culminated in his murder."

Party Strife : The Bahmani kingdom was divided into **Tarafs,** each under a **Tarafdar,** i.e. governor. While these provincial governors would enjoy great powers, they were under the control of the central government so long as there was a capable Sultan or an able Prime Minister like Mahmud Gawan. But in course of time two forces were in action, viz., the local governors, i.e., the **Tarafdars** were acquiring local power and influence, as also prestige with the people while the centre began to show signs of weakness due to absence of strong rulers or ministers and increase of party strife.

The inherent centrifugal forces that were in action in the Bahmani administration were all the more accentuated by the division of the Muslim aristocracy into two rival parties in the Sultan's court, the older ones, i.e., the domiciled Muslim aristocracy called the **Deccanis** and the new comers, called the foreigners or **pardesis.** The Deccanis were originally Muslim invaders, but their long stay in the Deccan and their marital relation with the Hindus carried Hindu blood in them. Many of them were also Hindu converts. Fathullah Imad Shah, founder of Imad Shahi dynasty of Berar and Ahmad Nizam Shah of Ahmadnagar were originally Brahmins. The **pardesis** came from outside for trade and ultimately found it to their advantage to take part in politics of the country and live in it permanently. They were from Turkey, Persia, Arabia, Afghanistan, Central Asia, etc. These foreigners were drafted to the Bahmani army. Mujahid Shah Bahmani even showed preference to the Persians and Turks in recruitment to his army. This created a feeling of dissatisfaction and grievance among the Deccanis. In course of time the number of the **pardesis** increased and they became a distinct community. They were more agile and enterprising than the Deccanis and many of them naturally rose to high positions of the state. The religious difference between the Deccanis who were Sunnis and the pardesis who were Shiahs, was a added cause of their mutual jealousy.

Towards the end of the fourteenth century the Deccanis realising that they were being ousted from power more and more, by the **pardesis** poisoned the ears of Ahmad Shah Vali (meaning saintly), when the king was declining both in physical and mental health. They succeeded in winning the favour of the Sultan and when the Bahmani army was defeated at the hands of the Gujarati army the blame of the defeat was claverly fastened to the **pardesis** by the Deccanis at the court. The result was that the Deccanis were raised to power in place of the pardesis. Once placed in power, the Deccanis treacherously massacred a large number of the pardesis. Soon after the Bahmani forces were defeated at the hands of the combined forces of Raja of Sangameswara and Raja Shankar Rao. The Bahmani forces under paradesis commander Khalaf Hasan had to retreat and take shelter in Chakan. The Deccanis represented to the Sultan that the debacle was due to the inefficiency of the pardesi commander Khalaf Hasan and the Sultan without realising the actual state of affairs, ordered the killing of all the surviving soldiers. A few paradesis who managed to escape the massacre reported the matter to the Sultan who held an enquiry and threw out the Deccanis from power and restored the pardesis to their former position in the administration. But the massacre at Chakan had set the seal on the mutual recrimination of the Deccanis and the pardesis and there was no question of any workable understanding between the two. Each party was out to destroy the other and this blind policy of extirpation of one by the other, led to the murder of the greatest of the medieval statesman Mahmud Gawan by the Deccanis in 1481. "The false accusation and violent death of this upright minister constitute one of the tragedies of medieval India."

KHVAJA MUHMUD GAWAN

By birth Khvaja Muhmud Gawan was a persian. He rose to the highest position in the Bahmani kingdom under Sultan Mahmud Shah III (1463-82). The Sultan recognised his honesty and ability, his statesmanship and administrative efficiency, and bestowed on him the title of **Malik-ut-Tujjar** and his followers were permitted to get precedence in the court over Hasan-ul-Mulk, the Deccani leader.

Gawan had welfare of the state nearest to his heart, and with a sense of strictest justice he held the scale evenly between the Deccanis and the pardesis by an equal division of office between the two parties, It goes without saying that Hasan-ul-Mulk was jealous of his power and eminence and was secretly waiting and wishing for the opportunity to overthrow the able minister.

Gawan initiated reforms which brought administrative efficiency in the state. Each of the four divisions of the state was sub-divided into two and regulations were promulgated for reduction of the powers of the provincial governors. But all this made him unpopular with the Deccanis and caused widespread resentment against him. Hasan-ul-Mulk instigated his followers to get rid of the author of the vexatious reforms and although Gawan tried his best to bring about a workable understanding between the Deccanis and the pardesis the attempt failed. Despite the high offices to which Gawan had appointed the Deccanis they were not satisfied and they began to hatch a plot for his destruction.

During the fifteen years of his administration Gawan enlarged the boundaries of Bahmani kingdom from Orissa to Goa. The entire Bombay-Karnataka area was brought under the Bahmani rule by him. He also consolidated Konkan and occupied Goa. Apart from the military exploits of Gawan that added to the territories of the Bahmani kingdom, Gawan worked for the welfare of the people. He established a **madrasah** and also a school which he had equipped with a good library. The school library was housed in a glittering building the outer walls of which were finished with glazed tiles.

When the conspiracy against Gawan was being hatched, he sent his righthand man Yusuf Adil Khan in an expedition against Telingana. This gave an opportunity to the conspirators and they wrote a forged letter to the king of Orissa inviting him to invade the Bahmani kingdom. Then as if the letter had been intercepted by them, they placed it before the Sultan, accusing Gawan of treachery. Muhammad Shah III without any enquiry ordered the immediate killing of Gawan (1481). This unmerited killing of Gawan was the immediate cause of the dissolution of the Bahmani kingdom, for, with the death of Gawan all hopes of maintaining political equilibrium were lost. Hasan-ul-Mulk who now became the Prime Minister monopolised all powers of the state and Muhammad Shah now due to moral compunction for shedding innocent blood tried to drown his remorse in wine and soon died (1482), uttering the name of Gawan in his last gasp for breath.

Muhammad Shah III was succeeded by his son Mahmud Shah.

MAHMUD SHAH (1482-1518)

Mahmud Shah was a minor and the affairs of the state were looked after by Malik-Naib Hasan-ul-Mulk. He was unpopular for his complicity in the murder of Gawan and the intrigues between the Deccanis and the pardesis assumed such serious proportions that Hasan-ul-Mulk had to flee for his life but was put to death by the Abyssinian governor of Bidar. By the turn of events the pardesis again came back to power. This time the Deccanis conspired to kill the Sultan himself but the attempt was thwarted by a Turkish body guard. The Sultan took reprisal by ordering mass killing of the Deccani conspirators.

Relieved of the trouble in his court, Mahmud Shah now continued to rule as a nominal Sultan, leaving the administration in the hands of Qasim Barid, till his death in 1518. The provincial governors refused to obey Qasim Barid and the son of Hasan-ul-Mulk was defeated. All this started the process of disintegration of the Bahmani kingdom. In 1490 Ahmad made himself independent at Ahmadnagar, named after himself. Bijapur and Berar followed suit. The sovereignty of Bahmani Sultanate became more or less a fiction.

Mahmud Shah rallied all **amirs** of the kingdom for proceeding in a war against Vijayanagar. The **amirs** and **wazirs** came to join in the **jehad** but the attempt brought repeated disaster on the Bahmani kingdom. The sense of unity did not work beyond the desire to defeat the idolators of Vijayanagar and the dissensions within the Bahmani kingdom were fully at work when in 1518 Mahmud Shah died. He was succeeded by four puppet rulers the last of whom was Kalim-ullah with whose death in 1538 the Bahmani dynasty came to an end and out of it five independent Sultanate emerged : Adil Shahi of Bijapur, Qutb Shahi of Golconda, Nizam Shahi of Ahmadnagar, Barid Shahi of Bidar and Imad Shahi of Berar.

Bahmani Administration : The Bahmani administration was modelled on the Islamic pattern. The highest power, administrative, judicial, military and religious rested in the king. King's duty was all-embracing and his authority was all-powerful. Mujahid Shah even claimed himself to be shadow of God on earth. Bahman Shah, founder of the Bahmani dynasty, acknowledged the supremacy of the Abbasid Caliphate and called himself the right hand of the Caliph.

Theoretically though the authority of the king was unlimited, in practice it was limited by the advice of the ministers in matters of administration and in determination of state-policy. The king had a Prime Minister called **vakil-us-Sultanat** and all orders of the king would pass through him. The finance minister, called the **amir-i-jumla** dealt with the finances of the state. **Wazir-i-ashraf** was the minister for external affairs. The judicial minister was called **sadr-i-jahan.** Apart from the major ministries, there were other minor ministers such as those of the **kotwal, nazir,** commander of the right wing and the commander of the left wing.

Ala-ud-din Bahman Shah divided his kingdom into four divisions, each under a trusted officer called **tarafdar,** i.e., governor. Tarafdar was the head of the provincial government both in civil and military matters. The posts of governors were transferable.

Mahmud Gawan divided each taraf into two parts and thereby there were eight subdivisions called **sarlashkarships.** This was done for more effective control of the tarafs. Each tarafdar held a command of 2,000 horses.

The subdivisions of a **sarlashkarshi** were called parganas which were again divided into villages. Village was the lowest unit of administration.

VIJAYANAGAR EMPIRE

The emergence of the Vijayanagar Empire was the result of Hindu reaction against the Turkish domination of the Deccan. Towards the end of the thirteenth century, that is, on the eve of Alaudin Khalji's invasion of the Deccan, the territories south of the Vindhyas were ruled over by four Hindu dynasties. The Yadavas of Devagiri ruled over whole of western Deccan from the Tapti to the Krishna, the Kakatiyas of Warangal were masters of eastern Deccan. The Hoysalas of Duarasamudra, and the Pandyas of Madura divided between themselves the rest of the peninsula. Economically all these great Hindu kingdoms were well off and the kings possessed immense riches, gold, silver, diamonds and pearls. Agriculture and commerce were in a flourishing state and the cities were beautiful and were centres of trade and culture. Every South Indian prince spent lavishly on temples and buildings.

Clash of interests of the rival dynasties hindered harmonious progress of the country. The Yadavas fought against the Kakatiyas, the Kakatiyas were at war with the Pandyas, the Pandyas fought with the Hoysalas and the Hoysalas against the Yadavas. This internecine quarrels rendered them weak against the Muslim invaders from the north, yet it took three decades to establish any Muslim hold on the south. The hold of the Central Government on the subordinate Hindu kingdoms of the south was lost almost after each conquest, and they paid tributes of Delhi only when it could be enforced.

In any case the triumph of the Muslims over the south was shortlived and when Malik Kafur intrigued to secure supreme power and eventually hastened Alauddin Khalji's death, and usurped power, the state was plunged into chaos. The Hindu kings of the south took advantage of the situation and immediately asserted their independence. But the set-back in imperial interests was only temporary and with the assassination of Malik Kafur within a short time, the south was recovered to the Delhi Sultanate.

The Hindu princes of the south did not rest in peace ; there were repeated attempts at independence and followed by repeated assertion of imperial authority over the south. It was under Muhammad bin Tughluq that the entire peninsula from Tapti to Cape Comorin came under Turkish rule and in 1327 the Sultan decided to transfer his capital from Delhi to Devagiri, renamed by him Daulatabad. The effects of the Turkish invasions were heart-rending for the Hindus. "Their land was ravaged, their accumulated riches were confiscated, and their rulers were humiliated. "Amir Khusrau in his **Khazainul Futuh** records that Malik Kafur destroyed several hoary shrines of the Pandyan kingdom, and plundered their riches."

Extension of the Turkish power in the south while disastrous to the Hindus, was lacking in any attempt at organising a permanent administration. "The incessant clash of arms and mutual misunderstanding gave no opportunity for the evolution of some system of government, which could reconcile the interests of the victors and the vanquished. The rule of Muhammad bin Tughluq was least fitted to hold together the vast areas under one sceptre."

All this had set the stage for a great revolution among the Hindu kingdoms. Barani and Ferishta give some description of the freedom movement of the Hindu princes of the south. Both of them however, gave wrong names to Kapaya Nayaka who was the real leader of the revolt at Telingana. The freedom movement spread westwards to Kampili. Harihara and Bukka, two of the five sons of one Sangama were sent by Muhammad bin Tughluq to quell the revolt. But the arrangement failed miserably. Harihara who had earlier taken to Islam, reverted to his ancestral faith and asserted his independence and laid the foundation of Vijaynagar under the inspiration of Madhava Vidyaranya, a sage and a scholar.

Foundation of Vijayanagar : There are several traditional accounts about the origin of the imperial city of Vijayanagar. Sewell deals extensively on the traditional accounts and accepts the tradition that the origin of Vijayanagar was the result of strenuous efforts of the five sons of one Sangama-Harihara I, Kampa I, Bukka I, Marappa and Mudappa, of whom Harihara I and Bukka I were the most prominent, laid the foundation of Vijayanagar, in 1336, on the southern bank of Tungabhadra facing the fortress of Anegundi.

HARIHARA I (1336-56)

When in 1336 Harihara's coronation was held, his kingdom comprised the region extending from Nellore in the south-east to Dharwar and Badami in the north Karnataka. Vijayanagar was not, however, secure as it was surrounded by powerful neighbours who were inimically disposed towards it. During the reigns of Harihara I and Bukka I most of the Hoysala territories came under the control of Vijayanagar. According to some scholars the two brothers did not assume any imperial title. The conquest of Hoysala kingdom was the most notable military achievement of the reign of Harihara. This conquest involved Harihara I with two other neighbouring kingdoms of the Kadambas on the coast of Konkan and Madura. Kadamba kingdom was annexed to the Vijayanagar territories. But after some initial success Harihara's designs on Madura failed due to the intervention of Bahman Shah of Bahmani kingdom which was a sworn enemy of Vijayanagar since its foundation. The last known date of Harihara I was 1356.

BUKKA I (1356-77)

Immediately on his accession Bukka I had to carry on war on two fronts, he himself fighting against Bahmani Sultan and his valiant son Kumara Kampana against the Sultan of Madura. Kumara Kampana's expedition against Madura and the south was rewarded with great success. Sambhuva Raya of Rajagambhira-rajya was overthrown and one of the Sultans of Madura was killed. Bukka reinstalled the images in the Rajasimheswara temple at Kanchi in 1364 and in Ranganathaswami temple at Srirangam in 1371. According to the **Pandyan Chronicle** "Kampanaduver (Kampana Odeyar), a native of Karnataka, having conquered the Musalmans, took possession of the kingdom. He opened the Siva and Vishnu temples which had been locked up. He opened the god's temple at Madura, and obtained a personal view of the god." Epigrahic evidence also shows that Kampana had cleared the Turkish garrison in the south. The **devadana** lands, that is lands dedicated to Gods were taxed under the Muslim rule but Kampana came on a campaign and destroyed the Turks and established a stable administration and worship in all temples was revived as of old. From records it appears that Kampana's influence extended from Mysore in the north to Ramnad in the south.

In 1374 Bukka I sent at embassy to China. After a fruitful career of more than twenty-two years he died in 1378 (1377?) and was succeeded by his son Harihara II.

HARIHARA II (1378-1404)

Harihara assumed the imperial titles of Maharajadhiraja, Rajaparamesvara etc. His authority was not acknowledged all over his kingdom at the initial stage. There were rebellious outbreaks in Konkan and other parts of the kingdom. "A widespread rebellion broke out in the Tamil country, in which the chiefs of Tundira, Chola and Pandya countries were involved." Harihara, however, succeeded in putting down these rebellions and uniting the Vijayanagar kingdom. His son Virupaksha whom he had appointed viceroy of the Tamil country brought the rebels there under subjection and it is believed that in further extension of his military exploits he invaded Ceylon and exacted tribute from its ruler. Harihara's eldest son Bukka II, in the meantime, had captured Pangal in Telingana. Harihara in his early campaigns had expelled the Musalmans from Goa and brought Kharepatan, Chaul and Dabhol, Trichinopoly and Kanchi within his dominion.

A greater challenge than the internal rebellions that threatened the stability of Harihara's rule came from the Bahmanis. Mujahid Shah, son of Muhammad Shah I, sent an envoy to the court of Harihara demanding abrogation of the treaty of 1365 and recognition of the Tungabhadra as the dividing line between the dominions of the Bahmanis and the king of Vijayanagar. On Harihara's turning down the demand, Mujahid Shah invaded Vijayanagar in 1377. Thus, in fact, Harihara had to ascend the throne amidst clash of arms.

Ferishta's account of the success of the Sultan's army is not confirmed by any other Muslim historian. According to Ferishta on the approach of Mujahid Shah's army near Adoni, Harihara fled and the former laid a siege of Vijayanagar and after some initial success he was ultimately obliged to raise the siege. On his return journey Mujahid Shah tried to take Adoni an important fort which guarded the road to Gulbarga. The siege lasted for nine months but had to be ultimately lifted. While returning to his capital he was assassinated in his camp in 1378. Ferishta's account has not found any credence with the historians although historians agree that Mujahid Shah I's invasion of Vijayanagar was quite probable, but it must have ended in his failure.

Death of Mujahid Shah had left the Bahmani kingdom defenceless and internal dissensions in the royal family made the kingdom all the more vulnerable. Harihara II took advantage of the situation and invaded Konkan and Northern Karnataka and occupied Goa and the neighbouring places such as **sapta Konkanas.** All this must have made him master of the entire west coast of the Deccan.

Now firmly established on the throne, Harihara turned his attention towards the eastern coast. It had been the policy of Vijayanagar since the time of Bukka I to seize the kingdom of Kondavidu. Appointment of Devaraya, son of Harihara marks the renewal of the attempt to annex Kondavidu. Death of the Reddi king Anavema of Kondavidu in 1382 offered Devaraya his opportunity and he at once annexed Addanki and Srisailam districts of the Reddi kingdom of Kondavidu to the Vijayanagar kingdom.

The success of Devaraya brought him in conflict with the Velma kingdom of Rachkonda and its ally the Bahmanis. Devaraya and his brother Immadi fought prolonged wars with the Velma king and Bahmani Sultan Muhammad Shah II and the upshot of the war was that neither the Velma king nor the Bahmani Sultan succeeded to achieve any victory.

Hostilities between Vijayanagar and the Velmas and the Bahmanis were renewed in 1398 taking advantage of the usurpation of the Bahmani throne by Sultan Firuz Tughluq. There are conflicting evidences about the success of the contestants in the war and "on the whole the fact seems to be that in spite of some initial successes gained by Firuz, he was ultimately forced to retreat and lost some territory to the north of the doab" and Harihara II succeeded in defeating the Velma as well as their Bahmani allies near Pangal in Nalgonda district.

Estimate of Harihara II : Harihara II is generally considered to be the greatest sovereign of his dynasty. With the Muslim power of Madura weakened enough to threaten his security and with Delhi Sultan Firuz Tughluq and the Bahmani Sultan Muhammad Shah II both without or very little taste for war Vijayanagar had nothing to worry about his northern frontiers. The north-eastern frontier was also made secure by a matrimonial alliance with the commander-in-chief and brother-in-law of the Reddi king. Harihara II thus had full decades of peace to consolidate his kingdom and to clothe it with imperial dignity. His vast empire was bounded in the eastern, southern and western sides by seas. The find spots of the inscriptions of his reign in Mysore, Dharwar, Kanchipuram, Chingleput and Trichinopoly give us a clear idea of the extent of his empire. He put his sons as viceroys in different parts of his empire.

Harihara II was a worshipper of Virupaksha i.e. Siva, but he was tolerant of other religious sects and patronised besides the Saivas, the Vaishnavas, Jainas and others. His patronage to learning and scholars earned him the epithets of **Rajavyasa** and **Rajavalmiki.** The Veda commentator Sayanacharya was for some time his chief minister and Irugapa, a Jaina and author of **Nanartha Ratnamala** was his general. Harihara was held so high in the estimation of his people that they often made grants and charities for his long life.

DEVARAYA I (1406-22)

Death of Harihara II was followed by a war of succession and on Devaraya I, the third son of Harihara II, emerging victorious he was formally consecrated as king and he ascended the Diamond throne and his coronation was held in 1406 (Now. 7). Devaraya I's reign of sixteen years was consumed in continuous hostilities with the Bahmani Sultans, the Velmas of Rachakonda, and the Reddis of Kondavidu. Despite this array of powerful hostile forces against him Devaraya not only succeeded in holding his own but actually extended his empire by fresh annexations.

Immediately upon the accession of Devaraya to the throne Firuz Shah invaded Vijayanagar. Firuz Shah and the Velmas were traditional allies. Besides Firuz Shah enlisted the support of the Reddis. While the Sultan Firuz invaded the **doab,** the Velmas and the Reddis invaded the eastern provinces of Vijayanagar. According to Ferishta, Firuz Shah marched on Vijayanagar unopposed. Devaraya sued for peace which was settled by cession of the fort of Bankapur, marriage of Devaraya's daughter with the Sultan and payment of much treasures. Nizam-ud-din's account more or less corroborates with that of Ferishta but there is no reference to the marriage of the daughter of Devaraya with the Sultan. Tabataba's account differs from those of Ferishta and Nizam-ud-din. According to him Firuz Shah's campaign was confined to Bhanur and Musalkal, two places situated in the Deodrug taluq in the north-west of Raichur district. In view of the conflicting statements of the Muslim historians it is rather difficult to form a correct opinion about the results of the campaign. Modern historians are of the opinion that the statement that Firuz Shah had marched upon the city of Vijyanagar unopposed is unlikely, nor do they agree with the view that there was a marriage between the Sultan and Devaraya's daughter.

Our information is more reliable with regard to the campaign in the east. The combined forces of the Velmas and the Reddis occupied Pottapi-nadu and Pulugla-nadu in the south-east of the Cuddapah district and held then for seven years when in 1413-14 they were expelled by Devaraya I. The Velmas and the Reddis failed to dislodge Devaraya from Pangal which in his hands was a source of danger to the safety of the Velma kingdom. From the Reddis of Kondavidu Devaraya recovered Udayagiri, and placed it under his son Ramchandra. According to Nuniz Devaraya took Goa, Chaul, Dhabal, Ceylon and all the country of the 'Coromandel'.

the Kondavidu province of Vijayanagar. The Vijayanagar army was expelled from Kondavidu and the important fort of Kondavidu, Vinukonda and Addanki together with territories dependent on them passed into his hands Kumara Hamvira one of Kapilendra's sons was placed on the newly acquired territories as governor.

Hamvira was a capable general and a great warrior and with his son Kumara Kapileswara Mahapatra captured all the important forts on the eastern coast of the Vijayanagar empire Udayagiri, Chandragiri, Padaividu, Kanchi, Valudulampatti-Usavadi, Tiravarur and Trichuropalli fell into the hands of Hamvira. He now prepared to advance upto the Keveri. It became obvious that Kapilendra the Orissa king elated by the success of his son and grandson Hamvira, and Kumara Kapileswara, now attempted to conquer the whole territory of Vijayanagar. He placed his grandson Kapileswar on an extensive area of the Vijayanagar empire which was conquered by himself and his father Hamvira.

But within two years the Orissa forces withdrew from their newly conquered territories for reasons only known to them. No light has yet been thrown on the real reason for which this unusual step was taken by the Orissa king. Except Udayagiri and Kondavidu all other places were lost to him.

Loss of these two strategic forts and the territories dependent on them weakened the empire and incapability on the part of the Vijayanagar king to beat the invaders lowered his prestige among the people. Mallikarjuna did not long outlive the invasion by Orissa and died in 1465. According to tradition Mallikarjuna was done to death by his cousin Virupaksha.

VIRUPAKSHA II (1465-85)

Virupaksha seized the throne through violence but failed to establish himself formally on the throne nor did he succeed in enforcing his authority over the empire which at that time only extended from Gundlakamma to the Kaveri and southern Karnataka. The bulk of the western Andhra districts were under the Saluvas who were virtually independent although seemingly acknowledging Vijayanagar overlordship. On the west coast the Tuluvas and the Konkan nobles, busy in internecine struggle cared little to obey the Vijayanagar king. Thus his authority was confined to Karnataka, parts of western Andhra. But the Diamond throne of Vijayanagar Rajas was in his possession.

The first few years of Virupaksha's reign passed without much events. But after Gajapati Kapilendra's death (1470) Orissa became rather weak. This gave an opportunity to the Bahmani Sultan, now free from the fear of Orissa King, invaded Vijayanagar territory in Konkan. Muhammad Shah III sent Muhammad Gawan against Vijayanagar. Gawan first attacked the king of Khelna and occupied the fort after two years struggle. Next he seized Goa giving Virupaksha little opportunity to take any defensive measure. Loss of Goa was a great blow to Vijayanagar empire for it was the principal port of the empire on the west coast. Virupaksha irreconciled to the loss of Goa made two attempts to recover it but failed. He then made a third attempt with the help of the ruler of Belgaum and the chief of Bankapur. Muhammad Shah and Gawan proceeded against the ruler of Belgaum and with his defeat expedition for recovering Goa collapsed. Yet another attempt was made in 1481 immediately after the execution of Gawan which was followed by confusion in the Bahmani Kingdom. But the invasion was repelled by Yusuf Adil Khan. The final result of the conflict between Muhammad Shah III and Virupaksha led to the loss of the sea board on northern Konkan but the bulk of northern Karnataka as well.

In the meantime the death of Kapilendra, Gajapati ruler of Orissa, threw his country into civil war. But Virupaksha could not take advantage of the opportunity, nor could he recover his prestige and affection of his people.

Ahmad Shah I died in 1436 and was succeeded by his son Ala-ud-din II who inaugurated his reign by declaring war against Vijayanagar. The war went in favour of Ala-ud-din and Devaraya II had to buy peace by surrendering twenty elephants, a considerable sum of money and two hundred females skilled in music and dancing.

Ala-ud-din's brother Muhammad Khan had led the expedition against Vijayanagar. His success turned his head and whetted his ambition. He now thought of revolting against his elder brother in order to seize the throne. He entered into a secret alliance with the king of Vijayanagar and with the assistance of Vijayanagar troops seized Mudkal, Raichur, Sholapur, Bijapur and Naldurg. Ala-ud-din proceeded against his brother defeated him and ultimately pardoned him. Next he sought to punish Vijayanagar king for his participation in the domestic quarrel of the Bahmanis. But the fact remains that there was no major war between the two. "Most probably defeat and conciliation of the rebel prince resulted in the automatic withdrawal of the Vijayanagar army." Ferishta is silent in this regard.

Devaraya's failure to succeed against the Bahmani kingdom led him to seriously consider the question of reorganising his army on the lines of the Bahmani forces. It did not lose his sight that the superiority of the Bahmani army was due to their better horses and archers. Devaraya, therefore, enrolled Musalmans in his service, allotted jagirs to them, built a mosque for their use and kept a copy of the Quran before his throne so that the Musalman horse men and archers might do him obeisance without violation of their religious laws. Soon Devaraya's army comprised two thousand Musalmans and sixty thousand Hindu skilled archers besides eighty thousand horses and two lakhs of foot. Having strengthened his position in this way Devaraya suddenly crossed Tungabhadra (1443) in his attempt to conquer the Bahmani kingdom, took the fort of Mudkal. His two sons laid siege of Raichur and Bankapur. In the three fierce battles that followed Devaraya was victorious in the first, the Musalmans in the second and in the third Devaraya lost his eldest son and his army fled the battlefield in panic and took shelter in the fort of Mudkal. A treaty was signed between the two parties and Devaraya agreed not to molest the Sultan's territories in future and to pay a stipulated amount as annual tribute.

The above account based on Ferishta has been doubted by modern historians. Silence of the Muslim historians about Mudkal, although they have given in details the terms of the treaty between the Bahmani Sultan and Vijayanagar, which was the most important stronghold in the Krishna-Tungabhadra doab, leave us in doubt that Mudkal was left in the possession of Devaraya. Devaraya's suing for peace when Devaraya was leading a victorious campaign against Orissa was rather unlikely, for "having a powerful army flushed with victory in the east coast in reserve, it is absurd to suppose that Devaraya would have sued for peace and concluded a treaty with the Sultan who was not strong enough to retake the fort of Mudkal which belonged to him." According to a Persian epigraph, the boundary of the Sultan's kingdom passed through a village in the present Bijapur district. This leaves us in no doubt that the Sultan's authority did not extend as far south as the Krishna-Tungabhadra doab.

In 1442 Abdur Razzak, an ambassador of Shah Rukh of Persia, arrived in Vijayanagar. According to him Lakkana Dannaik, the diwan and commander in chief of the king led a naval expedition to the frontier of Ceylon. The expedition was successful and the Ceylonese being completely defeated were compelled to pay tribute. Thus Devaraya's power extended over the southern ocean.

According to **Gangadasapratapavilasam** the Gajapati king Kapileswara sustained a defeat at the hands of Devaraya II. Kaileswara or Kapilendra had seized the throne of Orissa in 1434. In 1443 he launched an attack upon the Reddi kingdom of Rajahmundry. Devaraya II intervened and defeated Kapilendra who had to return to his kingdom. This saved the Reddi kingdom from immediate annihilation. Devaraya lived for two years more and died in 1446 after an eventful reign of twenty-five years.

Estimate : Devaraya II was a great monarch, the greatest among the rulers of the Sangama dynasty. In his inscriptions he is called **Gajabetakara** i.e. elephant hunter. He was the master of an extensive empire which extended "from the river Krishna to Ceylon and from the Arabian sea to the Bay of Bengal." According to Nuniz the kings of Ceylon, Quilon, Pegu, Pulicat and Tenasserim paid tribute to him. An inscription found at Nagar confirms Devaraya's levy of tribute on Ceylon. He had one thousand war elephants, and an army of eleven lakh men. Despite his constant engagement with his enemies Devaraya II found time to encourage and patronage men of learning in Sanskrit and vernaculars. He presided over philosophical and literary debates organised by himself. When Srinath succeeded his court poet Durdima in a disputation, he honoured the former with the title of Kavi-Sarvabhauma and "bathed him in gold coins."

From Abdur Razzaq we have an excellent account about the personality, military strength and economic condition of the country of Devaraya II. He remarks "one might seek in vain throughout the whole of Hindusthan, to find a more absolute rai (King). Next to him the Brahmans hold a rank superior to that of all other men." "The city of Vijaynagar is such that the pupil of the eye has never seen a place like it." The jewellers sell publicly in the bazar pearls, rubies, emeralds and diamonds. In this agreeable locality, as well as the King's palace one sees numerous running streams and canals, formed of chiselled stone, polished and smooth." Abdur Razzaq further states that persons of both high rank and of inferior class down to artisans of the bazar wear pearls, or rings studded with pearls.

About the administrative arrangements of Devaraya II Abdur Razzq refers to **dewan Khana** (Council chamber), **daftar Khana** (the archives) **Zorrab Khana** (the mint) and describes the splendour of **mahayyamy** i.e. Mohanawami festival.

VIJAYARAYA II (1446-47) AND MALLIKARJUNA (1446-65)

The political picture of Vijayanagar is rather blurred immediately after the death of Devaraya II. It is usually supposed that Mallikarjuna succeeded Devaraya II on the throne. But there are reasons to believe that Vijayaraya's brother of Devaraya II succeeded him and ruled for a short period as joint ruler with Mallikarjuna. Both literary and epigraphic evidences prove that Vijayaraya II and Mallikarjuna ruled over Vijayanagar simultaneously.

Vijayaraya a reign was particularly noteworthy for two attempts made by him to eradicate ministerial corruption and to establish an honest impartial and efficient administration. It is doubtful if his reform measures produced any permanent result.

From literary and epigraphic evidences, it appears that Mallikarjuna ruled Vijayanagar as a joint ruler initially. It was on Vijayaraya II's death that he became the sole ruler.

Mallikarjuna is referred to in the inscription as Immadi Devaraya III as well as Praudha Devaraya. He also assumed the title of **Gajbetekar.**

Mallikarjuna was rather an incapable and weak ruler and his accession as the sole ruler of Vijayanagar marks the beginning of decline of the Sangama Dynasty.

The rivalry between the Vijayanagar and Orissa for the possession of the coastal Andhra country came to a head under Mallikarjuna and after some initial victories, he suffered defeat which disrupted the Vijayanagar empire.

The Gajapati, King of Orissa and the Sultan of Bahmani Kingdom made a joint attack on Vijayanagar but were defeated.

But Kapilendra Gajapati king of Orissa again invaded the Vijayanagar empire and reduced the Reddi Kingdom of Rajahmundry and sent his forces across the Krishna into

In 1417 Firuz Shah made an unprovoked attack of fort of Nalsgonda belonging to Devaraya. From both Ferishta and Saiyyid Ali we know that the Sultan ultimately met with crushing defeat in 1419. This was mainly because the Velma king had defected and joined hands with Devaraya and Firuz's people "slaughtered without mercy and he was driven back to his country."

The remaining years of Devaraya's reign was peaceful and was undisturbed by wars. He bided his time in the company of learned men whom he patronised. Devaraya occupies a prominent place in the history of the Vijayanagar empire. He was not only a great military organiser but also a great diplomat. He effected a diplomatic revolution by winning over the Velma king from his traditional alliance with the Bahmani Sultans.

Devaraya was the first of his family to recognise the need for organising an efficient cavalry for which purpose he brought horses from Arabia and Persia. He also drafted Turkish bow-men to his army.

Devaraya was an ardent Saivite and was particularly devoted to Goddess Pompa of Hampi-tirtha. He was a patron of learning and men of letters, philosophers, poets and artists, lavished gold coins and pearls on them. "The Pearl Hall of the palace where he honoured the distinguished poets, philosophers and artists by bathing them in showers of gold coins and gems, is immortalised in literature and is still remembered in the Telugu country."

It was during his reign (1420) the Nicolo Conti, an Italian traveller visited his empire. He has left an account of some important social institutions of the country and graphically described the festivities on the New Year's day, holi, dipavali and mahanavami. According to Nicolo Conti "the circumference of the city is sixty miles; its walls are carried up to the mountains and enclose the valleys at their foot, so that its extent is thereby increases. In this city there are estimated to be ninety thousand men fit to bear arms. Their king is more powerful than all other kings of India." Devaraya I died sometime in April, 1422.

DEVARAYA II (1422-46)

Accession of Devaraya II to the throne of Vijayanagar synchronises with that of Ahmad Shah I on the Bahmani throne. Ahmad Shah did not forget the humiliation of Firuz Shah Bahmani at the hands of Devaraya I and immediately on his accession he proceeded to take full revenge on the king of Vijayanagar. He invaded Vijayanagar in December, 1422. At the initial stage of the war Vijayanagar troops penetrated upto Etgir in Gulbarga district, but they suffered defeat at the hands of the Bahmanis due to the desertion of the king of Warangal on the battlefield. To add to the discomfiture of Vijayanagar Bhanudeva IV of Orissa invaded and wrested from Vijayanagar the former territories of the Reddis of Kondavidu. Ferishta's statement that Devaraya II had to sue for peace when Ahmad Shah penetrated into the capital city is not accepted by modern historians. The fact that Ahmad Shah had to shift his capital from Gulbarga to the hilly tract of Bidar is a pointer to the fact that his attempts against Vijayanagar were not successful and transfer of capital to Bidar was considered a measure of security of the coastal areas from possible running over by Vijayanagar. Again mention of the victory of Devaraya II over the Turushkas in the record must have been the victory over Ahmad Shah I in 1423-24. From the same epigraphic record we come to know that Devaraya had won two other victories, one over the Andhras and the other over Orrisa. Devaraya then invaded the Velma ruler for his treachery in aiding Gajapati Bhanudeva king of Orissa in his invasion of coastal Andhra and in the wake of which he was occupying coastal Andhra country for some years. In 1428 Devaraya dislodged the Velmas from the coastal Andhra areas. Devaraya also did not forgive the Velmas, that is the Reddis of Kondavidu for their alliance with Firuz Shah Bahmani, and taking advantage of the weak rule annexed Kondavidu kingdom to Vijayanagar.

Opportunity thus lost was taken by a nobleman of the Saluva dynasty of the Vijayanagar empire, named Narasingha who emerged as the saviour of the empire and the protector of the power and prestige of the Udaynagar Rayas.

Saluva Narasimha son of the Chief of Chandragiri in Chittoor district used the confusion following Mallikarjuna's assassination to assume virtual independence offering lip homage to the rayas of Vijayanagar. Kapilendra's illness and eventual death gave him further opportunity to lead a campaign against Orissa and capturing Udayagiri which opened the coastal Andhra country to him. His progress was, however, checked by invasion by the Chola and the Pandya kings in the Tamil Country.

Narasimha expelled the invaders and chased them upto Rameswaram where he was honoured by the kings of Ceylon and other islands by sending him presents. He then proceeded in south-westernly directions and reached Trivandrum. Narasimha now resumed his campaign against Orissa. He conquered the whole of the coastal Andhra country south of the Krishna and captured Masulipatam and took possession of the fort of Kondavidu (1480). Further Isvara, the Commander-in-Chief of Narasimha defeated the Bahmani Sultan's army in a fierce battle. Muhammad Shah, sent Yusuf Adil Khan and Fakhr-ul-Mulk against Narasimha to recover his prestige which had been lowered by the defeat of his army at the hands of Narasimha and himself marched towards Masulipatam a dependent territory under Narasimha.

The Sultan succeeded in occupying Masulipatam, but the expedition under Yusuf Adil Khan and Fakhr-ul-Mulk failed miserably.

Under his capable command of Isvara Nayaka, Udayagiri, Chingleput, Srirangam, Bonagiri, Chenji, Coimbatore, Salem, Srirangapatanam, Nagamangalam, Bangalore, Anantapura, Cuddapali, were all conquered for Saluva Narasimha. Virupaksha II who was the Vijayanagar king failed to contain Narasimha Saluva, and Portuguese traveller Nuniz observes that he was not good for anything, Virupaksha was murdered by one of his sons in 1485 who renounced his claim to the throne in favour of Praudha Devaraya.

Praudha Devaraya was utterly unfit as a ruler and was not the type of a person that would effectively deal with the powerful and virtually independent vassal as Narasimha. Narasimha now made a bid to seize the Vijayanagar throne. The internal troubles in the Kingdoms of Orissa and of the Bahmanis made the time very opportune. He sent Narasa Nayaka son of his commander-in-Chief Isvara Nayaka to expel Praudha Devaraya from Vijayanagar capital, which he did without opposition, Praudha Devaraya having fled the country. With his flight the Sangama dynasty came to an end and Narasimha entered the capital and held his coronation towards the end of 1485.

SALUVA DYNASTY

NARASIMHA SALUVA (1485-90)

Although Narasimha had captured the throne rather easily, it was, however not so easy to enforce his authority over the captains and chiefs who lent him support for expelling Praudha Devaraya but now refused to submit to Narasimha's yoke.

Narasimha had, therefore, to fight against these chiefs and though apparently succeeded in imposing his authority yet many of the chiefs continued to remain unsubdued. In the meantime Muhammad Shah III, the Bahmani Sultan had died, Narasimha was preoccupied with subjugation of the disobedient chiefs. Taking advantage of the situation king of Orissa Purushottama Gajapati seized coastal Andhra country upto parts of Guntur district and captured the fort of Udayagiri.

Narasimha died early in 1490 after rendering immense service for the recovery of the Vijayanagar empire. His occupation of Vijayanagar throne was more for protecting "the Hindu kingdom, thereby save the Hindu Dharma from the neighbouring Muslim kingdom" than for lust for power. He befriended the Arab merchants, purchased Arabian horses and raised a strong cavalry. He contributed much to the glory of Vijayanagar and made Vijayanagar a nation of warriors and infused fresh vigour into the body politic and saved the empire from destruction.

NARASA NAYAKA (1490-1503)

Saluva Narasimha died leaving two minor sons. Before his death he appointed his minister Narasa Nayaka guardian of his two minor sons as well as the regent of the kingdom during the minority of the two princes. The Minister was also instructed to place one of the two princes on their attainment of majority, whom he would consider best suited, for the throne.

Narasa Nayaka on Narasimha's death placed Timma, the eldest prince on the throne, keeping the reigns of the Government in his own hands.

The task before Narasa Nayaka was by no means easy. The subordinate chiefs and nobles were least willing to acknowledge the supremacy of the sons of Narasimha. To add to this, there were two eternal enemies of Vijayanagar, namely the Bahmani Sultan and the Gajapati ruler of Orissa. But Narasa Nayaka proved equal to the task. He not only subdued Chera, Chola, Pandya and other territories in South India but also defeated the king of Orissa and took Adil Khan a powerful noble of the Bahmanis a prisoner for a time. Prime Minister Qasim Barid of Bahmani kingdom made Sultan Mahmud Shah a tool in his hands. Nobles like Adil Khan and Nizam-ul-Mulk assumed powers of independent rulers. Qasim Barid entered into an alliance with Bahadur Gilani ruler of Konkan and Narasa Nayaka in order to subdue Adil-Khan who had become a little too much overbearing.

Narasa Nayaka, Qasim Barid and Bahadur Gilani made a simultaneous attack on Bijapur. Narasa Nayaka marched into Krishna-Tungabhadra Doab and seized Mudkal and Raichur forts from Adil Khan. The latter soon after made a bid to recover these forts and declared war against Vijayanagar. But Narasa Nayaka signally defeated Adil Khan who took shelter in the fortress of Manava. Narasa Nayaka laid a siege of the fortress and finding the situation difficult, Adil Khan hit upon a stratagem and made a seeming offer for a conference with Narasa Nayaka for peace, the real motive being to kill Narasa Nayaka and his retinue when they would arrive. Adil Khan succeeded in his treacherous plan and while he put many of Narasa Nayak's followers to death, could not touch the persons of Narasa Nayaka and his young master Timma who made good their escape leaving Adil Khan to subdue the doab.

The Orissa Prataparudra also had invaded Vijayanagar but seems to have been beaten back.

Troubles brewed, in the meantime in Vijayanagar empire and nobles and chiefs were out to discredit and drive out Narasa Nayaka from power. One of Narasa Nayaka's enemies put Timma to death and tried to fasten the guilt of murder to Narasa Nayaka. But he cleared himself of the suspicion by placing the younger son of Narasimha on the throne. The younger Prince was Immadi Narasimha. But he soon after his accession went against his benefactor Narasa Nayaka.

Narasa Nayaka left the capital for a time on the pretext of hunting and after organising an army advanced against the capital city. Immadi Narasimha sued for peace and accepted Narasa Nayaka as his protector. Narasa Nayaka held sway over the empire more strongly than ever before and led an expedition against the nobles and chiefs of the south and defeated the Cholas, Pandyas and the Cheras who had asserted their independence on the death of Saluva Narasimha. He also captured Srirangapatam the stronghold of the rebels of western Karnataka. The Hoysala chief who led the rebellion was taken prisoner. Thus Narasa Nayaka's hold on Karnataka and the Tamil country was firmly established.

During the reign of the two sons of Saluva Narasimha, Narasa Nayaka was the real ruler and was called variously as protector, Prime Minister and agent of the king till he sat upon the diamond throne usurping it from Immadi Narasimha. But he kept up appearances. It goes to the credit of Narsa Nayaka that he finished the unfinished task of Saluva Narasimha. He restored the ancient boundaries of the Kingdom by reducing to subjection all the rebel chiefs and lords. He died in 1503 leaving the throne to his son Vira Narasimha.

Narasa Nayaka was a great patron of learning and of men of letters. A number of poets and scholars graced his court. He encouraged Telugu literature and invited Telugu poets to his court. Telugu literature which received patronage from the days of Harihara I and Bukka I, received further impetus from Narasa Nayaka.

VIRA NARASIMHA (1503-09)

Vira Narasimha succeeded his father Narasa Nayaka but he continued to rule as the regent of Immadi Narasimha who had come of age in the meantime. If Narasa Nayaka had kept up only appearances although he usurped the throne, Vira Narasimha had no inclination to keep the dynasty of Saluva Narasimha alive even as a legal fiction. He got Immadi Narasimha assassinated in the fort where he was kept confined, and thereby put an end to the Saluva dynasty.

Vira Narasimha assumed the title of king in 1505. For five years that Vira Narasimha had ruled over Vijayanagar was a period of turmoil. His open assumption of royal title by causing the death of Immadi Narasimha was a signal for widespread rebellion. Vira Narasimha, however, succeeded in subduing most of the rebels. Some of the important rebel chiefs subdued by him, as we know from epigraphic and literary evidences were the chiefs of Advani on the Tungabhadra and those of the Tulu district of the empire. His attempt against Karnataka failed but as he was preparing for a new campaign against Karnataka he fell ill and died.

During the short period of his rule which was mostly consumed in subduing the rebels. Vira Narasimha found time to improve his country and increase the efficiency of his army by introducing a new system of recruitment and training of soldiers. He infused a martial spirit among his people. Welfare of his rayats and alleviation of their distress were very dear to the heart of Vira Narasimha. He abolished marriage-tax which came as a great relief to the common people of his empire. To him belongs the credit of initiating popular reforms in Vijayanagar.

KRISHNADEVARAYA (1509-29)

Vira Narasimha was succeeded by his half-brother Krishnadevaraya on August 8, 1509. Vira Narasimha's success in subduing the rebellious lords and chiefs was not complete and some of them were yet to be put down. Eastern districts of the Vijayanagar Empire were still under the Gajapati king of Orissa and although the Bahmani kingdom existed only in name, yet Yusuf Adil Khan, founder of Bijapur Adil Shahi dynasty was pressing hard on the Vijayanagar boundary, in his attempt to extend his kingdom at the expense of Vijayanagar empire. These were the problems that Krishnadevaraya was faced with at the time of his accession.

Immediately on his accession, Krishnadevaraya found himself involved in a war with Adil Khan of Bijapur as well as with Bahmani Sultan Mahmud Shah. When the combined Muslim army arrived at Dony on the Vijayanagar border, its advance was checked by the Vijayanagar forces. The Muslim forces suffered a crushing defeat; Bahmani Sultan

Mahmud Shah was wounded and Yusuf Adil Khan (Shah) was killed in action. The result of the war was disastrous for the Bahmani Sultan and ruinous to the infant Bijapur state which fell into confusion and disorder.

Krishnadevaraya now invaded the Krishna-Tungabhadra doab and captured Raichur. He next annexed Gulbarga after defeating Barid-i-Mamalik. He pursued Barid upto Bidar and captured the fort. He then reinstated Sultan Mahmud Shah to power in commemoration of which he assumed the title **Yavana-raya-sthapanaacharya.** This was a shrewd diplomatic step, for he sought to weaken the Muslim neighbours by throwing an apple of discord in their midst, for as long as Bahmani rule would continue, there would be no peace among the Muslim rulers of the Deccan.

Krishnadevaraya's next step was against Gangaraja, Palaigar (chief) of Ummatur on the upper Kaveri valley which was regarded as impregnable due to the possession of the two strong forts of Seringapatam and Sivasamudram. For two years Krishnadevaraya's campaign lasted during which the fort of Srirangapatam was destroyed. Gangaraja fled the fort and took shelter in the fort of Sivasamudram which was also besieged by the Vijayanagar forces for long one year. When the situation became desperate Gangaraja in order to escape, left the fort but was drowned in the river Kaveri while attempting to cross it. The fort Sivasamudram also fell into the hands of Krishnadevaraya who dismantled its fortifications.

On his triumphal return to his capital Krishnadevaraya naturally felt bold enough to lead an expedition against the Gajapati ruler of Orissa who had earlier conquered two of the Vijayanagar provinces of Udayagiri and Kondavidu.

Krishnadevaraya's attack of Udayagiri was successful and the Orissa forces unable to hold the fort for long surrendered it and it was lost to them for ever. He now marched against Kondavidu burning and pillaging all that fell on the way. Kondavidu was a strong fortress and did not yield even after three months' prolonged siege by Krishnadevaraya's army. This necessitated the personal presence of Krishnadevaraya for conducting the siege operation. Ultimately the fortress gave in and it also fell into the hands of Krishnadevaraya.

The next campaign was against the fort of Bezwada which also fell into the hands of Krishnadevaraya. This was followed by a march on Kondapalli in the north-west of Bezwada when Gajapati king Prataparudra of Orissa attacked Krishnadevaraya only to be defeated. Kondapalli was captured by Vijayanagar forces. Conquests of Bezwada and Kondapalli opened the gate to Telingana and Vengi which formed parts of the Gajapati kingdom of Orissa. Krishnadevaraya reduced all the fortresses in the Nalgonda and Warangal districts and proceeded towards Rajahmundry. Attempt of the Gajapati king of Orissa to check the progress of Krishnadevaraya towards Rajahmundry, with the help of Shitab Khan of Bhogikula failed and Rajahmundry and Vengi fell into the hands of Krishnadevaraya.

Gajapati ruler was not reconciled to the loss of his territories to Krishnadevaraya and although he had sustained repeated defeats at his hands, he contemplated to recover them. But Krishnadevaraya now decided to conquer Cuttack, the very capital city of the Gajapati king.

According to Rayavachakam, Gajapati king was induced to sue for peace which was concluded in 1518 and which provided for the marriage of Gajapati king's daughter with Kirishnadevaraya who agreed to return all the territories conquered from Orissa. "Thus ended one of the most brilliant episodes in the military history of India in the 16th century."

A new enemy, however, emerged from the Qutb Shahi house of Telingana which now Vijayanagar had to reckon with. Defeat and loss of power and prestige of Orissa in the struggle with Vijayanagar was taken advantage of by Quli Qutb Shah who invaded and took possession of Kondapalli, Ellora and Rajahmundry and compelled the Gajapati king to cede to him the whole of the territories between the mouths of Krishna and Godavari. Elated by this success Qutb Shah advanced towards Vijayanagar only to be beaten back by the Vijayanagar forces.

Krishnadevaraya's war with Bijapur was a prolonged one and Ismail Adil Khan was completely defeated. As a diplomatic move, already referred to, Krishnadevaraya placed the eldest of the sons of Sultan Mahmud Shah Bahman whom Yusuf Adil Khan had kept in confinement in the Gulbarga fort, on his ancestral throne and took two other sons to Vijayanagar where they were granted pension of five thousand **paradaos** to each. Thus he ensured against future troubles from the Muslim rulers of the south as he might use of the three sons of Bahmani Sultan as he would find necessary. With this campaign against Bijapur, Krishnadevaraya's military campaigns came to an end.

Enjoyment of peace was, however, not the destiny of Krishnadevaraya. There was an outbreak of rebellion in the eastern provinces of the empire. Krishnadevaraya already much advanced in age and it was rather late in life that his chief queen bore a son to him named Tirumaladeva-Maharaya. Krishnadevaraya abdicated in favour of his son now about ten years of age and crowned him king, himself assuming the office of the prime minister. But the young king was poisoned to death by Timma Dandanayaka, son of Krishnadevaraya's minister Saluva Timmarasa. Krishnadevaraya put the minister, his son and his brother in prison. Timma Dandanayaka escaped from the prison and went to his cousins who were governors of Kondavidu and Gooty and induced them to raise the standard of rebellion. But Timma Dandanayaka was defeated and captured, his eyes were gouged which led to his death, Timmarasa and his brother were languishing in prison.

Krishnadevaraya had a second son only one and half years old, and a nephew, son of his brother Viranarasimha. But he did not consider them fit for the throne. He chose Achyuta, one of his half-brothers who was in prison, as his successor. Achyuta was set free and on Krishnadevaraya's death in 1529 succeeded to the Diamond Throne of Vijayanagar. The story of the career of Krishnadevaraya will not be complete unless a few words are said about his relations with the Portuguese. Krishnadevaraya maintained a friendly relationship with the Portuguese and purchased Arabian and Persian horses imported by them. There was a brisk trade between Vijayanagar and Portugal during the reign of Krishnadevaraya. Yet Krishnadevaraya spurned the suggestion of the Portuguese governor Alfonso Albuquerque to enter into an alliance with the Portuguese against the Zamorin of Calicut. In fact, when in 1523 the Portuguese conquered the mainland near Goa Krishnadevaraya sent a contingent of army against them under Saluva Timma. The expedition was, however, a failure and perhaps Krishnadevaraya did not put his mind seriously in fighting against the Portuguese. This war with the Portuguese was only a passing phase in the relation between the Portuguese and Vijayanagar and a large number of Portuguese merchants and travellers came to Vijayanagar to seek favour of Krishnadevaraya.

Estimate : Krishnadevaraya was an intrepid soldier and a capable general. He personally led his army in most of his campaigns. He turned the battle even in most desperate circumstances to his favour and won victory. "His triumphant armies entered the capitals of his enemies, and planted boar standard on the battlements of Cuttack, Bidar, Gulbarga and Bijapur." His bravery and skilful management of troops enabled him to overthrow the hostile forces. He commanded not only the obedience of his soldiers but their devotion. His care for the soldiers and his arrangements for those who would be wounded in battles won for him the affection of his army.

In spite of his military preoccupations Krishnadevaraya paid personal attention to civil administration. He himself and his ministers constantly checked and supervised the administration of the country. Maladministration of the provincial government was largely corrected by constant vigilance of the king and his ministers. Protection of the rayats and punishment of the wrong-doers were the basic principles of his administration.

For the development of agriculture, Krishnadevaraya constructed many irrigation tanks and excavated many canals. He brought more lands under cultivation. Abolition of marriage tax came as a great relief to the common people of the country, krishnadevaraya toured his empire every year listening to the complaints of the people and redressing their grievances.

Krishnadevaraya was a great builder and he beautified his new capital at Naglapur by constructing many temples and mansions. Thousand pillared **Mantapas** and **raya-gopurams** seen in South India were mostly built during his reign, he was also a patron of art and learning. He employed famous artists to decorate palaces and temples. His patronage of men of letters brought numerous poets, philosophers and scholars to his court. Krishnadevaraya patronised Sanskrit and South Indian vernaculars, but he favoured Telugu literature most. He was himself a poet and author of **Amuktamalyada** a great poem in Telugu. His court was adorned by **astadiggajas,** i.e., eight literary lumineries. His patronage of Telugu literature contributed much to the development of the language. Krishnadevaraya was a Vaishnava but he respected all Hindu sects alike. He endowed temples with fabulous wealth and the Brahmanas received liberal grants from him. He was the greatest of the South Indian monarchs.

Successors of Krishnadevaraya : Achyutaraya, half-brother of Krishnadevararaya succeeded him, but his accession was challenged by his brother-in-law Rama Raja. Ultimately the threatened civil war was averted by a settlement according to which Rama Raja was given a share in the governance of the country.

Both Prataparudra Gajapati and Ismail Adil Shah invaded Vijayanagar simultaneously with a view to recovering their lost possessions from Vijayanagar. Prataparudra was beaten back but Adil Shah occupied Raichur and Mudkal. To add to Achyuta Raya's discomfiture his minister Saluva Narasimha Nayaka led a rebellion with the help of the king of Travancore. Achyutaraya left Adil Shah alone for the time being and advanced against the rebel minister. The rebellion was crushed and the entire south was brought back to allegiance. In the meantime Ismail Adil Shah died and there was a struggle for the throne between his two sons Mallu and Ibrahim. Achyutaraya took advantage of the situation. Portuguese historian Barros as well as Rajanatha Dindima author of **Achutarayabhyudayam** give us the details of he campaign of Achyutaraya against Mallu Adil Shah who had to sue for peace. Nuniz observes that Raichur doab came under Achyutaraya as a result of this war. Achyutaraya now gave himself up to a life a sloth and luxury and Rama Raja taking this opportunity raised the standard of rebellion. But Achyutaraya's supporters put down this revolt. But Rama Raja kept Achyuta in captivity and sponsored the claims of Sadasiva son of the elder brother of Achyuta.

The disunity in the Vijayanagar empire encouraged Ibrahim Adil Shah who succeeded his brother Mallu Adil Shah, to the Bijapur throne, to march on Vijayanagar and raze Nagalapur to the ground. Rama Raja fled and retired to his jagir. Achyutaraya offered no resistance. But at point of time Burhan Nizam Shah attacked Bijapur which compelled Ibrahim to retreat but he compelled Achyutaraya to hand back Raichur as well as ten lakh gold **pardaos.** The rest of the reign of Achyutaraya saw progressive deterioration of the administration. Selfishness, brutality, violent despotism alienated the people from the government. In the midst of despair Achyutaraya died in 1542.

SALAKARAJU TIRUMALA, THE USURPER

Achyutaraya was succeeded by his son Venkata I but his maternal uncle Tirumala usurped all powers of Government. Queen mother's attempt to free her son from the clutches of her brother Tirumala only led to the murder of the young king. Rama Raja now planned the destruction of Tirumala who invited Ibrahim Adil Shah to his help. But the people resisted this national humiliation and joined hands with Rama Raja and the people feigned loyalty to Tirumala on condition that Ibrahim Adil Shah was asked to go away. This trick worked and Tirumala paid a large amount to Ibrahim as compensation and sent him back. Soon Rama Raja and the people attacked the Vijayanagar capital and Tirumala taken by surprise attempted to defend himself but was beheaded on the spot. Rama Raja placed Sadasiva on the throne in 1543.

SADASIVA (1543-67)

Sadasiva ruled over Vijayanagar from 1543-67 but the real power of the government was exercised by Rama Raja and his two brothers. Sadasiva was reduced to a mere titular head.

Sadasiva's reign was not free from conflict with the Muslim powers. Ibrahim Adil Shah hearing of the internal revolution in Vijayanagar sent Asad Khan to seize the fort of Adoni but the attack was beaten back. But soon after Asad Khan made a surprise attack and compelled Vijayanagar to sue for peace. But Ibrahim Adil Shah broke the terms of peace and with the help of Burhan Nizam of Ahmadnagar attacked and occupied some territories of Vijayanagar. Rama Raja relying not simply on military strength for defence of Vijayanagar, resorted to diplomacy and played the Muslim powers one against the other and by 1552 Ibrahim Adil Shah was completely crushed. Raichur and Mudkal were seized by Rama Raja but Kalyani and Sholapur were occupied by Burhan Nizam Shah.

On the death of Ibrahim Adil Shah his son Ali Adil Shah being pursued by Hussain Nizam Shah son of Burhan Nizam Shah (died in 1553) had to seek asylum in the Vijayanagar court. Rama Raja gave shelter and military support against Hussain Nizam Shah. Ultimately Hussain Nizam Shah was compelled to sign a humiliating peace with Rama Raja in 1559. The ruler of Golconda who always sided with Ahmadnagar has also to sign a similar treaty. For two decades Rama Raja decided the fortunes of the Deccan in every major conflict. But Rama Raja's frequent interference in the quarrels of the Sultans ultimately led to the formation of a "League of the faithful" against him. The combined armies of Golconda, Ahmadnagar, Bidar and Bijapur pitched their camp at Talikota in 1565 and in the battle the Hindu defenders lost the battle. The proud city of Vijayanagar was left defenceless and a victim of revengeful rapacity of the victors. The Sultans left the city in ruins carrying away immense booty after a sojourn of five months.

TIRUMALARAYA (ARAVIDU DYNASTY)

The battle of Talikota did not completely destory the empire of Vijayanagar. "The defeat in the battle simply reduced the empire's military prestige, economic prosperity and the extent of its territorial jurisdiction. The empire itself lingered for nearly a century more." Tirumala made peace with the Sultans surrendering all the places his brother had wrested from them. Son of Tirumala is said to have killed the lawful king. Inscriptions, however, indicate that he lived upto 1576. With the murder of the rightful king, Tuluva Dynasty came to an end and Tirumala now an acknowledged king founded that Aravidu Dynasty of Vijayanagar.

It was no smooth sailing for Tirumala after his formal accession to the throne as an usurper. His authority was not universally obeyed and Muslim rulers were again trying to acquire parts of Vijayanagar. Tirumala divided his empire into three parts, placing one of his three sons in charge of each. His three sons were Sri Ranga, Rama and Venkatapati. Thus relieved from the burden of administration Tirumala turned his full attention to the defence of his country and succeeded in putting down the rebels and warding off external attacks by Musalmans. In 1572 Tirumala died. He was succeeded by Sri Ranga I, his eldest son (1572), who in his turn was succeeded by Venkatapati II (1586).

Under Venkatapati, danger to Vijayanagar did not come from without, but from within. He had to fight incessantly against the rebellious lords and ultimately succeeded in bringing them back to his allegiance.

The latter part of the reign of Venkatapati was faced with two difficult problems, namely Akbar's imperialistic expansion in the south and the advent of the Dutch Traders. Venkatapati took precautionary measures against possible Mughal attack. Father Coutinho, a Jesuit at Venkatapati's court believed that the military preparations were intended "for driving back the army, of Akbar." Akbar and Ibrahim Adil Shah's envoys were waiting at Chandragiri the new capital of Vijayanagar for audience with Venkatapati in 1604 but things did not pass beyond diplomatic stage since Akbar died the following year.

Venkatapati showed much firmness in his dealings with the Portuguese for their hostility towards the Dutch which threatened to create disorder in Vijayanagar. He expelled the Dutch from their settlement Devanapatanam where they were permitted to build a factory and to carry on trade. He received an embassy from Philip III, King of Spain and Portugal, but he did not hesitate to put down unruly Portuguese at St. Thome. The Portuguese expelled the Dutch from Pulicat (1612) but Venkatapati helped them to come back and build a fort named fort Geldria. But the death of Venkatapati in 1614 put an end to further development in the matter of conflict between the Portuguese and the Dutch.

Venkatapati II was the greatest ruler of Aravidu dynasty and was a man of ability and character. He raised the status of his empire and several embassies from foreign countries visited his court, Venkatapati was a devout Vaishnava but he was tolerant of other religions. His court was attended by Jesuit fathers who had complete freedom to preach their religion. Eminent scholars, poets, philosophers graced his court. He was a great patron of the art of painting and engaged two Jesuit painters to paint some masterpieces of Christian theology. Venkatapati left his impress on the pages of history of Vijayanagar and his reign was the last flash of the glory of Vijayanagar before its final extinction.

Sri Ranga, Ramadevaraya, Venkata III who succeeded to the Vijayanagar throne were kings who saw the empie decline gradually.

It was Sri Ranga III who was the last great ruler of the Vijayanagar empire. His reign was consumed in establishing his authority which was challenged from within and without. While the provincial governors were behaving almost like independent rulers, apprehensions were there that the whole of the east coast might fall into the hands of the Muslims.

Jesuit records as well as English and Dutch factory papers show that Sri Ranga III took certain measures for the defence of his empire. He succeeded in defeating the Qutab Shahi Sultan of Golconda which gave his position some stability. But soon after three rebellious lords inflicted a severe defeat on Sri Ranga III. Mir Jumla, general of the Sultan of Golconda and the soldiers of Bijapur made a joint attack of Vijayanagar and Sri Ranga III had to buy peace by payment of a huge indemnity. The rebellious lords were, however, defeated by Muslim forces which compelled them to return to their allegiance to Sri Ranga III. But the prospect of offering a united resistance to Muslim invaders was spoiled by the invitation of Bijapur Sultan by Tirumala Nayaka one of the lords in order to conquer Gingee which was also coveted by the Sultan of Golconda.

But the selfish policy of Tirumala Nayaka spelt the ruin of Vijayanagar and paved the way for foreign domination over the South. Gingee fell into Muslim hands, Mir Jumla carved out a big jagir in the heart of eastern Karnataka, the only remnant of Vijayanagar empire. Sri Ranga III's appeal to the Mughal emperor for protection did not meet with any response.

Sri Ranga III did not, however, give up the hope of recovering his lost empire. He got the support and encouragement from the chief of Mysore and Ikkeri and having made some preparation, was in the wait for a favourable turn of events. This came to him when Mir Jumla quarrelled with his master and left for taking up service under the Mughals, Sri Ranga III seized the opportunity and recovered a considerable part of Karanataka. Vellore also came under his control.

But the jealously and treachery of Tirumala Nayaka who alarmed at the recovery of power and territory by Sri Ranga III, invited the help of Bijapur Sultan. The Sultan of Golconda also took the field against Sri Ranga III of his own. From Thevenot, we learn that the Sultan of Golconda overran Coromandal, and the Bijapur Sultan conquered territories upto Negapatam. After loss of Karnataka Sri Ranga III retired to Belur where he lived till 1678. Collapse of the empire was followed by an ugly scramble for power and territory among the local lords.

Gandeur of Vijayanagar : "The grandeur of the city, the splendour of the buildings, the wealth of the bazars, the volume of trade and the density of population are amply attested by a series of witnesses beginning in the fourteenth century, when Vijayanagar was only a few years old down to the date of its irremediable ruin, and also by survey of the existing remains."

According to Ferishta Vijayanagar rulers were superior in power, wealth and extent of their country to the Bahmani Sultans. Vijayanagar earned immense wealth from trade through the ports on the west coast as well as Goa.

Fortification of the city made it impregnable and construction of a dam in the Tungabhadra supplied water to the city fifteen miles away.

The Italian traveller Nicolo Conti who came to Vijayanagar in 1420, in the reign of Devaraya II thought that the extent of the city's circumference was about 60 miles. He was impressed by the strength of the fortifications of the city. The custom of **sattee** was prevalent and the "king who had 12,000 wives, of whom no less than 2000 to 3000 were required to burn themselves with him when he died."

In 1443 Abdur Razzaq of Herat, who was sent by Sultan Shahrukh, son of Timur to the court of the Zamorin of Calicut, visited Vijayanagar on the request of the king of Vijayanagar himself. He was so much impressed by the grandeur of the city that he observed : "The city in such that eye has not seen nor ear has heard of any place resembling it upon the whole earth. It is so built that it has seven fortified walls, one within the other." He then compares the city of Vijayanagar with his own city of Herat and remarks that the fortress in the centre of others occupied an area ten times greater than the chief market of Herat. By the palace of the king there are four bazars....the tradesmen of each separate guild or craft have their shops close to one another. The jewellers sell their rubies and pearls and diamonds and emeralds openly in the bazar. All inhabitants of the country, whether high or low, even down to the artificers of the bazar wear jewels and gilt ornaments in their ears and around their necks, arm, wrists and fingers."

We have also the account of the Portuguese traveller Dominigos Paes who visited Vijayanagar in 1522 during the reign of Krishnadevaraya, when the empire was at the height of its glory. According to Paes the city was as large as Rome. It was studded with numerous lakes, watercourses and orchards. The city had about 1,00,000 dwelling houses and according to him it was "the best provided city in the world." Paes who went round the enclosure of the Palace saw thirty four streets in it and one room of the palace that he was shown was all or ivory from top to bottom, with flowers and lotuses of ivory. Paes remarked that "it is so rich and beautiful that you would hardly find anywhere another such."

Nuniz, another Portuguese traveller who visited Vijayanagar thirteen years later observes that the king issued no written orders but his orders were noted down by Secretaries as was done at the Mughal court : According to Nuniz the king wore a cap of brocade and was dressed in fine silk cloth. "He was barefooted."

Administration : The raya i.e. the king was assisted by a council of ministers the composition and powers of which varies from time to time. Some of the offices became hereditary and particularly, that of **Pradhani.** In order to prevent concentration of power in the hands of the ministers Krishnadevaraya followed the policy of inducting new men so that control of too powerful ministers might be broken.

Besides the Council, there was a large secretariat as well as officials of royal household. The empire was divided into a few provinces each under a governor who was a member of the royal family and each province was subdivided into divisions each under a Naik or noble who held it on conditions of payment of a specified amount as revenue and of sending a contingent of troops to the emperor when demanded. The Naiks and the provincial governors enjoyed enough liberty of action within their respective territories but they were under the strictest control of the emperor who was an autocrat.

Punishment was extremely severe and as Krishnadevaraya remarked "The king maintains the law (Dhamma) by killing." Nuniz states that "for a thief, whatever theft he commits, however little it be, they forthwith cut off a foot and a hand; and if his theft be great one, he is hanged with a hook under his chin. If a man outrages a respectable woman or a virgin he has the same punishment." The traitors if belonging to the Nobility were impaled alive on a wooden stake thrushed through the belly. Traitors belonging to lower order would get their heads cut off in the market place.

Army : The Vijayanagar rulers maintained a vast army. In times of emergency a million fighting troops including 35,000 cavalry could be put in the field. The standing army, however, comprised one tenth of this number. According to Paes Krishnadevaraya in 1520 assembled for operation 7,03,000 foot and 32,600 horse and 551 elephants. Compared to the Muslim soldiers the Vijayanagar troops, although physically strong and individually brave, were inefficient.

Land Revenue : Vijayanagar kings assessed land revenue according to the nature of the land under cultivation. Assessment varied with reference to whether the land was wet, dry or garden land. According to Nuniz nineteenth of the produce used to be realised as land revenue. This is not, however, borne out by other evidences. The fact remains that the assessment of land revenue was very high. According to Wilks as well as other later writers, there were various vexatious cesses and levies on the peasants and the merchants alike. Heavy toll and city dues exacted from traders, hampered trade.

Condition of the People : The nobles used to live in luxury, but the common people lived a poor life in hovels. The Brahmans were mostly vegetarians but others used animal food freely. Brahmanas were held in high esteem by the authorities.

Paes refers to variety of meat of birds and beasts available in the market. Sheep killed daily were countless and the meat was clean, fat and looked like pork. Pork was also sold. Birds like partridges, quails, doves, pigeons and others were used for meat and were abundant and cheap. Nuniz writes that the kings of Vijayanagar eat all kinds of flesh but not of oxen or cows.

Religion : Some of the Vijayanagar king were devout worshippers of Vishnu. The kings of the Sangama dynasty however, had preference for Siva.

Animal sacrifice, inconsistent with Vaishnavism was performed. Sheep for sale of mutton in the market were killed at the gate of a temple. Blood and heads of the animals were left to the temple.

Literature, Art and Architecture : The Vijayanagar kings patronised Sanskrit and Telugu literature. Sayana the famous commentator of the Vedas was a minister of Harihara II and his brother Madhava Vidyaranya served Bukka II. Krishnadevaraya was himself an author and a liberal patron of Telugu writers. Alasani-Pedda was the poet-laureate of Krishnadevaraya. The tradition of royal patronage of literature was continued throughout the reigns of the kings of Vijayanagar.

The Vijayanagar kings were distinguished builders and they have many strong fortress and great works of irrigation to their credit. The palace of Vijayanagar was noted for its beauty and grandeur. The kings of Vijayanagar evolved a distinct school of architecture and had a large number of sculptors and painters in their service. Although no specimen of Vijayanagar painting has survived, enough of the sculptural remains show the excellent quality of the work. From the Portuguese travellers and Abdur Razzq we know that the painters in the service of the Vijayanagar kings had reached a very high degree of excellence. The basreliefs on the walls of Krishnadevaraya's chapel royal Hazara Rama Swami temple, depicting scenes of Ramayana built in 1513, are still admired.

REFERENCES

A Comprehensive History of India, The Delhi Sultanate : Habib & Nizami

The Delhi Sultanate : Bharatiya Vidyabhavan

The Oxford History of India : V. S. Smith, edited by P. Spear

An Advanced History of India : Majumdar, Roychaudhuri & Datta

Cambridge History of India, Vol. III : Wolseley Haig

8 Bengal Muslim Penetration and Settlement

MUSLIM PENETRATION AND SETTLEMENT

IKHTIYAR-UD-DIN MUḤAMMAD BIN BAKHTIYAR KHALJI (1201-1206)

There has been a good deal of confusion about the date, race and parentage of Muhammad bin Bakhtiyar Khalji. Raverty's theory about the race as well certain dates about Muhammad bin Bakhtiyar Khalji have been found to be incorrect by Sir Jadunath. Similarly R.D. Banerjee's theory that Muhammad bin Bakhtiyar Khalji was not a subordinate officer of Qutbuddin Aibak but held an equal status with the latter directly under the same sovereign at Ghur has been rejected by Sir Jadunath. The dates of Muhammad bin Bakhtiyar are also uncertain.

On the evidence of Taj-ud-maasir as in a Tibetan work, Sir Jadunath states that Muhammad bin Bakhtiyar was a subordinate officer of Aibak, for after the capture of Kalinjar Qutb-ud-din Aibak went to Badayun and on his return Muhammad bin Bakhtiyar waited on him with presents of elephants, jewels and cash. Again the Tibetan source refers to the visit of Sakya Sribhadra a Buddhist scholar of Kashmir to south Bihar in 1200 A.D. and he found Odantapuri and Vikramsila Viharas in ruins due to Turkish invasion and the monks of those Viharas had fled to Jagaddal monastery in Bengal. "This proves that Bengal had not yet been conquered by the Muslims."

From these sources it is found that Muhammad Bakhtiyar advanced towards Bihar and Munghyr in 1197-98, captured by walled city of Hisar in 1199. It was not until 1201 A.D. that he had surprised the city of Nadia.

This is in consonance with Minhaj-us-Siraj's account that "After being honoured by Qutb-ud-din Aibak with a special robe, Bakhtiyar returned and went towards Bihar (Province) and fear of him took a total hold of the hearts of the infidels on all sides of the countries of Lakhnauti, Bihar Bang and Kamrup. After returning from the court of Qutb-ud-din Bakhtiyar conquered Bihar. Raj Lakhmania sent out agents (to Mirzapur?) to find out if the personal appearance of Bakhtiyar agreed with those of the prophesied Turkish destroyer of his kingdom, and these spies reported that it was so. Then the Brahmans and rich traders began to leave Nadia and flee to Sylhet, Bang and Kamrup."

It is interesting to note that the soothsayers of Lakshman Sen prophesied that his kingdom would be destroyed by the Turks. They also gave a description of the Turkish destroyer. As the persons sent by Lakshman Sen to verify if the appearance of the Turkish destroyer really was similar to that dscribed by the soothsayers the Brahmans and many others advised Lakshman to leave the capital to some place of safety. But Lakshman Sen refused to listen to this cowardly advice.

"The year following this (1199-1200) Muhammad Bakhtiyar marched out of Bihar and suddenly entered the city of Nadia." Thus it is clear that the surprise of Nadia took place in 1201 A.D.

According to Minhaj only 18 of Bakhtiyar's horsemen could keep pace with him and the main army fell behind. He reached the palace gate without molesting anyone nor rousing any suspicion and the people imagined that he and his men were merchants and had brought horses for sale. But on their reaching the palace of the Rai Lakshman Sen, Bakhtiyar drew his sword and started an onslaught. "The whole of his treasures, his wives and other females, his domestic servants and his particular attendants were seized." A number of elephants and a vast booty fell into their hands. Lakshman Sen considering resistance impossible left Nadia barefooted by the back door for Sonargaon where he and his descendants ruled for some time more.

Bakhtiyar did not consider Nadia a place fit for the seat of his Government. He selected Lakhnauti on his capital both from political and geographical considerations. It was nearer to his base at Bihar. Bakhtiyar was correct in his decision for Nadia continued to be under Hindu control for decades. He however, consolidated his position both militarily and culturally in those portions of Northern Bengal that were under his occupation. He set up a number of mosques, madrasas, and Shanghas in those parts and established military stations in Nagar in Birbhum, and Devkot and Khutba was read in the name of Muizz-ud-din.

Bakhtiyar led a campaign against Tibet ignoring his possible victories ovef the Hindu principalities within his easy reach. It is suggested by Habib and Nizami that the Khalji spirit of adventure perhaps led Bakhtiyar to attempt at discovering a short route to Turkistan with a view to get uninterrupted supply of men and materials from Turkistan for expansion of his territories in Bengal. It might as well have been his intention to carve out a Kingdom independently of Delhi.

Bakhtiyar's Tibet expedition is rather interesting. According to Minhaj between Lakhnauti and Tibet there were three tribes of people : the Kunch, Mej and Tiharu. The Mej Chief fell into Bakhtiyar's hands and was converted to Islam. This Chief led Bakhtiyar and his army towards Tibet as a guide and on reaching a bridge over a hilly river left. Bakhtiyar crossed it and posted his men on two sides of the bridge in order to guard it till his safe return. The king of Kamrup at this point of time informed Bakhtiyar to wait till the end of the year and promised to help him in conquering the hilly areas. But Bakhtiyar rejected the suggestion and pushed ahead towards the mountains of Tibet. After sixteen days he reached Tibet. "The area was well-populated and well under cultivation. Ultimately the army reached a strong fort and started ravaging the area. The people of the fort as well as the adjoining areas assembled to give battle which started at daybreak and continued till sunset. Many Muslim soldiers fell in the field."

When Bakhtiyar discovered the difficult nature of the hilly terrain and found his soldiers thoroughly exhausted he retreated with his army. To his utter misfortune he found the bridge destroyed making it impossible to cross the hilly river. The king Kamrup surrounded Bakhtiyar and his men while they were preparing to improvise some raft-like things to cross the river. Bakhtiyar's men got drowned. Only one hundred of his horsemen and Bakhtiyar himself some how succeeded in crossing the river. Bakhtiyar some how reached Devkot with his fame and career completely ruined. At Devkot he was assassinated by Ali Mardan (1206).

Sir Jadunath observes that "Malik Ikhtiyar-ud-din Muhammad Bakhtiyar was indeed the maker of the medieval history of Bengal." His career was one of elevation from the slave market to the masnad of Bengal. Bakhtiyar began his life as a soldier of fortune but he excelled many of his contemporaries in soldierly skill, dash, resourcefulness and leadership. "Although a Plebeian by birth and deformed in body, he was a born leader of men, brave to recklessness and generous to a fabulous extent. His weaknesses were born of over-confidence and uninterrupted success." The Government that prevailed during the time of Bakhtiyar was more or less a sort of a clannish feudalism. It is believed that although Bakhtiyar did not assume the title of Sultan, he must have exercised the prerogatives of a Sultan, namely, reciting **Khutba** and striking coins in his own name. Mosques and Madrasas grew up through his beneficence.

ALI MARDAN (1206-07)

Ali Mardan occupied the Masnad of Bengal after assassinating, Ikhtiyar-ud-din Muhammad bin Bakhtiyar Khalji, in August, 1206. He unleashed a reign of terror in 'Lakhnauti'. But hardly the news of the assassination of Bakhtiyar reached Muhammad Shiran Khalji a trusted lieutenant of the former, he reached Devkot in north Bengal to punish Ali Mardan. Ali Mardan was defeated and captured and imprisoned, and the interregnum terminated with the election of Muhammad Shiran as a ruler of Lakhnauti (1207) by the Khalji Amirs.

MUHAMMAD SHIRAN KHALJI (1207-08) : HUSAM-UD-DIN IWAZ (1208-10)

In the meantime Muhammad Ghuri had been assassinated and Qutb-ud-din Aibak enthroned himself as the Sultan of Delhi. Muhammad Shiran found the time very much unsettled and the loyalty of his own Amirs was most uncertain as every one of them thought himself more suitable for the masnad than others. But Muhammad Shiran was man of extraordinary courage and sagacity. He maintained Status Quo within his dominions by confirming each Amir in his own jagir and showed no vindictiveness towards the partisans of Ali Mardan. He also avoided the wrath of Delhi by refraining from assuming any independent title while exercising, in fact, full independence. It is not certain if Muhammad Shiran exercised authority over Bihar.

Muhammad Shiran's peace was broken by Ali Mardan who managed to escape from prison and betook himself to Qutb-ud-din Aibak and instigated him to send an army against Muhammad Shiran. Alibak ordered Que-maz-Rumi, governor of Oudh to march against Lakhnauti. Muhammad Shiran who could not reorganise his army after the disaster of Tibet expedition of Bakhtiyar, found his position totally desperate due to the treachery of Husam-ud-din Iwaz, the premier noble of Lakhnauti. Muhammad Shiran evacuated Devkot and retreated with his army eastward beyond the river Punarbhava. Rumi occupied Devkot and it is not known if he had advanced against the city of Lakhnauti which had become an obscure city after its capture. Now, the position was that the Khalji principality was to be governed from Devkot by a protege of Delhi Sultan. Rumi now inflicted a defeat on Shiran who fled with the Khalji Amirs towards modern Bogra district. Thus ended the gloomy short rule of Izz-ud-din Muhammad Shiran. But there was no attempt on the part of Iwaz to pursue him. Shiran, in all possibility preferred to die a sovereign rather than submit to the vassalage of Delhi. Husam-ud-din Iwaz ruled over the greater part of Lakhnauti as vassal of Delhi Sultan (1208-1210) till Ali Mardan made his reappearance on the scene.

Qutb-ud-din found in Ali Mardan, a Khalji chief from Lakhnauti, a dare-devil soldier who might be put to good use. When Qutb-ud-din proceeded against his adversary Taj-ud-din Yalduz of Ghazni when the latter invaded Punjab, Ali Mardan accompanied him. Ali Mardan followed Qutb-ud-din to Lahore and thence to Ghazni in his triumphal train. But eventually fell a prisoner into the hands of Taj-ud-din who also found Ali Mardan a worthy courtier. But after one year's detention Ali Mardan rejoined Qutb-ud-din. His services and sufferings were recognised and rewarded by Sultan Qutb-ud-din who appointed him viceroy of Lakhnauti. But before his departure for the viceroyalty he must have raised an army of sturdy Turks and appeared on the scene of his viceroyalty in 1210.

Ali Mardan did not encounter any opposition. Iwaz welcomed the Delhi viceroy, Husam-ud-din also ostensibly accepted the rule of the Viceroy, retiring into the background waiting for the favourable turn of events.

Ali Mardan restored political unity of Lakhnauti by subduing the partisans of Muhammad Shiran. His strength lay in his army composed of foreigners who accompanied him from Lahore. The interests of these Turks naturally were agaist those of the Khalji oligarchs who were long domiciled in Bengal. "Owing to the influx of a fresh wave of immigrants the Muslim power in Bengal entered on a new phase of expansion. Hardly Ali Mardan had established his authority in Bengal, his master Sultan Qutb-ud-din Aibak died (1210, Nov.).

True, Muhammad bin Bakhtiyar and Muhammad Shiran had been independent ruler although they did not assume any royal title. But it was Ali Mardan who for the first time assumed the title of Sultan and styled himself as Sultan Ala-ud-din.

INDEPENDENT SULTANATE OF BENGAL

SULTAN ALA-UD-DIN (ALI MARDAN) (1210-13)

The sudden turn of fortune which made Ali Mardan Sultan of Bangal both in name and fact, completely turned his head. Unbridled power, inflow of wealth and all this made sycophants and sanctimonious hypocrites gather round him and he came to fancy that he was the sovereign of the then known Muslim world.

Ala-ud-din was doubtlessly, a soldier of great ability, of dare-devil courage, but he was extremely impolitic, blood-thirsty and of murderous disposition. He engaged his army to kill the greater part of the Khalji Amirs and the Hindus of the surrounding countries were terrified to send him tributes. "He began issuing orders of assignment of different parts of Hindustan, and his tongue uttered empty boastings. Both in public gatherings and open daroar he gave himself the airs of the lord of Khurasan, Ghazni and Ghor, and talked idle non-sense." (Tabakat-i-Nasiri). He even granted investiture for Ghazni, Khurasan and Ispahan to his flatterers and provided them with expenses to travel to those far off jagirs. But his own subjects were groaning under his ruthless tyranny. As a reaction to his tyranny the Khalji Amirs under the leadership of Husam-ud-din Iwaz entered into a conspiracy and killed Sultan Ala-ud-din Ali Mardan (1213). Husam-ud-din was elected by the Khalji Amirs as their ruler. Although there is no direct evidence as to the extent of the dominions ruled over by Ala-ud-din, yet there is no doubt that Bihar to the east of the river Son was annexed by him to Lakhnauti. The country of Lakhnauti under him must have extended in the south as far as the river Ajay, on the east to the river Bhagirathi, a little beyond Devkot in the north, river Karotoya in the east and the river Kosi in the west.

SULTAN GHIYAS-UD-DIN, HUSAM-UD-DIN IWAZ (1213-27)

Husam-ud-din Iwaz assumed the title of Sultan Ghiyas-ud-din. He was a fellow countryman of Bakhtiyar Khalji. In his early life he was an ass driver, but when Mohammad Ghuri conquered Delhi, he like many other adventurers came to India. He joined Bakhtiyar Khalji an equally destitute fortune hunter and by favourable turn of events eventually found himself lodged on the masnad of Bengal.

Ghiyas-ud-din came to the throne as the leader of the discontented Khalji Amirs of Lakhnauti. The initial years of his rule were, therefore, occupied in consolidating his authority in Lakhnauti and to win over the Turkish elements—the supporters of Ali Mardan to his side.

At this point of time Ganga Emperor Anangabhima of Orissa invaded Radh and carved out a portion, Laknor south of Radh. This success of Ganga Emperor damped the spirit of the Muslims for a time and they could not be easily roused to military action by the Sultan. Their religious frenzy had to be stirred by Jalal-ud-din.

Ghiyas-ud-din led an expedition to recover Laknor. The campaign was a prolonged one but ultimately Orissa army had to withdraw to their own territories clearing out of Laknor. According to Minhaj elephants and treasures fell into the hands of Ghiyas-ud-din when the Orissa army left Laknor.

Ghiyas-ud-din after having restored the prestige and morale of the Muslim arms by containing the imperialistic designs of the Ganga emperor of Orissa, pushed his southern frontiers from the bank of the Ajay river to that of the Damodar and the borders of Bishnupur. It is said that Jajnagar ruler paid tribute to Ghiyas-ud-din. But it is thought improbable in as much as Jajnagar was a tributary of Ganga dynasty. It is supposed that Vishnu the ruler of Jajnagar might have paid presents to Ghiyas-ud-din, but there is no evidence to show that he became a feudatory of Ghiyas-ud-din. Likewise, it is said that "Bang, Kamrup and Tirhut" paid tributes to Ghiyas-ud-din. But we have no source of information about Muslim inroads into these countries. But it is doubtless that Ghiyas-ud-din Iwaz made a definite bid for overlordship of Bengal and adjoining provinces by transferring the seat of his government to the city of Gauda-Lakhnauti the possession of which had been symbolic of the sovereignty of eastern India since the days of the Pala Dynasty.

Ghiyas-ud-din soon realised that for a country like river-interesected Bengal boats and foot-soldiers would command superiority over horsemen. The horse could guarantee only six months' security during the year but in rains, boats and footmen were the only reliable defence. Ghiyas-ud-din, therefore, raised a flotilla of war-boats which showed his military farsight.

Ghiyas-ud-din constructed a number of dykes with arched bridges to protect the capital city. He also connected the two frontier cities of Devkot and Laknor (in Birbhum) with the capital city, by an unusually wide and high-embanked Grand Trunk Road which survived the ravages of time and flood down to the close of the nineteenth century.

Under the beneficent yet vigorous rule of Ghiyas-ud-din the kingdom of Lakhnauti and Bihar enjoyed uninterrupted peace for nearly twelve years. The relation of vassalage of Lakhnauti to Delhi Sultanate was severed since the time of Ali Mardan (1211), Ghiyas-ud-din retained that independent status and read Khutba in his own name and struck his own coins, and assumed the title of Sultan. He, however, obtained honours and farman from the Caliph-al-Nasir.

In 1225 Sultan Iltutmish advanced against Ghiyas-ud-din to wrest Bihar and Bengal from him. Ghiyas-ud-din marched from his capital with his army while his war-boats proceeded up the river Ganges. Iltutmish's progress was arrested at some point in Bihar either at Monghyr or Sakrigally-Teliagarhi passes of the Rajmahal Hills. It is said that there was a peace treaty signed between Iltutmish and Ghiyas-ud-din whereby the latter had to pay 80 lakhs and 38 elephants as indemnity and accept the suzerainty to the Delhi Sultan. Ala-ud-din Jani was placed in charge of Bihar by Iltutmish before leaving for Delhi. But hardly Iltutmish had left Bihar Ghiyas-ud-din expelled Ala-ud-din Jani. It is doubtful if Ghiyas-ud-din respected the terms of the treaty with Iltutmish.

While Ghiyas-ud-din was apprehending reprisals from Iltutmish for driving out Ala-ud-din Jani from Bihar, the Delhi Sultan was embroiled in a rebellious situation in Oudh where the Hindu chief Prithu over-ran the whole of the country and killed "hundreds and thousands of Musalmans." Iltutmish sent his son Prince Nasir-ud-din Muhammad against Prithu. Ala-ud-din Jani also joined him. This came as a relief to Ghiyas-ud-din who now thought of conquering "Bang." He advanced east-ward with his army and his river-flotilla, leaving his capital without defence.

As he was advancing Nasir-ud-din made a sudden attack against Ghiyas-ud-din's capital. On hearing the news of this attack Ghiyas-ud-din rode back with as many troops as could accompany him. But the enemy had in the meantime entered the city and surprised the fortress of Basankot. But undaunted Ghiyas-ud-din fought a pitched battle outside his capital with the superior cavalry of Nasir-ud-din. The inevitable result was his defeat and capture with his men at the hands of his enemies who beheaded him and his men forthwith (1227, March).

Fairly long period of fourteen years that Ghiyas-ud-din ruled over Lakhnauti was pleasing epoch of peace and prosperity for his kingdom. Although he had begun his life as an ass driver, he proved a liberal patron of fine arts and learning. The news of his generosity and piety travelled beyond Hindukush and tempted Islamic learners to Lakhnauti. After the nightmarish reign of Ali Mardan, the rule of Ghiyas-ud-din came as a blessing of Almighty. On a later occasion when Iltutmish visited Lakhnauti, he showed respect to the memory of Ghiyas-ud-din.

"Sultan Ghiyas-ud-din in his exterior and interior graces was every inch a Padshah, just, benevolent and wise." One mistake that cost him his throne and life was his proceeding against 'Bang' leaving his capital defenceless. All the same he gave battle to the enemy and died a noble martyr to liberty. Ghiyas-ud-din was the first independent Sultan of Bengal whose coins have been found. But despite the fact that he was a great patron of architecture and the founder of several, benevolent institutions, no inscription of his time has come to light till now.

In absence of epigraphic evidence it is difficult to define the boundaries of the kingdom of Lakhnauti at the time of Ghiyas-ud-din's death. Within Bengal proper the Sultanate of Ghiyas-ud-din comprised Sarkars Lakhnauti, Purniah, Tajpur, Panjrah, Ghoraghat, Barbakabad, western part of Bazuha, (i.e. portions of Bogra and Rajshahi) parts of Sulaimanabad (i.e. Burdwan). Ghiyas-ud-din annexed South Bihar pushed his frontier upto the mouth of Gandak in South Bihar. It may be pointed out that the whole of Bengal was never conquered or even visited by Muslim army during the pre-Mughal period.

MAMLUK RULE IN BENGAL DURING ILTUTMISH'S SULTANATE (1227-87)

Sixty years following the death of Ghiyas-ud-din (1227) saw the rule of as many as fifteen chiefs over Lakhnauti and ten of them were Mamluks of the court of the Delhi Sultan. These Mamluks belonged to various Central Asian nationalities, such as Khitai Turk, Qipchaq and Uzbeg who were sold into slavery in early life but rose into the position of powerful Maliks before their appointment as governors of Bengal. Lakhnauti court became a copy of the court of the Delhi Sultan, in grandeur and magnificence as well as in administration.

The history of this long period of sixty years is one of unprecedented internal dissensions, usurpations and murders which the court of Delhi after Iltutmish's death could not punish or control. The governors of Oudh, Bihar, Kanauj and Kara-Manikpur became virtually independent. Even though Gaur-Lakhnauti lost independence to Delhi, it retained its status as a kingdom and its possession, practically made the possessor lord of the east. It was the political maxim that whosoever could occupy the throne by killing or ousting the reigning ruler must be acknowledged as the legitimate master. The result was frequent revolutions in the capital leading to changes of rulers. The Mamluks would show passive loyality to the Delhi throne, ruling in virtual independence. One of the most notable feature was that this period saw a rapprochement between the Muslim conquerers and the Hindu subjects, as a result of which the exodus of the upper class Hindus on a large scale from the Muslim territory stopped. "The Muslim rulers had no internal trouble with regard to their Hindu subjects even when the Hindus of Orissa threatened the capital with a siege." But the fact remains during this period the Muslim power of Lakhnauti was in relative decay in comparison with the Hindu powers in East Bengal and Kamrup. With the power of the Sena kings on the wane, part of East Bengal and South Bengal passed to a powerful Kayastha ruling house under Dasaratha-Danuja-Madhava of Chandradvipa i.e. modern Barisal district. Besides Chandradvipa, raya of Orissa (the Gangas), proved to be a menace to the power of Lakhnauti.

NASIR-UD-DIN MAHMUD (1227-29)

Prince Nasir-ud-din Mahmud who had defeated and killed Ghiyas-ud-din, united the provinces of Oudh and Bengal under one rule and shifted his residence to Lakhnauti, and distributed the accumulated treasures of Ghiyas-ud-din among the ulemas of Delhi. Sultan Iltutmish who had received **Khilat** from Caliph al-Mustanasir-Billah, sent a portion of the same, namely, a red umbrella and a red canopy of state as also the lofty title of **Malik-us-Sharq** i.e. Lord of the East for Nasir-ud-din. But Prince Nasir-ud-din died within a few days of the receipt of the honours. "The dead body of the Prince was taken to Delhi where it was buried and a mausoleum built on it, is known as Sultan Ghazi's **maqbara.**

IKHTIYAR-UD-DIN BALKA KHALJI (1229-30)

Hardly Nasir-ud-din breathed his last, Malik Ikhtiyar-ud-din Balka Khalji a trusted follower of Ghiyas-ud-din Iwaz Khalji expelled the imperial troops from Bengal and began to rule over Bengal as an independent king, for a period of one and half years during which he was not, however, distrubed by Sultan Iltutmish. A coin of the rebel chief Ikhtiyar-ud-din Balka reveals that he assumed the title of Daulat Shah Bin Maudud, but the coin also bears the name of the Delhi Sultan. Towards the end of 1230 Iltutmish advanced against Balka who met the imperial forces in an engagement but was defeated and captured. Under orders of the Sultan he was beheaded. Iltutmish placed Malik Ala-ud-din Jani, Governor of Bihar in charge of Bengal and the vacant governorship of Bihar was given to Malik Saif-ud-din Aibak.

MALIK ALA-UD-DIN JANI (1231-32)

Ala-ud-din Jani was a Shah-Zadah of Turkistan who had fled his country due to the Mongol menace. His demeanour his princely ability and administrative efficiency were proofs of his royal blood. We have no information about his activities as governor of Bengal for a short time. For reasons, not known, he was removed from his post and Malik Saif-ud-din Aibak governor of Bihar was appointed Governor of Bengal. Governorship of Bihar was given to Tughral-Tughan Khan governor of Badaun.

SAIF-UD-DIN AIBAK (1232-35)

Saif-ud-din was a Tartar by origin. He possessed all the noble qualities of his race and was one of the front-ranking Maliks of his time. Saif-ud-din rules over Bengal for three years with great efficiency and although his attempt at conquering Bang did not succeed, he captured some elephants which he sent to Iltutmish as present. The Sultan much pleased with Aibak for his presents and honoured him with the title **Yughan-tat.** Sultan Iltutmish died in 1236 (April 29) which was a signal for the rise of the forces of disorder and indiscipline all over Hindustan. According to Riyaz-ud-Salatin Saif-ud-din Aibak was poisoned to death soon after the death of Iltutmish.

Death of Iltutmish followed by that of Saif-ud-din Aibak, governor of Bengal, threw Bengal into disorder. The situation was taken advantage of by Aor Khan Aibak a Turk of great daring and impetuosity who seized power of Lakhnauti.

AOR KHAN AIBAK (1236)

Aor Khan Aibak's usurpation of power at Lakhnauti was challenged by Tughral-Tughan Khan, governor of Bihar who demanded surrender of the province of Lakhnauti, from Aor Khan. Failure of Aor Khan to surrender the province made Tughral Khan to lead an expedition against him to enforce his claim. In the battle that was fought between Aor Khan and Tughral Khan in the place between the fortress Baskot and Lakhnauti, Aor Khan lost his life as an arrow from Tughral Khan pierced through him. "The partisans of the vanquished chief evacuated the capital and Tughral-Tughan became the master of both the wings of the Muslim territory, Radha and Varind, in addition to his own province of Bihar."

TUGHRAL TUGHAN KHAN (1236-45)

Tughral Khan was also a Turkish Mamluk trained in the royal household of Sultan Iltutmish. He began his career as a cup-bearer, **Saqi-i-Khans,** of Iltutmish. His promotion to the post of the custodian of the royal pen and ink (sar-dawat-dar) brought him to grief. For he lost the bejewelled pen of the Sultan and got a round beating for the offence and demoted to a post in the royal kitchen. But Tughral regained his master's confidence and was promoted to the post of Amir-i-Akhur, i.e. in charge of the royal stable. Minhaj-us-Siraj speaks highly of the personal qualities of Tughral. "He was adorned with all sorts of humanity and sagacity, and graced with many virtues and noble qualities; and liberality, generosity and power of winning men's hearts, he had no equal." Even after making allowances for the possible exaggeration, for Minhaj was bestowed by Tughral with many favours, it can be safely accepted that Tughral was far superior to the contemporary Maliks whose selfishness and tyranny made people suffer terribly under their rule.

Tughral Tughan Khan ruled over Bengal and Bihar for nearly nine years in virtual independence. But he obtained formal recognition of his authority from Sultana Raziyah. He received from her the insignia of office—a red canopy and standards in return for his protestations of loyalty to the Sultana and the rich presents that he had sent her through his personal envoy. Tughral Tughan kept himself aloof from the court politics at Delhi and would read **Khutba** and strike coins in the name of the member of Iltutmish's family whoever might happen to occupy the Delhi throne. He kept every Delhi Sultan pleased by sending presents after his accession.

Tughral now launched upon a career of conquest. He began with a successful campaign against Tirhut which resulted in acquisition of rich booty but no submission. Tughral Tughan was particularly mindful of reorganising his army and navy. While he raised a large number of horse and infantry, he also built a flotilla of warboats. It is rather interesting to find that he did not use his military strength to extend his dominions within Bengal by occupying the nearby Hindu rulers' kingdoms, but conserved his energy for trial of strength with his fellow Mamluks of Oudh, Kara-Manikpur, and Ganga-Jamuna doab in order to make himself the defacto sovereign of eastern India. It is said that his Syrian minister Baha-ud-din Hilal instigated him to this ambitious scheme. That Tughral Tughan was a highly ambitious person can easily be understood from his adoption of high-sounding title to be found in his inscription discovered at Bihar. **Majlis-i-Ala Ghiyas-al-Islam wa al-Musalmain Mughis-al Muluk wa al-Salatin Abi-al-Fatha Tughral-al-Sultani.**

In 1242 Tughral advanced towards Bihar by river route and without any opposition succeeded in proceeding in a victorious march through Chunar, Benaras, Allahabad and Kara. Ala-ud-din Mahmud Shah was the Sultan at Delhi. Tughral obtained Khilat from him (1243) an umbrella and a red canopy of state. But soon after his triumphant return to Lakhnauti Narasimhadeva king of Orissa led an expedition into Radha and the frontiers of Vanga. Narasimhadeva took advantage of the time consumed in the withdrawal of the army and the fleet from Lakhnauti to distant places like Kara, Allahabad etc. The result was that "The Muslims, sustained an overthrow, and a great number of those holy warriors attained martyrdom."

Situation at Lakhnauti was also very critical. Tughral sent Sharf-ul-Mulk and Jalal-ud-din Kashani to Delhi to seek military assistance. Sultan Ala-ud-din Mas'ud Shah ordered Malik Qara-Qash Khan governor of Kara-Manikpur and Malik Tamar Khan of Oudh to at once proceed to "exterminate the infidels of Jajnagar" (Orissa). The Orissa King Narasimhadeva, in the meantime, had occupied Laknor and was advancing towards Lakhnauti. He advanced upto Rajmahal Hills but finding the combined forces of Kara-Manikpur and Oudh arrayed against him he fell back and retreated. Tughral Tughan wanted the forces of Qara-Qash Khan and Tamar Khan to return to their places. But Tughral had to share the unhappy fate of a prince that calls more powerful ally for military assistance.

Tamar Khan now contemplating to dispossess Tughral from Bengal laid seige of Lakhnauti and fightings between the forces of Tamar and Tughral continued. One day when after an engagement both sides were busy in taking their mid-day meal, Tamar Khan surprised Tughral Tughan who was left with few troopers with him in the camp near the gates of his city. Absolutely unprepared for the attack Tughral saved himself by fight within the city.

Through the good offices of Minhaj-us-Siraj negotiations were opened between the two Khans and Tughral was allowed to leave his city unmolested "with his treasures, elephants and followers", giving up Lakhnauti and Bihar to Tamar Khan. Tughral left for the imperial court with his Amirs, Malik Qara-Qash, Minhaj, Taj-ud-din etc. and reached there on July 11, 1245'.

Sultan Ala-ud-din Masud was too weak to punish Malik Tamar Khan and it was not until Prince Nasir-ud-din Mahmud II occupied the Delhi throne that some relief was given to Tughral. He was appointed governor of Oudh, the province over which Malik Tamar himself was also the governor. Tughral reached Oudh to make good his claim but he was removed by death before he could do anything.

Malik Tamar Khan was also not destined to enjoy his usurped rule for more than two years and by a divine coincidence died on the same night (March 9, 1247) that Tughral died in Oudh.

JALAL-UD-DIN MASUD JANI (1247-51)

On the death of the usurper Tamar Khan Jalal-ud-din Jani was appointed governor of Bengal and Bihar by the imperial court. He ruled for about four years assuming the high-sounding title **Malik-us-Sharq.** Although he acknowledged the supremacy of the Delhi Sultanate, he assumed the title of **Shah** also.

SULTAN MUGHIS-UD-DIN YUZBAK (1251)

Ikhtiyar-ud-din Yuzbak (later Mughis-ud-din Yuzbak) governor of oudh, was transferred to the governorship of Bengal and Bihar. He was a disloyal, habitual rebel and twice he revolted against Sultan Nasir-ud-din but Ulugh Khan Balban secured his pardon twice. As Minhaj puts it "rashness and imperiousness were implanted in his nature and constitution. Ikhtiyar-ud-din was, however, a man of great ability both as a soldier and a ruler. He aimed at retrieving the prestige of the Turkish arms. He led an expedition to Radha but a very valiant chief of the Orissa king Narasimhadeva, who was also latter's son-in-law has occupied the north-eastern corner of the Hooghly district and made Madaran his capital. In the three battles that were fought during the expedition, Ikhtiyar-ud-din was signally defeated. He implored military assistance from Delhi in vain. But he was not to be daunted. He made another attack on Madaran and this time fortune smiled on him and he succeeded in capturing it. Gradually the whole of Radha came under his sway. Ikhtiyar-ud-din Yuzbak now rebelled against Delhi for the third time and declared himself independent assuming the title of Sultan Mughis-ud-din Yuzbak.

Next Mughis-ud-din conquered Oudh, thus making him sovereign over Bengal, Bihar and Oudh. In 1257 the imperial court was embroiled in a struggle of powerful nobles. This gave Mughis his opportunity. He proceeded on his expedition against Kamrup which was an unknown land to the Turks except only the bordering areas. He advanced with his army through Ghoraghat in modern Rangpur district, and Goalpara. The king of Kamrup offered on resistance to Sultan Mughis and fled his capital. He sent proposals for paying tribute to Mughis-ud-din. Mughis-ud-din in the flush of success refused the offer. While Mughis-ud-din and his army were staying in kamrup the rains set in which made departure difficult. The Hindu subjects of the king of Kamrup laid an economic siege of Kamrup stopping all ways through which supply of food and other requirements of the army could reach. Supply of fodder for the horses was also stopped. When Mughis ud-din and his men were in dire distress the Hindu subjects of the king of Kamrup took arms against them and in a desperate bid to leave Kamrup when Mughis-ud-din and his men began to flee the city they were attacked by the Hindu subjects of Kamrup king. While fighting his way back Mughis-ud-din was fatally struck by an arrow in his breast and finding that death was approaching he surrendered with his army and his own family who were with him, to the king of Kamrup. As Sultan Mughis breathed his last (July, 1257) Bengal reverted to its allegeance to the Delhi Sultanate.

RULERS OF BENGAL BETWEEN 1257 AND 1268

Mughis-ud-din's rashness brought the disaster on the Turkish soldiery and broke the spell of the invincibility of the Turkish arms. The Mamluk rulers that ruled Bengal during the period from 1257-1268 were not of much importance either from the point of view of personality or that of administrative efficiency.

Among these rulers the names of Izz-ud-din Bolkan-i-Yuzbaki, Malik Taj-ud-din Arslan Khan, Tatar Khan etc. ruled over Bengal in virtual independence.

MUGHIS-UD-DIN TUGHRAL KHAN (1268-81)

Mughis-ud-din Tughral Khan was the last and the greatest of the Mamluk Maliks that ruled over Bengal. He was originally a household slave who rose into the position of Bengal governor during the reign of Sultan Ghiyas-ud-din Balban. All the characteristic virtues of a Turk, namely, rackless bravery, boundless ambition and resourcefulness were abundant in his character. Mughis-ud-din Tughral Khan was first appointed a **naib** i.e. deputy of Bengal Governor Amir Khan who was also governor of Oudh. As Amin Khan had to look after the governorship of Oudh, which was his original appointment, the affairs of Bengal were largely left into the hands of Mughis-ud-din, his deputy. Mughis-ud-din Tughral Khan was a soldier of great ability and also an efficient administrator. He extended the boundary of Lakhnauti well within East Bengal and Built a fort named after himself Qila-Tughral at a place twentyfive miles from Dacca.

Tughral's aggressions were not confined to East Bengal, he also perhaps extended the boundary of the Muslim dominion in the Radha tract and carried raids into the territory of Jajnagar (Orissa) whose northern boundary extended from Chotanagpur to the delta of the Bhagirathi river including portions of Birbhum, Bankura and Burdwan districts, and western half of Hooghly district. Tughral's raid into Jajnagar brought him immense booty in elephants and treasures. But Tughral did not care to send to the imperial court the accoustomed share of one-fifth of the booty.

Sultan Ghiyas-ud-din Balban preoccupied with the Mongol menace could not turn his attention to Bengal. When on the occasion of a Mongol invasion he betook himself to Lahore and fell sick, rumour was afoot that the Sultan was dead, Tughral Khan took advantage of this situation and thinking that he had no obligation towards the Delhi Sultanate, absolved himself of his allegeance to Delhi. Amir Khan who was the governor of Oudh and was also placed in charge of Bengal where Tughral was a naib i.e. deputy governor, at once sought to put down Tughral Khan. In the hostilities that began Amir Khan was defeated in a battle outside Lakhnauti.

From **Tarikh-i-Mubarakshahi** we learn that Sultan Balban kept a diplomative silence during his illness and on his recovery asked Tughral to celebrate the Sultan's recovery in a befitting manner. Tughral was in no mood to retreat to the position of surveillance and replied by reading Khutba in his own name and assuming the title Sultan Mughis-ud-din. He made his court a rival of the imperial court at Delhi in grandeur and magnificence. "He was more popular with the people and better served by them than Sultan Balban who was more feared than loved by his subjects." According to Barni Tughral Khan "was profuse in his liberality ; so the people of the city (of Delhi), who had been there, and also the inhabitants of that place (Lakhnawati) become very friendly to him. The troops and the citizens having shaken off all of the Balbani chastisement, joined Tughral heart and soul." On the authority of Barni we learn that Tughral Khan made a gift of five maunds of gold for the maintenance of an establishment of **Darwishes** in Bengal. His kingly virtues and liberality made him loved and respected by both Hindus and Muslims alike.

Sultan Balban when he came to know of Tughral's assumption of sovereignty in Bengal "lost his sleep and appetite." The Delhi Sultan at that time had no standing army and was obliged to depend on feudal and provincial levies. In 1278 an army composed of provincial levies marched against Tughral but after it had crossed the river Sarju on its way to Tirhut its progress was checked by Tughral's forces which although weak in cavalry, was numerically superior to the imperial army.

The two armies remained encamped facing each other for a pretty long time which was used by Tughral in winning over some of the officers of the imperial army by payment of money. In the battle that eventually took place the army under Malik Turmati, governor of Oudh was miserably defeated ; some of his men fearing the terrible punishment that would come upon them from Sultan Balban preferred to accompany Tughral to Lakhnauti. According to **Futuh-us-Salatin** Sultan Balban got Turmati gibetted in the gateway of Oudh.

Next expedition against Tughral was sent under the next governor of Oudh who was also defeated by Tughral. It is said Balban also ordered the defeated governor who commanded the army against Tughral to death. Now Balban had no other alternative but to take the field against Tughral personally. Bengal compaign necessitated three years' absence of Balban from the capital. One year was consumed in making the preparation and two years in actual campaign. Balban placed the imperial administration in charge of Malik-ul-Umara, the Kotwal of Delhi and required his younger son Bughra Khan to leave the charge of Samana and Sunam and to follow up the expeditionary force. According to Barani Sultan's expeditionary force comprised two lakhs men including cavalry, infantry, paiks (i.e. Hindu footmen), Dhanaks etc. To this two lakhs was added one lakh that accompanied Bughra Khan. Such a huge army never assembled under the banner of any Muslim emperor other than that of Muhammad bin Tughluq when he made a project for conquest of Khorasan. Needless to say Bengal was likely to be crushed under the sheer wight of numbers.

Tughral stealthily watched the crossing of the river Sarju by the imperial army from a fleet at the mouth of the river and then sailed back to Lakhnauti. In the meantime rains set in, the Balban's army was slow in proceeding through mud and water. Tughral thinking defence of the city impossible against a force so vast, evacuated the city of Lakhnauti with more respectable section of the civil population to escape from the barbarous cruelty of the Sultan. He took the road to Jajnagar.

Balban reached Lakhnauti, stayed there till the end of the rains and left for Delhi in September, 1280 leaving Hisham-ud-din as Commandant of Lakhnauti. Balban led two more campaign against Tughral one in the winter of 1280 and another after the rains of 1281. In 1281 expedition his army advanced far into East Bengal very near to Qila-i-Tughral. Tughral's march towards Jajnagar in 1279 was "a mere bluff" to divert the attention of Balban from the fort of Narkila where his family was staying. In 1281 again Tughral gave Balban slip.

According to Barani, Balban declared in public that "I have put half the empire of Delhi at stake for the pursuit of Tughral ; if he would sit down on sea, I will pursue him." This implacable resolve of the Sultan must have been born of his failure to touch Tughral and also perhaps of his realisation of his possible escape by boats into the sea if necessary.

At this point of time Balban entered into an agreement with Rai Danuj of Sonargaon according to which Rai Danuj undertook to watch the Brahamputra and the Padma down to Narkila as also other river ways to prevent Tughral's escape when the Sultan would march upon the stronghold of Tughral. Tughral had in the meantime left Narkila suspecting that the enemy got information of his hideout. Tughral successfully baffled the Sultan till now keeping his movements secret. One day a few merchants were found to return to their village. Suspecting that they might know the whereabouts to Tughral were caught hold of by some scouts of the imperial forces. Two of the merchants were at once beheaded, and being thus terrified others revealed the place where Tughral and his army were encamping.

This was followed by Malik Sher-Andaz and his desperadoes' stealthy march on the camp of Tughral who was found drinking while his horses were grazing and elephants kept tied to trees. They attacked Tughral, who puzzled by the surprise attack thought that the entire army of the Sultan was upon him, fell into the nearby river to swim across in a bid to escape but was struck by an arrow from an enemy and another cut off his head.

Thus came to an end the stormy career of Sultan Mughis-ud-din Tughral whose achievements both as a soldier, strategist and a ruler the contemporaries admired and the posterity must as well admire.

Balban stayed at Lakhnauti for some time during which he reorganised the administration and put his youngest son Bughra Khan on the masnad as governor of Bengal granting him all insignia of royalty.

One day in a private meeting Balban administered an oath to his son Bughra Khan that he should thereafter exert himself in conquering Diyar-i-Bengal and establishing his authority there firmly, not to drink wine or idle away his time in childish amusement.

Balban exhorted his son : "Remember my son what amount of blood I have drunk in subduing **Iqlim-i-Lakhnawati** and **Arsh-i-Bangala** (Satgaon region) for the sake of the durability of the government of this country, I have acted like a Pharaoh and hanged people from gallows....But I know as soon as I shall travel away five or six stages, from Lakhnauti in the direction of Delhi, you will plunge yourself in voluptuous pleasures and merriment."

BUGHRA KHAN (1281-1300)

Prince Nasir-ud-din Mahmud Bughra Khan, youngest son of Sultan Balban was appointed viceroy of Bengal after the death to Tughral. There was a note of despair in the advice that Balban had administered to his son Bughra Khan and he made no secret that despite his advice, Bughra Khan would act in its full disregard. "I know" wrote Balban "that whatever principles of government I may enforce on this son of mine, he through his devotion to pleasure, will disregard them."

Bughra Khan ruled over Bengal as viceroy, for six years from 1281-87 during which he lived a care-free life of pleasure. But his capable lieutenants true to Balban's advice to his son Bughra Khan, were carrying out the conquests of Satgaon and Sonargaon which had been only partially conquered before. As Balban felt that his death was nearing he sent for Bughra Khan so that he might assume the imperial robe on his death, the eldest son Muhammad having been killed during a Mongol raid. Bughra Khan preferred to remain the viceroy of Bengal with all its pleasures to the prospect of an imperial throne and stealthily left for Bengal. Balban died in July, 1287 having settled the succession on his minor grandson Kai-Khusru. But the wazir, Nizam-ud-din set aside Kai-Khusru and placed Kaiqubad, son of Bughra Khan on the imperial throne with the ulterior motive of usurping the government.

Bughra Khan after observing a week's mouring of his father's death assumed full independence under the title Sultan Nasir-ud-din (Sept. 1287). The crafty wazir Nizam-ud-din at Delhi induced the young Sultan of 18 years who had been brought up by his grandfather in a puritanic atmosphere, shielding him from the prevalent vices, to give himself up to voluptuous pleasures and wine. This was done to reduce him to a puppet in order to make himself (wazir) the real master of the State. Bughra Khan wrote a series of letters to his son to mend his ways and when his advice proved unavailing he himself marched against Delhi.

In the plains of Ajodhya father and son met, and Kaiqubad sent his own son Kaimurs, a baby in arms with his minister to Nasir-ud-din (Bughra Khan). At the sight of his grandson Nasir-ud-din forgot himself, fondled the baby prince without noticing anything around. Sultan Nasir-ud-din wanted to see his son Kaiqubad. Crafty Nizam-ud-din set certain pre-conditions to the interview of Sultan Nasir-ud-din Bughra Khan with his son Sultan Kaiqubad. When Nasir-ud-din reached the camp of the Delhi emperor by boat Kaiqubad was seated on the imperial **masnad** set up in the camp, the father felt like leaping out of the boat and the son coming down from the masnad. Ultimately Kaiqubad "ran barefooted to his father and was about to fall at his feet, when the weeping father caught him in his embrace." Nasir-ud-din gave certain wholesome advice to his son and recommended Nizam-ud-din and Quam-ud-din to his special favour but in an opportune moment whispered into his son's ears that these two should be put to death at the earliest opportunity.

Politically speaking, independence of Bengal was recognised by the Delhi Sultanate. Nasir-ud-din, however, handed back Oudh to Delhi but kept his hold on Bengal and Bihar.

The political scene in Delhi was fast changing, Nizam-ud-din was poisoned to death but Sultan Kaiqubad himself was killed by the Khalji Maliks. Kaimurs a child, son of Kaiqubad was placed on the Delhi throne a few days before the murder of his father. Kaimurs was given the title of Sultan Shams-ud-din but he also met with cruel death at the hands of Arkali Khan within a nominal reign of three months and a few days. The House of Balban thus came to an end at Delhi. The imperial throne was now occupied by Jalal-ud-din Firuzshah Khalji (April, 1290).

Nasir-ud-din on receipt of the news of the death of his son and grandson was much mortified. He discarded the royal insignia in disgust for life and abdicated placing his son Ruku-ud-din Kaikaus on the throne of Bengal. He died perhaps some time in 1290.

From the advice given by Bulban to his son Bughra Khan, later Sultan Nasir-ud-din Muhammad, gives us a clear idea about the latter's character. Sultan Nasir-ud-din was of weak temperament, although wise in consel and was given to pleasures which kept him unmindful of his responsibilities as Sultan. His geniality of temperament, his affection for his children and his subjects earned him the esteem of his people.

SULTAN RUKU-UD-DIN KAIKAUS (1291-1301)

From the coins and inscriptions of the reign of Kaikaus we find that his rule extended over Bengal and Bihar. Under his father Nasir-ud-din Mahmud the Sultanate of Bengal was divided into four governorships of Bihar, Satgaon, Bang and Devkot. Tradition of local independence was deep rooted in Bengal and whenever there was weak government at the capital of Bengal, the centrifugal forces came into play. This force of local independence was working since the fourteenth century and ended up with the parcelling out of portions of Bengal among the Bara Bhuniyas in the sixteenth century.

Kaikaus held his sway over a number of the Bengal feudatories including Firuz Aitigin who was the most powerful among them. The reign of Kaikaus synchronised with that of the Delhi Sultan Jalal-ud-din Firuz Khalji and initial years of the reign of Ala-ud-din Khalji. There is no evidence of any intercourse friendly or otherwise, between Delhi and Bengal during this period except that Jalal-ud-din who was unwilling to shed Muslim blood banished boat-loads of **Thugs** into Bengal. Invasion on Mongols and the distance of Bengal from Delhi precluded Jalal-ud-din's attempting conquest of Bengal. Kaikaus was succeeded by Sultan Shams-ud-din Firuz.

SULTAN SHAMS-UD-DIN FIRUZ (1301-22)

Sultan Shams-ud-din Firuz was the most capable and powerful ruler of Bengal among the descendants of the house of Balban. The greatest achievement of the reign of Shams-ud-din Firuz was the expansion of Muslim power over Mymensingh and Sylhet districts.

Shams-ud-din Firuz ascended the throne pretty late in life when he had already a few grown up sons each of whom was impatient to get the kingly power. His reign for the first seven years was peaceful but after this his sons became rebellious, the most turbulent among whom was Bahadur who began to rule as Sultan Bahadur Shah. Shams-ud-din was a ruler of exceptional ability which saved him from the tragedy of Emperor Shahjahan during his life time because of his rebellious sons. He had a fad for naming cities after himself. Tribeni in Hooghly district was named Firuzabad. Pandua was found by Firuz-ud-din to be suitable from strategic and health points of view than Lakhnauti, and named it Firuzabad where the capital was transferred. Firuz-ud-din died full of years.

Successors of Firuz-ud-din : Death of Shams-ud-din Firuz was a signal for a civil war between his five sons. Of the five sons Ghiyas-ud-din Bahadur had rebelled during his father's life time and was ruling over Eastern Bengal with Sonargaon as capital since

1310 A.D., another son Shihab-ud-din Bughra Shah succeeded his father Shams-ud-din Firuz to the throne of Bengal with Lakhnauti as capital. Ghiyas-ud-din Bahadur defeated Bughra Shah and seized the throne of Bengal. Another son Nasir-ud-din who coveted the throne of Bengal appealed to the Delhi Sultan Ghiyas-ud-din Tughluq. The opportunity was readily availed by the Sultan ; he marched towards Lakhnauti in 1324 captured Ghiyas-ud-din Bahadur and sent him to Delhi as a prisoner. Nasir-ud-din was placed on the throne of Bengal as a vassal of Delhi. East Bengal was made a province of Delhi Sultanate. On his return journey to Delhi, the Sultan captured Tirhut which became of fief of Delhi. But Ghiyas-ud-din Tughluq did not long survive his Triumph in Bengal. He died the next year (1325).

Under Muhammad bin Tughluq, son of Ghiyas-ud-din Tughluq the Delhi Sultanate's authority remained unchallenged in Bengal. He, however, placed Qadr Khan to the government of Lakhnauti, Izz-ud-din to that of Sonargaon and reinstated Ghiyas-ud-din Bahadur Shah to the government of Sonargaon but Tartar Khan a half-brother of Ghiyas-ud-din Bahadur was associated with him in the administration. But this arrangement did not work. Bahadur soon revolted, killed Tartar Khan and made himself sole governor of Sonargaon, Satgaon and temporarily of Lakhnauti. Such unsetftled condition continued till Iliyas Shah ascended the throne of Bengal. But since 1335 fortunes of Muhammad bin Tughluq began to wane. Provincial governors began to assert their independence. Fakhar-ud-din Mubarak Shah governor of Bengal whose loyalty to Delhi Sultanate was never beyond doubt threw off allegance to it and began to strike coins in his own name in 1338. Sultan being pre-occupied with more pressing problems could not make any move to subdue Bengal and it became an independent province.

SULTAN SHAMS-UD-DIN ILIYAS SHAH (1342-57)

Sultan-Shams-ud-din Iliyas Shah foster-brother of Ala-ud-din Adil Shah who had made himself independent in Northern Bengal reigned during 1339-1345. Fakhr-ud-din Mubarak Shah was the ruler of Sonargaon.

In 1342 a new chapter was opened in the history of Bengal with the accession of Iliyas Shah to the throne of Lakhnauti. The entire Northern India was in turmoil at that time due to the impracticable plans put into hurried execution by Muhammad bin Tughluq. The Hindu Chiefs had thrown off the allegiance to the Delhi Sultan, the governor of provinces carved out independent position for themselves. Lack of unity among the Hindu chiefs and absence of Delhi Sultan's authority over the provincial governors made Iliyas Shah to take advantage of the situation.

Iliyas Shah took advantage of the struggle between the Hindu Rajas of Tirhut area and easily conquered Tirhut. He then advanced towards Nepal and destroyed many cities, entered Katmandu burnt and destroyed the holy Swayambhunath stupa and the sacred standard of Sakyamuni. His success whetted his military ambition and he sought to bring the long stretch of alluvial plain from Suvaranarekha to Godavari under his sway. The wealth and numerous temples of this area namely of modern Bhuvaneswara, Cuttack, Puri and Konarak long excited the cupidity of the Muslim invaders. Iliyas Shah exacted tribute from Orissa and advanced as far as Benares. In 1353 he further strengthened his position by overthrowing Fakr-ud-din Mubarak Shah's son, the rival Sultan of Sonargaon. But within a year his conquests began to melt away. On the death of Muhammad bin Tughluq Firuz Tughluq, the new Sultan of Delhi quickly set the affairs of the state in order, then proceeded to chastise Sultan Iliyas Shah. His army comprised 90,000 horsemen, a vast number of infantry and archers, and one thousand war-boats. On the evidence of Siraj-Afif we learn that the flotilla of Iliyas Shah proceeded upto the confluence of the Ganges and the Gogra to oppose the imperial navy. But Firuz Tughluq overcoming all oppositions occupied Pandua, the capital of Iliyas Shah. Iliyas Shah took shelter in the Ekdala which could not be reduced to submission by the imperial forces despite prolonged efforts. Firuz then had recourse to a strategem and sent a saint as a spy who represented to Iliyas Shah that confusion and disorder broke out in the imperial forces and it would be easy for Iliyas Shah to defeat them. Relying on the false representation of the spy Iliyas Shah felt encouraged to emerge from the fort to fight the imperial army in open engagement Firuz Shah's stratagem having succeeded, he inflicted a severe defeat on Iliyas Shah who again repaired to the fort Ekdala. Firuz Shah laid seige of the fort but to no purpose. According to Sirat-i-Firuz-Shahi it is said that the imperial army was determined to raze the fort to the ground "but the piteous lamentation and supplications of Muslim women who came unveiled to the parapet with dishevelled hair, so moved the Sultan that he forthwith quitted Ekdala for Delhi." Zia-ud-din Barani, however, says that the Sultan would not listen to the demand to make an all out attack on the Ekdala and proceeded towards Delhi with Bengali prisoners, forty-seven elephants and other booty. Iliyas Shah was left to rule over Bengal as an independent Sultan. In 1355 and 1356 Iliyas Shah sent presents to the Delhi Sultan as token of friendship. In 1357 Sultan Firuz Shah requested Iliyas Shah to send him a few elephants which Iliyas Shah gladly sent through Malik Taj-ud-din. Firuz Tughluq reciprocated by sending Iliyas Shah a few Turkish and Arabian horses, some fruits brought from Khorasan and other valuable presents. After having ensured the friendship of the Delhi Sultan. Iliyas Shah started preparations for conquest of Kamrup. Conquest of Kamrup was the last military achievement of Iliyas Shah.

We have no historical records about the character, administration and life of Iliyas Shah. It is said that he had built a city named Hajipur and excavated an aqueduct in Firuzabad, i.e. Adina. It is also not known for certain the year in which his reign came to an end. There is difference of opinion about the date of his death. According to the coins of his reign the date of his death has been placed at 1357 whereas Twarik-i-Mubarakshahi and Sirat-i-Firuz-Shahi put the date as 1358.

It goes without saying that Iliyas Shah was one of the greatest independent Sultans of Bengal. Under his rule Bengal knew peace and order which again resulted in overall prosperity. He patronised architecture, and various other cultural activities.

SIKANDAR SHAH (1357(58 ?)-89)

On the death of Iliyas Shah, his son Sikandar Shah became Sultan of Bengal. He was an equally capable monarch like his father Iliyas Shah. For the three decades that he ruled over Bengal, he protected the independence of Bengal against the attacks of Delhi. Unfortunately we have no records of his long reign except a few inscriptions and brief reference in contemporary Persian chronicles which refer to his engagement with imperial forces.

In order to consolidate his position on the throne, Sikandar Shah made diplomatic overtures to Delhi by sending an envoy Alam Khan to the imperial court in the year of his coronation. A second embassy was sent some months afterwards with a present of five elephants. But all this did not neutralise the hostilities of the Delhi Sultan towards Bengal.

Firuz Tughluq won a great military victory over Iliyas Shah, but could not reduce the latter to his vasslage. Independence of Bengal was naturally a challenge to the pride of Firuz Tughluq as also an affront to his pride and prestige. Firuz Tughluq was, therefore, looking for a favourable opportunity to deal with Bengal adequately.

Sultan Fakr-ud-din of Sonargaon and his family had been massacred by Iliyas Shah in 1532 while conquering Sonargaon. Fakr-ud-din's son-in-law Zafar Khan, a Persian, held a high post in the revenue department of Fark-ud-din, but was reduced to insignificance by Iliyas Shah. Zafar Khan went to Delhi to seek redress. Firuz soon after the accession of Sikandar Shah sent an ultimatum demanding the latter's allegiance and the demand was supported by marching an army 80,000 strong cavalry, 470 elephants, and an enormous body of infantry.

Sikandar Shah followed the same strategy as did his father. He avoided any open battle and took shelter in the fort Ekdala. There were only skirmishes between groups of imperial and Bengal troops. The imperial army dashed itself in vain against the fort and could not detect a single weak point in the defences of the fort nor a split in the ranks of the Bengalis who kept the imperial army on the defensive.

According of Afif a tower of the fort crumbled down due to the sheer weight of Sikandar's men and when the imperial army wanted to enter the fort through the breach Firuz Tughluq desisted them in order to save the honour of the women within the fort.

Negotiations were started and brought to a successful close due to a Bengali officer Azam Humayum Haibat Khan whose readywit and mastery over speech ended in the signing of a treaty of friendship between Firuz Tughluq and Sikandar Shah and there was exchange of presents. Firuz Tughluq left for Delhi (1359). From this year, for a period of about two centuries Bengal maintained her independence.

Sikandar was a capable ruler and under his rule peace and order prevailed, which led to much prosperity. He was a patron of architecture and the famous Adina Mosque which can be seen even to-day. This mosque is 507 feet in length and 285 feet in breadth. A mosque so large cannot be found any where else in India. "This sumptuous mosque extending 507 ft. north to south and 285 ft. east to west surpasses in sheer dimension any other building of its kind in India. The central quadrangle inside the mosque forms a rectangle 400 ft. long by 150 ft. wide and is enclosed within ranges of pillard aisles five feet deep on the western side and three on the remainder, consisting of 400 pillars in all."

In **Riaz-us-Salatin** it is stated that the mosque took four years (1364-68) to be built. This statement is also corroborated by an inscription on the western side of the wall of the mosque. This magnificient structure which rivals in size the Great Mosque of Damascus was built with the spoils of the Hindu and Buddhist shrines. R. K. Chakraborty observes that "a Buddhist stupa was dismantled to secure materials for its building." Remains of Hindu images, carved head of a lion said to have formed the part of the throne of a Hindu Raja, mutiliated figures of Hindu deities are found in the door sills and all over to hall. "It is not improbable" remarks Percy Brown "that the finest monuments of the Hindu capital Lakhnauti were demolished in order to produce this one Muhammedan mosque. Adina mosque apart, the mosque of Akhi Siraj-ud-din, the Kotwali Darwaza built in the centre of the city of Gaur as also two other mosques built by Maulana Ata (1363) at Gangarampur in Dinajpur District and the other at Molla Simla in Hooghly district belong to this period. The famous saint Shaikh Alaul Haq lived at Pandua during Sikandar's reign.

The last years of Sikandar's reign were disturbed by the plots of his sons. Sikandar had seventeen sons by his first wife and only one by his second. His too much love for the only son of his second wife excited the jealousy of the first wife who poisoned Sikandar's ears. The young Prince Ghiyas-ud-din Azam had to escape for life to Sonargaon where he took up arms against his father in 1388 and conquered Sonargaon and Satgaon. The war ended in the victory of the prince Ghiyas-ud-din Azam but Sikandar lost his life in action against his son (1389). According to tradition Sikandar was buried in a chamber attached to Adina mosque.

GHIYAS-UD-DIN AZAM SHAH (1389-1409)

Ghiyas-ud-din Azam Shah was a patricide no doubt but he was driven to that state by the jealousy of his stepmother. According to Sir Jadunath, Ghiyas-ud-din Azam Shah was an attractive figure among the Sultans of Bengal.

Two anecdotes which got currency among the people of Bengal and assumed the character of proverbs are worth mentioning. One was Sultan Ghiyas-ud-din Azam Shah's great regard for law and justice. On one occasion the Sultan while practising with bow and arrows, an arrow accidentally killed the son of a widow who sued the Sultan before the Qazi. On being summoned by the Qazi the Sultan appeared before him and accepted the punishment, namely to compensate the widow for the death of her son. After the trial was over the Sultan told the Qazi that if he would have shown favour towards him (Sultan) he would have been beheaded, the Qazi promptly replied, if his Royal Majesty would not obeyed the law Qazi would have scourged him.

The second anecdote was that the Sultan when fell ill and thinking that the illness would prove fatal, asked his three concubines named Cypress, Tulip and Rose to wash his body after his death. The Sultan recovered but the three concubines were now shown greater favour by the Sultan which made jealous the other inmates of the harem. When the matter reached the ears of the Sultan he wrote a poem praising the three concubines, but he could write only one line of the poem but failed to complete it. He wrote to poet Hafiz who supplied him the second line of the poem. This is how he corresponded with Hafiz, but its truth is questioned by many.

From Assamese Buranji it is learnt that the Ahom King Sudangpha led an expedition against the Raja of Kamta for harbouring a noble in his court who had given offence to Ahom King. When the Ahom King invaded kamta kingdom, Ghiyas-ud-din Azam Shah thought it be a good opportunity for him to carve out a portion of the Kamta kingdom. Faced with the double danger the Kamta Raja concluded a peace with the Ahom King and the combined forces of the Ahom and Kamta Kingdoms forced the Bengal army to retreat beyond the river Karatoya.

According to Ferishta Ghiyas-ud-din cultivated friendship with Khwaja Jahan ruler of Jaunpur to whom he sent elephants and other gifts. There was also friendly intercourse between Ghiyas-ud-din and the contemporary Chinese ruler. In 1406 a Chinese mission visited Bengal and Mahuan came as an interpreter of the mission. Mahuan has left a brief but interesting account about Bengal. In 1409 Ghiyas-ud-din reciprocated by sending his own envoys with presents to the Chinese emperor. Ghiyas-ud-din was murdered in 1409 for which a tradition holds Raja Ganesh responsible.

SAIF-UD-DIN HAMZA SHAH (1409-10)

On the murder of Ghiyas-ud-din his son Saif-ud-din Hamza Shah was placed on the throne by the army chief in 1409, with the title Sultan-us-Salatin i.e. King of Kings. But his accession was a signal for a civil war between himself and his Kinsmen. During the confusion Ganesh, the Zamindar of Bhaturia and Dinajpur and an influential officer of Iliyas Shahi rulers of Bengal, declared his independence and assumed the title Raja and made himself the virtual dictator during the reign of the puppet rulers like Saif-ud-din Hamza Shah.

RAJA GANESH

Ganesh was Hindu Zamindar of Bhaturia and Dinajpur, and according to some was a Barendra Brahmin with the surname of Bhaduri. Taking advantage of the weakness of the rule of the Iliyas Shahi ruler like Saif-ud-din, he declared his independence. Saif-ud-din Hamza Shah was succeeded by his adopted son or perhaps a slave Shihab-ud-din Bayazid Shah and the latter by his son Ala-ud-din Firuz Shah. The quick succession of weak and incompetent rulers to the throne of Bengal offered opportunity to Raja Ganesh who seized the throne of Bengal for himself early in 1415. Ganesh restored Hindu rule over Bengal.

We have references to Raja Ganesh's assumption of authority over Bengal in Tabaqat-in-Akbari as well as in Ferishta's writings. Raja Ganesh help sway over Bengal for seven years. Tarikh-i-Ferishta states that the son of Saif-ud-din Hamza Shah was succeeded by his son Byazid who was "of poor intellect" and one of the nobles a Hindu attained to great power and predominance taking advantage of the weak, inefficient rule of Byazid, and assumed the title of Raja. In 1415, he seized the throne of Bengal.

It may be noted here that Ganesh was not only the most powerful of the nobles of Ghiyas-ud-din Azam Shah's reign. He was the Zamindar of Dinajpur who had an independent and hereditary source of strength in his ancestral estate, and personal contingent of troops, not in the pay of the Sultan. He made good use of his power when the successors of Iliyas Shah were weak and incapable. Raja Ganesh's usurpation of the throne of Bengal outraged the Muslim sentiments, and an invitation to Ibrahim Shah Sharqi, Sultan of Jaunpur was sent for delivering Bengal from the **Kafir** on the throne.

Ibrahim Sharqi on his way to Bengal with an expeditionary force reduced Shiva Sinha of Mithila who had dethroned his father Devi Sinha and threw off the allegiance of Jaunpur. Shiva Sinha was also a friend of Raja Ganesh. In Bengal Raja Ganesh could not withstand the onslaught of the vast Jaunpur army and had to abdicate. Raja Ganesh's son Jadusen out of lust for power agreed to embrace Islam. Ibrahim Sharqi placed Jadusen on the throne of Bengal under the title Jalal-ud-din. But on sooner than Ibrahim Sharqi had left Bengal Raja Ganesh recovered his authority as ruler of Bengal and assumed the title Danujamardana Deva. It is also said that he got his son reconverted to Hinduism, but as **Suddhi** was not acceptable to the Hindu society, Jadusen remained an out-caste.

Raja Ganesh now ruled over whole of Bengal till the middle of 1418. He was a wise an able ruler and according to Beveridge, Ganesh was the most interesting figure among the kings of Bengal. He broke the bonds of Islam for a time and "must have been a man of vigour and capacity." Ferishta also praises the qualities of Ganesh as a ruler. He ruled over his kingdom in the best manner and his treatment of the Muslim subjects was genial but he tried to "reduce the overgrown and unruly Muslim monastic orders to obedience." Raja Ganesh died in 1418. From coins issued in the same year from Pandua and Chittagong by Mahendra Deva, younger son of Raja Ganesh, it appears that he was placed on the throne by some of his partisans. But within a few months Jadusen, re-embracing Islam occupied the throne under the title Jalal-ud-din Muhammad (1418).

JALAL-UD-DIN MUHAMMAD—JADUSEN (1418-31)

From the coins issued by Jalal-ud-din it may be confidently said that he ruled over whole of Bengal including East Bengal and Chittagong. According to tradition, recorded by Ghulam Hussain Salim, Jalal-ud-din transferred his capital from Pandua to Gaur. He had, however, built many splendid buildings at Pandu, and one mosque, two tanks and a sarai in Gaur. Jalal-ud-din's rule was a period of peace and prosperity for Bengal. According to Ghulam Hussain the Eklakhi tomb at Pandua contains the mortal remains of Jalal-ud-din, his wife and son. Cunningham considers this sepulchre as an excellent example of Muslim architecture of Bengal in the pre-Mughal days. Many of the stones of this tomb clearly show that they once formed parts of Hindu and Buddhist shrines.

Jalal-ud-din was succeeded by his son Shams-ud-din Ahmad in 1431, but his reign was a catalogue of crimes and follies. The nobles, at last, got rid of this ruler by getting him assassinated (1442).

For a time the assassins of Shams-ud-din Ahmad held the power of the State, but under them situation did not improve. On the contrary the two assassins Shadi Khan and Nasir Khan fell out in a struggle for power in which Shadi Khan was first killed but Nasir Khan was also assassinated within a week. A descendant of Iliyas Shahi dynasty—Nasir-ud-din, was chosen by the people to be the new sovereign.

Restored Iliyas Shahi Dynasty : Abyssinian Rule : Nasir-ud-din Abul Muzaffar Mahmud was chosen by the people to the throne of Bengal, thus was the dynasty of Iliyas Shah restored to the throne of Bengal.

As Nasir-ud-din was the choice of the people themselves, he had their willing obedience, as such he enjoyed a peaceful and prosperous reign. He was a good administrator, just and liberal, "the people, both young and old, were contented and the wounds of oppression inflicated by Ahamad Shah were healed."

The major interest of Nasir-ud-din lay in the arts of peace. Many inscriptions of his time bear testimony to his building of mosques, bridges, tombs etc. He himself laid the foundations of the citadel and palace of Gaur which had become the capital of Bengal since the days of Jalal-ud-din (Jadusen). The **Kotwali darwaza**, five arched stone bridge and parts of the massive walls of the fort have survived. Needless to say, Nasir-ud-din's pursuit of the arts of peace was possible due to the security that Bengal then enjoyed against external aggression. As Ferishta states this was facilitated by the deadly struggle that was going on between the Lodis and the Sharqis. The Sharqis had made inroads into Bengal twice in récent past. But in the contest with the Lodis the Sharqis were finally worsted.

Nasir-ud-din's reign was not entirely without military achievement. From epigraphic evidence it is learnt that parts of Jessore and Khulna districts were annexed to Bengal under his rule.

In an inscription dated 1447 it is found that Kapilendradeva, king of Orissa styles himself as "Gaurêswara." It is possible that during the uncertainties of the past few reigns Orissa pushed its frontier upto Bhagirathi river. From an extensive number of coins and inscriptions of Nasir-ud-din's reign found at Bhagatpur, Satgaon, Bagherhat, Faridpur, Nusratabad testify to his fairly extensive and well-knit kingdom. His death took place probably in the year 1459.

RUKH-UD-DIN BARBAK (1459-74)

Before his accession to his father's throne Rukh-ud-din Barbak was a viceroy of Satgaon. He is regarded as a sagacious, law-abiding sovereign in whose reign the citizens and soldiers enjoyed security and contentment alike.

In Risalat-us-Shuhada by Pir Muhammad Shattari exploits of Barbak are narrated. Hostilities with Orissa were perhaps an unending process and these hostilities related to the occupation and recovery of the fortress. Mandaran in the Arambagh subdivision which was captured by Gajapati king Kapilendra but was ultimately recovered by Ismail on behalf of Barbak.

Ismail was then sent to recover the cis-Karatoya regions which had been lately over run by the Kamrup forces. Kamtapur kingdom was then in most flourishing state and progress of Ismail was severely contested. Kamtapur king Kameswar fought the battle near Santosh in Dinajpur and was severely defeated. But the saintly character of Ismail so impressed him that he is reported to have surrendered and embraced Islam. So long as Ismail was alive the frontiers of Bengal ran along the Karatoya. But the success of Ismail excited the jealousy of Bhandsi Rai Commandant of the fort of Ghoraghat. He poisoned the ears of Barbak who ordered Ismail's execution (Jan. 1474).

On the authority of Ferishta we come to know that Barbak collected a large number of Abyssinian slaves and employed them in the army as also in the palace guard. He is said to have employed about eight thousand Abyssian slaves to such posts who gradually monopolised all the key positions of the state.

Dinajpur inscription of Barbak indicates that his dominions extended north of the Ganges. But the districts of west of Monghyr belonged to the Sharqis of Jaunpur. Sylhet belonged to Bengal Sultan, the possession of Chittagong was disputed by the Arakanese but Barbak's authority was re-established there. Occupation of Bakhargunge which linking the recently conquered Jessor-Khulna regions gave Muslim dominion in Bengal a continuous frontier.

Barbak took great interest in Bengali literature and patronised Maladhar Basu who wrote his **Shri Krishna Bijay** in 1473 and honoured him with the title **Gunaraj Khan.** Maladhar Basu records gratefully the patronage he received from Barbak. Maladhar Basu's son was likewise conferred the title of **Satyaraj Khan** by Barbak.

SHAMS-UD-DIN YUSUF (1474-81)

Barbak was succeeded by his son Yusuf. According Ferishta and Nizam-ud-din, Shams-ud-din Yusuf was an able administrator and a vastly learned man. He dispensed strictest justice according to law and insisted on impartial application of law to all his subjects. He would often assist the judges to come to correct judgement in difficult cases. He refrained from taking wine. The inscriptions on the wall of the **Baisdarwaza** mosque show that he extended his dominion to the south, perhaps at the cost of Orissa. His dominion over Sylhet continued as is evident from an inscription near the mosque of Shah Jalal at Sylhet. Yusuf perhaps died in 1481.

JALAL-UD-DIN FATH (1481-86)

According to Salim, Yusuf was succeeded by his son named Sikandar but on his accession he showed signs of lunacy and after three days of his accession the crown was offered to another son of Yusuf named Hussain who assumed the title of Jalal-ud-din Fath.

Jalal-ud-din Fath is said to have been a liberal, intelligent and capable ruler under whom people "enjoyed happiness and comfort." The Abyssinians through the continued patronage of Barbak and Yusuf were holding positions in the government. They now swarmed in the palace and the city. Power made them arrogant and their behaviour with the people was characterised by violence. As their arrogance exceeded all tolerable limits Fath decided to punish them and curb their power. As Ferishta states, more defiant among them were punished "with the scourge of justice." This led to discontent among them and they entered into a conspiracy with chief eunuch of the palace Sultan Shahzada who commanded the palace guards and at a time when the loyal Abyssinian commander of the forces Amir-ul-umara-Malik Andil, Shahzada murdered Fath (Dec. 1486).

With the murder of Fath Iliyas Shahi dynasty finally disappeared from the history of Bengal. This dynasty had produced with remarkable consistency able rulers who were tolerant, enlightened and contributed much to the economic and intellectual life of the people of Bengal for nearly a century.

It certainly goes to the credit of the Iliyas Shahi Sultans of Bengal that although they belonged to an alien faith, ruled over the people of Bengal and enjoyed people's trust and allegiance. Tolerance was their greatest asset and when this dynasty was out of power for about twenty-five years and situation fast continued to deteriorate people of Bengal restored this dynasty to power. "It was a singular proof of their popularity—a popularity which rested on their past services. The dynasty had almost become an integral part of Bengal's political and social life and its passing boded ill for the country."

ABYSSINIAN RULE

BARBAK SHAH (1487)

Rukh-ud-din Barbak's too much latitude towards the Abyssinian slaves and employing them in high positions of the government, army and palace guards, cost the life of Fath. The blind policy of placing reliance on the Abyssinian slaves had resulted in so total destruction of old nobility that there was not a sign of opposition when the murderer Abyssinian slave body-guard assumed sovereignty. Bloch-mann observes "from protector of the dynasty, the Abyssinians became the master of the kingdom."

Murderer of Fath, Shahzada sat on the throne, assumed the title of Barbak Shah. Malik Andil, the loyal commander of Fath's army returned to the capital. This un-nerved Barbak Shah. He persuaded Malik Andil to take an oath not to place his hand on him so long as he would be on the throne. Malik Andil with the help of the paiks, one night secretly entered the palace but finding Barbak Shah sleeping on the throne, he remembered his oath not to place his hand on Barbak so long as he was on the throne, and stopped. But nemesis dragged Barbak Shah to his end. Due to the influence of too much drinking he slipped down from the throne. This gave Malik Andil his opportunity to kill Barbak.

It is difficult to say how long Barbak Shah's sovereignty lasted. Salim assigns to him a reign of six months only.

SAIF-UD-DIN FIRUZ (1487-90)

Malik Andil was loyal to his assassinated master Fath. True to his salt he offered the throne to Fath's infant son, but Fath's widow declined it. The Abyssinian general, then was persuaded by the nobles led by Wazir Khan Jahan to assume the sovereignty. Malik Andil ascended the throne in 1487 with the title Saif-ud-din Firuz.

Saif-ud-din Firuz's attachment to Iliyas Shahi dynasty and his reputation as a capable soldier inspired awe and respect and people soon forgot his racial origin. His benevolence, his charity kindness were highly praised by the historians. According to **Riyaz** the largeness of his gifts "once confounded his treasury officials." Firuz's inscription found at Sherpur on northern Mymensingh, shows the continued inclusion of that part of Bengal within the kingdom of Gaur. Saif-ud-din's rule terminated with his murder at the hands of the paiks, (Abyssinian Troops) who now became the King-makers.

NASIR-UD-DIN MAHMUD II (1490-91)

The antecedents of Sultan Nasir-ud-din is not known. In coins and inscription of his time he described himself as "king, son of a king"—an unprecedented and unusual description of the parentage of a ruling monarch. Mahmud was very young as such the government was carried on by Habsh Khan, an Abyssinian. But Sidi Badr, nick-named Diwana (i.e. mad), became jealous of Habsh Khan and assumed the regency and was planning to usurp the throne. He entered into a conspiracy with palace guards and murdered Mahmud and occupied the throne himself. Mahmud's reign ended within one year of his accession.

SHAMS-UD-DIN MUZAFFAR (SIDI BADR DIWANA) (1491-93)

Sidi Badr, assassin of Mahmud assumed the style Shams-ud-din Muzaffar. The rule of three years and few months of this Abyssinian was the climax of the infamous reign of tyranny and disorder which caused widespread discontent among officers, soldiers, including the wise minister Sayyid Hussain who was of Arab descent. In order to root out opposition, he did not rest content by purging the administration of all suspected of disloyalty but commended a ruthless destruction of Hindu nobility and princess suspected of least opposition to his sovereignty. His greed for money led him to make extortionate demands from the people. The reign of terror unleashed by Sidi Badr ultimately drove the people to armed resistance. The Wazir Sayyid Hussain secretly joined the insurgents. Sidi Badr was beseiged in Gaur for four months during which he died. Nobles of Bengal raised Sayyid Hussain to the throne of Bengal in 1493 under the title Ala-ud-din Hussain Shah.

HUSSAIN SHAH DYNASTY (1493-1538)

Ala-ud-din Hussain Shah marks the beginning a new dynasty which ruled over Bengal for nearly half a century. After the Habshi interregnum had violently disturbed the social, economic and cultural progress of Bengal, there was the need for a capable person who would meet the Hussain, an Arabian. One of the first things that Hussain Shah did was to transfer his capital to Ekdala.

Hussain Shah was a wise, far-sighted capable administrator, a liberal-minded, just and honest ruler. He was a great patron of art and culture. The creative genius of the Bengalis reached its Zenith under the liberal patronage of Hussain Shah.

On the accession to the throne Hussain Shah's task was to bring peace and order out of the prevailing confusion and disorder into which the country had been thrown by the Abyssinian usurpers. In order to save Bengal and her people from the Habshi beneful political influence Hussain Shah drove the Habshis i.e. the Abyssinians from Bengal. The palace guards had become unruly during the Habshi rule. Hussain Shah put them down with a strong hand and then disbanded and dispersed them. He sent efficient district officers to different parts of his dominions and all the disloyal elements were suppressed and removed from office. In 1494 Sikandar Lodi defeated Sharqi Sultan Hussain of Jaunpur and the kingdom of Jaunpur was annexed to the Delhi Sultanate. Hussain of Jaunpur took refuge in Bengal. Occupation of Jaunpur, the entrance to Bihar and Bengal by the Lodi Sultan of Delhi was a threat to the security of Sultanate of Bengal. Hussain Shah received his name sake with all honour and hospitality. Sikandar Lodi saw in this undue liberal treatment of the Sharqi Sultan by Hussain Shah some secret political motive. He, therefore, advanced towards Bengal frontiers. Hussain Shah had anticipated it and sent his son Daniyal to intercept the invaders. Whether for fear of the Bengal army or exhaustion of war and long march, the Lodi generals hesitated to start fighting. Sikandar Lodi was obliged to open negotiations. The result was that the whole of North Bihar and trans-Gandak region came within Hussain Shah's sway.

Next, Hussain Shah proceeded towards north-east. Barbak had lost considerable territories on the eastern bank of Karatoya to the king of Kamtapur. Hussain Shah invaded Ahom kingdom of Assam and captured Kamtapur. A colony of Afghans was left in Kamrup, but Kamrup was recovered by its Ahom king.

From Riyaz-us-Salatin and an annonymous historical writing we know that Hussain Shah extended his territories upto the borders of Orissa. He could not succeed in his military campaign against Orissa. When Hussain Shah ascended the throne Bengal was involved in a war with Tipperah. Hussain Shah annexed portions of Tipperah and recovered Chittagong from the Arakanese possession. Recovery of Chittagong is also indicated in **Rajmala.** Tipperah and Chittagong campaigns were in all probability led by the crown-prince Nusrat. He was assisted by Paragal Khan who was appointed military governor of the newly acquired territory. Paragal Khan and later, his son Chhuti steadily pushed the Arakanese southwards and kept a vigilant watch on the Tipperah king. Hussain Shah died in 1519.

Character and Estimate of Hussain Shah : Hussain Shah was decidedly the best, if not the greatest of the medieval rulers of Bengal. He was a true statesman and with a deep insight he realised that the hopes and aspirations of Bengal and her people were his task to fulfil. Courteous and affable, modest and kind he naturally earned the love and respect of the people. "He had almost become a national institution." He identified himself with the hopes and aspirations of the people of Bengal and his foreign origin was soon forgotten.

Hussain was a great conqueror and extended the boundaries of Bengal by "annexation of Kamrup, Saran and part of Tipperah. No rebellion disturbed the peace and security of his well-knit dominions which comprised all the territories bounded by Saran and Bihar on the north-west, Sylhet and Chittagong on the south-east, and Hajo on the north-east and 24 parganas on the south-west."

Posterity remembers Hussain Shah not for the material benefits he conferred on the people, "but for his liberalism and catholicism of mind of which it is hard to find a parallel in Muslim India until the age of the great Akbar." He appointed Hindus to high offices, but this was nothing new but to appoint Hindus in charge of highly confidential work was something more than more diplomatic expediency. His wazir was Gopinath Basu, later entitle Purandar Khan, his private physician was Mukunda Das, the chief of his body-guards was Kesava Chhatri and the master of the mint, Anup. In **Rajmala** it is found that Gaur Mallick was his general in charge of the second Tipperah expedition. Two brothers Rup Goswami and Sanatan Goswami held high offices under him and one of them was his secretary.

Hussain Shah was a great patron not only of Arabic and Persian literature but also of Bengali. Most of the works produced during his reign have perished, but among the Bengali writers Maladhar Basu, Bijay Gupta, Bipradas, Jasoraj Khan, mention Hussain Shah's name with gratitude.

Hussain Shah's reign constitutes an epoch in the history of independent medieval Bengal. His liberal policy administrative efficiency and territorial expansion brought internal peace and security which in consequence brought economic prosperity.

It was during the reign of Hussain Shah that Chaitanya preached his religion which ushered in an era of social and religious reform among the Hindus of Bengal which again constituted an important factory in this renaissance of Bengal.

NASIR-UD-DIN ABUL MUZAFFAR NUSRAT SHAH (1519-32)

Of the eighteen children of Hussain Shah, Nusrat Shah was the eldest. He was nominated to succeed Hussain Shah during the latter's life time and as was customary in Bengal, the crown-prince was permitted to strike coins in his own name.

Nusrat Shah inherited his father's quality of liberalism and humanism. He was equally just and impartial administrator. On his accession to the throne, he, contrary to the prevalent custom, instead of putting his brothers to death, raised their status and dignity and enhanced their allowances. He practically settled double the estate each of them had actually inherited.

Nusrat Shah had inherited his father's qualities in full and by working with his father as the crown-prince he had imbibed the administrative and military abilities of a high order and got a thorough grasp of the political problems of the state. He also possessed subtle diplomatic ability which stood him in good stead as a ruler.

Accession of Nusrat Shah to the throne of Bengal synchronised with the decline and fall of the Delhi Sultanate. The **Lohani** and **Formuli** Maliks appropriated the country from Jaunpur to Patna. Hussain Shah's non-aggression pact with Sikandar Lodi gave Bengal peace but no security. Occupation of North Bihar later by Hussain Shah gave protection to only one flank of Bengal but no military barrier separated Delhi from

Monghyr. Nusrat Shah entered into an alliance with the Lohani and Formuli Maliks and thereby strengthening his frontiers against possible attack from Delhi, advanced against Tirhut and brought whole of it under his sway. He placed his two brothers-in-law in charge of administration there. He set up a military out-post at Hajipur on the confluence of the Ganga-Jamuna rivers, thereby gave security to his kingdom. In 1526 when Babur won victory in the battle of Panipat, Nusrat Shah formed and **entente** with the Afghan chiefs who had flocked to the East. The Afghans sustained a defeat at the hands of Humayun in August 1526, this made Nusrat Shah to realise the strength of his adversary and he thought it prudent to maintain neutrality in order to disarm Mughal hostility. Babur sent his envoy to Nusrat Shah's court to know his attitude towards him. Nusrat Shah kept the envoy in his court for one year avoiding any answer as to his attitude. As this roused suspicion, Nusrat Shah sent an envoy to Babur with presents and assurance of loyalty. He, however, lent secret support to the Afghans. Thus by feigning loyalty to the Mughals at times and supporting the Afghans against the Mughals, Nusrat played his diplomatic cards well. Death of Bahar Khan Lohani, the main organiser of Afghan resistance against the Mughals had practically disrupted the Afghan confederacy in the East. Sher Khan who obtained a **jagir** from the Mughals was trying to enhance his power and interest with the assistance of the governor of Jaunpur all the more disrupted the Afghan unity. The task, therefore, fell on Nusrat Shah who with his subtle diplomacy kept appearances of friendship with the Mughals and at the same time tried to reorganise Afghan resistance against the Mughals.

By 1529 Mahmud of the Lodi dynasty, Nusrat Shah and Sher Khan for a time formed a confederacy against the Mughals but the purpose of the confederacy did not succeed due to utter incompetence of Mahmud.

On the death of Babur, Nusrat shah again formed a confederacy and Sher Khan for a time the Mughals. Humayun was about to march against Nusrat Shah when news reached him that Bahadur Shah of Gujarat had rebelled. Nusrat Shah sent his envoy Malik Marjan to Gujarat to establish contact with rebel Bahadur Shah. In the circumstance, Humayun has to first proceed against Bahadur Shah leaving Bengal alone.

During the reign of Nusrat Shah there were several engagements between Bengali and the Ahom Troops in which the Bengal was defeated. Even after Nusrat Shah's death conflict with the Ahoms continued.

Nusrat Shah lost his life at the hands of an assassin who was one of his own slaves whom he had punished on an earlier occasion.

Like his father Hussain Shah, Nusrat Shah patronised Bengali literature. He ordered the translation of the Mahabharata into Bengali, which was the earliest of its kind. His military governor of Chittagong, Chhuti Khan ordered the translation of Mahabharata to be done by yet another writer named Srikara Nandi, Nusrat Shah was also a great builder. The **Kadm Rasul** and the **Bara Sona Masjid** of Gaur were built under his orders.

ALA-UD-DIN FIRUZ (1532-33)

Abdul Badr brother of Nusrat Shah seem to have been nominated heir-apparent during the life time of Nusrat Shah. But his nomination was perhaps opposed by a section of the nobles headed by the governor of North Bihar. Governor of Bihar Mukhdum, brother of Nusrat Shah, declared his young son as the ruler of Bengal under the title Ala-ud-din Firuz. He, however, ruled a few months. But although young and ruled for a very short time, Ala-ud-din's name is remembered for his patronage of literature, for it was on his request poet Sridhara composed the versified life story of Vidyasundar.

GHIYAS-UD-DIN MUHAMMAD SHAH (1533-58)

Usurpation of throne by Ala-ud-din Firuz Shah, contrary to the nomination of Abdul Badr led to an unfortunate struggle not consistent with the ideas and attitudes of the Hussain Shahi kings. Ala-ud-din was killed by his uncle Ghiyas-ud-din Muhammad Shah who occupied the throne in 1533. It was during his reign that Afghan chief Sher Khan, later Sultan Sher Shah defeated and expelled Ghiyas-ud-din Muhammad from Bengal. Thus Hussain Shahi dynasty of Bengal came to an end.

LITERATURE, ECONOMIC CONDITION, ART AND ARCHITECTURE UNDER THE INDEPENDENT SULTANATE OF BENGAL

During the first one and half centuries of the Muslim rule in Bengal, there was no development of any literature. But with consolidation of Muslim rule and return of peace and prosperity, greater attention to old learning—a sort of an early renaissance in Brahmanical lore and Sanskrit started during the 14th-15th Centuries. Krittivasa Ojha Mukhati was the most popular Bengali poet who translated Sanskrit Ramayana into Bengali in 1418. Sanskrit Ramayana of Valmiki, translated into Bengali by Krittivasa brought the heroic deeds of Rama, the god-incarnate, within the reach of the simple people of Bengal. The poem of Krittivasa is saturated with the spirit of **Bhakti.** Krishna legend was likewise taken up by Maladhar Basu who earned the title Gunaraj Khan for his Sri Krishna Vijaya in 1473 based on Sanskrit Bhagavat Purana. The story of Behula Lakhmindhara—a great tale of wife's love and devotion which secured the life of dead husband from Manasa. The theme of the story older than the Muslim rule in Bengal and the first poet to write on this theme was Kana-Haridatta. Two other poets Vijaya Gupta of Barisal and Bipradas Pipali of Baduria wrote on the same theme.

A great lyrical poet of medieval Bengali literature was Chandidasa, "who is considered by many to be the greatest lyric poet of Bengal prior to Rabindranath Tagore." He composed over 1250 poems over the love of Radha and Krishna. Exact time of Chandidasa is not known to us, but Chaitanya used to find pleasure in listening to the singing of the poems of Chandidasa. This naturally places Chandidasa before Chaitanya (1486-1533) and his date is supposed by some historians as 1450.

Three different sobriquets such as **Badu, Dvija** and **Dina** by Chandidasa naturally have raised the problem of Chandidasa. It is supposed that there were as many as three Chandidasas. The first was Badu Chandidasa who was responsible for composing Sri Krishna-Kirttana. He was of pre-Chaitanya period. The second one—Dvija Chandidasa was of post-Chaitanya period who composed the poems on which the popularity of Chandidasa rests to-day. The third one Dina Chandidasa lived after 1600 A.D. But the fact remains that both Badu Chandidasa and Dvija Chandidasa were great poets and often these personalities were mixed up.

Fifteenth century Bengl is marked by great religious, literary and cultural activities. Hussain Shah was a great patron of Bengali literature, besides of Arabic and Persian literature. Maladhar Basu, Bijay Gupta, Bipra Das, Jasoraj Khan—all celebrated writers of Bengali literature flourished under Hussain Shah's liberal patronage. Paragal Khan and his son Chhuti Khan, governors of Chittagong under Hussain Shah and his son Nusrat Shah, caused translation of Mahabharata into Bengali, first by poet Kavindra whose book was named Pandava-Vijaya Katha and the second one by Srikara Nandi. Stories of Ramayana and of Lord Krishna of Mahabharata were the themes of many literary works in Bengali from the fifteenth down to the nineteenth century.

Sanskrit works of the fifteenth century were of high standard. Works of jurist like Raghunandan Bhattacharya, logician like Raghunatha Siromani, poet like Chaturbhuja

Misra enriched the fund of the Sanskrit literature of the time. Colleges of Sanskrit learning grew up everywhere, particularly, in Navadvipa in Nadia district, Vishnupur in Bankura district, in Vikrampur in Dacca district, and at various places in Maldah, Rajshahi, Chittagong, Faridpur etc. There were close contacts and exhange of scholars between Bengal Sanskrit colleges and centres of Hindu culture and learning such as Mithila, Gaya, Banaras. Orissa, and Vrindavana.

"Chaitanya, who flourished from 1486 to 1533, rode at the crest of the wave of the fifteenth century Brahmanical renaissance and gave a new turn to Hinduism in Bengal through a reviving of Vaisnavism with Krishna and Radha as symbols for the Divinity and its innate power of bliss." Chaitanya represented the cultural and spiritual life of late medieval Bengal. His deep influence on the people of Bengal, particularly his followers and devotees, from king to beggar, from Brahmana to the social outcaste and to Muslim, brought a new spirit of liberalism and catholicity in the Hindu society. A contradiction is, however seen in the works of the social organisers like Devivara Ghataka who set certain rules of conduct for Hindu marriages to help to keep the Hindu society against the onslaught of Islam.

HINDU-MUSLIM RELATIONS IN BENGAL DURING THE 15TH AND 16TH CENTURIES

An idea about the Hindu-Muslim relations can be obtained from the contemporary Bengali literature. Jayananda, author **Chaitanya-Mangala** states. "The king seizes the Brahmanas, pollute their caste, and even take their iives. If a conchshell is heard to blow in any house, its owner is made to forfeit his wealth, caste and even life. The king plunders the houses of those who were sacred threads on the shoulders and put sacred marks on their foreheads. He breaks the temples and Tulasi plants, and the residents of Navadvipa are in perpetual fear of their lives ... Misled by the false report that a Brahmana was destined to be the king of Navadvipa... the king of Gauda ordered the destruction of Nadiya (Navadvipa) Sarbabhauma Bhattacharya left Gauda with his family and Kinsmen and fled to Orissa where he was honoured by its ruler Prataparudra." Some time later the king of Gauda changed his attitude and caused the broken temples and houses to be rebuilt. But the mischief had already been done. The Brahmanas whose caste had been polluted continued to remain as outcastes.

Communal relation became even worse under the benign rule of Hussain Shah who is regarded as the most liberal-minded Muslim ruler of Bengal. From Vijaya Gupta who eulogises Hussain Shah narrates how the Hindus were outraged by the two Muslim Qazis Hasan and Hussain.

Isana Nagara, another contemporary writer describes the condition of the Hindus under Hussain Shah. "The wicked mlechhas pollute the religion of the Hindus every day. They break the images of gods into pieces and throw away the articles of worship." Two famous biographies of Chaitanya, namely, **Chaitanya-Charitamrita** and **Chaitanya-Bhagavata** contain many stories about the religious bigotry and intolerance of the Muslims and the consequent persecution of the Hindus : **Kirtan** parties of the devotees of Chaitanya were disrupted and participants beaten up by the qazis. The qazi of Navadvipa prohibited Kirtan but Chaitanya defied the order and when the qazi wild with anger, thought of descrating the caste of all Hindus of Navadvipa, he had to contain himself seeing the vast concourse of people determined to oppose the qazi. The angry crowd wrecked the house of the qazi and when Chaitanya sent for the qazi, the latter came before Chaitanya and there a cordial relation was established between the two. Soon after Chaitanya visited a village called Ramakeli near Gauda. When Hussain Shah came to know about the vast concourse of people following Chaitanya, he order the qazis not to injure him and to allow him to go anywhere he liked unhindered, for a person whom huge number of people follow for no expectation of material benefit, he must be a saint.

Even after issuing this order Hussain Shah had destroyed numerous temples in Orissa. He had kept Sanatana confined as the latter was one day found engaged in religious discourse with thirty Vaishnavas. But some time afterwards when Hussain Shah was about to advance in a compaign against Orissa he asked Sanatana to accompany him. But Sanatana refused on the ground that the Sultan would torment the Hindu gods and break the temples and he could not be a party to such sacrilegious activities. Sanatana's forthright answer stands in striking contrast to the fulsome praises of Hussain Shah by contemporary eulogists like Vijaya Gupta.

This is but one side of the shield. The Vaishnava literature also shows a brighter side of the Hindu-Muslim relation in Bengal during the 15th and 16th centuries. When the qazi had met Chaitanya, referred to above, the latter pointed out to the qazi that his (Chaitanya's) maternal grandfather was the qazi's uncle according to customary usage in regard to the relation between the communities and in that way Chaitanya was the qazi's nephew. It shows that the two communities had good neighbourly relationship and one community would regard the members of the other community as their relations. It goes without saying that good neighbourly relation naturally developed between them by their living together in the same village, town or city.

Economic Condition : In Eastern India, Bengal was particularly noted for the manufacture of abundant quantity of finer textiles of different varieties. In 1346 when Ibn Batuta visited Bengal finest cotton piece goods were being sold in Bengal markets at extra-ordinarily cheap price. The Chinese traveller Ma Huan writing in the middle of the fifteenth century listed six varieties of fine cotton stuffs produced in Bengal. Two other Chinese writers Wang Ta-Yuan and Fei Hsin of the 14th and the 15th centuries as also Barbosa in the 16th century give similar lists of cotton goods produced in Bengal. French scholar Paul Pelliot gives us the list contained in the writings of Ma Huan of the finer cotton goods of Bengal. These were : white glossy stuff, Chintz, cotton gauze called Shana-baf, fine stuff used for turban, chowtar, and velvets of cotton. According to Barbosa Bengal cloths found a good market in two great international ports, Malacca in the East and Ormuz in the West. Famous muslins of Bengal and good white sugar-cane were exported by Muslim merchants in their own ships to Cambay and other places. Trade with international port was so brisk that traders both Hindu and Muslim from Bengal, established a colony in Malacca.

We have full details about the economic prosperity of Bengal from the writings of foreign travellers during the period from the fourteenth to the sixteenth centuries. Ibn Batuta said that commodities in Bengal were cheaper than in any other country in the world. He quoted a long list of current prices of commodities such as rice, paddy, cows, hens, pigeons, lambs, sugar, ghee, sesame oil, finest cotton cloth as well as female slaves. A family consisting of husband and wife and a servant would need only 8 dirhams (small silver coins) for its maintenance for one full year. Nicolo Conti sailing up the Ganges saw on two sides villages and plantations with gardens of various fruit trees. Chinese traveller Fei Hsin observes that "men dressed themselves in cotton garments, sheep skin shoes with gold thread while women wore garments of cotton, silk or brocade, and adorned themselves with ear-rings of precious stones, gold necklaces, gold bracelets, and rings on fingers and toes." Barbosa states that respectable Muslims wore white cotton smocks with silk scarves, and carrying jewelled daggers with gold and silver in their girdles. They lived a life of luxury eating well and spending freely. Muslim women of respectable families had a great store of gold and silver and were dressed in fine silk.

A Chinese ambassador Huang Sheng-Tseng from the Chinese imperial court came to Pandua the capital of the ruler of Bengal in 1415. The embassy was received in the audience Hall with pillars plated with brass figures of animals and flowers. More than a thousand men in shining armours and hundreds of soldiers mounted on elephants, stood at the reception. The king sat on a high throne inlaid with precious stones, was under an umbrella of hundreds of peacock-feathers. The embassy was presented with rich gifts of various things including gowns of white hemp and silk.

Art and Architecture : History of Muslim architecture in Bengal dates from the time of Ikhtiyar-ud-din Muhammad bin Bakhtiyar. Minhaj-us-Siraj in his Tabaqat-i-Nasiri mentions that Bakhtiyar himself caused the establishment of mosques, colleges and rest-houses at Lakhnauti. Likewise Husam-ud-din Iwaz one of Bakhtiyar's successors also had built mosques, madrasahs, rest-houses in his capital and constructed roads across low and marshy country to facilitate movement of people and trade.

From epigraphic evidence we come to know that Sultan Iltutmish erected mosques at Pinchhli a few miles west of Malda. Zafar Khan Ghazi built a mosque with a mausoleum at Tribeni in Hooghly district in 1298, and another mosque at Gaulmati near Gaur in 1311.

The style and technique of Muslim architecture in Bengal while represented the characteristic forms of Muslim architecture, in the details of construction and design there was evolved a local individuality. There were various types of mosques such as single-domed, multi-domed and oblong type vaulted construction. Barrel shaped vault-type construction is to be found only in Bengal. Adina mosque at Pandua, and the Gunamant mosque and Darabari mosque, both at Gaur belong to this type and are still extant.

Sultan Sikandar Shah's famous Jami mosque at Adina, according to Marshall "was also the most ambitious structure of its kind ever essayed in Eastern India." It is "almost as big as the great mosque at Damascus."

Lotan Masjid at Gaur, the Eklakhi tomb, smaller mosques at Chhota Pandua in Hooghly district, at Goaldihi in Sonargaon, at Molla Simla in Hooghly district were other mosques built during the Muslim rule in Bengal. Chika masjid is virtually a copy of Eklakhi tomb. The Chhoti Sona Masjid at Gaur, built by Wali Muhammad during Hussain Shah's reign and the Bari Sona Masjid at Gaur, built by Nusrat Shah, Sat-Gumbad mosque at Bagerhat are of special interest as architectural works of the period. Qadam Rasul at Gaur built by Nusrat Shah in a type by itself and represents a single specimen of architecture.

Difficulty in obtaining stone in Bengal made it necessary to use bricks for building of mosques, palaces and mausoleums. This gave rise to a new style. Thickness of the walls and heaviness of the structure were due to the desire to give permanence to the construction. All this led Percy Brown to remark that "Islamic architecture of Bengal is not a style of building of a very impressive kind." Yet Percy Brown sums up the achievements of the architects of Muslim Bengal thus : "What they achieved may not have been a great art but its constructive principles were sound, its appearances were inventive and original, and it was peculiarly suitable to the climate and to the purpose for which it was intended."

REFERENCES

The Delhi Sultanate : Bharatiya Vidya Bhavan

The Delhi Sultanate : Md. Habib & K. A. Nizami

History of Bengal (D. U.) : Jadunath Sarkar

History of Bengal, Muslim Period 1200-1757 : J. N. Sarkar

An Advanced History of India : Majumdar, Roychaudhuri & Datta

The Oxford History of India (4th Edn.) : V. A. Smith (Revised by T. G. P. Spear)

9

Mughal-Afghan Contest [1526-1556]

A RETROSPECT

Hardly Nusrat Shah was on the throne of Bengal (1519), the Lodi empire of Delhi began to crack. By 1522, Lohani State was set up in Bihar, and the entire territory from Jaunpur to Patna became virtually independent under Lohanis and Formuli Afghans. The Lohani state and Bengal's common interest of security bound them into friendship. As the eastern part of the Lodi empire began to fall apart and Lohanis and Formulis became independent in the tract from Jaunpur to Patna, Nusrat Shah, Sultan of Bengal annexed the whole of Tirhut by which he rounded off his conquest in North Bihar. He placed his two brothers-in-Law Ala-ud-din and Makhdum Alam in Hajipur on the confluence of the Gandak and the Ganges which occupied a strategic position controlling all the river entrances into Bihar. His control of Saran gave him control over the reverine tract upto the Gandak as far as Azamgarh.

This military and strategic sefeguards made Nusrat Shah well-nigh complacent about Babur's victory at Panipat in 1526. The Afghan chief flocked together in the East and Nusrat Shah exerted himself to build up an Eastern entente against possible inroad of the Mughals and to make Bihar a centre of resistance. In 1526, Prince Humayun defeated the Afghans and drove Maruf and Nasir Lohani from Qanauj and Jaunpur annexing the Gangetic tract upto Ghogra south of the river Tons. Nusrat Shah found that it was not really a security to rely on the fickleness of his Afghan Allies and disarmed the Mughals by professing neutrality in the Mughal-Afghan conflict. Babur sent his envoy to Nusrat Shah's court for knowing if Nusrat would owe Babur's allegiance. Nusrat kept the envoy waiting in his court for more than a year which roused Babur's suspicion to allay which Nusrat sent the envoy back with his own envoy with presents and protestations of loyality to Babur. In 1528, Babur decided not to advance against Bengal.

Nusrat Shah's loyalty to Babur was a diplomatic move, his secret support was behind the Afghans who attempted to recover Qanauj but retreated on Babur's approach. Death of Bahar Khan Lohani of Jaunpur deprived the Afghan confederacy of one of its strongest supporters and Babur marched in triumph across the Ganges upto Buxar. Sher Khan Sur accepted the Mughal jagir in south Bihar and with the help of the governor of Jaunpur began to further his own interest at the cost of that of the Afghans. Jalal Khan son of Bahar Khan Lohani, a minor could hardly lead the Afghan confederacy. Nusrat took over the leadership secretly, ostensibly keeping his friendship with the Mughals.

In the meantime, a Lodi pretender Mahmud succeeded in rallying the Afghans once again under him. He seized Bihar from the powerless Jalal Khan who fled to Hajipur to ask for Nusrat's intervention. But Nusrat's hesitancy threw Jalal into the arms of the Mughals and he established contact with them. Nusrat prevented Jalal to leave Hajipur and in the meantime preparations went on for Mahmud Lodi's military enterprise against the Mughals. Sher Khan was also persuaded to join the confederacy against the Mughals. The joint army moved along the two banks of the Ganges under Sher Khan and Mahmud Lodi, but due to latter's incompetence the whole strategy was frustrated. Mahmud fled on the news of Babur's approach. Sher Khan also withdrew from the contest, as a result of which the confederacy totally collapsed leaving Nusrat alone in the field. Jalal Khan and his party evading Bengalis submitted to Babur in Buxar. Deserted by all allies Nusrat had to sign a treaty dictated by Babur (1529) to Nusrat's envoy. The draft treaty contained one clause which demanded free passage across the Ghogra. Nusrat was left with no choice but to agree yet he delayed in giving his consent to the draft. Babur waited for a month, sent another envoy and in the last resort decided on military action. In the three day battle that followed the Bengali forces supported by war-flotilla had to give way due to superior tactics of the Mughals. But Nusrat's diplomacy succeeded where his army failed, he retained the friendship of the Mughals.

Babur's death in 1530 presented an opportunity to Mahmud. He with Sher Khan and others moved out of Bihar and drove out the Mughal garrison from Jaunpur, and threatened Lucknow. Mahmud received much material assistance from Bengal. But Mahmud was abjectly defeated at the battle of Dadrah more due to the treachery of Sher Khan than to his own incompetence. With Sher Khan's acceptance of the vassalage of the Mughals for the fort of Chunapur the Afghan confederacy against the Mughals was dead. Humayun, it was now rumoured, was preparing for advancing against Bengal. Nusrat Shah had to look out for allies and sent his emissary to Bahadur Shah of Gujarat, the only determined enemy of Humayun, son of Babur, now succeeded to the Delhi Sultanate. But before the alliance could take shape Nusrat Shah died at the hands of an assassin, but Humayun had to stop his march against Bengal to meet the hostile moves of Bahadur Shah of Gujarat.

It was unfortunate for Bengal that Ghiyas-ud-din did not pursue the diplomatic move initiated by Nusrat Shah for an alliance against Humayun. There was also a chance to revive the Afghan confederacy, for neither Jalal Khan Lohani nor Sher Khan were friends of the Mughals. But Mahmud Lodi lacked imagination and failed to take advantage of the situation. He banked on the alliance with the Lohanis whose fickleness and political impotence he failed to understand. Mahmud despatched Qutb Khan of Monghyr, his ally, ostensibly for conquering Bihar but in reality aimed at destruction of Sher Khan ally of Makhdum who was in charge of Hajipur on the confluence of the Gandak and the Ganges. Sher Khan tried to dissuade Mahmud but Qutb Khan proceeded as asked by Mahmud only to be defeated and killed by Sher Khan.

Mahmud even now failed to realise that Sher Khan was a far more powerful ally than the Afghans of Patna. In the meantime Jalal Khan secretly accepted Mahmud's suzerainty in order to save himself from his over-bearing minister Sher Khan. Mahmud kept Jalal Khan Lohani detained in Hajipur and occupied Bihar. Now being in occupation of Bihar he had a technical right to put down Sher Khan. He made preparations and organised a formidable force comprising cavalry, artillery and the Bengal Paiks. Sher Khan who lacked artillery and sufficient foot-soldiers resorted to surprise tactics. He held the army of Mahmud, commanded by Ibrahim Khan in the plain of Surajgarh. But eventually the two armies met and Sher Khan by his brilliant use of cavalry routed the great army of Mahmud.

The battle of Surajgarh, from the political point of view, was one of the most decisive battles of medieval India. It placed Sher Khan on the way to Kingship. Mahmud and Sher Khan were now confirmed in their hostility to each other. But Sher Khan determined his policy with an eye to Humayun's attitude towards him. As Humayun advanced against

Gujarat, Sher Khan had a breathing time which he used for annexing Bihar territory as far as Bhagalpur. His march (1536) towards Bihar was sought to be prevented by Mahmud at Teliagarhi which was ably defended. Sher Khan left his son Jalal Khan to keep the enemy engaged at Teliagarhi and turned aside, took Jharkhand and suddenly appeared before Gaur. Mahmud bought off Sher Khan by paying thirteen lakhs and the latter withdrew from Bengal.

Mahmud in order to recover his power and prestige sought help of the Portuguese, but Sher Khan forestalled Mahmud by besieging Gaur. Humayun roused by these proceedings of Sher Khan now advanced against the East. He first laid a siege of Chunar. Sher Khan left operations against Gaur to his generals Jalal and Khawas Khan, hurried to Chunar, strengthened its defences and removed its treasures and his family to safety. After a few months Chunar fell to the mughals but Sher Khan sent another general to Bengal to force a decision. The Bengal forces gave battle but was routed and Sher Khan's army entered the capital of Bengal and carried with him "60 millions in gold."

Following his capture of Chunar Humayun advanced against Bengal. On his arrival he found the city of Gaur emptied of all Afghan troops and treasures.

BENGAL UNDER THE AFGHANS : MUGHAL-AFGHAN CONTEST FOR SUPREMACY

Rise of the Afghans to the imperial throne in the fifteenth century and the Mughal-Afghan contest in the sixteenth century form an interesting chapter in the Indo-Muslim history. The Afghans were enlisted in the army of Muizz-ud-din but they attained prominence under Balban when they were placed as garrisons in disaffected Hindu centres of Patiali, Kampila and Bhojpur. They became rebellious during the reign of Muhammad bin Tughluq under their leaders Malik Shahu Lodi in Multan, Quzi Jalal in Gujrat and Ismail Mukh in the Deccan. But elevation of the Afghans on the imperial throne was due to Bahlul Lodi who had united the Afghan Chiefs into a confederacy. But within a hundred years of Bahlul Lodi's death the Afghans became divided among themselves and made room for the Chaghtai Turks, known as Mughals on the Delhi throne.

The change of the imperial crown was followed by a bitter Mughal-Afghan contest in which an Afghan of extra-ordinary ability and genius occupied the imperial throne at Delhi and built up a transient Pathan empire. He was Sher Khan, son of a humble assignee of a jagir at Sasaram in Bihar. He rose by gradual steps to be the tutor and guardian of Jalal Khan, minor son of Bahar Khan Lohani, the ruler of Bihar and ultimately, on the death of Bahar Khan, became the ruler of the kingdom (1534). His star since then was in the ascendant and he annexed all territory of Bengal Sultan west of Teliagarhi and made a bid for the crown of Bengal in 1536.

Rise of Sher Khan became a matter of concern for the Mughal Emperor, Humayun who had in the meantime succeeded his father on his death in 1530. He advanced against Sher Khan from Delhi in 1538 with a large force supported by a war-flotilla. He first captured Chunar, an ancient castle. Humayun thought of entering into a treaty with Sher Khan and opened negotiations but Sayyid Mahmud Shah Sultan of Bengal who was a fugitive having been driven out of his kingdom by Sher Khan invoked Humayun's protection against the Afghan. Humayun at once broke the negotiations and advanced against Bengal. Sher Khan found himself, then only master of a strip of land from Bharkunda to Rhotas in great difficulty. He hurried to Gaur with 500 men by river route by-passing Humayun and seized and removed the treasure "60 million gold coins", that had fallen into the hands of his lieutenants Jalal Khan (his son) and Khwas Khan at Gaur. He also assumed sovereignty of Bengal and struck coins in his name. He sent

Jalal Khan and Haji Khan to hold Teliagarhi pass. Jalal Khan, on removal of the treasure from Gaur met his father Sher Khan in Sherpur in modern Birbhum and Humayun found Gaur emptied of the Afghans and entered the city without opposition.

Humayun, immediately on occupation of the city took up residence at the palace and got the roads cleansed and walls and villas repaired. "It was the month of May ; nature was now in a very gay mood in Bengal ; here woods were decked with luxuriant foliage : the rivers swollen with rain water, banks of clouds raced over the sky. The heat of the day was no doubt unpleasant, but gusts of wind accompanied by showers would often arise and then there would be a glorious freshness in the air. Such an agreeable place with its quiet, pure air, enraptured Humayun who in a mood of ecstacy conferred upon Gaur (meaning graveyard) the name Jinnatabad (the heavenly city). He apportioned the different parts of the country among his officers, placed garrisons at important points, and then abandoned himself to pleasure."

Sher Khan emerged from his retreat and during the time when Humayun was resting in Gaur, occupied south Bihar and ranged across Mughal territory from Benares to Bharaich. His cavalry worsted 5000 Mughal horse and preyed upon supplies to the capital. To add to the discomfiture Emperor Humayun, his brother Hindal revolted at Agra. When Humayun required of his brother Askari to support his cause against Hindal, Askari demanded perquisites as muslin, eunuchs and elephants of Bengal ; his officers demanded higher rank and enhanced salaries.

Humayun now woke up to the realities of the situation and leaving Jahangir Quli Beg with a body of 5000 horse, as governor, he left Bengal. But he again under-estimated his enemy. "Humayun failed to see that the shrewd Afghan had bowed his head, even as the cane branch of Bengal bends before the breeze, only to lift its head after its fall. He had allowed him to enter Gaur, and to march back unopposed only to meet him at an hour suited to him and on a ground of his own choice."

Humayun first reached Monghyr where Askari joined him, thence he marched along the south bank of the Ganges to Maner for four days he proceeded westward from Maner when Sher Khan began to attack his flanks. When Humayun reached Chausa on the bank of the Karamnasha Sher Khan intercepted him. But instead of fighting him openly he had recourse to diplomacy. He wrote to Humayun "What am I but the humble Farid, a servant of Majesty and where could I find resources enough to measure swords with the ruler of Hindustan?" He offered to relinquish all his possessions if only the Emperor would permit him to hold Bengal under the Emperor's suzerainty. Tired due to long march and the loss of his guns and non-arrival of much hoped for reinforcement from Delhi, Humayun condescended to accept the terms, on one condition that Sher Khan should feign a flight and Humayun would make a mock pursuit of him after which the Emperor would return to his capital and grant a **farman** according to the suggestions made by Sher Khan. All this was obviously to save the prestige of the Emperor.

Sher Khan agreed to the condition and signed the agreement with his seal and sent it to Humayun. When there was friendly atomosphere prevailing between the two camps Sher Khan made a surprise attack on Humayun's camp and the entire army of the Emperor fell into confusion. Sher Khan won a smashing victory over the Mughals at **Chausa**. According to Abul Fazl 8,000 Mughals including Mirza Muhammad Zaman, Maulana Jalal and many others perished in the water of the Ganges in their attempt to cross it to escape. Humayun was saved from a watery gave with the support of the water-bag of a water-carrier (visthi).

Sher next turned his attention to Bengal to deal with the Mughal viceroy Jahangir Quli who was defeated in several engagements and eventually inveigled him to a private interview and put him to death with many of his followers. The port of Chittagong was still under the officers of the Bengal Sultan Sayyid Mahmud Shah. Taking advantage of a dispute between these officers Sher Khan's deputy Nawzish Khan captured Chittagong but was himself captured by Portuguese chief Fernandiz Freire. Nawazish Khan somehow escaped and reconquered Chittagong. Thus Sher Khan's authority over Gaur, Sharifabad, Satgaon, and Chittagong was re-established. Eastern Mymensingh and Sylhet remained outside the ambit of his territory.

In the interval of making administrative arrangements for Bengal Sher made massive military preparation for the inevitable contest with Humayun. Sher reached Kanauj in 1540 and foiled the Mughal attempt to cross the river at Bhojpur by destroying the bridge. Humayun marched to Kanauj along the bank of the Ganges.

Humayun's vast army had four division, the van under Hindal, right under Askari, left under Nasir Mirza, and the centre under Humayun and his **dost** (friend) Mirza Haidar. The army was variously computed between 40,000 and 90,000. Sher began the assault before the enemy could take their appointed places and drew up the artillery. The battle was lost for Humayun. "No wonder in these circumstances Mirza Haidar's indignation mixed with grief broke out in such words as these : "the Chagtai army 40,000 strong was defeated by 10,000 Afghans on a battle field where not a man, either friend or foe was wounded ; not a gun was fired and the Chariots were useless." But the Mughals running helter-skelter to escape, plunged into the Ganges and an immense number of them perished. Humayun himself reached the other side of the stream on the back of an elephant and had to be lifted to the bank by making a noose of turbans. Such was the battle of **Kanauj or Bilgram** (1540) which transferred the imperial sceptre of India from the hands of the Mughals to the Afghans.

Sher now became Sher Shah, Emperor of Delhi, from the ruler of Bengal, the Emperor of Delhi was an elevation which was the reward of Sher's finesse, military strategy and the treasure of Bengal which enabled him to support a vast, strong army "as numerous as ants and locusts."

BABUR (1483-1530)

Zahir-ud-din Muhammad Babur, better known in history as Babur was the son of Umar Shaikh Mirza, ruler of Farghana a small kingdom in Russian Turkestan. He was born in 1483 (Feb. 14). He carried in his veins the blood of two Central Asian warriors, namely Timur the Turkish hero and Chinghiz Khan the hero of the Mongols. True to his blood Babur also grew into the traditions of his forebears and became a valiant warrior, adventurous and boundlessly ambitious. He was a descendant of Timur from his father's side and Chinghiz from his mother's. But he and his dynasty is known in history as **Mughal** perhaps derived from Mongol thereby showing preference to the maternal line.

Babur's childhood was spent under the influence of his wise, learned grandmother and mastered his mother tongue Turki as also Persian even in his childhood. He developed unusual power of appreciating significance of political events and judge human character. Umar Shaik Mirza and some other contemporary writers who saw Babur in his childhood have spoken highly of his keen intelligence and insight into men and things. He had military training, experience of administration and of war and diplomacy.

Babur succeeded to the throne of Farghana at the age of eleven in 1494 when his kingdom was invaded by enemies from two directions. His grandmother Aisan-i-Daulat Begum hurriedly performed the coronation ceremony of her grandson and set his house in order. Two enemies were Babur's paternal uncle Ahmad Mirza and meternal uncle Mahmud Khan. Babur first reconciliation with Ahmad Mirza by offering to hold Farghana as his vassalage. But this offer was rejected and in the war that followed Ahmad Mirza was routed and he had to retreat to his country Samarqand.

Mahmud Khan also was disheartened at the determination of Babur and the strong resistance put up by him. Mahmud Khan also retired to his country, Farghana was thus saved from the invasions of two enemies. Babur turned his attention to administration of the country and the honesty and efficiency that he breathed in the administration of Farghana as also his lovable personality won him popularity of his subjects.

Samarqand with its mosques, colleges, baths palatial buildings and charming gardens and particularly, its being the capital of Timur, the ancestor of Babur, had always fascinated him and he harboured an ambition to occupy it. In 1494 Ahmad Mirza died which was a singal for a civil war between his sons. Babur took advantage of the situation and attacked Samarqand in 1496 but the attempt failed. He repeated the attempt in 1497 and succeeded and sat on the throne of Timur thus fulfilling his life's ambition. But after three months when he fell sick at Samarqand, a rebellion broke out in Farghana. Babur hurried to Farghana ; he found most of Farghana had already fallen into the hands of the rebels. He Hastened back to Samarqand to find it had also slipped from his hands. Babur was now left with no territory except a small hilly district of Khojend. His followers also began to desert him and he had only two to three hundred men with him. He was a wanderer. In his diary the entry of the time was that "It came very hard on me. I could not help crying a good deal." His attempts to recover Samarqand and Farghana failed. In 1498 he won back Farghana only to lose it within a short time. In 1500-1 he tried to conquer Samarqand which was under Shaibani Khan, defeated him and took possession of Samarqand but could not keep hold on it for long. Shaibani Khan defeated Babur and took him prisoner. He had to purchase his freedom by giving his sister in marriage to Shaibani Khan and become a wanderer again with a handful of followers. He was in utter distress, although he always retained buoyancy of spirit and never gave in to despair.

After his defeat at the hands of Shaibani Khan by a sudden turn of events Babur's fortune began to smile on him. Shaibani Khan had defeated the governor Khusrav Shah of Qunduz and disbanded his army about four thousand of whom joined Babur. Babur now proceeded against Kabul to wrest it from Muqim who had seized it from Babur's uncle. In 1504 Babur succeeded in occupying Kabul and Ghazni with their dependent districts without a fight. Next few years he spent in strengthening his army and consolidating his conquests. In 1507 Babur assumed the title of **Badshah** or emperor and his eldest son was born to him next year (1508).

Babur, although a Badshah now, could not reconcile himself to the loss of Samarqand. He sought the assistance of Sultan Hussain Mirza of Herat to deliver a blow to Shaibani, but he returned disappointed. In 1511 Shaibani Khan died. This gave Babur an opportunity to regain his ancestral dominions. He entered into an alliance with Shah Ismail Shafavi of Ivar and recovered Samarqand, and occupied Bukhara, and Khurasan. Babur's territories now included Tashkhent, Qunduz, Hisar, Samarqand, Bukhara, Farghana, Kabul and Ghazni. In the following year (1512) the Uzbegs under their leader Ubaid-Ullah Khan defeated Babur and he had to abandon the whole of Trans-Oxiana. The only territory that still remained in possession of Babur in central Asia was Badakshan.

From the early age Babur learnt the art of defensive and offensive war. He had occasions to fight against the Turks, Mongols, Uzbegs, Persians as also Afghans. He in his great military acumen learnt their peculiar military tactics and modes of fighting. From the Uzbegs he learnt to attack the enemy in the flanks, in the rear and in the van with break-neck speed. He also learnt the tactics of laying ambuscade luring the enemy to a place of danger, only advantageous to himself. Babur evolved a system of warfare of his own which was the result of a synthesis of various modes of fighting known to the central Asian people. It meant an effective combination of highly trained mobile cavalry, scientific artillery, use of brilliant tactics such as **tulghuma**, as well as use of **balista**.

Babur used the period from 1514 to 1519 for raising a strong artillery under Ustad Ali, a Turkish artillery-man. Ustad Ali also raised a considerable body of musketeers. Babur acquired the knowledge of the use of fire-arms from the Persians who had learnt in form Constantinople. Babur got a number of pieces of cannon cast and maskets manufactured for his army. This powerful artillery was largely responsible for Babur's success against Hindustan.

In 1503 when Babur was the guest in the house of a village headman in the course of his wanderings in Tans-Oxiana, he heard from the hundred and eleven years old mother of the headman, the story of Timur's invasion of India. This kindled in him the ambition of repeating the exploits of his great ancestor Timur.

Babur led his first expedition against India in 1519 which was in the nature of a reconnaisance. He subjugated the Yusufzai tribe, then occupied the fort of Bajaur and proceeded upto the town of Bhera on the Jhelum. Babur believed that Punjab belonged to him as it was conquered by Timur in 1398-99. Babur wrote in his memoirs, "As it was always in my heart to possess Hindustan and as these several countries had once been held by the Turks, I pictured them as my own, and was resolved to get them into my hands, whether peacefully or by force."

Babur sent his envoy to Delhi to demand the countries that once belonged to the Turks. Daulat Khan Lodi detained the envoy at Lahore. Babur waited for some time but received no reply to his demand. He placed Bhera under his follower Hindu Beg and returned to Kabul. Soon after his departure Hindu Beg was driven out of Bhera by the people. This necessitated Babur's second expedition. Toward the latter part of 1519 he reduced the Yusufzai Afghans to submission and was about to attempt at fortification of Peshawar. But he had to return to Kabul on receipt of the news of rebellion in Badakshan.

Next year (1520) Babur led his third expedition to Hindustan and recovered Bhera and Bajaur. He next occupied Sialkot. The people of Sayyidpur refused Babur's supremacy without a fight and Babur had to subdue them by force. As trouble started at Qandahar babur had to return to recover Qandahar. The rebel governor of Qandahar abandoned Qandahar no doubt, but set himself up as the ruler of Sind.

Now Babur made himself secure in the rear and the strong fort of Qandahar was in his possession. When he was thus free from internal troubles, Daulat Khan Lodi, governor of the Punjab being discontended with Ibrahim Lodi for the cruel treatment meted to his son Dilwar Khan, joined hands with Alam Khan, an uncle of Ibrahim Lodi and a pretender to the Delhi throne, went to the extent of inviting assistance of Babur to invade India. Babur who had been cherishing the ambition of invading India, finding the opportunity coming of its own to him, readily accepted the invitation and marched towards Lahore with a formidable force in 1524. This was exactly the time when Ibrahim Lodi, the Delhi Sultan had despatched imperial army to punish Daulat Khan Lodi who was defeated and expelled from Lahore. The imperial army now tried to obstruct Babur's progress and met him when he had reached within a few miles of Lahore. Babur attacked the imperial army and succeeded in scattering it. Next Babur captured Lahore, entered the city, plundered and burnt it. He then occupied Dipalpur, the modern Montgomery district and put the imperial garrison to sword. Practically the whole of Punjab, was now under Babur. Daulat Khan Lodi now emerged from his exile and joined Babur who kept Punjab for himself giving Jullundar and Sultanpur to Daulat Khan Lodi as fiefs. Both

Daulat Khan and Alam Khan now realised their mistake that in inviting a friend, they had brought in a new master. They turned against Babur who was compelled to retire to Kabul but to reappear with a more formidable force, next November (1525).

In the meantime Daulat Khan and Alam Khan proceeded against Ibrahim Lodi who, however, succeeded in defeating them.

Babur began his march from Kabul in November and having occupied the Punjab, he compelled Daulat Khan Lodi to submit and was sent to Bhera to be imprisoned there. Daulat Khan died on the way. The Lodi pretender came to Babur in the mood of a supplicant and he was taken care of by Babur to take political advantage of his presence with him.

As Babur advanced towards, Delhi, he was receiving encouraging offers from a number of court nobles of Delhi. Perhaps it was at this stage that Rana Sanga of Chitor proposed to Babur to make a joint assault on Delhi. Ibrahim Lodi collected a large force and proceeded towards the Punjab sending two advance parties towards Hisar one of which was routed by Humayun. The other was also beaten back. Babur then reached Panipat and set up his camp. Ibrahim met him on the historic field of Panipat on April 21, 1526 with an army of 100,000 men. Babur had a large park of artillery and an army of 12,000 men.

While Babur had the strength of character and experience of a veteran general, Ibrahim Lodi, in the words of Babur himself "was an inexperienced man, careless in his movements who marched without order, halted or retired without method and engaged without foresight." After a desperate fight, fell on the field of the battle with the flower of his army yielding victory to inferior number but superior strategy and generalship and the use of artillery. Babur quickly occupied Delhi and Agra, thus the sceptre of Delhi passed into the hands of the Mughals from those of the Lodis i.e. the Afghans.

CAUSES OF BABUR'S SUCCESS : SIGNIFICANCE OF THE FIRST BATTLE OF PANIPAT (1526)

Compared man to man, Ibrahim Lodi was no match for Babur either in force of personality and character or of military acumen and soldierly abilities.

Secondly, while Babur had been chastened in the school of adversity and suffered many viccitudes of fortune which gave him a practical training in matters of warfare, Ibrahim, in the very words of Babur himself was an inexperienced man who knew little about movements in war.

Thirdly, Babur's army was not only well-disciplined by knew the art of attack on flanks, front and rear simultaneously. The Persian system of artillery was copied by him and he had a large park of artillery of guns and muskets. Ibrahim's army lacked discipline as it was organised on clanuish basis each group of soldiers obeying only its immediate superior but not the supreme commander. Although the army was huge, on Ibrahim's side, the smallness of number on Babur's side was covered up by its greater skill and efficiency. Ibrahim had no artillery.

Fourthly, Babur's army shared his zeal and enthusiasm and the hope of occupying a new and wealthy country held out a great prospect to them, the army of Ibrahim lacked homogeneity and discipline. As Babur observed, the Indian soldiers knew how to die but not how to fight.

Lastly, Ibrahim Lodi did not try to secure assistance of other Indian rulers, particularly of Rajput Sangram Singha in order to make a combined resistance to the common enemy. If such a joint front could be raised, perhaps the decision of Panipat would have been different.

As to the significance of the battle of Panipat (1526), it must be observed that it was one of the most decisive battles of the Indian history. Apart from the immediate result, namely, the death of Ibrahim Lodi himself on the battle field, and loss of twenty thousand soldiers on the imperial side, the battle was the last peg in the coffin of the Afghan sovereignty at least for a temporary period. All the same with a short break the dynasty of Babur ruled India for a period of nearly two hundred years after its restoration. From that point of view the first battle of Panipat had broken the back of the Afghans and their temporary revival was the prize of the extra-ordinary ability of an extra-ordinary Afghan, namely Sher Shah.

More important significance of the battle was that the foundation of the Mughal rule in India as a result of the victory of babur, was the beginning of the evolution of a composite culture reached its culmination under Akbar the great.

Conquests of Babur (1526-30) : The short rule of Babur was consumed in war of conquests and subjugation of rebellions of local chiefs, and kings. Ibrahim Lodi's death and the founding of a new foreign dynasty at Delhi led to a confusion in the country for a time, the advantage of which was taken by the Afghan chief who assumed independent status and fortified their strongholds. Independent rulers emerged in Sambhal, Bayana, Mewat, Dholpur, Gwalior, Rapri, Etwa, and Kalpi. Lohani, Formuli and other Amirs held Kanauj, Bihar, Mahaban and the territory along the Ganges. There were many Afghan chiefs and non-Afghan chiefs who had been sitting on the fance, found it expedient to come over to the side of Babur once it became clear that he had come to stay in India and rule over the country. They joined him with their troops and those who still held out were easily forced to submission. The Afghan chiefs except those of Awadh and Bihar and Rana Sangram Singha remained the only formidable enemies to be dealt with. As Rana Sanga i.e. Sangram Singha was at a long distance from Delhi, Babur took up sword against the Afghans first. Prince Humayun easily took Kanauj, Jaunpur, Ghazipur and Gwalior from the Afghan chiefs.

Battle of Khanua (1527, March 17) : Rana Sanga expected that Babur would retire after plundering the country, as his ancestor Timur had done. But when it became clear that Babur not only occupied Delhi but had decided to stay on permanently. Rana Sanga, a veteran and intrepid soldier, for the first time in the medieval Indian history, organised a confederacy of most of the medieval Indian history, organised a confederacy of most of the kings of Rajasthan. He was also joined by a number of powerful chiefs including Silahadi of Raisin, Husan Khan Mewati and Mahmud Lodi, brother of the Late Sultan Ibrahim Lodi : Rana Sanga recognised Mahmud Lodi as king of Delhi. Thus the Rajputs and some of the Muslim chiefs allied themselves with the determination to prevent the imposition of another foreign rule in India. Yet unfortunately all the Afghan chiefs did not join with the Rajputs at this critical juncture. If all the Afghan and non-Afghan chiefs would have combined with the Rajputs to oppose the foreign invader the history of India would have been different. It is a misfortune that Rana Sanga did not apply his mind to the question of putting up a joint defence with Ibrahim Lodi in the first battle of Panipat. However, the confederacy that Rana Sanga now could organise was more formidable that the army of Ibrahim. The combined army comprised 25 chiefs, had 80,000 horse, 550 elephants and the rulers of Marwar, Amber, Gwalior, Ajmer, and Chanderi ; and Sultan Muhammad Lodi brother of Ibrahim Lodi joined it.

Rana Sanga hero of a hundred battles was now ready to meet Babur. The Rajputs being "energetic, chivalrous, fond of battle and bloodshed, animated by a strong national spirit, were ready to meet face to face the boldest veterans of the camp and were at all times prepared to lay down their life for their honour."

Babur's small army became un-nerved at the sight of large, determined army under Rana Sanga. Babur broke all his drinking cups and poured the liquor on the ground and by an impassioned speech appealed to his army to take courage. This instilled fresh courage and enthusiasm into the hearts of his men. All his soldiers swore by the Holy Quran to fight for him.

In the battle that followed in the village of khanua due west of Agra, the Rajputs fought with desperate valour but Babur repeating the tactics of the battle of Panipat triumphed over the combined forces of Hindustan. Rana Sanga escaped with the help of some of his followers but died broken-hearted within two years. This victory was immediately followed by capture of the fortress of Chanderi by Babur despite gallant opposition by the Rajputs.

The battle of Khanua was another decisive battle of India which removed from the field the only other adversary without whose defeat the occupation of Delhi could not be regarded as complete.

Babur now turned to subjugate of Afghan chiefs who had repudiated their allegiance on the eve of the battle of Khanua, Rapri, Chandwar, Etwa were recovered. He met the allied Afghans of Bihar and Bengal at the junction of the rivers Gogra or Ghagra and the Ganges. In the battle of **Ghagra** (1529, May 6) he inflicted a crushing defeat to the Afghans. Thus by the three battles, **Panipat**, **Khanua** and **Ghagra** a considerable portion of Northern India was reduced to submission by Babur. His kingdom now extended from the Oxus to the Ghagra or Gogra and from the Himalayas to Gwalior.

Babur could not enjoy the fruits of his conquests for long. It is said that when his son Humayun fell ill Babur by a fervent prayer to God, had his son's disease transferred to himself. Humayun began to recover gradually but Babur fell sick and died in 1530 (Dec. 26) at the age of 47 or 48. Abul Fazl observes : Babur died as the result of the sacrifice he performed for his son. A modern writer Ram Sharma, remarks that "there is no reason to believe the fantasy told by Abul Fazl" about Babur's death.

BABUR'S MEMOIRS

Babur left a detailed record of his impressions about the country, climate, people, fruits, animals etc. of Hindustan. The book is written in Babur's mother tongue—Turki and styled **Tuzuki-i-Baburi** better known as **Memoirs of Babur**. It has been translated into several languages and there are three important English translations of the work, the best of which, however, is that of Mrs. A.S. Beveridge, who translated it from the original Turki.

The book, which is Babur's autobiography has been written in a facile style and reads almost like a romance. His flawless style and economy of words with penpictures of the contemporary celebrities, his candid descriptions of human virtues and vices, description of Nature, birds, flowers and trees etc. make the work one of the "most enthralling and romantic works in the literature of all time." The book has, however, gaps of several years at different stages.

Babur possessed an extra-ordinary power of observation and he took notes of the natural peculiarities, climate, fauna and flora of the country and the social, economic and cultural condition of the people.

Babur observed in his memoirs that Hindustan "is a country of few charms." About the people his observation is that they were of no good looks, were averse to social intercourse, had no genius or capacity, no good manners. There were no good horses, good dogs or grapes, muskmelons or good fruits, no ice or cold water, no good bread, no cooked food in the bazars, no hot baths, no colleges, no candles, torches or candlesticks.

They had a dirty gang of people who used to hold lamps fed by oil. Except their large rivers there was no running water in gardens or residences. The people of low standing and peasants went about naked wearing a **languta**. But he admired the country for its masses of gold and silver.

Babur, however, praised the climate, as it was not so hot as in Bakh or Qandahar. In the rainy season the rain-soaked wind was very pleasant. But the fault was that the air was very damp and humid so that bows, armours, books, clothes, utensils etc. did not last long.

Another good thing Babur mentioned was that there were enough number of skilled workers of every type of work, say stone-cutters, or any other type of work. He engaged 1491 stone-cutters for his buildings at Agra from Agra-stone cutters only.

Although some of the observations of Babur appear to be rather too much hasty and perhaps fear of the conqueror kept the people away from Babur and his followers, his memoirs generally speaking was influenced by his indigenous ideas as also from his observation from a conqueror's point of view.

Character and Estimate : Historians are unanimous in their opinion that Babur was decidedly one of the most fascinating and romantic personalities, in the history of Asia. In **Tarikh-i-Rashidi** it is said about him that he was "adorned with various virtues and adorned with numberless excellences above all of which towered bravery and humanity." In her **Humayun Nama,** Gulbadan Begum speaks in the same strain. According to Havell, Babur was "one of the most attractive figures in the history of Islam."

Babur was a dutiful son and a loving father. His love for his mother and his grandmother was very great. Although he was not free from all the faults inherent in persons of aristocratic birth in that age, Babur was a steadfast friend and kind to those who needed his help. His personal life was marked by a standard of morality that was rare in the country of his birth.

Trained in the school of adversity and gone through many viccissitudes of life, Babur developed a rare quality of courage and tact, and an ability to face upto any danger which normally cannot be expected in sons of kings. His education, military and administrative experience made him eminently suited for the problems of life that he was faced with. He was a man of great physical powers and of high ambition, cherishing in his bossom the thought of conquering Hindustan as did his forefather Timur.

"Babur emerges" observes V.A. Smith "as immensely likeable, a vigorous, artistic personality, as able to 'rough it' over the Hindu Kush in winter as to write most excellent Turki verses."

Babur was a great scholar and knew Turki and Persian to a degree of excellence. His culture and urbanity, his love of art and architecture and above all his aesthetic sense and power of appreciation of the beauties of Nature places him above his contemporaries. A devout **Sunni** Musalman Babur was by no means a bigot nor a religious fanatic. He treated the **Shiahs** of Samarqand with liberality. As he was a conquer or belonging to an alien faith he encouraged his terror-striken soldiers by declaring a **Jihad** against Rana Sanga and by inciting them to fight against Sanga as a religious duty. Against Medini Rai of Chanderi his call to his men was of a holy war. He also abolished the stamp duty for all Muslim traders but not for the Hindus. Yet, it may be said that his attitude to the non-Muslims was not as bad as it had been under the Sultanate.

Babur was a soldier all his life. He was an excellent horse-man and a good short. He could ply his sword effectively and hunt as a mighty hunter of the age. Babur was a good general and knew how to lead his men to success. He organised his army with the modern weapons of the time, namely the guns and maskets. He developed a park of artillery.

Although Babur had a very short period of rule which was mostly covered by wars of conquest and subjugation of rebellious chiefs yet he used the intervals for the maintenance of peace and discipline among his subjects and protecting them from the oppression of the free-booters. But he did not take any step for setting up any new and more workable administration. He allowed the antedated and outmoded administration of the decadent Sultanate days to continue. He divided his dominions among his followers upon whom he entrusted the task of administration. This gave rise to "a congeries of little states under prince than one regular and uniformly governed Kingdom. Many of the hill and frontier districts yielded a little more than a nominal submission"—as Eskine puts it. This feudal structure of the state developed centrifugal tendencies and whenever there was a weak ruler at Delhi the local governors and chiefs would become, or at least try to become independent. Babur's revenue as also judicial administration were haphazard and un-uniform. His financial administration likewise was poor.

Rushbrook Williams remarks that "As it was he bequeathed to his son a monarchy which could be held together only by continuance of war conditions, which in times of peace was weak, structureless and invertebrate."

HUMAYUN (1530-56)

Nasir-ud-din Muhammad Humayun was born in Kabul in 1508 (March 6) and although he had received education due to the arrangements made by Babur and acquired knowledge of Turki, Arabic and Persian he does not seem to have developed any scholarly interest in anything. He learnt Hindi after Babur's conquest of northern India. He acquired exprience of battle in Panipat and Khanua when he was barely eighteen. In 1526, he was assigned Hisar Firuza and afterwards he was given Sambhal as Jagir. After the battle of Khanua, he was put in charge of Badakshan where he fell sick and was brought to Agra. Babur nominated him as his successor while on death bed.

Difficulties : Humayun's accession to the throne was delayed by four days (Babur's death Dec. 26, Humayun's accession Dec. 30), during which attempts were made to set aside his claim and place Mahdi Khwaja on the throne. Situation at the time of his accession was not an easy one as there were hostile forces on all sides and as these were disguised, so were more dangerous. Prime Minister Nizam-ud-din Muhammad Khalifa had sustained a very poor opinion of Humayun and preferred to support Mahdi Khwaja, brother-in-law of Humayun to the throne. What prevented the prime Minister to place Mahdi Khwaja, at the last moment was, according to **Tabakat-i-Akbari,** that the loud thinking of Mahdi Khwaja "God willing my first act (as king) would be to flay you (meaning Prime Minister Nizam-ud-din) and other traitors" was overheard by the Prime Minister himself. The situation therefore, was intriguing. There was also no unity in the royal family and Humayun's cousins Muhammad Zamari and Muhammad Sultan were pretenders to the throne.

Among the Muslims, the theory of primogeniture was not strictly followed which made Humayun's three brothers Kamran, Hindal and Askari aspirants to the throne. "The sword was the grand arbiter of right, and every son was prepared to try his fortune angainst his brother" (Erskine).

Humayun's court was full of nobles who were busy in engineering plots for occupation of the throne. His empire which included the provinces of Balk, Qunduz, Badakshan in Central Asia, and Multan, the Punjab, the modern Uttar Pradesh, Bihar, Gwalior, Bayana, Dholpur and Chanderi in India was not completely reduced to submission and was ill organised. The Afghan chiefs within the empire were not subdued. Mahmud Lodi, brother of Ibrahim Lodi, the last Sultan of Delhi was still a claimant to the Delhi throne. Sher Khan was trying to weld the Afghans into a powerful community in order to set up an independent kingdom with their help. Bibban and Bayazid were looking for the opportunity to recover the territories from which they had been expelled. Nusrat Shah, Sultan of Bengal was trying hard to organise an Afghan confederacy to contain the Mughals. Alam Khan who along with Daulat Khan had invited Babur to invade India, collected an army with the help of Bahadur Shah of Gujarat, sent his son Tarta Khan to invade Agra. Humayun's near relations, the Mirzas were his rivals. Besides, his brothers Kamran, Askari and Hindal were all ambitious to occupy the throne. Kamran who was in charge of Kabul and Qandahar turned his covetous eye on the Delhi throne.

The situation demanded a ruler of much political wisdom, military skill and diplomatic ability. But Humayun lacked all these qualities. His lack of these qualities proved to be the major cause of his undoing. He was no doubt a man endowed with intellectual taste and love of culture, but he hopelessly lacked the determination, perseverance, practical wisdom and above all, discretion which were the need of the hour.

Humayun, immediately on accession to the throne, took a step which showed some brotherly feeling and liberality of mind, but no political wisdom. He divided his empire between his brothers, thinking that it would be possible for him to disarm his brothers by making them partners of his empire. Kamran was not only confirmed in his possession of Kabul and Qandahar but was allowed to keep in his possession the Punjab and Hisar Firuza which had been forcibly seized by him. Askari was given Sambhal in assignment. Hindal was given jagir in Mewat instead of Badakshan. Mewat comprised the extensive territories of Gurgaon, Mathura and part of Agra and Alwar which was his capital. Humayun's cousin Sulaiman Mirza was given Badakshan.

Possession of Kabul and Qandahar by Kamran who was openly hostile to Humayun, deprived the latter of excellent recruiting grounds for his army. Further, by confirming Kamran's forceful occupation of the Punjab and Hisar Firuza Humayun not only revealed his weakness but also sturck at the root of the integrity of the empire. Possession of Hisar gave Humayun command of the road connecting Delhi and the Punjab. Apart from dividing the empire between his brothers, Humayun also increased the jagi of every Amir.

Humayun's Wars : As the ruler of Bundelkhand was in league with the Afghans, who were enemies of the Mughals, Humayun first advanced against fort of Kalinjar in 1531. But he could not bring his campaign to any satisfactory conclusion as he had to hurry towards the east to deal with the Afghan menace. He made peace with the Raja of Bundelkhand, accepted a huge indemnity and left.

Mahmud Lodi, brother of Ibrahim Lodi who was advancing with his Afghan followers towards Mughal province of Jaunpur, easily took it and marched on the modern town of Nawabgunge in Barabanki district. Humayun defeated Mahmud Lodi in **Dauhria** in 1532. Next he laid siege of Chunar fort which was under the most powerful Afghan of time, namely Sher Khan. After four months' siege, Sher Khan made "a purely perfunctory submission." Humayun allowed Sher Khan's son Qutb Khan with Afghan troops to remain in Chunar under Mughal disposal (1532).

The year 1533-34 was wasted by Humayun in holding feasts and festivities and distribution of rewards to the nobles in Agra and Delhi allowing time to Bahadur Shah of Gujarat to increase his power and territory.

Humayun's policy of conciliating ambitious fief-holders like Muhammad Zaman Mirza and Muhammad Sultan Mirza having failed to completely win them over Humayun followed the path of further conciliation by confirming, Muhammad Zaman Mirza as governor of Bihar. This was taken by the Mirzas as sign of weakness on the part of Humayun and with the assistance of Wali Mirza these two Mirzas raised a standard of rebellion (1534). Muhammad Zaman Mirza was subdued, taken prisoner and blinded. But he escaped from the prison and took shelter under Bahadur Shah of Gujarat. Bahadur Shah refused to hand over the prisoner to Humayun, in fact, he gave shelter to many Afghan enemies of Humayun, including Alam Khan Lodi. Bahadur Shah had in the meantime annexed Malwa, besieged and defeated the Rana of Chittor and captured Raisin fort. He secured the services of Rumi Khan a skilled gunner from Constantinople and strengthened his armed forces by raising a troop of musketeers. Bahadur Shah had helped Alam Khan Lodi's son Tartar Khan to occupy Bayana from the Mughals. All this was too much for Humayun to tolerate. He sent Askari and Hindal against Tartak Khan who was defeated and killed. Humayun, himself marched against Bahadur Shah who was now engaged in second assault on Chitor. The queen mother of Rana Vikramaditya sought Humayun's help, calling that latter her brother. But this did not yield any result, for Humayun preferred not help a non-Muslim against his brother-in-faith, although his enemy. This cost him the Rajput support. Chitor fell to Bahadur Shah after a heroic defence and the women escaped dishonour by resorting to jauhar i.e. self immolation in a pyre. Bahadur Shah although triumphant did not venture to face the Mughal army and took shelter in Mandu which Humayun besieged. As the city fell Bahadur Shah fled to Champaner which was also besieged by Humayun. Bahadur Shah fled to Cambay and therefrom to Diu. Humayun then returned to Champaner, captured the city which was the respository of the treasures of Bahadur Shah. As Humayun was spending his time in pleasure at Gujarat, Bahadur Shah sent his trusted office Imad-ul-Mulk to collect revenue from Ahmadabad. But Askari defeated him. Humayun appointed Askari as governor of Gujarat and was preparing for the pursuit of Bahadur Shah in Diu. At this stage, Gujarat fell in confusion and Bahadur Shah taking advantage of the situation recovered some of the towns from the Mughals. Askari who lost courage was busy in his personal safety. In the meantime, Bahadur Shah proceeded towards Ahmadabad and reached very near it which necessitated Humayun's march against him. Askari finding that he could expect no help from Humayun fled from his post which gave Bahadur Shah to stage a come back to Gujarat which was now lost to Humayun (1536). Humayun finding it impossible to retain Malwa as alarming news from different parts of the empire began to pour in, left Mandu and started for Agra.

War with Sher Khan : We have already seen that Humayun's accession to the imperial throne was followed by a bitter Mughal-Afghan contest for sovereignty in which Sher Khan an humble assignee of a jagir in Sasaram succeeded in occupying the imperial throne by the dint of his ability, finesse and military tactics. Sher Khan was a tutor of Jalal Khan, son of Bahar Khan Lohani of Bihar, but after the death of Bahar Khan he became the ruler of Bihar himself in 1534. He then annexed Bengal.

Humayun advanced against Sher Khan in 1538, captured his stronghold, the fort of Chunar. Humayun was willing to negotiate a peace treaty with Sher Khan when Sayyid Muhammad Shah fugitive Sultan of Bengal sought his protection. This changed the mind of Humayun and immediately breaking the negotiations which had already been started with Sher Khan, he marched against Bengal. Sher Khan left Bengal with the treasure which had fallen into the hands of his son Jalal Khan and by passing Humayun proceeded towards south Bihar. Humayun entered the city of Gaur unopposed and was given to rest and pleasure. Sher Khan occupied, in the meantime, south Bihar, Benares to Bharaich.

Humayun did not realise that Sher Shah had only made a perfunctory submission to him and requested that he might be allowed to retain only Bengal as a vassalage. Humayun agreed. But when a friendly atmosphere prevailed between the two sides Sher Khan made a surprise attack on Humayun at **Chausa** (June 26, 1539), defeated him, and Humayun was saved from a watery grave by a water-carrier (visthi).

Sher Shah knew well, that more wars with Humayun lay in the logic of history. He made massive military preparations. Humayun met Sher Shah in the battle of **Kanauj or Bilgram** (May 17, 1540), but Humayun was defeated again. Such was the nature of the surprise attack that according to Mirza Haider "not a cannon was fired, not a gun. The artillery was totally useless." Humayun had to flee the field and cross the Ganges on the back of an elephant and hoisted on the bank by an improvised rope made of turbans. Many of his men perished in the Ganges in their attempt to escape by crossing it.

Humayun hurried to Agra, but the city did not afford any safety or security to him, on the contrary the news of the pursuit of the Afghans after him reached him. He therefore, repaired to Lahore where Kamran anxious to retain hold on the Punjab and Afghanistan did not feel inclined to earn the wrath of Sher Khan by either giving asistance or asylum to Humayun. Finding Kamran in secret correspondence with Sher Khan to whom he promised assistance if left in possession of the Punjab and Kabul, and also finding the prospect of recovering Delhi either from a base in Kashmir or Gujarat was bleak, flight was the only course open to Humayun. (for details see sec. Mughal-Afghan contest for supremacy).

HUMAYUN IN EXILE (1541-55)

It appeared that the work of Babur in India was undone and the sovereignty of India reverted to the Afghans. For fifteen years Humayun lived the life of a wanderer. It was during the course of this wanderings that he married Hamida Banu (1542) aged only 14 and much younger to him in age. Humayun for a time found shelter with Rana Prasad of Amarkot who promised to help him to conquer Thatta. But ultimately backed out. It was while at Amarkot that Akbar was born on November 23, 1543. Thus driven from pillar to post Humayun left India and ultimately found both asylum and assistance in the court of Persian emperor Shah Tahmasp. On his promise that on conquering Qandahar Humayun would hand it over to Persia that Shah provided him military help. But once Qandahar and Kabul were conquered, Humayun kept Qandhar to himself, contrary to his promise Shah Tahmasp (1545). Humayun took Kamran prisoner, blinded him and sent him to Mecca. Soon after Hindal was killed in a night encounter. Askari fled to Mecca. Having thus relieved of his unkind brothers' opposition, Humayun prepared to reconquer Hindustan. He began his march from the north-west in November 1553 and took full advantage of the civil war among the successors of Sher Shah who had died in the meantime.

Mughal Rule Restored : Humayun captured Lahore in 1555 without difficulty. Then he proceeded towards Delhi. During the civil war after Sher Shah's death the rebellious Afghan chiefs had declared Sikandar Sur, governor of the Punjab as the Sultan. Humayun defeated Sikandar Sur in the battle of Sirhind in 1555 and recovered Delhi and Agra and reoccupied the throne of Delhi after an interval of fifteen years. Thus by a favourable turn of fortune Humayun succeeded in recovering a part of the empire which he had lost due to his indiscretion, weakness and lack of diplomatic skill. He died on January 24, 1556 due to an accidental fall from the stairs of his library in Delhi.

Character and Estimate : Humayun, compared to his father, was a far too inferior personality, thoroughly unsuited to the needs of the time. He lacked that personality and force of character, that determination and discretion which were very much needed for the state which was in a formative stage when his father died and the central authority challenged almost every where, within the royal family, among the nobles and the rulers. Lacking in military genius, diplomatic skill and political wisdom, he was often a prisoner of indecision. True, he wanted to be kind to his brothers to a degree of fault, he was of amiable disposition and a patron of learning, art and literature. But his fifteen years wanderings and his experience in the school of adversity made him somewhat capable of tackling the problems that faced him from a practical stand point. But before he could do anything beyond recovering his lost throne, he died leaving his minor son Akbar to succeed him.

Humayun had succeeded to an empire which comprised Kabul, Qandahar, the Punjab, north Bihar, modern Uttar Pradesh ; Mewar, the foremost of the Rajput states also owed allegiance to the Mughals. Babur had conquered this vast empire, but was not destined to consolidate it. The task naturally fell on his son Humayun. But Humayun lacked the qualities that would only be able to help him to perform the task.

His difficulties were numerous. The Afghans were only half subdued. The same could be said of the Rajputs. Bahadur Shah of Gujarat was the inveterate enemy of the Mughals. Humayun's brothers and cousins were also aiming at the throne. Humayun began with the initial mistake of making his three brothers virtually independent rulers in three parts of his empire. Although the policy was commendable for the brotherly feeling shown in it, in reality it was impolitic and ruinous for the empire. Kamran was given Kabul and Qandahar. Soon he occupied the Punjab and Hisar Firuza, thus depriving Humayun of his territories and also recruiting grounds for his army. Humayun instead of punishing Kamran for this rebellious conduct, confirmed him in the authority of these newly conquered places. Such impolitic steps were not only suicidal for the security and integrity of the empire but also for his own position as the emperor.

While investing the fort of Kalinjar he had to abandon it half way in order to meet the Afghan menace. Similarly, he did not complete his seige of Chunar on the perfunctory allegiance of Sher Khan and allowed the latter to take full advantage of his impolitic step.

Humayun spurned the hand of friendship extended to him by Rani Karnavate of Mewar against the common enemy Bahadur Shah of Gujarat. But Humayun preferred to remain a passive spectator to the defeat of the Rajputs at the hands of Bahadur Shah, to sworn enemy of the Mughals. Humayun proceeded against Bahadur Shah not when he was embroiled in hostilities with the Rajputs, but only after he had emerged stronger after defeating them. Although for a time he succeeded against Bahadur Shah, yet he could not prevent him to reoccupy Malwa and Gujarat.

Against Sher Khan also, Humayun's policy was characterised by indecision and lack of foresight. Instead of attacking Sher Khan in Bengal, he spent time in the siege and occupation of Chunar and when he proceeded against Bengal, Sher Khan bypassed him leaving Gaur unprotected. Humayun occupied Gaur, spent his time there in pleasure and enjoyment the advantage of which was taken by Sher Khan who reoccupied Chunar, conquered Rohtas, Benares and marched upto Kanauj. Humayun coming to know that the way to his return to Agra was being occupied by Sher Khan hurried to Agra, but on the way was defeated in the battle of **Chausa** by Sher Khan.

Now Humayun made full preparation for a war with Sher Khan and both sides met near Kanauj in the village of **Bilgram**. In this battle Humayun met with a crushing defeat. He lost his throne in Delhi. Both Delhi and Agra passed into the hands of the Afghan chief Sher Khan now Sher Shah, emperor of Delhi.

Refused any asylum or assistance by his brothers and driven from pillar to post Humayun ultimately found asylum and military support from Shah Tahmasp of Iran and recovered his lost throne. The civil war among the successors of Sher Shah facilitated his recovery of the imperial throne after fifteen years. It, however, goes to his credit, whatever might have been the advantages of the circumstances of the time, Humayun, at least succeeded in regaining the throne that he had lost. This was to a large extent to the chastening of his personality and political sense due to his experience in the school of adversity during the fifteen years of exile. But Humayun did not live to consolidate his regained empire, for he died as a result of an accident, in 1556 (Jan.).

IMPORTANCE OF SHER SHAH'S ECONOMIC AND ADMINISTRATIVE REFORMS.

Sher Shah's Administration : Panipat and Gogra or Ghagra humbled, but did not annihilate the Afghan chiefs. They needed a personality of ability and imagination, diplomatic skill and military acumen who could coalesce their isolated efforts into a national resistance. This they found in Sher Khan, who succeeded in recovering the Delhi throne for the Afghans, at least, temporarily.

Sher Shah's career is as fascinating as that of Babur and as instructive as that of Akbar the great. About his administration, some three decades ago, scholars of medieval Indian history would regard Sher Shah essentially as a soldier and only secondarily an administrator of average ability. But as early as mid nineteenth century Erskine in his History of India under the First Two Sovereigns of the House of Timur (Vol. ii) called Sher Shah more a legislator and the guardian of his people than a successful military adventurer. Dr. K. R. Qanungo went to extent of calling him a greater constructive genius and better nation builder than even Akbar. But other writers such as Dr. Tripathi and Dr. Saran argue that Sher Shah's achievements as administrator have been highly exaggerated and he was, to speak the truth, a reformer but not an innovator. But it must be said without fear of contradiction that Sher Shah is regarded, by and large, as one of the greatest administrators of medieval India. He retained much of the old system but breathed a new spirit in it and transformed the medieval administration into an instrument of service to the people. Sher Shah's character showed a unique mixture of military genius and administrative efficiency. "His reign of five years was marked by introduction of wise and salutary changes in every conceivable branch of administration. Some of these were by way of revival and reformation of the traditional features of the old administrative systems of India, Hindu as well as Muslim, while others were entirely original in character, and form, indeed a link between ancient and modern India." According to Keene "No Government, not even the British has shown so much wisdom as this Pathan."

True, Sher Shah's government was personal government but it was autocracy without despotism. He was the repository of all powers of the State but, in practice he exercised his powers for the benefit of his people. His was an "enlightened despotism" which did not give the people any share in the governance of the country but recognised their rights to be well governed. He "attempted to found an empire broadly based upon the peoples will."

There were four ministers who were in change of daily routine work of administration, but they had no right to initiate any policy, which was within the power of the emperor only, to determine. These ministers were : **Diwan-i-Wazirat**, called **Wazir**, was in charge of revenue and finance. He held the status of Prime Minister and as such exercised a supervisory power over all other ministers. The next minister was **Diwan-i-Ariz** under **Ariz-i-Mamalik**. He was the minister in charge of the armed forces. Recruitment, organisation and discipline of the soldiers, payment of their salaries, their deployment in the battle field wee the duties of Ariz-i-Mamalik. He fixed the salaries of soldiers and officers and looked after their welfare.

The next, was **Diwan-i-Rasalat** or **Diwan-i-Muhtasib**. He was the foreign minister and was to be in close touch with the envoys and ambassadors sent to or come from foreign countries. Diplomatic correspondences were carried on by him under instruction of the emperor.

The fourth minister was **Diwan-i-Insha** who would draft royal proclamations, despatches, communications to governors of provinces and maintain records.

Other departments next to the above four, the heads of which were also sometimes called ministers, were **Diwani-i-Qaza**. Under the chief **Qazi** who would hear appeals from all provincial courts of Qazis ; **Diwan-i-Barid** under **Barid-i-Mamalik** who was the head of the intelligence department. It was the duty of Barid-i-Mamalik to report on every important incident happening throughout the empire, to the emperor. He would have a network of spies under him.

There was also a high official who was in charge of the imperial household. He would manage and superintend the work of the large number of royal servants and keep watch on them.

Sarkars and Parganas : Sher Shah divided his empire into forty seven **Sarkars** each of which was again subdivided into Parganas. There were few military governorships also. The provinces or Sarkars were, however, not uniform in size and income. These were under the Delhi Sultanate, not called **provinces** or **subahs**, but **iqtas** each of which was assigned to an importnt chief. Sher Shah introduced the systems of **Sarkars** and **Parganas**. Above each Sarkar was placed an Afghan officer. There were also military governors appointed in units higher than Sarkars, these were the governorships of Lahore, Punjab, Malwa and Ajmer. Thus there were a few provinces each under a military governor with a large force under him, and forty seven sarkars which were smaller units each under an Afghan Chief.

Sarkars were subdivided into Parganas, each of which had one **Amin**, one **Shiqdar**, one treasurer, one Hindu writer, and one persian writer to keep accounts. In every Pargana there was one **Shiqdar-i-Shiqdaran** and one **Munsif-i-Munsifan** to supervise the work of the pargana officers. Munsif was primarily a judge and had to decide civil cases. In order that officers might not develop any vested interest in the place of their work, Sher Shah introduced the system of periodical transfer of officials.

Sher Shah maintained autonomous villages and always kept himself in touch with the villages through village officials like **Patwaris** and **Chowkidars**. The village **Panchayat** which was composed of the village elders looked after elementary education, sanitation, irrigation, watch and ward, and other matters related to rural life. The petty disputes were also settled by the **Panchayat**.

Military Organisation : Sher Shah realised the need of a strong army and in his fight against the Mughals he relied mostly on the Afghans whom he invited from different parts of the country and employed them to positions suitable to every body's ability. He also appointed Hindus in his army. He realised the weakness of a feudal army based on occasional contingents supplied by the feudal chiefs. He, therefore, followed the policy of raising a permanent army partly by grant of jagirs and partly by payment from the royal treasury. Salaries of the troops and officers were fixed in accordance with their skill and ability. Sher Shah revived Ala-ud-din's system of branding horses to prevent fraudulent muster of horses or their clandestine sale. Promotion in the army depended entirely on merit and actual service rendered.

Sher Shah's army comprised 150,000 cavalry, 25,000 infantry, 300 elephants and artillery. At different strategic points of the empire garrisons were maintained. Each garrison was called a **fauj** and was under a **faujdar**. He took personal interest in the training and discipline of his soldiers. Transport and commissariat were in the charge of soldiers and commanders.

Police : Sher Shah reorganised the Police system in order to secure peace and order in the country and the responsibility for local crimes had to be borne by the local people.

The village headman was responsible for maintenance of peace, deteotion of crime and apprehension of the criminals. According to Nizam-ud-din "such was the state of safety of the highway that if any one carried a purse full of gold (pieces) and slept in the desert (deserted places) for nights, there was no need for keeping watch."

The chief shiqdar's duty was to maintain peace and security in the Sarkar. He was the guardian of peace within his jurisdiction. The shiqdar of the pargana discharged the same function. The efficiency of Sher Shah's police system can be realised from Abbas Sarwani's observation that "travellers and wayfarers during Sher Shah's reign were relieved from the trouble of keeping watch, nor did they fear to halt in the midst of a desert...they turned out their mules to graze, and they slept with minds at ease and free from care, as if in their own house...."

Sher Shah revived the systems of **dak chauki** and espionage of the time of Ala-ud-din Khalji. **Daroga-i-Dak Chauki** was the head of this department. Royal **dak** was carried by runners posted at **Sarais**. Sher Shah kept himself informed of every incident taking place in the empire through the network of spies. Daily report on the prices of commodities would reach Sher Shah. It has been said that much of the success of Sher Shah's administration was due to the efficiency of his espionage system. Sher Shah introduced the system of sending **dak** by horse men for quick service.

Justice : Honest and efficient administration of justice had also earned for Sher Shah the reputation of being a good administrator. Efficient judicial service is by itself a welfare measure for the people, and Sher Shah ensured this, He himself heard the final appeal as well as original cases. He would sit in his court for judicial purpose every Wednesday. Chief Qazi was the highest judge below the emperor and heard appeals from Qazis of district courts. There was a Qazi in every district. The munsif administered civil justice in district while the amins did the same function in parganas. **Mir Adl** was another judicial officer.

Sher Shah's Revenue Administration : Sher Shah's revenue reform is of abiding importance in the administrative history of India and provided a model for future agrarian system of the country. He made a great improvement upon the revenue administration of the Sultanate period and it constituted his chief title to fame. His experience of the working of the revenue system of his father's jagir in Sasaram stood him in good stead on his accession to the imperial throne.

Sher Shah made arrangements for the survey of lands, and the area of land under cultivation was ascertained village by village. Cultivable land was divided into three classes in accordance with their quality-god, middle and bad. The produce of these three kinds would be added up and divided by three to get the average quantum of produce which was fixed as revenue, Government revenue could be paid either in kind or cash, the latter being preferred. Sher Shah settled revenue directly with the cultivators. For the collection of revenue he utilised the services of the officials like the **Amins**, the **Maqadams**, the **Shiqdars**, the **Qanungos** and the **Patwaris**. Punctual and full payment of the assessed revenue was insisted upon by Sher Shah.

The state granted **Patta** i.e. the title deed to each cultivator specifying the state demand, i.e. the revenue that the cultivator had to pay, and each cultivator on his part had to sign a **qabuliat** i.e. argeement deed signifying assent to pay the stipulated revenue. Both in the **Patta** and the **qabuliat** the land under the cultivator is specifically defined with its area. While Sher Shah's principle was lenient revenue assessment, collection of revenue was very strict and if necessary enforced. Remission of rent and grants of loans to tenants would be made if crops were damaged during war or when there was failure of crops due to drought or flood. Sher Shah's revenue reforms enhanced the resources of the state and also conduced to the well-being of the people.

It may be mentioned on the basis of recorded evidence that Sher Shah did not insist on a uniform survey of lands in every part of his empire. For instance Multan and Rajasthan lands were not surveyed. It is supposed by some historians that Sher Shah also retained the traditional three types of assessment in some parts of his empire. These types or modes were known as (i) **ghallabakhi** or **batai**, (ii) **nasq**, **muktai** or **Kankut**, and (iii) **naqdi**, **Zabti** or **jamai**.

The first type of assessment had three variants such as determining the landlord's share as soon as the land was sown. The second variant is that the landlord's share is determined as soon as the crop was collected on the threshing ground. The third variant was a rough estimate of the produce of the soil on the basis of which the landlord's share would be determined.

The second type was in the nature of a contract between the cultivator and the Zamindar or the State by which the rent per bigha of land would be determined independently of the fertility or situation of the land.

The third mode was largely popular. The peasants were required to pay one third of the produce as revenue as well as the cost of collection of revenue and survey of the land.

Over and above the land revenue every cultivator was required to pay a cess of $2^1/_2$% of the revenue payable.

Apart from Firuz Tughluq no other medieval ruler had been so much solicitous of the welfare of the peasants except Sher Shah. He meted out punishment to those who used to oppress the peasants and compelled the oppressor to pay due compensation.

The revenue reforms of Sher Shah has been criticised by some on the ground that by fixing the average of the produce of the three types of lands, the best land was under-assessed while the worst land was overassessed. But Moreland points out that variation of crops grown in different types of land must have adjusted this apparent inequity.

Second defect pointed out, of the revenue reforms of Sher Shah was the additional cess of $2^1/_2$% of total revenue which was burdensome to the peasants.

Thirdly, the revenue officials, despite Sher Shah's keen and vigilant eye were not all above corruption and Sher Shah's system of transferring officers after every one or two years from one place to another is in itself an indirect admission of the existence of corruption.

Fourthly, annual assessment was both vexations and inconvenient and did not give the peasants security of hold on the land under his cultivation.

Lastly, the jagirdars must have been exercising their own rights on their cultivators and the latter were likely to have been suffering under them (the jagirdars).

Yet Sher Shah's anxiety to look after the welfare of the peasants and his anxiety to enhance their interest and punish those who would oppress them must have gone a long way to improve the condition of the peasants.

Finance, Trade and Commerce : The government under Sher Shah derived its revenue from land revenue, taxes on production and consumption of various articles, duties on trade and transport. Properties without any heir, presents, inheritance, salt, customs, Jizya, mint etc. were other sources of revenue. The feudatories, the jagirdars, nobles, vassals etc. had to make presents to the ruler which constituted an important source of revenue. **Khams**, i.e. one fifth of the booty taken in times of war went to the coffers of the ruler.

Currency and Tariff reforms of Sher Shah were also intended for the improvement of the general economic condition of the people. Sher Shah removed vexatious internal customs and levying the same only at forntiers and in the places of sale. This reduced the prices of commodities which conduced to the development of Trade and Commerce.

Communication : Sher Shah saw the importance of good roads both for military as also for commercial purposes. Roads also helped the movement of the people. He, therefore, connected his empire by a network of good roads, the most important of which was however, the Grand Trunk Road which extended from Sonargaon in East Bengal to the Indus, a length of 1500 Kos. Other roads ran from Agra to Burhanpur, from Agra to Jodhpur, Agra to Chitor, and from Lahore to Multan. Rest-houses and or Sarais were built on the road-sides at stages and trees planted on both sides of the roads for the benefit of the travellers and merchants.

Forts And Buildings : Sher Shah was a great builder. His buildings were of both military and civil interests. The magnificient fort at Rohtasgarh was built by him to provide defence to his north-western frontier. The **Purana Qila** at Delhi within the enclosure of which Sher Shah built a grand mosque which is considered to be an excellent example of Indo-Islamic architecture. Fergusson calls it the "most perfect of his buildings." According to Dr. Smith Sher Shah's mausoleum at Sasaram "built on a lofty plinth in the midst of a lake, is one of the best designed and most beautiful buildings in India, unequalled among early buildings in the northern provinces for grandeur and dignity." Cunningham preferred this mausoleum to the Tajmahal, Shahjahan's masterpiece. Not only Dr. Qanungo but Percy Brown as well, lavishly praised the buildings of Sher Shah.

Sher Shah's Religious Policy : Sher Shah was a devout **sunni** Musalman and strictly obeyed the injunctions of Islam. He said his five daily prayers kept fast of **Ramdan**.

About his religious policy opinions are at variance. While Dr. Qanungo is of opinion that Sher Shah's policy towards the Hindus "was not contemptuous sufference but respectful deference." But there are other scholars, for instance Prof. Sharma, asserts that Sher Shah could not raise himself above the Turko-Afghan rulers in his religious policy. He declared his war against the Rajputs as **Jihad** i.e. holy war. His war against Jodhpur was essentially a political and military step but it had doubtlessly a religious overtone and after victory he demolished the temples within the fort of Jodhpur and built a mosque on that site. But on a dispassionate consideration we cannot equate Sher Shah with pre-Mughal Sultans of Delhi. He was, on the whole, a tolerant ruler who did not resort to the policy of Hindu persecution, nor was there any determined attempt to demolish temples or any anti-Hindu propaganda. Leaving out certain special occasions, generally speaking, Sher Shah was tolerant to religions other than his own.

Character and Estimate of Sher Shah : Sher Shah's rise from the position of an assignee of Sasaram in Bihar to that of the emperor of Delhi was the reward of his perseverence, military skill, finesse, political foresight and the lessons learnt in the school of adversity in early life.

Well-educated and possessed of good knowledge of Arabic and Persian as also of history, he was a patron of learning although he did not extend his patronages to any individual scholar or writer.

He acquired military skill and experience while subduing the rebellious zamindars of his father's jagir. He understood what made a good soldier and a capable commander. His military tactics lay in surprising the enemy, crash attack and avoiding open battle till the enemy is lured into a position of advantage for him. The battles of Chausa and Bilgram exemplified his skill in command and his military strategy. He was a good military organiser and his personal magnetism kept his soldiers loyal to him under conditions of stress and trouble.

Sher Shah's solicitude for the peasants, for the improvement of the economic condition of the people by introducing utilitarian reforms such as improvement and construction of roads, abolition of internal customs etc. made him popular with his subjects. His religious policy although at times revealed his want of tolerance, it must be conceded, that his reign was generally free from the religious intolerance of the pre-Mughal Muslim rule.

From the points of view of strength of personality; actual achievements as a conqueror and an administrator, Sher Shah rivals Ala-ud-din, the greatest medieval Delhi Sultan, but stands for superior to him in constructive statesmanship. In his administrative activities, Sher Shah anticipated Akbar, the great Mughal emperor. Sher Shah's devotion to duty, his revenue and other reforms, love of justice and above all his tireless energy and indefatigable industry made him the best of the Turko-Afghan Sultans of Delhi. If we may not agree with Sir Wolseley Haig that Sher Shah was the "greatest of the Muslim rulers of India", he was certainly the greatest of the Turko-Afghan Sultans.

REFERENCES

An Advanced History of India : Majumdar, Roychaudhuri & Datta

The Oxford History of India (4th Edn.) : Dr. V. A. Smith

History of India, Vols. IV, V, VI : Elliot & Dawson

Cambridge History of India, Vols. IV, V

Mughal Rule in India : Edwardes & Garret

Studies in Mughal India : J. N. Sarkar

Later Medieval India : A. B. Pandey

Mughal Empire : A. L. Srivastava

10

Akbar the Great

MUGHAL EXPANSION UNDER AKBAR

EARLY LIFE : HIS ACCESSION

Born in Amarkot on October 15, 1542, when his father was a fugitive, Akbar's childhood was spent in adversity. When Humayun was on his way to Persia to implore Shah Tahmasp's assistance he received the news of Askari's march against him. Humayun was at Mustang then. He fled with Hamida Banu, Akbar's mother leaving Akbar, a baby of one year, behind, to his fate. Askari picked the baby and sent him to his wife who looked after the baby with motherly affection. In 1545 after recovering Qandahar from Askari and Kabul from Kamran he sent for his son whose whereabouts he came to know in the meantime. Akbar was then three years of age and when brought to Hamida Banu, he easily recognised his mother and jumped into her arms.

Akbar was now being looked after by a number of nurses, the chief of whom was Maham Anaga, wife of Atga Khan who has saved Humayun from drowning after the battle of Kanauj or Bilgram.

Akbar was a truant boy and all attempts of his tutors to teach him to read write failed. He bided his time in horse and camel riding, and looking after his pet dogs, pigeons etc. Although endowed with extraordinary memory he would not even sit down to learn the alphabet. Even in his childhood he became an expert swordsman, horse-rider and also expert in other martial exercises.

In 1551, on the death of Hindal, Akbar was made the governor of Ghazni, with Munim Khan as his guardian. After Humayun succeeded in defeating Sikandar Shah Sur in 1555, he formally declared Akbar as the heir-apparent, and after occupation of Delhi Akbar was appointed governor of Lahore and the famous Bairam Khan, a friend of Humayun, was appointed Akbar's guardian.

At the time of Humayun's death in 1556, Akbar was in camp with his guardian Bairam Khan, in the pursuit of Sikandar Sur, nephew of Sher Shah. The news of the death of Humayun was kept concealed in order to facilitate Akbar's peaceful accession. Bairam Khan took immediate step to enthrone Akbar, then a boy of thirteen on a brick platform improvised on the occasion and proclaimed him emperor on February 14, 1556. His accession to the throne had already been proclaimed in Delhi on February 11, 1556 the day of which Humayun died.

INDIA AT THE TIME OF AKBAR'S ACCESSION

India "presented a dark and complex picture." Akbar's half-brother Mirza Muhammad Hakim was governing Kabul almost in full independence. Kashmir, Multan, Orissa, Malwa and Gujarat as also the local chieftains of Gondwana had become virtually independent. In the south, the vast Vijayanagar empire, the Muslim Sultanates of Khandesh, Berar,

Bidar, Ahmadnagar and Golconda etc. felt little interest in North Indian politics. The Portuguese were in possession of Goa and Diu.

Humayun had succeeded in recovering only a small part of the Mughal territories in Hindustan. The Afghan Surs were still in occupation of the greater portion of Sher Shah's dominions. "The country from Agra to Malwa, and the confines of Jaunpur owned the sovereignty of Adil Shah ; from Delhi to the smaller Rohtas on the road to Kabul, it was in the hands of Shah Sikandar ; and from the borders of the hills to the boundaries of Gujarat, it belonged to Ibrahim Khan."

After Akbar's accession, Adil Shah's general Himu came forward to oppose the Mughals. He defeated the Mughal governor of Delhi Tardi Beg, and occupied Delhi and Agra. Himu betrayed his master, assumed the title of Raja Vikramjit or Vikramaditya and advanced to meet Akbar and Bairam Khan in the historic field of Panipat.

SECOND BATTLE OF PANIPAT (1556)

Bairam Khan with Akbar advanced through Thaneswar to the plain of Panipat, where thirty years earlier, Akbar's grandfather, Babur had routed and slain Ibrahim Lodi. Himu lost his park of artillery in a preliminary engagement yet he faced his adversary with 15,000 war-elephants and a vast number of troops far superior in number to those of Akbar.

The battle was fought on November 5, 1556, and at the initial stage Himu successfully attacked the enemy on both wings. Bairam Khan commanded the ten thousand strong army from the rear, placed Ali Quli Khan, later appointed Khan Zaman, in charge of the centre, Sikandar Khan Uzbeg in charge of the right wing and Abdullah Khan Uzbeg in charge of the left wing. Akbar was kept by Bairam Khan at a safe distance in the rear by his guardian Bairam Khan.

After a successful attack on the two wings, Himu launched an attack on the centre of the Mughal army, Himu appeared to be on the point of winning victory. But the defeated Mughal troops on two wings collected themselves and made a counter offensive on Himu's flanks. Ali Quli Khan made a cavalry charge on the centre of Himu's army. While fighting was raging with all fury between the two sides, Himu was struck by an arrow in his eye and he fell fainted. Himu's elephant driver took him out of the battlefield but was pursued by the Mughal army and brought before Akbar. Bairam Khan insisted on his young master to sever the head of Himu by his own hand and become a **Ghazi**, i.e. slayer of infidel, which Akbar complied with. Abul Fazl gives us a different story. According to him Akbar refused to kill a dying man. Dr. Smith, however, points out that "the commonly accepted story that young Akbar exhibited a chivalrous unwillingness to strike a wounded prisoner is a later, courtly invention."

Significance of the second battle of Panipat (Nov. 5, 1556) lay in the fact that it marked the real beginning of the Mughal empire in India and the history of its expansion began. The political significance of this battle was all the more far-reaching, for it shattered the military power of Himu on the one hand and put an end to the Afghan pretensions to sovereignty in Hindustan for ever. The victors occupied Delhi on the day of victory. Agra was also captured soon after. Himu's aged father was taken prisoner and put to death on his refusal to embrace Islam. Attempt to capture Himu's widow, however, failed. Sikandar Sur Afghan, pretender to the Delhi throne, was compelled to surrender in May, 1557, and was assigned a jagir in Bihar only to be expelled therefrom soon after. Muhammad Adil, another Afghan pretender, was killed in 1557. The third pretender Ibrahim had to flee and take refuge in Orissa. Within two years of the second battle of Panipat there remained no Sur claimant to the throne of Delhi and Akbar's sovereignty over Delhi was confirmed.

AKBAR FREED HIMSELF FROM HIS GUARDIAN BAIRAM KHAN (1660)

In 1660, Akbar had attained the age of eighteen and began to resent the galling tutelage of Bairam Khan. Bairam Khan was a man of extraordinary personality and of imperious nature. He would have no regard for other people's feelings. Akbar's impatience of the guardianship of Bairam Khan was all the more accentuated by the encouragement by his mother Hamida Banu Begum and his foster-mother Maham Anaga. Further all persons who were not pleased with Bairam Khan or were inimically disposed towards him seized every opportunity to exaggerate his faults. Coolness grew between Bairam and his royal ward which gradually developed into open breach. Bairam Khan's order of execution of Tardi Beg wounded the religious feelings of the **Sunnis**, particularly so due to the appointment of Shaikh Gadi in his place. Bairam Khan had also committed certain acts of indecision by punishing a **Mahaut**, i.e. elephant-driver whose elephant ran through the ropes of the tents of Bairam Khan when the elephant was engaged in an elephant-fight witnessed by Akbar himself, and by dismissing Mulla Pir Muhammad, Akbar's tutor. Akbar was egged upon by **harem party** headed by Maham Anaga which drew some of the governors to its cause. Akbar yielded to their pleadings and in a letter couched in polite language written by Abdul Latif, Akbar acknowledged the services of Bairam Khan and conveyed his intention to assume the affairs of the State into his own hands and desiring the Bairam Khan should make a pilgrimage to Mecca. A suitable assignment was made for Bairam's maintenance, the revenue of which would be transmitted to him from time to time.

Bairam Khan, despite well-wishers advice, after some hesitation complied with the royal command, relinquished his office and was making arragements to collect his treasures in the Punjab, but as he was not moving sufficiently fast as desired by those who wanted him to be finally out of India, i.e. the court party, sent Pir Muhammad with an army to hasten him out of the country. Pir Muhammad was the former ungrateful protege of Bairam Khan. This was too much for Bairam. He expressed this affront to his personal dignity and status held by him so long by standing up for armed resistance. He was defeated Akbar, with his generosity and gratitude to his former guardian, granted him pardon. He was offered the governorship of Chanderi, and Kalpi, alternatively to become Akbar's confidential adviser or leave for Mecca. Bairam Khan chose the last alternative, after all he was too high-minded and dignified a person to accept any position inferior to one that he had been occupying for long. He decided to start for Mecca. But on his way he was assassinated by an Afghan named Mubarak Khan whose father was killed by Bairam Khan in a battle in 1555. Akbar gave shelter to the now destitute family of Bairam Khan. Bairam Khan's infant son, Abdul Rahim, was brought up under Akbar's care and in 1584 was honoured by his father's title of **Khan Khana**.

Taking a dispassionate view of the services rendered by Bairam Khan when Akbar's position on the Delhi throne was precarious, his able guidance of his royal ward and the court party's setting of Pir Muhammad to hasten him out of the country, one cannot but come to the conclusion that Bairam Khan was a person more sinned against than sinning. Akbar's generosity towards him when he had revolted was not certainly commensurate with the services rendered by him in restoring the Mughals on the Delhi throne.

Akbar's freedom from the tutelage of Bairam Khan did not make him completely a free man in regard to his administration. He was now under the new tutelage of his chief nurse Maham Anaga, her son Adham Khan, Pir Muhammad, Shiab-ud-din Ahmad Khan etc. of the **harem party**. In 1561 when Akbar appointed his foster-father Shams-ud-din Atga Khan as his Prime Minister, the harem party, particularly, Maham Anaga and Adham Khan were extremely displeased. The intransigence and high-handedness of Adham

Khan and Pir Muhamman began to exceed all bounds of toleration. On May 16, 1562, Adham Khan stabbed Atga Khan to death while he was attending to his official duties. He also tried to enter the room in which Akbar was then sleeping in order to make his peace with Akbar. But the guard prevented his entry by bolting the door from inside. Akbar awakened by the noise caused by the murder of Atga Khan came out and asked Adham Khan why he had killed Atga Khan. Adham Khan had the temerity to threaten Akbar himself and even held his hand and sword but Akbar's severe blow stunned him and at once he was put under arrest, bound hands and feet and thrown down from the palace terrace under orders of Akbar. Maham Anaga who was ailing was informed of the incident by Akbar himself which evoked a reply from her "Your Majesty has done well." Soon after Maham also died. This was how Akbar freed himself from the influence of the **harem party**.

EXPANSION OF MUGHAL EMPIRE UNDER AKBAR

When Akbar ascended the Delhi throne the Mughal empire comprised the Punjab, Delhi and Agra. During the years 1558 to 1560 when Akbar was under the tutelage and protection of Bairam Khan Mughal dominion in Hindustan was on the road to expansion by the occupation of the strong fort of Gwalior in Central India, Ajmer, the key of northern Rajputana and Jaunpur province in the east.

With the emancipation of Akbar from the tutelage of the **harem party**, called the petticoat government (1560-62) by Dr. Smith, began his personal rule in the fullest sense of the term. Akbar "was the most ambitious of men who loved power and wealth, brooking no rival near his throne", now set himself to the conquest of north-western and central India, to be followed by the conquest of the east and the south. He would say that "A monarch should be ever intent on conquest, otherwise his neighbours rise in arms against him." Akbar acted on these avowed principles all throughout his reign.

During the petticoat government, Adham Khan and Pir Muhammad had conquered Malwa, but its ruler Baz Bahadur recovered it and held it till he was compelled to submit some years later.

In 1564 Akbar emancipated himself from the influence of the harem party and now he was both in fact and name to make himself the sole master of Hindustan. Akbar knew well that capture of the leading fortresses was a *sine qua non* to the overall authority over Hindustan. During the course of his conquest it will be noticed that he was taking particular care to acquire important fortresss.

(a) In 1564, Akbar despatched Asaf Khan, governor of Kara and eastern provinces to conquer the kingdom of Garh-Katanga, i.e. *Gondwana,* comprising the northern districts of the Central provinces. Vir Narayan, the reigning king was a minor and the queen-mother Durgabati, a Rajput lady of great charm and valour was ruling the kingdom as the regent of her son. He had a powerful army of 20,000 horses, 1000 elephants and a large infantry. Durgabati had valiantly defended her kingdom against Baz Bahadur and his Afghan followers of Malwa. Akbar's attack on Gondwana was an unprovoked one, a part of his policy of imperialistic expansion. Asaf Khan's army had 50,000 troops. Durgabati ably resisted Asaf Khan with an inferior force for two days. Vir Narayan was wounded in the battle and his mother got him removed from the scene of the battle. Durgabati continued to fight till she herself got struck by two arrows from the enemy side. She stabbed herself to death in order to avoid dishonour at the hands of the Mughal army. "Choosing death rather than dishonour she stabbed herself to the heart so that her end was noble and devoted as her life had been useful." Vir Narayan, despite his being wounded now offered resistance and fell fighting. His women immolated themselves by performing **jauhar** to escape dishonour. Asaf Khan collected immense booty in jewels, gold and silver, and 1000 elephants out of which he sent on 200 elephants to Akbar retaining the rest of the booty for himself.

At this point of time Abdullah Khan Uzbeg, governor of Malwa, and Khan Zaman, governor of Jaunpur, rebelled. Taking the cue from these rebellions, Mirza Hakim, brother of Akbar, also proclaimed himself emperor of Hindustan. Akbar quelled all the three rebels with a heavy hand and meted out adequate punishment to the rebels.

(b) Akbar's next move was for the conquest of **Chitor**, the capital of Mewar. Akbar's sense of imperialism deeply resented the independent status assumed by Rana Udai Singh of Mewar, who was acknowledged as the head of the Rajput clans.

It may be recalled here that even after the defeat of Sangram Singha in the battle of Khanua, the Rajput power was not totally disrupted. Akbar's far-sightedness gave him to realise that friendship and support of a valiant race of people like the Rajputs would be very much valuable for putting the Mughal rule over Hindustan on permanent basis. This apart, Rajput friendship and assistance would immensely help Akbar to expand the Mughal empire and render security to it. It was through Rajputana again that commercial route between north-western India and the rest of the country passed. Akbar's political wisdom, his far-sighted statesmanship revealed these political and economic advantages of friendly relationship with the Rajputs. In 1562 Beharimal of Amber (Jaipur) accepted Akbar as his suzerain and gave his daughter in marriage with Akbar. In this a matrimonial relationship was established between the Mughals and the Rajputs. Behari Mal, his son Bhagawandas and grandson Man Singha accepted high military posts in Akbar's army and helped him in expanding his empire. It may be mentioned here that Rana Sangram Singha who represented the spirit of Rajput valiance and independence and who staked his claim for the throne of Hindustan fought against Babur, the grandfather of Akbar. But neither that spirit of independence and dignity nor the valliance and fighting strength now remained among the Rajputs.

Rana Udai Singha was as incapable as craven-hearted. He, however, did not stoop so low as to buy Mughal neutrality or friendship by giving his daughter in marriage to Akbar or to accept his vassalage. In 1567 when Akbar invested the famous fort of Chitor, Udai Singha fled and took shelter in the hills. Jai Mal and Patta or Fatha—two Rajput chiefs fought valiantly up to the last and laid their lives down in fighting against the Mughals. A large number of the Rajputs lost their lives in defence of their capital. When all hopes of victory were lost the Rajput women performed **jauhar** in order to avoid dishonour. Akbar was victorious, Chitor fell and Akbar inflamed by the stiff resistance offered to his arms ordered a general massacre which led to the killing of 30,000 Rajputs. "The gates of the fortress (Chitor) were taken off their hinges and removed to Agra. The huge kettledrums which used to proclaim for miles around, the exit and entrance of the princes, and the massive candelabra which lighted the shrine of the Great Mother, also were carried away to adorn the halls of the victor. Chitor was left desolate, so that in the eighteenth century it became the haunt of tigers and other wild beasts. In these latter days it has partially recovered, and the lower town is now a prosperous little place with a railway station."

(c) Next year, in 1568, Akbar advanced to reduce **Ranthambhor**. Raja Surjan Rai Hara was a vassal of the Rana of Mewar. But before the siege was laid the army was recalled as the rebellious Mirzas invaded Malwa. It was in 1569 that Akbar could again advance against Ranthambhor. The siege of the fort lasted for a month during which there were heavy casualties on both sides. It was on March 18, 1569 that the fort of Ranthambhor fell despite most valiant resistance put up by Surjan Rai Hara. Tod refers to a visit by Bhagawandas to Surjan Rai along with Akbar in disguise. The Rajputs having recognised Akbar, the latter personally conducted negotiations. Some historians including Dr. Smith accepts the narrative of Tod, but according to badauni Surjan Rai Hara, a vassal of the Rana of Mewar, considering the fact that an impregnable fort like Chitor had failed to resist the Mughals thought that resistance would be useless and as such sent his sons Danda and Bhoja to Akbar for negotiating peace with him. Akbar granted lenient terms and returned to his capital.

(d) The capture of two strong Rajput forts, namely, Chitor and Ranthambhor, while adding to the military strength of the Mughal, empire, enhanced the military prestige of Akbar. Now the only fort of importance that was yet to be occupied was **Kalinjar in the modern Banda district** of Uttar Pradesh. Sher Shah could not reduce it. Raja Ramchand of Rewa had watched with consternation the fate of Chitor and Ranthambhor. So when in 1569 Majnun Khan Qaqshal was sent by Akbar against Kalinjar, Ram Chand made a seeming defence and submitted. Raja was assigned a jagir near Allahabad and Kalinjar was put in charge of Majnun Khan.

(e) Akbar's visit to Nagaur in 1570 brought more Rajput principalities under his control without any war. It was through Bhagawandas, brother-in-law of Akbar, that the rulers of **Bikaner** and **Jodhpur**, Rai Raiyan Mal and Chandra Sen respectively, waited upon Akbar. They were received with all courtesy, in audience, and they made their submission to Akbar's sovereignty. Likewise Rawal Hara Rai of **Jaisalmer** submitted. Akbar married a princess of the ruling family of Bikaner and also the daughter of the ruler of Jaisalmer. By 1570, the entire Rajsthan except Mewar with its feudatory States—Banswara, Pratapgarh and Dungarpura—accepted the suzerainty of emperor Akbar.

(f) Akbar's attention was now turned towards **Gujarat**. It had been conquered and possesed by Babur for some time, but it regained its independence. Gujarat was a rich centre of commerce between India, Turkey, rich ports on its coasts, Gujarat had an attractive commercial position and possessed rare economic advantages. Gujarat also lay on the way through which Indian Muslims in those days would journey to Mecca. Akbar, naturally, realised the importance of occupying Gujarat for the interests of his empire. The ruling king Muzaffar Shah III was only a nominal ruler and the distracted condition of Gujarat due to a bloody feud among the nobles for extension of their powers and interests, offered an excellent opportunity to Akbar. Besides, Akbar's rebellious relatives, the Mirzas, had taken shelter in different parts of Gujarat. This gave an added cause to Akbar's invasion of Gujarat. In the meantime one of the leaders of the civil war that was raging in Gujarat, Itimad Khan appealed to Akbar for intervention. Akbar at once sent Khan Khana with 10,000 horses as advance guard and himself followed with the main army in September, 1572. Akbar easily took possession of Ahmedabad and took Muzaffar Shah III prisoner. Itimad Khan and other chief nobles came and waited on Akbar. Khan Azam was appointed governor of Gujarat and Muzaffar Shah III was pensioned off. Akbar next proceeded to Cambay where the merchants from Turkey, Syria, Persia, Trans-Oxiana, portugal etc. waited on him. Akbar next captured **Surat** (Feb. 28, 1573) and the Portuguese who had come in touch with him courted his friendship.

Hardly Akbar had returned to Fathpur Sikri in Agra when news reached him of insurrections breaking out in Gujarat. Akbar hurried to Ahmedabad vanquished the insurgents and annexed **Gujarat** as an integral part of his empire. According to Dr. Smith, "The conquest of Gujarat marks an important epoch in Akbar's history. The annexation gave his government free access to the sea with all the rich commerce passing through Surat and other western ports. The territory and income of the State were vastly extended, so that the viceroyalty of Gujarat became one of the most important posts in the gift of the sovereign."

Towards the last part of the reign of Sher Shah, Sulaiman Karrani was the governor of Bihar. But with the fall of the Sur dynasty he made himself independent and extended his authority over Bengal and Orissa. Sulaiman Karrani was circumspect enough to disarm Akbar by acknowledging his suzerainty. But the rashness of his son Daud Khan, who considered himself more than a match for the imperial power, prompted him to openly defy Akbar. In 1574, Akbar undertook an expedition to chastise the presumptuous prince. He expelled him from Patna and Hajipur during the rainy season of the year. Mumin Khan was then left in charge of the Bengal campaign and Akbar himself returned to Fathpur Sikri. Daud Khan retreated towards Orissa but was defeated by the imperial forces at Tukaroi on the eastern bank of the river Suvarnarekha early in 1575 (March 3). But towards the end of the same year Daud made an attempt to recover Bengal. But near Rajmahal he was finally defeated and killed in July, 1576. **Bengal** was thus finally annexed to the Mughal empire. But some local chiefs, the most important of whom were Kedar Rai of Vikrampur, Pratapaditya of Jessore, Kandarpa Narayan of Chandradvipa, i.e. Bakarganj and Isa Khan of East Bengal, continued to resist the authority of the emperor for long. Akbar annexed **Orissa** finally in 1592.

(g) Chitor and the eastern part of Mewar had been occupied by Akbar in 1568, but the major portion of Mewar continued to be under Rana Udai Singh. His son, the indomitable **Rana Pratap**, ascended the throne of Mewar at Gogunda on March 3, 1572. He swore uncompromising resistance to the Mughals and recovery of Chitor. The magnitude of his task can be better understood when we note that without a capital and with only slander resources he had to oppose the organised strength of "immeasurably the richest on the face of the earth." His fellow Rajput chiefs and neighbours and even his brother Shakti Singh who lacked the high Rajput ideals of chivalry and independence had allied themselves with the Mughals. No obstacle was too alarming for this national hero of Rajputana, who was of a much nobler stuff than his relatives. The magnitude of the peril confirmed the fortitude of Pratap, who vowed, in the words of the bard to make his mother's milk resplendent and he amply redeemed his pledge.

Akbar, on the other hand, was bent upon wresting the remaining portions of Mewar from Rana Pratap. He sent Man Singh assisted by Asaf Khan, with a powerful army to invade the remnant of Mewar in April, 1576. Man Singh reached the plain at the northern end of the pass of Haldighat. Here the imperial army was attacked by Rana Pratap and a furious battle was fought in which the arrows and the bullets were shot indiscriminately as the Rajputs proved too much for the Sisodia heroes. Pratap was surrounded by the enemy and was about to be cut off. Bida Jhala, a faithful follower of Pratap, cleverly seized the crown from the head of the Rana which gave an impression to the enemy that he was himself the Rana. As he was pursued, Pratap was taken out of the battlefield by some faithful soldiers. Bida Jhala proved his loyalty to Pratap by laying his life down in the battlefield. Pratap took shelter in the hills.

Next morning, **Gogunda** was occupied by Man Singh and Pratap's strongholds fell into the hands of the Mughals one by one. The indomitable Sisodia king Rana Pratap, although reduced to starvation at times, would neither condescend to lower his pride and acknowledge Akbar's suzerainty, nor to agree to any matrimonial alliance with the Mughals. It is wrongly supposed by some that Akbar due to chivalrous regard for Rana Pratap, his great adversary, left him unmolested for the rest of his life. That fact is otherwise, Pratap was hunted from hill to hill and he and his family had to live on the fruits of the hills of his own native land. Instead of giving himself up to despair, Pratap continued the war with the Mughals and before his death in 1597 (Jan.) succeeded in recovering many of his strongholds. Before he breathed his last he exacted a pledge from his chief, for he had no faith in his son, that "his country should not be abandoned to the Turks."

Tod's observation about Rana Pratap is worth quoting : "Thus closed the life of a Rajput whose memory is even now idolised by every Sisodia...Had Mewar possessed her Thucydides or her Xenophon, neither the wars of Peloponnesus nor the retreat of the Ten Thousand would have yielded more diversified incidents for the historic muse than the deeds of the brilliant reign amid the many vicissitudes of Mewar. Undaunted heroism, inflexible fortitude, that sincerity which 'keeps honour bright', perseverance—with fidelity such as no nation can boast of—were the materials opposed to a soaring ambition, commanding talents, unlimited means and the fervour of religious zeal ; all, however, insufficient to contend with one unconquerable mind." Rana Pratap's death provided Akbar with an opportunity to reduce the remaining portion of Mewar, but his preoccupation in other quarters prevented him from doing so. Though Akbar did not stop sending more than one expedition against Amar Singh, son of Pratap, yet Mewar defied total annexation to the Mughal empire.

(h) **North-west frontier** had been occupying a position of strategic importance to every goverment in India and the problem of maintaining control over the region drew the most pointed attention of all rulers. "The Hindukush range, separating Central Asia from Southern Afghanistan, Baluchistan and India, becomes 'much less forbidding' in the north of Herat, and through this vulnerable point an external invader from Persia or Central Asia may easily enter the Kabul valley and India." At a time when Kabul was within the Mughal empire, Qandahar was India's first line of defence. Qandahar was also a very important commercial centre where merchandise of different parts of Asia used to come for marketing. Qandahar in enemy hands would, therefore, mean a dagger pointed to the heart of the Mughal empire. The turbulent Afghan tribes of the frontier—the Yusufzais and the Uzbegs—were dangerous in the fastnesses of their native hills and fanatically attached to their liberty. They were least friendly to the Mughals. Akbar had suppressed the turbulence of the Uzbegs and Abdullah Khan, their leader became friendly to him. The Yusufzais were reduced to submission by Raja Todor Mal and Prince Murad. Simultaneously with the expeditions against the tribesmen, Akbar despatched Bhagawan Das and Qasim Khan for the reduction of Kashmir. The Sultan of Kashmir, Yusuf Shah, and his son Yaqub were defeated and **Kashmir** was annexed to the Mughal empire (1586). Sind was conquered in 1590-91 and Baluchistan in 1595. Being harassed by his own relatives the Persian governor of Qandahar, Muzaffar Hussain Mirza, surrendered it to Akbar, thus **Qandahar** came peacefully into the possession of Akbar. In this way Akbar made his north-west frontier secure and at the same time made important additions to his territories. By 1595 Akbar's empire extended from Hindukush to the Brahmaputra and from the Himalayas to the Narmada except a few tracts.

(i) After making north-west frontier secure and having consolidated his authority over northern and central India, Akbar turned his attention towards the **Deccan**. Akbar's imperialistic ideal necessarily included extension of his hegemony over the Deccan Sultanates—Khandesh, Bijapur, Ahmadnagar and Golconda. Akbar's farsightedness also made it clear to him that the Portuguese merchants must be pushed back to the sea in order to prevent them from interfering in the politics of the country.

The Deccan Sultanates were frittering their strength in mutual hostilities and except on a solitary occasion when they united against the Vijayanagar empire they did not realise the wisdom of offering a joint front against the common enemy. Thus when Akbar sent his emissary to demand their peaceful submission, all except Khandesh sent evasive answers. Diplomatic missions having failed, Akbar decided to use force. He first appointed Prince Danial to lead an expedition to the Deccan but changed his mind and recalled him after he had already left Lahore. Mirza Abdur Rahim was appointed in the place of Danial to command the invading force. Abdur Rahim, Bairam Khan's son, assisted by Murad, the emperor's second son, marched against Ahmadnagar. Ahmadnagar, the premier kingdom of the Deccan, was rent with internecine feuds and dissensions at this crucial time. Though the operations of the Mughal army were hindered because the two general did not pull on well with each other, yet the siege of Ahmadnagar was laid in 1595. The city was heroically defended by the gallant Chand Bibi, the Dowager-Queen of Bijapur and an aunt of the reigning king Muzaffar of Ahmadnagar. Torn by internal dissensions the imperial general raised the siege and made peace with Chand Bibi according to which **Berar** was ceded to the Mughals and Ahmadnagar agreed to recognise the suzerainty of the Mughal emperor, Bahadur, a minor, was placed on the throne of Ahmadnagar. Soon after Chand Bibi resigned her authority and contrary to her advice and in violation of the peace signed between the Mughals and Chand Bibi, a militant section of the nobles at Ahmadnagar expelled the Mughals from Berar. This brough the Mughal army against Ahmadnagar once again and the Mughals gained a signal victory in a battle on the bank of the Godavari (1577). Internal dissensions led to the murder of Chand Bibi and the city was stormed by the Mughals in 1600. It was, however, not until the reign of Emperor Shah Jahan that Ahmadnagar was finally annexed to the Mughal empire.

In 1598, Abdulla Khan Uzbeg died, which brought relief to Akbar from the anxiety of a possible invasion of India from the north west. The Sultan of Khandesh, Miran Bahadur Shah, repudiated the Mughal authority and prepared to defend himself in his strong fortress of **Asirgarh**. Akbar marched to the south in July, 1599 and easily captured **Burhampur**, the capital of Khandesh. He laid siege of the fortress of Asirgarh. "It was impossible to conceive a stronger fortress or a more amply supplied with artillery, warlike stores and provisions." While the siege was being valiantly resisted by the army of Khandesh, the news of the fall of Ahmadnagar reached them. It caused much disappointment and dejection among them. An unexpected calamity had also fallen on the Mughal camp, for Prince Salim had risen in open revolt. Thus both sides had enough reasons to come to terms.

Akbar himself took the initiative, he sent an invitation to Bahadur to meet him on the assurance of safe return. Bahadur arrived at Burhampur camp with a scarf round his neck which was a sign of submission. But as he stood before the emperor, an imperial officer rudely threw Bahadur prostrate on the ground. Akbar then ordered Bahadur to send a written communication to his garrison at Asirgarh to surrender the fort. This Bahadur refused to comply, and he was put under detention. As the news of this treachery reached the Abyssinian commandant of the fortress of Asirgarh, he sent his son Mukarrib Khan to protest. Mukarrib was also asked, when he came to protest, if his father would surrender the fort. Mukarrib's answer was flat refusal couched in a language full of taunts which stung Akbar deeply. He ordered Mukarrib to be stabbed to death.

Akbar turned desperate. He wrote to Father Jerome and Benedict of Goa to write to the Portuguese of Goa to send him heavy artillery to reduce the fort to submission. When the Portuguese refused, Akbar flew into a rage. Although there are contradictory versions of the means applied for securing the surrender of the fort, both from the accounts of Sirhindi and Abul Fazl, it is clear that unfair means such as distribution of gold and silver among the officers of the garrison as well as the outbreak of pestilence within the fort led to the surrender of Asirgarh in 1601. "There can hardly be any doubt that the ignoble methods by which the strongest fort in India was captured by Akbar must for ever remain as a slur on his reputation."

AKBAR'S ATTITUDE TO STATE

Akbar's conquest of Bengal in 1576, twenty year after his accession, made him master of the whole of Hindustan and the most important administrative reform effected by him in that year was the division of the empire into twelve **Subahs** or provinces : Agra, Ajmer, Allahabad, Oudh, Bengal, Bihar, Delhi, Kabul, Lahore, Malwa, Multan and Gujarat. After Khandesh, Berar and Ahmadnagar were conquered, the number of the Subahs rose to fifteen.

Akbar's attitude to the State went through a process of evolution closely connected with the gradual change in his religious policy as well as his theory of kingship. At the initial stage of his reign, Akbar was an orthodox Muslim ruler, the **Amir-ul-Mummin,** i.e. the commander of the faithful, a defender of Islam and entrusted to carry out God's will as expressed in the Holy Quran, and as such responsible to God alone. In theory, if not in practice, he was subordinate to the **millat**, i.e. the whole Muslim population. The **millat** was, however, controlled by the **ulemas**, i.e. the Muslim divines.

Akbar was wise enough to understand that his growing empire based on military conquests would not ensure permanence. The experiences of the Sultanate of Delhi as also of the military success of his grandfather were not lost on him. He realised that a strong political system and an efficient administrative machinery based on the habitual allegiance of all Subjects irrespective of caste, creed or religion were imperatively necessary for an enduring empire. He, therefore, set about in his characteristically forthright manner to achieve them. Akbar sought to remove the check upon his will by the millat or the ulemas and to that end promulgated his **Infallible Decree** (Mahzar) in 1579 (Sept.) by which he assumed power of interpreting law which in his opinion was likely to be beneficial to the State or adopte any line of action for the benefit of his subjects, provided he could quote any verse of the Quran in support of his action. In practice, however, this meant that Akbar combined in his person both the secular and ecclesiastical authorities. The next logical step was to establish his claim as the impartial ruler of his people, Muslims or non Muslims. Not that Akbar's policy of setting up an administration which would be personal by all means, but would be fully devoted to the welfare of the people and the State, went without any opposition. The Sunni ulemas and the Muslim nobility who had been enjoying a privileged position in the State combined to raise a standard of rebellion, for they found Akbar's policy to be a virtual establishment of common citizenship on the basis of complete toleration. With the help of the Persians and the Rajputs as well as the tacit acquiescence of the bulk of the Sunni population Akbar triumphed. The rebellion of the Sunni ulemas and a section of the Muslim nobility convinced Akbar that the concept of an Islamic State had to be given up completely and welfare of the diverse creeds within the empire was the only right course to be followed. The scholarly secretary of Akbar, Abul Fazl, propounded the theory of Divine Right of Kingship, which was subscribed to by Akbar. According to Abul Fazl the king was God's representative on earth and his shadow. Greater knowledge and wisdom are given to him by God than to any other human being. Akbar maintained that "the very sight of kings had been held to be a part of divine worship." "Divine worship in monarchs consists in their justice and good administration. Tyranny is unlawful in everyone, especially in a sovereign who is the guardian of the world."

It is thus clear that Akbar's attitude to the State and government was one of personal despotism, but enlightened and solicitous of the welfare of the subjects. As the supreme head of the State, he was the supreme commander of the army, the highest executive, the highest law-giver and the fountainhead of justice. He believed in a paternal concept of the State and considered himself as the father and guardian of his people. As the head of the State and government Akbar worked hard for the discharge of his manifold duties. From **Akbarnama** we know that Akbar would appear before the public early at sunrise when he was accessible to the common people and would hear their complaints and transact State business. In the second session he would hold an open court which would generally last for four and a half hours. Huge crowds of all descriptions of people of both sexes would collect and present their petitions to the emperor. Akbar would listen to them and would dispose of many of the cases on the spot. The third session when he would again appear in the afternoon and hold a full durbar in the **Diwan-i-Am**. This session lasted usually for an hour and a half when daily routine business, particularly matters related to the imperial forces, **Karkhanas**, appointments and promotions of **mansabdars**, granting of **Jagirs** etc. were attended to. At night he would meet his ministers and advisers in the private audience hall, i.e. **Diwan-i-Khas** where affairs relating to foreign relations and internal administration were looked after. Late at night confidential matters relating to war and foreign policy or internal administration would be attended to with important ministers in a room called **Daulat Khana**.

From Abul Fazl we come to know that Akbar would spend hours of night in his private audience hall with philosophers and sufis. There would also be present "unprejudiced historians." Akbar devoted about sixteen hours of a day in the business of the State.

The above discussion will not leave us in any doubt that Akbar's solicitousness for the welfare of the people, his paternal attitude towards his duties to his subjects made him both an enlightened and benevolent despot, for, while he would not share his supreme authority with the people, he believed in their right to be well-governed. He earned the habitual obedience of his subjects, both Muslims and non-Muslims and made himself the first Muslim ruler who could be reasonably regarded as the national emperor of India.

COMPOSITE NATURE OF ADMINISTRATION : CENTRE

Under Akbar the structure of administration continued to be more or less of the time of the Sultanate, although changes in names as well as in details were brought about by him. Under Akbar, the central government as it had evolved comprised the Prime Minister (Vakil), Finance Minister (Diwan), Paymaster General (Mir Bakshi), Chief Sadr (Sadr-i-Sadur). The ministers were appointed by the emperor himself and held office during his pleasure. Ministers were subordinate to the Prime Minister. The Mughal ministers did not constitute any cabinet, they were rather glorified clerks than ministers.

As long as Bairam Khan was the **Vakil**, he exercised the powers of appointing and dismissing other ministers and was the virtual head of all the different departments of the government. But with his removal, the post of Vakil was gradually bereft of much of its real power and the department of finance was taken out of his hands and given to a separate minister called Diwan. Gradually, the Vakil's position became an ornamental one and did not possess more power than advising the crown. Later, under shah Jahan Diwan was actually made the Grand Wazir, i.e. the Prime Minister.

The **Diwan** or the finance minister also called wazir, was the head of the finance department and was in charge of the revenue and expenditure of the empire. Muzaffar Khan was Akbar's first Diwan but was replaced by Raja Todar Mal who was a skilled financier and a first rate administrator.

The main duties of the Diwan were to formulate rules and regulations for land revenue settlement, to fix the rates of revenues, to scrutinise and control disbursements. Important transactions were scrutinised and passed for payment by the Diwan. The provincial Diwans were appointed on his recommendations and were under his control and supervision.

All important revenue transactions, grants of assignments became valid only when his seal was affixed. Diwan was the most trusted person of the emperor and enjoyed wide powers and discretion. His duties were so heavy and multifarious that he had a few important officials to assit him. These were : Diwan-i-Khalsa, who looked after the crown land, Diwan-i-Jagir, who looked after assignments of land for service or free gifts of land, Sahib-i-Taujih who was in charge of military accounts, Diwan-i-Bayutut who supervised the accounts of various workshops (karkhanas) and Mushrif-i-Khazana who was the treasury officer, all assisting the Diwan in the discharge of his duties.

Akbar fully realised the importance of the revenue and finance department and took a personal interest in its working. He appointed a board of five experts to review the work of the department from time to time.

Mir-Bakshi or Paymaster General was in rank next to the imperial Diwan. He was in charge of recording the names, ranks and salaries of **mansabdars**. Salaries of all officers were disbursed through this office. Mir Bakshi had to keep himself in touch with every head of the military department and every mansabdar. He was required to attend the imperial Durbar and his position was on the right side of the throne. He had to present the candidates for service in the military department as also to present all horses and mansabdars before the emperor. He maintained the list of the palace guards. Although not the commander-in-chief of the army, he was at times sent in command of forces. Muster of troops, branding of horses, issue of certificates for grant of mansabs under his seal and signature were among his important duties. With the increase in the number of troops more than one Bakshi had to be appointed.

Sadr-us-Sadur or the chief Sadr was also an important minister and had to perform three types of duties : To act as the religious adviser to the emperor, to disburse royal charities, and to function as the chief justice of the empire. Under Akbar the chief Sadr enjoyed great power and prestige in regard to all the three types of functions that he discharged. At the initial stage of his administration Akbar allowed the chief Sadr to function as the religious adviser to the crown. But after he had reorganised his administration in his own concept and rejected the Islamic theory of government the chief Sadr ceased to be his chief religious adviser. Even with regard to the chief Sadr's power of granting scholarships and religious jagirs Akbar allowed him only the right to recommend. From **Ain-i-Akbari** we know that before such steps were taken by Akbar much corruption had crept into the department of the chief Sadr. Akbar also appointed Sadrs in provinces which also reduced the power of the chief Sadr. After all these measures, the department of chief Sadr began to function efficiently.

Apart from the above four principal ministries there was the ministry of royal harem, kitchen guards and workshop under a minister called **Mir Saman**.

PROVINCES

Akbar divided his empire into a number of **Subahs** or provinces for the sake of administrative efficiency. In 1602 the total number of provinces was fifteen. There were a number of subordinate States belonging to chiefs who had accepted Akbar's sovereignty. The States were strewn all over the empire and were of different sizes and the chiefs enjoyed different degrees of status and prestige. They were required to enlist themselves as **mansabdars** in the imperial service and to be present at the court on important occasions.

In each Subah or province the head of the administration as also the commander of the provincial force was the **Sipah Salar** i.e. the governor, popularly known as **subahdar**. He was the viceroy of the emperor and appointed by him. The subahdar was to administer even-handed justice in criminal cases, maintain peace and order, look after the welfare of the people. He was responsible for punishing the disaffected and the recalcitrant elements. He was to appoint loyal persons for police and intelligence service. The Mughal system was one of checks and balances. The provincial **diwan** was next to the subahdar and he was in charge of revenue collection, disbursement of salaries of the provincial officers, to keep accounts, meet the expenses of the subahdar and despatch the balance to the imperial treasury. The diwan was appointed by the emperor on the recommendation of the imperial diwan and was not subordinate to the subahdar. The system was devised so as to make the subahdar a check on the diwan and the latter a check on the subahdar. The mutual checks and balances were thought to be the only way to curtail the powers of either of these provincial officials. In fact, the subahdar and the diwan occupied equal status. Besides his financial duties such as revenue collections, disbursements of salaries and meeting other expenses of administration, the diwan was also in charge of civil justice. It goes without saying, cooperation between the subahdar and the diwan was the only condition of smooth administration of a province.

The provincial **sadr** and **qazi's** duties were combined in the same post. While as sadr, it was his duty to recommend persons for free grant of land or cash scholarship to the imperial sadr, his duty as qazi was to try cases as the head of the judicial department of the province. The district and town qazis worked under his supervision.

The provincial **Bakshi** was in charge of recruitment, organisation, discipline and efficiency of the provincial armed forces. Under the command of the **Sipah Salar**, the provincial Bakshi was appointed on the recommendation of the imperial Mir Bakshi.

Waqi Navis or **Waqaya Navis** was in charge of posting news writers and spies in all important places in the province including the offices of the Sipah Salar, diwan, qazi, faujdar, police officer etc. Much of the security and efficiency of the administration depended on the secret intelligence, as such great attention was paid to this branch. There are instances when news writers were appointed in provinces and in parganas by the central government.

Qotwal was in charge of internal defence, health, sanitation and peace of the provincial captial. He was the head of the entire police administration and thanas of the province.

Mir Bahar was in charge of the customs and boats and ferries, collections made there as well as of port duties realised in coastal towns.

DISTRICTS OF SARKARS

Each province was divided into a number of districts or sarkars. The head of the district was the **Faujdar** who was a military officer. He had to maintain peace and order in the district, to ensure safety of travel by road by keeping them free from robbers and dacoits, and enforce imperial regulations. He was also in charge of the local militia comprising of a small force. It was his duty to keep this army always well-equipped and in readiness for service. It was also his duty to assist the amal-guzar, i.e. the revenue collector in his function. Central Government would from time to time inspect the work of the Faujdar by sending officers from the centre.

Amal-Guzar was next in importance to Faujdar in the district administration. He was in charge of revenue collection and was assisted by a large subordinate staff. He was authorised to advance loans (Taqavi) to the cultivators, grant partial remissions when necessary or otherwise redress the grievances of the peasants. He was to supervise the work of the treasurer of his district and send monthly report on collection and expenditure to the court and remit regularly surplus revenue to the royal treasury.

Bitikchi is a Turkish word meaning writer. But in the Mughal district administration he prepared necessary papers and records relating to the nature, produce etc. of the land on the basis of which amal-guzars made the assessment.

Khazandar's (treasurer's) main duty was to receive the revenue, to keep it and despatch it from time to time to the central treasury. In order that money collected was kept in safe custody, one key was kept with the collector and another with him. He had no authority to make any disbursement.

PARGANAS

Each sarkar was divided into several parganas each of which was the lowest fiscal and administrative unit. The chief officers of each pargana were **shiqdar**, **amil**, **fotadar**, and **karkun**. There were a few other semi-official functionaries such as **qanungos** and the **chaudharis**. Shiqdar was the executive officer of the pargana. His duties included maintenance of peace and order, to receive money when the cultivators brought the same for payment to the treasury. He would also administer criminal justice. Amil also called Munsif had the duty of making assessment and collection of land revenue. He was required to deal with the cultivators directly and not through the village headmen. **Fotadar** was the treasurer of the pargana and discharged the same function as did **Khazandar** of the district. The Karkuns kept records of the arable lands, kinds of crops raised, revenue payable by the cultivators, actual collection, arrears etc. **Qanungo** was the head of the **Patwaris** in the pargana. His duties were akin to those of the Karkun. The Qanungo was the repository of knowledge of various kinds of land tenures and other peculiarities relating to the nature of the soil, assessment and collection of revenue. Abul Fazl termed him "the refuge of the husbandman." He was originally paid a commission on collection, but Akbar made his post a salaried one and assigned land for his personal maintenance.

CHARACTER OF AKBAR'S ADMINISTRATION

The Mughal administration under Akbar acquired an efficiency which rendered it brilliant in the Indo-Islamic history of India, but it was not national in the sense that it was mostly foreign in personnel. The Turks, Mongols, Uzbegs, Persians, Arabs and the Afghans with a small percentage of Indian Muslims and Hindus comprised the administrative personnel under Akbar. Most of the foreigners had of course settled in the country for one or two generations and many of them accompanied Babur or Humayun and were related to the royal family. According to Blochmann, 70 per cent of the high officers of the State had been occupied by them. Akbar threw higher services open to the Hindus, although their number was small both in the civil and the military services. Among the Hindus who held high civil or military offices, the Rajputs predominated. Thus from the point of view of administrative personnel, both civil and military, under Akbar the Mughal administration assumed a composite character.

Structurally, the Mughal administration basically continued to be what it was under the Delhi Sultanate, but with reforms in details, Akbar gave it a secular character which raised it from the narrow sectarian nature of the Sultanate days. Akbar's establishment of a common citizensip of his subjects irrespective of their castes and creeds and his solicitousness for their welfare and his eagerness for meteing out even handed justice to the people gave him the unstinted loyalty of his vast composite people.

MANSABDARI SYSTEM

Under Babur and Humayun the army consisted mostly of foreigners such as the Mongols, Turks, Uzbegs, Persians and the Afghans. The commanding officers were granted assignments in lands in lieu of salaries. Weaknesses as in the ruler, for instance in Humayun, made these commanders corrupt, inclined to insubordination, often avoiding to maintain the number of troops under them, which they were duty bound to do. Akbar clearly understood the malady of the armed forces and attempted reforms which were resisted by the commanders. He had to subdue numerous rebellions of the Mughal and Uzbeg officers. All this convinced Akbar that the only way out of the sorry and dangerous state of affairs was to assume absolute power of control and direction over the army into his own hands. The army needed to be organised in such a manner that corruption would be stamped out and army would become a disciplined force on which the State could safely rely on. The result was the **mansabdari system**.

A mansab means a rank and a mansabdar a holder of rank in the imperial service. A mansabdar had to maintain a definite number of troops. There were mansabs from ten to ten thousand. The ranks above 5,000 mansabs were, to begin with, kept reserved for the princes and relatives of the blood royal. But later these were given to others, as for instance, Man Singh was made a mansabdar of 7,000. Mansabs above 7,000 were now reserved for members of the royal family.

These mansabdars formed the official nobility and their appointment, promotion, reduction or dismissal depended on the emperor.

Complaints constantly poured in throughout the reign of Akbar that officers did not maintain the required number of horses and necessary equipment out of the revenues allotted to them. Badaoni writing in 1573-74 observed, "In cases of emergency they (Jagirdars) came themselves with some of their slaves and Mughal attendants to the scene of war, but of really useful soldiers there were none." Badaoni also refers to measures like branding of horses, preparation of minute muster rolls etc., even these did not totally prevent fraud, for "the amirs", remarks Badaoni, "put most of their servants and mounted attendants in soldiers' clothes, brought them to the musters and performed everything according to their duties. But when they got to their jagirs they gave leave to their mounted attendants....After enquiry it was found that they were all hired and that their very clothes and saddles were borrowed articles."

Some mansabdars had no duty except waiting upon the emperor and performing the work they might be called upon to do. Services of the mansabdars might be both civil and military or any of the two. All imperial officers except the sadr and the qazi were enrolled as military officers. Each mansabdar had a fixed rate of pay out of which he had to defray the cost of his establishment and the salary of his troops.

The Mughal army comprised cavalry, infantry, artillery and elephants, but no navy. Cavalry was, however, the flower of the Mughal army. The infantry comprised matchlockmen, archers, Mewatis, swordsmen, wrestlers, macebearers, porters, slaves etc. According to **Ain-i-Akbari**, the total number of matchlockmen under Akbar was 12,000. Akbar's artillery was not by any means strong or efficient, although there were pieces of ordinance which were carried by elephants and hundreds of bullocks. There were also different kinds of guns. The artillery was in charge of an officer called **mir atish**. The elephants were also trained to fight offensive battles by dashing the enemies to the ground and trampling them under foot. Elephants were furnished with defensive armours. Some elephants used to carry **ganjals**, i.e. light guns on their back which were ignited and fired from their back during battles.

Blochmann's statement that Akbar's standing army was only 25,000 strong is not regarded as correct by modern historians who point out that while the standing army under Jahangir and Shahjahan was not less than three lakhs in strength, Akbar's standing army could not be in all reasonableness any less than this figure, including of course the contingents of the mansabdars.

It may, however, be pointed out that despite Akbar's giving a great deal of thought and attention to his military establishment, his army was inherently weak and on the evidence of Badaoni we know that corruption in the mansabdari system could not be totally eradicated in spite of various measures undertaken by Akbar.

REVENUE SETTLEMENT—TODAR MAL

The fiscal sources of the empire were divided into two parts : central and local. The central revenue comprised income from commerce, mint, presents, salt, inheritance, customs and land. The land revenue, of these, was the most important source. Akbar had abolished the pilgrims' tax, **Jizya**, which were previously charged from the Hindus. Zakat which was a religious tax on the Muslims was also allowed to lapse. It may be mentioned that Akbar did not believe in the Islamic theory of taxation, namely, **kharaj**, **khams**, **zakat** and **jizya**. Land revenue, according to Moreland, during the laster years of Akbar's reign amounted to ninety million rupees. Revenue derived from other sources constituted only a fraction of the total amount of land revenue.

The land revenue was charged on the basis of the government records prepared after ascertaining the average produce of various kinds of lands for ten years. The system was evolved as a result of a series of experiments undertaken during the early years of the reign of Akbar. The first experiment was undertaken in 1563 by Aitmad Khan under orders of Akbar. Aitmad Khan divided the **Khalisa** land of Agra, Delhi and a part of Lahore into several areas, each yielding two and a half lakhs of rupees as revenue. But this did not mean any fundamental change in the system of land revenue assessment. As such in 1566, the second experiment was undertaken when Muzaffar Khan was the Diwan and Todar Mal his assistant. It was noticed that fictitious roll rent was maintained and the State demand was converted into cash on the basis of a fixed price of the produce for all parts of the empire without reference to their actual market price, whereby the State received much less than what it was entitled to. Muzaffar Khan made new rent roll but without measuring the lands of villages or referring to the records of the village patwaris. But Muzaffar Khan's attempt was only partially successful. In 1569 a third experiment under the new Diwan Shiab-ud-din Ahmad abandoned Sher Shah's schedule of assessment and introduced the system of assessing the revenue, when the crop would ripen and would be standing in the field. This was rather an arbitrary and cumbersome system which often led to higgling and bargaining between the cultivator and the revenue collector. This system was known as **Kankut**.

In 1570-71 the fourth experiment was made when revenue assessment was made on the basis of the actual produce of the soil. This system was extended to the jagir lands which were so long kept out of all revenue experiments and revenue systems. The Kankut or Nasq as it was previously introduced was abandoned. Land was measured by the government officials and revenue was settled on the actual produce of the land. This system was the work of **Raja Todar Mal**. This experiment proved very successful and the assessment schedule prepared by Todar Mal continued to be in force till 1580. Towards the end of his reign Akbar fixed the rate of revenue in cash.

The revenue settlement made by the ordinance called **Ain-i-Dahsala** established certain fixed processes. (i) The land of the empire was surveyed by Sikandar Lodi's **gaz** or yeard, measuring 33 inches. Akbar used bamboo **jarib**, instead of hempen rope as was done in Sher Shah's time as the rope was liable to expansion and contraction. 3600 square yards would make a unit called a **bigha**. The actual area of land under the cultivation of a cultivator was recorded. In this way the lands of all villages, districts, provinces and the empire had been measured. (ii) Lands which were under cultivation or cultivable were classified into four types according to fertility. (a) **Polaj** belonged to the first category and was always cultivated. (b) **Parauti** was cultivated almost always but would be left fallow for some time occasionally to recuperate fertility. (c) **Chachar** was land that had to be left fallow for three or four years, and (d) **Banjar**, the land which had to be left fallow for five or more years. The first three types of lands would be divided into three kinds according to their produce and on the basis of their average produce revenue would be assessed. The State's demand was one-third of the produce of the land as revenue. The produce payable as revenue was commuted into cash. Akbar divided his empire into several **dasturs** and all places within a dastur would have a uniform price of corn. In fixing the price of corn in a dastur the average of past ten years' prices would be the basis.

Although there has been divergence of opinions about the interpretation of Ain-i-Dahsala among scholars like Dr. Smith, Moreland, Prof. Sri Ram, Dr. R. P. Tripathi etc., it must have been in all probability a ten years' settlement.

The revenue collection was done by government officials, i.e. the parganas, districts and villages by **amil** or **amal-guzar** assisted by qanungos patwaris and village headmen. About the merit of Akbar's revenue system Smith observes that "the system was an admirable one. The principles were sound and the practical instructions to officials all that could be desired."

In criticism of Akbar's revenue system it has been said that there was no strict or searching supervision. The assessment having been one-third of the produce was very high. It is also said that there was a good deal of corruption in the revenue department.

AKBAR'S RELIGIOUS POLICY

Akbar had in his veins the blood of the orthodox father, Mughal **Sunni** and the orthodox mother, Persian **Shia**. His guardian and protector Bairam Khan was also a Shia, who as well as Abdul Latif, Akbar's tutor, a liberal-minded person and termed "a Sunni in the Shia country of Persia and a Shia in the sunni-ridden northern India" influenced the religious views of Akbar and taught him the principle of universal peace—**Suleh-i-Kul.** Thus both hereditary and environmental influences moulded his religious views in the direction of liberalism. He was by nature incapable of religious fanaticism and although even after the fall of Bairam Khan he was on occasions persuaded to sanction measures of persecution against certain notable Muslim heretics, he did never give evidence of narrow religious bigotry. He abolished the system of enslaving the prisoners of war and their conversion of Islam even before he had attained the age of twenty. As Akbar himself remarked "On the completion of my twentieth year, I experienced an internal bitterness from the lack of spiritual provisions for my last journey, my soul seized with exceeding sorrow." This shows the spiritual awakening in Akbar rather early in his life the consequences of which could be seen in the liberal measures like abolition of pilgrims' tax on the Hindus in 1563 all over his empire. In 1564 he took a more liberal and what might be termed as a revolutionary measure of abolishing the poll tax called **jizya** on all the non-Muslims of his empire, a tax which was systematically realised by all the Turko-Afghan Sultans as well as Akbar's father and grandfather in pursuance of the Quranic laws.

Akbar's inquisitive mind led him to hold regular religious discussions in **Ibadat Khana**, a building built for the purpose at Fathpur Sikri in 1575. Although, to begin with, discussions were confined to Muslim Shaiks, Ulemas, Sayyids and where only Muslim nobles were allowed to be present, Akbar was soon disillusioned at the bickerings between the Ulemas who while failed to explain the fundamental doctrines of Islam to Akbar's satisfaction behaved most irresponsibly in the presence of the emperor. Akbar now threw the discussion open to Hindus, Jains, Zoroastrians, Christians etc.

In 1579 (June 22) Akbar read the **Khutba** from the mosque of the Fathpur Sikri. The Khutba was drafted by the poet-laureate Faizi. In September, same year Faizi's father Shaikh Mubarak and Abul Fazl produced at Akbar's instance a **Mahzar** i.e. a formal document, The Infallible Decree—which gave Akbar the supreme authority of an arbiter in all controversial matters concerning Islam whether civil or ecclesiastical. This document was endorsed by All Muslim divines of the time.

The crux of the **Mahzar** was that "should his Majesty see fit to issue a new order in conformity with some text of the Quran, and calculated to benefit the nation, all shall be bound by it, and opposition to it will involve damnation in the next world, and loss of religious privileges and property in this. "Thus Akbar appropriated to himself the privileges which had been hitherto enjoyed by the Ulemas. According to Dr. Smith and Wolseley Haig, promulgation of this order virtually made Akbar both the "Emperor and the Pope."

Discussions in the **Ibadat Khana**, however, continued as before, but Akbar would also arrange private meetings with holy men and scholars of different faiths. After Akbar had lost faith in **Sunni** orthodoxy we find Mulla Muhammad Yazdi and Hakim Abul Fateh—two **Shia** scholars won great ascendancy with Akbar. But Shiaism also did not bring much solace to him and the turned to **Sufism**. Shaikh Faizi and Mirza Sulaiman of Badakshan initiated Akbar into the mysteries of Sufi principles and practices like direct communion with God. But Akbar's intense curiosity was not satisfied by Sufism alone, he turned to Hindu Sannayasis, Christian missionaries and Zoroastrian priests. He held discussions with Brahmin scholars Purushottam and Devi, as well as Buddhists, Jains etc. Akbar was a rationalist and carried on search for truth in a scientific spirit.

Not satisfied with tradition and authority in matters of religion, Akbar prescribed reason to be the sole basis of religion and it was reason that dictated him to extend complete toleration to every creed and sect within his empire. The religious discord distressed him and to do away with it he attempted to effect a synthesis of all the various religions known to him and styled it **Din-Ilahi** or Divine Monotheism. Truly speaking, it was not a religion but a socio-religious order or brotherhood, designed to weld the diverse communities of the empire into a broad brotherhood. It was based on the principle of **Suleh-i-Kul**, i.e. universal toleration. It believed in the unity of Godhead and some of the important Hindu, Jain and Parsi doctrines found place in it. It was Akbar's policy not to impose his religion by force on his subjects. **Din-Ilahi**, therefore, remained confined to a few thousands of his court circles and followers. Akbar allowed full religious toleration to his subjects, for he believed that there was truth in every religion and the same God was everywhere. Akbar permitted men and women converted to Islam earlier; to return to their former religion. The Christians were allowed to build churches and proselytize Hindus and Muslims into Christianity. All these steps as also Akbar's religious innovations were looked upon by the orthodox Ulemas as apostacy, and in 1580 Mullah Muhammad Yazdi, Qazi of Jaunpur issued a **fatwa** declaring that Akbar had ceased to be a Muslim and a rebellion against him was lawful. The time synchronised with Akbar's step to resume Jagir lands and to convert them into Khalisa. This added to the cutting down of the allowances of the imperial officers led to rebellions in Bengal, Bihar and in some other parts. Akbar put down the rebels and severely punished the malcontents.

Dr. Smith, Wolseley Haig and some other scholars of their thinking are of the opinion that Akbar was fully tolerant to other faiths no doubt but he persecuted Islam. This is based on the statements of Badaoni and the Jesuit missionaries. Badaoni took umbrage because Akbar gave up Islam as a State religion. According to Badaoni, a bigoted Muslim as he had been, Akbar's equal treatment to all religions was tantamount to unorthodoxy and hence was denounced as persecution of Islam. The Jesuit missionaries were busy in proving to their superiors in Goa and Lisbon that the emperor was well on the road to be converted to Christianity. This exaggeration they made purposely to magnify their achievements. But on a dispassionate consideration it has been found that the charges of apostacy brought against Akbar were untenable, for saying of prayers five times a day, pilgrimage to Mecca, celebration of Muslim festivals throughout the empire, etc. continued as before during Akbar's time. What Akbar did was to bring Islam at par with all other religions within the empire.

AKBAR AND THE RAJPUTS

Akbar's Rajput policy was born of enlightened self-interest, the result of a deliberate policy dictated by far-sightedness, political wisdom and exigencies of the situation rather than the outcome of a sentimental recognition of the valour, patriotism or a mere chivalrous recognition of their merit.

Even at an early age Akbar had experience of contumacy of the highly placed Muslim officials who were more mindful of their own interests, mutual jealousies and when opportunities came proved even traitors. The lessons of the refusal of Shah Abdul Mali to attend Akbar's coronation, prime minister Shah Mansu's conduct in traitorously backing Mirza Muhammad in his rebellion against Akbar were not lost on Akbar. Likewise, Bairam Khan's rebellion, Adham Khan's and Pir Muhammad's unprincipled and selfish conduct, the rebellions of Asaf Khan, Abdulla Khan Uzbeg and Khan Zaman showed Akbar how highly placed officials and his kinsmen menaced his throne and his life. The Afghans were never reconciled to the Mughal rule, for they regarded the Mughal rule as usurpation of their rightful claim. Bihar, Bengal and Orissa were still under the domination of the Afghans.

Akbar's farsightedness made it clear to him that the Rajputs who held a vast tract of territories under them and had legions in their army, taken the race as a whole, all renowned for the valour, loyalty to their masters, fidelity to their words of honour, if converted into friends, would become the strongest pillars of the Mughal empire both for offence and defence purposes. Akbar, therefore, decided to earn their friendship, seek their cooperation and use them as a counterpoise against the self-seeking Mughal, Uzbeg, Afghan and Persian officials and nobility.

In pursuance of this policy Akbar accepted the submission of the Raja of Amber (Jaipur) and entered into a matrimonial alliance with that Kachhawaha ruling family and took Bhagawandas and his son Man Singh into his service. It did not take long for Akbar to discover that these Rajputs were more loyal and serviceable than the most of his top-ranking Muslim nobles. Akbar now decided upon the policy of inviting the other Rajput chiefs to accept his suzerainty but to be left undisturbed in possession of their land. One after another most of the Rajput States accepted Akbar's suzerainty and entered into alliance with the Mughals retaining their autonomy. Marwar, Bikaner, Jaisalmer submitted. Metra fell in 1562, Ranthambhor in 1568. Mewar was the only State that did not submit. Chitor fell, parts of Mewar fell into the hands of the Mughals, but Rana Pratap, the indomitable Rȧjput patriot fought from the wilds of his native lands in utter distress and before death recovered a number of fortresses from the Mughals.

Akbar found in the Rajputs not only reliable friends but fighters who helped in the expansion of the Mughal empire. The confidence reposed in Man Singh by Akbar showed the changed picture compared to the one seen under the Turko-Afghan Sultans. Not looking upon them as political inferiors and being free from religious narrowness, Akbar treated the Rajputs with the honour and equality which the latter recompensed by their loyal service. The broad-mindedness of Akbar, his-total tolerance to all subjects his great trust in the Rajputs made the latter fight for the Mughals, against the same Rajputs who had for more than three centuries fought stubbornly against the Turko-Afghan Sultans of Delhi. This miracle was performed by Akbar by his statesman-like appreciation of the situation, his political wisdom and his far-sightedness and above all his rational mind.

SOCIAL REFORMS OF AKBAR

Despite his multifarious activities Akbar found time to undertake several reform measures for weeding out the evils of both the Muslim and non-Muslim societies. His principle of religious toleration did not, however, make him blind to certain evils in the Hindu society.

In his first regnal year Akbar abolished all inland customs and taxes on trades and professions. The removal of these impositions while gave economic relief to the people by bringing down the prices, free movement of goods produced indirectly a sense of oneness among the people.

In 1562 Akbar prohibited the age-long custom of enslaving the prisoners of war, selling their wives and children etc. This pernicious custom followed during centuries past was abolished saving many innocent unfortunate people from being reduced to slavery.

In 1563 Akbar was hunting near Mathura. He noticed that a tax was being realised from the people who had gathered there on pilgrimage. Akbar had no idea of the tax that was realised from pilgrims form all places of Hindu pilgrimage. On enquiry Akbar was told that it had been the custom of every Muslim ruler to realise pilgrim tax from the Hindus at every place of Hindu pilgrimage. The tax was not a fixed one. It was determined arbitrarily according to rank and wealth of the pilgrim. Akbar found that the pilgrim tax was morally wrong both because it was imposed on people who came "in search of the light of God" and because it was not uniform but arbitrary, variable according to the whim of the collector of the tax. He abolished the pilgrim tax all throughout his empire.

Akbar also abolished **jizya**, the poll-tax which was imposed on the non-Muslims, for its imposition, to his mind, hindered emotional integration of his subjects into one united brotherhood. There was considerable opposition to the abolition of this tax from an influential section of the court on both religious and financial grounds. But Akbar stuck to his order.

From 1581 several reform measures were undertaken in quick succession. In the same year on his way to Kabul expedition Akbar passed an order from Sirhind that a census of population should be taken. The Jagirdars, Siqdars, Daroghas of all provinces were to record the number of the people, their trade, occupation, income, and also the residents, i.e. not permanent inhabitants of the area. The good inhabitants were to be classified from the bad. It is difficult, in absence of detailed evidence, the extent to which this order for census was actually executed in those days when there was lack of proper communication, conveyance etc.

In 1582 an order was passed appointing a number of officers to regulate the transactions of sale and purchase of a certain number of listed articles.

In the same year (1582) a very important proclamation was made liberating all the slaves in the empire. Akbar observed in the proclamation. "How can it be right to call those seized by force by his (Akbar's) name and to order them to serve?" By a third order in the same year it was declared that the day of his accession would be a day of public festival.

The governors of the provinces were ordered not to inflict capital punishment without Akbar's confirmation. This had the effect of stopping random hanging or killing of accused persons under orders of the governors. Small birds and creeping animals were prohibited to be killed. **Sarais** were opened throughout the imperial territories. People were induced to give something to charity once a week or a month or a year. To encourage this, charities were instituted in the Palace. Public hospitals were also established.

Akbar was against child marriage which was prevalent both among the Hindus and the Muslims. Orders prohibiting marriage before the age of 12 and between cousins though permissible under Muslim law, were passed by Akbar. Later the lowest age for marriage was raised to 16 for the boys and 14 for the girls. Akbar seemed to have possessed a very modern mind. Consent of the parents of the boy and the girl to be married and also their mutual consent were made obligatory before marriage was performed. A token marriage tax at varying rates was realised.

It is interesting to note that under the influence of the Jaina teachers Akbar declared his preference to abstinence from meat eating (1578). In fact, he gave up hunting on Jumma days (Fridays) and abstained from meat taking on these days. He even remarked "It is not right that a man should make his stomach the grave of animals." A decree was passed by him recommending that his subjects should refrain from eating meat on the day of his accession as thanks-giving to almighty in order that the year may pass in prosperity. Badaoni deplored Akbar's certain orders by observing that he "promulgated some of his new-fangled decrees. The killing of animals on the first day of the week was strictly prohibited, because the day is sacred to the Sun, and during the eighteen days of the month of Fawardin, the whole month of Aban (the month in which his Majesty was born) and on sacred days to please the Hindus."

Badaoni observed elsewhere that Akbar discouraged study of Arabic, Mahommedan Law and the exegesis of the Quran. "Astronomy, philosophy, medicine, mathematics, poetry, history and novels were enclivated and thought necessary." It has to be noted that Akbar's emphasis on secular studies was not liked by orthodox school of thought, and there was no intention on Akbar's part to destroy Arabic literature as is made out by some of his orthodox contemporaries like Badaoni. The Imperial Library in fact, contained a great many works in Arabic. Akbar not only widened the curriculum of studies but also threw open the gates of educational institutions which had hitherto before been exclusively reserved for the Muslims. For the first time under him Hindu and Muslim children sat side by side in the same educational institutitons. Sialkot was a famous seat of learning during his time. Such was Akbar's fervour for education that Abul Fazl wrote in appreciation that "All civilised nations have schools for education of youths, but Hindustan is particularly famous for its seminaries. A big college was founded at Fathpur on the hill, the like of which few travellers can name." A number of Madrasahs flourished in Agra and that of Gujarat was specially famous. Beides the Madrasahs and educational institutions set up by Akbar and the nobles, there were many private schools.

Akbar took special care for the education of his sons. Mirza Abdur Rahim and Qutb-ud-din Khan, both known for their liberal outlook, were amongst the tutors of Salim. Shaikh Faizi and Sharif Khan were the teachers of Murad. Monserrate taught Murad the Christian doctrines. Sayyid Khan Chagtai was Danial's tutor. Abul Fazl and a Brahmin Pandit were engaged to give lessons to Akbar's grandsons. Female education was also encouraged. It was customary for Muslim nobility to send their daughters to schools. Princess Gul Badan wrote the famous **Humayun-Nama** as a contribution to Abul Fazl's **Akbarnama**. Salima Sultana was a poet of repute in persian and Maham Anaga, Akbar's chief nurse was also an educated lady.

One of the most memorable reforming step taken by Akbar was against the inhuman practice of Suttee. Jaiman, a cousin of Raja Bhagawan Das died prematurely. His widow was unwilling to become a **Suttee**, i.e. to burn herself in the funeral pyre of her dead husband but her step son Udai Singh and other relations almost forced her to agree to become a suttee. As the news reached Akbar he hurriedly appeared in the scene and taking the risk of being misunderstood by his Rajput relations intervened and got those who were forcing the widow to become a Suttee, arrested (Akbarnama). In another case Akbar intervened to persuade the young widow of Birbhadra of Panna not to immolate herself in her husband's pyre. Although Akbar did not pass any formal decree against the practice of **Suttee** he thoroughly discouraged the practice.

Akbar recognised the evils of intoxicants, drinks or otherwise, but he also realised that it would be impossible to enforce total prohibition and he made a compromise. He permitted wine-taking by only those whom doctors would certify it to be neccssary. Excessive drinking, disorderly behaviour after drinking or to booze were made punishable. The names of the purchasers of wine had to be recorded in the shop at the time of buying wine.

To meet the problem of beggary Akbar set up dormitories called **Khairpura** for the Muslim beggars, **Dharampura** for the Hindu beggars and **Jogipura** for Jogis where free food was served to them at the cost of the state.

Akbar recognised the evil of gambling but it was so wide spread that he found it impossible to suppress the evil. Gambling brought ruin to families, resulted in strifes, yet it was almost universal. Akbar set up a state bank from which loans might be taken by the gamblers and every gambling den was made liable to pay a fixed charge.

The measures that Akbar had introduced give us an impression of a new world or modernism.

PRINCE SALIM'S REBELLION

Akbar's last years were unhappy and passed in anxiety due to the unfilial conduct and eventual rebellion of the eldest Prince Salim. He was the child, much sought for and the result of many prayers born of the Kachhawaha Princess, daughter of Bherimal of Amber. He was born in Fathpur Sikri at the hermitage of the Muslim Saint Shaik Salim Chisti on August 30, 1569. Akbar took great care for the education of his son and engaged most learned persons as his teachers. But contrary to all expectations of his father, Salim grew into a headstrong, ease-loving youngman. He was appointed governor of Ajmer and given the charge of reducing the Rana Amar Singh of Mewar. Salim gave up the campaign and failed to perform the task given him by Akbar. This displeased Akbar who placed Danial, the third Prince in charge of the task in preference to Salim. Murad the second son died in the meantime. Abul Fazl who was not pleased with Salim used his influence on Akbar against him. Salim who flet rather impatient for the throne took all this as deliberate steps to denigrate his power. He decided to rise in rebellion. Salim seized the immense wealth of Shahbaz Khan a wealthy noble of Ajmer who had died and proceeded towards Agra. He by-passed his grandmother Hamida Banu who had started to meet him in order to persuade him to give up his rebellious intention. He seized the imperial treasure at Bihar and appointed his own officers in Allahabad, Bihar and Awadh and began to rule as an independent ruler.

After the fall of Asirgarh Akbar returned to Agra and opened negotiations with his son Salim. But the latter's demands were so extravagant that Akbar despite all his filial affection and willingness to come to a settlement with his erring son, found it impossible to comply. He now sent for Abul Fazl, his friend from the Deccan to consult him what course might be followed with regard to Salim. But Salim got Abul Fazl murdered on the way. Soon after there was a temporary rapprochement between the father and the son but as Akbar directed Salim to lead an expedition against Mewar he stopped short of reaching the place and went to Allahabad on the plea of collecting a park of artillery.

But there he was given to profuse drinking and orgies of cruelty and murder. In 1604 Danial died and Akbar was already 77. The year before (1603) Salim's first wife, mother of Khusrav died by taking an over dose of opium due to the maltreatment meted to her by Salim. She was the sister of Man Singh.

All this had a sobering effect on Salim. He visited his father in November 16, 1604 to offer condolences to his father for the two deaths in the family. As Salim presented himself before Akbar, the latter did not betray any sign of displeasure, but later chided him for his misdeeds and slept him in the face and kept him confined in the bathroom under the charge of Raja of Salivahan who was a phsycian of great repute for the treatment of Salim. Akbar sincerely believed that his son was suffering from a mental imbalance and needed medical treatment. Salim's principal followers were all arrested and thrown into prison. For ten days Salim was kept without any liquor, opium or any other intoxicant after which he was released and given residence in a suitable place. Salim was reconciled to his father. He humbly accepted the governorship of the western provinces of the empire and deputed his deputies there himself remaining at Agra by the side of his father who was nearing his death.

AKBAR'S DEATH (OCTOBER 25-26, 1605)

In 1605 autumn, Akbar fell ill perhaps due to acute dysentery or diarrhoea. Emperor's physician failed to diagnose the disease for about eight days during which no medicine was administered. Akbar's condition became worse. He realised that his end was nearing and nominated his son Salim as his successor (Oct. 21) and the day on which Salim visited his ailing father, the latter had lost power of speech. He made signs indicating that the royal turban should be placed on the head of Salim and Humayun's sword to his gird. In the midnight of October 25-26, 1605 Akbar breathed his last. Majumdar, Roychaudhuri and Dutta, however, put the date of his death as October 17, 1605.

AKBAR'S CHARACTER, PERSONALITY AND ESTIMATE

Jahangir in his Memoirs observes that his father Akbar "in his actions and movements was not like the people of the world, and the glory of God manifested itself in him." Both Abul Fazl, a dear friend of Akbar and Badaoni who was definitely a hostile critic of the emperor, were unanimous on one point that Akbar possessed an extra-ordinary commanding personality and "looked every inch a king." Contemporary writers both indigenous and foreign testify to Akbar's uncommon dignity, and there was none who would be left unimpressed by his presence.

Father Monserrate who had the privilege of close association with Akbar writes that "he was in face and stature fit for the dignity of king, so that any body even at the first glance, would easily recognise him as the king." Physical description of Akbar given by father Monserrate tallies with that of Jahangir.

Akbar had a very charming personality yet possessed extra-ordinary valour, remarkable courage and uncommon physical strength. "Like Alexander of Macedon, (he) was always ready to risk his life, regardless of political consequences." "An intrepid soldier, a benevolent and wise ruler, a man of enlightened ideas, and a sound judge of character, Akbar occupies a unique position in the history of India." He was a good conversationalist, witty and frank, always willing to hear cases of the people and to respond graciously to their requests. Akbar was a dutiful son, a liberal brother, an indulgent father and a loving husband.

His food habits were very moderate. He avoided meat from his diet at first on fridays, then on certain months of the year. Writers saw influence of Jainism on his food habits.

Akbar was a truant child and was illiterate. Recent discoveries have, however, shown that Akbar was not altogether unlettered. But on the evidence of Jesuit Missionaries Monserrate and Jerome Xaviere as well as Jahangir's **Memoirs**, although Akbar was illiterate, yet he was so intimately connected with various branches of knowledge that no one could imagine that he was illiterate. He was not ignorant. He had acquired deep knowledge of theology, literature, poetry, history and some other sciences by coming into touch with learned men. Akbar had a wonderful memory which largely compensated his illiteracy.

Abul Fazl who was always a close companion of Akbar says that he wrote daily with his own pen in numerals the number of pages read to him and to whom he paid accordingly. Abul Fazl also says that Akbar took special interest in calligraphy and the several modes of writing then prevalent. All this leads to one conclusion that Akbar must have not been illiterate. There is evidence that he could compose poetry, recite poems of Hafiz and fables of India. Lastly, Jahangir observed that although his father was **ummi** i.e. unlettered, "he himself wrote on the front page of **Zafarnamah**, a work treasured by the Mughals, testifying to the signature of Akbar on that page." "There are references to the specimens of Akbar's handwriting in the manuscripts preserved in the India office Library, London, and the Victoria Memorial Hall Calcutta" (Indian Historical Quarterly, Vol. 22, No. I, 81).

Akbar was deeply religious and as it often happens with such persons, he was at times torn between doubts and beliefs and to remove which he would spend days and nights in discussions with learned men. He came to a firm belief that God is omnipresent and each person according to his condition and understanding gives the Almighty a name but to name the "Unknowable" in vain, he would often say.

In his presonal life, Akbar was not given to profligacy, but he did not rise completely above the standard of his age. His **harem** comprised 500 women and making allowances for the presence of female relatives, servants etc. the number of his wives must have been quite numerous. Although Akbar would burst out in violent paroxysm of rage, at times, such occasions were very rare and it will be only fair to credit him with amiability, moderation, gentleness as also to say that he was never a slave of any kind of weakness.

Akbar was out and out an imperialist and believed in a policy of conquest. It was his principle that "a monarch should always be intent on conquest otherwise his neighbours rise in arms against him." His career was actually one of continuous conquest. By his indefatigable energy, soldierly skill, diplomacy and finesse he built an empire which comprised whole of northern India, a part of the Deccan. He brought this vast empire under one uniform government and one political system. He gave the country one official language, a uniform administrative system, coinage, a common system of weights and measures. He introduced certain most modern systems in his government, such as transfer of officers from one place to another without upsetting the work of administration. Barriers of imposts, customs, tolls etc. between one Subah and the other were removed bringing down prices at the same time encouraging expansion of trade. "This led to a growing sense of oneness of territory and a common fountain of all authority." By giving the country one official language (Persian) Akbar attempted to give a sort of a cultural unity to the empire. His patronage of Sanskrit, Arabic, Persian and causing translation of the Sanskrit works like the Vedas, Persian, Arabic, Greek and works on Sciences showed his eagerness for cultural activities. His attempt to prevent child marriage as also the inhuman practice of Suttee, and to restrict other social vices like prostitutions, overdrinking, drunken brawls etc. showed his highly reformed mind.

He was a great military organiser and he devised the mansabdari system with payment from the imperial treasury besides assignment in land, and his reliance on the Rajputs made his army an invincible force.

Akbar's revenue system rivals in interest and merit the system under the British rule. Akbar's spirit of toleration, his genial treatment of the Rajputs and the non-Muslims earned him the habitual allegiance of his subjects.

Akbar was also a great builder. His greatest architectural achievement was the new capital at Fathpur Sikri within which he built the Record office, Diwan-i-Am, Diwan-i-Khas, Panch-Mahal, Maryam's palace, Birbar's palace, emperor's sleeping chamber, Library and Jodha Bai's palace. Outside the enclosure of Fatpur Sikri stands the Jami mosque with its portal called Bulanddarwaja. Within the enclosure of the mosque in the tomb of Shaikh Salim Chisti. Most of the buildings of Akbar's time betray a mixture of Hindu-Muslim architectural styles.

For the benefit of the people, we are told by Abul Fazl, Akbar built numerous sarais and dug many wells and tanks. "Every where also sarais have been built which are the comfort of travellers and asylum for poor strangers" (Abul Fazl). From the same source we know of the founding of schools by Akbar.

The internal peace and prosperity coupled with the benevolent patronage of Akbar led to the development of art and letters during his reign. It was a period when as many as fifty-nine top-ranking Persian poets flourished. The list had been given by Abul Fazl. Abul Fazl in his **Insah-i-Abul Fazl**—a collection of Persian letters set up a model of epistolary composition in Persian. The most important Persian poet of Akbar's time was Abul Fazl's elder brother Abul Faizi.

Akbar sought to effect a fusion of Hindu-Muslim cultures and to this end arranged for providing a common literature to the intelligensia of the country by translating Persian, Arabic and Sanskrit works. For this purpose a translation department was opened which functioned under Akbar's personal supervision. Amir Fatehullah Shirazi, Mirza Abdur Rahim Khan Khana, Mullah Ahmad, Qasim Beg, Shaikh Munnavvar, Naqib Khan, Abdul Qadir Badauni, Haji Ibrahim Sarhindi, Shaikh Sultan, Faizi, Abul Fazl, Maulana Sheri etc. did the work of translation.

Of the renowned composition of the historical literature in Persian in Akbar's time were Abul Fazl's **Ain-i-Akbari**, and **Akbar-Nama** ; Nizam-ud-din Ahmad's **Tabqat-i-Akbari**, Gulbadan Begum's **Humayun-Nama**, Abbas Sarwani's **Tohfa-i-Akbar Shahi** alias **Tarikh-i-Sher Shahi** and Jauhar's **Tazkirat-ul-Waqayat** ; other works were Abdul Qadir Badauni's **Muntakhab-ul-Tawarikh**, Faizi Sarhend's **Akbar-Nama** etc.

Akbar's reign was also a golden age of Hindi poetry. Many first-rate Hindi poets produced Hindi poetical works which became classics. The most notable of the Hindi poets were Sur Das, Tulsi Das, Abdur Rahim Khan Khana, Ras Khan, Birbar, Tulsi Das produced serveral works of high standard the most important and popular of which is **Ramcharit-manas**. His other important work is **Vinaya Patrika**. Sur Das's important work is **Sur Sagar**. It is supposed that Sur Das was one of the court poets of Akbar, his father Ram Das was also Akbar's court poet. Muslim poet of Hindi, Ras Khan was a worshipper of Lord Krishna and a friend of Tulsi Das. He was responsible for a large number of first-rate Hindi poems.

Akbar was a lover of painting. He believed that painting far from making a person irreligious turns him to God. Like the Persian emperors of the Safavi dynasty Akbar liberally patronised painting disregarding the injunctions of Quran. Akbar's patronage attracted a number of painters to his court of whom as many as thirteen were Hindus. It is interesting to note that two styles—Persian and Indian styles of painting during Akbar's time got gradually fused into one. Akbar opened a separate department for painting under Khwaja Abdus Samad, one of the best painters of his court.

Akbar was an emperor of diverse interests. He was not a literate person but he had a great taste for calligraphy. He appointed many skilled calligraphists in his court. There were eight kinds of calligraphic writings prevalent in Akbar's time, the eighty variety called **Nastaliq** which was favoured by Akbar.

From Ain-i-Akbari we know that there were thirty-six top-ranking musicians in Akbar's court. They were divided into seven groups, each group was to entertain the emperor on one day of the week. Akbar, early in his reign sent for Tansen the notable musician from Rewa and gave him a position of great honour in his court. According to Abul Fazl "a singer like him had not been in India for the last thousand years." Tansen received training in a school founded by Raja Man Singh Tomar at Gwalior. He is said to have invented a number of ragas. Baba Ram Das was next to Tansen. Another equally famous singer was Baba Hari Das.

Akbar by virtue of his rare personality, force of character, his achievements and lofty ideas occupies a place in the history of India which shines in its own brilliance making him for ever as the first national emperor of medieval India. His high sense of patriotism, intellectual superiority and his liberal attitude to religion and his principle of universal toleration entitle him to a lofty place among the kings and emperors of all countries and of all time.

REFERENCES

An Advanced History of India : Majumdar, Roychaudhuri & Datta
The Oxford History of India (4th Edn.) : V. A. Smith
Akbar the Great Mogul : V. A. Smith
Akbar, Vols. I & II : J. N. Shelat
The Mughal Empire : A. L. Srivastava
History of India as told by its Own Historians, Vols. IV, V, VI : Elliot & Dawson
Mughal Administration : Sir Jadunath Sarkar
Later Medieval India : A. B. Pandey
Some Aspects of Mughal Administration : A. Roy

11

Jahangir to Shah Jahan [1605-1658]

JAHANGIR (1605-27)

Jahangir ascended the throne on November 3, 1605, a week after his father's death. He assumed the title of Nur-ud-din Muhammad Jahangir Padshah Ghazi. We have seen how his impatience for the imperial throne made him a rebel and he was about to lose his inheritance as the successor to his father. But his father had ultimately pardoned him and declared him to be his heir to the throne.

On his enthronement Jahangir granted general amnesty to his oppositions and released many prisoners and struck coins in his own name. He promulgated twelve edicts which he ordered his subjects to obey. (a) He prohibited the levy of cesses (Zakat), (b) Ordered the building of mosques, sarais and hospitals along the roads and appointment of physicians to attend the sick, (c) Prohibited the seizure of property and cutting of ears or noses of criminals, (d) confirmed all mansabs and jagirs of Akbar's time, (e) Animal slaughter was prohibited on certain days, including Sundays and Thursdays for the former was Akbar's birthday and the latter was Jahangir's accession day, (f) Prohibited manufacture and sale of wine and intoxicants, (g) Prohibited forcible occupation of cultivator's land, (h) **Aima** land i.e. lands devoted to prayer and praise were confirmed, (i) Free inheritance of property of the deceased was permitted and in case where there was no heir of the deceased, the property was to escheat to the state, (j) Theft or robbery, was checked by passing of regulations, such as making opening of merchants bales without their knowledge punishable, (k) No government collector or jagir was to inter-marry with the people of the pargana without royal permission, and (1) Government hospitals were to be established in big cities for the treatment of the poor people.

Jahangir also caused a gold chain with bells to be hung, between the Shah Burz in the Agra Fort and a post on the bank of the Yamuna to enable the suitors seeking justice to pull the chain which would enable him to approach the emperor without any officers mediation.

The edicts promulgated by Jahangir do not seem to have had much practical effect. He now made certain changes in the official positions in order to ensure the support of a group of high officials. He made Bir Singh Bundela through whom he had caused the murder of Abul Fazl a commander of 300 horse, Abur Rahman son of Abul Fazl and Maha Singh, son of Man Singh were also placed in the rank of commander of 2000 horse each. Father of Nur Jahan, famous as Itimad-ud-daulah was made a commander of 1500 horse. Both Man Singh and Mirza Aziz Koka who had backed the claim of Kushrav to the throne, were pardoned and allowed to retain their posts but they did no longer exercise the same influence on the court as under Akbar. Further, out of a sense of gratitude which was innate quality in his character, Jahangir promoted to high offices those who supported him, but such persons did not really deserve such high appointment.

Father of Nur Jahan Ghiyas Beg, later Itimad-ud-daulah and Zaman Beg later Mahabat Khan belonged to this category.

REVOLT OF KHUSRAV (1606)

Jahangir's "early pleasant dreams" received a rude shock within a few months of his accesion. His eldest son Khusrav had been forgiven by Jahangir for his earlier conduct due to the intercession of Man Singh, his maternal uncle, but Khusrav was kept confined as soon as Man Singh had left for Bengal. Khusrav whose relations with his father was far from friendly since the closing years of Akbar's reign and having enjoyed the love and affection of his grandfather and the prospect of the imperial throne, he became the most popular prince in the Empire.

Now that he had been kept as a state prisoner in thc Agra Fort, Khusrav could not reconcile himself to the indignity, nor could he forget the prospect of occupying the imperial throne which was once within almost his grasp.

On April 6, 1606, Khusrav slipped out of the Agra Fort with 350 horses and on the pretence of visiting Akbar's mausoleum at Sikandara he marched towards Delhi. He was joined on the way by Hussain Beg and soon his army became 12,000 strong. He was also joined by Abdur Rahman Diwan of Lahore. At Taran, the fifth Sikh Guru Arjan Singh gave him benediction. The Governor of Lahore, Dilwar Khan defended the fort of Lahore which was raided by Khusrav and beat him off.

In the meantime Jahangir having learnt of the escape of Khusrav, marched without delay with a huge army against his son. Khusrav was defeated near Jullundur and was captured with his principal followers. Khusrav was brought before Jahangir in chains, was severely reproached by his father and imprisoned. His supporters were cruelly punished. In the words of Jahangir himself "I gave Khusrav into custody and I ordered these two villains (Hussain Beg and Abdur Rahman) to be enclosed in the skins of a cow and an ass, and to be placed on asses, face to the tail, and so to be paraded round the city."

Jahangir now turned to Guru Arjan who had bestowed benediction on Khusrav and fined him two lakhs of rupees. On his refusal to pay he was put to death. This was an act of indiscretion on the part of Jahangir and made the Skikhs inverterate enemies of the Mughals.

Rising of Khusrav encouraged a few more risings. Rai Singh of Bikaner raised a standard of revolt. The rising was put down. Rai Singh was pardoned and restored to his mansab and his dignity. A petty chief of Bihar, Sangram by name, rose in rebellion taking advantage of Khusrav's revolt. But Quli Khan governor of Bihar put him down. But what was the most serious consequence of the rebellion of Khusrav was the encouragement it gave to Shah Abbas, Shah of Persia to attempt conquest of Qandahar.

Qandahar occupied a strategic position, hence it was a bone of contention between India and Persia. Revolt of Khusrav and the consequent disturbances in the country gave Shah abbas, the Persian Shah to instigate the chiefs of Khurasan to attack Qandahar. But Jahangir sent reinforcement (1607) to assist the Mughal governor Shah Beg Khan of Qandahar. As the reinforcement under Mirza Ghazi approached Qandahar the besiegers retreated and Shah Abbas disclaimed any knowledge of the siege of Qandahar by the Khurasan chief, rebuked the Khurasani nobles and offered apology to Jahangir, who accepted the explanation.

Jahangir now thought of visting the north-western frontier of his empire to see the arrangements for himself so that similar attacks might not occur in future. He visited Kabul and on his return journey as he had set out for Lahore a conspiracy to assassinate him was hatched. Khusrav was the central figure among the conspirators. Khusrav's beautiful presence, polished manners, his attractive way of speaking and his spotless private life won him supporters in Nur-ud-din, Fateh-Ullah Sharif, Itibar Khan etc. who conspired to place Khusrav on the imperial throne after assassinating Jahangir. Khurram (later Shah Jahan) got scent of the conspiracy and informed his father Jahangir. The ring leaders were put to death, Khusrav was blinded and imprisoned in the Agra Fort. Later Jahangir out of filial affection ordered the physician to treat the eyes of Khusrav. One of his eyes regained sight.

NUR JAHAN

In 1611 Jahangir married the widow of Sher Afghan named Mehr-un-nisa subsequently given the name of Nur Jahan or Nur Mahal. There are many romantic legends centring round Nur Jahan but modern researches have discarded most of them. The account of Mutamid-Khan, named **Iqbal-Nama-i-Jahangiri** has been found by modern scholars to be reliable in regard to the early life of Mehr-un-nisa. She was the daughter of a Persian immigrant. Mirza Ghiyas Beg who rose to high position during the reigns of Akbar and Jahangir. She was married to Ali Quli Beg Istajhi a Persian adventurer who was given jagir in Burdwan in Bengal in the beginning of the reign of Jahangir and given the title of Sher Afghan.

Sher Afghan was suspected of treasonable designs and Jahangir ordered the new governor of Bengal Qutb-ud-din Khan to send Sher Afghan to the imperial court and in the case of his disobedience to punish him. Qutb-ud-din summoned Sher Afghan to his camp at Burdwan and the latter came with two of his servants to meet the governor. When the troops of the governor surrounded Sher Afghan an affray began in which the latter was killed. But before death Sher Afghan had struck the governor Qutb-ud-din and one of his retainers fatally. Jahangir got Sher Afghan's widow Mehr-un-nisa and daughter Ladli Begum taken to Delhi were he married Mehr-un-nisa in May 1611.

Jahangir was forty-two and Mehr-un-nisa thirty-four at the time of their marriage. Mehr-un-nisa, now **Nur Mahal** and later **Nur Jahan**, kept excellent health and beauty. She was endowed with exceptionally strong intellect, quick understanding, a versatile temper and sound common sense. But the most important and dominant trait of her character was her indomitable ambition and domineering personality which led her to establish an unlimited ascendancy of Jahangir. She strengthened her position by appointing her father Itimad-ud-daulah and brother Asaf Khan to important positions in the court. She also got her daughter by her earlier marriage, married to Prince Shahryar, the youngest son of Jahangir. Asaf Khan's daughter Arjumand Banu Begum was married to Prince Khurram, later Shah Jahan.

It must be noted that Itimad-ud-din, Nur Jahan's father, was an able administrator and her brother Asaf Khan was a good financier and a diplomat and were very reliable and capable pillars of Nur Jahan's party in the imperial court.

Nur Jahan's influence upon Jahangir was not at all unhealthy, in fact, she looked after the administration of her husband's empire with care and devotion. Her influence on her husband personally was for the latter's good. Excessive drinking to which Jahangir had given himself to, was considerably reduced due to Nur Jahan's personal influence. Much of his administrative drudgery and anxiety had been relieved by her. She had definitely enhanced the splendour of the Mughal court and rendered every assistance to her husband in bestowing patronage to art and learning. She distributed charity in profuse quantity and patronised the women and extended protection to them.

All the same, the influence of Nur Jahan on Jahangir's administration was not all for good. During the period of her personal ascendancy she was guided by an extraordinary ambition for power to retain which she of necessity resorted to party politics. She placed her near relations in important positions in the court and in order to perpetuate her authority, she sought to divert the inheritance from Prince Khurram to Prince Shahrayar, the youngest son of Jahangir, and her son-in-law (husband of the daughter by her earlier marriage). This interference in the affairs of the normal course of inheritance convulsed the empire in a civil war. Her too much indulgence in party-politics in order to maintain her supremacy, her disregard of the loyal services of some of the top-ranking officials, her suspicion of all those who either did not see eye to eye with her or ventured to spell out different opinion brought about an estrangement between herself and some of the most meritorious and devoted servants of the state. Mahabat Khan who was the Amir-ul-umrah and was one of the most capable and devoted servants of the state was driven to desperation and rebellion by the imperious conduct of Nur Jahan.

Jahangir's Conquests : Jahangir was not without the imperial ambition of his father, and early years of his reign saw some important military successes. Bengal had never been reconciled to the vassalage of Delhi and the frequent change of governors gave the local Afghans opportunity to rebel. Under the governorship of Islam Khan, the Afghans of Bengal under the leadership of Usman Khan rebelled but the rebellion was suppressed and Usman Khan died of the injury inflicted on his head in the fight (1612). Jahangir saw the need of earning the good will of the Afghans in order to disarm them against the Mughals. He, therefore, followed a conciliatory policy towards them which succeeded in making the Afghans of Bengal friendly to the Mughals.

Most noteworthy military success of Jahangir was his triumph over the Rajputs of Mewar. We have seen that despite his best efforts Akbar could not completely reduce the Rajput State of Mewar. Rana Pratap had succeeded in recovering many of his fortresses before his death in 1597. Amar Singh, son of Pratap although devoid of his father's unflinching resolution, continued his father's policy of resisting the Mughals and the several expeditions sent by Akbar towards the end of his reign failed due to the stiff resistance of the Sisodias. Jahangir on his accession sent an expedition against Mewar under Prince Khurram but the battle proved indecisive. The imperial army had to be recalled due to Prince Khusrav's rebellion. In 1608 Jahangir again sent an expedition against Amar Singh under the command of Mahabat Khan but he also failed to make much head way. Mahabat Khan was replaced by Abdulla Khan who defeated Amar Singh's son Karan Singh but was himself defeated by the Rajputs at Ranpura. In this way Raja Basu, Mirza Aziz Koka who were placed in charge of the expedition against Mewar failed to make much headway. In 1613 Jahangir personally proceeded to Ajmer to guide the expedition the supreme command of which was given to Prince Khurram. The campaign began in 1614. Khurram conducted the campaign with consummate ability and ruthless severity. Though the Rajputs displayed dauntless heroism, they suffered heavy losses. Famine and pestilence also fought in favour of the Mughals and Amar Shingh was compelled to oepen negotiations for peace with Khurram. Amar Singh met Prince Khurram who received him cordially and warmly embraced him. Amar Singh presented the Prince with a ruby, Prince Karan Singh, son of Amar Singh also met Khurram and was received with honour. The treaty that was signed between the Rana and the Emperor (1615) recognised Jahangir as the suzerain of Mewar. The Rana was reinstated to his territory including Chitor but it was not to be fortified. The Rana was not required to be personally present in the Imperial Durbar, but could be represented through his son. A contingent of troops had to be provided by the Rana to the emperor in times of need. There was no matrimonial alliance between the two sides.

Jahangir wanted to complete the Deccan conquest of Akbar who had before his death succeeded in conquering whole of Khandesh and part of Ahmadnagar. Jahangir now attempted to complete the conquest of Ahmadnagar as well as of Bijapur and Golconda. In 1608 Khan Khana marched against Ahmadnagar but could not make any impression against Malik Ambar, the Abyssinian Prime Minister of Ahmadnagar. Jahangir sent Prince Parvez with Asaf Khan as his guardian to strengthen the Mughal army. Parvez was appointed governor of Khandesh and Berar (1610) but he fared no better than Khan Khana. One after another important Mughal commanders failed against Malik Ambar till 1612.

Jahangir bent on retrieving the prestige of the Mughal army severely damaged by their repeated failure replaced Prince Parvez by Prince Khurram whom he appointed to the governorship of Khandesh and Berar and command of the expedition against Ahmadnagar in 1616. Khurram was given the title of Shah Sultan. Khurram opened negotiations with Malik Ambar and the latter being overawed by the superior force of the Prince agreed to cede the territories recently occupied by him from the Mughals and to surrender the fort of Ahmadnagar. Jahangir confirmed the terms of the agreement in 1617.

But in 1620 Malik Ambar threw off the treaty of 1617 and after making a common cause with Bijapur and Golconda rose in revolt. Jahangir sent Khurram (Shah Jahan) to punish Malik Ambar. On his approaching Patan, Malik Ambar offered submission and Shah Jahan finding Nur Jahan inimically disposed towards him hurriedly signed a peace treaty with Malik Ambar in 1621 and the Kingdoms of Ahmadnagar, Bijapur and Golconda paid tributes of twelve lakhs, eighteen lakhs and twenty lakhs respectively to the Emperor. Subjugation of the Deccan added another laurel to Prince Shah Jahan. In the same year news reached him of his father's illness and in order to make his prospect to the throne clear he got Khusrav murdered, falsely representing that he died of a serious attack of colic. Jahangir already sick became very much upset at the death of his eldest son Khusrav who was most popular with the subjects.

In 1621 Shah Abbas taking advantage of the illness of Jahangir and the estrangement between Nur Jahan and Shah Jahan sent a large force for the capture of Qandahar. Siege of Qandahar began in 1622 and there was s rumour that another Persian army was marching towards Thatta. Jahangir was then convalescing in Kashmir. He at once ordered Shah Jahan to march against Shah Abbas to relieve Qandahar. Shah Jahan who was suspecting that his absence would be utilised by Nur Jahan to ensure the succession of her son-in-law, the youngest brother of Shah Jahan— Shahryar did not obey his father's order and was in fact in a mood to rise in rebellion. Shah Abbas in the meantime occupied Qandahar. Jahangir sent Parvez to recapture Qandahar but this could not materialise as Shah Jahan had in the meantime raised the standard of rebellion. He was preparing for a surprise attack on Agra before Jahangir had recovered from the shock of the loss of Qandahar and the news of his own revolt. But Nur Jahan got the news of the impending surprise attack by Shah Jahan through her spies and made prompt preparations to frustrate the rebel's design. Parvez was recalled from Allahabad, Rajput chiefs of Mewar, Amber, Bundi, Kota, Orchha and other states were urgently summoned to come to the defence of the imperial throne. Mahabat Khan was appointed to the command. Jahangir and Nur Jahan returned from Kashmir and reached Ajmer in May 1623.

Shah Jahan made a dash against Fathpur Sikri but failed to take the fort and was badly beaten back from the gates of Agra by the imperial force. In this battle Shah Jahan lost his staunchest friend and supporter Rai Rayan Bikramjit, one of the greatest generals in the country. On the approach of the imperial army Shah Jahan was obliged to flee to fort Asirgarh. Many of his supporters defected to the imperial side, Parvez was now raised to the rank of 40,000 Zat and 30,000 Sarwar in order to exalt him above Shah

Jahan. Shah Jahan's piteous appeal for help to his erstwhile enemy Malik Ambar evoked no response.

Shah Jahan then after much detour reached Orissa, the craven-hearted governor of which fled to Cuttack thence to Burdwan and finally to Dacca. Shah Jahan occupied Orissa, Burdwan, and then marched on to Rajmahal where Ibrahim Khan governor of Bengal was killed in resisting Shah Jahan. The governor of Orissa, Ahmad Beg who had fled to Dacca surrendered to Shah Jahan. Thus both Bengal and Orissa came under the possession of Shah Jahan. Next Shah Jahan seized Bihar, Awadh, Allahabad and even Agra. His valiant commander prince Bhim of Mewar occupied whole of Bihar including the impregnable fortress of Rohtas which passed into Shah Jahan's hands. Jaunpur also fell to his hands.

But his attempted siege of Allahabad was frustrated by the timely intervention of Parvez and Mahabat Khan who inflicted a severe defeat on Shah Jahan who had to flee to the Deccan where he was pursued by Parvez and Mahabat Khan. As Shah Jahan fell ill at this point of time, he had no other alternative but to submit to his father.

Shah Jahan with depleted strength of his supporters due to death and defection, personally exhausted both mentally and physically due to long-drawn struggle and hounded by the imperial army, thought out his only course of action to be an unconditional surrender and asking for father's forgiveness. Jahangir forgave his erring son and appointed him governor of Balaghat. The civil war which convulsed the empire for three years thus came to an end in 1626.

Mahabat Khan, an Afghan by birth was at the beginning of the reign of Jahangir a mansabdar of 500 but was rapidly promoted to higher and higher rank because of his conspicuous service to the emperor. He was in fact, the greatest soldier, and most clever diplomat of the empire during Jahangir's reign. His services in putting down the rebellion of Prince Shah Jahan had enhanced his power and status in the government. All this had excited the jealousy of Nur Jahan and her brother Asaf Khan and they were not willing to tolerate the indomitable personality and extra-ordinary ability of Mahabat Khan. Nur Jahan, in particular, decided to reduce Mahabat Khan to submission. Mahabat Khan had, naturally a high sense of personal dignity and would not accept orders from any body other than the emperor himself. But as soon as Shah Jahan had surrendered, Nur Jahan got Mahabat Khan transferred to Bengal and Khan Jahan Lodi was appointed in his place and also the adviser of Parvez.

Mahabat Khan was prepared to start for Bengal in obedience to the imperial order, but Nur Jahan and Asaf Khan brought charges of insubordination and disloyalty against him for no better reason than their personal jealousy for him. He was asked to account for money said to have been collected by him and to send the elephants to Delhi which he was said to have received in Bihar and Bengal. Mahabat Khan thought of placing his case before the emperor and seek justice and if he would fail he would by a **coup de main** deprive Nur Jahan of her power. He proceeded to Punjab where the emperor was supposed to be then. As he approaching Punjab, Jahangir had returned from Kashmir and was on his way to Kabul. Mahabat Khan had a few thousand Rajput soldiers with him. There Nur Jahan, in her hautiness hurled more insults on Mahabat Khan which led him to open rebellion. In a **coup d'etat** he took possession of the person of the emperor but forgot to take into custody Nur Jahan who escaped and with her brother Asaf Khan, made preparations against Mahabat Khan. Jahangir sent information to Nur Jahan to refrain from that course. But Nur Jahan would not listen to reason. She proceeded against Mahabat Khan only to be defeated and compelled to surrender, to Mahabat Khan, who permitted her to join Jahangir. Asaf Khan's surrender was also secured.

Jahangir now reconciled to the domination of Mahabat Khan left the administration in his hands. But although a great soldier and a diplomat Mahabat Khan was no administration. Administration soon began to fall into decay, the advantage of the situation was taken by Nur Jahan and she now began to regain her lost supremacy. Mahabat Khan had ultimately to run away and make peace with Shah Jahan. Nur Jahan's triumph, however, was short-lived, for Jahangir died soon after on October 28, 1627. His body was buried at Shahdara were a beautiful tomb has been built. It is on the river Ravi.

Character and Achievements of Jahangir : Jahangir has been regarded as a very complex personality of Medieval Indian history and in the words of Terry "Now for the disposition of that king, it ever seemed to me to be composed of extremes : for sometimes he was cruel and at other times he would seem to be exceedingly fair and gentle." Beveridge's remarks also confirm Terry's observations about Jahangir's character and personality. According him "Jahangir was indeed a strange mixture. The man who could stand by and see man flayed alive ...could yet be a lover of justice and could spend his Thursday evenings in holding high converse... He could procure the murder of Abul Fazl and avow the fact without remorse, and also pity the royal elephants because they shivered in winter."

According to Francis Gladwin Jahangir's disposition towards his subjects was humane and considerate. His biographer has called him a sensible, kind-hearted man, with strong family affections and unstinted generosity for all, with a burning hatted of oppression and a passion for justice." His chain of justice was a novel device and spoke eloquently of his great sense of doing justice to one and all without any consideration of rank.

Jahangir was a patron of art and literature and his own memoirs **Tuzuk-i-Jahangiri** illustrates his great literary attainment. Although not so much rational in his religious outlook like his father, yet Jahangir loved to hold philosophical discourses with Hindu and Muslim saints, Zorastrian priests and Christian missionaries. He was sincere in his belief in God and was eclectic in matters of religion.

He rebelled against his father no doubt but he has cherished a loving memory of him and would often visit Akbar's mausoleum at Sikandara where he would throw himself down to rub his forehead on its threshold.

Jahangir was a highly educated and cultured Prince and was an adept in Turki and Persian. He was also a patron of painting, music etc. He had deep interest in subjects like Biology, Medicine and Zoology, and was a great lover of the beauties of Nature. It was during the reign of Jahangir that a new intercourse between India and Europe had begun. In 1608 Capt. William Hawkins came to the court of Jahangir with a letter from James I of Great Britain requesting trade facilities for the English merchants. But the embassy failed due to the opposition of the Portuguese. Sir Thomas Roe came to his court as the second accredited ambassador of the king James I. Jahangir often invited Roe and Terry into his private audience hall called **Ibadat Khana** during Akbar's time and **Ghusal-Khana** during Jahangir's time for serious philosophical discussions, along with others.

In his personal life he was polygamous, but he was all the same a loving husband. His love for Nur Jahan was very near doting.

He was a great patron of building. Akbar's tomb at Sikandara, Itimad-ud-daulah's tomb near Agra and the great mosque at Lahore that rivals in beauty and interest that at Delhi built by Shah Jahan are among the most remarkable architectural specimens of Jahangir's time.

Jahangir received training in soldierly pursuit and in the art of warfare under his father, but although he had developed into a capable soldier he did not display that ambition, skill or energy that might be reasonably expected of him. The notable military success of Jahangir's reign was the capture of Mewar and the strong fortress of Kangra. But the exultation resulting from these successes was soon followed by the disaster of the loss of Qandahar and the rebellion of Shah Jahan and eventually of Mahabat Khan.

Jahangir was a fairly successful administrator and had the wisdom to continue the administrative system and policy of his father. Although he did not possess the constructive statesmanship of his father he at least left his father's administrative system unaltered and tried to mete out justice to the people irrespective of their rank.

In matters of religion Jahangir at the initial stage of his reign fell under the influence of the **Ulemas** who sought to persuade the new emperor to reverse the secularising of the state done by his father. But soon he realised the folly of such a policy, for with his liberal mind it became impossible for him to go back on the path of toleration which Akbar had traversed and left open before him. But it is possible to cite instances where he punished Hindus for marrying Muslims and converting them into Hinduism and of demolishing Hindu temples in Mewar and Kangra, ordering closure of churches in his empire. At Ajmer he ordered the idol of the Baraha temple to be thrown into the tank. But such steps were only occasional and did not constitute a determined policy. In fact, he was tolerant to all faiths. Even he did not charge any pilgrim tax from the Hindus going to the places of their pilgrimage, maintained Christian service at the expense of the court and participated in some of the Hindus festivals. He would visit Yogis during Shivaratri festivals and allowed the Christians to hold Easter and other Christian festivals. But as we have seen in case of the Hindus and Christians he was at times repressive, so also with the Muslim heretics. He sanctioned severe repression on the Muslim heretics at times, for instance Shaikh Rahim of Lahore a religious leader was thrown into the prison, Qazi Nurullah a Shiah writer was put to death.

Jahangir's relation with the Sikhs became very bitter and inimical because of the murder of fifth Sikh Guru Arjan for his granting benediction to Prince Khusrav. Guru Arjan was brought before Jahangir asked to accept Islam or die. He chose the latter alternative. This act of indiscretion on the part of Jahangir made the Skihs avowed enemies of the Mughals with disastrous consequences in the reign of Aurangzeb.

Jahangir's discussions with Hindu and Muslim saints, the Varshaves and the Sufis, the Zorastrians and Christians led him to one final conclusion that the Hindu Vedanta and Muslim Sufism were almost identical.

Jahangir continued his father's policy of maintaining the composite character of the bureaucracy by appointing also Hindus to high posts. Man Singh, Kalyan Singh, son of Todar Mal and Vikramadit were three Hindu governors besides many high Hindu officials under Jahangir.

Like his father Akbar, Jahangir also issued orders that Hindu widow must not be burnt in the funeral pyre of her deceased husband as **Suttee** against her will. He also prohibited female infanticide. Charity to the proof, free kitchen for the **Fakirs** etc. were his other social reform measures.

If not a great ruler, nor a great statesman or a conqueror or even an administrator of any outstanding calibre, yet he deserves to be remembered as a successful and benevolent ruler who was solicitous of the welfare of his subjects. "He stands in the roll of the Indian monarchs as a man with generous instincts, fond of sport, art and good living aiming to do well to all and failing by the lack of the finer intellectual qualities to attain the ranks of great administrators"—as Sir Richard Burn puts it.

SHAH JAHAN (1628-58)

Jahangir at the time of his death in October 1627 was survived by two of his sons, Prince Khurrâm or Shah Jahan the elder and Prince Shahryar the younger son. Both Shah

Jahan and Shahryar were related to Nur Jahan, the former married Mumtaj Mahal daughter of Asaf Khan, Nur Jahan's brother and the latter married daughter of Nur Jahan by her first husband Sher Afghan. At the time of Jahangir's death Shah Jahan was in the Deccan and Shahryar was at Agra. Shahryar hastened to Lahore where Nur Jahan was still staying after Jahangir's death, and assumed imperial title. Shah Jahan took a few weeks to reach the capital from the Deccan, the advantage of the delay was taken by Nur Jahan. But Asaf Khan, Shah Jahan's father-in-law and brother of Nur Jahan wanted his son-in-law to inherit the imperial throne. He placed Dawar Baksh, son of Khusrav on the throne as a stop-gap and was waiting for the arrival of Shah Jahan. Shahryar who was an worthless prince and no match for Asaf Khan was captured by the latter and blinded. Shah Jahan ordered for the execution of all male relatives who had any chance of putting up any claim to the throne.

As Khusrav, the eldest son of Jahangir lost favour with his father Shah Jahan was marked for the throne. In 1607 Shah Jahan was made a mansabdar of 8000 Zat and 5000 Sarwar and in 1611 he was raised to the status of 10,000 Zat and 5000 Sarwar. Next year he married Asaf Khan's daughter **Arjumand Banu Begum** better known as **Mumtaj Mahal**. Later Shah Jahan became mansabdar of an unprecedented rank of 30,000 Zat and 20,000 Sarwar. As a Prince Shah Jahan reduced Mewar to submission as also brought Ahmadnagar's Abyssinian general Malik Ambar to return Balaghat, surrender the fort of Ahmadnagar and other forts. Jahangir bestowed the title of Shah on the Prince and added Gujarat to his viceroyalty.

Nur Jahan's willingness to see her son-in-law Shahryar succeed to the imperial throne led to estrangement between Nur Jahan and Shah Jahan. This led to a fratricidal struggle referred to above and it was due to the astuteness of Asaf Khan that accession of Shah Jahan was secured on February 14, 1628, assuming the title of Abul Muzaffar Shihab-ud-din Muhammad Sahib-i-Qiran II, Shah Jahan Padshah Ghazi. Dawar Baksh the "sacrificial lamb" as described by the contemporaries was put into the prison.

Rebellions : To begin with every thing appeared to move smoothly. Asaf Khan and Mahabat Khan the architects of Shah Jahan's fortune were raised to high offices of the state. But soon clouds of distrubances began to gather. Several rebellions distrubed the reign of Shah Jahan, the first was that of Khan Jahan Lodi, a capable but turbulent officer who was appointed adviser to Prince Parvez who was placed in charge of the Deccan. The other rebellion was of Jujhar Singh Bundela. Shah Jahan easily Suppressed the two rebellions. Jujhar Singh was chased out of the country and was ultimately killed in a skirmish with the Gonds. Khan Jahan Lodi was likewise chased from place to place by the imperialists and was ultimately defeated near Kalinjar and cut to pieces along with his sons, Aziz and Aimal (1631).

DEATH OF MUMTAJ MAHAL (1631)

We have already seen that Mumtaj Mahal whose original name was Arjumand Banu Begum was the daughter of Asaf Khan, Nur Jahan's brother. She was married to Prince Khurram, later Shah Jahan when the latter was twenty years of age (1612). This marriage was successful to a degree rare in a polygamous family. She bore fourteen out of eighteen children of her husband, eight sons and six daughters between 1613 and 1631. "Husband and wife were devotedly attached to each other, and during her life time nothing is heard of the scandalous licentiousness which dishonoured Shah Jahan's later years." Mumtaj Mahal was an accomplished lady, kind and charitable, pious and deeply religiousminded. Her religious views are said to have been very much orthodox, bodering on bigotry and the harsh treatment of the Hindus and the Christians by Shah Jahan is ascribed to her influence. The Taj Mahal at Agra which is built on the earthly remains of Mumtaj is the noblest monument of conjugal love and fidelity unique in the world. Mumtaj's death was a blow from which Shah Jahan could not ever recover in his life time.

Famine : During the years 1630-32 a devastating famine stalked the Deccan and Gujarat. During these years when the emperor was usually encamping in Burhampur in Khandesh intent on his scheme of imperialist aggression upon the Sultans of Bijapur and Golconda, the people of the Deccan and Gujarat were reduced to the direct extremity "Life was offered for a loaf but none would buy; rank was to be sold for a cake, but none cared for it.... Destitution at last reached such a pitch that men began to devour each other, and the flesh of a son was preferred to his love. The numbers of the dying caused obstructions on the roads.... (Abdul Hamid). Peter Mundy a merchant gave a picture of the famine and said that at Surat "out of twenty-one English traders seventeen died."

Jahangir generously remitted the revenue to the tune of 70 lakhs of rupees and the jagir holders were expected to make similar remission. From the English and the Dutch traders we come to know that there was long distrubance to trade and production of commercial crops caused by the famine.

The famine of 1630-32 in the Deccan and Gujarat may be compared to the great famine of Bengal of 1770 when identical miseries were seen.

Shah Jahan and the Portuguese : About 1579 the Portuguese traders obtained an imperial **farman** on the strength of which they established their settlement in Hughli. They started exacting heavy duties from the Indian traders and even carried on piracy. Under Jahangir they went unpunished and their arrogance went on increasing to the extent of their Kidnapping Hindu or Muslim children for slave trading or conversion into Christianity. Before accession to the throne when two slave girls were being sent for Mumtaj, the Portuguese kidnapped them. After accession to the throne there were added cause of complaint, against the Portuguese. The Portuguese missionaries were converting Indians to Christianity. Further the governor of Bengal Qasim Khan reported to the emperor that they were fortifying their settlements in Bengal, levied tool on ships and practically destroyed Satgaon. Further, they failed to send the emperor the usual **Nazarana** on his accession. For these reasons Shah Jahan ordered Qasim Khan to punish the Portuguese. Qasim Khan's son besieged Hughli and captured it after three months. According to Abdul Hamid Lahori many Portuguese were killed in action and a huge number of them taken prisoners and sent to Agra where they were punished cruelly.

Shah Jahan and the Deccan Policy : Akbar had in his imperial conquest of the south only succeeded in conquering Khandesh and Berar. Jahangir's attempt to capture Ahmadnagar was thwarted by its Abyssinian general Malik Ambar. Bijapur and Golconda continued to enjoy independence. On Malik Ambar's death, his son Fath Khan became the Prime Minister of Ahmadnagar. In 1630 the imperial force laid siege of the fort of Parenda in Ahmadnagar but was compelled to withdraw it. Soon after Fath Khan quarelled with his own sovereign Sultan Nizam-ul-Mulk of Ahmadnagar and seized and confined his own sovereign. He opened negotiations with Emperor Shah Jahan who instructed him to kill his Sultan. Fath Khan promptly complied with the instruction and placed the ten year old son of Nizam-ul-Mulk, Hussain Shah on the throne of Ahmadnagar. But Fath Khan soon proved faithless to the Mughals and when the Mughal besieged the fortress of Daulatabad (1631), he at first defended it against the imperial forces but was bribed to surrender the fortress. He was taken into imperial service on a liberal salary. Hussain Shah, the boy king of Ahmadnagar was confined in the Gwalior fort in lifelong imprisonment. Thus the Nizam Shahi kingdom of Ahmadnagar came to an end in 1632, and annexed to the Mughal empire.

Shah Jahan was not reconciled to the independence of Bijapur and Golconda states both from his imperialistic and anti-shiah zeal. The independent attitude of these two Deccan states was a standing offence in his eyes. There was also another complication that had arisen due to the appearance of the Marathas in the political scene of the Deccan from 1630.

Shah Jahan demanded of the Sultans of Bijapur and Golconda recognition of imperial suzerainty and payment of tributes and abstention from supporting Shahji or Sahu (father of Shivaji). The craven-hearted Sultan of Golconda (Hyderabad) a staunch Shiah who regarded the Shah of Persia as his suzerain submitted after a show of resistance and read the Khutba in the name of Shah Jahan who was a devout Sunni. The Sultan agreed to pay an annual tribute of two lakhs of **hun** equivalent of six lakhs of rupees. He also agreed to help the Mughals in their war against Bijapur.

Sultan Adil Shah of Bijapur was less complacent and was determined to resist the imperial aggression. Khan Jahan, Khan-i-Dauran and Khan-i-Zaman marched against Bijapur from three directions cutting off the supplies and poisoning the wells of drinking water. Bijapur soldiers fought against all these odds and valiantly defended the city. Shahji was prepared to come to the defence of Bijapur but at that point of time had been made by Bijapur Sultan with the Mughals. Bijapur Sultan tried to persuade Shahji to surrender the fort of Junnar to the Mughals which he refused to do. Mughals invested the fort and after a tough fight Shahji surrendered Junnar to the Mughals. Shahji had to hand over the boy whom he had enthroned as the king of Ahmadnagar.

Sultan of Bijapur had to yield obedience to the Emperor, pay a war indemnity of 20 lakhs of rupees and to abstain from aiding Shahji in his hostile measures against the Mughals. For a time the affairs of the Deccan were settled to the satisfaction of Shah Jahan.

Aurangzeb was appointed viceroy of the Deccan. His viceroyalty comprised four provinces, namely, Khandesh, Berar, Daulatabad including the imperial portion of the former Ahmadnagar Sultanate, and Telingana, regions between Berar and Golconda state and parts of Hyderabad. These provinces contained as many as sixty-four fortresses, a few of them under the Maratha chief Shahji. Aurangzeb was the viceroy of the Deccan for nine years from 1636 to 1644.

Conquest of Qandahar (1638) : We have seen before that the strategic fortress of Qandahar was for decades the bone of contention between the Persian Shahs and the Mughal Emperors of Delhi. It was under the Mughals during early years of the Mughal rule, but was lost to Jahangir towards the end of his reign, for his attempt to send Shah Jahan, then prince Khurram against the attacks on Qandahar by Shah Abbas due to the estrangement between himself and Nur Jahan, failed. Soon after Shah Jahan's accession to the throne Shah Abbas died and was succeeded by a minor who was embroiled in a war with the Turks. Shah Jahan was looking for an opportunity to recover the strategically important fortress. The opportunity came of its own. The Persian minister Saru Taqi who was not on good terms with the governor of Qandahar Ali Mardan, demanded of him accounts of income and expenditure and sent troops to Qandahar to back his demand. Ali Mardan put himself in touch with the Mughals and offered to surrender Qandahar to Shah Jahan. In 1638 he changed side and formally transferred his services to the Mughals and admitted Mughal troops into the fortress. Qandahar fortress thus came into Mughal hands once again.

Policy Towards Central Asia and North-West Frontier : It had been the ambition of the Mughals to occupy trans-Oxiana, their ancestral homeland in Central Asia. While Babur and Humayun's attempts failed Akbar and Jahangir's ambition could not materialise for they did not venture to make any attempt to occupy the inhospitable regions.

Shah Jahan, however, was determined to make an attempt on Samarqand which was ruled over then, by the Janiad family of Astrakhan. The ruling Shah at that time was Imam Quli who on his side was casting his covetous eye on Kabul. He made repeated raids and even was able to make some progress. All this naturally infuriated the Mughals and Nazir Muhammad brother of Imam Quli, who led the expeditions offered apology and bitterness between the two countries was removed.

In 1639 Samarqand was torn by internal dissensions and there were rebellions resulting in wide-spread confusion. Shah Jahan instructed the governor of Kabul to take every advantage of the situation to fulfil the traditional Mughal ambition of occupying Samarqand. Murad was given the overall command of the expedition. Murad captured Narin and Qunduz. It was Shah Jahan's policy to render assistance to Nazr Muhammad who had occupied the throne of Samarqand by deposing his brother Imam Quli, but his own son rebelled against him and put him to flight, so that Nazr Muhammad might recover Bukhara and Samarqand and then to wrest the places from him. But Nazr Muhammad was clever enough to see through the game of the Mughals and he pretended to hand over all his territories to the Mughals and was making for Mecca. But Murad was also that much intelligent to understand this trick. He attacked Balkh, Nazr Muhammad took to flight, Balkh fell into Mughal hands (1646). Next he captured Tirmiz on the Oxus. Nazr Muhammad was defeated at Shivarghan and fled to Persia.

Murad who was accustomed to a life of pleasure and enjoyment was unwilling to remain in the barren country with inhospitable climate and sought Emperor's permission to return to India. Shah Jahan replaced Murad by Aurangzeb but the latter had to fight his way against the Uzbegs and could not proceed beyond the Oxus as his soldiers were unwilling to stay in the dry inhospitable rigorous climate of Trans-Oxiana and even Aurangzeb wanted to return to India. His willingness to return was also motivated by his anxiety to succeed his father to the throne. In the meantime Nazr Muhammad attacked Afghanistan with the help he received from the Shah Abbas II of Persia and Aurangzeb had to hurriedly fall back to Kabul. It was found necessary for diplomatic reason to accept a seeming apology from Nazr Muhammad and his country Samarqand was returned to him. All this demonstrated the weakness of the position of the Mughals and in 1648 he stood up openly for the cause of the Uzbegs and demanded restoration of Qandahar from Shah Jahan. Balkh was also demanded of the Emperor to be restored to Nazr Muhammad. The Mughals had to abandon Balkh. Central Asian campaign caused much loss of men and money to the Mughals. "Thus ended Shah Jahan's fatuous war in Balkh—a war in which the Indian Treasury spent four crores of rupees in two years and realised from the conquered country a revenue of $22^1/_2$ lakhs only ...... five hundred soldiers fell in battle and ten times that number (including camp-followers) were slain by cold and snow on the mountains." (J. N. Sarkar)

Shah Abbas invested Khurasan and advanced towards Qandahar. Daulat Khan who was in charge of Qandahar lost heart and surrendered the fortress to the Persians, before Aurangzeb could reach Qandahar from Kabul. Shah Jahan himself also marched to Kabul to infuse courage and discipline among the Mughal forces.

By the middle of 1649 Shah Jahan with Wazir Sadullah Khan marched with 50,000 troops and reached near Qandahar and laid siege of the fortress. The Mughals could not make much impression on the fortress which received reinforcement from Persia. Due to lack of supplies and ammunitions, the Mughals suffered greatly. Ultimately the siege was abandoned in September, 1649.

In 1652 Shah Jahan made a second attempt to recover Qandahar and sent Aurangzeb in charge of the expedition. The siege proved infructuous and not only that the Uzbegs threatened Ghazni which lay on the route between Kabul and Qandahar. Shah Jahan had to order the abandonment of the siege.

Yet another, that is the third siege of Qandahar was laid in 1653 by Dara under Shah Jahan's instruction. Dara had some initial success and captured Bist and Girishk which lay immediately on the west of Qandahar. But against the more powerful Persian artillery the Mughals could not make any headway in the siege operation. Yet the tenacity of the Mughal soldiers struck terror among the Persians but as winter set in and supplies fell short the Mughals had to lift the siege in October 1653.

With loss of about twelve crores of rupees and huge number of Mughal army and without acquisition of not an inch of territory the three sieges of Qandahar in 1649, 1652 and 1653, the Mughal emperor finally accepted the loss of the impregnable fortress of Qandahar and also the loss of the political and military prestige of the empire. The relation between India and Persia during the rest of the reign of Shah Jahan was extremely strained.

Minor Conquests : The Mughals wanted to conquer Tibet. Jahangir's attempt was beaten back. Shah Jahan decided to renew his father's project and in 1634 sent an expedition against Balkistan or Little Tibet then ruled over by Abdal who earned the displeasure of the Emperor by giving shelter to the fugitives from Kashmir. The expedition was successful, for Abdal made timely submission. But he threw off allegiance soon after, which necessitated another expedition. Abdal was compelled to pay war indemnity and to hand over the leader of the fugitives. Hardly a year passed when Tibet proper rebelled and by a third expedition Tibet was defeated and peace restored in the northern frontier of the empire.

In 1637 Baglan in the Nasik district was conquered. The Portuguese of Diu and Daman were subdued. The governor of the fortress of Kangra having rebelled was forced to submit in 1642. Champat Rai, the Bundela chief of Bundelkhand rebelled but although on the approach of the imperial force Champat Rai fled and his adopted son Prithvi Raj was captured and imprisoned, yet ultimately Champat Rai was persuaded to submit. He was taken into Mughal service. Places like Bundelkhand, the aboriginal tribes like the Cheros of Palamau, the Gonds and Bhils of Malwa were subjugated and made to submit to Mughal sovereignty.

Aurangzeb's Second Viceroyalty of the Deccan (1652-1657) : On his return from Qandahar Aurangzeb did not find the atmosphere in the court congenial due to the hostility of Dara Shukoh. He, therefore, preferred to be sent to the Deccan as its viceroy for the second time. During the few years that elapsed between his first and the second viceroyalties, administration of the Deccan had fallen into utter confusion and the finances were in a ruinous state. The deficit has to be constantly met from the central treasury.

One of the first concerns of Aurangzeb, therefore, was to improve the finances of the Subah. He was, however, fortunate to have Murshid Quli Khan an able Persian who was an expert revenue officer. Murshid Quli Khan came to the Deccan with Aurangzeb as diwan of Daulatabad and Telingana, and subsequently of Berar and Khandesh.

Deccan had been ill-governed by a succession of incompetent administrators and frequently changed officers who instead of repairing the damage done by war and famine only hastened the decrease in cultivated area, oppressed the people and abandoned the villages to their fate. Aurangzeb naturally did his best to restore cultivation and improve revenue. But before he could complete his task, although when much had been accomplished, war of succession broke out.

Murshid Quli introduced the principle of Todar Mal's systems of revenue, measured the lands and fixed the revenue on the basis of the produce of the soil. Of course, he appreciated that a uniform system could not be introduced all over the country as such he allowed local tradition and usage to remain undisturbed. Side by side with **Zabti, batai** and **nasq** were allowed to continue.

For the purpose of revenue collection the Deccan subah was divided into two parts, namely **Painghat** or the Lowlands, and **Balaghat** or the Highlands each having its revenue minister or **diwan** as he was called.

The revenue demand was made in a rough and ready manner. Thus in thinly populated or backward areas revenue was fixed on a lump sum basis on land cultivated by each plough. Elsewhere the batai system was introduced where the share of the state varied according to the nature of crop raised and source of water for irrigation. In other areas state claim was fixed per bighas on a uniform rate of one-fourth of the produce after a careful survey of the lands and on consideration of the quantity of the produce. Advances of cash to the cultivators for restoration of cultivation were freely granted. These wise measures taken by Murshid Quli restored prosperity in the Deccan within a very short time. J. N. Sarkar refers to the observation of Bhim Sen Burhampure, author of **Nuksha-i-Dilkhusha** that in 1658 there "was not a single piece of waste land near Aurangabad; wheat and pulse sold at $2^1/_2$ maunds a rupee, jawar and bajra at $3^1/_2$ maunds, molasses at half a maund, and yellow oil (ghee) at 4 seers."

After having set the revenue of the Subah in order, and reorganised its internal organisation Aurangzeb set himself to carry on the traditional policy of his family, namely to destroy the independence of Golconda and Bijapur, to play the part of "a great pike in a pond" as chaplain Terry puts it. Both imperialistic expansion and religious bigotry supplied the motive force behind Aurangzeb's policy of war against these two Sultanates. Aurangzeb was a bigoted Sunni Muslim and took special pleasure in war against the two Shiah sultanates of the South.

Since 1636 Golconda was a tributary state and tribute always fell into arrears. Muhammad said, better known in history as **Mir Jumla** was a Persian adventurer who amassed immense fortune by trading in diamonds and precious stones and by virtue of his military genius and administrative ability became like Muhammad Gawan under the Bahmani Sultan, the virtual master of Golconda, as the chief minister of Sultan Abdullah Qutb Shah. His ambition was too high to be satisfied with the position of the chief minister which was nothing more than the chief servant of the Sultan. He conquered Karnataka and began to rule there almost as an independent ruler. Qutb Shah wanted to coerce Mir Jumla to submission, and arrested his son. Mir Jumala in self-defence entered into intrigues with Shah Jahan and Aurangzeb. Aurangzeb saw in Mir Jumla a great source of strength in dealing with the Sultan of Golconda. Mir Jumla accepted a high office under Shah Jahan, thus proving a traitor to Qutb Shah.

Aurangzeb demanded of Qutb Shah the release of the son and other members of Mir Jumla's family and without waiting for any answer, declared war and deputed his son Prince Muhammad at the head of a large army to invade Golconda. Prince Muhammad attacked Hyderabad in 1656 and Aurangzeb himself proceeded towards Golconda. Prince Muhammad defeated the Golconda army and besieged Hyderabad. Intention of Aurangzeb was nothing short of complete annexation of Golconda. Meanwhile Golconda was also besieged by Aurangzeb which compelled the Sultan Qutb Shah to sue for peace. When negotiations were going on Qutb Shah's agents were waiting on the Emperor Shah Jahan. Prince Dara and Princess Jahanara. When negotiations between Qutb Shah and Aurangzeb were continuing and the latter was about the press the siege, he received orders from Shah Jahan to withdraw from Golconda. Aurangzeb, however, lifted the siege only after Qutb Shah made payment of the arrears of the tributes and restored the properties, of Mir Jumla. Qutb Shah gave his daughter in marriage with Prince Muhammad when a dowry of ten lakhs of rupees was paid. Qutb Shah promised never to default in payment of tribute and paid an idemnity of fifteen lakhs of rupees.

Next came the turn of Bijapur after the death of its capable Sultan Adil Shah towards the end of 1656. This gave Aurangzeb his opportunity to proceed against Bijapur. But remembering his experience in his campaign against Golconda, Aurangzeb asked for Shah Jahan's permission before-hand on the ground that the successor to Adil Shah was not his son but really an imposter. But this could be no legal ground for interference from the Mughals for Bijapur was an independent ally and not a vassal of the Emperor. But the real ground was the confusion that was going on in Bijapur on the death of Adil Shah over the question of succession.

Assisted by Mir Jumla who had a clear idea of the strategic points of the area, Aurangzeb invaded Bijapur in 1657 and laid siege of the fortress of Bidar and reduced the fortress after its valiant commandant Sidi Marjan died in action. Next the Bijapur army was defeated by Mahabat Khan at Gulbarga which enabled Aurangzeb to advance to Kalyani. Here again Aurangzed prevented from proceeding against Bijapur any further due to the sudden intervention of Shah Jahan due to the advice of Dara Shukoh and other opponents of Aurangzeb in the imperial court. Aurangzeb, however, arrived at peace with the Bijapur Sultan and the latter was compelled to surrender the forts of Bidar, Kalyani, Parenda as well as those in Konkan and Vengi and pay an indemnity of one and a half crores of rupees. Shah Jahan approved of the settlement but reduced the indemnity by half a crore.

In the meantime the news of Shah Jahan's illness made Aurangzeb more mindful of the impending war of succession, the advantage of the confusing political situation that soon ensued was taken by the Sultan of Bijapur who declined to fulfil the terms of settlement with the Mughals (1657).

We have already seen how Shahji had made his appearance in the Deccan. When Aurangzeb was busy in his campaign against the Deccan Sultanates of Golconda and Bijapur, Shivaji, the indomitables son of Shahji, captured Junnar and raided Mughal territories west of Ahmadnagar, Aurangzeb made arrangements to subdue Shivaji and a Mughal contingent put down Shivaji's raids on the western flank of the Mughal territories in the Deccan. When Aurangzeb withdrew his forces from Golconda and Bijapur that Shivaji stopped raiding the Mughal territories for a time.

Aurangzeb : The War of Succession (1657-59) : Towards the latter part of 1657 Shah Jahan fell ill and it was rumoured that he was dead. Shah Jahan when he had fallen sick, thinking that his end was near, called upon Dara Shukoh, his eldest son, to conduct the business of the state. Dara Shukoh was in the confidence of his father and he actually desired him to succeed to the throne.

By an irony of fate the war of succession among the four sons of Shah Jahan broke out even before his death, as soon as he fell ill in September, 1657. All of his four sons were of mature age at that time. Dara Shukoh (43) was the governor of Punjab and Delhi, but he usually stayed with his father at Agra, Shuja (41) was the governor of Bengal, Aurangzeb (39) was the governor of the Deccan, and Murad (33) governor of Gujarat. Of the two daughters, Jahanara sided with Dara, and Raushnara with Aurangzeb.

Although all the brothers had acquired enough experience of civil and military administration, yet there was considerable difference in their personal qualities, capabilities and mental make-up. Dara Shukoh was "a man of eclective views, liberal disposition, and of scholarly instincts, Dara Shukoh mixed with the followers of other faiths and studied the doctrines of Vedanta, the Talmud, the New Testament and the works of Sufi writers...." But too much fondness that his father bestowed on him and his stay in the court and particularly his scholarly pursuits prevented the development of the qualities of an astute statesman, political wisdom or diplomatic insight into men and things or any soldierly ability that made a good general. He grew somewhat Proud and intolerant of sane advice when it came from others. But he was tolerant to all religions and friendly to the Hindus and the Rajput aristocracy.

Shuja was a capable administrator, brave soldier, and an intelligent commander. But all these good qualities were given in him in vain, for he was excessively indolent and pleasure-loving, incapable of sustained effort, perseverance, and use of caution.

Murad, the youngest was no doubt brave, frank and liberal but too much drinking made him utterly incapable of action and often made him light, laughable and bereft of leadership.

Aurangzeb, the third son was the most capable as a soldier and a diplomatic, crafty and cruel about whose character we shall discuss in details in proper place.

When Shah Jahan fell ill (Sept. 1657) Dara Shukoh was in Agra and it was suspected by other three brothers that their father had actually died, but the news was purposely suppressed by Dara Shukoh. This gave rise to confusion within the empire and a fratricidal struggle began. Shuja who had been the governor of Bengal and ruled the subah with success proclaimed himself emperor at Rajmahal, then capital of Bengal, and proceeded towards Agra at the head of a large army to fight Dara Shukoh and wrest the Delhi throne. Murad had in the meantime assumed the title of the Emperor at Ahmadabad on December 5, 1657 and struck coins in his name. Murad entered into correspondence with Aurangzeb who cleverly concealed his real intention and made an agreement with Murad ultimately to overpower all the brothers and occupy the throne himself. According to the agreement, after the occupation of the Empire Afghanistan, Kashmir, Punjab and Sind would consititute an independent kingdom under Murad, one-third of the booty would go to Murad and two thirds to Aurangzeb.

In the meantime Shuja having completed his coronation at Rajmahal proceeded against Dara at the head of a large army and advanced upto Banaras early in February, 1658. Dara planned to defeat Shuja and Murad first and then to proceed against Aurangzeb. He sent his eldest son Sulaiman Shukoh and Jai Singh of Amber against Shuja who was defeated at Bahadurpur (Feb. 24, 1658) and was hotly chased upto the borders of Bengal.

Aurangzeb having entered into the agreement with Murad, conciliated both Golconda and Bijapur as well as Shivaji. He also encouraged the Persian Shah to invade Afghanistan which was a Mughal province then, in order to distract Dara's attention. He then proceeded against Dara and was joined by Murad at Dipalpur. The combined army advanced upto **Dharmat** where Dara's army under Jaswant Singh of Jodhpur and Qasim Khan met there. The imperial army badly led and organised was beaten back with great slaughter (April 25, 1658). Victory at Dharmat enhanced both the political and military prestige of Aurangzed. "The hero of the Deccan wars and the victor of Dharmat faced the world not only without loss but with his military reputation rendered absolutely unrivalled in India" (J.N.Sarkar). Aurangzeb founded the town of Fatehabad at the site of the battle.

Aurangzeb then crossed the Chambal and arrived at **Samugarh** where Dara had reached to give battle to his victorious brothers. He had with him an army of 50,000 soldiers formidable in number but weak in quality for the number was collected hastily from different localities and diverse classes and not trained to work in unison and discipline. Dara Shukoh made the intial mistake of not attacking Aurangzeb's troops immediately who were exhausted due to the long march, and postponed the battle for the next day. When the battle began next day, the 8th June 1658, Dara seated on an elephant and commanded the army in person. He fought gallantly, but unluckily his elephant got severely wounded and Dara had to dismount from the elephant and ride on a horse. According to V. A. Smith "That action settled the fate of the battle." As the troops of Dara found the howdah of the elephant on which Dara was seated vacant, thought that he had fallen in the battle and dispersed from the battle-field in utter confusion. Dara, greatly dismayed escaped leaving 10,000 of his men dead on the battle ground. many more perished due to heat and exhaustion. He returned to Agra but did not meet his father out of shame and left for Delhi with his family and some followers to raise an army to oppose Aurangzeb and Murad.

It may be pointed out the political significance of the battle of **Samugarh** was that it decided the issue in the war of succession. Aurangzeb at once marched to Agra and seized the fort (June 8, 1658) defying Shah Jahan's attempt to come to an amicable settlement with his son.

Shah Jahan was deprived of his throne and confined in the Agra Fort without even the most common conveniences.

Aurangzeb proved most unfilial to his old father and every effort made by Shah Jahan and Jahanara for conciliation went unheeded by him. Shah Jahan lived in the Shah Burj of the Agra Fort for long eight years as a prisoner, closely watched by Aurangzeb's men and disallowed to have any contact with outsiders. He was, however, attended by his favourite daughter Jahanara. On rare occasions he was permitted to correspond or allowed to meet with people from outside in presence of Aurangzeb's agents. In the correspondence that passed between Aurangzeb and imprisoned Shah Jahan the former charged his father of partiality towards Dara Shukoh while the latter in anger and distress called Aurangzeb a robber, an usurper and a hypocrite. The old Emperor was subjected to extreme humiliation and agony till his exit from the world. His life in the prison of his son was unhappy beyond measure and beggars description. "Like a child that cries itself to sleep, ceased to complain, he found solace in religion, and in a spirit of resignation, passed his last days in prayer and meditation." It is said that he kept on gazing at the Taj Mahal till his last moment which came at the age of seventy four on January 22, 1666. He was denied the funeral due to an Emperor and his bier was carried by eunuchs and menials and interred by the side of Mumtaj Mahal in Taj Mahal at Agra.

In the meantime coldness developed in the relation between Aurangzeb and Murad who had by this time seen through the designs of Aurangzeb. Murad was enveigled into a trap. He was given some gold and was asked to advance against Dara who had fled to Lahore in the meantime. Before his departure Murad was invited to a grand feast allowed to drink heavily and imprisoned first in the fort of Salimgarh and then in the fortress of Gwalior (1659). He was put to death there in 1661.

After imprisoning Murad in 1658, Aurangzeb marched to Delhi and formally crowned himself Emperor on July 21, 1658. Aurangzeb now advanced against his remaining rivals, Dara and Shuja.

Shuja noticed with interest the defeat of Dara in the battles of Dharmat and Samugarh. He made a bid for power but was defeated by Aurangzeb at **Khajwah** on January 5, 1659. Mir Jumla persued him through West Bengal and Dacca and he fled to Arakan (May 1660). Prince Muhammad, son of Aurangzeb who joined Shuja was captured and imprisoned for life. Nothing was known of Shuja after his flight into Arakan and it is believed that he with his family had been done to death by the Arakanese.

Having failed to raise troops in Delhi Dara Shukoh fled to Lahore where also he could not rally any force against Aurangzeb. He went to Gujarat and was kindly received by the governor of Ahmadabad who gave ten lakhs of rupees to him with which he raised an army. His attempt to enlist the support of Jaswant Singh did not succeed as he had been won over through the intercession of Jai Singh of Amber. Aurangzeb, now Emperor, sent the imperial army to pursue Dara. In the battle of **Deorai** near Ajmer Dara was signally defeated by the imperial force and was compelled to take refuge in Ahmadabad. But the governor who assisted him earlier now refused to give him shelter and Dara had no way out but to make for Afghanistan. He took shelter at Dadar in the house of one Malik Jiwan whom he had once saved from Shah Jahan's wrath. Nadira Begam wife of Dara and his second son Siphir Shukoh accompanied him. In Jiwan's house Nadira died of illness and Dara was also ill due to the shock of the death of his wife. But Jiwan treacherously handed Dara and his second son to Aurangzeb's men (Sept. 1, 1659). Aurangzeb paraded Dara who was then in a dirty, wretched dress, in the streets of Delhi seated on an elephant. Bernier, an eye witness narrates the pity the tragic plight excited among the citizens of Delhi. "The crowd assembled was immense, and everywhere I observed the people weeping, and lamenting the fate of Dara in the most touching language...... From every quarter I heard piercing and distressing shrieks...... men, women, and children wailing as if, some mighty calamity had happened to themselves." "But not a single hand could be raised to rescue the unfortunate prince, as he was girt round by cavalry and archers." Then a riot broke out which was particularly directed against Malik Jiwan, and Aurangzeb found it dangerous to keep Dara alive any longer. He was tried of apostacy by a special tribunal, found guilty and beheaded. Aurangzeb thus became the unquestioned master of Hindustan.

Personality and Character of Shah Jahan : Contemporary writers Thomas Roe, Chaplain Terry, Francois Bernier and De Laet as also Dr. Smith consider Shah Jahan as not essentially unrelenting or unduly pleasure-loving ruler. But as Dr. Smith observes "Shah Jahan who received from most modern historians, and especially from Elphinstone, treatment unduly favourable." Shah Jahan's Character was partly liberal and progressive, and also partly severe and reactionary. He may be looked upon as a sort of an admixture of Jahangir and Aurangzeb. His acquisition of the throne certainly left unpleasant memories but Alexander Dow ramarks that "we lose half our rage in the pressure of circumstances that drove him to such a ghastly step" due to the ceaseless intrigues of Nur Jahan. While Majumdar-Roychaudhuri and Datta observe that "Though not as great a warrior as some of his ancestors, Shah Jahan was not devoid of military qualities." But Dr. Smith says he had little skill as a military leader. The loss of Qandahar and failure of his three attempts showed his inefficiency as well that of his army.

Shah Jahan learnt to read and speak Turki from Ruqayya Begum who brought him up and read with eminent teachers like Mulla Qasim Beg Tabrezi, Hakim Dawai, Shaikh Abdul Kahir and Shaikh Sufi. He acquired proficiency both in Persian and Hindi. The brightest feature of his character was intense love for Mumtaz Mahal who had a restraining influence on him so long as she was alive. But after her death Shah Jahan disgraced himself by gross licentiousness.

Eulogists have written flatteringly about Shah Jahan's justice, but examination of concrete facts shows it to be crude and cruel. He took pleasure in personally witnessing shocking punishments inflicted on the criminals. Heads of thieves were gibetted in **chor-minars** and Peter Mundy saw 8,000 heads in Cawnpore District gibetted in **chor-minars**.

Shah Jahan's administration was severe which was also reflected in the provincial administration. There was no serious challenge to the Emperor's authority till the outbreak of the war of succession, and there was no external invasion of India during his reign. Shah Jahan succeeded in restoring the efficiency of the Mansabdari system which had deteriorated in the later years of his father's rule. But his military exploits were nil. If his Qandahar expeditions had failed, his Central Asian policy had no better success. The Mughal army under Shah Jahan had definitely become weaker than before.

Climax of Mughal Empire : Golden Age ? : Dr. Smith is of opinion that irrespective of the view that we may hold about the character of Shah Jahan or the efficiency of his administration, "his reign marks the climax of the Mughal dynasty and empire." This claim he justifies on the grounds (i) that for thirty years from 1628-1658 the Mughal Emperor's authority was not seriously challenged, (ii) the Empire was not invaded by any external enemy, (iii) loss of Qandahar and failure to recover it did not have any adverse effect in India, (iv) the period also saw development of export trade with western Asia and the begining of trade with Europe as also improvement of the state finances.

It is also customary to regard the reign of Shah Jahan as a golden age, looked at from the total output of art, architecture painting, patronage of literature etc.

It was a period of Pomp and splendour. The brilliant productions of architecture such as the **Taj mahal**, the **Pearl Mosque** of Agra, the **Diwan-i-Am** and **Diwan-i-Khas** and the **Jami Masjid** of Delhi will certainly lead one to believe that the reign of Shah Jahan was the golden age of the medieval Indian history. The celebrated **Peacock throne** studded with pearls and jewels added to the splendour of the reign.

The Indo-Persian architecture under Akbar and Jahangir was more virile then, than under Shah Jahan, according to some critics. "But the world is agreed in preferring the Taj, with its feminine grace, to all its predecessors or successors." The Hindu style of architecture which was so pronounced in the buildings of Akbar and Jahangir had been considerably diminished under Shah Jahan.

Shah Jahan had lavished patronage on the art of painting but the work of the time was somewhat crude imitation of Persian work of painting of the days of Akbar and by the time of Shah Jahan had become antedated and gone out of fashion. Yet some of the paintings of Shah Jahan's time were wonderfully free from the stiffness of the previous reigns and even of the succeeding reigns and were perfectly charming and life-like. Artists of Shah Jahan's time were largely influenced by the old Hindu tradition and European art.

Shah Jahan's reign also saw the contimation of historical works mostly in Persian language. Elliot and Dawson as well as J. N. Sarkar specially mention the historical works like **Badshah-nama** by Abdul Hamid Lahori, and the **Muntakhab-ul-Lubab** of Muhammad Hashim of Khwaf better known as Khafi Khan. Most eminent Hindi poet was Bihari Lal, but none of the numerous Hindi poets that had flourished under Shah Jahan can be compared to Tulsi Das or Sur Das.

Looked at superficially the reign of Shah Jahan is sure to dazzle the eyes as the reign of Louis XIV had done of the contemporary Europe. Shah Jahan's reign has been regarded by many as the golden age of the medieval Indian history. But this is an uncritical and partial, one-sided statement which does not stand scrutiny. Any reign in order that it may constitute a golden age must essentially be welfare state and it is not simply the superficial splendour and pomp but the totality of the intrinsic benefits derived by the people at large that makes a reign really golden.

The gloomy side of the reign of Shah Jahan has been brought out by Bernier, a highly trained observer who was also reputed to be the most learned man of Asia. His observations were free from personal bias. While he enthusiastically admired the fertility and commerce of Bengal, he spoke also of the despotic tyranny of the local governors of the empire. Their tyranny was often so excessive that the peasants and artisans were deprived of the necessaries of life and were left to die in misery and exhaustion. "... a tyranny in fine, that drives the cultivator of the soil from his wretched home to some neighbouring state, in hopes of finding milder treatment, or to the army, where he becomes the servant of the trooper." Lands were not properly tilled, irrigation ditches and canals never repaired, houses were left in dilapidated condition, there were very few to build new houses or repair those which were tumbling down.

"The country is ruined by the necessity of defraying the enormous charges required to maintain the splendour a numerous court, and to pay a large army maintained for the purpose of keeping the people in subjection. No adequate idea can be conveyed of the sufferings of that people, cudgel and the whip compel them to incessant labour for the benefit of others, and driven to despair by every kind of cruel treatment, their revolt or their flight is only prevented by the presence of a military force."

The picture of extortionate state demand is largely borne out by the early revenue farmans of Aurangzeb as we find in J. N. Sarkar's studies in Mughal India.

According to J. N. Sarkar, Shah Jahan, despite his fondness for pleasure, pomp and splendour was a hard-working ruler. It was during his reign that the seeds of reaction which became the most important cause of the downfall of the Mughal dynasty had been sown.

REFERENCES

An Advanced History of India : Majumdar, Roychaudhuri & Datta

The Oxford History of India (4th Edn.) : V. A. Smith

The Mughal Empire : A. L. Srivastava

History of India, Vols. IV, V, VI : Elliot & Dawson

Cambridge History of India, Vols. V, VI

Mughal Administration : J. N. Sarkar

Mughal Rule in India : Edwardes & Garret

Studies in Mughal India : J. N. Sarkar

Later Medieval India : A. B. Pandey

12

Crisis of the Mughal Empire

CRISIS OF THE MUGHAL EMPIRE : AURANGZEB (1658-1707)

We have seen earlier that Aurangzeb had enthroned himself on July 21, 1658 after his occupation of Agra. But he held his second enthronment after his success in the battles of Khajwa and Deorai, on May 15, 1659 after entering Delhi in a grand procession. There was prolonged rejoicings, and lavish expenditure was incurred to make the occasion memorable. There were large-scale illuminations and grand feasts. **Khutba** was read and coins struck in his name. He assumed the title of **Alamgir Padshah Ghazi**.

Aurangzeb's first concern was to take steps to win the confidence, particularly of his co-religionists and to alleviate the distress of the common people who had suffered considerably due to the war of succession and loss of production of every kind. He discontinued the Ilahi era introduced by Akbar and reverted to the lunar calendar followed by the Muslims. He remitted certain vexalious taxes and cesses, such as transit duty, octroi duty, **awabs** which were extra levies and special awabs which were licence tax, gift tax, fees and commissions realised for the state. But as was usual with all previous rulers, these remissions were not effective in reality except in one or two cases. The local officers continued to collect all the taxes for their own benefits. According to Khafi Khan the local officers actually collected transit duties often twice the cost price of the commodities.

In order to bring peace and repair the damages done during the war of succession, particularly in northern India, Aurangzeb brought the governors and officers under strict control.

Aurangzeb was the champion of the Sunni Muslims and in order that he might conform to orthodox precepts of the Quran, he issued several regulations. Formerly **Kalima** used to be embossed on the coins. This practice was abandoned by Aurangzeb as it was un-Islamic. He also gave up, the practice of observing the Persian New Year's day. Cultivation of **Bhang** in the empire was prohibited, gambling, drinking and prostitution were also strictly prohibited and censors of public morals were appointed to see to it that orders were strictly obeyed. Every Muslim was required to say prayers five times a day and keep Ramdan Fast. Heresy and blasphemy were strictly punished. Many Shiahs were beheaded for abusing the first three Caliphs i.e. Khalifas. The Ismailia and Bohra communities of Gujarat had to suffer bloody persecution at the hands of Aurangzeb.

Expansion of Territories : Imperial expansion under Aurangzeb ran apace and if the loss of Qandahar and Central Asia under Shah Jahan is not taken into account the extent of the empire remained intact under Aurangzeb at the time of the accession. Daud Khan, Governor of Bihar conquered Palamau in 1661 and it was fortunate for Aurangzeb that his enterprising officers added to the empire of their master.

Assam Campaign : On the eastern frontier of the Empire the Ahoms, a Mongoloid dynasty that ruled over Assam and Cooch-Behar seized the Mughal district of Kamrup that lay between their territories. Mir Jumla, the governor of Bengal was directed to advance against the Ahoms to check their aggression. The Mughals had already to fight the Ahoms when they raided the eastern frontier of the Empire under Shah Jahan and a peace was arrived at between the two in 1639. But the war of succession gave the Ahoms the opportunity to occupy Gauhati in 1658, seize 140 horses, 40 pieces of cannon, 200 matchlocks and much booty.

Mir Jumla marched at the head of 12,000 cavalry and 30,000.infantry, a large flotilla and sufficient artillery from Dacca in 1661 to punish the aggressors. Mir Jumla rapidly over-ran Cooch-Behar in December 1661 and pursued the Ahom Raja up the Brahmaputra valley. Fort after fort fell to him and Assam was also captured. Mir Jumla entered Garhgaon, the capital of the Ahom Raja in March 1662. The Raja left the capital defenceless at the mercy of the invader and Mir Jumla collected immense booty. But with the onset of the rains Nature fought for the Ahoms. Mir Jumla's troops suffered heavily from the inclimencies of the climate and fell sick—both for want of provisions and medicines the army of Mir Jumla was in a hopeless state of disorder and confusion. The Ahoms who had avoided open conflict with the Mughals now fell upon them. The Mughal governor despite the famine and pestilence in his camp held his own till the rains were over, and then resumed offensive in full scale. The Ahoms were now compelled to sue for peace. Thus "judged as a military exploit, Mir Jumla's invasion of Assam was a success" (J.N. Sarkar). Jayadhvaj, king of Assam agreed to pay an annual tribute to the Mughals and pay a huge indemnity, a part of which was paid immediately and the balance was to be paid in twelve equal monthly instalments. It must, however, be noted that compared to the loss sustained, particularly death of Mir Jumla (April, 10, 1663) himself on his way to Dacca due to illness caused during the Assam Campaign and loss of men and money, the gain was too insignificant and of no permanent advantage to the empire.

Mir Jumla was succeeded by Shayista Khan, son of Asaf Khan and maternal uncle of Aurangzeb, as governor of Bengal. The Portuguese at that time made themselves a veritable menace in Bengal for they carried on piracy in coastal Bengal in the name of trade and even carried off people and sold them as slaves. Shayista Khan raised a flotilla or 300 vessels and captured the island of Sandvip as well as Chittagong. Sandvip was the stronghold of the Portuguese pirates. Shayista Khan released thousands of slaves. Chittagong belonged to the king of Arakan, who was an ally of the Portuguese. Shayista Khan placed a commandant in charge of Chittagong to deal with evil of the Portuguese piracy, but it could not completely eradicated.

North-West Frontier War : Aurangzeb was a champion of Muslim orthodoxy, but he had to face equally orthodox Muslim Afghan tribes in the north-west frontier of his empire who had always been a menace to the north-western borders of the empire. The Afghan tribes were hardy people who lived by high way robbery and blackmailing the rich cities of the north-western Punjab. The Mughal emperors found it difficult to conquer or tame the tribesmen and resorted to the system of bribing them. But these tribes euphemistically called political pensions were not always effective in securing obedience. In 1667 a leader of the Yusufzai clan rose in arms and a large number of them crossed the Indus and raided the Mughal district of Hazara. A section of the Yusufzais plundered Attock and Peshawar and attempted to hold the ferry and Harun to prevent the Mughal army to cross into the tribal areas. They were, however, defeated by the Mughal commandant Kamil Khan of Attock (April, 1667). Shamsher Khan another Mughal commander crossed into the tribal area and defeated the Yusufzais tribals. Aurangzeb also sent Muhammad Amin Khan to punish the Yusufzais within a few months.

In 1672 another revolt in the frontier region took place under the Afridi chief Akmal Khan who declared himself independent, assumed the crown of king himself and declared a holy war against the Mughals calling upon all the the Pathans to join him. In May, 1672, they inflicted a crushing defeat on the Mughals under Muhammad Amin Khan at Ali Masjid. Amin Khan made good his escape leaving his camp and property including his women who were turned into slaves by their Pathan captors. This victory enhanced the power and prestige of Akmal Khan and recruits began to flock into his army. The success also fired the ambition of the tribesmen who were joined by Khushal Khan of the Khattak clan and the rising spread throughout the entire frontier region. The whole of the Ptathan land from Attock to Quandahar rose in arms. Aurangzeb appointed Mahabat Khan as the governor of Afghanistan with the specific instruction to put down the rebellion. The new governor arrived at a secret understanding with the rebels and there was no improvement in the situation. Aurangzeb was very much displeased and sent Shujaat Khan, supported by Jaswant Singh to deal with rebellious tribesmen. Shujaat Khan was defeated by the Pathans in February, 1674 and he himself was killed with a large number of his soldiers. The remnant of his army was rescued by the Rathor contingent of Jaswant Singh.

The situation at the frontier was fast going out of control. Aurangzeb, therefore, personally proceeded to Hasan Abdal, (1674) a place near Peshawar and by both diplomacy, bribing and use of force achieved much success. He succeeded in bringing many Afghan tribes to submission by grant of pensions, jagirs and presents as also offices, while more recalcitrants were subdued by use of force. By December 1675, the frontier became almost quiet and Aurangzeb left for Delhi. Amin Khan, the governor of Afghanistan was a capable man who by his tact, diplomacy and friendly behaviour towards the Afghan tribals succeeded in further quietening the frontier during the term of his office from 1677 to 1698 the year of his death. His success was to a very large extent due to the wise advice and able support of his wife Sahibji, daughter of Ali Mardan Khan.

Amin Khan while paid subsidies·to the tribal chiefs sowed dissensions among them and gradually broke up the Afghan Tribal confederacy organised by Akmal Khan. On the latter's death the Afridis submitted and made peace with the Mughals. Khushal Khan, the Khattak hero, however, carried on hostilities for a few years more till his own son betrayed him and went over to the Mughals. Khushal Khan was captured and imprisoned. The frontier war came to an end. The war against the Afghan tribals proved to be a very costly affair and as Sir J. N. Sarkar puts it, their indirect effects were prejudicial to the interests of the empire, for it was ruinous to imperial finances and even more harmful in its political effects. It made employment of the Afghans in the ensuing hostilities with the Rajputs impossible, although Afghans were the fittest soldiers to fight in the barren country of Rajputana. It also relieved pressure on Shivaji by directing the Mughal troops from the south to service in the north-west. The advantage was taken by Shivaji who took possession of Karnataka and Raigarh. "The Maratha chief took advantage of this division of his enemys strength to sweep in a dazzling succession of triumphs through Golconda to the Karnataka and back again through Mysore and Bijapur to Raigarh during the fifteen months following, December 1675. It was the climax of his career; but the Afridis and the Khattaks made his unbroken success possible."

Aurangzeb and the Deccan : Aurangzeb's attention during the first half of his reign was engrossed in the affairs of the north. Affairs of the Deccan were left in the hands of the governors who had not much difficulty in dealing with the Bijapur and Golconda sultanates as they were decadent. They had not been able to recover from the blows they received from the imperial troops and their weakness was taken advantage of by the rising Marathas whose appearance in the Deccan complicated the political situation in the south and posed a great challenge to the Mughal power.

For the first twenty years of Aurangzeb's reign his governors in the Deccan could not achieve any success against the sultanates or against the rising Marathas, nor could the Emperor himself realise the full significance of the rise of the Marathas at first.

Abdulla Qutb Shah, sultan of Golconda was as indolent as pleasure-loving. He spent most of his time in the company of women leaving the affairs of the state in the hands of his favourite officers. Abdul Hasan who succeeded him was no better. He also left the administration of the state to his two Brahmin ministers, Madanna and Makkanna. He entered into a defensive alliance with Shivaji promising him an annual subsidy of five lakhs of rupees. Bijapur was more defiant than Golconda and imperial troops had to be sent against it several times. Aurangzeb, as soon as he emerged successful in the war of succession, turned his attention towards the Deccan.

Aurangzeb sent Jai Singh of Jaipur (1665) to chastise Bijapur for violating the terms of 1657. Jai Singh was also instructed to subdue Shivaji. Jai Singh first dealt with Shivaji and compelled him to surrender the fort of Purandar and forced Shivaji to accept the treaty of Purandar in June, 1665 by which he had to give up twenty-three forts and extensive lands, and to become a Mughal vassal, and promised a contingent of 5,000 horses. Jai Singh persuaded Shivaji to go to Agra where he was received by Aurangzeb, but refused to be treated as a mansabdar of 5,000 horses, Shivaji refused to comply with the etiquette of the imperial court and demanded respect due to a sovereign prince. Shivaji, consequently was kept under surveillance from which he managed to escape with his son, with the connivance of Ram Singh, a son of Jai Singh, returned to his country after many adventures, in December, 1666, after an absence of nine months.

Next year Jai Singh died (1667) in the Deccan having been poisoned by his son Kirat Singh. Aurangzeb was glad that Jai Singh was dead, for he felt he had now greater liberty in pursuing his policy of persecution. "He availed himself of the liberty so gained by destroying the large temple at Mathura."

Raja Jaswant Singh of Marwar (Jodhpur) now took over Jai Singh's position in the Deccan where he had served before. But his previous experience and assistance received from Prince Muazzam did not help him to make any improvement in the situation for the imperialists. Both Jaswant Singh and Prince Muazzam accepted large sums of money from Shivaji and refrained from taking effective steps against him. On the contrary they persuaded Aurangzed to confer on Shivaji the title of Raja (1667). Next two years were devoted by Shivaji in organising his internal government and in 1670 resumed active hostilities against the Mughals and **Chauth** was realised from certain parts of Khandesh. Smith says that "we may date the first imposition of Maratha on a province immediately subject to the Mughals." This was indeed a conclusive proof of the feebleness of Aurangzeb's government even early in his reign. In October, 1670 Shivaji pillaged the city of Surat although was not able to damage the European factories. He also conquered Ramnagar and Jawhar. At Raigarh, Shivaji celebrated his formal coronation as an independent **Chatrapati** on June 16, 1674. He then conquered Karnataka and a part of Mysore, helped Sidi Masud, regent of Bijapur against the Mughals (1678). Soon after he fell ill and died on April 14, 1680.

Death of Shivaji did not mean any improvement in the imperial position in the Deccan. Prince Akbar fled and took shelter with Shambhuji and an alliance between "disturber of India" (Akbar) and the "infernal son of an infernal father" (Shambhuji) as Aurangzeb termed these two, called for a change in Aurangzeb's Deccan policy. He now personally marched toward, the Deccan leaving Ajmer (1681) after having patched up a peace with Mewar. He reached Burhampur in November 1681 and Ahmadnagar early in 1682. "His mind must have been full of high hopes, and he could not foresee that destiny was dragging him to the south to dig the graves of himself and his empire." From 1682 to 1685 were spent in vain pursuit of Prince Akbar and although a few of the Maratha forts had been conquered by the imperial forces the sturdy Marathas could not be suppressed.

Aurangzeb's policy towards the Deccan sultanates was guided by both imperialist interest and religious consideration. Siege of Bijapur which had been in decadence due to internal dissensions began in 1685 and Aurangzeb arrived there in person in 1686. The garrison held out gallantly and it was not until lack of provisions, and huge toll taken by pestilence and famine of countless men and horses that it surrendered to the Mughals and the Adil Shahi dynasty came to an end. Aurangzeb entered the city of Bijapur in triumph and perpetrated the act of vandalism by destroying all the fine paintings and frescoes of Sikandar Shah's palace. Bijapur not only lost its independence but was left a desolate and plundered city. "A few years later Bhimsen noticed how the city and its equally large suburb Nauraspur looked deserted and ruined, the population was scattered, and even the water-supply in the city-wells had suddenly grown scanty."

Next, Aurangzeb turned his attention to the Qutb Shahi kingdom of Golconda which had enjoyed immunity from Mughal attacks for the past thirty years during which the Sultan paid the tributes regularly. Predominance of Hindu influence at Golconda and its alliance with Shambhuji were particularly offensive to Aurangzeb. The immediate cause of hostility between Golconda and the Mughals was the interception of a letter of Abdul Hasan to his agent in the Mughal camp in which he called Aurangzeb "a meanminded coward for attacking a helpless young orphan like Sikandar Adil Shah" and mentioned that he would render military support to Bijapur. This letter infuriated Aurangzeb who at once despatched Prince Shah Alam to invade Hyderabad (July, 1685). The Prince was held up at Malkhed by a Golconda army and attained no success. Soon after, Mir Muhammad Ibrahim, the commander-in-chief of Golconda army was bribed to join the Mughals. The Sultan Abul Hasan thus betrayed, fled from the Golconda fort, Hyderabad was captured by Shah Alam. Abul Hasan had to sumbit and was pardoned on condition of surrendering Malkhed and Seram, to dismiss his Hindu ministers Madanna and Akkanna and to pay an indemnity of one crore twenty lakhs of rupees.

But independent Golconda was by itself an offence in Aurangzeb's scheme of things. He, therefore, resumed operation against Abul Hasan after conquest of Bijapur and himself appeared before Golconda early in 1687. The fort was besieged but it held out valiantly for about eight months. Prince Shah Alam in the meantime accepted presents from the Sultan Abul Hasan and was about to get him pardoned. Aurangzeb got information about the secret negotiations between Abul Hasan and the Prince and put the latter with his family under arrest and confiscated his property. Aurangzeb now pressed the siege but due to rains and lack of provisions the Mughal army could not make much impression. On the contrary the chief of the Mughal artillery Chairat Khan and some other high military officers of the Mughals were taken prisoners by the Golconda troops. Aurangzeb ordered three mines to be dug under the bastions of the fort but when ignited these were misdirected and killed 1,100 Mughal troops. Now, Aurangzeb following the example of Akbar at Asirgarh had resort to bribery and through the treachery of one Abdullah Pani an Afghan soldier of fortune employed in the service of Abul Hasan got the main gate of the fort thrown open to the Mughals. The only Golconda officer who spurned Aurangzeb's tempting offer of money and fought valiantly in defence of the fort was Abur Razzaq Lari till he fell down after receiving as many as seventy wounds on his person. He was nursed to recovery by the Mughals and given a high rank in the imperial service. Abul Hasan was sent to Daulatabad fortress with a pension of Rs. 50,000 a year and Golconda was annexed to the Mughal empire (1687).

We have seen that Aurangzeb's earlier attempt to conquer the two Deccan Sultanates was prevented by the intervention of Dara Shukoh and Jahanara. But Aurangzeb imperialistic policy and religious bigotry would not tolerate independent Sultanates of the Deccan. According to Dr. Smith, Elphinstone and others, the annihilation of the Southern Sultanates was an impolitic step on the part of Aurangzeb. Extinction of these Sultanates "freed the Maratha chief from any fear of local rivalry" which could have been used by the Mughal Emperor to his advantage against the Marathas. But historians have doubted if the decadent deccan Sultanates would be in a position to check the rise of Marathas. Sir J. N. Sarkar observes that "since Akbar had crossed the Vindhyas, the Deccan Sultanates could never forget that the sleepless aim of the Mughal Emperors was the final extinction and annexation of all their territories." It is, therefore, idle to speculate that if the Deccan Sultanates were allowed to exist they would serve as good opposition to the rise of the Marathas.

In the extinction of the Deccan Sultanates Aurangzeb's policy of imperialistic expansion towards the south and subduing the Shiahs was successful. His other policy remained yet to be fulfilled, namely the subjugation of the Marathas. His attempt at suppression of the renascent Maratha power met with initial success and in 1689 (March 11) Shambhuji was executed at Raigarh, the Maratha capital which was captured by the Mughals. Rajaram, brother of Shambhuji managed to escape, but Shambhuji's son, Shahu and the rest of his family were taken captives by Aurangzeb. Next, the imperial authority was extended further south and the Hindu states of Tanjore and Trichinopoly were made to agree to pay tributes to the Emperor. By 1690 Aurangzeb's empire comprised whole of India from Kabul to Chittagong and from Kashmir to Kaveri. Insofar as the expansion was concerned, Aurangzed was at the Zenith of the Empire. "All seemed to have been gained by Aurangzeb now, but in reality all was lost. It was the beginning of his end. The saddest and most hopeless chapter of his life was now opened." The vastness of the empire precluded its being ruled from one common centre and by one man. Recalcitrant forces raised their heads everywhere throughout the empire. Lawlessness, rebellions, disorder and confusion reigned in many places which the corrupt officials of the state could not control. The chiefs, the Zaminders defied local authorities, the province of Agra especially became the scene of disorder and disobedience. Learning decayed, treasury was exhausted due to the prolonged Deccan war, Emperor's absence from capital in the Deccan for long years threw the whole of northern India in disorder. The army in arrear of pay for long mutinied. Murshid Quli the diwan of Bengal sent the revenue of Bengal to the centre which was the only source of income. It the **"Spanish Ulcer"** had ruined Napoleon Bonaparte I, it was the **"Deccan Ulcer"** that ruined Aurangzeb. The Marathas recovered their losses by 1691 and began a national resistance.

Aurangzeb and Rajasthan : Aurangzeb in his lack of statesmanship and too much regard for religious bigotry failed to realise the value of the alliance of the Rajputs who had previously contributed to the expansion and strength of the Empire. He introduced a radical change in the policy of the state towards them. So long as Jai Singh of Amber and Jaswant Singh of Marwar were alive Aurangzeb was not feeling completely free to put his religious policy into effect. Death of Jai Singh in the Deccan in 1667 was a matter of public rejoicings to Aurangzeb. This removed a powerful leader of Rajput opposition to Aurangzeb's policy. Aurangzeb suspected, Jaswant Singh of marwar formerly a partisan of Dara Shukoh, might stand forth as the leader of the Rajput opposition. This apart, Aurangzeb had in his mind the conquest of Marwar very much necessary for the empire, as it occupied a strategically important position both from the military and commercial points of view. Soon an opportunity to give effect to his designs against

Marwar arose. Raja Jaswant Singh died in 1678 at Jamrud while serving as the commander of the Mughal posts in the Khyber pass and the Peshawar district. Immediately on the death of Jaswant Singh Aurangzeb brought Marwar under Mughal rule and appointed his own officers as Faujdar, Qiladar, Kotwal and Amin. On the same day he imposed Jizya on the Hindus. The Rathors shocked and thrown into confusion at the sudden death of their Raja failed to rally a national resistance and a grand-nephew of Jaswant Singh—Indra Singh Rathor, the chief of Nagor got himself recognised as the Rana of Jodhpur on payment of thirty six lakhs of rupees as succession fee. He was only a phantom ruler, surrounded by Mughal officers. Aurangzeb's designs on Marwar thus seemed to have crowned with success.

Aurangzeb's hopes of quiet rule over Marwar was belied soon, for every Rajput family now became determined to undo what Aurangzeb had done to Marwar. In February 1679 two posthumous sons of Jaswant were born to two Ranis, at Lahore. One of the two died, the other, Ajit Singh survived. The loyal followers of Jaswant Singh took the child to Delhi and appealed to Aurangzeb to recognise him as the successor of Jaswant Singh. The Emperor offered to bring up the child in his harem. It is also said that the throne of Jodhpur was offered to Ajit Singh provided he would accept Islam. This wounded the religious susceptibilities of the Rajputs who preferred to lay their lives down rather than to allow the child of Jaswant Singh embrace Islam. At this critical hour of the Rathor national life Durgadas the son of Jaswant Singh's Minister Askaran, took up the leadership of the Rathors and a new chapter in the Mughal-Rajput hostilities began.

Durgadas rescued the Ranis and child Ajit Singh and when an imperial force was sent to seize the Ranis and the child, a band of Rajputs defying death fell upon the Mughal troops and in the prevailling confusion rode away with the Ranis disguised in male attire and reached Marwar. Baffled in his designs Aurangzeb substituted a milkman's son in place of Ajit and proclaimed that Durgadas' protege was an imposter. In Marwar the People rose in rebellion against the Mughal oppressors. Aurangzeb sent Prince Akbar to reconquer Marwar, who after prolonged warfare captured the country, plundered the towns, destroyed the temples. The Rathors fled to take shelter in the hills and deserts.

Aurangzeb's next target was Mewar. He ordered Maharana Raj Singh to pay Jizya for his entire state. Raj Singh did not miss the real intention of Aurangzeb which was nothing less to extirpate the Rajput states, and he at once decided to join hands with Durgadas in the cause of Ajit Singh of Marwar. With Rathor-Sisodia alliance the Rajput war assumed the character of a national rising in defence of liberty. Aurangzeb forestalled Maharana's designs by sending 7000 of his chosen troops under Hasan Ali Khan to invade Mewar. Raj Singh fled his capital Udaipur and took shelter in the hills with all his subjects, considering it unwise to face the superior strength of the Mughals. The Mughal troops easily occupied Chitor and Udaipur. The Emperor, now sure of success, placed Prince Akbar in charge of Chitor and left for Ajmer. Now the Mughals had their disillusionment. The Rajputs fell upon the Mughals as guerilla troops and did havoc to the Mughal outposts. The command of Mughal outposts fell vacant as officer after officer declined to undertake the responsibility on one or the other pretext. In early 1680 the Rajputs surprised the Mughal army under Prince Akbar and carried off their provisions, reducing the Mughal army to starvation. Aurangzeb got infuriated at Prince Akbar and handed over the command of Chitor to Prince Azam and ordered Akbar to go to Marwar. Prince Akbar took it as an insult thought of entering into an alliance with the Rajputs whose worth he had sufficiently realised during his war with them. The Rajput chiefs also pointed out to him how the faulty policy of his father was destroying the stability of the Empire and hoping to "place a truly national king on the throne of Delhi, they promised to back him with the armed strength of the two greatest Rajput clans, the Sisodias and the Rathors."

With 70,000 strong army which included the best blood of Rajputana, Akbar arrived near Rajputana in 1681 (Jan. 15). Aurangzeb's army was at that time separated in two divisions one in Chitor and the other at Rajsamudra Lake. Akbar instead of taking advantage of this critical situation of Aurangzeb's army deployment wasted his time before attacking the imperial force. Aurangzeb resorted to a strategem and wrote a letter to his rebellious son contriving it so as to fall into the hand of the Rajputs. The purpose of the letter led the Rajputs desert Prince Akbar, suspecting treachery. The Rajputs soon after discovered the fraud and the Rathor hero Durgadas chivalrously saved the Prince from his father's wrath and escorted him through Khandesh and Baglana to the court of the Maratha King Shambhuji. But Shambhuji an unworthy successor of Shivaji could little afford to help the Prince in realising his dream of an Empire based on Hindu-Muslim unity and reconciliation. After a few years Akbar left for Persia where his death occured in 1704.

Prince Akbar's rebellion and the support that was rendered initially by the Rajputs to his cause, at least had one advantage. Temporary success of the Mughals was largely set off by the loss sustained by them due to the guerilla action of the Rajputs. Suffereings of the Mughals had been considerable and Aurangzeb thought it would be wise to enter into a treaty with Jay Singh, son and successor of Raj Singh in 1681 by which the Mughals withdrew from Mewar and Jay Singh ceded a few districts in lien of Jizya. Marwar continued to fight the Mughals thirty years more. Under Durgadas leadership the Rathors ceaselessly harassed the Mughals and the Mughal officers of some outposts were compelled to pay Chauth to their unrelenting foe to save themselves from their aggression. The war went on unabated till Aurangzeb's death in 1707 and it was his son and successor Bahadur Shah I that recognised Ajit Singh as the Rana of Marwar in 1709.

Like the Deccan policy, the Rajput policy of Aurangzeb also produced disastrous consequences for the Mughal Empire. Loss of life, loss of money in the Rajputana desert did not bring any lasting benefit to the Empire. The imperial prestige was lost and added to this was the huge material loss to the empire. "It was an act of political unwisdom on the part of Aurangzeb to provoke the Rajput hostility and thus forfeit the devoted service of gallant chiefs and soldiers, so long friends of the empire......"

Religious Policy of Aurangzeb : At the very outset it has to be clearly understood that religion with Aurangzeb was no pretence and his religious policy was not influenced by any consideration of wordly gains. He was a devout Sunni Muslim and a champion of Sunni orthodoxy which prompted him to strictly enforce the Quranic laws accordings to which, to his mind, every pius Muslim must carry on Jhad i.e. holy war against dar-ul-harb i.e. the lands of the non-Muslims till they were turned into dar-ul-Islam i.e. realm of Islam.

Aurangzeb's narrow bigotry made him taciturn, and extremely puritanic in his temperament and took steps to translate his own ideas of morose seriousness of life conforming to punctilious orthodoxy. He issued several ordinances to make the Muslims conform to the orthodox rules of conduct prescribed by the Quran. He prohibited the practice of inscribing the **Kalima** on the coins. Observance of the Persian New Year's Day (Nauroj) was discontinued as, to his mind, it was un-Islamic. He appointed **Muhtasibs** or censors of Public morals in every important town and city to enforce Quranic law and to see to it that drinking, gambling and prostitution etc. were effectively put down. Muhtasibs were also to see that the muslims said their five daily prayers and kept Ramdan or Ramzan. They were empowered to punish those who were guilty of heresy or blasphemy. Aurangzeb prohibited cultivation of **bhang** throughout the empire. He simplified the customary celebrations on his birthday and the day of his coronation. In the eleventh year of his reign Aurangzeb discontinued the practice of appearing before the people from the balcony of the palace every morning to receive their salutation. He also prohibited music in the court and dismissed the old musicians and singers. But secret practice of music went on despite the imperial prohibition and it was only in the imperial court and in prominent towns that the order forbidding music could be put into effect. Aurangzeb's puritanism led him to discard the practice of weighing him in gold and silver on birthdays and to dismiss the astrologers of the court.

Aurangzeb did not hesitate to punish the Sufis because of their liberal religious views bordering on pantheism. Sarmad who was a close associate of Dara was put to death by Aurangzeb on charge of apostasy. Many converts to Islam who were suspected of having reverted to their original faith were killed under orders of Aurangzeb. Likewise many Shiahs were beheaded as they denounced the first three Caliphs. Aurangzeb ruthlessly persecuted the Ismailia and Bohra sects of Gujarat.

Aurangzeb did not stop by issuing religious orders and ordinances for others, in fact, he practised what he professed and sought to enforce on others. He was above the contemporary vices and kept himself clean of all that had a remote touch of irreligiocity or immorality. To the devout Muslims he was a **"dervish** born in purple", he was venerated as a living saint, a **Zinda Pir**.

From the official guide book of the reign of Aurangzeb, we come to know that he prohibited the practice of **Suttee** (1633), but from the accounts of the European travellers of the time we learn that this prohibitive order was seldom obeyed.

In 1679 Aurangzeb issued farman reimposing Jizya on the non-Muslims. The inauguration of a new religious policy with regard to important sections of the people made a deep adverse reaction on the minds of the people affected by his regulations and ordinances. Without denying the Emperor the credit of being a conscientious and sincere exponent of the faith he professed, it must be mentioned that his over zealousness made him oblivious of the composite character of the people over whom destiny had placed him to rule, not a homogenous people but a population that included diverse religious traditions and ideals that needed tact, understanding, friendliness and equality of treatment to be won over. But Aurangzeb made the colossal mistake of identifying his personal religion with the state of which he was the head and that had the ruinous effect of generating a feeling of discontent among different sections of the people which even during his life time distracted his energies and was the major cause of the decline and fall of the Empire which Babur and Akbar had built up.

Aurangzeb's Administration : Aurangzeb's administration was a centralised personal despotism where every minister took orders from the Emperor into whose hands all authority was concentrated. In his despotic control over the administration he could only be compared with European contemporary Louis XIV, king of France.

Aurangzeb was, like Louis XIV of France, was his own prime minister and would never share counsel with any of his ministers or officers. The policy of the government and the principles administration were all determined by him personally. He was extremely industrious and looked into the minutest details of administration. He personally went through the petitions submitted to him and either dictated orders or himself wrote them. There was an element of suspicion in Aurangzeb's excluding all his ministers and officers in initiating or formulating plans or policies of the government. He could not reconcile himself to the presence of rival authority within the state or in the administration and was even suspicious of superior intellect.

Aurangzeb took punctilious care to see that rules of etiquette and royal prerogatives were observed and not transgressed by any body. For instance Prince Muazzam was taken to task for saying prayers by putting up canvas screen which was only the imperial prerogative. Likewise when he was informed that Ibrahim Khan governor of Bengal held his court by sitting on a couch while the Qazi, diwan etc. were sitting on the farash i.e. floor, Aurangzeb caused a sarcastic letter to be written to the governor that if his illness precluded his sitting on the floor with others he would better soon get him medically treated.

The system of administration under Aurangzeb remained substantially the same as in the days of Akbar or his immediate predecessors. But too much concentration of power in the hands of the emperor resulted in great administrative degeneration and helplessness. Aurangzeb canalised his political, administrative, economic, in one word, every effort to convert India into a Muslim state. The result was that he effected a great change in the manner, principle and the spirit in which his predecessors had worked the instrument of the government.

In the latter years of Aurangzeb's reign the total number of subahs of the Mughal empire numbered twenty one. Under Akbar the number was fifteen. From the reign of Aurangzeb must be dated the wide extension of farming of revenues, an inordinate increase in the revenue demand which compelled the peasants to flee their land or resort to passive resistance. According to Sir Jadunath Sarkar the revenue of the empire under Aurangzeb amounted to 33 crores and 85 lakhs of rupees. Besides land revenue other principal sources of revenue were **Zakat** or tithe payable by the Muslims, **Jizya** or a poll tax payable by all Hindus, a salt tax, customs duties, income from the mint and spoils of war. Aurangzeb, immediately on assumption of the imperial throne had abolished certain taxes and cesses which were realised above the legally payable taxes. Aurangzeb allowed the system of revenue assessment and revenue collection introduced by Raja Todar Mal under Akbar, to fall into disuse and introduced the system of revenue farming, that is allowing contractors, that is, the middleman, to realise revenue from the peasants, instead of entrusting the state officers to do so under the supervision of the state government. The revenue farmers would be required to pay a stipulated amount to the imperial treasury and the balance after meeting the expenses of collection would be enjoyed by them. Foreign trade did not constitute an important source of revenue to the state under Aurangzeb. Agriculture and manufacture of cotton piece goods and cloth were the occupations of most of the people and the items of export were mainly indigo and cotton goods. Imports were mainly horses from Persia, spices from the Dutch India, wine, glass ware and curiosities from European countries, superior king of tobacco from America and slaves from Abyssinia. Considered by the total amount of customs duties collected during Aurangzeb's reign in a year, of only 30 lakhs of rupees, it is easy to realise that the volume of foreign trade was small.

Dr. Smith observes that under Aurangzeb "The army which made a brave show on paper or in camp, was of little military value." He agrees with Manucci's remark that "30,000 good European soldiers could sweep away the imperial authority and occupy the whole empire." Sir Jadunath's estimate of Aurangzeb's total force as in 1674 was: cavalry 2,00,000 mansabdars 8,000, ahdis and barqandazes 7,000, troops under princes, nobles and mansabdars, 40,000 infantry armed with muskets and guns. During the Deccan war the number was further increased. The expenditure for the army under Aurangzeb was twice as much as under Shah Jahan and its efficiency was not half as much as under Akbar. The navy was also utterly inefficient.

Aurangzeb and the Nobility : Party Politics in the Court : The organisation of the nobility under the Mughals was one of the most important institutions devised by them, upon whom depended in a very large measure the functioning of the administrative system, due discharge of civil and military as well as political functions of the state.

The Mughal nobility in its institutionalised form has a long history of evolution. The nobility played and extremely important part in the founding, expansion, and consolidation of the Mughal empire during the latter half of sixteenth and the first half of eighteenth century.

Before Akbar the nobility had no definite organisation. Under the Sultanate period the Zamindars were not included in the list of nobility and therefore, the Hindus had nothing to do with what was known as "nobility" during that period. It was under Humayun that an elaborate classification of the nobles was made and the nobility was divided into three classes or sections, each section subdivided into twelve grades. We have no definite information as to the order of precedence of the different sections.

Under Akbar we find the famous **mansabdari** system was given a definite form and order and a number of new elements were introduced into it. It will be a mistake to suppose that Akbar was first to introduce mansabdari system. In fact the system was not entirely new. It had long existed in rudements. Akbar institutionalised it giving it a definition and form. Akbar classified the mansabs, i.e. the nobles on the basis of the number of the **sarwars** to be maintained by them. The lowest rank was of 10 and the highest 5,000 sarwars. Soon, however, mansab became an index of rank and official status and salary received not connected with the actual number of sarwars maintained by a mansabdar. For instance, mansabdars of 1,000 and above were called amirs. At times even mansabs below 500 or less were also regarded as amirs, although generally speaking only higher mansabs carried the name of amir with them. Zamindars and small mansabdars formed separate groups. Subdivisions of mansabs or the ranks of mansabs might be increased. For instance Akbar raised the highest mansab from 5,000 to 7,000 and later to 8,000.

The Mughals did not show any ethnic preference in admitting persons of different racial orgin into its nobility. Hence it included Iranis, Turanis, Uzbegs, and even Afghans. The descendants of the earlier Muslim immigrants from western and central Asia and the Indian converts to Islam also found place in the Mughal nobility. Akbar's mansabdari system was an attempt to weld the hetrogenous elements of the Mughal nobility into a harmonious whole. Akbar was wise enough to recognise the position of the Rajputs rulers and chiefs in the Hindu society and gave them a special position in the imperial service. The actual number of the Rajputs included in the nobility was not very large but inclusion of gifted individuals like Jai Singh, Man Singh, Jaswant Singh etc. benefitted both the Mughals and the Rajputs. With the expansion of the empire in the Deccan the Mughal imperialism lacking its essential humanism and generosity as also its high sense of purpose as under Akbar, allowed religious and sectarian differences to affect the nobles.

It appears that from 1666 Aurangzeb began to adopt a policy, if not directly opposed to, certainly was different in spirit from his predecessors with regard to the nobility. Consistently with his emphasis on the Islamic character of the Empire Aurangzeb began to follow a discriminatory policy towards the Hindus copuled with an attempt to associate Muslim orthodoxy as closely as possible to the Empire. Muslim divines were called upon to support his every political action and in this he went so far as to provoke protest from the saner section of the nobility. Mahabat Khan expressed his surprise at the Emperor's policy in the late 70s that he termed his action in a letter as making "fowlers into captives and sparrows into huntsmen. The experienced and the able officers of the state are deprived of all trust and confidence while full reliance is placed on hypoeritical mystics and empty headed scholars. Since these men are selling their knowledge and manners for the company of kings, to rely upon them was neither in accordance with the divinely prescribed path, nor suited to the ways of the world. Thus these men are robbers in every way. The country is being laid waste; the army disheartened; the peasantry ravaged; the lowly crying of distress; the higher ones seeking to raise disturbances. (As the saying is) the finances are given over to the Qazi and the Qazi is satisfied only with bribes." According to Manucci all the high-placed and important men at the court opposed themselves to this measure. They besought the king most humbly to refrain. Aurangzeb in pursuance of his new policy of military orthodoxy offered the jagirs of the Rajputs to his Muslim nobility in order to rally it more firmly behind the throne. On the whole his policy succeeded in consolidating his position against the Rathors and rebellious Prince Akbar due to the indifference of the rest of the Rajputs, at least temporarily, although in the long run his Rajput policy proved harmful for the Empire.

In northern India Mughal conquests had been quickly consolidated, but not so in the Deccan due to, among other causes, the peculiar attitude of the Muslim nobility towards the question of the annexation of the Deccan. According to Bernier the failure of the Mughals to annex Bijapur was largely due to the langour with which every general conducted the operation and availed themselves of every pretest of prolongation of war which was alike the source of their emolument and dignity. Both Beriner and Fryer called "Deccan, the Bread of the military men".

Owing to constant revages of war the Deccan had suffered heavily in its economic resources which were progressively diminishing. Mughal nobles who were posted in the Deccan, therefore, found it difficult to raise enough revenue to maintain their contingents and ceased to be militarily superior to their Deccan opponents. Circumstanced as this, the Mughal generals inevitably were in collusion with the Deccanis. Mahabat Khan too seems to have done the same thing. From Khafi Khan, we know that his cynicism about Aurangzeb's efforts in the Deccan was revealed in a report to the Emperor's suggestion that it was necessary to crush Shivaji. Mahabat Khan reported that there was no need to send any army to the Deccan only a Fatwa of the Qazi would suffice. In 1671 report reached the Emperor that Mahabat Khan had entered into an alliance with Shivaji and was not exerting himself against the Marathas whereupon he was replaced by Bahadur Khan.

In the war against Golconda the Persian nobles were suspected of sympathising with Qutb Shah as the latter was a Shiah as themselves. But during the twenty five years from 1682 to 1707 Aurangzeb remained in the Deccan and in the first part of this period he succeeded in smashing three centres of political power, namely, Bijapur, Golconda and capturing and executing Shambhuji. He declared his war against the Marathas as a Jihad i.e. a holy war. The long drawn Deccan war created a profound political crisis to which the nobles did not remain indifferent. The noble of the old families were against influx of the Deccan nobles into Mughal nobility and sought to revive their former power and prestige as well as their dominant position. Other nobles desired an agreement with the Marathas, so that both parties might live in peace in the Deccan or alternatively the return of the Emperor to north India leaving the Deccan war to subordinate military officers. But all these suggestions were indignantly spurned by Aurangzeb and the nobles carried on the Deccan war in a half-hearted fashion requiring personal presence of Aurangzeb in the Deccan imperative. The Deccani and Hyderabadi nobles who had been taken in the Mughal nobility recently caused great damage to the imperial cause in the Deccan.

In such circumstances intrigues in the imperial court and mutual jealousies and pursuit of selfish ends went on freely. For instance Tarbiyat Khan was jealous of Fathullah Khan. Muqarrab Khan who captured Shambhuji could not be given promotion by the Emperor due to the stiff opposition of other nobles. There was rivalry between Sayyid Lashkar

Khan and Zulfiqr Khan. In this atmosphere surcharged with suspicion, cliques and factious quarrels groups of nobles pulling in different directions was inevitable. Every noble and every group looked to its own interest. The princes, Kings, governors and generals began to follow their own lines of policy with a view to securing success of their own designs. Important groups among the great nobles naturally arose and typified the new factionalism in the Mughal court. The Irani, Turani and Hindustani groups of nobles by their jealousies, rivalries and factionalism indicated the serious political crisis that the Mughal Empire was to face in the immediate future. The factionalism among the nobles while revealed their internal contradictions, also showed their lack of confidence in the Emperor and the imperial policy and above all in the ability of the Emperor to reduce them to order and discipline.

PARTY POLITICS IN THE COURT

In a monarchical system of despotic nature as the Mughal rule had been, the future, i.e. the prospects and promotions of all officers depended directly or indirectly on the approbation of Emperor. It was the court towards which the eyes of all nobles were turned.

Towards the latter part of Aurangzeb's reign and early in the eighteenth century two groups of nobles came into forefront in the court. We have seen that the descendants of the earlier immigrants from Western and Central Asia as also the Indian converts into Islam found place in the Mughal nobility which therefore, comprised Iranis, Turanis, Uzbegs, Afghans and the Indian converts into Islam known as Hindustani nobles. Under Aurangzeb the Hindu nobility—Rajputs or the Marathas had been excluded.

The two groups that came into the forefront from towards the latter part of the seventeenth century in the imperial court were the **Irani** and **Turni** parties. The leading figures of the first party were Asad Khan and his son Zulfiqar Khan. This family belonged to a well known family of Iran. Asad Khan's father had migrated to India towards the end of Jahangir's reign. Asad Khan whose original name was Muhammad Ibrahim was a favourite of Emperor Shah Jahan and married the daughter of Asaf Khan. He was also a great favourite of Aurangzeb and in 1669 was made the **wazir**. He took part in the siege of Bijapur, in Rajput campaign and in the capture of Golconda. He was promoted to the rank of **masnad of wazirat** which meant that he was entitled to sit on a **masnad** in presence of the Emperor, and made a mansabdar of 7,000. Asad Khan's son Zulfiqar Khan made his mark by commanding the Mughal Troops in the capture of Jinji from the Marathas. His services were recognised by Aurangzeb by promoting him to the position of **Mir Bakshi** in 1702.

When Aurangzeb died in 1707, Asad Khan was the Wazir while his son Zulfiqar Khan was Mir Bakshi two top posts under the state. Besides Zulfiqar was a great general and had Daud Khan Panni, Rao Dalpat Bundela and Rao Ram Singh Hara as his staunch supporters.

The second party, namely the **Turani** party was led by Ghazi-ud-din Firuz Jang, his sons Chin Qilich Khan (Later Nizam-ul-Mulk) and Hamid Khan, and his cousin Muhammad Amin Khan. Father of Firuz Jang, Khwaja Abid had migrated to India from Bukhara towards the end of the reign of Shah Jahan. Khwaja Abid took part in the war against Dara Shukoh, Shuja and Jaswant Singh and was made **Sadr-i-Kul**. He died at the siege of Golconda in 1687. Chin Qilich Khan participated in the early compaigns of his father. In 1699 he was appointed governor of Bijapur. His half-brother Hamid Khan also served under his father Firuz Jang. Amin Khan, cousin of Chin Qilich Khan came to India in 1687 and served under Firuz Jang, and earned a name as a valiant warrior. He was appointed by Aurangzeb as Sadr in recognition of his merit. As this group came from Turan this party was known as Turani party and the Turanis formed a large part of their following. There was greater solidarity in this party than in the Irani party. But cold relation between Firuz Jang and Chin Qilich Khan and the blindness that developed in the former became a serious weakness of this party.

Between the Irani and the Turani Parties there had been a sense of competition and rivalry from the very beginning and each was vying with the other for the royal favour. Particularly the rivalry between the two younger nobles of the two parties—Zulfiqar Khan and Chin Qilich Khan soon turned into mutual jealousy and naturally the two did not get on well together.

The third party known as Hindustani party comprised the Muslims born in India although their forefathers had come from outside. This party had supporters among the Jats, Rajputs and many Hindu lords. According to Prof. Satish Chandra the general assumption that the parties and politics at the Mughal court were based on ethnic or religious groupings among the nobility is not borne out by facts. The groups which were formed towards the end of the reign of Aurangzeb, were essentially based on family relations and personal affiliations and interests. "Hence it would appear" remarks Prof. Chandra "that the slogans of race and religion were raised by individual nobles only to suit their convenience, and that the actual groupings cut across ethnic and religious divisions."

The rise of the parties at the Mughal court was facilitated by the (a) decline of the power and prestige of the Emperor due to Aurangzeb's failure to deal effectively with the oppositions of the Marathas, Rajputs, Jat etc. and the wars of succession after the death of Aurangzeb and every one of his successors, (b) absence of competent ruler after Aurangzeb, (c) System of the grant of jagirs steadily worsened, grant of jagirs was unnecessarily delayed, discrepancies in the income of the jagirs shown and the actual income received, grant of jagir exceeding the total amount of Khas land, (d) scramble for the best and the most profitable jagir among the nobles, (e) competition between different parties for leading position in the court, particularly by securing the posts of the **Wazir** and the **Mir Bakshi**, (f) lack of mutual trust between the parties and individual nobles at the court.

It must be particularly pointed out that the struggle for the wazirat was no less a struggle for implementing of policies. The question of the attitude to be taken towards the Rajputs, Marathas, Jats etc., the status of the Hindus and imposition of jizya became issues of party politics. Factually the question was whether the state was to rest on racist and religous foundations and on Muslims alone or on Hindu-Muslim loyality and allegiance in a spirit of secularism.

For a quarter of a century to follow, the rivalries and jealousies of the three parties, particularly the Iranis and the Turanis, as also conflict of personalities and their struggle to clear the way to the supreme power constituted the main historical theme.

Personality and Character : Success and Failure of Aurangzeb : It has become more or less fashionable to acclaim any heterodox view about any historical personality of his doings, whether it stands to reason or not. There is a section of writers who have been at pains to prove that Aurangzeb was not a religious bigot and in fact he made liberal grants to Hindu temples and wherever he had destroyed Hindu temples this was necessitated by the exigencies of war. This view is a laboured view unrelated to historical facts and so palpably incorrect that one need not have to refute it. It should, however, be made clear in order to avoid confusion that there were instances of bestowal of grants of lands on a few priests or their temples, but these grants were in the nature of renewal or confirmation of the grants made by his predecessors or made with the purpose to win the grantees over to his side. Hence these were not instances of liberality but strokes of diplomacy. Further, to contend that the destruction of Hindu temples was only a measure of wartime necessity is a pure and simple invention unsupported by any historical evidence. History is respecter of no person and it is based on truth and nothing but truth.

Sir Jadunath Sarkar in his History of Aurangzeb (5 vols.) has given us a correct balanced picture of the personality and character of Aurangzeb and it is doubtful if modern researches will be capable of altering the conclusions drawn by Sir J. N. Sarkar about Aurangzeb.

Aurangzeb's private life was above the comtemporary vices and unquestionably ideal. He was an indefatigable worker, of disciplined habits, and methodical in his ways. He had a few wives but never did he transgress the Quranic injunction of having more than four wives at a time. His food habits were simple and did not touch wine. He had acquired proficiency in Arabic and Persian and could speak Turki and Hindi with ease. He inherited the scholarly temper of his house and lover of books and patron of scholars. In matters of religion he was a bigot, strictly adhering to Quranic law, saying his daily prayers five times a day and kept Ramzan. Too much regard for religiocity made him taciturn, puritanic and intolerant not only of Hinduism but also of Shiahism. He enforced Jizya on the non-Hindus. All this earned for him the reverence of the devout Muslims. The chief defects of his character were his obstinacy, over-ambition, narrow religious bigotry, unfilial attitude to his father and his betrayal and inhuman treatment of his brothers. Yet he was not a parricide.

Khafi Khan also tries to draw a balanced picture of the character and personality of Aurangzeb and while calling him the most distinguished sovereign of Delhi for devotion, austerity and justice, he criticises him for his intense suspiciousness and lack of trust in any body. His reliance on mere cunning as the principal instrument of statecraft was born of the smallness of his mind.

As a soldier and a general, Aurangzeb ranked with Babur and Akbar. He possessed great physical strength, coolness of temperament and great courage.

Success and Failure : When we judge Aurangzeb as a sovereign, his failure more than set off his success. To judge the measures of his success and failure as also his policy is rather perplexing. The manner of his securing accession to the throne was nothing new in the tradition of the Muslim history in India and his success in the war of succession was more in the nature of the survival of the fittest and if he would have lost some one of his other brothers would seize the throne. His military campaign showed him to be not only a capable soldier but also a general of great ability who knew how to thwart his enemy by diplomacy and stratagem. He possessed a wonderful memory and remembered every detail of the administration and issued orders to his ministers accordingly. He was a pastmaster in diplomacy and statecraft. He was of indefatigable energy and went through the petitions of the people himself and passed orders on them. Gemelli-Careri, an Italian physician who visited India during Aurangzeb's reign saw the Emperor when he was seventy five years old (1695) and "admired to see him endorse the petitions with his own hand without spectacles and by his cheerful, smiling countenance seemed to be extremely pleased with the employment.

Yet with all the vitality, strength and physical fitness Aurangzeb proved a failure as a sovereign, for he failed to realise that the greatness of India depended on the unity, as well as the progress of the people of India as a whole. The lessons of the past history of India, that political progress and permanence of the state in India depended on the policy of religious toleration and the ability and the foresight in the ruler to create a sense of harmony and unity among the various discordant elements, were lost on him.

Further, despite his intelligence and shrewdness Aurangzeb failed to devise a correct policy to meet an emergency or even to meet the normal legislative needs of the empire. His study of political problems as well as remedies that he sought to devise were coloured by religious prejudices which naturally vitiated the measures taken by him. Little did he realise that more than eighty percent of the population of the empire was non-Muslims and to make things worse he systematically persecuted the Muslims of the Shiah, Ismaili, Daudi and Bohra communities.

Aurangzeb's over-confidence in his industry, strength and ability which generated a distrust and suspicion of officers in his mind led to a policy of holding all local officers in strict, perpetual tutelage produced administrative degeneration, lack of initiative, sense of responsibility and efficiency in the administration.

One of the major causes of Aurangzeb's failure was the alienation of the sympathy and friendship of the Rajputs who played so important a part in the expansion and organisation of the Mughal Empire under Aurangzeb's predecessors. This is nicely stated by Mulla Shirin that "The Hindu wields the sword of Islam."

Aurangzeb also had alienated other material elements in the Hindu population such as the Jats, Bundelas, Sikhs and the Marathas who by their rebellions drained the empire of its blood and money, and distracted the Emperor's attention in times of crisis. His long absence in the Deccan threw northern India in disorder and confusion from which it could not be recovered. Disintegration of the Empire had begun during the latter part of his rule.

So Emperor Aurangzeb lived and died. The famous letters written shortly before his death to his son. "express the weariness of a man who lived too long, had failed in cherished plans, and was tormented by morbid fears about his fate in the next world..." Aurangzeb wrote "My years have gone by profitless. God has been in my heart yet my darkened eyes have not recognised his light...... There is no hope for me in the future......when I have lost hope in myself, how can I hope in other?" The Emperor died in the morning of March 3, 1707. None need have to sermonise on the pathos of these lamentations for none, even the sternest critic of the Emperor so mighty, can but feel deepest sympathy for him during the humble moments of his lonely deathbed.

REFERENCES

History of Aurangzeb, Vols. I-V : Sir J. N. Sarkar

Cambridge History of India, Vols. IV-V

The Oxford History of India (4th Edn.) : Dr. V. A. Smith

The Mughal Empire : A. L. Srivastava

An Advanced History of India : Majumdar, Roychaudhuri & Datta

Parties and Politics at the Mughal Court : Satish Chandra

The Mughal Nobility under Aurangzeb : A. Athar Ali

13

Rise of Regional Powers

A. THE RAJPUTS : NATURE AND CONSEQUENCES OF RAJPUT REBELLION UNDER AURANGZEB

Aurangzeb in his narrow, bigoted, short-sighted policy did not see the need for maintaining the traditional friendly relation with the Rajputs who had previously contributed so much to the expansion, administration and defence of the Empire. He introduced a change in the policy of the state towards them. His policy was guided both by his imperialist ambition and religious intolerance. But he used the Rajput services in the early years of his reign. When Shayista Khan, Aurangzeb's maternal uncle failing to deal with Shivaji asked for his recall from the Deccan, Aurangzeb sent Jai Singh of Jaipur associated with Prince Muazzam to the Deccan. Jai Singh succeeded in capturing the fort of Purandar and forcing Shivaji to accept a treaty by which the latter surrendered twenty-three forts and extensive lands to the Mughals. Jai Singh also persuaded Shivaji to surrender to the imperial authority and visit the Delhi Court (1666).

Jai Singh died in the Deccan due to poisoning by his son Kirat Singh and it is suspected that this was done at the instigation of Aurangzeb who "publicly rejoiced at the news of the raja's death." So long as Jai Singh was alive, Aurangzeb did not feel at liberty to follow his policy of persecution. Aurangzeb replaced Raja Jai Singh of Jaipur by Raja Jaswant Singh of Jodhpur in the Deccan with no improvement in the situation there.

But conquest of the Rajput states was not ventured upon by Aurangzeb so long as the other Rajput hero Raja Jaswant Singh of Jodhpur (Marwar) was alive. Jaswant Singh was the foremost Hindu chief in the Empire and had fought against Aurangzeb in the battles of Dharma and Khajwa. He was transferred from the Deccan to Jamrud to protect the Mughal outposts in north-west frontier. Jaswant Singh died in December 1678. The death of Jaswant Singh removed from the field two valiant figures during whose life-time Aurangzeb did not venture to place his hands on Rajput states. Immediately on Raja Jaswant Singh's death, Aurangzeb ordered the annexation of Marwar and himself proceeded to Ajmer to meet any possible national resistance the annexation of Marwar might give rise to. After occupation of Marwar Aurangzeb, on his return to Delhi reimposed **Jizya** on the Hindus which had been abolished by Akbar.

Meanwhile the two queens of Raja Jaswant Singh were on their way to Delhi from Jamrud and while at Lahore the two queen gave birth (Feb. 1679) to two posthumous sons of Jaswant Singh. One of the babies died. Soon after, the other, was christened Ajit Singh. Some of the supporters of Raja Jaswant Singh, the queen mother and the baby Ajit Singh came to the court of Aurangzeb and pleaded for recognising Ajit Singh as the successor of Raja Jaswant Singh. Aurangzeb agreed to do so on condition that the baby should be brought up in the Mughal harem and must embrace Islam. The offer was spurned by the Rajputs and the queen and the baby were sought to be seized by Aurangzeb. It was the pluck and courage of a Rathor chief, Durgadas, son of a loyal associate of Raja Jaswant Singh that the queen and the baby were rescued from the Mughal troops who came to besiege the place where the queen and the baby took residence in Delhi. Aurangzeb put up a milkman's son as an impostor and sought to pass him off as Ajit Singh, declaring that Ajit Singh whom Durgadas was supporting was a bogus prince. Durgadas took possession of Marwar by removing Indra Singh a protege of Aurangzeb who was placed on the throne by Aurangzeb after its annexation. Aurangzeb marched towards Ajmer and despatched three Princes Muazzam, Azam and Akbar with a large army divided into three commands to recover Marwar. The Mughals had to fight a prolonged war during the course of which they plundered towns, destroyed temples but were themselves harassed by the Rathor troops who took shelter in deserts and hills. But Jodhpur was captured and pillaged. But the conquest of Marwar was far from complete and continued for next about thirty years.

In this policy of agression of the Mughal army against the Rathors of Marwar, Rana Raj Singh of Mewar joined the Rathors in defence of Marwar. Ajit Singh was related to Raj Singh whose mother was a Sisodia princess. As a result of the Rathor-Sisodia alliance the Rajput defence assumed the character of a national defence against the Mughal imperialism. Raj Singh also considered that annexation of Marwar exposed Mewar to the danger of Mughal annexation. Reimposition of Jizya was a matter of great disappointment for him and this step highly incensed him.

Aurangzeb at once marched against Mewar and Rana Raj Singh finding defence useless against the vast military strength of the Mughals deserted Chitor and took shelter in the fastnesses of the hills. Chitor was easily captured by the Mughal forces. Prince Akbar was placed in charge of Chitor and Aurangzeb made for Ajmer. The Rajput guerillas began to harass the Mughal outposts inflicting such damage that Mughal outposts could not be filled in by commandants for none was willing to take the risk of accepting the posts due to the Rajput onslaught. Aurangzeb held Prince Akbar responsible for the Mughal failure and replaced Akbar by Prince Azam. Akbar was sent to Marwar. Akbar took it as an insult and contemplated seizing the crown of Delhi from his father, with the help of the Rajputs. The Rajputs who found that Aurangzeb was destroying the stability of the Empire by his policy of religious fanaticism and distrust of one and all, promised to support Akbar with the Rajput armed strength of the rathors and the Sisodias.

In 1681, Akbar marched on to Ajmer at the head of 70,000 strong army including the flower of the Rajput troops. Akbar would have had a sure win, if he had attacked the Mughal army for its divisions were stationed at two different places. But Akbar spent his time in pleasure and merriment and thereby allowing his father time to bring his army together and arrange it in war posture. Aurangzeb also had resort to a stratagem. He wrote a letter couched in a language which showed that Akbar was playing false with the Rajputs with Aurangzeb's knowledge and under his instruction, and contrived the letter to fall into the hands of the Rajputs. This had the desired effect. The Rajputs suspected treachery on the part of Akbar and forsook him. Deserted by the Rajputs Akbar fled and reached the court of the Maratha chief Shambhuji. The Rajputs discovered the fraud played on them by Aurangzeb when it was too late.

Shambhuji could ill afford to render help to the fugitive Prince and his dream of building an Indian Empire of the basis of Hindu-Muslim unity proved a failure. He left for Persia after a few years and died there in 1704.

The hostilities between Mewar and the Mughals meant great sufferings for the subjects of the Rana and of the Emperor. None could gain success against the other. Jai Singh son of Raj Singh therefore, concluded a treaty with the Mughals in 1681 by which the Rana ceded some of his districts in lieu of Jizya to the Emperor and the latter withdrew all Mughal troops from Mewar. The war with marwar, however, continued for further period of thirty years and after the death of Aurangzeb, his son Bahadur Shah I recognised Ajit Singh as the Rana of Marwar (1709).

The Rajput war proved disastrous to the Mughal Empire in more than one way. While it had taken a toll of a huge number of the Mughal troops and an enormous sum was spent in the pursuit of the wars in the deserts of Rajputana, it brought no permanent success to the Empire or to the Emperor. What was worse, was the shattering of the military prestige of the Emperor. For Aurangzeb it was an unstatesman like policy to provoke Rajputs hostility and thereby lose the support of the valiant and trusted race which rendered devoted service to Empire, in its expansion, in its security, administration, in holding north-west frontier of the Empire under control and even in the wasting wars in the Deccan.

Occupation of Marwar because of its strategic position controlling the military and commercial routes from Delhi to the rich ports of Western India was certainly not enough argument to provoke Rajput hostilities for a friendly Marwar would have met the strategic needs of the Empire.

It was Aurangzeb's desperate bid to convert India a land of Islam that made him follow the unwise policy of occupying Marwar. To him existence of a powerful military state in northern India was annoying. Likewise, Mewar whose chief Jaswant Singh, formerly a partisan of Dara Shukoh was to Aurangzeb, a person too dangerous to be allowed to continue as chief of a powerful Rajput state. Religion and imperial consideration led Aurangzeb to push Marwar and Mewar to stand forth as leaders of Rajput national resistance.

B. RISING OF THE SIKHS (RETROSPECT)

During the religious revival that marked the history of India of the fifteenth and sixteenth centuries, Sikhs emerged as a distinct community. Sikhism* was founded by Guru Nanak (1469-1539) who was of a saintly character from his early life. He was born in a Khatri family of Talwandi, modern Nankana. He was a reviver of the pure monotheistic doctrine of the Upanishads and laid stress on the unity of Godhead. He emphasised the fundamental truth underlying all religions and the chief features of the religion he spread were its (i) non-sectarian character, and (ii) its harmony with secular life. He spent his life in preaching the gospel of universal toleration. Nanak died in 1539 nominating Angad as the next Guru. The fourth Guru Ramdas (1574-1581) was held in great veneration by Emperor Akbar who granted him a plot of land at Amritsar containing a pool which was improved and extended and on the side of it the famous Golden Temple was constructed.

Under the fifth Guru Arjan Mal, the Sikh community was organised and expanded. It was he who compiled the Adi Granth, the "First Sacred Book" as the original Sikh scriptures are called. This is a collection of "select verses from the works of his four predecessors as well as from those of the Hindu and Muhammadan saints who had appeared since the days of Jaidev". From the writings of a contemporary we know that "Emperor Akbar and kings bow before him". Guru Arjan also organised the finances of his church by levying compulsory spiritual tribute.

* 1st Guru Nank (1469-1539), 2nd Guru Angad (1539-1552), 3rd Guru Amardas (1552-1574), 4th Guru Ramdas (1574-1581), 5th Guru Arjan Mal (1581-1606), 6th Guru Har Govind (1606-1645), 7th Guru Har Rai (1645-1661), 8th Guru Har Kishan (1661-1664), 9th Guru Teg Bahadur (1664-1675), 10th and the last Guru Govind (1675-1708).

Guru Arjan incurred the displeasure of Emperor Jahangir by bestowing benediction to Prince Khusrav who had rebelled against his father. Jahangir already suspicious of Guru Arjan for his wealth and influence got him arrested and tortured him to death. (1606), on a charge of treason. Next Guru Har Govind, son of Arjan was a man with great organising ability. He raised an army, obviously to take revenge of the death of his father. He was imprisoned for a time in the Gwalior fort for his refusal to pay the fine that was levied on his father. During the reign of Shah Jahan he rose in revolt and defeated the imperial army near Amritsar in 1628. The ninth Guru Teg Bahadur settled at Anandpur a few miles from kiratpur in the Kashmir Hills where Har Govind had earlier shifted his head quarters in 1634.

While staying at Patna Teg Bahadur's son Govind, the last Guru was born in 1666. The religious persecution of Aurangzeb roused Teg Bahadur to revolt. He encouraged the Kashmir Brahmins to resist the measures passed against the Hindus by Aurangzeb. Teg Bahadur was captured in 1675 and offered the alternatives of either accepting Islam or death. Teg Bahadur chose death to conversion to Islam and in consequence was executed.

The martyrdom of Teg Bahadur roused the Sikhs to a feeling of revenge against the Mughals and made Sikh-Mughal hostilities inevitable. Govind Singh the tenth and the last Guru and the son of Teg Bahadur was one of the most remarkable personalities of Indian history. He set himself earnestly and with determination to organise his followers in Spartan discipline. He was the real founder of the Sikh military power which organised to oppose the Mughals. He bound the Sikh fraternity together by instituting the cermony called **pahul** or baptism by pouring water with a dagger or a sword. The members of the fraternity would be seated in a circle and partake of a mixture of flour, butter and sugar. The ceremony was obviously designed to break caste. The brotherhood so constituted was termed **Khalsa** or pure. Guru Govind required the members of the brotherhood to abstain from taking tobacco, wine, Indian hemp. The initiated members of the brotherhood were commended to wear the five **K's** namely **Kes** long (hair), **Kanga** (Comb), **Kachcha** (short drawers), **Kara** (steel bangle) and **Kripan** (sword). Every one that received the new baptism had to use the appellation Singh. A supplementary **Granth** containing the compositions of Guru Govind was compiled after his death.

Guru Govind fought against the Mughals and in a long war with the hill rajas and the Mughal officers in which he lost two of his sons who were executed by the governor of Sirhind, he stood in support of Shah Alam I (Bahadur Shah) in the war of succession and accepted service under the Mughals when the Prince became the Emperor. While in the Deccan Guru Govind was assassinated by an Afghan fanatic at Nandur in 1708.

After Guru Govind's assassination Banda gave out that the soul of Guru Govind had entered his person. The imposter-Govind organised a large number of Sikhs and took revenge on Wazir Khan Faujdar of Sirhind murderer of Guru Govind's children with appalling ferocity. Irvene gives us a full picture of the ferocity of Banda. "For the space of four days the town (Sirhind) was given up to pillage, the mosques were defiled, the houses burnt, and the Muhammadans slaughtered, even their women and children were not spared...... The Hindus who had not joined the sect were not exempt from those oppressions."

Banda then captured the countries between the Sutlej and the Jumna. He established the stronghold of Lohgarh i.e. Blood and Iron Fort at Mukhlispur where he assumed regal state and struck coins in his own name. The Emperor marched against Lohgarh and besieged the fort. Banda fled into the hills with his men. After Bahadur Shah I's death Banda came out of his hiding and recovered Lohgarh and pillaged the town of Sirhind once again. In 1715 Banda was besieged in the fortress of Gurudaspur and although the Sikhs fought valiantly for the defence of the fortresses but many of them were killed and many more captured. Banda and his followers were sent to Delhi where his son was killed before his eyes, his followers tortured inhumanly and Banda crushed to death under the feet of elephants. By 1716 the fortunes of the Sikhs sank very low.

But Sikhs could not be destroyed for good. The Sikhs—peasants and people nursed the tenets of Guru Nanak and of Guru Govind ardently in their heart and began to recover their strength and organisation in quick paces. Kapur Singh of Eyzullapur started an organisation which soon developed later into what is known as **Dal Khalsa** or the theocracy of the Sikhs. Taking advantage of the confusion consequent upon the invasion of Nadir Shah, the Sikhs augmented their military strength. Now it became difficult to suppress the resurgent Sikhs. They built a fort at Dalewal on the Ravi and carried on depredations in areas around Lahore. Ahmad Shah Abdali's invasion further helped them to acquire further strength and power.

C. JAT AND SATNAMI REBELLIONS

In 1669, the Jat peasant population of Mathura district, close to Delhi rose in rebellion under the leadership of Gokla and killed the Mughal faujdar i.e. commandant for his over zealous implementing of the policy of persecution. In a fierce battle in which 5,000 Jats and 4,000 imperial troops were lost, the imperialists restored order. But the Jats were only temporarily subdued. In 1681 and for a third time in 1688 the Jats renewed their rebellion and the rebellion continued till the end of the reign of Aurangzeb. In 1691 the Jat rebels inflicted the gravest affront to the Mughal Emperor by plundering the grave of Akbar and burning his bones. Such affront on the ancestor of the Mughal Emperor very near to Delhi was symptomatic of the weakness of the empire towards the latter part of Aurangzeb's reign. It is only to be imagined what would be the effectiveness of the imperial control over the distant Deccan and other parts of the Empire if in Mathura the Jats could prove themselves to be so powerful. The second insurrection against Aurangzeb's persecutory policy was headed by Prince Chhatrasal Bundela. During the early years of the reign of Aurangzeb Champat Rai, father of Chhatrasal had rebelled against he Emperor. But Aurangzeb's strong military action against him left him no other alternative but to commit suicide to avoid torture at the hands of Emperor. Chhatrasal for some time served under the Emperor and during the course of his service in the Deccan he was inspired by the patriotic example of the Maratha hero Shivaji. He therefore contemplated to have a life of independence and taking the discontent of the Hindu population of Budelkhand as his opportunity he raised the standard of rebellion. He stood as the champion of Bundela liberty in 1671 and after gaining several victories against the Mughals succeeded in carving out an independent principality in Eastern Malwa for himself with his capital at Panna in 1731.

Another Hindu sect called the Satnamis rebelled in 1672. Khafi Khan describes the Satnamis as "a gang of bloody miserable rebels, goldsmiths, carpenters, sweepers, tanners and other ignoble beings" who had their centre of work at Narnaul now in Patiala district of the Punjab. The rebels were about five thousand in number and captured Narnaul and fought desperately and seemed to be proof against human weapons. To begin with they had some success, but ultimately they were beaten back with heavy slaughter, only a few escaping sword.

D. SHIVAJI AND THE RISE OF THE MARATHAS

We are indebted to the contemporary Europeans, the English, French, Dutch, Portuguese and Italian writers who left in their accounts references to the exploits of Shivaji. For the earliest biographies of Shivaji also we are indebted to such visitors. It is true that their accounts have been full of inaccuracies, for instance, the English factors of Rajapur wrote to their official superiors at Surat that "Sevagy, a great Rashpoote" (Shivaji was a great Rajput) and an unknown French writer wrote that Shivaji had descended from the ancient emperors of India and was a relative of the Great Moghul. Most of these visitors were educated and intelligent men. Fryer was a physician, Bernier, Dellon also belonged to the same profession. Thevenot was a highly cultured person and Carre, Navarette and Ovigton were clergymen. But all of them made serious factual mistakes in their accounts. Yet we cannot ignore their testimony for some of them had recognised Shivaji more than a rebel chief and called him a great general and a greater statesman. There need not be any hesitation in saying that even modern British historians, at least most of them, have not been able to raise themselves above the British imperial outlook and called Shivaji "a robber chief" (as Dr. Smith had done). Cosme da Guarda, a Portuguese was the first European to attempt a systematic biography of Shivaji. He was an admirer of Shivaji, although he made many inaccurate statements in his work. From Guarda's writing we find that the Portuguese held a very high opinion about Shivaji's generalship and statesmanly qualities. Francois Martin Furnishes us with the best contemporary account of Shivaji's Karnataka expedition.

We can glean considerable historical materials about Shivaji and his exploits from the writings of the foreigners of different European nationalities.

Shivaji was born in Shivner near Junnar in 1630. According to some historians, for instance Dr. Smith, he was born in 1627. His father Shahji was at first in the service of Ahmadnagar and when the Kingdom was in the process of dissolution, he carved out a territory for himself from Poona and Chakan to the neighbourhood of Ahmadnagar and Nasik. He set up a boy as the king of Ahmadnagar with the help of Bijapur in 1633 and for a few years carried on the government of Ahmadnagar in the name of that boy king. But in 1636 he was forced to surrender the boy to the Mughals. There after he took service under the Bijapur Sultan and carved out a vast estate for himself in the Mysore plateau and the Eastern Karnataka and came to be reckoned as the foremost vassal or jagirdar under Bijapur Sultan.

While at Poona, Shivaji was born of Shahji's first wife Jijabai in the Shivner fort. Shahji's personal life was not beyond reproach. He married a second wife Tukabai Mohite, a lady of great beauty and began to neglect his first wife Jijabai and her son Shivaji who were first left at Shivner and then at Poona under the guardianship of Dadaji Konda-Deva.

Father's neglect of his mother had a deep reaction on the growing child Shivaji whose love for his mother became akin to veneration for a deity and the forlorn lady poured all her love and affect, and all that she had thought best to train up the boy's mind. The exploits of the heroes of the Ramayana and the Mahabharata as he heard from his mother kept him spell bound and generated in him an ambition to emulate those heroes. Dadaji Konda-Deva gave him training in the art of military exercises and horse riding and the boy grew into a fearless, intolerant of subordination to authority and with the rare sense of dignity and power of organisation. The rugged nature of the hilly country of Maval in Maharashtra, studded with forts made Shivaji strong in physique, capable of enduring inhuman strain and made him a leader of the naturally sturdy Marathas who were destined to play so important a part in the history of India.

The decay of Ahmadnagar and Bijapur gave Shivaji an opportunity to carve out for himself a kingdom in full sovereignty, but it is doubtful, if the building up of a Hindu dominion by liberating the Hindus from the Muslim domination actually occurred in his mind at that time.

Shivaji's first acquisition after having raised an army of the local Mavalis, was the fort of Torna from its commandant under the Bijapur Sultan was in 1646. He found a treasure of two lakhs **huns** in the fort which he utilised in building the fort of Raigarh five miles away from Torna which was to be his capital in future. He also used a part of the treasure in further strengthening his army. In 1647 Dadaji Konda-Deva died which removed the only person who could stop Shivaji from following any desperate course. In 1648, Shivaji acquired the forts of Chakan, Kondana, Bangalore etc. from their hereditary owners or local officers of Bijapur Sultan. Bijapur Sultan suspecting Shahji having a secret hand in his son's proceedings, put him under arrest and this for a time induced Shivaji to stop his aggressive activities. Shivaji restored the forts of Bangalore and Kondana to the Sultan in 1649 whereupon Shahji was released by the Bijapur Sultan. Meanwhile Shivaji had captured the fort of Purandar from Nilkanth whose father had made himself independent from the Bijapur Sultanate and this was not altogether unwelcome to Bijapur Sultan.

In 1656, Shivaji annexed the small Maratha Principality of Javli which lay at the north-western corner of Satara district. Javli was in possession of Chandra Rao More who was a semi-independent prince. Chandra Rao had entered into an anti-Shivaji coalition with the Mughal Governor of that region in order to check the progress of Shivaji. Chandra Rao's murder was secured by Shivaji by a hired assassin and as Sir Jadunath remarks "the conquest of Javli was the result of deliberate murder and organised treachery on the part of Shivaji. His power was then in its infancy and he could not afford to be scrupulous in the choice of the means of strengthening himself...... The only redeeming feature of this dark episode in his life is that the crime was not aggravated by hypocrisy."

The conquest of Javli was important to Shivaji in more than one way. It added to his military strength due to the inclusion of the troops of Chandra Rao to his army; it opened the gateway to further conquest of territories towards the south and west of his kingdom; and placed the immense treasures of Chandra Rao to Shivaji's disposal.

It was in 1657 that Shivaji came in direct clash with the Mughals for the first time. In that year when Aurangzeb as the viceroy of the Deccan invaded Bijapur Shivaji's troops raided that Mughal districts of Ahmadnagar and he himself attacked Junnar and looted the city of Junnar and carried away three lakhs **huns** in cash. Aurangzeb promptly reinforced the Mughal contingent fighting against Shivaji which was defeated. When Adil Shah of Bijapur had made peace with the Mughals, Shivaji also submitted to Aurangzeb. But Aurangzeb never trusted Shivaji, but a peace had to be patched up as the news of Shah Jahan's illness had reached him and his presence in the north was necessary.

Aurangzeb's departure for the north, offered both a respite and an opportunity to Shivaji to prepare and begin fight for the extension of his dominions. Shivaji conquered Kalyan, Bhiwandi and Mahuli, and proceeded as far as Mahad. Absence of Aurangzeb from the Deccan also gave the Sultan of Bijapur an opportunity to strike at the power of Shivaji and in 1659, he sent Afzal Khan one of the noted and capable generals of the kingdom to deal with Shivaji. Afzal Khan was ordered by the Sultan to bring Shivaji as "a captive in chains without having one to dismount from his own horse" and tried to seduce officers of Shivaji by bribes and some were actually won over. Afzal reached Wai, twenty miles north of Satara and realised a fine of two lakhs of rupees from Bajaji Nayak Nimbalkar for siding with Shivaji. Then instead of choosing to fight openly with Shivaji he hit upon a stratagem. He opened negotiations with him through a Maratha Brahmin named Krishnaji Bhaskar, and invited him to a conference. Afzal promised to get Shivaji confirmed in his possession of Konkan and other forts held by him. The message also added. "I shall secure for yourself further distinctions and military equipment from our government. If you wish to attend the court, you will be welcomed. Or, if you want to be excused make personal attendance there, and you will be exempted." Krishnaji was received cordially by Shivaji and in the name of religion appealed to him to disclose the real intention of Afzal in asking for the conference. Krishnaji, moved by Shivaji's appeal hinted that Afzal had mischief in his mind. This put Shivaji on the alert.

The Maratha court was divided on the policy to be followed towards Afzal. Some officers suggested a policy of no-confrontation. But Shivaji dismissed this advice as cowardly and decided to confront Afzal in a manner befitting a sovereign.

A pavilion was set up within a mile of Pratapgarh to receive Shivaji. Shivaji kept his picked troops concealed in the forests on both sides of the pathway leading to the pavilion. Shivaji went to meet Afzal wearing a coat of chain-armour under his tunic and a steel helmet under his turban, and iron claws **(baghnakh)** in his sleeve and a sword called **bichhwa** i.e. scorpion.

Afzal Khan came accompanied by an escort of a thousand musketteers. Shivaji's envoy insisted on Afzal's keeping his escorts at safe distance lest their huge number would make Shivaji refuse to come for the meeting. This being done, Shivaji came to the pavilion with two of his followers. As Shivaji was appearing before Afzal he bent a little in salutation, Afzal embraced him and attempted to strangulate him and taking out a sword struck Shivaji on his side. But as Shivaji was wearing an armour the blow had no effect. Rallying himself from the sudden attack, Shivaji tore Afzal's bowels open with the steel claws and plunged the iron scorpion by the side of Afzal. Attracted by the cries of Afzal, Sayyid Banda stepped forward and struck Shivaji on the head with his sword but it produced no effect as he had worn a helmet below his turban. The incident took place on November 2, 1659. Questions have been raised as to who had struck the first blow. Mir Alam, the Wazir of Nizam-ul-Mulk gave the details as follows : "... the Khan intoxicated with pride of being a hero gripped Shivaji very hard in the art of embracing and struck him with the beltdagger." This sets at rest the question, and there is hardly any doubt that Afzal Khan gave the first blow.

The Maratha troops who were hiding themselves in the jungles on two sides of the path-way fell on the troops of Afzal and three hundred of them were slaughtered and the rest made good their escape. To Shivaji fell an immense booty of ten lakhs of rupees in cash and jewels, and considerable number of elephants, horses, camels, artillery and ammunition.

Khafi Khan and Grant Duff have charged Shivaji with treacherously murdering Afzal Khan, and that it was Shivaji who struck the first blow. The Maratha writers have justified the killing of Afzal as an act of self defence, and as to who struck the first blow the controversy has been set at rest by Mir Alam.

Shivaji followed up his victory over Afzal Khan by entering south Konkan and Kohlapur district. He also captured the fort of Panhala and defeated another Bijapur contingent under Rustam Zaman and Fazl Khan. The forts of Khelna, Vasantgarh, Pangua and some others in the surrounding areas also fell into the hands of Shivaji. Early in 1660 Shivaji returned in triumph to his capital at Raigarh with immense booty.

Sultan of Bijapur was greatly alarmed at the progress of Shivaji and directed Sidi Jauhar who was in charge of Kurnool to proceed against Shivaji. Sidi Jauhar was assisted by Baji Ghorpade, Rustam-i-Zaman, Fazl Khan and several other officers and Shivaji was invested in the fort Panhala in July 1660. Shivaji was forced to evacuate Panhala. To add to his danger the new Mughal governor of the Deccan Shayista Khan was commissioned by Aurangzeb to chastise Shivaji. Shayista Khan occupied Poona, Chakan and drove the Marathas from the Kalyan districts. In the critical juncture Shivaji compounded his hostilities with the Bijapur Sultan through the good offices of his father Shahji and thus made him free to turn his full attention towards the Mughals. For about two years he fought indecisively with the Mughals when one day he secretly entered Shayista Khan's camp with 200 followers. Shivaji was first to enter Shayista Khan's bedroom and made an attack on him. Shayista Khan, however, made good his escape losing his thumb. His son was killed. A number of women of Shayista Khan's harem were put to the sword in the darkness without recognising whether they were men or women. Shayista Khan lost 40 of his attendants, 6 of his wives and slave-girls, one son dead two other sons and 8 other women wounded. Shayista Khan's prestige suffered badly and Aurangzeb in anger transferred him to Bengal. The night attack on Shayista Khan took place on April 15, 1663.

Next year Shivaji marched on Surat, the richest port in the country and plundered it. He kept his plan of his march on Surat a closely guarded secret and declared he was moving to the south, while he was moving to the north. After reaching Nasik he made a sudden dash for Surat. The governor of Surat Inayat Khan fled the town and took shelter in the fort and sent his agent to negotiate with Shivaji who kept the envoy detained and plundred the city for four days. Inayat Khan engaged an assassin to murder Shivaji but he failed and lost his own right hand by the sword of one of Shivaji's body-guards. The booty from Surat amounted to more than a crore of rupees.

Failure of Shayista Khan annoyed Aurangzeb very much. He sent Raja Jai Singh of Amber and Dilir Khan with whom was associated in command Prince Muazzam to chastise Shivaji. Jai Singh had seen action both in India and Central Asia and had an unbroken record of victories. He was a brave general, tactful, and calculating with political cunning, military foresight besides diplomatic skill and power of cautious manoeuvering. He was the fittest person to deal with the clever Maratha hero Shivaji. He formed a ring of enemies round Shivaji, then laid siege of the fort of Purandar. The fort offered a heroic resistance during which there was considerable casualties on Shivaji's side including Munar Baji Deshpande. Meanwhile Jai Singh had sent columns of his army to ravage the villages around Raigarh, Singhgarh and Rohira and to strike an economic blow to Shivaji's state by destroying the cultivation there. The Mughal troops devasted the villages to the complete satisfaction of Jai Singh, looted and burnt the villages and not a trace of cultivation was left in the villages. The siege of Purandar continued in the meantime. Considering the cost of further resistance Shivaji decided to make peace by offering to submit. After some negotiations through envoys Shivaji agreed to come to Jai Singh in person on the latter's promising him safe conduct. A treaty was concluded between the two on June 22, 1665 known as treaty of Purandar by which Shivaji was compelled (i) to cede twenty-three of his forts to the Mughals, (ii) retaining only twelve for himself, (iii) He also promised to assist the Mughals with 5,000 cavalry in their Deccan campaign, (iv) but he was permitted to compensate himself for his territorial losses by collecting **chauth** and **sardeshmukhi** from certain districts of Bijapur, (v) Shivaji was, however, exempted from personal attendance to the imperial court.

After the conclusion of the treaty of Purandar Jai Singh proceeded to invade Bijapur and Shivaji joined the imperialists in fulfilment of the conditions of the treaty of Purandar. Jai Singh had no artillery with him and thought of capturing Bijapur by a sudden coup. But his progress was halted by the Bijapuri troops ten miles in advance of Bijapur fort and after waiting there for several weeks Jai Singh abandoned the campaign. Meanwhile Shivaji was sent to invest the fort of Panhala but failed to take it. In this way Jai Singh's Bijapur campaign proved a failure. But he succeeded in prevailing upon Shivaji to visit the Emperor at Agra with a view to removing him temporarily from the Deccan lest he would again turn against the Mughals. Jai Singh also had in his mind the thought of retrieving his prestige with the Emperor which suffered somewhat due to the failure of his Bijapur campaign by showing that he was able to send a person like Shivaji to the imperial court who had abhorred bowing to any ruler, however great. Jai Singh is also supposed to have hinted the prospect of Shivaji's being appointed governor of the Deccan and conferred on him Janjira from the Sidis, an Island coveted by Shivaji. Shivaji accepted Jai Singh's offer after long hesitation and started for Agra on March 10, 1666 with his son Shambhuji, reaching there on May 9th.

As Aurangzeb had already withdrawn from the Diwan-i-Khas to Diwan-i-Am, Shivaji was presented there by Asad Khan the Assistant Mir-Bakshi. Shivaji paid a **nazarana** of one thousand **mohurs** and two thousand rupees and a **nisar** of five thousand rupees. Aurangzeb received the nazar and nisar, looked at Shivaji but uttered no word. Shivaji was then led to the row of the Mansabdars of 5,000, the third line of the nobles and made to stand there. When Shivaji came to know that Raja Jaswant Singh was standing in the front row he burst out "Jaswant Singh whose back my soldiers have seen! I have to stand behind him? What does it mean?." Then at the time of the presentation of the robes of honour Jaswant Singh, the Princes, Wazir and others were presented with the robes but not Shivaji. Here again Shivaji burst out in anger, "You have seen what sort of man I am, and yet you have wilfully made me stand so long. I cast off your mansab." Shivaji at once turned round, rudely walked away and wrenching his hand which Ram Singh, son of Jai Singh caught hold of, he sat down behind the pillars.

The matter was promptly reported to Aurangzeb who sent three nobles with a robe of honour to pacify Shivaji but the latter refused to receive the robe or to return to the Durbar. To avoid imperial wrath the nobles reported to the Emperor that rustic Shivaji had fallen sick due to the heat of the hall to which he was unaccustomed. Aurangzeb ordered Ram Singh to take Shivaji back to his residence. Even next day Shivaji refused to go to the imperisl Durbar and after prolonged persuasion his son Shambhuji was sent to attend the Durbar. Aurangzeb now decided to imprison Shivaji and to put him to death at a convenient moment for he had to be cautious not to rouse any suspicion. Immediate murder of Shivaji was also difficult because Jai Singh and his son Ram Singh were pledged to the safety of Shivaji, further Sisodia-Rathor rivalry also made the situation all the more complex. The Rathors headed by Jaswant Singh wanted to see Jai Singh disgraced *in war* against Shivaji. Wives of Shayista Khan and Wazir Jafar Khan, and also Aurangzeb's sister Roushnara wanted Shivaji's blood.

Aurangzeb, therefore, decided to keep Shivaji confined in a fortress or to get him killed at the right moment. At first Shivaji was kept closely guarded in his residence, but Aurangzeb next ordered him to be kept confined in the house of Radandaz Khan notorious for his cruelty to state prisoners in Agra fort. It was due to strong protest of Ram Singh that Aurangzeb had to ultimately relent and Shivaji was allowed to remain in Jaipur house on Ram Singh's signing a bond regarding the Maratha chief's conduct at Agra. Now Shivaji was a prisoner under strict surveillance. He hit upon a plan and possibly with the connivance of some of the guards he managed to escape and reach Raigarh on September 22, 1666 after twenty five days of his escape from Agra.

The fight of Shivaji was known at Agra two days after it had actually taken place i.e. on August 30, 1666. Faulad Khan in reporting the matter to the Emperor said that Shivaji had suddenly vanished in the sky. Aurangzeb, naturally, did not believe this story and ordered a through search for the Maratha chief and suspecting Ram Singh in having complicity in the matter dismissed him. Jai Singh, now worried about himself as well as his son wrote to Aurangzeb that he would invite Shivaji to an interview and get him killed. But Aurangzeb who was to regret the escape of Shivaji all his life, was not satisfied at the assurance of Jai Singh and removed his from the Deccan. Jai Singh handed over charge to Prince Muazzam and started for Agra and died on the way at Burhanpur on September 7, 1667.

Jaswant Singh now succeeded Jai Singh in the Deccan. He was friendly towards Shivaji who had meanwhile was keeping indifferent health due to his imprisonment at Agra and strenuous journey from Agra to Raigarh. Prince Muazzam being a peace-loving man and Jaswant Singh friendly towards Shivaji were not, naturaly, in any mood to wage any war of aggression in the south. Shivaji was also tired in flesh, preferred a respite and three years that followed was utilised inorganisation of his internal administration. Aurangzeb with his hands full due to the revolt of the Afghan tribes in the north-west and the fear of Persian invasion did not have any time to turn his attention to the south. Aurangzeb granted Shivaji the title of Raja and a Jagir in Berar and raised his son Shambhuji to the rank of a mansab of 5,000. Shivaji took the peace with the Mughals as a truce and Aurangzeb not sincere in his intentions, and suspicious of Shivaji's friendship with Muazzam, planned to entrap Shivaji a second time failing which to capture Shambhuji and keep him as a hostage.

The rupture betwen Shivaji and Aurangzeb occured because the former appointed the disbanded troops from the Mughal army in the Deccan for financial reasons. This apart, Aurangzeb in dire financial distress tried to recover rupees one lakh advanced to Shivaji in 1666 to meet the expenses of his journey to Delhi and to this end he attached a portion of Berar which was granted to Shivaji as jagir. Shivaji began hostilities in 1670 and recovered several forts that had been surrendered by him according to the terms of the treaty of Purandar. This was facilitated by the bitter quarrel between the Prince and Dilir Khan which had weakened the imperialists. In the same year (1670) Shivaji plundered Surat for a second time and carried away immense booty. Purandar was next to fall. One by one Kalyan, Bhiwandi, Mahali and other forts fell into the hands of Shivaji. Shivaji himself had plundered fifty-one villages around Ahmadnagar, Junnar and Parenda.

Shivaji suddenly irrupted into Berar, Bengal and Khandesh and captured some of the forts in Baglan district. By 1671 a few more forts fell into Shivaji's hands. He then carried on daring raids into Mughal provinces and defeated the Mughal generals in several engagements. In 1672 he demanded chauth from Surat. From 1672 to 1678 the Mughal commandants had no success against the Maratha chief and Shivaji was in full-tide of power.

On June 16, 1674 Shivaji held his coronation ceremony with great pomp and grandeur at Raigarh, his capital, and assumed the title of **Chhatrapati**. The day on the eve of the coronation was spent by Shivaji in self-restraint and mortification of the flesh and made gifts of gold pieces to Brahmanas and learned men. He also repeated similar gifts on the day of the coronation. Shivaji had seated himself on a gold-plated stool, his queen sitting on his left and their son Shambhuji sitting close behind. The **Astapradhans** i.e. the eight ministers stood at eight points with gold jars full of sacred water which they poured over the heads of the king, queen and the prince in accompaniment of hymns and music.

Having spent lavishly in the coronation the state finances become very weak to replenish which Shivaji plundered the headquarters of the Mughal general Bahadur Khan at Pedgaon and obtained a booty of one crore of rupees in cash and two hundred horses. Shivaji continued his aggressive war and captured Kohlapur. Mughal attempt to recover Kalyan was beaten back by the Marathas although Shivaji was lying ill at that time. Shivaji secured the friendship of the Sultan of Golconda and in 1677 captured Jinji, Vellore and the neighbouring districts. In the same year he took possession of Bijapur, Karnataka. All this greatly enhanced the prestige of Shivaji and gave him possession of a vast territory in the Madras, Carnatic and the Mysore plateau which yielded a revenue of 70 lakhs of huns and contained 100 forts.

Shivaji died in 1680 (April 14) at the premature age of fifty (or fifty three) leaving a kingdom extending from Ramnagar in the north of Karwar in the south excluding of course the European trade settlements, and on the east from Baglana in the north covering Nasik, Poona, whole of Satara to Kohlapur in the south, western Carnatic : a large part of present Mysore were also within his kingdom.

Shivaji's Administration : Shivaji's administration was a centralised despotism, all authority of the state was concentrated in the hands of Shivaji himself. Yet he used his authority for the benefit of his subjects, as such, he may be regarded as a benevolent despot. Shivaji developed a bureaucratic administration with eight Pradhans or ministers collectively called Astapradhans who did not formaly cabinet but simply an advisory body insofar as the formulation of state policy was concerned. They were, however, given specific duties for which they were responsible to the Chhatrapati alone. Shivaji did not normally interfere in the function of each of the Pradhans :

(i) The **Mukhya Pradhan** or the Prime Minister who was better known as **Peshwa** enjoyed a higher status than that of other Pradhans but had no supervisory power over others. The Peshwa was a man of royal confidence.

(ii) **The Majumdar** or **Amatya** was the auditor whose duty was to check all accounts of income and expenditure and countersign all statements of accounts of the state.

(iii) **Waqia-Nawis** or **Mantri** compiled daily records of royal activities and keep a watch over plots and conspiracies, maintain lists of invitees in times of important occasions, meals to be served, etc.

(iv) **Sachiv** or **Shuru-Nawis** was in charge of all correspondences. He drafted letters to be sent out and revise letters written by others. He had the additional duty of checking the accounts of parganas.

(v) **Dabir** or **Sumant** was the foreign Secretary and dealt with matters relating to foreign states and peace and war. He would receive envoys and ambassadors from foreign countries.

(vi) **Sar-i-naubat** or **Senapati** was the Commander-in-chief. Recruitment of troops, their training, discipline, deployment of soldiers in battles were his reponsibilities.

(vii) **Pandit Rao** or **Danadhyaksha** i.e. **Sadr** or **Muhtasib** was the head of religion. Fixing the dates of religious ceremonies, disbursement of gifts to Brahmanas, to set apart adequate fund for royal charity and to punish heresy were among his duties.

(viii) **Nyayadhish** or the chief justice of the kingdom was responsible for meteing out civil, criminal and military justice of the kingdom.

All the Astapradhans except the Pandit Rao and the Nyayadhish were required to command troops and lead expedition whenever required. All letters, charters, treaties etc. would require the seals of the Chhatrapati and Peshwa and the endorsements of ministers, other than the Commander-in-chief, Head of religion and the Chief Justice.

For administrative convenience Shivaji divided the kingdom into a number of provinces or **prants** each under a viceroy who held office during the pleasure of the king. The viceroy of Karnataka enjoyed a little higher status than that held by those of other provinces. Recently occupied provinces were kept under army control.

The viceroy had a supply of subordinate staff to assist him in administering the province. The Provinces were subdivided into **Parganas** each of which had a collector and a contingent of troops.

Besides the provinces there were territories which were conquered and were under Shivaji's suzerainty and paid him tributes.

Each pargana was subdivided into **tarafs** and village was the lowest administrative unit.

Revenue System : Shivaji based his revenue settlement on measurement of land according a uniform system and on the basis of the expected produce per bigha. Two-fifths of the produce was taken by the state as revenue. He abandoned the system of tax-farming and introduced the system of direct collection from the cultivators through state officials. The cultivator would know the amount of his dues and would pay the same to the government without any oppression. Cultivators who were new in the trade would be helped with draught animals the price of which would be realised in instalments. Land revenue could be paid either in cash or in kind. Shivaji avoided as far as practicable the grant of jagir in lieu of service to the state. Even when he would grant any jagir in lieu of service to the state. Even when he would grant any jagir, Shivaji would see that the jagirdar did not acquire any political power or influence.

One important source of income of the Maratha state, besides land revenue was the collection of **Chauth** and **Sardeshmukhi**. **Chauth** was one-fourth of the revenue of the country belonging to the neighbours which Shivaji realised every year as a buy-off money. The other was Sardeshmukhi which was one-tenth of the revenue realised from the neighbouring states. The practice of levying Chauth was nothing new in Western India. Raja of Ramnagar levied Chauth on the Potuguese of Daman.

According to Ranade, Chauth was no buy-off money but its levy meant a corresponding responsibility of the state or king levying it, to render protection to the country from which chauth was realised. It was therefore in the nature of the Subsidiary Alliance of Lord Wellesly. Sir Jadunath, however, does not agree with this view. According to him Chauth only kept the Marathas' unwelcome presence away from the country paying the Chauth. Thus it was nothing more or less than buy-off money with no corresponding duty or responsibility to render protection to the country from which Chauth was realised. "The Chauth was only a means of buying off one robber ; and not a subsidiary system for the maintenance of peace against all enemies." (J. N. Sarkar). Mr. Sardesai calls it a tribute realised from hostile or conquered territories. Dr. S. N. Sen argues that Chauth was a contribution exacted by a military leader which was justified by the exigencies of the situation. Sardeshmukhi was an additional claim of 10 per cent which Shivaji claimed as the chief headman, i.e. **Sardeshmukhi** of the whole of the country of Maharashtra. Leaving aside the controversy about the real meaning of the terms Chauth and Sardeshmukhi, the fact remains that their realisation gave the Marathas a great influence over the district which lay beyond their jurisdiction.

ARMY

Shivaji was not simply a great soldier, but he was a military genius and one proof of which was his organisation of the Maratha army. Before Shivaji the Maratha army consisted mainly of cavalry who would keep themselves engaged in cultivation for half the year and only in the dry season when the kings or chiefs would be out on military expedition, they would render active service. Shivaji introduced the system of a standing army which he retained on pay all the months of the year. At the time of his death Shivaji's army comprised 45,000 paga and 60,000 silahdar cavalry and one lak Mavli infantry. There were 32,000 horses in his stable in addition to 5,000 with the Bargirs. The number of his elephants variously computed by him were 1,25,300 and 1,260. According to **Sabhasad Bakhar** Shivaji's elephant corps comprised 1,260 elephants and camel corps 3,000 or 1,500 camels. The strength of the Shivaji's park of artillery is not known for certain. According to Orme he had previously purchased 80 pieces of cannon and lead sufficient for his match locks from the French at Surat.

Paga or the state cavalry was the most important part of the army. Twenty-five troopers of **Bargirs** would form a unit and was placed under one **havaldar**. Over five havaldars, there was one **Jumladar** and over ten jumladars on **hazari** who received 1,000 huns a year. Over the hazari were **panjhazaris** and at the command of the cavalry was **sar-i-naubat** or supreme commander. The bargirs were provided with pay and equipment by the state while the silahdars had to equip themselves at their own cost and supply the equipment and pay of the troopers under them whom they would bring to the service of the state. The government would pay a stipulated sum to meet their expense of service in the field.

In the infantry the lowest unit was of nine **paiks** i.e. privates under one **naik**, five naiks would be under one **havaldar**, over two or three havaldars there would be one **jumladar** and over ten jumladars one **hazari**. In place of five hazaris as in the case of cavalry seven hazaris would be under the command of **sar-in-naubat of the infantry**. In most cases it was Shivaji himself who led the army in a war or expedition, the army was formally under a commander-in-chief or Senapati who was one of the **Astapradhans**.

Forts played an important part in Shivaji's scheme of defence and the garrisons of the forts were carefully constituted and special precautions. were taken against the commandants being corrupted. He, therefore, introduced a policy of checks and balances and appointed three officers, **sabnis**, **havaldar** and **sar-i-naubat** of equal status who served as a check on one another. Further, in order to prevent treachery on the part of the garrison, Shivaji took care to see that each garrison was a mixture of people of different castes.

Shivaji's army was highly mobile and disciplined and was not fettered by heavy luggages. At the time of marching for military action lists were prepared of the belongings of each soldier and officer. The standing army was engaged in action during the dry season and for four months of rains they were kept in cantonment. Unlike the Mughal army, Shivaji's army was not permitted to take any woman, female slave or dancing girl with it. The army was required to conform to high moral standard. During a campaign Brahmins were not to be molested or taken prisoners, goods of the poor people were not to be touched, places of worship not defiled, holy Quran if fell into the hands of the soldiers were to be handed over to the Muslims, women and aged or the children were not to be molested. Gold and silver, jewels etc. that would fall into the hands of the soldiers would be state property while copper and brass vessels etc. would belong to the finder.

Shivaji also built a considerable fleet and stationed it at Kolaba in order to check the power of Sidi or the Abyssinian private chief of Jinjira as well as to plunder the Mughal ships laden with rich merchandise.

JUSTICE

Shivaji followed the traditional Hindu system of **panchayat** system of adjudication, i.e. the jury of the neighbours at the village level. At the higher level justice was meted out by **Nyayadhish** with cooperation of officers and Brahmanas learned in the Sastras "in a manner that no blame may be laid at the King's door". It is obvious that impartial justice was done to the people.

Shivaji's Estimate : As a man, soldier, military organiser and a ruler Shivaji distinguished himself as one of the geniuses of Indian history. European as well as Muslim historians have done scant justice to Shivaji who raised himself from the humble position of a **faujdar** to a **chhatrapati** by the dint of his bravery, diplomacy, his unswerving pursuit of ideal. Khafi Khan who called Shivaji "the reprobate", "son of a devil", "father of fraud" was obliged to honour him by saying "But he made it a rule that wherever his followers went plundering, they should do no harm to the mosques, the Book of God, or the women of any one. Whenever a copy of the sacred Quran came into his hands, he treated it with respect and gave it to some of his Muslman followers." All this speaks abundantly of his great personal influence over his army and its discipline. Shivaji was a born leader of men and his greatest achievement was the welding of the Maratha people which was "scattered like atoms" into a mighty nation "in the teeth of the opposition of four great powers—like the Mughal Empire, Bijapur, Portuguese India and the Abyssinians of Janjira." It goes to the credit of Shivaji that the Maratha power that he had built up defied the Mughal Empire both during his life time and after his death.

To Khafi Khan and some modern writers Shivaji was the "Hindu edition of Ala-ud-din or Tamarlene." But nothing could be more contrary to the facts of life and activities of Shivaji. He was a great genius who possessed all the essential qualities that are needed for a national regeneration. Whether in civil or military administration he left marks of his unparalleled power of organisation and his creative genius. His administration was his own creation and not a copy of any other. His ideal was the restoration of an indigenous empire and revival of Hinduism.

Shivaji was above the contemporary vices to which most of the rulers were subject and his moral virtues were exceptionally high. He was a devout Hindu and sincerely religious. But he was tolerant of other religious. He never forgot the lofty ideals instilled in him by his pius mother Jija Bai and his guru Ramdas. "Religion remained with him an ever-fresh fountain of right conduct and generosity ; it did not obsess his mind or harden him into a bigot." He venerated both Hindu and Muslim saints and granted lands to meet the expenses of illumination of Muslim shrines. He was like wise respectful towards the Capuchin fathers even when Surat was plundered.

Shivaji took steps to encourage Vedic scholarship and set apart adequate funds for the encouragement of learned Brahmanas.

Shivaji's statesmanship made him instinctively perceive the possibilities of his time and gather the best elements in the country of Maharashtra round him to establish a Hindu **Swaraj** in Maharashtra. He breathed a new life, new spirit of nationalism among the Marathas. "He taught the modern Hindus to rise to the full stature of their growth. Shivaji has shown that the tree of Hinduism is not really dead, that it can rise from beneath the seemingly crushing load of centuries of political bondage, that it can put forth new leaves and branches. It can again lift up its head to the skies" (Sir J.N. Sarkar).

Maratha historian Sardesai holds that Shivaji's vision was not restricted to Maharashtra alone. He wanted to secure freedom for the Hindus of the entire Indian Sub-continent. According to him Shivaji's main object was religious freedom, not acquisition of territory. **Chauth** and **Sardeshmukhi** were instruments of expansion all over India. Sardesai also refers to a Jaipur poets belief that Shivaji aspired after the imperial throne of Delhi, and Shivaji agreeing to visit the Agra court was for the purpose of obtaining first-hand knowledge whether North India was prepared to shake of the Mughal yoke. Shivaji's building of navy and his belief in strengthening the Maratha sate both by land and sea showed his freedom from Hindu prejudice against sea voyage and his accepting Hindu converts from Islam into the Hindu society showed his high ideal of political and moral regeneration of the Hindu society. His Hindu-philosophy was abundantly clear from his refraining from fighting against the Rajputs.

The aboves arguments of Sardesai have not been found to be convincing by most of the modern historians. Although it is possible to show that Shivaji protested against the levy of jizya and appealed to Jai Singh and Jaswant Singh's Hindu sentiments yet it is difficult to show that the attempted to rouse the Hindus as such against the Muslim rule or prepared any scheme of alliance with the Rajputs to overthrow the Mughals.

Yet Shivaji stands forth in Indian history as an inspirer of the people, an inspiration wchich did never die out and even envigorated the fighters for Indian freedom against the British. He occupies a distinguished place in the history of India.

We need must refer to the causes of his failure to build up an enduring state. These were (i) the short reign mostly occupied in fighting with his enemies as the Mughals, the Sultan of Bijapur, etc., (ii) Casteism among the Marathas of the seventeenth century made permanent national solidarity difficult and as soon as lesser personalities came upon the throne the fissiperous tendencies found fullest play, (iii) Sir Jadunath remarks that "Shivaji's political success sapped the main foundation of that success. In proportion as Shivaji's ideal of Hindu Swaraj was based on orthodoxy, it contained within itself the seed of its own death." (iv) Division of inheritance in land **(watan)** led to disputes which Shivaji had to settle as the head of the state. Those who lost in the adjudication went against Shivaji who had, therefore, to fight not only against his enemies but also against his own people. (v) Although the people of Maharashtra had gained considerably due to the political independence that Shivaji ensured for them, lack of interest of the bulk of the people in the destiny of the country due to lack of general education was the basic failure of the Maratha Kingdom and contributed to its decay within a few years of the death of Shivaji whose untiring labour had built it up.

REFERENCES

New History of the Marathas : G. S. Sardesai

Rise of the Sikh Power : N. K. Sinah

Shivaji and his Times : Sir J. N. Sarkar

Siva Chhatrapati : S. N. Sen

The Oxford History of India (4th Edn.) : Dr. V. A. Smith

An Advanced History of India : Majumdar, Roychaudhuri & Datta

Cambridge History of India, Vol. IV

History of Aurangzeb, Vols. I-V : Sir J. N. Sarkar

The Mughal Empire : A. L. Srivastava

Foreign Biographies of Shivaji : S. N. Sen

14

Social, Economic and Cultural History

TOWN AND COUNTRY IN MEDIEVAL AGE : TOWNS AND CITIES

History of the people, their social, economic and cultural life are certainly of great interest to the students of history than the political events or the military campaigns of any period. This is particularly true of the medieval period of Indian history. The real history of Mughal India consists in the socio-economic cultural condition of the people of the period.

During the Mughal period, particularly under Akbar's rule India had as many as 120 cities and 3,200 towns. These cities and towns differed in origin and history of their growth as well as in character from those of the Western world. While the towns and cities in the West grew centering round industry and commerce those in India, except, the port towns, most of the cities and towns grew on rural bases, that is, rural areas gradually developed into towns or cities due to residence of rulers, governors or high officials or because due to garrisoning of soldiers or encampment of royal army for long at times of expeditions. Some towns, as has been mentioned above grew in port areas because of the growth of warehouses and influx of indigenous and foreign merchants. Some towns also originated as business marts. What distinguished the Indian towns and cities was that the bases of these towns and cities were rural and not only the food-stuff but also all other consumer goods would come into the towns and cities from the rural areas. There were a few **Karkhanas** in the capital cities in which articles specially needed by the kings and Emperors, nobles and high officials, such as dresses, used to be manufactured. With the change of time, however, and in particular with the advent of the European merchants Indian towns and cities also gradually began to assume industrial and commercial character.

We have interesting observations of Ralph Fitch about the plenty and prosperity in the major Indian cities of India during the Mughal period (1585). He observes "Agra and Fatehpore are two very great cities, either of them much greater than London and very populous. Between Agra and Fatehpore are twelve miles, and all the way is a market of victual and other things, as full as though a man were in a market." Similarly Edward Terry refers to Punjab as a large province and most fruitful. "Lahore is the chief city thereof, built very large and abounds both in people and riches, one of the principal cities of trade in all India." According to C.D. Monserrate, Lahore was not second to any city in Europe or Asia. Abdul Fazl describes Ahmadabad as a "noble city in a high state of prosperity" and in climate and production of choicest things unrivalled in the world.

The ancient capitals like Kanauj, Vijayanagar, etc. where in a state of decay and the modern cities like Calcutta, Bombay and Madras had not come up. The more flourishing towns and cities besides the ones already referred to above, were Delhi, Allahabad, Benares, Multan, Ajmer, Patna, Ujjain, Rajmahal, Dacca, Burdwan, Hughli, Chittagong, etc.

Different parts of the country and important towns and cities were connected by roads which were **Kacha**, i.e. not metalled. Roads were shaded by trees on both sides and dotted with Sarais for the merchants and the travellers. The city of Agra which was capital of the Mughals for a long time was connected with the rest of the empire by a network of roads. The Grant Trunk Road ran from Dacca in the east to Kabul in the north-west passing through Patna, Allahabad, Benares, Agra, Mathura, Lahore, Attock. Another important road ran from Agra to Asirgarh in the south and a third from Agra to Ahmadabad. Apart from the roads, rivers afforded excellent means of communication both for human and mercantile traffic. The Ganga, Jamuna, Ghagra, Indus, the rivers of the south and of Bengal were navigable and frequently used for the transport of commercial goods and troops.

Society : India of those days as even of today, lived in villages and the society was broadly divided into Hindus and Muslims. The Hindus needless to say formed the great majority of the population; they included the Jains, the Buddhists and the Sikhs among them. The upper classes of the Hindu society mostly belonged to the Brahman, Kayastha, Rajput and Vaishya castes and did neither inter-dine nor inter-marry between them. There were many other mixed classes in the society. The Baidyas were a mixed class next to the Brahmanas. These apart there were various other castes and sub-castes which grew up as a result of social mixture i.e. intermarriage between castes. There was much conservatism among the Hindus of upper classes.

The Muslims were divided into two major sections, viz. (a) those who came with the conquerors or for trade and commerce or employment from countries like Arabia, Persia, Afghanistan, Abyssinia etc. and (b) the converts from the indigenous Hindu population and their descendants. As the country was open to foreign traders and travellers, there were also people of various nationalities from Europe, such as the Portuguese, English, Parsis, Chinese etc.

The history of the medieval period of India like that of the Middle Ages of the European history is largely occupied by the story of warfare of the kings and emperors. The common people and their condition were by and large beyond the attention of the historians except insofar as they hrust themselves, into history by their activities in relation to the kings or emperors. Abul Fazl and some European travellers of the Mughal period have refferred to the contemporary people of India and their condition. Among the European tavellers Ralph Fitch, William Hawkings, Sir Thomas Roe, Francisco Paelsart, Bernier, Tevernier, Thevenot etc. deserve special mention.

The society during the Mughal period was feudal in nature. Nobility and the officials of the state were entitled to high esteem in the society. Their standard of living was very high. Luxury, debauchery, drinking etc. were their special characteristics. Apart from the kings and emperors the nobles also had their harem. From Abul Fazl it is known that the imperial harem had five thousand women. The nobility was characterised by mutual jealousy, conspiracy and recrimination.

Below the nobility, we find the existence of the middle class whose number was comparatively small. Their standard of living was moderate and far below that of the nobles and state officials. Middle class was above the contemporary vices of dinking, debauchery and lavity. But the merchants of the west-coast of India was fabulously rich and their standard of living was also very high.

The condition of the common people, compared to the nobility and the middle class was miserable. They had not the wherewithal to purchased warm clothes, shoes etc. which were luxury items to them. Francisco Paelsart remarked that in normal years although they would have no difficulty in maintaining themselves, in times of natural calamities like flood, drought and famine their condition would beggar description. Paelsart who lived in India for long seven years during the Mughal rule remarked that the labourers, the grocers, the bearers or servant classes were three sections of the society who were nominally free men but in reality their condition was no better than that of the slaves.

The common people lived in huddless of mud and reeds. They were poor yet they were subjected to exactions by the state officials. From the time of Shah Jahan there was much repression on the common people, particularly the peasants. Gradually their condition became desperate. The provincial governors and officials realised as much money as they could from the peasants by repressing them.

About the social habits and practices Edward Terry remarks that "None of the people there at any time seen drunk (though they might find liquor enough to do it but the very offal and dregs of that people, and these rarely or very seldom." In the diet and food habits the Indians were temperate; and they were polite to the strangers. The prominent social practices of the time among the Hindus were **Suttee**, **Kulinism** etc. and among both the Hindus and the Muslims, child-marriage and dowry-system. Akbar sought to check the evil practices of **Suttee** and child-marriage. From the writings of Bolt, Scrafton and Crauford we come to know that social evils increased in Bengal during the eighteenth century. In Maharashtra dowry-system was discouraged. Widow re-marriage was prevalent in certain parts of India.

Among the various types of deterioration in the social life in the eighteenth century, one redeeming feature was the continuity of Hindu-Muslim reapproachment and growth of understanding and amiability between the two great Indian communities. The reign of Akbar was remarkably important in this regard, even under Aurangzeb a Muhammadan poet Alwal wrote many Hindi poems and translated **Padmavat** into Bengali. While the Hindus showed reverence to Muslim **Pirs** (saints), the Muslims did likewise to the Hindu **Yogis** (Saints).

One of the demoralizing institution of the society was slavery and there was a regular slave trade. Likewise eunuchs were bought and sold. Akbar's attempt to prohibit it did not succeed.

The upper classes dressed themselves in a long coat and light trousers and turbans. Many wore a silk or cotton scarf round the waist and slung down the ends of the scarf down the leg. Poor Hindus wore **dhotis** one end of which was tied round the waist. Poor Muslims put on **pyjama** and long shirt.

Perfumes and oils were used by men and women, both Hindu and Muslim. **Pan** served as a sort of lip stick. Hindu women wore **saris** while the Muslims women wore **pyjamas** or **ghagras**. Soap made of pulses or soap berry was used. Muslim men and women used collyrium in their eyes and women coloured their palms and feet with **Mehdi**.

Among the indoor games chess, cards, games of guites, satranj and among outdoor games hunting, polo (Chaugan) etc. were popular with the high ranking people. Wrestling, juggler's feats, magic shows etc. were enjoyed by all. Games like tiger hunting, elephant snaring were the privileges of the Emperor. Music both in the court and in private residences, fairs and festivals, specially those sponsored by the state, for example Nauroj were occasions for enjoyment by all people. Hindu festivals like Dasserah, Vasant, Dipavali (prohibited during Aurangzeb's reign) and Muslim festivals of two Ids, Shab-i-barat etc. were festivals of great enjoyment by the respective communities. Occasional fairs were held at Hardwar, Prayag, Mathura, Kurukshetra and many other places of Hindu pilgrimages and also in places of Muslim Pilgrimages like Ajmer, Panipat, Sirhind etc.

The position of women under the Mughals marked a definite deterioration. Purdah system of the Muslim women and the growing conservatism in the Hindu family life precluding Hindu women except of the low castes from coming out of their houses made the life of the women rather unenjoyable. Polygamy was permitted by the Quranic law and a Muslim could take four wives at a time. A Shiah Muslim has no restriction as to the number of wives. While the Hindu ruling class indulged in polygamy the Muslims almost as a rule would have more them one wife. The Emperors and nobles maintained harem i.e. a number of women not formally married.

ECONOMY : AGRICULTURE

The most remarkable feature of the economic system of the Mughals was the gap that kept the producers and the consumers far asunder. The producers were agriculturists, workers in the cottage industries, artisans, producers of consumers goods like oil, cloth, sugar etc. workers in the Karkhanas. The consumers were the rulers, nobles, officers both civil and military, professional and religious classes, slaves, servants and other sundry people. The result was, particularly in view of lack of every transport, that the producers received only marginal profits whereas the middlemen and traders got the lion's share of the profit. This is largely true even today.

Another important feature of the Mughal economic system was the unnecessary burden that the state economy was made to bear due to the huge number of servants and slaves retained by the emperor, nobles and high officials, who practically served more as decoration rather than actual service-hands. This was a great waste of the state income.

The riotous living by the nobles and the officials, their costly jewels, dresses, lavish expenses during the marriage of their children, maintenance of horses, elephants and retainers needed enough money which compelled them to extort the same from the peasants.

Under Aurangzeb agriculture, industry, trade and commerce were very adversely affected by his incessant wars and slack administration. "Thus ensued the great economic impoverishment of India, not only a decrease of the national stock, but also a rapid lowering of mechanical skill and standard of civilisation, a disappearance of art and culture over wide tract of the country" (Sir J. N. Sarkar).

Agriculture depended on rainfall and naturally failure of seasonal rain fall of heavy down pour resulting in flood would result in failure in agricultural crops which meant famine. There were frequent outbreaks of famine in Mughal India during which the sufferings of the peasants and common people would know no bounds.

Lack of any systematic effort to provide relief to the famine stricken people or to allow remission of revenue collection from the peasants made the condition of the people, the peasants in particular, indescribably miserable. Famine was followed by pestilence which was an additional scourge of the people. During 1556-57 a terrible famine broke out in the north-western India followed by pestilence which took a heavy toll of life. Badauni who saw the famine-stricken people with his own eyes remarks that "men ate their own kind and the appearance of the famished sufferers was so hideous that one could scarcely look upon them.... The whole country was a desert and no husbandman remained to till the ground." During 1573-74 Gujarat suffered from similar famine and pestilence and still another in Kashmir in 1595-96. Bengal was visited by famine in 1575 and the Deccan and Gujarat during 1630-32. A number of famines broke out during the reign of Aurangzeb. From Akbar downwards, the Mughal emperors tried to relieve the distress of the people, but as there was no systematic effort, nor any famine policy nor any easy means of transport the relief measures were inadequate.

INDUSTRIES : TRADE

During the Mughal period the most important economic activity besides agriculture was the varied industrial production by the people of India. The industrial products could not only meet the internal needs of the country but also supply the demands of the

European merchants as well as merchants from different parts of Asia. Manufacture of cotton cloth was the most important industry during the period under discussion. The principal centres of cotton manufacture were distributed all over the country, for instance, the coromandel coast, Patan in Gujarat, Khandesh, Burhampur, Jaunpur, Benares, Patna, some other places in United Provinces, Bihar, many centres in Orissa and Bengal. "The whole country from Orissa to East Bengal looked like a big cotton factory, and Dacca district was especially famous for finest cotton fabrics called muslin—"the best, the finest cloth made of cotton." According Paelsant, in Chabaspur and Sonargaon in East Bengal", all lived by weaving industry and the produce has the highest reputation and quality. "Bernier called Bengal store-house of cotton and silk not only of Hindustan but also of Europe. Edward Terry refers to the flourishing condition of dyeing industry of Bengal. Dyeing and printing were of such high quality that these would not be washed out.

Silk industry, however, was limited in scope compared to the cotton industry. Abul Fazl tells us that silk industry was patronised by Akbar. Bengal was the most important centre of silk production and silk manufacture. Other centres of silk manufacture were Lahore, Fathepur Sikri, Agra, Gujarat, Benares, Bhagalpur, Kashmir etc. From Tavernier we know that Bengal produced silk and silk goods worth two and half million pounds. Three-fourth million pounds worth raw silk used to be exported to foreign countries by the Dutch.

Woolen goods such as blankets, shawl, carpets etc. were woven at Kashmir, Lahore, Alwar, Jaunpur and Agra. The shawl industry flourished due to the patronage of Akbar. The state encouraged manufacture of various articles particularly for the use of the Emperors, nobles and the state officials in **Karkhanas** to which many skilled workers were engaged.

Saltpetre was manufactured in Bihar and was exported by the European traders to their countries. It was used for the manufacture of gun-powder. Copper mines existed in Central India and Rajasthan. Iron was found in many parts of India. Red stone quarries were there in Rajasthan and Fathepur. Marble came from Rajasthan. Opium, an agricultural produce, was exported after meeting internal consumption. Gold mines were found in Kumayun and in the hills and rivers of the Punjab.

From Abul Fazl and other contemporary writers, we learn that prices of articles such as rice, oil, ghee, spices, vegetables, milk, meat, live-stock were very low. Terry remarks that there was "plenty of provisions" and people "eat bread without scarceness."

From what we know from the foreign travellers and the contemporary writers, we may observe that the people did not grovel in misery since the prices were low, although in times of natural calamities they had to suffer.

DISTRESS OF THE PEASANT : PEASANTS' REVOLT

The Mughal revenue system according to Prof. Habib suffered from two infirmities. First, the revenue was set at the highest in order that the military contingents to be supplied by the mansabdars could be met out of the revenue collection of the jagir. Secondly, the revenue was fixed at so high a level that it left only the marginal surplus, that is enough margin for the survival of the peasants, which was the barest minimum needed for his subsistence. This meant while the appropriation of the surplus produce constituted the great wealth and the wherewithal of the Mughal imperial government to maintain its pomp and splendour as also its military strength, it left the actual producers of the wealth in a state of utter poverty. As Paelsart observed, the contrast between the rich and the common people was so great that "the rich in their great superfluity and the utter subjection and poverty of the common people" was the economic picture of the Mughal times.

But this was not a static situation, with the passage of time there was a progressive increase in the revenue demand with the rise in prices. Bernier gives us a resonable explanation of this situation. According to him, "The country is ruined by the necessity of defraying the enormous charges required to maintain the splendour of a numerous court and to pay a large army maintained for keeping the people in subjection. No adequate idea can be conveyed of the sufferings of the people. The cudgel and the whip compel them to incessant labour for the benefit of others." A jagirdar who was liable to be transferred from his jagir at any moment or after three or four years was not likely to follow a far-sighted policy of development of the condition of the peasants under him, rather he would allow oppression on the peasants for his personal benefit even if it would ruin the peasantry or destroy the revenue yielding capacity of the land for all time in future.

This narrow selfish outlook of the jagirdars has been nicely described by Bernier in the following lines : "Why the neglected state of this land create uneasiness in our minds ? and why should we expend our money and time to render it fruitful ? We may be deprived of it in a single moment and our exertions would benefit neither ourselves nor our children. Let us draw from the soil all the money we can though the peasant should starve or abscond and we should leave it. When commanded to quit, a dreary wilderness." Similar observations are to be found also in the writings of Xavier, Hawkins, and Manrique. Indian writer Bhimsen observes that unpredictable and constant transfer of Jagirdars made the agents of the jagirdars to help the **rayotwari** or **istiqlal** arrangements. The **amils** of the jagirdars were also not sure of the tenure of service and as such were unrelenting and tyrannical in revenue collection. What was even worse, the jagirdars even resorted to farming out revenue instead of appointing their own agents for tax collection. Sadiq Khan, writing during Shah Jahan's reign observed that lands were being laid waste through bribery, revenue farming the result of which was impoverishment of the peasantry who were literally plundered and robbed.

Thus the system of jagir transfer in the 17th century led to reckless exploitation of peasant population of the country. The imperial administration could check this evil partially for some time only but not permanently, for the imperial regulations left much liberty to the jagirdars, for it was within the discretion of the jagirdars to assist the peasants by granting loans, remission of revenue in times of famine or other calamities or to insist on payment even before harvesting of the crops. Aurangzeb's **farman** in regard to the revenue demand in Gujarat and his regulations prohibiting realising certain taxes remained effective on paper, but not in practice. In the circumstances the burden on the peasantry became so heavy in certain areas that they were even left without the means of subsistence. As Manrique observes where the raiyats, peasants could not pay the exhorbitant revenue were "beaten unmercifully and maltreated" Manucci, who on this, occasion assumes the view point of the rulers, declares that it is the peasants habit to go on refusing payment, asserting that they have no money. The chastiments and instruments (of torture) are very severe. They are also made to endure hunger and thirst.... They feign death (that some times really happens)... But this trick secures them no compassion."

The misery of the peasants were such and torture so inhuman that they were obliged to sell their women, children and cattle to meet the revenue demand. The villages which could not pay the full amount of the revenue-farm were put on a charge of rebellion and the wives, the children of the peasants were sold or carried off and attached to heavy iron-chains sent with their wives and children to various markets and fairs to be sold.

Even when robbery took place within the jurisdiction of a jagirdar or faujdar, the villagers were to find out the culprits and recover the lost properties or compensate the loss. This was also a pretext for the jagirdar or faujdar to sack the village or villages, kill the men folk and sell the women to slavery. Akbar's ordinance not to seize or sell women or children of combatants was directed to stop the avaricious men who would on false imputation of disloyalty or on mere suspicion would sack and plunder villages and carry away the women.

From the narrative of J. Xavier we know that Mughal conquest of Kashmir and Gujarat resulted in fall in cultivation, and the number of runaway peasants grew due to oppression of the peasants. Under Jahangir's reign the peasants were "so cruelly and pitilessly oppressed" that the agricultural fields often lay "unsown and grow into wildernesses." The poor labourers also deserted the villages as a result these were poorly populated. A historian of the reign of Shah Jahan remarks that "owing to natural calamities, the rebellions of seditious zamindars and the cruelty of ill-fated officers "vast areas were depopulated and despite best efforts of the Emperor and his well-meaning ministrers the land looked more deserted than it had been under Jahangir. In Gujarat a Dutch traveller in 1629 noted that "the peasants are more oppressed than formerly (and) frequently abscond." The same thing was noted by an Indian writer with regard to Sind which according to him "was the land of the forsaken, of the cruel and the helpless." This was due to the oppression of the jagirdars. In the Deccan the period before the second vice-royalty of Aurangzeb, desolation was stalking the land and the peasant population dispersed due to the oppression of the governors.

During the early years of Aurangzeb's reign a great portion of good cultivable land remained uncultivated for want of labourers a large number of whom had perished due to the bad treatment and oppression of the governors, or had left the country.

Khafi Khan gives us a clear picture of the condition of the peasantry under Muhammad Shah. According him all experienced and thoughtful persons who used to manage the offices of the state, protect peasantry and encourage the prosperity of the country had departed, the revenue-farmers became veritable sewerage of the revenue-paying pesantry. As these revenue farmers had no guarantee of being confirmed in their office next year would extort as much as possible from the peasants and sell away both the state's share and peasants share. They even sell away the fruit-bearing trees and the hereditary lands of the peasants. Many of the parganas had been so ruined and devasted due to the oppression by the revenue-farmers that these turned into deep forests infested by tigers and wild beasts. "Oppression and injustice of the officials, who have no thought of God, has reached such a degree that if one wishes to describe a hundreth part of it, it will still defy description."

There were, however, certain areas, for instance deltaic Bengal, particularly its eastern portions, parts of Terai etc. where there were extensions of cultivation. But these constituted an insignificant part of the Empire.

Certain points which require to be specially stressed are that (1) flight of peasant population was a common phenomenon during the 17th centrury of the Mughal period. Famine was an added cause to the oppression by the jagirdars, revenue farmers etc. Accumulation of arrear of revenue demand was another cause of absconding. There were cases where peasantry gave up cultivation as a profession altogether. As Bernier observes "some left country to seek a more tolerable mode of existence either in the towns or in the camps, as bearers of burdens, carriers of water or servants of horsemen." As under the Mughal rule the urban population was numerous there were needs of innumerable peons, menials, labourers and slaves in the towns and cities. According to Manucci in southern India where oppression was equally severe, the lot of people leaving rural areas was only to accept slavery or to resort to armed resistance.

PEASANTS' REVOLTS

Considered from the general inclination of the common people during the period under review, there was no trend toward rebellion, In Malwa the artisans and the peasants used to carry arms with them, but that was no indication of their war-like inclination. Paelsart writing about the third decade of the seventeenth century observed "that despite much misery and poverty the people endure patiently, professing that they do not deserve anything better."

But patient endurance also has its limit and the way in which the peasants knew to show defiance was by stoppage of the payment of land revenue. When saturation point was reached under oppression, even a small act of oppression might lead them to rebellion. Villages or areas protected by ravines, forests or hills are naturally convenient for rebellions. Rebellious villages or peasants who ceased to pay land revenue were called **Zortalab** and **mawas** as distinguished from revenue-paying villages called **raiyati**. When the rebellion would be put down the fate of the rebels could only be imagined. "Every one is killed that is met with and their wives, sons and daughters and cattle carried off."

It goes without saying that the intensity of oppression varied from place to place as also due to the variance in the character of the jagirdars and their agents or revenue-farmers. As such while the rebellion in the village or group of villages when put down and men were butchered and their wives and children carried away, the neighbouring areas remained placid and unconcerned. But this was always not the thing. The community of caste often played a cementing factor and in extending the scale of rebellion out of an urge to collectively defend common interests. According to Prof. Habib "In the Jat revolt we have, perhaps, the clearest instance of how an essentially peasant rebellion proceeded along caste lines. The same influence is visible also in the 'lawless' activities of such seditious castes as the Mewatis and the Wattus and the Dogras."

Religious community is another factor that was responsible for extension of the scale of rebellion. Kabir, Nanak, Dadu did not preach militancy but humility and resignation. Their approach to a caste-less society made a deep appeal to the hearts of the masses. They provided inspiration for two powerful revolts, namely, the Satnami and Sikh revolts against the Mughals. A third factor was that the Zamindars had their own objects in opposing the Mughal ruling class. They at certain stage of the peasants' revolt assumed leadership or the leaders of the peasants became themselves Zamindars or in desperation the peasants provided recruits for the rebellious zamindars.

ZAMINDARS : THEIR EVOLUTION, CATEGORIES : THEIR REVOLTS

The term zamindar connotes holders of certain rights based on revenue collection and there are degrees of zamindars from those who have rights over to small portions of a village upwards to the ruler of a kingdom. The zamindars have certain features in common. The rights of zamindars did not originate from imperial grants although there were some exceptions to this. Zamindars were commanders of retainers under them and often they were leaders of caste groups.

Literally the term zamindar means 'holder' of land. According to Moreland in North India, it meant "a chief, that is a landholder with title or claim antecedent to Moslem rule, commonly a Raja Rao, or some other Hindu king or ex-king, who had become tributary to the Moslem state." But as there were zamindars in other areas directly administered by the Muslim Emperors which were not within tributary states, the definition of Moreland is not wholly correct. In Bengal, the term zamindar had a wider meaning. There were landholders the Rajas, whose title to land was antecedent to Moslem rule' and there were other great landholders not holders of so large estates as those of the Rajas, who traced their origin to fourteenth and fifteenth centuries. Even under Murshid Quli Khan a number of zamindari families had originated.

Reference to **sanad** that is formal grant, patent by the Board of Revenue during early years of the East India Company's rule does not find corroboration in Ain-i-Akbari. A

sanad was, as John Shore stated, a confirmation of rights and also an honourable distinction issued to "principal zamindars who enjoyed extensive jurisdiction and the right to be admitted to the presence of the sovereign or his viceroy." Smaller zamindars did not enjoy that kind of formal acknowledgement of their rights. Under the Mughal Emperors, there was, however the system of confirmation of the proprietory right on the soil to zamindars, or inheritance of zamindari. According to Shore the Mughal principle of finance established the practice that the "rents belong to the soveriegn, and the land to the zamindar."

It goes without saying the zamindars were a class of intermediaries between the peasants and the state, their primary function being collection of rent. There were three main categories of intermediaries. The first was, those who paid tributes. These zamindars were rulers and often called Rajas, Raos etc. The tributes might be in cash or only symbolic payment by way of presentation say of an elephant or horse etc.

The second category comprised the zamindars who paid peshkash that is the revenue payable to the state. In revenue payable the peshkash was also included.

Ordinary zamindars formed the third category and they occupied a position inferior to those of the first two categories namely the tribute paying and **peshkash-paying** zamindars.

The zamindars derived their right and title to the management of the zamindari from a **sanad** which was in the nature of a contract emphasising the obligations of the zamindars. Default in payment would render a **sanad** revoked. A zamindari might be leased out that is given of **ijara** or even sold out. With the increasing weakness of the imperial administration there was a progressive increase in the autonomy of the Zamindars.

There was a gradation among the landholders. The first among the rank were the **zamindars**. Next to the **zamindars** were the **chaudhuris** below whom in rank were the **talukdars**. The Talukdars were of two groups the **huzuri talukdars** who had to pay a fixed revenue to the state. The other groups was of the **mazkuri talukdars** who paid their rent to the zamindar or chaudhuri. Zamindars during Akbar's reign were revenue farmers on annual contract basis, with ten percent of the revenue demand as commission and small estate. There were also some hereditary proprietors of zamindari estates.

The ryots were under obligation to pay **mal** i.e. land revenue, **sair** i.e. other taxes, **abwabs** i.e. irregular and extra exactions by the state officials, zamindars or their agents.

The zamindars, during the Mughal period, maintained an attitude of hostility towards the imperial administration and often sided with whoever appeared to be powerful and tumult-raising. This is known from Abul Fazl. He also praises Raja Beharimal who "out of wisdom and good fortune, aspired to leave the ranks of zamindars and become one of the select of the Court." Prof. Habib very rightly questions if zamindar's position and when become one of the court were mutually incompatible. Abul Fazl as well as the chroniclers of Aurangzeb mentions of the opportunism and disloyalty of the zamindars.

Prof. Habib states that "In documents written from the official point of view, it is assumed as a matter of course that the main danger to law and order came from the zamindars who refused to pay the revenue and had to be cowed down or destroyed by force either by the faujdar or the jagirdar. Erection of fort by any zamindar immediately aroused the suspicions of the authorities and could apparently be a sufficient justification of punitive action against him." The correspondence from Radandaz Khan faujdar of Biswara reveals the condition arising out of non-payment of revenue in an area in the very heart of the empire by the zamindars against whom expeditions had to be sent. The zamindars were also engaged in robbery. Appointment of zamindars direct from the court under Aurangzeb was a method adopted for the purpose of counter-balancing the power of the old houses of zamindars.

One of the important political features of the period under review was the struggle between the zamindars and the imperial administration, often breaking out into open hostility. Manucci, writing in 1700, says "usually the viceroys and the governors are in a constant state of quarrel with the Hindu princes and zamindars—with some because they wish to seize their lands, with others, to force them to pay more revenue than customary...... usually there is some rebellion of the rajahs and zamindars going on in the Mughal kingdom."

As the zamindars were weaker in comparison with the imperial government, they always tried to adopt a conciliatory attitude towards the peasants whose support was very much needed both for defence and fight as well as for finance by way of timely payment of revenue. The zamindars having been conversant with the local customs could make their relation and arrangements with the peasants more flexible than what the imperial administration could do in Khalisa lands or the assignees could do in the lands under them. The imperial administration in Khalisa lands and the assigness were more interested in realising more and more revenue. Bernier observed that the peasants found "less oppression and allowed greater degree of comfort in the territories of the Raja. Even the court chronicler of Aurangzeb observed that the zamindars" for winning the hearts of and conciliating the peasants, in order that may not cease to obey or pay revenue to them" conducted themselves gently. Frequently it happened that peasants fleeing the lands under the imperial administration were attracted to the lands of the zamindars. In this way the peasants and the zamindars were often associated in the struggle against the Mughal authorities. The peasants added to the resources of the zamindars by engaging in cultivation and also to their fighting strength by providing recruits. Although such ill-equipped and ill-trained troops were no match for the imperial force, yet the difficult terrain, interspersed by rivers gave some advantage to such troops and they could continue their struggle. During Aurangzeb's reign a new feature was added to the nature of the struggle of the zamindars. It was not only defensive, but now assumed also an offensive character.

Peasants Revolts in the 17th and 18th Centuries : It is customary for the seventeenth and eighteenth century writers to emphasise economic and administrative causes behind the upheavals, against the Mughals. It has also been argued by some authors that opposition to the Mughals was due to Hindu reaction or national awakening. Prof. Habib, however, emphasies religious reaction and national consciousness as the motive force behind the opposition to the Mughals.

Jat Revolt : From Abul Fazl it is known that the peculiar climate of the province of Agra made the peasant masses of the area notorious in the whole of the country "for religion, bravery and courage." The two sides of the Jumna figured constantly in military operations against the rebellious peasantry of the area. The Emperor had once to lead personally, an expedition against a Raja of a pargana in Kanauja who used to engage robbers and peasants to defend himself when attacked. During the reign of Jahangir it was reported that "ganwars and cultivators" on the east of Jumna, near Mathura "do-not cease to commit highway robbery, and protected by dense jungle and fastness, live in rebellion, have no fear of anyone and do not pay the revenue to the jagirdars." In an expedition which was sent against them resulted in the death of a number of rebels and captivity of their wives and children. This happened in the twelfth regnal year of Jahangir. In 1634 a larger expedition had to be despatched against the rebels on both sides of the river Jumna who committed robberies on the Delhi-Agra route. Ten thousands of the "human looking beasts were slaughtered" and their women, children and cattle beyond computation were seized. In the year of the death of Sadullah Khan, wazir of Shah Jahan, the peasants of the villages near Agra rose in arms. They were suprised by Abdul Nabi, faujdar of the deceased Sadullah Khan, who put to sword or imprisoned all those who could not flee in time. This was the history of the cradle of the Jat rebellion in the reign of Aurangzeb. It is noteworthy that the rebels were not named as Jats, but called ganwars or villagers and in a few cases they were perhaps led by the Rajputs. Manucci who wrote about Aurangzeb's time and knew about the Jat revolts called them as peasants. The Jats are "a peasant caste", who inhabited the villages between Delhi and Agra, and were entered as zamindars in many **mahals** in the Doab. The Jat rebellion, speaking properly, dates from the time of Gokla Jat, the zamindar of Talpat near Mathura. He collected a large number of Jat soldiers and other villagers and raised a rebellion. He was killed in 1669, but the leadership passed to his son, Raja Ram Jat and then his nephew, Churaman Jat who is said to have been the son of a zamindar of eleven villages. Over wide areas the peasants refused to pay revenue and took to arms. From a grant of a zamindari it is found that the new zamindar was required to expel the "evil-mannered rebels", who inhabited the 25 villages near Mathura. In 1681 the Faujdar Multafat Khan of the district around Agra lost his life while leading an attack on a village that refused to pay the revenue. In the same decade for three years a jagirdar failed to get anything by way of revenue payment from his jagirs near Agra due to rebellion.

Leadership of the Jat rebellion was provided by the zamindars and capture of the estates of other zamindars was the aim of the leaders of the rebellion. In the mid-eighteenth century much of the lands under the possession of the Jats was not in their own hands. The king or Raja who wanted to render assistance to the old zamindars, would bring him inevitably in conflict with the Jats. One net result of the Jat rebellion was extension of Jat zamindari in the middle of the Doab.

About the character of the Jat rebellion it may be said that it was a huge plundering movement. "This was, perhaps, inevitable under the narrow caste-horizons of the peasants and the plundering instincts of their zamindar-leaders." Gokla plundered the pargana of Sadabad, the pargana around Agra was plundered by Raja Ram and all the parganas under Agra and Delhi had been sacked and plundered by Churaman. "So far as we know", says Prof. Irfan Habib, the Jat rebels (in spite of Haridas) had no connection with any particular religious movement.

Satnami Revolt : While the Jat rebellion was unconnected with religion the Satnami (as also the Sikh) rebellions were entirely based on religion and not on casteism.

The Satnamis were a sect of the **Bairagis**, which was founded in 1657 at Narnaul by a native of the place. They were believers in monotheism and abhorred formal rituals and superstition. They did not believe in caste distinctions and would not live on the charity of others. Sympathy with the poor and hostility towards authorities and wealth were their commandments. "Do not harass the poor, ...Shun the company of an unjust king and wealthy and dishonest man, do not accept a gift from these or from kings." Naturally such a religion appealed to the conscience of the poor and the lower classes of the people. A contemporary historian describes the **Satnamis** as a group of Hindu mendicants also called **Mundiyas**. In the parganas of Narnaul and Mewat they numbered four or five thousand householders. "Although those Mundiyas dress like mendicants, yet their livelihood and profession are usually agriculture and trade in the manner of grain-merchants with some capital. Living according to the ways of their own community, they aspire to reach the status of a good name (nek-nam), which is the meaning of the word **satnam**. But if any one should want to impose tyranny and oppression upon them as a display of courage or authority they will not tolerate it ; and most of them bear arms and weapons." From another contemporary writer we come to know that they were extremely dirty, foul, filthy and impure. They did "not differentiate between Muslims and Hindus, who eat pig's flesh and other disgusting things."

The Satnamis were habitually of rebellious conduct and even before they had rebelled they did not appear to have been loyal to authorities. They brought the cultivators and their families and possessions in the pargana of Bhatnair under their control and they were "not free from the thoughts of sedition and robbery." The revolt of the Satnamis in 1672 began as a village affray. One Satnami while working in a field had hot exchange of words with a trooper who was guarding the corn-heap which led to a fracas and the trooper struck the satnami with a stick breaking his skull. Other Satnamis gathered and beat the trooper almost to death whereupon the Shiqdar sent a contingent of troops to chastise the Satnamis and the hostilities began.

That the rebellion was that of the lower classes of people which gave it a plebeian character can be clearly understood from the composition of the rebellious force of the Satnamis. They were the destitute gangs of carpenters, peasants, sweepers, tanners who suddenly burst forth in the region of Mewat and fell upon the imperial troops like locusts. But after their initial success and capture of Narnaul and Bairat they were finally destroyed by the large army sent from the court. Masir-i-Alamgiri compares their valiant defence against the imperial army by remaking that "despite the lack of all materials of war, they repeated the scenes of the great war of Mahabharat."

Prof. Habib would even feel like calling the rising of the Sikhs a peasants revolt on the grounds that Sikhism is a peasant religion and the verses of Guru Nanak were all in the language of the Jats which means, in the dialect of the Punjab village. But these facts as well as the plebeian character of the rebellion, for "most of the chiefs of the highest dignity among the Sikhs", he points out, "were low-born persons, such as carpenters, shoe-markers and Jats", prove that the rise of the Sikhs was a peasants' revolt. On similar arguments Prof. Habib regards that other revolts in northern India as well as the Maratha rise in the south were mainly due to agrarian reasons.

While these revolts had contributed to the fall of the Mughal empire, to characterise all of them as mainly due to oppression of the peasants from economic or religious points of view will be over simplification of the causes of the fall of the empire. Oppression of the lower classes constitutes an important factor in the ruin of empires as it definitely did in case of the Persian empire and the poet Sadi in his immortal poem wrote a sort of an epitaph to the falling Persian empire by saying that the glory and empire of the Emperors are gone the same way as the oppressor emperors themselves and their tyranny over the peasants had also thus ended. All the same, there is a risk in taking Sadi literally in case of the fall of the Mughal empire.

The failure of the peasants' revolts which took place during the Mughal period was due largely to (i) historical environment of the time, (ii) particular correlation of class-forces existing at that time. Lack of new class relation or class force, lack of any new economic relation and lack of capable political leadership led to the failure of the peasants. China's past history offers a parallel instance.

MARITIME TRADE—INDIAN MERCHANTS vs. EUROPEAN TRADERS

The route through which India maintained maritime contact with the Red Sea area was rendered unsafe due to the Turkish control over the area from the Persian Gulf to the Near East. The Red Sea route itself was also interfered with by the Egyptian Government. Early in the seventeenth century Aden was more a garrison under its "rapacious and treacherous" Turkish governor. Aden and Moch—two leading sea ports—were important commercial centres due to influx of pilgrims and traders from Egypt who purchased eastern products, in return for gold and silver. These ports were main outlets of the maritime activities of the traders of Gujarat, Cambay and Diu. The same ports were frequented by pilgrims and merchants from Lahari Bandar port in Sind, Mughal port of Surat, Bijapur port of Dabhol and the Vijayanagar ports of Cannanore and Cochin.

Indian ships of States commanding the sea coast from the Cape of Good Hope and Madagascar to the East Indies and the Far East brought vast wealth and resources to the Turks. When the Turkish officers came down heavily on the English merchants, the masters of the Indian ships often played the role of mediators of intermediaries; the Turks evidently derived considerable profit from the trade carried on by the Indian ships.

In Mocha there was an Indian colony. The Indians built for themselves "a petty town of slight cabins, along the strand." Some of the masters of the ships of Nakhuda of the great ships, had their own houses at Mocha. Such houses were occasionally venues of discussions between the Indian Nakhudas and Turkish officers. Malik Ambar, a thirty year old name sake of the famous Malik Ambar of Ahmadnagar, used to style himself as "Nakhuda of the great ship, captain of Dabul, the port of Bijapur." This great ship had the capacity to carry 4,000 Khandies (one Khandi = 20 maunds) of goods. Mahomet, i.e. Mohammad of Cannanore is referred to in the East India Company papers as another influential Nakhuda from Vijayanagar.

Although there were constant frictions between the English merchants and the Turkish authorities, the relation between the English and the India ships were on the whole tolerably good. From the Indian merchants the English traders obtained information of the progress which their predecessors like William Hawkins, Jourdain and Sharpeigh had been making with regard to the development of trade in Surat and Cambay. The Indian Nakhudas played an important role in the release of the Englishmen imprisoned by the Turks at Mocha.

Sir Henry Middleton, the General of the 6th Voyage of the English East India Company towards India, who received great help from the Indian Nakhudas when he and his men were imprisoned at Mocha by the Turkish authorities, reached Surat on September 26, 1611. Denied trade privilege by the Mughal emperor due to the opposition of the Portuguese, Middleton sailed from Surat on February 11, 1612. He decided to return to the Red Sea and avenge himself on the Turks, Mughals and the Portuguese. Nicholas Downton gives in detail the plan the Enghlish contemplated of following. "Our best way is to lie in the way of the Red Sea 'where the English would find' ships of Surat and Cambay with diverse others, the subjects of the great Mogul but also men of Diu, subject to the Portuguese." The idea was that the capture of these ships would not only injure the Mughals and the Portuguese, but would be "no small distrubance to the Turks at Mocha, for though there were no goods of theirs thereon, the loss of customs would greatly pinch and vex them and spoil the Turks' scale' at Aden and Mocha. The ships of Dhabol, Malabar and other places would be permitted to proceed unmolested. This would have the effect of warning the Mughals that the English were not a nation "to be coarsely treated." Thus, the measures of reprisal would compel the Mughals to duly honour and respect the English. Middleton's party actually captured two ships—one from Cochin bound for Chaul laden with dried coconut, raw silk etc. and another from Chaul, bound for Ormuz. Some bales of raw silk were taken away from the Cochin ship and a few bags of rice from the Chaul ship, and the ships were let off. Next Middleton's fleet lay in wait in the traits of Bad-el-Mandeb to intercept all ships entering the Red Sea. This was to be done in order to avenge the wrong done to the English at Mocha by the Turks, and indirectly warn the Mughal emperor that the subjects of the king of England would not put up with so great abuses unavenged and captured goods from the Indian ships for compensating their loss in India. They were also determined to seize the Portuguese ships of Diu.

Downton remained at Aden to intercept all Indian ships and divert them into the straits of Bab-el-Mandeb, where Middleton lay in wait. Downton intercepted a ship from

Lahari Bandar and took away some of its merchandise. Another ship of 200 tons from Diu and a large ship named Muhammadi from Dabhol were intercepted. The latter being from friendly State was not despoiled. Although Malik Ambar, the Nakhuda of the ship, was thought to be too much proud and insolent and Downton thought of attacking the ship, the large ship's speed was too great for Downton's ship Peppercorn to reach her. Downton in desperation fired as shot at her. From the ship of Diu, which the sailors gave out to be a ship from Cutsnagana, Downton took away a few bales of cotton, cloth, butter and oil. In the meantime, Middleton intercepted as many as eleven Indian ships, Rahimi (1500 tons), Harsonee (600 tons), Mohammadee (450 tons) of Surat, Sullamettee (450/60 tons), Caderee (200 tons), Agancany (208 tons) of Diu, and Caudree (400 tons) of Dabhol, a big ship from Cannanore, 3 ships from Malabar—altogether eleven ships.

The English employed a thorough method of plunder of the Indian ships which was the daily business of the men under him. All Indian merchant ships were searched one after another. All commodities suitable for the market in England, such as indigo, packs of cloth, etc. and the spoils were divided between Middleton and another Saris who joined him. The Indian merchants were forced to exchange their goods for the English merchandise. No transit charges of the Indian goods were added to the value of the Indian commodities whereas all rates and taxes etc. were added to the value of the English goods while exchanges were made. The unusual delay in settling the exchange accounts or sale of Indian goods was so sickening to the Indian merchants that many of them left the goods at the prices dictated by the English, even at a great loss in order to return home.

The Gujarat and Diu ships which were targets of attack being of Mughal and Portuguese ownership were kept under surveillance and ransom was demanded for their release. Even Downton found the process of realisation of ransom "a most troublesome and heart-relenting business" because of the cries of the poor people, difficulty in their getting money and the pressure put on them to pay the ransom with haste and the exhorbitant rate of interest charged by the Turks for lending money to the Indian merchants and sailors. Every ship had to pay a huge amount as ransom.

The news of the fate of the Indian merchants and the ships in the Red Sea reached Surat toward the latter part of 1612. A Mughal ship returning from Mocha in September, 1612 gave out the information of the treatment of the Indian ships by Henry Middleton. There was great nervousness among the English merchants such as Thomas Aldworth, William Biddulph, and Nicholas Withington as to what might befall them. But "influential men came to those Englishmen, assured them that the news need not disturb them and that in spite of the injury done by Middleton to the Indian ships, they would continue to show "honest respect" to the Englishmen. "This is a curious but sad commentary on the naval weakness of the Mughals" and set naval vigilance to sleep and naval expansion unattended.

INDUSTRY : EUROPEAN TRADERS

The seventeenth century and the major part of the eighteenth, exhibited almost similar industrial organisation and features although a marked process of decline was noticeable.

There were extensive and diverse manufactures the premier manufacturing industries being cotton and silk textiles. Orme observes that "on the coast of Coromandel and the province of Bengal, where at some distance from the high road or a principal town, it is difficult to find a village in which every man, woman or child is not employed in making a piece of cloth." The manufacture of cloth and silk fabrics was on domestic basis and every weavery's house was a little textile manufactory. What was specially noteworthy was that the tillers of the soil could spend their time and the agricultural vacations such as after sowing and harvesting seasons in the manufacture of cloth or some kind of work in the loom.

From Bernier we come to know that there was rigid specialisation. For instance, a goldsmith would not work on silver and the hereditary nature of the craftsmanship gave an extraordinary specialisation. A weaver would weave only a particular staff which would naturally give him a special proficiency at work through repetition. The family traditionally followed the same trade.

Foster, Bernier and Abul Fazl referred to **Karkhanas** which manufactured the articles needed by the impeial household, the aristocracy, the official dom. These manufactories employed a large number of workers who worked for the manufacture of the items of luxury. But these began to disappear gradually.

Metallic industries such as iron, glass, brass, weapons, gold and silver vessels and ornaments etc., other industries like salt petre, salt, jute, sugar, opium, etc. were highly developed. But with the decline of agriculture due to lack of initiative and enterprise, oppression by the overlords, other industries also began to decline.

With the advent of the European merchants the cotton and silk textile industries received an initial fillip. Textile industry was scattered all over India. Surat was noted for the manufacture of finest Indian brocades, calicoes and muslins. Ahmadabad also manufactured brocades of gold and silver, carpets, satins, taffetas, silk linen and cotton cloth. Burhanpur in Khandesh, Chanderi in Malwa were also important centres of textile manufactures. Masulipatam, Chicacole, Ellore, Burrampore, Vizagapatam etc. were noted for manufacture of cotton piece goods, muslins, silk calico prints etc. Jaunpur, Benares, Allahabad etc. were important centres of calico manufacture, manufacture of chintz, gȧzi, cotton piece goods. Bihar and Orissa also were centres of manufacture of cloth. Bengal "produced cloth of all kinds, most beautiful muslins, silk raw or worked." Dhaka held the premier position in Bengal for the manufacture of delicate cloth and muslin Dhaka also famous for embroidery and flowering works.

The Mughal commercial policy was an unwise as bankrupt of economic foresight. The most important illustration is the farman of Farruk Shiyar of 1717 by which the English traders were granted an unqualified right of trading in Bengal and Gujarat, denied to other foreign and even to indigenous merchants, to carry on duty-free trade on an annual payment of a meagre sum of Rs. 3,000/- only. This while meant a huge loss of revenue to the government, virtually conceded a sort of an extra-territorial right to the English which affected the sovereignty of the Mughal emperor and paved the way for the commercial and eventually the political supremacy of the English in India. The English merchants were permitted to carry on export and import trade only but not to participated in the internal trade of the country. They were issued **dustaks**, i.e. discharge certificates to cover their export and import trade without having to pay duties at check-points. This English merchants later began to abuse these **dustaks**.

Nawab Murshid Quli Khan was sufficiently shrewad and wise to see the implications of the concession granted to the English and disobeyed the farman.

In the meantime, the Portuguese decline, particularly after the sack of Hughli in 1632 continued without any hope of recovery. The Dutch, the most formidable rivals of the English in India in the first half of the seventeenth century had lost their position. Lack of foresight of the Dutch directors, their ignorance of the actual state of things in India and the prospect the Indian trade held out made them keep themselves preoccupied in Indonesia, Cochin, Travancore, Malabour, Ceylon etc. and neglect Bengal. The result was their ultimate ouster.

More powerful and aggressive than the Dutch were the French traders. The only European trading company that contended with the English was the French East India

Company. The first half of the eighteenth century saw the ouster of the French and the exclusive commercial supremacy and political accession of the English in India.

The advent of the European trading communities and the eventual supremacy of the English in the matter carried with it also, the subjugation of the Indian trade and industries and conversion of India into a raw material producing and supplying country. All this had its impact on the Indian trading community.

India had trade relations with Basra, Muscat, Ormuz, and other ports of the Persian Gulf, China, Arabia, Java, Malacca, Sumatra, Madagascar, Cornorro Islands, Mozambique and other ports of East Africa. Bengal had flourishing trade in Bengal sugar, cotton cloths, silk stuffs. "The immense commerce of Bengal was the central point to which the riches of India were attracted. Specie flowed in by thousand channels.... the Gulfs (of Mocha and Persia) poured in their treasures into this river (the Ganges)" (Verelst). Bengal had trade relations with Laccadives, Maldive, China, Pegu, Manilla, Malaya, Philippines, Persia, Red Sea, African coast, Tibet etc. Persian, Abyssinian, Chinese, Turkish, Arabian, Jewish, Moorish, Armenian traders flocked to Bengal.

In the seventeenth century individual Indian merchants like Baharji Borah of Surat and Malaya Coast controlled the wholesale trade of particular regions. Such merchants were both investors and carriers of the then flourishing internal and external trade. In the east coast merchants like Kanakaraya Mudali, Ananda Ranga Pillai, Seshachala Chetty and others were of great repute as investors and carriers of internal and foreign trade. Bengal merchants had trade relations with Kashmir, Punjab, Gujarat, Malabar, Coromandel, Assam, Cachar etc. In Bihar the European traders purchased salt petre through contact merchants i.e. **dalals** like Omichand, Digchand, Khwaja Wajid etc. Some of the Indian merchants and bankers even took part in active politics, for instance Jagat Seths and Umichand in Bengal, Arjunji Nathji in Western India.

Seventeenth century and first few decades of the eighteenth was bright both for Indian trade and traders. But the process of drainage of Indian economy started with the growing commercial power of the English and with gradual transformation of the East India company into a political power in the post-Plassey period the Indian trade and Indian traders began to suffer till the latter were ousted from the field due to unfair competition of the English. The invasion of the English into the private trade of the country, their abuse of Dustaks etc. had the effect of the ouster of the Indian merchants from the field. Scramble for riches and scandalous misuse of dustaks after Plassey unleashed the forces of economic decline and emergence of commercial and political supremacy of the English.

The main principle of the British commercial policy in India was to protect the textile industry of Britain against the competition of the Indian textile manufactures. An Act was passed in 1700 prohibiting use of silk goods and calico-prints of Bengal, Persia, China and the East Indies in England. Raw silk was allowed to be imported into England in 1701. Added to all this was the cruel treatment of the weavers and tenders which hastened the decline of the Indian trading community and the destruction of the manufactures. The political disintergration of the Mughal Empire sapped the economic vitality of India. External invasion and internal disruption affected easy transit of goods from one part of the country to the other. Inter provincial trade gradually came to a stand still. What still lingered was due to the fact that the Mughal Empire took some length of time to die. When it had become incapacitated the economic reins were assumed by the English merchant community.

LITERATURE

The Timurid rulers were great patrons of literature and under them literature in its different branches received considerable impetus. Babur was himself a gifted poet in Turki and Persian as also the writer of his own memoirs. Humayun, if not a scholar himself, was a patron of learning and had a great interest in literature. He bided his time in his library. By far the greatest patron of scholars, learning and literature was Akbar under whom many scholars of repute flourished and by their works brought about a cultural renaissance in medieval Indian history. Akbar's tolerant and benevolent policy, his liberal patronage of learning and the learned, the peace and prosperity of his reign naturally led to an exuberance in the works of literature and art. No wonder that scholars of outstanding ability flourished under his reign and enriched the fund of medieval Indian literature by their immortal works.

During the Mughal rule Bengali literature was deeply influenced by the Neo-Vaishnava movement the result of which could be seen in the emergence of one of the richest treasures of the Bengali literature which may be broadly termed as Vaishnava literature.

Vaishnava literature divides itself into **biography** and **padavali**. Among the biographical literature we have the earliest biography of Chaitanya by Murari Gupta one of the oldest followers of Chaitanya. The work was in Sanskrit. The oldest biography of Chitanya in Bengali is Brindavandasa's **Chaitanya-bhagavata** or **Chaitanya-mangala**. Brindavanadas was Chaitanya's classmate. The work stresses on the human qualities of Chaitanya and gives an interesting picture of the social life of Bengal at the time of Chaitanya. Krishnadas Kaviraj's **Chaitanya-Charitamrita** was the next important biography of Chaitanya. Krishnadas looked upon Chaitanya as the incarnation of both Krishna and Radha. Jayanandas **Chaitanya-mangal** was another important biography of Chaitanya. Another **Chaitanya-mangal** was written by Lochandas. Churamanidas wrote Gauranga-Vijaya another biography of Chaitanya. But Chaitanya-Charitamrita of Krishnadas Kaviraj is regarded by many scholars as the most important of Vaishnava literature. Lochandas was one of the best lyricists and introduced the folk song called **Dhamali** or **Dhamail**. There were many other minor biographical works on Chaitanya.

Lyrical poems, known as **Padavali** occupies the next important place in Vaishnava literature. These poems dealt with love outside web-lock i.e. **Parakiya prem**, of Radha and Krishna. Besides Lochandas, Basudev Ghosh, Narahari Sarkar, Yasoraj Khan, Kavisekhara, Narottamdas, Balaramdas and Jnanadas were lyrical poets of the sixteenth century. Govindadas Kaviraj wrote his lyrics in **Brajabuli** which was a mixture of Bengali and Maithili. Among the later poets the name of Gopaldas deserves mention. There were also professional **Kathakas** i.e. story-letters who wrote narative poems dwelling on love of Radha and Krishna. The Vaishnava lyrics flourished mainly due to the patronage of both Hindu and Muslim rulers. The Hindu rulers of Tripura and Cooch Behar were liberal patrons of the lyrical Vaishnava poets.

Important works of Vaishnava doctrine and philosophy, Vaishnava history, biography of Vaishnava leaders were written by Gosains of Brindavan. Nityanandadas, Narahari Chakravarti, Ramgopal Das, Pitambar Das were some of them.

There emerged a literature of the Vaishnava sect which later came to be known as **Sahajiya**. This sect was somewhat akin to the **Tantrics**. They carried to excess the practice their theory that love of woman, not one's own wife was the easiest way to salvation. The philosophy behind this theory was ably and skilfully expressed in a number of treatises which belong to Sahajiya literature.

Next in importance to the Vaishnava literature were the **Mangala-Kavyas** which were poetical compositions describing the glories of many popular gods such as **Manasa** (snake goddes), Chandi (a form of goddess Durga), Siva, Kalika, etc. The Manasa-mangal Kavyas of Bijayagupta, Bipradas Piplai, Narayanadeva deserve mention. In Chandimangala Kavya a merchant Kalketu became king through the favour of goddess Chandi, and similarly a merchant Dhanapati after many reverses of fortune due to disfavour of the king of

Ceylon was ultimately restored to the King's favour through the blessings of Chandi and was married to the king's daughter. Manasa-mangala Kavya depicts the conversion of the merchant Chand Sadagar who was at first unwilling to pay respect to Manasa, the snake goddess to a worshipper of the goddess after his seven sons were killed by snake bites. The most beautiful part of the story is the resurrection to life the dead body of the seventh son by his widow Behula who took the snake-bitten dead body on a raft to the abode of gods and restored him to life with their blessings. The best work of this class is the **Kalika-mangala** commonly known as **Vidya-sundara Kavya** a **Annadamangal** composed by poet Bharat Chandra. The theme is the secret love of princes Vidya and Sundara. Goddess Kali appeared at the ultimate stage of the story when Sundara was condemned to death and saved his life. There are a number of mangala Kavyas glorifying gods and goddesses like Sitala, Lakshmi, Shashthi, etc. **Raya-mangala** is a poem which glorifies **Dakshin-raya** the Tiger-god. It is commonly believed in the tiger infested parts of Bengal, in Sundarbans, in particular, that worshipping of Dakshinrava would save the people from the tigers.

Reference to the translation literature during the medieval period, under the Sultanate has been made earlier. In the 16th and the 17th centuries the great Sankaradeva of Assam and two other poets translated parts of the **Bhagavata**.

Influence of the Bengali Literature on Arakanese Literature : Asylum given to the king of Arakan in Bengal after he was driven out of his kingdom by the Burmese king, and his long stay of 26 years in Bengal as also Bengal's occupation of Chittagong led to the establishment of close contact with Bengal and Arakan, and in consequence Bengali literature flourished in that region and Bengali became virtually the cultural language of Arakan. Daulat Qazi was the earliest Bengali poet in the Arakanese court. He translated into Bengali some romantic stories current in various languages such as Hindi, Gujarati, Rajasthani etc. His poem **Sati Mayana** was completed by the great Sufi poet Alaol in the Arakanese court. Padmavati, the best work of Alaol was written on the request of Magan Thakur a friend of the foster son of the sister of Arakanese king. **Padmavati** was a romantic composition on the conquest of Chitor by Ala-ud-din who is said to have been infatuated by the beauty of Padmini. Nizami's Persian work Saiful-mulk-badiujjamal was rendered into Bengali verse by poet Alaol. Padmavati the best work of Alaol was written at the instance of Madan Thakur who wanted to have a rendering of Padmavati of Jayasi into Bengali. Alaol's book was not a translation but an abridged version to which Padmini episode has been incorporated. Other less famous Muslim poets also flourished in Bengal. They were Sabirid Khan author of Vidya Sundar Kavya, Saiyad Sultan of Chittagong, Muhammad Khan etc. Rajamala, a chronicle of the Tripura kings was the only historical work in Bengali during this period. Champakavijaya was the other historical work.

Assamese Literature : During the period under discussion Sankaradeva about whom reference has already been made, ushered in a new era in Assamese literature. His disciple Madhavadasa was an able follower of the trend set by his guru. His chief works include Bhakti-ratnavali, Nama-ghosa, Bara-gitas and Anikiya Nats (nine in number). One important feature of the Assamese literature of this period was that the works produced only dealt with the childhood and early life of Krishna but excluded the episode of the love of Radha and Krishna which formed the theme of the Vaishnava movement and Vaishnava literature in Bengal, Mithila, Braj, Gujarat, Rajasthan etc.

One of the important writers of the Vaishnava movement was Rama Saraswati who translated four cantos of the **Mahabharata** under the patronage of Naranarayan, king of Cooch Behar. He also translated some stories from the Puranas into Assamese in which the stories ended with the death of a hero or of a demon. These are known as **Vadha-**

Kavyas. Another author Gopal Chandra Dvija wrote in Assamese verses Lord Krishna's life story from **Vishnu Purana**, **Bhagavat Purana** ; and **Bhagavat Gita** were rendered into Assamese prose by Bhattadeva.

One important feature of the Assamese literature of the Mughal period was that the Assamese prose was influenced by the Sino-Tibetan speech of the Ahoms who wrote their history in Sino-Tibetan language. These historical writings are known as **Buranjis**. The Assamese Buranjis throw valuable light on the socio-political and economic condition of north-eastern India from the 17th to the 19th century.

Oriya Literature : During the Mughal period many writers in Oriya flourished who distinguished themselves by producing literary works based on Sanskrit literature. Oriya literature of the period echoed the spirit of the Sanskrit literature and mainly consisted of translation, adaptation from and imitation of the Puranas, the Ramayana etc. Sanskrit religious works as well as technical literature were thus made available in Oriya language. Works of outstanding merits based on the Puranas were produced by poets Madhusudana, Sadasiva, Bhima, Dhivara, Sisu Isvaradasa. On non-Puranic themes, such as love romances were the bases of the writings of the prolific Oriya writer Dhananjay Bhanja. Dina-Kushna Dasa was one of the greatest Oriya poets who was responsible for many works the most important of which is **Rasa-Kallola** dealing with the love of Radha and Krishna. Every line in this work begins with the letter 'K'. Brindavana Dasa's Gitagovinda adaptation in Oriya has retained the music in its original form. A few other distinguished works are **Ushavilasha** of Sisu Sankara Dasa, **Rahasyamanjari** of Devadurlava Dasa, **Rukminibibha** of Karttika Dasa. Among the distinguished poets, the names of Bhupati Pandita and Lokanatha Vidyadhara may be mentioned. Ramchandra Pattanayaka took the life of a common house holder and an ordinary peasant as the theme of his novel named **Haravali** in which the hero was an ordinary householder and heroine, daughter of a peasant.

Marathi Literature : The Marathi literature during the period under review was greatly indebted to three famous saints Santa Eknath, Santa Tukaram and Swami Ramdas. They "revolutionised the tone of religious writing, provided forms of artistic writing and set high standards of aesthetic expressions." Their contributions were as voluminous as varied. Their works inspired many Marathi writers and enriched the Marathi literature to an extent that the period is generally regarded as the most glorious in the literary history of Maharashtra.

The writers of the period were followers of **Bhakti** cult initiated by Jnanesvara and Namadeva but the literature of the period reveals an awareness of the socio-political as well as religious environment of the time. Janardan Swami, the guru of Ekanath illustrated in his personal life that worldly life and spiritual life were not antithetical but complementary. He served as the governor of a fort under the Muslim ruler and acquired fame as a statesman, but dedicated himself to religious pursuits as well. "Thus he demonstrated in that difficult age how the worldly life and the spiritual life can be reconciled to the advantage of the both, the individual and the Society." Works of Ekanath reveal his mastery of Bhagavata in the **Ekanathi-Bhagavata** which is a commentary of the eleventh canto of the **Bhagavata**. Next in importance is his **Bhavartha Ramayana** and **Rukmini Svayamvara**. He also composed hundreds of **abhangas**, **gavlanas bharudas**. Ekanathi-Bhagavata is a spiritual treatise while abhangas are narration of his spiritual experience. In Rukmini Svayamvara he dwelt on the philosophical theme of equating Jiva with Siva. He made the ideas of Vedanta popular through his works. The struggle between Rama and Ravana has been seen by him as the perennial conflict between the soul and the ego. He propagated the path of Bhakti which leads, as he believed, man to the service of the society. In this way he combined religion with social service. Ekanath's profound love for Marathi is revealed in his assertion : "My language Marathi, is worthy of expressing the highest sentiments, and is rich, laden with the fruits of divine knowledge." To him Marathi is as good as Sanskrit as a language to express oneself to God. Ekanath was a great saint as well as a great poet. Ekanath was the initiator of a literary movement in Maharashtra and according to tradition there was a group of five writers known as **Eknath-Panchaka**—Eknath, Rama Janardana, Jnani Janardana, Vitha Renukanandana, and Dasopanta. Dasopanta has left a rich legacy of 45 works comprising two hundred thousand verses in all. He also composed songs and verses in Kanada and Telegu languages as well. His dynamic thinking and profound scholarship in many philosophical and religious problems and his profound faith in religious and cultural tradition of Maharashtra are revealed in many of his works.

Vishnudasanama a senior contemporary of Ekanath produced the first Marathi version of the Mahabharata. **Budhbavani** and **Sukakhyana** are his two other important works. He is supposed to have hailed from Goa.

Sivakalyana, Mrityunjaya, Ranganatha Mogarekar, Tryambakaraj, Ramavallabhadasa, Mahalingadasa, Lolimbaraja were some of the many other poets that flourished during this period. Santalingappa was a Lingayat poet and made an exposition of the Lingayat sect in his poetical work **Karanahastaki**.

Shaikh Muhammad, Mutoji Vazir-ul-mulk, Hussain Ambar were Muslim Marathi authors. Mutoji Vazir-ul-mulk was also author of a Sanskrit treatise.

The literary movement of the period brought people of all castes and creeds of Maharashtra under its influence. The Christian missionary father Thomas Stephen found the Puranic form of the Marathi literature very helpful for the propagation of Christianity and his work **Khrista Purna** of 11,000 verses in chaste Marathi is still considered as a fascinating work in Marathi language. Likewise another priest father Croix composed **Peter-Purana** in which the author went out of his way to ridicule Hindu gods and goddesses.

Tukaram gave a more vigorous momentum to the Marathi literary movement. A Kunabi (Sudra ?) by caste, Tukaram began his life as a small merchant and married two wives—Rakhuma Bai and Jija Bai. He lost his first wife and his eldest son as also his business in the famine of 1619 when he was only twenty-one years old. What he lost in the wordly life, he sought to gain the spiritual world. He studied the works of Ekanath Jnanesvar, Namdev, Kabir etc. and is said to have received initiation from Guru Babaji in a dream and the mantra received by him was **'Rama, Krishna, Hari'**. His spitirual attainments and literary genius found expression in the abhangas composed by him. Scholars have computed his abhangas to be 4,500 in number. His accepted mission was to propagate religion, "to advance religion and to destroy atheism is my business"— he would say. Tukaram was forced into the spitirual world by his adversities, as such there is a touch of pessimism and melancholy in his teachings. His emphasis on a detached life was taken as total renunciation of worldly life and social obligation. But the political and social conditions of the period needed an activist philosophy rather than a negation of social responsibility. Swami Ramdasa for whom Tukaram had great reverence, propagated the need for a positive, activist role by the people.

Samartha Ramdas Swami (1608-1682) renounced the world at the age of 12 and practised autere penance for 12 years when he had the vision of Rama. He wandered for 12 years all over India visiting all holy places and during the course of his wandering, like Swami Vivekananda later, he was moved by the miserable conditions of the people and he decided to dedicate himself to the service of the people. He began to preach the cult of Dhanurdhari Rama and Balabhima, established **maths** in different places which became centres of religion, education and culture. He also popularised physical culture and training of the youth for military purposes. The most important work of Ramdas is **Dasabobha**. It is the outcome of the experience of the world by a person who attained the highest spiritual experience. It is a guide to all people for all time who desire happiness as also spiritual joy simultaneously. In his **Anandavana Bhuvana** he gives as inspiring vision of the state which is. the protector of the pius and destroyer of the wicked. His works deal with the conditions of the people, the evil nature of the Pseudo-saints etc. His works deal with the conditions of the people, the evil nature of the Pseudo-saints etc. His **Karunashtake** and **Manache Sloka** along with the **Ramayana** and **Ramavaradayini** are still regarded as the best in Marathi literature for properly moulding the minds of the young.

Tukaram and Swami Ramadasa were more concerned with the religious and ethical teaching. But there were other writers who paid greater attention to aesthetic value of literature in the tradition of Eknath.

Muktesvara, a grandson of Eknath, Vamana Pandit, Raghunath Pandit, Anandatanaya, Nagesa and Vithal Bidkar were poets who enriched the poetical literature of Maharashtra in the seventeenth century. Raghunath Pandit and Nagesa were contemporaries of Shivaji. These writers of long narrative poems adopted themes from the epics and the Puranas and followed the traditional techniques of classical Sanskrit. Gradually a new style and new themes were introduced by Sridhara and Krishnadayarnava. The scholar-poets of this period popularised narrative form of poetry.

Under the direction of Shivaji **Raja-Vyavahara-Kosha** which contained the useful political administrative terms, is even now considered to be a mine of useful information and source of coining new administrative and political terms. This period is also noted for the composition of Pavadas i.e. ballads in very exciting style on historical events. A few of the Pavadas have survived. One of such ballads by Agindas narrates Shivaji's encounter with Afzal Khan. The capture of Simhagarh by Tanaji is the theme of another ballad by Tulsidas.

Gujarati Literature : Bhakti cult founded by Chaitanya in Vrindavana had a deep influence on the Gujarati literature of the Mughal period. Miranbai (Mira Bai) and Narasimha Mehta were the two greatest Gujarati poets who were influenced by the Virndavan School of Bhakti Cult. "A pattern of poetic rapsody developed, imbibing its inspiration from the legacy of Sri Krishna's pastoral romance in the woodlands of Vrindavan and combining lyrical verse, musical symphony and a responsive dance, movement (rasa). The sweet strains of Sri Krishna's magic flute were heard time and again and the glimpses of his eternal rasalila repeated in the poetic composition of these two great bhaktas of Sri Krishna."

Mira Bai dedicated herself to Lord Krishna whom she fancied her bridegroom. Her earlier songs all addressed to Girdhar Gopal were composed in Rajasthani which is the parent of modern Gujarati, Mevadi and Marwadi. Her later songs were, however, in Braj-bhasha, the sweet language of love and devotion. Her songs breathed a rare "intensity of feeling and sensitiveness of emotion." In poetic-fervour, divine love and saintliness Mira's contribution is matchless in Vaishnav literature.

Narasimha Mehta who also lived in the 16th century ushered in a philosophical poetry and gave a fresh impetus to Bhakti cult. **Vaishnava jana to tene Kahiye** is the most welknown Bhajan composed by Narasimha and Mahatma Gandhi said, "That one song is enough to sustain me even if I were to forget the Bhagavad Gita."

Narasimha composed about 740 padas which are collected in Sringaramala. His large volume of poems is an elaborate exposition of rasa as depicted in the Bhagavata and collected in Rasasahasrapadi. Charm of language and rich diction are special features of his poems. He was the finest representative, besides Mira Bai, of Bhakti cult in Gujarat.

Along with religious literature secular literature such as popular fiction, stories in imitation of those Gunadya, the author of **Brihat Katha** in Prakrit, love, affairs of men and women, etc. attracted the attention of many authors. Bhakti cult which from its very nature was the privilege of the few and lost appeal and a reaction was noticed in the essentially Vedantic philosophy in the simple language of poet Akho or Akha Bhagats' works. He was popularly known as **Vedantakaviseromani** and was a seeker after ancient wisdom.

Premanand was a born poet and his work would alone make any language or age brilliant. He was the greatest medieval poet and was responsible for as many as 57 works. His works were mainly Akhyanas from Epics and the Puranas. He also wrote poems on the life of Narasimha Mehta. Samalbhatt, next to Premchand was the most notable poet of the period. He was gifted with a matchless style and wounderful power of story-telling. His works are a welcome escape from the morbid influences of his times and often dealt with stories on worldly wisdom.

The Jaina Sadhus of the period composed Charitas of their Tirthankaras, Chakravartins and Saints. Most notable Jaina writer of the 16th Century was Lavanya Samay who had 29 works to his credit. Nayasundara, a successor of Lavanya Samay was a versatile writer who acquired knowledge of Sanskrit, Prakrit, Hindi and Urdu literature, Rishavadas was another Jaina writer.

Hindi Literature : Hindi literature received a fresh vigour from the writings of Malik Muhammad Jayasi who flourished in the mid-sixteenth century. His Padmavat which was a fine philosophical epic and refers to the story of queen Padmini of Mewar "in an allegorical setting." The patronage extended by Akbar to Hindi poetry encouraged Hindi literature. Raja Birbar (Birbal) was a Hindu poet of repute and Akbar conferred on him the title of Kavi Priya. Raja Man Singh was a Hindi versifier, while Khan-i-Khanan Abdur Rahim, Narahari, Harinath, Ganj etc. were other Hindi writers.

The greatest Hindi writer of the period under review was Goswami Tulasidasa who was born in Gonda district of U.P. (1523). His **Ramacharitamanasa** (1574) is a Hindi masterpiece and considered to be "the Bible of the Hindu masses of North India." It relates the life story of Rama and propounds the philosophy of Bhakti cult. Its exquisite language, devotional spirit, poetic charm and popular and purely native Hindi with borrowings from Sanskrit words have made the work an immortal piece of Hindi literature. Tulasidasa was supporter of orthodox Brahmanical Hinduism and "his advent with this and other books did the greatest service in strengthening the Hindus of Northern India in their religion, their old ways, and their culture, which seemed to be overwhelmed in the floodtide of an aggressive Islam. "Among many other works of Tulasidasa **Vinaya-Patrika** is the most well-known and the best. Besides devotional spirit that permeates his writings, his belief in a personal God—Rama, his purely humanistic approach based on the knowledge of men and things gave his works a universality to mankind. He wrote in highly Sanskritised Awadhi.

Devotional poems dwelling on Krishna-lila was earlier produced by poets in Braja-bhasa, that is a Hindi dialect prevalent in the Braja i.e. to the Jumna valley. Bhakti-cult dwelling on the legends of Rama or Krishna was already highly developed due to the contributions of the writers in **Brajabhasa** who drew inspiration from Bhagavat Purana. Surdas, the blind poet of Agra, the follower of Vallabhacharya was the most famous of such devotional poets. His **Surasagar** dwelling on the life-story of Krishna in Braja-bhasa is a famous work. Nanddas, Vithal Nath, Kumbhan Das, Parmanand Das, Mira Bai who belonged to the same school were predecessors of Tulasidas. But as it has already been stated that the greatest exponent of the Ram cult was Tulasidas.

The Awadhi dialect of Hindi was greatly enriched by a number of Sufi writers who composed romantic tales of the folk lore type into beautiful allegorical poems by way of elucidating Sufi doctrines. Maulana Daud and Kutban, Manjhan, Malik Jayasi etc, belonged to this school. This tradition was continued in the 17th and the 18th centuries by a number of other Muslim poets like Usman, Shaikh Nabi, Kasim and Nur Muhammad. The latest writer in the line was Nazir Ahmad of Pratapgarh.

Kabir's tradition was continued by the mystic poet Dadu Dayal who was considered to be a later counter-part of Kabir and his works show a mixture of **Brajabhasa** and **Khari-boli** as we find in the writings of Kabir.

This period also saw the emergence of a rhetorical and artistic type of literature in lyrical verses. This type of literature was introduced by Kesavadasa. The poets of this school described the beauty of women, different types of women in love, married or unmarried, moods of lovers and sweethearts, various Ragas and Raginis, as well as the seasons. Their poems also dealt with **biraha** (separation) and **milan** (union) and various other sentiments of the lovers. Hindu, Muslim, Brahmans, low-castes, Rajput, Orissan, Dakhni, men and women composed on the above themes. Paintings depicting the above moods and sentiments were produced by artists of different schools of painting of Medieval India.

The Hindi literature of the 17th century was not characterised by any originality. It merely followed the old tradition of showing an under current of Rambhakti or Krishna-bhakti or Sufism. The lack of originality and decline in the standard of Hindi literature in the 17th century was to an extent due to the absence of the patronage of the imperial court under Aurangzeb. Mention may, however, be made of Biharilal, the court poet of Jay Singh, Raja of Amber who produced the famous **Satasai**—collection 700 verses. Bhusana was another author who distinguished himself by writing verses in praise of Shivaji in **Brajabhasa**. Works of Biharilal and Bhusana are noted for their melody, poetic imagery patriotic spirit. The last great Hindi poet during the period under discussion was Lal Kavi or Gorelal Purohit who composed **Chhatra-prakasa**, an epic biography of Chhatrasal the Raja of Bundelkhand.

Guru Govind Singh, the 10th and last Sikh Guru is included among the writers of Hindi for his auto-biographical poem **Bichitra-Natak** in old **apabhramsa** style of Hindi.

Hindi literature before the 18th century was wholly in verse and although Hindi prose such as Brajabhasa and Khari-boli (Delhi-Hindi) goes back to the 16th century modern Hindi prose did not appear earlier than the 18th century. In the 16th century Hindi prose style is to be seen in some sufi works and biographies by the Krishna-bhakti school.

Sanskrit Literature : Growth of Sanskrit literature was retarded due to the Muslim occupation of large areas of North India. Emperor Akbar tried to create an atmosphere of tolerance and Shah Jahan and Dara extended some patronage to Sanskrit scholars. But that atmosphere of peace and security that was needed for the progress of Sanskrit literature was generally speaking lacking during the Mughal period. Even Kashmir which was a reputed centre of Sanskrit learning and culture, hardly produced any Sanskrit work worth naming after the end of the Hindu rule. In Bengal also Jaydev was the last name in Sanskrit literary history. Gujarat, Bihar etc. which were important centres of Sanskrit culture did not produce any scholar of repute. It was only in Hindu states that Sanskrit literature continued to prosper.

In South India Sanskrit literature and learning prospered and the renaissance movement initiated by Madhavacharya and Savana continued for centuries to inspire both rulers and scholars to help in enriching the Sanskrit culture of the south. Vijayanagar empire continued to nourish Sanskrit language and literature even after the disaster of Talikota. The Nayakas of Tanjore, chiefs of Cochin and Travancore, Zamorin of Calicut not only patronised Sanskrit scholars, but many of them were themselves poets of repute.

Mahakavya, **Kavya**, **Drama**, **Slesha-kavya** (sarcastic poetry), **Historical Kavya**, **Champu Kavya**, lyrics and smaller poems in Sanskrit were produced in the south. In

Mahakavya Literature Raghunath Nayaka of Tanjore and his court poets made important contributions. Raghunath was not only a zealous patron of letters but a well-known poet himself. Among his works **Achyutarayabhyudaya** a biography of his father Achyutaraya, **Rukmini-Krishna-vivaha** deserve special mention. Madhuravani a poetess in Raghunath's court was a talented lady and produced a **Kavya** of 14 cantos on the Ramayana.

Srinivasa Dikshita, a minister of the Nayakas of Gingee was a prolific writer. He wrote eighteen dramas and sixty Kavyas. Nil Kantha Dikshita, son of Srinivasa Dikshit was a great Saiva scholar. His Sivalilarnava is a mahakavya of 22 cantos. His **Gangavatarana** is a story of Bhagirath and descent of Ganga on earth. Chakravarti was another contemporary poet of rupute.

Narayana was one of the greatest scholar-poets produced by Kerala. He was a friend of Mahadeva Zamorin, king of Kozhikode, and his works covered the fields of **Kavya** and **Mimansa**.

Slesha-Kavya with a device having double meaning or treble meanings of the same text was the works of Venkatadhvarin, Rajachuramoni Dikshit, Chidambash etc.

Achyuta Rayabhyudaya of Dindima, Rajanatha III is an important **historical Kavya**. Tirumalamba, was an accomplished lady who produced **historical Kavya**. Somanatha throws much light on the scholastic and cultural achievements of Vyasaraja the rajaguru of Krishnadevaraya. Jayarama Pande in his **Radhamadhavo-Vilasa Champu** gives an account of the poets who graced the court of Shahji, father of Shivaji. Shambhurajacharita of Bhanubhatta, Rajaram-charita of Kesava Pandit are historical Kavyas. Likewise Gangadhara wrote a Kavya dealing with the Bhonsle family. Bhuminatha wrote a Champu-kavya called Dharmavijaya-champu on the life of his patron Shahji son of Ekoji. Sridhara also wrote a work on Shahji's life. **Rajatarangini** of Kalhana, the famous history of Kashmir was continued by different authors in different periods, and the history of the Mughal period in Prajyabhatta's Rajavalipataka. Similarly history of Khandesh, of the ruler of Bikaner, praise of Dara Shukoh, Asaf Khan, achievements of Jahangir were preserved in Sanskrit historical Kavyas.

Reference to Champu-Kavya has already been made and Dindima, Chidambara, Tirumalaba etc. were authors of Champu-Kavya.

Geetagovinda of Jaydeva was the model on which many lyrics and small poems were composed during the period. Jagannatha Panditaraja was one of the greatest lyricists of the period. He was the court poet of the Rajputs, Mughals and the rulers of Kamrupa. Mention may be made of Duta-Kavya on the model of Kalidasa's Meghaduta, was produced during this period Subhagasandesa, Bhramarasandesa were such **Duta-kavyas**.

Mythological plays by Jagajyotimalla of Nepal, Madhava, Ramabhadra, Bhuminatha dealt with subject like the marriage of Hara-Gauri, Sita in Lanka, marriage of Subhadra and Arjuna were some of the many mythological plays produced during the period. Historical plays, allegorical plays as also erotic plays were also produced during the period.

Alankara, musical works, works on philosophy and epigraphical literature in Sanskrit were also written during the period under study.

Arabic Literature : Arabic literature during the Mughal period as in the pre-Mughal days, was mainly based on religious subjects such as the Quran, Hadith, Fiqh (jurisprudence), Grammar and Sufism. Purely literary writings in Arabic were very few. Almost the entire Arabic literature of the time comprised commentaries, supercommentaries, glossaries, and annotations of the Quran.

Study of Islamic theology received impetus due to visits of Indian Ulemas to centres of religious instructions in Hejaz. This was facilitated by the safe journey ensured by the Portuguese voyages between India and Arabia in the 16th century. This was further added to by the Knowledge the scholars acquired by occasionally visiting Mecca and Madina.

Akbar was not a follower of orthodox religious views, but there was no dearth of Ulemas and theological writings during his reign. Abdullah Sultanpuri and Shaikh Abdal Nabi were among the leading Ulemas of the time and Shaikh Sadullah Bani Israil of Lahore was a scholar of repute who translated **Bahr-i-Mawwaj** of Qadi Shahab al Din Daulatabadi into Arabic. Shah Fathullah Shirzi, Mir Sadr-al-Din, Mir Ghyath-al-Din Mansur and Mirza Jan Mir dealt with Islamic learning, logic and philosophy. The most outstanding author was, however, Abdul Haqq Dihlawi who was a prolific writer both in Persian and Arabic. His Arabic works of repute were commentary on Hadith, on science of biography, and a treatise on Hanafite Jurisprudence.

Akbar's court poet Faizi who was the greatest Persian poet was also an Arabic writer of amazing ability. His commentary **Sawati-al-Ilham** in two volumes shows his wonderful mastery over Arabic language. In rhetorical device, this book has been regarded by many scholars as a most outstanding work. Faizi's other works in Arabic also show a great intellectual and literary skill. Akbar's another court-poet Hakim Jilani wrote an Arabic commentary on Avicenna's al-Qanun as also many treatises on theology in Arabic language. Akbar's unorthodox religious policy produced Islamic reaction through the writings of the theological-scholars like Khwaja Baqibillah, Ahmad Sirhindi, and Shaikh Farid. Shaik Taj-al-Din Sambhali wrote several Arabic works in the reign of Jahangir. Mughal literary patronage and pursuits in Arabic reached it culminating point under Shah Jahan. Numerous scholars and theologians flourished under him but Mulla Abdul Hakim Sialkuti received special regard and patronage from the Emperor. Mulla Mahmud Jaunpuri was another outstanding scholar who worte many glossaries on classical works as also books on Philosophhy in Arabic. Shaikh Nur al-Haqq was a jurist, historian, worked all his life for the course of Hadith literature. Abdul Baqi and Abdur Rashid were two contemporary philosophical writers. A popular work on dialectics was written by Sayyid al-Shariff Ali bin Muhammad Jurjani. Muhbibullah Illahabadi was a Sufi of renown and wrote a commentary on the Quran from the Sufistic point of view.

The most enthusiastic of Mughal Emperor who patronised Islamic studies was Aurangzeb. **Fatwat-i-Alamgiri** a compendious six-volume on the Hanafi Law. Mulla Jiwan was another commentator of the Quranic verses. Mir Muhammad Zahid and Muhibbullah Bihari were two writers of philosophical treatises. Sayyid Ibn Masum was a writer on secular subjects. He was the author of several poetic compositions. He compiled a biographical dictionary of Arabic poets. During the Mughal period Gujarat was an important centre of Arabic studies. Through the ports of Surat and Cambay many scholars in Arabic travelled by sea to Hejaz for higher studies. Haji Dabir of Gujarat wrote a valuable history of Gujarat in Arabic. Likewise Al Din Abdul Qadir wrote a chronology of sixteenth century and also contemporary accounts in a lucid, simple style. Al Din Alwi wrote on various subjects of Islamic learning.

Muhammad Tahir of Pattan in Gujarat immortalised himself by his invaluable works on the Quran and Hadith, Jalal bin Muhammad al-Bukhari better known as Badr-i-Alam was leading traditionalist and divine during Jahangir's reign who wrote a commentary on the Hadith.

In Golconda, the Qutb Shahi Sultans were enthusiastic patrons of Arabic learning and literature. Muhammad Ali Karbalai, Muhazzim al-Din Damamini, Hakim Nizam al-Din Gilani etc. were the writers of renown in Arabic in Golconda during the period.

Persian Literature : The Mughals ushered in a glorious period of Persian literature and Persian is said to have enjoyed the status of Latin in central Asia. Babur had written his Tuzak i.e. memoir in Turki but he was an accomplished poet in Persian. He wrote a **Mathnavi** i.e. a didactic poem in Persian and there were quite a few Persian scholars, poets and writers among his followers, most notable among them were Farighi, Nadir Samarqandi, Atishi Qandhari and Tahir Khawandi.

Coming of the Persian intellectuals into India from Iran in the 16th and the 17th centuries was the most important contributory factor in the development of Indo-Persian literature. While Persian literature, particularly poetry declined in Persia the same thrived in India. Under Humayun a host of Persian poets migrated to India where the Mughal court offered them a congenial atmosphere for the expression of their talents. "The literary efforts of these immigrants coupled with similar efforts of indigenous litterateurs created in India an intellectual tradition which sometimes seemed to outshine that of Iran itself both in output and quality." India continued to remain the El-Dorado of Persian emigrants during the 16th and 17th centuries.

The summer days of the Persian literature in India were brought about by efforts of Akbar. Jahangir and Shah Jahan. A long and distinguished chain of poets both Indian and Iranian brought about a cultural synthesis which gave rise to the body of poetry called **Sabk-i-Hindi** which was a distinct Indian style of the Persian poetry. This poetry was characterised by the use of puns, chronograms, similies, satires and concepts. Humayun was fond of poetry as well as poets and himself composed verses of quality and wrote a Persian **diwan**. Shaikh Amanullah Panipati, Maulana Jalali, Mir Waisi, Damiri Bilgrami, Qasim Khan Mauji were poetic geniuses of the time of Humayun. Khwandamir wrote a general history **Habib al Siyar** and composed a versified history of Humayun. Qasim Kahi of Kabul who was the court poet of Humayun and Akbar was a poetic genius. Yusuf bin Muhammad wrote several Persian works when he was attached to Humayun's court. Jauhar Aftabchi Humayun's ewer-bearer wrote a memoir of Humayun. Gulbadan Begum, Humayun's sister wrote an intimate account of the reigns of Babur and Humayun. Bayazid Bayat wrote a useful history of the reign of Humayun and the early years of Akbar.

With the accession of Akbar to the throne in 1556, the era of an unprecedented blossoming of the Persian prose and poetry began. Akbar's liberal patronage to poets, writers, philosophers, historians, thinkers, theologians etc. led to a literary effloroscence unrivalled in the history of medieval India. Akbar's nobles also bestowed liberal patronage to writers and poets, scholars and historians of the time. According to Abul Fazl thousands of poets thronged the court of Emperor Akbar of whom at least fifty produced **diwans**. Ghizali Mahshhadi was the first poet-laureate of Akbar among whose many works were one **diwan** and an anthology of poems dedicated to Akbar. Faizi succeeded Ghizali as Akbar's poet-laureate who according to Badaoni and others was the author of hundred Persian works many of which have, however, not reached us. Abul Fazl mentions some of the principal works of Faizi, such as **diwan** entitled **Tabashir-al-Suba**. **Diwan** comprises, **qasidas**, **ghazals**, **tarkib-bands**, **targi-bands**, elegies, **qitas** and **rubias**. Faizi also wrote in Arabic. Abdur Rahim Khan-i-Khanan son of Bairam Khan besides having been a talented poet was a great patron of learning and men of letters. Jamal-ud-din Urfi Shiraji was the most famous of the writers that had enjoyed his patronage. Faizi's **Nal Damal** (Nal Damayanti) was written in imitation of **Laila Majnu** of Nizami. "Faizi was a true representative of a great age" and as Dr. Rida Zada Shafaq asserts, his reputation travelled beyond the confines of India and his reputation was very high in Ottoman Turkey and the popularity of the Persian literature in that country was due to his influence. Abdur Rahim Khani-i-Khanan was a veritable embodiment of erudition and culture during the reign of Akbar and Jahangir and was a large-hearted patron of a host of talented scholars, the brightest luminary among whom was Urfi Shiraji.

Mughal period was particularly noted for Persian prose literature which flourished in the historical works of the period. It was under Akbar that the practice of commissioning chroniclers for writing systemic dynastic history was introduced. Abul Fazl, the celebrated author of official history **Akbar-nama** and an encyclopaedic directory of the contemporary administration **Ain-i-Akbari**, was the Emperor's confidant and minister. His **Insha** was a collection of official despatches sent to foreign rulers and his **Ruqaat**, a collection of his own private letters. Abul Fazl's works are not only important from historical point of view but are of much importance from the point of literary interest. Selections from Abul Fazl's letters have always formed part of Persian syllabi at colleges and universities in India. **Tarikh-i-Alfi** a work by Mulla Ahmad Thattawi was compiled at the royal command and dealt with Akbar's religious views. Mulla Abdul Qadir Badauni's unofficial historical work **Muntakhab-al-Tawarikh** was an authentic, thorough, sincere and competent writing. **Tabakat-i-Akbari** by Nizam-ud-din Ahmad Bakshi is a work which serves as an important source book for the history of the period of Akbar. Faizi Shirhindi's **Tarik-i-Humayun-Shahi**, Shaikh Abdul Haq. Abdul Baq's **Ma' asir-i-Rahimi**, Dihlawi's **Tarikh-i-Haqqi**, are other minor historical works of the period. Shaikh Baqi was responsible for writing on theology and has to his credit the famous work **Akhbarul Akhyar**, containing, short biographies of all Sufi saints in India. Amir Fathulluh Shirazi, was another most distinguished scholar of Akbar's time whom Badauni called "the most learned man of his times."

Many Sanskrit works were translated into Persian under orders of Akbar. **Mahabharata** was translated in parts by different scholars and included in a work entitled **Razamnama**. Translation of the Ramayana by Badaoni, **Atharva Veda** by Haji Ibrahim Shirhindi, Hindu Mathematics **Lilavati** by Faizi, on Hindu Astronomy **Tazak** by Muhammad Khan Gujarati, **Bhagavat-Purana** by Todar Mal are some of the important translation literature of the time. Translation of Greek and Arabic works into Persian was also done during this period.

While in Northern India Persian literature flourished due to the liberal patronage of Akbar and his nobles, in the south the Persian literatures developed due to the encouragement of Adil Shahi rulers of Bijapur. The Adil Shahi period is particularly noted for the celebrated **Tarik-i-Firishta** written by Abul Qasim Firishta (Ferishta) during the reign of Ibrahim Adil Shah in 1611. Likewise Qutb Shahi rulers of Golconda were also liberal patrons of Persian literature. Tawarikh-i-Qutb-Shahi, Hada-iq-Al-Salatin, Burhan-i-Qati are a few of the numerous Persian works of the period.

Jahangir maintained his forefathers' tradition of munificent patronage of Persian literature. He himself wrote his autobiography Tuzuk-i-Jahangiri a work of great historical and literary merit. Mutamad Khan's **Iqbal Nama-i-Jahangiri** is an important source of history for the reign of Jahangir, **Ma-athir-Jahangiri** of Kamgar Khan, **Mawaiza-i-Jahangir** of Baqir Khan. **Akhlaq-i-Jahangiri** of Qazi Nuruddin Beg are other important historical writings of the time. Jahangir's court was adorned by a galaxy of learned men and poets such as Shikabi, Ghyas Beg, Hayati, Rasmi, Thanai, Naui, Nagib Khan, Niamatullah, the most noted among whom was Talib Amuli.

Shah Jahan was munificent towards the verisifiers "in the true manner of an Eastern monarch." Abu Talib Kalim, Shah Jahan's court poet composed his epic poem Padshah-nama. Kalim described India as a second paradise and "whoever quits the garden departs with regret." The greatest Persian poet of the time was Ali Saib of Tabriz who was the creator of a new style in Persian poetry. Ali Saib was attached to the court of Shah Jahan's noble Zafar Khan, Governor of Kashmir, and he left for his home at Ispahan but he recorded his indebtedness to India in a number of verses and compared his love for India as a lover's love for his lady-love. Some of the many other versifiers and lyricists of Shah Jahan's time were Qasim Khan Juwaini, Muhammad Hussain Sharqi, Shaida Akbarabadi, Hadhiq Fathepuri etc. Sufi writer Sarmad was noted for his mystic themes.

Historical works in Persian prose were **Padshanama** of Abdul Hamid Lahori, Amina-i-Qazwani and Muhammad Warith. All the three works of these three historian bore the same title. Md. Sadiq Isfahani an official of Bengal in Shah Jahan's time was a noted historian. His **Subh Sadiq** and **Shahid-Sadiq**, the former a detailed historical-cum-geographical work and the latter an encyclopaedic work were dedicated to Shah Jahan's son Prince Dara Shukoh. The Prince Dara Shukoh himself was an erudite scholar and an orthodox mystic of Qadiriyah order. **Yoga-Vasishtha**, **Bhagavat Gita** and **Upanishads** were got translated into Persian by him. His **Majmaul Bahrain** is a collection of correspondence between the Sufi and Hindu cosmologies. A biographical work on Khvaja Muin-ud-din Chisti entitled **Munis-al-Arwah** by Jahan Ara Begum was remarkable for its dignity and chaste scholarship. Lexciographical works like **Farhang-i-Jhangiri** and a revised version of preceding lexicon **The Farhang-i-Rashidi** were produced during the period.

The Persian poetry lost its place of honour in the imperial court due to the withdrawal of patronage by Aurangzeb. The Emperor's daughter Zibun Nisa was herself a gifted poetess and under the assumed name Makfi wrote poems, the **Diwan-i-Makfi** being the great monument of her poetic genius. Several historical works were produced during Aurangzeb's time, the best being Khafi Khan's **Muntakhab al-Lubab**. Muhammad Kazim's **Alamgir-nama**, Saqi Mustad Khan's **Mathnavi-i-Alamgiri** are two other important historical works. **Miratul Alam** of Bakhtawar Khan is a biographical account of the intelligentsia of the time.

Hindu scholar's contribution to the development of the Indo-Persian literature need more than a passing comment. In the reign of Akbar, Hindu scholars participated in the literary efforts of the time in full measure. Scholars like Kishujoshi, Gangadhar, Mahesa, Mahananda, Devi Misra, Madhusudan Misra, Bhavan and Chaturbhuja were engaged by Akbar to collaborate with Faizi, Abul Fazl, Badauni and Ibrahim Sarhindi and others in the programme of translation of Sanskrit works into Persian. Jahangir continued this patronage of translation of Sanskrit works into Persian. Some Hindu scholars also achieved literary greatness in Persian was Chandra Bhan whose poetic name was Brahman who enjoyed the patronage of Prince Dara Shukoh. Jaswant Rai Munshi, Bhupat Rai also known as Bhigam Vairagi were other Hindu scholars in Persian.

In epistolography the Hindu scholars surpassed the Muslim writers. Historiography which began with Abul Fazl's **Ain-i-Akbari** was further enriched by the works of Hindu chroniclers like Bhagwan Das, Rai Vrindaban, Munshi Sujan Rai. Hindu historiography began with Chandra Bhan's *Chahar-Chaman* was excelled by Bhagawan Das, **Shah Jahan-nama**, Vrindavan's **Lubb-ut-Tawarikh**, and Sujan Rai's **Kulasat-ut-Tawarikh**. Hiraman Lal, Narayan Kaul, Lakshmi Narayan Shafiq were minor Hindu chroniclers. According to Dr. S.M. Abdullah "at the end of the 18th century the contribution of Hindus to Persian literature was equal to that of their Muslim compatriots." Punjabi, Pushtu, Sindhi, Baluchi and Kashmiri languages were modelled on Persian tradition and these used Persian script. Influence of Persian language is felt largely on Urdu but in varying degrees on Rajasthani, Gujarati, Marathi, Bengali and Hindi as well.

Urdu Literature : The world Urdu is derived from the Turki Ordu which meant a military camp. This language, to speak the truth, did not come into existence during the period under review, but it was essentially a dialect current among the Muslim in the Deccan and South India from the fourteenth century and came to be known as Dakhni or the South Indian speech which was the literary language which emerged in the 15th century. It was employed in literature in the south by the Muslims who were not much influenced by local Hindu dialects, or languages of northern India. The script used was Perso-Arabian and the literature became more and more Muslim and Persian in spirit although "a good deal of its Indian vocabulary and Indian literary **catchets** and **cliches**" were retained till the end of the 17th century.

Gujarat, Bijapur, Aurangabad, Golconda and Bidar were the main centres of Dakhni literature. Sayyid Banda Nawaz Gesu-Dara was the most famous Sufi saint who was the oldest writer in this Muslim-Hindi tradition. He is said to have produced more than a hundred works. Shah Ali Muhammad and Shaikh Khub Muhammad were two great poets in **Dakhni** language in Gujarat.

Qutb Shahi Sultans of Golconda were liberal patrons of Dakhni literature. Qutb Shah was himself a gifted poet. His court poet Mulla Wajhi wrote a romantic poem **Qutub Mustari** on the theme of the Sultan's love while still a Prince, for a Telugu Hindu girl named Bhagmati. This girl was later married by the Sultan and built a city in her honour first called Bhag-nagar, then renamed Haider-Begum the Muslim name given to Bhagmati. This Haider-Begum later became the famous city of Hyderabad.

Sultan Adil Shah of Bijapur was a munificent patron of letters who wrote a book on music in Dakhni. Hasan Shawqi, Rustumi, Malik Khusnud were other poets. A Hindu Dakhni (Urdu) poet who was one of the greatest of the time wrote under a Muslim pen-name Nusrati.

Dakhni literature flourished upto the end of the 17th century but it decayed with the conquest of the south by Aurangzeb. In the 18th century **Dakhni** gave place to Urdu speech of Delhi, and Urdu became well-established by mid-eighteenth century.

Punjabi Literature : Although on written record of Punjabi literary works is found prior to the time of Guru Nanak (1469-1539), the founder of Sikhism, Punjabi language is however, much older and derived from Sauraseni apabhramsa and followed the same grammatical lines of Brajabhasa, Pahari and Rajasthani.

The earliest authentic record of Punjabi language and literature is the Sikh scripture—an anthology known as **Adi Granth** compiled by Guru Arjan Dev the fifth Sikh Guru in 1604. As scholar point out, the **Adi Granth** "is an unparalleled treasure house of northern-Indian medieval literature."

Adi Granth is the greatest work in Pubjabi, the sacred book of the Sikhs. The language of this work only in part is in pure or nearly pure Punjabi. The rest is in some variety of Hindi or combined Hindi-Marathi.

The hymns in the Adi Granth are arranged in accordance with the musical measures i.e. ragas in which the hymns are sung. The traditional medieval devotional lyrical poetry had been adopted by the Gurus.

Guru Arjan compiled the hymns of the first five Gurus in the **Adi Granth** (1604) as also the devotional compositions of many non-Sikh **bhagats.**

Besides the composition of the Sikh Gurus, highly poetical work on the principles of the Sikh faith was made by Bhai Gurdas. The thought, tradition and philosophy contained in the various forms of Hindi and Bengali in Northern India had been transferred to his won language by Bhai Gurdas.

A good deal of devotional poetry relating to Sikh faith grew in this period. Prose literature in Punjabi mainly are of two broad categories—biographies called **Janam-Sakhi** i.e. testament of birth of Guru Nanak, and exposition of the principles and texts of the Sikh faith.

Among other writers of Punjabi prose was the great martyr Bhai Mani Singh a direc disciple and school-mate of Guru Govind. His **Gian Ratnavali** contains Guru Nanak' life-story and other issues relating to his faith and spiritual life. The language used i Punjabi with an admixture of Hindi.

Many Muslim writers were responsible for a good deal of literary productions i Punjabi during the Mughal rule. Their works in Punjabi are known as **Qissas** i.e. tale Damoda Ghulati was a Hindu who was one of the earliest writers of Punjabi Qissa. Hi tale was the most popular story of the Punjab—the love episode of Hir and Ranjha. War

Shah was also a gifted poet whose Hir Ranjiha version is most popular. Another Punjab country-side romance is the story of the Muslim lovers Murza and Shahiban. Another version of the same story by Peelu is most popular, A Hindu poet Aggra composed the saga of Haqiqat Rai Sikh-Hindu martyr during the reign of Shah Jahan.

There were some folk Sufi poets in Punjab. Sufi poetry was very popular in Punjab for its appeal to the heart. Among the Sufis of this period Hafiz, Bankhudar Vajid, Ali Haidar, Shah Hussain and Bulhe Shah were particularly noted.

Kashmiri Literature : Except some doubtful specimens of stray verses, the composition of a fourteenth century poet Lalla Didi, nothing is practically known of the Kashmiri literature before the 15th century. Lalla Didi was a Sanyasini who wandered about singing her little mystic poems on Siva. Sir George Abraham Grierson edited and translated more than a hundred of her poems.

Next came the Muslim saint Shah Nur-ud-din, another mystic poet. It was under Zain-ul-Abidin the enlightened Sultan of Kashmir that a number of writers in Persian and Sanskrit flourished in Kashmir in the fifteenth century. But these works which were mostly biographical and panegyrical in nature are lost.

In the 16th century excellent lyrical poems of Human love and life were composed by Habba Khatun. She is one of the most popular poetesses and occupies a place of honour in Kashmiri literary world. Khwaja Habibullah Naushari, Hindu poet Sahib Kaul, and poetess Rupa-bhavani were other writers of the period.

Tamil Literature : The period under review was one that marked the decadence of the Tamil literature. The inroads of the Mughals in the south and the restrictive rule of the petty local chiefs gave rise to a stifling situation which was just not conducive to the production of creative literature. Scores of poets sedulously aped Sanskrit and classical Tamil models and courts of Tamil kings and Saiva Maths were the centres of such literary activities. But although the flame of literary activities burnt dim yet it was kept lit and was not allowed to go out altogether.

Varathungan Pandayan and Athivirarama Pandyan were two royal cousins who were Tamil poets of great renown of the Pandya Kingdom. Varathungan was a devout Saiva and his principal work reveals his great devotion of Lord Siva. Athivirarama's most successful poetical work is on the love story of Nala and Damayanti. The Saiva maths were the beehives of Tamil literary activity. Most of these works were religious, ethical or theological but several of them are of great value as poetry. Kumara Guruparar born of Saiva parents grew into an austere ascetic and produced a large number of Tamil works, the most important and popular two are **Needi Neri Vilakkam** and **Madurakkalambakam**. Sivaprakasar and Paranjoti, Viraraghava Mudaliar were other Saiva poets of repute.

There was also a Vaishnava poet named Pillaipherumal Iyengar, also called Divya Kavi Pillaipherumal who was not only a staunch Saiva but also a fanatical devotee of Ranganatha of Srirangam. Padikka Suppuluvar was another Tamil poet who was the court poet of a local king at Ramnad. Sixteenth and the seventeenth centuries were a period of decadence of Tamil literature in which verbose style and fluency kept in hiding the real poverty of literary thought and imagination. There was too much of superficial gloss but little trace of genius.

Telugu Literature : Early years of the sixteenth century constitutes a new era in the Telugu literature under the reign of Krishnadevaraya, Emperor of Vijayanagar. The hitherto prevalent features of the Telgu literature which were mainly translation, adaptation and imitation of classical Sanskrit models, particularly Sanskrit epics, yielded place to new elements neo-classicism and romanticism under Krishnadevaraya. **Prabandh** essentially of **Kavya** type now occupied eminence in Telugu literature. The courts of Krishnadevaraya and of the kings of Rajahmundry were adorned by poets who were held in high honour. Vijayanagar imperial court was adorned by **astadiggajahs**—the eight great court poets. Peddana was the best of the lot and was the author of **Manu Charita.** There were many other poets who flourished at that time among whom Dhurjati, Madayagari Mallana deserve special mention. Tenali Ramalinga and Pingali Surana were very popular Telugu poets of those times.

After the fall of the Vijayanagar empire in 1565 a decadence had set in the Telugu literature. But a few poets of renown flourished during the period. Early in the seventeenth century four of the Nellore Friends' Circle flourished whose works were of high quality and classical dignity, and acquired great popularity. Kankanti Paparaju author of **Uttara Ramayanamu**, Tikkana author of **Vishnumaya Vilasamu**, Tekaumalla Ranga Sayi composed Vanavilasa Vanamalika and Pushpagiri Timmakavi author of **Samira Kumara Vijayamu** and Ramamantri composer of **Dasavatara Charita** were poets worth the name.

Never before or after Telugu literature could claim so many royal poets as during this period. Malli Ananta, Kumarananta, Damera Ankabhupala, Bijjala Timmabhupala were poets and play-wrights of the period. Kavi Chaudappa a poet of the Sidhout court became very popular for his amatory and didactic fun and frolic. Elakuchi Venkata Krishanayya reputed by the title **Balasaraswati** was the court poet of Jataprolu and became a Mahamahopadhyaya i.e. a great scholar and a teacher. He was the author of many works out of which mention may be made of his great book a triple entendre named **Raghava Yadava Pandaviyamu** in which the stories of three epics, the Ramayana, the Bhagavata and the Mahabharata and the translation of three Satakas of Subhashita of Bhartrihari have been put together in Telugu.

Two historical naratives were also produced for the first time during this period. A work on grammar was also produced by the great grammarian Appakavi. Another phase of the Telugu literature in the 17th century was that Telugu literature was produced also in places outside Telugu country. Royal courts of Tanjore and Madura extended patronage to Telugu literature and poets and scholars coming from Telugu countries were welcome in these courts. This Telugu colonial literature unlike its decadent counterpart in Telugu countries, was noted for its vigour and freshness. Tanjore court patronised a number of Telugu poets and poetesses as also dramatic literature in Telugu. Tanjore court was also famous for musical composition of lyrical nature in Telugu.

Madura rivalled Tanjore as a centre of Telugu literature and Madura royal court encouraged the development of Telugu prose literatured and a new type of **Prabandha** called **Sringarh-Prabandha**.

A few works in Telugu were also produced in places like Mysore and Gingee during the 16th and the 17th centuries. The 17th century Telugu literature had its individuality no doubt was "on the whole a huge foliage with few flowers when compared with its counterpart in the 16th century."

Kannada Literature : From sixteenth to early eighteenth century Kannada literature was passing through a transitional period and literary works were mainly produced by the Virasaivas and Haridasas. Their works were of didactic and polemic nature. Poets of great eminence were, however, few the most prominent of them being Lakshmisa, Shadakshara, Ratnakara Varni and Sarvajna.

The Virasaivas were primarily concerned with Puranic themes. The Brahmana authors of the time were mostly concerned with the epics and the Puranas. Nityamasuka Yogi rendered the Mahabharata and Bhagavata into Kannada but the latter appears to be the work of several writers. Chikkadeva Raya of the Wodeyar family of Mysore is said to have composed **Binappa**, **Gita Gopala**, **Bhagavata** in Kannada prose. The Gita Gopala is an imitation Jaydev's **Gita Govinda**. Mallikarjuna wrote **Sriranga Mahatmya**.

Under the patronage of Chikkadeva Ray two women authors Sringaramma and Sanchi Honnamma flourished. Jaina author Chidananda was also patronised by Chikkadeva Raya.

Story of Kumara Rama by Nanjunda and Ganga was a semi-historical work. There were several such semi-historical works written during this period.

The Haridasas composed a large number of devotional songs. The Haridasas belonged mostly to Vaishnava and Madhva sects. The great poet Lakshmisa flourished during the last quarter of the 16th century. His **Jaimini Bharata** is considered to be a work of great worth and is highly popular. **Markandeya Purana**, the **Ramayana**, **Brahmottarakhanda** etc. were rendered into Kannada prose during this period.

There were many poets who composed **Satakas** or centuries of verses which contained didactic matters. Technical works either on arts or sciences were comparatively few. There were works on rhetoric and prosody, on grammar, on lexicography, astrology, prognostics etc. Mathematics also was the subject-matter of the works of Bhaskara, Timmarasa and Bala Vaidya. Bhaskara's **Behara Ganita**, Timmarasa's **Kshetra Ganita** and Bala Vaidya's Kannada **Lilavati** were good works on Mathematics.

Malayalam Literature : The period under review saw the emergence of a new type of devotional literature and the traditional Malayalam language and literature underwent a sort of metamorphosis. Thunchathu Ezhuthachan initiated this change and is regarded as the father of modern Malayalam. Two trends of development are noticeable in the Malayalam literature during this period one keeping close dependence on Sanskrit and another on Tamil. The earliest literary work in Malayalam prose was a commentary on Kautilya's **Arthasastra** during the 13th century. A poetical work and a Champu Kavya were also produced during that century.

But it was Thunchathu Ezhuthachan who flourished in the sixteenth century, breathed modernism in Malayalam language and literature and the literature of this period is primarily devotional literature for which the period itself is called **Bhakti-Yuga**. The first work of Ezhuthachan was a translation of **Adhyatma Ramayanam** from Sanskrit. What Tulsidas did for the North Indian language of the people, Ezhuthachan did for the Keralities. Devotional element blended with the Vedantic thoughts most artistically linked the story of Rama, opened a new chapter in the literary history of Malayalam. The next work of the author was the **Mahabharatam**. It is regarded as a classic written in modern Malayalam language.

Many other works of devotional nature were written by several authors during and after the 16th century but these were inferior to the works of Ezhuthachan. Puranas written in Malayalam during this period closely imitated his style. Melapattur Narayana Bhattatiri was a contemporary of Ezhuthachan and was the author of the immortal Sanskrit works **Bhakti-Kavya**, **Narayaniyam**. He stood as a living monument of Sanskrit erudition, and Sanskrit attained such a place of honour that its knowledge was counted as a symbol of scholarship not only during the contemporary period but for four centuries that followed. But the ascendancy of Sanskirt as the language of the scholars was challenged by Poontharam Nambudiri, author of **Jnanappana**, a philosophical work in simple Malayalam without using a single Sanskrit technical term.

In the 16th and the 17th centuries Champukavyas were composed. Punam Nambudiri, Mahishamangalam Nambudiri were the most noted Champu writers of the period. The Champu-Kavya's speciality was that it contained both Sanskrit and indigenous elements of poetry.

Attakkatha literature following the **Champu** style in using both Sanskrit and Malayalam. **Atta** in Malayalam means 'dance or drama' and Katha means 'story'— Attakkathas therefore are written for a type of dance-drama indigenous to Kerala, known as **Kathakali** which enjoys international reputation today. It is a dance-drama that represents a fusion of Aryan and Dravidian cultural elements. Bharata's Natya sastra had become by the time a hand-book of the traditional actors of Sanskrit dramas in Kerala temples. Interesting variations of dramas staged in temples developed. Dance-drama based on Jaydeva's Gitagovinda, and those based on the story of Lord Krishna and on a Sanskrit work called Krishnagiti were composed and staged within the temple precincts. Dance-drama based on **Krishnagiti** was known as **Krishnanattam**.

Raja of Kottarakkara was himself, a poet and wrote the story of **Ramayana** in Malayalam in imitation of Krishnagiti, and it came to be called **Ramanattam**. Ramanattam also paved the path for the development of the art of **Kathakali**. Another Prince Raja of Kottayam composed the story of **Mahabharata**, for same purpose. Unnayi Varyar is most popular even today as the writer of **Attakkatha** and he was not only the most prominent of the Kathakali writers but also among the classical poets of Kerala of the 18th century.

ARCHITECTURE AND PAINTING

Patronage of art and architecture by individual Mughal emperor has already been discussed while discussing their respective period of rule. A running summary of the entire period's activities in art and architecture will therefore suffice under this head.

Architecture : With the advent of the Mughals, Indo-Muslim architecture reached its fullness and unity specially under the patronage of Emperor Akbar. The Mughal emperors were by tradition lovers of nature and art, and as such they showed a marked interest in art and culture of the time in which their personality itself was reflected, so to say.

Babur and Humayun had uncertain times which did not conduce to the development of art and architecture. Babur had, however, a keen sense of perception of nature and art as we know from his memoirs, and even during the very short period of his rule consumed mostly by warfare, he did not fail to undertake certain ambitious building projects at Agra, Sikri, Gwalior, Dholpur, Kiul and Biana. In his memoirs there is reference to his employing 680 workmen daily working on his buildings at Agra while "1491 stone-cutters worked daily on my buildings at Arga, Sikri, Biana, Dholpur, Gwalior and Kiul." Considered from the number of workmen employed, the ambitiousness of the scheme of buildings may be imagined. It is difficult to determine the style and architectural features of his buildings as hardly any monument definitely attributable to Babur has survived today. About one mosque built within the Lodi Fort at Agra, Babur himself remarked that "it is not well done" and "it is in Hindustani fashion." Obviously, Indian architecture at that time had not acquired anything to commend to his inherent artistic taste. He was however, very much impressed by the workmanship and beauty of the palaces of Man Singh and Vikramjit within the Gwalior Fort.

Humayun was as aesthetically inclined as his father and in the early years of his reign undertook the building of a new city at Delhi which he named **Dinpanh** i.e. an asylum of the wise and intelligent persons. But it is doubtful in the city which was to consist of a magnificent place of seven storey with gardens, orchards etc. was ever completed, even if it were, the first Mughal city might have been destroyed during the Mughal-Afghan contest. The material records which have survived of both Babur and Humayun's contributions to art and architecture are negligible and only contribution they made was to leave behind them an aesthetic sense to be followed up by their successors in more favourable times.

Interruption of the Mughal rule by Sher Shah was also an interruption in the history of Mughal art and architecture but the intervention of the reign of Sher Shah was welcome chapter in the history of art and architecture and as Percy Brown remarks. Sher Shah was "a man of marked constructional propensities and architectural ideals." Few architectural illustrations of his reign are of exceptional character and clearly exemplifies his ideals of and attitude towards building art. In the history of Indo-Muslim architecture Sher Shah's buildings are important link between earlier Indo-Muslim style under the Delhi Sultanate and the later Indo-Muslim style under the Mughals. At Sasaram and in its neighbourhood there are five monuments, majority of which in all probability were built during Sher Shah's reign. Of these the Mausoleum of Sher Shah stands out prominently as the best, supreme in conception and extra-ordinary in architectural interest. Under Sher Shah a forceful architectural movement expressive of his versatile nature was initiated at the capital **Purana Quila** on the site of Indraprastha exhibited exceptionally elegant treatment at once of massive vigour and refined grace. Quila-i-Kuhna Masjid, Sher Shah's chapel royal, is the only surviving monument of his time and serves as a specimen of the qualities of the various buildings Sher Shah had erected.

It was from the time of Akbar that the Mughal architectural style as a distinctive tradition may be said to have begun. He undertook an elaborate programme of building projects in different parts of his empire and initiated and gave direction to a vigorous architectural activity.

The mausoleum of Humayun at Delhi is a landmark in the history of the art of building of the Mughals and it heralded the new movement in the architectural style. This mausoleum erected by Humayun's widow Humayun Haji Begam (Akbar's step-mother) during early years of Akbar's reign is one of the most striking monuments of Indo-Islamic architecture. Both the exterior and interior arrangements of the structure are equally pleasing. The white marble dome of the mausoleum shows new features in shape and new structural conception. Percy Brown in assessing the various elements contributing to the conception and execution of this noble mausoleum remarks that "perhaps the nearest definition of the architectural style of this monument is that it represents an Indian interpretation of a Persian conception, as while there is much in its structure that is indigenous, there is at the same time much that can only be of Persian inspiration." The tomb of Muhammad Ghaus at Gwalior is a nearly contemporary architectural work of the mausoleum of Humayun. This tomb has certain features characteristic of Gujarat and Malwa Muslim architecture.

It may be said, that during the early years of the Mughal rule several forces were at work which attempted a revivification of the moribund art of building of the previous epoch. Only a new, intelligent direction of the new forces was what was needed for a refined architectural movement.

Akbar, as we know from Abul Fazl, planned his splendid edifices and "dresses the work of his mind and heart in the garment of stone and clay." Akbar was a man of profound culture and of fine literary and aesthetic tastes as could be seen in his patronage of literature and initiation of ambitious architectural projects. Akbar's architectural projects differed from earlier architectural styles and instead of drawing on the Persian style he evolved an indigenous style only where the Indian conceptions and techniques were found wanting to give fullest expression to his own ideas. By using the Indian artistic and architectural skill and indigenous materials he gave architecture during his period an Indian character.

Of the buildings during Akbar's reign the fortresses occupied an important position. These were built to render protection to the timid "to frighten the rebellious and to please the obedient." "Delightful villas and imposing towers" as Abul Fazl observed were built to "afford excellent protection against cold and rain, provide for the comfort of the princesses of the harem, and are conductive to that dignity which are so necessary for worldly power." Saris, schools, places of worship were also built for utilitarian and cultural benefits of the subjects. Thus Akbar's building activities had political military, utilitarian and cultural objects in view.

The most noteworthy building projects of Akbar's early years of reign are the palace—fortressess of Agra and Lahore. Akbar's buildings at Agra occupied the southern angle of the fort and were linked with the parapet of the eastern wall over-looking the river Jumna. Most of these buildings have not survived. Among the few that have escaped ravages of time and destruction **Akbari Mahal** and **Jahangiri Mahal** are two important palaces. The former was completed in 1571 and the latter was presumably built for the heir apparent Jahangir towards the end of Akbar's reign. The fort at Lahore, the construction of which was started almost at the same time and at Allahabad two decades later were also carried out on a grand scale.

It may be pointed out that the place-fortress at Agra was built of fire-red hewn stones linked by iron rings and joints are so even and close that it is difficult to insert a hair in-between the two stones. The Akbari Mahal and Jahangiri Mahal in general, resemble Man Singh's palace-fortress at Gwalior built early in the 16th century. The palace-fortress at Allahabad is also a very elegant structure.

The most magnificent and ambitious architectural project of Akbar is the new capital built on the ridge at Sikri 26 miles west of Agra. This city was later named Fathpur-Sikri (city of victory) after Akbar's conquest of Gujarat in 1572. The conception of the new imperial headquarters is linked with circumstances connected with the birth of Salim, the later emperor Jahangir. Saint Shaikh Salim Chisti lived in Sikri who predicted the birth of a son to Akbar who would survive to succeed him as emperor. The queen was kept at Sikri where a magnificent place now stands, known as Rangmahal near the residence of the saint. There the queen gave birth in 1569 to a son, who was named Salim. This new capital city with its grand mosque, delightful palaces and pavilions, spacious official buildings and other edifices bears Akbar's magnificent achievement as a patron of the art of building. In Fathpur Sikri we have one of the finest groups of Mughal buildings, majority of which still survive. "Conceived and built as a single unit, the work was pushed on with such phenomenal speed that, as if by magic, palaces, public buildings, mosques, and tombs, gardens and baths, pavilions and water-courses were called into being beneath the sandstone ridge of Sikri." Jahangir in his memoirs writes "in the course of fourteen or fifteen years that hill full of wild beasts became a city containing all kinds of gardens and buildings lofty edifices and pleasant palaces attractive to the heart." Father Monserrate and Ralph Fitch praised the splendour and prosperity of the city. The latter described it as greater than the city of London with its teeming population and wealth of merchandise.

The monuments of Fathpur Sikri fall under two distinct categories, religious and secular. The most splendourous creation of this new capital is the grand **Jami Masjid**. Fergusson has called it the glory of Fathpur Sikri, Hardly surpassed by any in India. It served as the model for great congregational mosques usually associated with the chief cities of the Mughal empire. Jami Masjid was conceived as a balanced and harmonious composition.

The city of Fathpur Sikri occupies a rectangular area enclosed by bastion walls running round its three sides, one side being protected by the lake. The wall was of little military value compared to the solid and massive walls of Agra or the Lahore fort. "Nine gate-ways" are there "in the fortress wall" the Agra gate being the principal entrance to the city. Each gateway was built in such a fashion as to accommodate a large number of troops. From the Agra gate the road leads to **Diwan-i-Am** and further to **Jami Masjid**. The southern entrance to the Jami Masjid where the original entrance was replaced by the construction of a massive portal known as **Buland Darwaza** with its immense bulk towering above the buildings of the city represents one of the most striking compositions ever known. This gateway served a double purpose of a triumph arch and an imposing gateway to a grand mosque Jami Masjid. Buland Darwaza represents a perfect co-ordination of structural and ornamental aspects of architectural art.

Two additions made within the mosque enclosure were the tomb of Shaikh Salim Chisti the patron Saint of Sikri. It is a small but very attractive building of marble, erected in 1571 by Nawab Qutb-ud-din Khan with its delicate ornamental work has a soft effiminate grace. It stands in definite contrast to the robusi style of Akbari architecture. Close to the saint's tomb stands the mausoleum of Islam Khan, grandson of the saint, built of red sand-stone. But this building retains Akbari style.

The secular buildings within the Fathpur Sikri are by far the most numerous. There were palaces, offices, private residences, Daftar Khana on the office, **Diwan-i-khas**, the audience hall, Jodha Bai's palace, Raja Birbal's palace were secular buildings. The secular buildings had some markedly Hindu and Jaina features and obviously copied from the Hindu and Jaina styles of architecture. **Panch Mahal** in Fathpur Sikri has been described by art critics as a "fantastic creation." It consists of a tall pyramidal structure of five storeys each designed as an open pavilion supported by pillars of excellent design.

Jahangir's reign served as a period of transition insofar as the art of building was concerned, from the phase of Akbar's time to that of Shah Jahan. The tendency towards decorative and ornamental architecture at the cost of grandeur and boldness of conception is discernible from the time of Jahangir. Akbar's genius for constructive ideas and conceiving architectural projects was now giving place to use of costly materials to clothe creative ideas of the past. There was little creativeness and intellectuality in structural designs, more of lavish use of costly materials to create a sumptuous decorative effect.

The most important transition was the substitution of red-sand stone by white marble. In Akbar's buildings marble was used in order to lend relief and colour contrast to red-sand stone. This gave a most charming feature in the ornamentation of the surfaces of the buildings. But this sense of value and beauty of contrast of colour and ornamentation were undermined in the subsequent period when the buildings were made of white marble only. This transition took place towards the end of the reign of Jahangir. It goes without saying that marble has some what effeminate quality and beauty and lacks the boldness, solidity and strength imparted by red-sand stone.

Jahangir was fond of colour and this was imparted to his buildings. The system of **pietra dura** i.e. the inlaid mosaic work of hard and precious stones of various hues and shades which gave colourful and picturesque effect to the buildings was introduced. Jahangir completed Akbar's tomb at Sikandara near Agra, the foundation of which was laid by Akbar himself. Although completed by Jahangir its conception, its layout etc. were of Akbar. Jahangir's own tomb at Shahdara near Lahore was more or less built on the same lines at Akbar's tomb.

It may be pointed out that Jahangir did not leave any personal impression on the architecture of his time. His palace at Lahore in which he lived during most of his life has nothing distinctive from architectural point of view. **Shalimar Bagh** in Kashmir is one of the most charming of Jahangir's undertakings.

Two tombs built towards the end of the reign of Jahangir are rather successful achievements from the points of view of design as well as execution. One is the tomb of Itimad-ud-daula, father of Jahangir's famous consort Nur Jahan and the other is the tomb of Abdur Rahim Khan-i-Khanan at Delhi. Itimad-ud-daula's tomb is significant in the Mughal architectural history for it is the link between the two important phases of architecture namely of Akbar and Shah Jahan. Itimad-ud-daula's tomb is the first notable building made of white marble with rich ornamentation in **pietra dura** which reached culmination under Shah Jahan.

The tomb of Abur-Rahim supplies the link between Humayun's tomb at Delhi and Raj Mahal built by Shah Jahan. It is, however, worthwhile to mention that during the reign of Jahangir Akbari style of architecture lost its substance and vigour.

Shah Jahan occupies a high place in the history of Mughal building art and his extraordinarily liberal patronage of this art. The Mughal architecture during Shah Jahan's reign showed two distinct departure from the Akbari style. Shah Jahan's predilection for marble is graphically illustrated by the replacements of the earlier sand-stone buildings of Akbar at Agra which a court panegyrist author of **Badshah-nama** described as "barbaric abomination" by marble palaces pavilions which were praised as masterpieces of the "august reign" of Shah Jahan "when lovely things reached the zenith of perfection."

Architecture during Shah Jahan's reign had three special features, (i) the extensive use of white marble instead of red sand-stone. Marble of a pure white texture and delicate grains was procured from the quarries of Makrana in Jodhpur. The costly fabric required costly decoration and **pietra dura** i.e. gilding and mosaic of precious stones which constituted a special feature of Shah Jahan's buildings. Tendency to lavish display of pomp an ornamentation give ample expression to the exaggerated sense of luxury and magnificence of Shah Jahan's court. Although not endowed with that originality and nobility of imagination which his grandfather Akbar possessed, Shah Jahan was doubtlessly a great builder. He not only replaced the sandstone buildings at Agra and Lahore forts, by marble palaces and pavilions but he projected a new capital city at Delhi, that of Shahjahanabad where he built a fortress of unusual dimension and erected splendid palaces, administrative buildings and other structures. Both at Agra and Delhi he built two grand congregational mosques. At Agra he built his far-formed "dream in marble", the mausoleum, Taj Mahal to enshrine the mortal remains of his beloved consort Arjumand Banu Begam better known as Mumtaj Mahal. Under Shah Jahan, Mughal architecture produced a plentiful crop, but beneath this plenty was hidden the forces of degeneration. Efforts were made to build pretty structures, ornamented and refined in appearence rather than to make new experiments in structural conception or in design. Eulogy of panegyrists does not apply to all the buildings of the time of Shah Jahan although a few are not of mean artistic beauty.

At Lahore fort Shah Jahan's buildings consist of the **Diwan-i-Am**, a hall with forty pillars, the Musamman Burz, the **Khwabagh**, the **Shish Mahal** and few other buildings. Emphasis was laid on the **pietra dura**. The buildings of Shah Jahan at Delhi and Lahore originally appeared to be of the same style and character. Remodelling of former buildings was undertaken on an extensive scale at Agra fort and no where is the contrast between Akbar's style of architecture and that of Shah Jahan is so pronounced, "The former noble and robust and the latter, elegant and, to a certain extent, feeble." The Diwan-i-Am in Agra fort as well as Delhi fort are of red sand stone and because of the use of the red-sand stone some scholars ascribe these to Akbar-Jahangir period, "it is definitely known to have been" the work of Shah Jahan most possibly at the earliest period of his architectural undertakings when marble was yet to become the sole material for the purpose.

Behind the **Diwan-i-Am** stood the **Diwan-i-Khas** and in between was the **Machchhi Bhavan**. Diwan-i-Khas (1636-37) is entirely built of marble. Close to the south is situated the building called **Khas Mahal** with a spacious court of **Anguri Bagh** (grape-garden) in the front. According to Abdul Hamid Lahauri, author of Padshah-nama, the ceiling of the building was originally inlaid with patterns in gold and colour, traces of which are still discernible. In the north-east corner of the court stands **Shish Mahal** (palace of mirror) with two chambers with arrangements for bath.

A little apart from the group of buildings described above is situated the **Moti Masjid** (Pearl mosque) which according to Fergusson is "one of the purest and most elegant buildings of its class to be found anywhere." Moti Masjid of Agra has a remarkably restrained grandeur which stands in sharp contrast to the floral beauty of other buildings of Shah Jahan.

In 1638 Shah Jahan started construction of Shahjahanabad at Delhi. The city is on the right bank of the Jumna. With a grand palace and a congregational mosque called **Jami Masjid** the city is a splendid architectural work of a splendid of the Mughal emperors. The palace fortress, the **Red Fort** as it is called because of the red-sand stone fabric of its rampart walls was designed on a massive scale with all amenities of a luxurious life of an imperial house and court. It has two main gateways, one in the middle of the western wall and the other in the south.

Two buildings, the Diwan-i-Am and Rang Mahal give us an idea of the grandeur and brilliance of conception of these two palaces. Diwan-i-khas, the private audience hall, was an indispensable part of the Mughal court etiquette and court life. The Rang Mahal was the palace of pleasure used by the emperor after a busy and tiring day's work. The Diwan-i-Khas is built entirely of white marble and every available space in the facade is wrought in brilliant colour, lusturous gold and costly **pietra dura** which have now disappeared due to pilferage. Fergusson thinks that "if not the most beautiful, certainly the most highly ornamented of all Shah Jahan's buildings" Rang Mahal is also one of the most sumptuous conceptions of Shah Jahan's architectural undertakings.

Jami Masjid at Delhi is the largest and the most well-known mosque in whole of India. It forms the essential element of Shahjahanabad.

The other important building is the Diwan-i-Am i.e. the public audience hall which was also designed in a stately manner. It is built of sand-stone but was originally shell-plastered which gave it a white look to fit in with the white marble structures that stand around. It is a colonnaded hall open on three sides covered only at the rear and the facade consists of nine foliated arches rising from double columns. It has a canopied platform of white marble richly inlaid with precious stones. The magnificence of this throne platform known as **Nashihman-i-Zill-i-Ilahi** (seat of the shadow of God) is an excellent example of the splendour and pageantry of the grand Mughals at the time of their supreme briliance. The **pietra dura work** is attributed to one Austin de Bordeaux.

Arrangements for constant supply of water from the Jumna, seventy miles up the river, brought to the fortress by the canal of Ali Mardan and brought into the palace through an artificially scalloped marble cascade placed near Shah Burz was a rare feat of hydro-engineering.

Before concluding Shah Jahan's works of building it is worthwhile to write a few words about the grand mausoleum the Taj which with its luminous beauty and picturesque setting has been attracting millions of enamoured visitors from different parts of the world far and near. With its milk-white beauty the Taj has its beauty of texture and lineaments that leaves an abiding impression on the mind of the visitor. This grand mausoleum to enshrine the mortal remains of his beloved consort Mumtaj Mahal took many years from 1631 to 1653 to complete and entailed an expenditure of four and half million pound sterlings and continued labour of twenty thousand men and artisans.

The chief craftsman who gave shape to this noble mausoleum was **Ustad Isa** who lived in Agra at that time and historians have found father Manrique's statement that the model of the mausoleum was prepared by Geronimo Verronea, a Venetian resident of Agra to be incorrect. Dr. Smith's statement that the Taj, is the product of "European and Asiatic genius is not borned out by scrutiny of the style and structural design and techniques of the Taj. In fact, it is the culmination of the architectural style and trend noticeable in the tombs of Humayun and Abdur Rahim Khan-i-Khanan. The writer of the inscriptions of the wall surface Amanat Khan Shirazi came from Qandahar while architect of the dome Ismail Khan Rumi came from Constantinople. According to modern historians the craftsmen from Kanauj and Multan and not the French jeweller Austin de Bordeaux did the work of the **petra dura**. The garden was planned by Ranmal, a Kashmiri garden-planner. Taj, it must be said in conclusion, does not show any European intervention and is entirely Indian in look and in style and technique. Its flawless execution, its ornamentation and its picturesque setting, its luminous beauty and purity of lineaments make it a rare product of ingenuity of man.

Yet critics have seen in it an effeminacy and an inherent weakness of strength and "lack of variety in its architectural forms." Aldous Huxley finds in it a "poverty of imagination" when the monuments is viewed more closely. "The Taj is not so much a triumph of architecture as of splendid decorative setting, and to this the monument owes much of its charm and beauty."

Aurangzeb's accession marks the end of the rich tradition in the building art of the Mughals and the beginning of a period of decline. His reign saw a rapid dissolution of the Mughal architectural style.

Under Aurangzeb, the Mughal empire reached a dizzy height and symptoms of disintegration became visible in his life time and the inevitable crash was not long to come. Naturally enough, when the empire was reaching to its tollering height, forces of decline were already at play although unnoticed. Such circumstances are not conducive to cultural activities. Cultural activities in all forms, architecture not excluded, naturally began to languish. Added to this political reason was the personal puritanic character of Aurangzeb himself. Aurangzeb's intolerance of other religions precluded his extending that aesthetic patronage to Hindu and other non-Muslims which is essential for development of art and culture. While both Jahangir and Shah Jahan recognised the technical skill and efficiency of indigenous artists and craftsmen and utilised their services, Aurangzeb stopped this and the indigenous style and technique were nipped at the roots. When the indigenous source dried up the architectural art was rapidly disintegrated. The economic pressure due to military undertakings of Aurangzeb's reign was also unhelpful to the building art of the reign. Productions of Aurangzeb's time are therefore few and definitely of an inferior quality. Two mosques, namely the Moti-Masjid inside the Delhi fort built for Aurangzeb's personal prayers and Jami masjid at Lahore built by Fidai Khan Kuka a provincial officer, deserve mention. The Moti Masjid is a small but graceful structure of marble of most polished variety. The Jami Masjid also known as Badshahi Masjid is an imposing and vigorous compostition. It is built of red-sand stone with three white marble dome. These mosques although bear some semblance of former achievements due to their orthodox character, reveal undoubtedly the symptoms of approaching decline. The tomb of Aurangzeb's queen Rabi-a-ud-Daurani at Aurangabad is a pathetic illustration of the deteriorated Mughal architectural style under Aurangzeb. According to Fergusson it "narrowly escapes vulgarity and bad taste." With the death of Aurangzeb (1707) the grand empire vanished and with it collapsed the Mughal architectural style. The Mughal architectural style was long dead when the last of the dynasty of the Great Mughals was bereft of his titular sovereignty.

MUGHAL PAINTING

Mughal painting represnts one of the most important phases of Indian art of painting. The imperial Mughals introduced a new concept in Indian art. In conception and execution Mughal miniatures show something never seen in India before, and their impact could be noticed throughout the Deccan. Rajasthan, the Punjab Hills and northern India even when the grand Mughals had vanished.

The Mughal art of painting was the product of combination of Hindu and Persian ideas. The Persian painting had been influenced by the Mongols who after conquering Persia introduced there the Chinese art of painting which was the product of Indian Buddhist, Bacterian, Iranian and Mongolian influences. In Persia eventually the Mongolian and Chinese styles of art vanished leaving the field to Indian and Persian styles in which colour predominated.

The Mughal painting adopted the materialistic aspects of the court life such a hunting scenes, elephant fight, royal procession, durbar scene etc. The contemporary Hindu artists, however, depicted scenes from Indian classics, lofty thoughts about life and motherland and its creeds.

Foundation of Mughal painting was laid by Humayun who inherited his father's love of Nature and beauty. While at Persia he secured the services of two of Persia's greatest master artists, Mir Sayyid Ali and Abdus Samad who could not receive Shah of Persia Shah Tahmasp's patronage due to his lack of interest in art because of his religious bigotry. These two artists were persuaded by Humayun to join his court at Kabul before his recovery of Delhi. Young Akbar received lessons in painting from them. Both these master artists followed Humayun to Delhi. Humayun had also recruited a large number of talented artists from different parts of the country and his court became soon the centre for fine and sophisticated productions. The most important work of art produced by the Mughal studio is known as **Hamzanama** which consisted of nearly 1200 paintings drawn in bold and vivid colours. Unfortunately a small fragment of this massive work of art has survived which is now included in the collections in Europe and America. There is a controversy among the historians about the emperor who actually had initiated the work. According to Badauni and Shahnawaz Khan it was Akbar who initiated it, but according to others it was Humayun. Modern historians are of opinion that it must have been initiated by Akbar and completed by 1575-76 A.D.

Till 1562 we notice the influence of the Persian art predominant on the Mughal art of painting. But from that we notice a marked change which showed itself in the fusion of Persian and Indian (Hindu) styles and techniques of painting. The first product of this combination was the painting depicting the arrival of the famous musician Tansen in Akbar's court (1562).

With Akbar's increasing interest in diverse religions and his insatiable desire to go into the depth of these religions led to the production of sumptuous manuscripts, original and translations but also many illustrations painted by the painters of the imperial atelier. Abul Fazl mentions the names of fifteen painters both Hindu and Muslims, such as Daswant, Basawan, Kesav, Lal Mukund, Mishkin, Farrukh, Madhu, Jagan, Mahes, Khem Karan, Tara, Sanwala, Haribans and Ram. These painters were recruited from various centres of Indian art such as Gujarat, Gwalior, Kashmir, Lahore, Rajasthan and eastern Uttar Pradesh. According to Abul Fazl Daswant was the 'first master' of the age and "did not trail behind those of Bihzad and the painters of China." The only manuscript in which the painting of this celebrated painters can be seen in **Razmnama** now preserved in the Museum of Maharaja Sawai Man Singh II of Jaipur. Farrukh also assisted in illustrating this manuscript. Lal, Tulsi, Mishkin were also responsible for some five paintings during the reign of Akbar. Baswan's painting of Majnun on an emaciated horse now preserved in Calcutta Museum, is a masterpiece.

According to Abul Fazl more than a hundred painters became famous during Akbar's time out of whom a number had attained perfection. Akbar took personal interest in the work of the artists providing them with every facility including costly materials needed for painting. He would reward the works which would be of excellent workmanship. The painters working in Fathpur Sikri were conferred military rank of **mansabdars** or **ahadis**.

The paintings of the artists of the imperial atelier have been preserved in various museums all over India, Asia and Europe : for instance, Fogg Museum of Cambridge, Bodelian Library of Oxford, Watters Gallery of Baltimore, Albert Museum of London, British Museum, London, Imperial Library at Tehran and various Indian Libraries and Museums. Some of the finest paintings of the last decades of the 16th century to be found in **Akbarnama** are preserved in fragments in the Victoria and Albert Museum, London.

Under Jahangir the art of painting received a new turn and a fresh life and trend had been infused in the style of Mughal painting. Even before his accession to the throne Prince Salim set up a new studio under an emigre Harati painter Aqa Riza, which worked in full swing at Agra even when Salim was in rebellion against his father. The paintings of the period, i.e. before Salim's accession of Jahangir contained in manuscripts of Raj Kumar, collection of **Ghazls** and **Rubais** by Hasan Dihlvi in those of **Anwar-i-Suhaili** by Aqa Riza are now preserved in foreign libraries and museums.

The trend begun in his Princely days reached its culmination during the reign of Jahangir as emperor and freed the painting from its bond with the text of manuscripts. Jahangir wanted his master painters to specialise in different branches of the art so that they might paint pictures of persons or groups or themes selected by the Emperor himself.

Initially he instructed his artists to illustrate certain interesting parts of the manuscripts kept in the imperial archives. Later he got interested in portraits and had a large number portraits of the numbers of the royal family, dignitaries of the imperial court, men of religion, and persons important in the fields of literature and music etc. It may be pointed out, that portrait painting was practised in Akbar's time also.

In some paintings preserved in Jahangir's albums the names of the persons were noted by Jahangir himself and certain cases names of the painters, the dates of the works are also to be found. Artists Manohar, Nanha and Farrukh Beg were at first entrusted with the work of painting, but later Manohar, Abul Hasan and Bishndas were engaged to paint the portraits. Their style and technique were copied later during the reigns of Shah Jahan and Aurangzeb.

From the time of Akbar the Mughal painting began to feel the impact of European painting. Jahangir while a Prince began to appreciate the European paintings and engravings of Christian subjects and some of the Mughal artists began to copy designs and details of works from them. Baswan and Abul Hasan's works clearly show influence of European art.

Jahangir was keen on preserving the record of the important events of his reign in paintings. Records of his coronation, important festivals, assemblies, rare birds, animals, holi festival, birthday weighing etc. in painting were prepared by the artists during his reign.

In the next stage of development the Mughal painters introduced occasional European scenes and figures in their work. They used with enough efficiency the technique of light and shade, modelling and perspective.

Although Shah Jahan was interested in good miniatures and illustrated manuscripts, the glamour and refinement of Mughal painting were lost after Jahangir's time. At the early stage of his reign the artists were allowed to work as was usual under the reign of Jahangir, but soon he reduced the number of the painters and only one Persian artist was in his employ. Deprived of royal patronage the artists would sell their work to earn their livelihood. The result was that the artists lost their status of dignity and were relegated the position of artisans.

Shah Jahan, however, loved himself to be portrayed as a universal monarch under divine care—the angels carrying the crown for him. Standing or sitting on his peacock throne in the best of attire or on horse back etc. were the portraits that he loved to be painted of himself.

Decay of the art of painting under Shah Jahan was also noticeable in the use of loud and extravagant colours in place of harmonious blend of colours and the freshness and vigour of the paintings of the period of Jahangir. Dara Shukoh was, however, patron of master painters who under his patronage produced exquisite portraits of young princes and beautiful maidens.

Although a decadence had set in, the portrait painting in general was practised more abundantly under Shah Jahan. Muhammad Nadir Samar-qandis' works were abundant and had fine draftsmanship and a feminine touch.

The process of decline was hastened by Aurangzeb by his bigotry and hatred against art of painting. Towards the end of his rule he might have developed some interest in painting for a number of good quality miniatures, showing the Emperor engaged in hunting, in court, in war, were produced. The art of painting which did not receive royal patronage naturally shifted from the imperial capital to regional centres.

During the sixteenth and seventeenth centuries and particularly from the time of Aurangzeb the art of painting developed in centres like Mewar, Amber, Bikaner, Bundi etc. in Rajasthan, in Golconda, Bijapur, Ahmadnagar in the Deccan. As many Rajput rulers served under the Mughals and spent much of their time in the Mughal court, they naturally were influenced by whatever development that had taken place there. The impact of this Mughal influence was also noticeable on the Rajasthani art of painting and the paintings of the 16th and the 17th centuries of Rajasthan betrays a close knowledge of Mughal art of painting within the broader Rajasthani frame-work.

In the Deccan the style and technique of painting had been very refined and sophisticated. Brilliant colour scheme, rich decorative details differ considerably from the Mughal art. Musical painting, that is, depiction of **ragas** and **raginis** in painting prepared in Bijapur is unique in history of Indian art. **Hindola Raga** painted in Bijapur in the 16th century, now preserved in the National Museum, New Delhi is the finest example of musical painting. A set of ten exquisite pieces of such work, show indebtedness to Mughal painting. The enchanting figure of an unknown lady, sometimes identified as the Queen of Sheba prepared at Bijapur is another piece of rare artistic product.

The peacock throne of Shah Jahan referred to before was a masterpiece of art of gold and silver smithy and finest jewellery.

REFERENCES

The Mughal Empire, Vol. VII : Bharatiya Vidya Bhavan
The Mughal Empire : A. L. Srivastava
The Agrarian System of Bengal : A. C. Banerjee
Studies in Economic Life in Mughal India : J. N. Sarkar

15

Impact of Islam

SUFISM

Sufi or Sufism is derived from **Suf** which means undyed garments of wool worn as a mark of personal penitence and poverty. The Sufis originally drew their ideas from certain verses of the **Quran** and **Hadith** i.e. traditions of the prophet. Their difference with orthodox Muslims lay in the fact that while the latter interpreted the Quran and Hadith in a literal way, the Sufis gave a mystic interpretation to them.

Sufism flourished in Persia where from the Sufi saints had fled to Kabul due to Safavi persecution. It may be recalled that Akbar's mother who was the daughter of a Persian scholar and was influenced by Sufism sowed the seeds of toleration in the mind of her son Akbar. His early life in Kabul also brought him in contact with Sufism.

Sufism believed in communion between man and God through loving devotion. It is somewhat akin to **Bhakti cult**. Sufism had its own practices and did not always conform to the rituals of orthodox Islam. For instance singing, dancing etc. not permitted by the Muslim Ulamas were considered by the Sufis as methods of reaching an ecstatic stage which would bring them nearer to God. Although the Sufis accepted Muhammad as prophet and the authority of the Quran in course of time they drew diverse religious practices from different religions such as Gnostic Christianity, Zoroastrianism, **Buddhism**, Neo-Platonism and Indian philosophical system—the Vedanta and Yoga. Sufism had been likened to a stream that gathered volume by joining of tributaries from many lands.

Sufism found its way into India during the eleventh and twelfth centuries when many Sufi saints came to India particularly in Multan and Lahore of the Punjab. The most celebrated of these Sufi saints was Khwaja Muinuddin Chisti who came to Lahore from Ghazni in 1161 and settled in Ajmer under Prithviraj. Muinuddin Chisti is the greatest Sufi and holds the highest position of honour in the history of Sufism. He died in either 1235 or 1236 at Ajmer where his tomb is still today a place of pilgrimage for many. Muinuddin Chisti founded the Chisti order of the Sufis in India. Shaikh Farid Shakarganj (1175-1265) belonged to the Chisti order of the Sufis, Shaikh Farid was one of the earliest contributors to Punjabi language and his writings are regarded as the earliest specimens of Punjabi. Some of his contributions were incorporated in the **Adi Granth** by Guru Arjan and Shaikh Farid is known in Sikh tradition as Baba Farid. Shaikh Nizamuddin Auliya (1238-1325) settled near Delhi where his tomb is also a shrine and centre of devotion and proselytism.

Apart from the Chisti order another Sufi order that dominated the Muslim thought during the thirteenth and early years of the fourteenth centuries was **Suhrawardy** order founded by Shaikh Bahauddin Zakariya. In the fourteenth century, however, the influence of the Sufis declined due to anti-Sufi attitude of Muhammad bin Tughluq and Sunni orthodoxy of Firuz Tughluq which gave opportunity to the Ulamas to oppose the Sufi heterodoxy with greater vehemence. The result was that greater emphasis was laid on religious ceremonies and rituals thus reducing religion into a mere formalism. The predominance of the **Ulamas, Mullas, Pirs** continued from the latter half of the fourteenth century to the first half of the sixteenth.

Besides the **Chisti** and **Suhrawardy** orders two more Sufi orders were founded, namely the **Qadivis** by Sayyid Ghaus Wala Pir and the **Shattaris** by Shaikh Abdul Shattari in the fifteenth century. In the sixteenth century Khwaja Baqi Billa founded the **Naqsbandi** order.

During the sixteenth and earlier part of the eighteenth the Sufi poets made great contribution to Punjabi literature. Sufi poetry appealed to the heart of the common people and became very popular among all classes of people of the Punjab. Spiritual urges are expressed in terms of simple objects familiar to common folk, such as the spinning wheel, the Persian wheel, the dancing **Dervishes**, Characters drawn from popular mythology Hindu as well as Muslim.

Among the Sufis of this period the names of Hafiz Barkhudar Vajid, Ali Haidar, Sultan Bahu, Shah Hussain and Bulhe Shah deserve mention. Sultan Bahu was a mystic dervish. He expressed himself in passionate poetry of devotion and renunciation. Shah Hussain was a fakir given to free way of life, loved by the people for his sincerity of passion and devotion, but reproved by the orthodox Muslims. The song-lyrics practised by Hussain and other Sufi poets is known as **Kafi**. Bulhe Shah was, however, the prince of the Sufi poets. Some sects were founded in the seventeenth century which emphasised the unity of religions between the Hindus and the Muslims. The name of Dadu (1544-1603) stands foremost among the founders of such sects. Dadu founded the **Parabrahma Sampradaya** with a view to uniting different faiths in one bond of love and comradeship. A Kshatriya of Malwa named Baba Lal gave seven interviews to Dara Shukoh in 1648 and their conversations are recorded in a Persian work named **Nadu un Mikat** which is an admixture of the Vedanta and Sufi doctrines. A few other sects apart from Parabrahma Sampradaya were those of **Qalandar** and **Jangam**. The followers of the latter were **fakirs** who like Hindu **Sannyasis** kept long matted hair and wandered about.

Under Shah Jahan the renowned Sufi and author Muhibbullah Illahabadi wrote a commentary on Quarn from sufistic view point, entitled **Maratib al-Arbaah**.

Lastly, it may be pointed out that Sufis helped the spread of Islam in India by emphasising social equality of all men. Many of the Sufis were men of great learning, they were guides to good life. They are "thought of as forming a bridge of understanding with the Hindu **Bhakti** movement, with their emphasis on the inner life and the unity of all believers in one God."

BHAKTI CULT

Bhakti is intense devotion to God conceived as personal, a Saviour worthy of trust and ready to be gracious, it is an important element of Vaishavism and Saivism as expounded in the Gita and **Svetasvatara Upanishad**. Followers of Bhakti cult preached the fundamental equality of all religions and the unity of Godhead, and held that dignity of man depended on his actions and not on his birth, protested against too much ritualism and formalities in matters of religion as also the domination of the priesthood. They emphasised simple devotion and faith as a means of salvation for one and all. Substance of Bhakti cult lies in loving devotion to the supreme Diety variously named Krishna, Vishnu, Narayana etc. and communion with Him.

Bhakti was propagated by Ramanuja in the eleventh century and during the period twelfth to fourteenth centuries it was propagated in South India by the Vaishnava teachers like Nimbarka, Lokacharya, Vedantadesika, Madhava Pillai etc.

The Bhakti movement in the period between the sixth and the twelfth centuries was raised above caste restrictions in the Tamil country where the Alvars and Adiyars introduced this revolutionary social equality. One of the preachers arose from the lower caste. Likewise, the Bhakti movement in the sixteenth and seventeenth centuries tended to raise the status of non-Brahmanas. Some of the non-Brahmanas became the spiritual preachers of the Brahmanas.

During the Mughal period a considerable Bhakti literature grew up in Hindi, Bengali, Oriya, Gujarati and Assamese languages.

SPREAD OF BHAKTI MOVEMENT

With the establishment of the Turkish rule in North India, Islam came as a challenge to Hinduism and Hindu society. **Bhakti** cult met this challenge of Islam by introducing a liberal character in the society under Ramananda's leadership. He is said to have been born in Mysore by some and at Allahabad by others and perhaps lived during the end of the fourteenth and early years of the fifteenth centuries. Ramananda served as "the bridge between the Bhakti movement of the South and the North." He preached in the language of the common people, i.e. Hindi. He rejected castes and admitted men of all classes as his disciples, among whom were a cobbler, a barber and a Muhammadan weaver, namely Kabir. Ramananda was a worshipper of Rama and his followers are still numerous in the Gangetic plain. Mira Bai, a Rajput princess renounced the palace life of Chitor and became a disciple of the follower of Ramananda. Ramananda's doctrines were embodied by her in Hindi and Gujarati devotional verses of high quality. Some of Ramananda's hymns have been included in the **Adi Granth** by Guru Arjan.

Ramananda is supposed to have been connected with the great Vaishnava Ramanuja. But Ramananda substituted Ram and Sita for Vishnu and Lakshmi of Ramanuja sect as objects of devotion. Ramananda propagated his **Bhakti** cult in Hindi and not in Sanskrit as did Ramanuja sect, and thus his appeal to common people was great as they understood his language. Ramananda raised his movement above caste prejudices, unlike Ramanuja sect, allowing people of all castes high or low to eat and drink together, thus get emancipated from the restrictions of caste prejudices. The followers of Ramananda were therefore, known as **Abhadhuts**, i.e. emancipated.

Ramananda considered formalities of worship as immaterial and superfluous, for, "supreme reward" would come to the devotee by incessant taking of the name of God. One who loves God, is loved by God Himself. "Whoever adores God is God's own" he would say, hence there was no question of any one's identification by his caste or birth.

The liberal idea propagated by Ramananda appears to have been to an extent due to the impact of Islam. This was most likely for he lived during the period of Muslim rule in India. But his liberalism in matters of castes and inter-dining was regarded as a great threat to Hindu orthodoxy. But despite a section of orthodox Hindus who would like to cling to traditional class restrictions in social behaviours, the need for acceptance of the challenge of Islam and socio-religious adjustment was felt by a liberal section of the Hindus and as such Ramananda's movement was welcomed by them. Ramananda did not leave any organised sect behind him and this was the reason why while his influence had flowed into different channels it lost its momentum in its original form.

KABIR

The most significant figure among the religious reformers who followed the ways of Ramananda was Kabir. He was undoubtedly the greatest of the pupils of Ramananda. According to tradition he was the abandoned child of a Brahmin widow, but grew up as the foster-child of a Muslim weaver named Niru and his wife. He flourished perhaps in the end of the fourteenth and early fifteenth centuries. He composed numerous verses in Hindi which are still familiar in Northern India. His compositions unmistakbly show "a mind of profound inner sensitiveness and daring utterances." Kabir called himself "at once the child of Allah and Ram." In fact he was the most cosmopolitan of all the **bhagats** that flourished during medieval India. The works of Kabir reveal such an approach to God that persons of any religious denomination can accept it and if pursued without bigotry, will be advantageous for salvation. Rules of caste, religious observances of the Hindus and the Muslims were considered by him as worthless. It was constant utterance of God's name that was needed for salvation.

It is supposed that Kabir's cosmopolitanism was the result of the expreience of his own life. He is said to have been a born Hindu, brought up as a Muslim, and weaver by profession. He worked at Benares. He lived in Hindu surroundings, associated himself with Muslim saints, was a disciple of Ramananda—all these diverse influences contributed to his cosmopolitanism.

It is supposed that Kabir lived when Sikandar Lodi (1489-1517) was the Sultan of Delhi, and had occasion to meet Guru Nanak. His indebtedness to Ramananda was very great, yet it must be conceded that he was undoubtedly a great adherent of the Bhakti cult. While ancient philosophy had little influence on him, he drew inspiration from both Hindu and Muslim scriptures. His mystic love for Godhead was derived from Sufism. His followers go by the name of **Kabirpanthis**.

Kabir's conviction was that God is "omnipresent" for he would often say : "Whichever way I look there is he contained." Repetition of God's name would lead to communion with God, was his firm conviction.

Kabir's conviction of Allah and Rama being one and same God gave him a clue to Hindu-Muslim unity in religion and society. Humanity, according to him, happen to be God's children, so the Hindu and the Turk have one path, and whether they are **Pandits** or **Shaikhs** their religion is the same. Strife between the Hindus and the Muslims was very much distressing to him. "Hindus call upon Rama, the Musalmans on Rahim, yet both fight and kill each other, and none knows the truth."

Kabir in his numerous **dohas** (small poems) emphasised that God is omnipresent, He is everywhere, beside everybody. God need not be sought either in temples or in mosques, in Kaba or in Kailash, in rites and ceremonies or yogas, but if one is a devoted lover of God a true seeker of God he will see Him everywhere. "O Sadhu God is the breath of all breath"—Kabir would say.

Kabir's teachings are closely akin to those of the Persian mystics like Jalal-ud-din Rumi, Hafiz etc. whose doctrines were embraced by Abul Fazl and Akbar in the 16th century. Nanak, the founder of Sikhism got his spiritual inspiration from Kabir.

Theology of Kabir was meant to unite the Hindus and the Muhammadans in the worship of one God. None of Ramananda's followers except Kabir seemed to have been conscious of the evil consequences of strifes between the Hindus and Muslims and none of them with the sole exception of Kabir made any conscious effort to effect a socio-religious rapprochment between the two great Indian communities. But unfortunately the "seed to the message of unity of Hari and Allah was not evidently sown on a fertile soil and did not sprout." Yet Kabir had done his best if the Hindus and the Muslims paid no heed to the practical utility and fundamental truth underlying all religions the fault lay with them.

Kabir was also a poetical genius besides his having been a religious teacher. His dohas, bhajans in simple Hindi appealed to the heart of the common people who understood his language easily. His poetry enriched the Hindi devotional literature. Parts of his compositions were later included in Adi Granth by Sikh Guru Arjan. Kabir did not nominate any successor and his son refused to accept the position of his father on the ground that his father (Kabir) was not in favour of sectarianism. In fact, he fought against sectarianism all his life. The result was that the followers of Kabir formed small groups or subsects under different religious leaders. So there arose twelve groups of Kabirpanthis the two major divisions having their centres at Chattisgarh in Madhya Pradesh and Benares in Uttar Pradesh.

When Kabir died, the story goes, that both the Hindus and Muslims contended for his corpse, but when they raised the shroud that covered the deadbody they were amazed to find that there was no dead body but some flowers—all that remained under the shroud in place of the corpse of Kabir. The Hindus took half of the flowers and cremated it at Varanasi and the Muslims who took the other half and buried it at Gorakhpur.

VALLABHACHARYA

Another offshoot of Bhakti movement was the Krishna cult of Vallabhacharya a Telugu Brahmin born in 1479 in Varanasi while the family was on pilgrimage to the holy city. Even as a child he was looked upon as a prodigy. After his education was over he was on his travels. He arrived at the court of Krishnadevaraya of Vijayanagar where he defeated the **Saivas** in a public debate. He then went to Mathura, Vrindaban and other places of pilgrimage and ultimately he settled at Varanasi. Vallabhacharya taught **Suddha-advaita** which recognised no distinction between Brahman and an individual soul and regarded **Bhakti** as the means for soul to escape the bondage due to worldly delusions. Vallabhacharya emphasised the doctrine of self-control and renunciation yet it came to be known as **pushti-marga** under his successors who laid stress on the physical aspects of Krishna's sports, hence the creed came to be known as 'Epicureanism of the East."

CHAITANYA

The greatest and the most popular Vaishnava saint was Chaitanya (1485-1533) who propagated a sublime variety of **Bhakti** cult. Chaitanya was born in Nadia in Bengal in 1485 in a Brahmana family that had migrated to Nabadwip, in Nadia, from Sylhet now in Bangladesh. His father was jagannath Misra, and mother Sachi Devi. He was known variously as Nemai, Gouranga, Gora, etc. Chaitanya displayed a wonderful literary acumen in his early life and his soul soon aspired to rise above the fetters of the world. He showed a great love for Hari and would often take that name. He married at an early age but his first wife died not long after when he married Vishnupriya. But nothing could keep him away from his pursuit of emancipation from worldly life.

He had in the meantime acquired mastery over different branches of Sanskrit sastras and proved his scholarship in a number of dialectical controversies with eminent Sanskrit scholars. He toured all over East Bengal and visited his ancestral home at Sylhet. In 1508 while he had been to Gaya for performing the **Sradha** of his father who had died earlier, he met the famous Isvara Puri, disciple of Madhava Puri founder of the Madhava Sect in South India. He was initiated by Isvara Puri in **dasakshara** Krish-mantra. It is said, on his way back to Bengal he had a vision of Lord Krishna in a village. This effected a total transformation of his mind and he gave up his occupation of running a tol and teaching scholars. He became deeply engrossed in the thought of Lord Krishna and began to sing the praise of Krishna in **Sankirtan** and while doing so, he in fits of ecstacy shed tears in profusion. All this was taken at first as signs of mental imbalance by some people, but soon they came to realise the magnetic influence of his preachings and Vaishnavas of Nabadwip were attracted to him. People of all classes, Hindus and Muslims, high and low became his disciples. The Qazi took alarm at the great popularity of the movement and particularly as Chaitanya movement attracted even followers from the Muslim community. He sought to suppress the movement with a strong hand. Hussain Shah, the Sultan of Bengal, on hearing all about the large number that congregated at the Sankirtan of Chaitanya remarked that a person who could draw so many people must have something very special about him. The Qazi was ordered not to oppress him or to put impediments to his Sankirtan.

In 1510 Chaitanya renounced the world and got initiated by **Kesava Bharati** at Katwa in West Bengal. Kesava Bharati christened him as Sri Krishna Chaitanya. Soon after his initiation he left Nabadwip and took residence at Puri where he converted and took Vasudeva Sarbhavauma, a great scholar in Vedanta and Nyaya as disciple of his Bhakti cult. Ramananda, the Governor of Rajahmundri also became his disciple. Chaitanya proceeded through Rameswaram, Cape Comorin, and the states now called Kerala, Karnataka, Maharashtra, Andhra Pradesh and returned to Rajahmundri. He is said to have also visited Dwarka, Pravasa and Saurashtra. On his return to Puri from Rajahmundri, Prataprudra king of Orissa became his disciple.

In 1514 on his way to pilgrimage to Vrindaban Chaitanya passed through Bengal when he converted Rup and Sanatan—two ministers of Hussain Shah as well as their nephew Jiva. This led to the progress of Vaisnavism in Bengal. Two years later (1516) Chaitanya returned to Puri and lived his remaining life in monastic seclusion. It is common belief that Chaitanya disappeared in the temple of Jagannath and merged in the diety.

Chaitanya is regarded by his followers as an incarnation of Vishnu. The essence of Chaitanya's Bhakti cult has been expressed by Krishnadas Kaviraj, the author of **Chaitanya Charitamrita** in the following sentence "if a creature adores Krishna and serves his Guru, he is released from the meshes of illusion and attains to Krishna's feet'.

Chaitanya was against priestly ritualism and preached faith in Hari. "He believed that through love and devotion and song and dance on ecstasy could be produced in which the personal of God would be realised." Chaitanya's influence on the common people was deep and wide.

Chaitanya did not leave his teachings or views in writing. His disciples Rup, Sanatan, Jiva, Gopal Bhatta, Raghunath Das and others correctly explained and arranged the teachings and views of Chaitanya in their works. "Just as we know of Socrates and his teachings not from his own writings but through the writings of his disciples like Plato, so also we know of Chaitanya's philosophy principally through the writings of his spiritual disciples."

Chaitanya adhered to essentially orthodox philosophical traditions yet his religion had an immensely liberal character. He did not recognise any caste limit in following his Bhakti cult which according to him was the only way to salvation. Vaishnavism in Bengal was responsible for the removal of social disabilities of the lowest castes of the society by giving them equal footing with his other disciples. The traditional monopoly of the Brahmanas in guiding the society was by admitting non-Brahmanas to the ministry of the Vaishnava congregation for spiritual guidance. Chaitanya and his followers had simplified the traditional socio-religious ceremonies like marriage, sradh, etc.

The liberal socio-religious trend that had developed as a result of the propagation of Bhakti cult by Chaitanya would have transformed the Bengali society. But the traditional orthodoxy that existed within the Vaishnavas themselves due to the incoming of converts of high caste Hindus like the Brahmanas, Vaidyas and Kayasthas, led to adherence to high social position by these people. Thus the unorthodox system of a casteless unified Vaishnava sect could not fully develop. The general socio-religious laws and practices of the Hindu society continued to be followed by the Vaishnavas who came from the upper castes. The Vaishnavas of Bengal, in this way, were split into two sections one adhering to traditional Hindu laws and practices and the other following the liberal Vaishnava socio-religious laws and practices, the latter being gradually looked upon as lower than the former in social position.

Hindu orthodoxy also prevailed in the theological aspect of Vaishnavism. Image worship came in and there was a wide prevalence of image worship by the Vaishnavas. A very small section of the Vaishnavas could conceive of a spiritual body which was conceived to be the Supreme Diety.

Chaitanya did not leave any nominee nor any organised body for propagation of his cult. Nityananda, Advaitacharya who were his associates were also regarded by the Vaishnavas as incarnation of Vishnu in a limited way. The descendants of these associates of Chaitanya who are living in Navadvip and Santipur are regarded as the spiritual heads of the Vaishnavas of Bengal. Chaitanya's life ended in 1533.

NAMDEV

In Maharashtra Bhakti cult was preached by Namadeva or Namdev. Namdev belonged to a family of tailors or calico-printers and flourished during the earlier half of the fifteenth century. He believed in the unity of Godhead and was against religious rituals and formal observances as well as idol worship. According to him salvation was attainable through love of God. The love of God must be like the love of the child for its mother, he would often say.

In Maharashtra worship of Vithoba took the form of Bhakti cult. Vithoba worship had three great leaders namely Jnanesvar, Namdev and Tukaram. They were the leaders of the Pandharpur movement, i.e. Bhakti movement in Maharashtra. Their influence on society and religion in Maharashtra was very great and also helped the development of Marathi literature. "modification of caste exclusiveness, sanctification of family life, elevation of the status of women, spread of humaneness and toleration, partial reconciliation with Islam, Subordination of ritual and learning to love and faith, and limitation to the excesses of polytheism" (Ranade). People from lowest professions the tailors, carpenters, goldsmiths, potters and even slave girls and prostitutes were taken as followers of the sect.

The Pandharpur movement was originally a regional one but gradually it spread to Northern India.

SANKARDEV

Sankardev was born about 1487 in a Kayastha family of feudal chiefs of the Brahmaputra valley. He introduced Vaishnavism (Bhakti cult) in Kamrupa and Cooch Behar. According to his biographers, Sankardev did not find the atmosphere in Assam congenial under the Ahom King Svargodeo for the propagation of his Bhakti cult and he fled to the domains of Raja Nara Narayan of Cooch Behar who gave him fullest liberty to preach his religion.

Sankara studied sanskrit in his early life and led the life of a house-holder with his wife and children. It is said that the death of his wife turned him into a Yogi and became a devout Vaishnava and began to preach Bhakti cult.

Madhavadeva was the greatest of Sankardev's disciples and accompanied him to Cooch Behar. Both Sankardev and Madhavadev attained much success in their mission of the propagation of Bhakti cult in Cooch Behar. Rulph Fitch who visited Nara Narayana's Kingdom of Cooch Behar in the sixteenth century testifies to the influence of Vaishnavism on the people. "There they be gentiles and they will kill nothing. They have hospitals for sheep, goats, dogs, cats, birds and for all the living creatures." The Bhakti movement of Sankardev and Madhavadev attracted some tribal people also. The rulers of Heramba principalities of Cooch Behar became disciples of Sankardev. Madhavadev, the greatest disciple of Sankardev writes in his **Nama-Ghosha** that "Garos, Bhutias, Muslims take the name of Hari, it is a pity such Hari-nama is criticised by some of the learned." Some Brahmanas also became the disciples of Sankardev.

The sect founded by Sankardev and Madhavadev is known as **Mahapurushias**. Some European writers considered them to be followers of Chaitanya. But although Sankardev propagated Bhakti cult like Chaitanya there were some fundamental differences between the two (i) Sankardev believed that God is formless, hence there was no question of image worship according to him. But the followers of Chaitanya consider it essential. (ii) While salvation is the ultimate objective of the spiritual life the school of Sankardev, the followers of Chaitanya yearn for only loving servitude of Radha and Krishna eternally. (iii) Sankardeva does not recognise Radha at all. (iv) Bengal Vaishnavas recite **Hare-Krishna** but the Assam Vaishnavas recite **Ram-Krishna**.

Sankardev's centres of religious propagation are **satras** or the refuge of the devotees and at the centre of satra lies the **Nam Ghara** where **Gita** or the **Bhagavata** is kept on a pedestal and holy name is recited.

Sankaradev followed the **Visishtadvaita** philosophical system of Ramanuja, but as we have mentioned above he would not recognise the female counterpart of the Supreme Diety, such as Radha, Lakshmi or Sita. He emphasised **Nishkama Bhakti**, i.e. devotion with no yarning for getting any benefit. Sankardev denounced caste-system and preached in tongue of the people.

NANAK

Sikhism was founded by Nanak who was reviver of the monotheistic doctrine of the Upanishads. Born in a Khatri family of Talwandi in modern Nankana about thirty-five miles south-west of Lahore city in 1469, Nanak spent his whole life in preaching his gospel of universal toleration based on all that was good in Hinduism and Islam. He was a religious preacher of saintly disposition.

Nanak received elementary lessons from his village teacher but his lack of interest in earning a living and his munificence without the thought of his own needs, made his parents somewhat unhappy. His religiocity revealed itself in his early life. He married and had two children, but nothing increased his attraction to the world.

In 1485 he got appointment as a store-keeper of the Government granary at Sultanpur which was the administrative centre of Jullundur Doab. But even this appointment did not divert his mind from spiritual pursuits and he spent the time other than what he was required to spend for official duties, in singing the praise of God. One morning he was found missing and it is said that he was taken to the presence of Supreme Being. But shorn of the exaggeration of the traditional story, the fact remains, that he had obtained the mystic-experience which was the fruit of his long spiritual pursuit. Three days later he returned to preach. "There is no Hindu, there is no Musalman" and when local **Qazi** took exception to this statement Nanak explained that a Musalman is one "who effaceth himself and make the truth and contentment his only creed." The local Muslim Governor was pleased at this explanation.

Nanak now left Sultanpur and visited different parts of India and also the countries in West Asia. This travelling like an **Udasi**, i.e. recluse, continued till 1526 during the course of which he visited most of the present states of India, but also Ceylon, Mecca, Madina, Baghbad etc.

When Babur invaded India and North West India was in turmoil, Nanak was in Punjab and it is said that he once met Babur. From 1526 to 1539, the year of his demise Nanak settled in a village named Kartarpur in Sialkot, now in Pakistan preaching his own gospel. He nominated Angad as his successor, before his death.

Guru Nanak's teachings are to be found in the hymns composed by him and included in the **Adi Granth** compiled by Guru Arjan in 1604. **Japji** one of the hymns contained in the Adi Granth is the sumtotal of Nanak's spiritual realisation, as also an inimitable literary work. In **Japji** Nanak gives in a succint way his conception of God. "There is one God. His name is Eternal Truth, He is the Maker of all things, He fears nothing and is in enmity with nothing. His Image is Timeless. He is not begotten, being of His own being." Nanak teachings were based on the unity of Godhead. Nanak did not believe in the appearance and reappearance of God on earth in human form.

Nanak's ideal of religious pursuit is union with God. It is by raising the soul to the level of spiritual excellence which will free it from the cycle of birth and death, a level of perfection which will enable the individual soul **(atma)** to find dissolution in the Supreme Being **(Paramatma)**.

Nanak rejected religious ceremonies and cautioned his followers against five evils namely : lust, anger, covetousness, pride and attachment. He was against formal observance of rituals, fasting, penance, prayers according to set schedule, pilgrimage, feeding people, putting religious marks on forehead, smearing the body with ashes. He recommended modesty, civility, right conduct, devotion to truth, etc. He criticised worship of many gods and idolatry. According to him neither the Vedas nor the Quran but by deep devotion to God that can bring salvation. One has to be hungry for God, and that means **Bhakti**.

Nanak, however, believed in the Brahmanical doctrine of **Karma**. "As a man soweth, so shall he reap; as he earneth, so shall he eat." In other words man determines his fate through deeds done by him. Rebirth can only be stopped by Gods' blessings, attainable by men by meditating on the **Nama**.

Guru Nanak was a religious reformer but the contemporary political and social evils did not miss his sight. In his poem known as **Babur-Vani** Nanak referred to the sufferings of the men and women at the hand of Babur's troops. He was not a social reformer in the accepted sense, but in his spiritual propaganda he did not make any distinction between high-caste or low-caste. He said that "There is no Hindu and no Musalman", it was an accident that one was born in one family or in the other. Thus Nanak conceived of a human society based on universal brotherhood and which has nothing to do with castes. Honest labour and pursuit of truth were, according to Nanak the ways to find 'release'.

It is worth while to discuss the influence of Hinduism and Islam on Nanak and his religious ideas While Nanak's hymns reveal the influence of the **Rig Veda**, the **Upanishads**. particularly **Chhandogya**, **Mandukya**, **Katha**, **Prasna** and the **Bhagavad Gita**, he rejected the Brahmanical doctrine of incarnation of God, and caste-system which had its origin in the Vedas and developed in the times of the **Puranas**. Nanak, however, uses expressions of the Hindu sashtras, such as **yuga**, **guna**, **nad**, **maya**, **mukti**, **karma** etc. as well as Brahmanical names such as Hari Krishna, Rama to denote the Supreme Being. It may therefore, be said that Nanak adopted Brahmanical ideas on selective basis.

The Sikh religion, according to Toynbee "is creation of an ex-Hindu religious enquirer who adopted monotheism and rejected caste under the influence of Islam." The great Indian savant Radha-krishna is of the opinion that Nanak was greatly influenced by the monotheism of Islam and strove to bring the Hindus and Muslims together. Similar opinion has been expressed by Carpenter. Yet it must be remarked that Nanak's religion was not synthesis of Hindu and Islamic beliefs. It is also difficult to accept the view that Nanak's monotheism was the result of the influence of Islam. In fact, it was drawn from the Upanishads. Again Nanak's ideas about transmigration of soul, and deliverance from the cycle of birth and death as a result of the merger of **atma** with **Paramatma** constitute major points of difference between Nanak's religion and Islam. Although Nanak had come into contact with the Sufis, **Sufism** had little influence on his religion.

Nanak was the founder of Sikhism and his religion remains essentially the same in fundamentals although annotations, supplementary additions have been made, but no modification has been made and to the Skihs it is inconceivable.

REFERENCES

The Mughal Empire, Vol. VII : Bharatiya Vidya Bhavan

An Advanced History of India : Majumdar, Roychaudhuri & Datta

Oxford History of India (4th Edn.) : V. A. Smith

The Sikh Gurus and the Sikh Religion : A. C. Banerjee

Akbar the Great Mughal, Vols. I-III : A. L. Srivastava